Provence
and the Côte d'Azur

THE ROUGH GUIDE

There are more than one hundred Rough Guide titles
covering destinations from Amsterdam to Zimbabwe

Forthcoming titles include
Bangkok • Barbados • Central America
Israel • Japan • Jordan • New Zealand • Syria

Rough Guide Reference Series
Classical Music • European Football • The Internet • Jazz
Opera • Reggae • Rock Music • World Music

Rough Guide Phrasebooks
Czech • French • German • Greek • Hindi & Urdu • Indonesian • Italian
Mandarin Chinese • Mexican Spanish • Polish • Portuguese
Russian • Spanish • Thai • Turkish • Vietnamese

Rough Guides on the Internet
http://www.roughguides.com

Rough Guide Credits

Text Editor:	Lemisse Al-Hafidh
Series editor:	Mark Ellingham
Editorial:	Martin Dunford, Jonathan Buckley, Samantha Cook, Jo Mead, Amanda Tomlin, Paul Gray, Sarah Dallas, Kate Berens, Chris Schüler, Helena Smith, Julia Kelly, Caroline Osborne, Kieren Falconer, Judith Bamber, Alan Spicer (UK); Andrew Rosenberg (US)
Online:	Kate Hands (UK); Geronimo Madrid (US)
Production:	Susanne Hillen, Andy Hilliard, Melissa Flack, Judy Pang, Link Hall, Nicola Williamson, Helen Ostick, Maxine Burke
Finance:	John Fisher, Celia Crowley, Catherine Gillespie
Marketing and Publicity:	Richard Trillo, Simon Carloss, Niki Smith (UK), Jean-Marie Kelly, Sorelle Braun (US)
Administration:	Tania Hummel, Alexander Mark Rogers

Acknowledgments

The author would like to thank François and Mireille Provansal, Monique Provansal, Tim Salmon, Michel and Yves in Nice and Steve Saint Leger for their invaluable help in researching and writing this edition; Peter Polish for his support throughout; Lemisse Al-Hafidh for her sympathetic editing; and the Production team for swift typesetting. A special debt of gratitude is owed to the much loved friends Anne Provansal and Lotfi Ben Othmane in Marseille, Jean and Margaret Llasera in Le Muy, and the Ivaldi-Magnani family in Nice – Roland, Cerise, Thomas, Véronique, Florian and Valentine. In addition, the editor thanks Andrew Tibber for proofreading and Micromap Ltd for map production.

Many thanks also to all the **readers** who have written in with their comments, information and suggestions, including: M Aldridge, AJB Allen, Valerie Aronovici, Lisa Ausden, Lucy Barker, Jean-Paul Battaglia, Andrea Brusch, Kit Cameron, RW Coleman, Paul Commins, Alistair Cooper, Anna Crane, David Crowe, Mrs G Doherty, Michelle Dubouchet, Katherine Duncan Jones, Margaret Fisher, JM Goldbloom, Brian Gordon, Martin Harrap, Peter Huxford, Alan Jeffreys, Susan Jones, Jean Kramer, Pamela Kinlock, David Leslie, Billy Macmillan and family, Lee Marshall, Margaret Martin, Ian McFie, Ida Miller, Nigel Newman, Chris and Kaya Oakley, Michael Oldcorn, Mr R Papasdaro, Gilly Phillips, Antonia Pitchford, Mike Poulard, Jill Prime, Carol Rahn, Anna Raisin, Robert Sandelson, Michael Shane, LJ Scott, Mrs Maureen Sharkey, Julia Simmonds, Nadine Steele, Carrie Supple, Sia Sarkic, Jean Thomas, Irwin S Turbitt and Clare Williams. Please keep writing! (address on p.427).

This third edition published April 1996 by Rough Guides Ltd, 1 Mercer Street, London WC2H 9QJ.
Reprinted in January 1998.

Distributed by The Penguin Group:

Penguin Books Ltd, 27 Wrights Lane, London W8 5TZ
Penguin Books USA Inc., 375 Hudson Street, New York 10014, USA
Penguin Books Australia Ltd, 487 Maroondah Highway, PO Box 257, Ringwood, Victoria 3134, Australia
Penguin Books Canada Ltd, 10 Alcorn Avenue, Toronto, Ontario, Canada M4V 1E4
Penguin Books (NZ) Ltd, 182–190 Wairau Road, Auckland 10, New Zealand.

Typeset in Linotron Univers and Century Old Style to an original design by Andrew Oliver.
Printed in the United Kingdom by Cox & Wyman Ltd (Reading).
Illustrations in Part One and Part Three by Ed Briant.
Basics and Contexts illustrations by Henry Iles.

496pp
includes index

A catalogue record for this book is available from the British Library.

ISBN 1-85828-127-X

Provence

and the Côte d'Azur

THE ROUGH GUIDE

Written and researched by

Kate Baillie

THE ROUGH GUIDES

LIST OF MAPS

MAP SYMBOLS

Motorway
Road
Minor road
Steps
Path
Railway
Ferry route
National border
Chapter division boundary
River
Airport
Campsite
Hostel
Point of interest
Viewpoint
Cliffs
Waterfall
Mountain range
Mountain peak
Tourist office
Post office
Métro station
Wall
Building
Church
Cemetery
Park
National park
Beach

CONTENTS

To the memory of Nicole Beckerman
who died in Oxford in 1979
and who, I suspect, had some of the
happiest moments of her life in Provence.

INTRODUCTION

The ancient Provençal version of Genesis maintains that prior to introducing Adam, the Creator realized he had several materials left over: large expanses of celestial blue, all kinds of rocks, arable soil filled with seeds for a sumptuous flora, and a variety of as yet unused tastes and smells from the most subtle to the most powerful. "Well", He thinks, "why don't I make a beautiful resumé of my world, my own special paradise?" And so **Provence** came into being.

This paradise encompasses the snow-peaked lower Alps and their foothills, which in the east descend to the sea's edge, and to the west extend almost to the Rhône. In central Provence the wild high plateaux are cut by the deepest cleft in the surface of Europe – the Grand Canyon du Verdon. The coastal hinterland is made up of range after range of steep forested hills in which the warm scent of pines, eucalyptus and wild herbs intoxicates the senses. The shore is an ever-changing series of geometric bays giving way to chaotic outcrops of glimmering rock and deep, narrow inlets, like miniature Norwegian fjords – the *calanques*. In the Camargue, the shoreline itself becomes an abstraction as land and sea merge in infinite horizons. Away from the Rhône delta there is nowhere that does not have its frame of hills, or mountains, or strange sudden eruptions of rock.

But all these elements would be nothing without the Mediterranean light, which is at its best in spring and autumn. It is both soft and brightly theatrical, as if each landscape had lighting rigged up by an expert for maximum colour and definition with minimum glare. It is no surprise that of all the arts, painting should be the one that owes so much of its European history over the last hundred years to the beauty and escapism of this world.

The Genesis legend doesn't go quite as far as siting the Garden of Eden in Provence. The truth is that Provence and its coast were far from being a paradise for their **early inhabitants**. As with most mountainous regions, the soil is poor and cultivation away from rivers (prior to the extensive irrigation systems) only possible where there were springs. The low-lying areas of the Camargue and Rhône valley were marshes or rubbly plains subject to inundation. The coast had no natural defences of rough seas and high cliffs to dissuade invaders. Communities clustered on easily defensible hilltops – the *village perchés* – with the position of outlying farms determined by the availability of water.

For hundreds of years, Provence remained a prime target for foreign invaders. The **ancient Greeks** established bases on the coast and on the Rhône, including *Massalia* and *Nikea* – Marseille and Nice, and when the **Romans** came along later, they cleared a route all along the coast to their cities on the Rhône. Belligerent foreigners came from all over northern Europe and from across the Mediterranean, and if this wasn't enough, Provence's independence was also contested with **France**, the **Holy Roman Empire**, **Burgundy**, **Savoy** and the **Popes**, with internal feuding between rival fiefdoms aggravating the insecurity of daily life. After just fifty years of reunification with France (1481), Provence was again invaded, and within a hundred years was suffering the bloodiest of French civil wars, the *Guerres de Religion*.

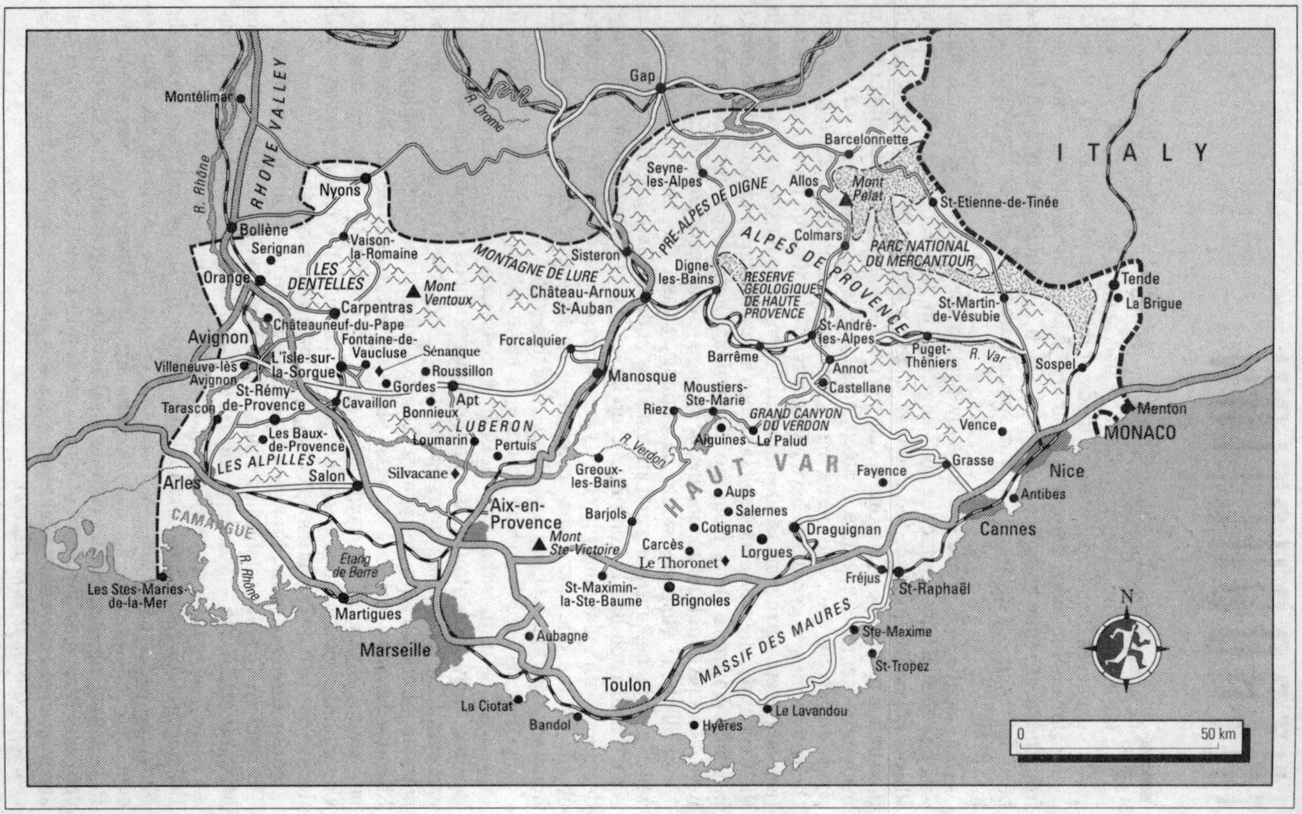

ITALY
MONACO
Menton
Tende
La Brigue
Sospel
Nice
Antibes
Cannes
St-Raphaël
Ste-Maxime
St-Tropez
Fréjus
Le Lavandou
Hyères
Toulon
Bandol
La Ciotat
Marseille
Martigues
Etang de Berre
Aubagne
Les Stes-Maries-de-la-Mer
CAMARGUE
R. Rhône
Arles
Tarascon
St-Rémy-de-Provence
Les Baux-de-Provence
LES ALPILLES
Salon
Avignon
Villeneuve-lès-Avignon
Orange
Montélimar
Bollène
Serignan
RHONE VALLEY
Nyons
R. Drome
Châteauneuf-du-Pape
L'Isle-sur-la-Sorgue
Cavaillon
Fontaine-de-Vaucluse
Carpentras
LES DENTELLES
Vaison-la-Romaine
Mont Ventoux
MONTAGNE DE LURE
Gordes
Sénanque
Roussillon
Bonnieux
Apt
Lourmarin
LUBERON
Silvacane
Pertuis
Forcalquier
Aix-en-Provence
Mont Ste-Victoire
Château-Arnoux
St-Auban
Sisteron
Manosque
Greoux-les-Bains
R. Verdon
Barjols
St-Maximin-la-Ste-Baume
Carcès
Le Thoronet
Brignoles
Cotignac
Salernes
Aups
Lorgues
Draguignan
Fayence
HAUT VAR
MASSIF DES MAURES
Riez
Moustiers-Ste-Marie
Aiguines
Le Palud
GRAND CANYON DU VERDON
Castellane
Barrême
Digne-les-Bains
RESERVE GEOLOGIQUE DE HAUTE PROVENCE
Gap
Seyne-les-Alpes
PRE-ALPES DE DIGNE
ALPES DE PROVENCE
Allos
Colmars
Barcelonnette
Mont Pelat
St-André-les-Alpes
Annot
Puget-Théniers
PARC NATIONAL DU MERCANTOUR
St-Etienne-de-Tinée
St-Martin-de-Vésubie
R. Var
Vence
Grasse
N
0
50 km

Yet Provence has remained remarkably unscathed by the vicissitudes of time. It preserves the best **Roman monuments** of any region in France, and has substantial traces left by earlier colonizers at Glanum, and some still-visible outlines of indigenous Ligurian settlements. More romantic, however, are the numerous surviving *villages perchés* and old town quarters – the *vieilles villes* – with their tight labyrinths of medieval streets, passageways and winding stairs leading inexorably up to a **château fort**, and which have visually hardly changed in centuries. A great many have had no major restoration work and may well not even have a bar or restaurant; just a food shop and perhaps a petrol pump. That said, almost all have a later addition to their medieval church towers or gateways. Others, including all those on or near the coast, have been manicured and coiffed into chic and expensive models of the picturesque. But even with the Monaco licence plate Porsches parked on the streets, the closed shutters outside holiday time of *résidence secondaires*, and the designer boutiques, the history is there in the pattern of the buildings and in their basic structures.

There are other great reminders of the medieval age: the **palace of the Popes in Avignon**; the three great **monasteries** of **Silvacane**, **Thoronet** and **Sénanque**, built by the Cistercian order in the twelfth century; the **ruined city** of **Les Baux**; the **border fortresses** of **Tarascon** and **Sisteron**; the **frescoes and paintings** in the village churches north of Nice.

While life in the mountain villages evolved slowly, a turbulent process of change, of revolution and decline, was played out in the **main cities**, all by the Rhône or the sea. The contrasts here, between the formal splendour of **Avignon** and the vivacious warmth of **Nice**, between smug, bourgeois **Arles** and **Aix** and down-to-earth, proletariat **Marseille**, are another of the region's great attractions. The greatest polarity of all, however, is between the Côte d'Azur, which runs east from Toulon incorporating the Riviera from Cannes to the Italian border, and the rest of Provence.

The **Côte d'Azur** has to be the most built-up, overpopulated, over-eulogized, and expensive stretch of coast anywhere in the world. There are only two industries to speak of – tourism and building, plus the related services of estate agents, yacht traffic wardens, and *Rolls Royce* valets. Posters for the *Front National* go undefaced and construction companies pick their labourers from lines of North African immigrants just as galley owners once chose their slaves. Meanwhile a hotel serves tender meat morsels to its clients' pets in a restaurant for dogs.

Yet in every gap between the monstrous habitations – in the **Esterel**, the **St-Tropez peninsula**, the **islands** off **Cannes** and **Hyères**, and the **Massif des Maures** – the remarkable beauty of the hills and land's edge, the scent of plant life, the February mimosa blossom and the strange synthesis of Mediterranean pollutants that make the water so translucent, devastate the senses.

These elements were once the glory of the whole coast when Cannes and Villefranche, Le Lavandou and St-Tropez were tiny fishing villages. Foreign aristocrats and royals who had turned Nice into Europe's most fashionable winter watering hole in the eighteenth century, spread east and westwards in the nineteenth. **Avant-gardists** in art and lifestyle and successions of celebrities gradually discovered how much simple and sophisticated pleasure this coast could provide. The 1950s saw the advent of mass tourism on an upmarket scale in these parts, the Sixties brought the starlets and the hippies in their droves, and in the 1970s the French government began to realize the horror that their greatest tourist asset was threatening to become.

In the decades either side of 1900, **artists** seduced by the light and relative ease of living bade farewell to the gloom of northern winters. The Côte d'Azur became as much a part of the European art scene as Montmartre and Montparnasse. The great names of the Modern period who painted and sculpted on this coast include **Matisse**, **Renoir**, **Signac**, **Léger**, **Dufy**, **Miró**, **Bonnard**, **Chagall**, **Cocteau**, **Dérain**, **Modigliani**, **Soutine** and **Picasso** all of whom came in summer and shocked the natives by swimming in the sea. Many of their works are permanently exhibited in superb **museums** from St-Tropez to Menton; reason in itself for a visit to the Côte today.

The one great artist native to Provence is **Cézanne**, who was born in Aix in 1839. Many of his canvases were inspired by the landscapes around his home town but very few remain in the region. Because of his relationship with his subjects, a pilgrimage to the **Mont Ste-Victoire** and other favourite scenes is still compelling. The man whose works on show outnumber any other artist is Hungarian-born **Vasarely**, who chose **Aix** and **Gordes** as centres for his studies into an all-embracing concept of art, science, architecture and social life. In and around **Arles** and **St-Rémy** you can follow the sad passage of **Van Gogh**, but again there are hardly any original paintings to be seen.

Food and wine are the other great inducements to bring you to Provence. This is the one French region where fruits and vegetables, fish and seafood, are on an equal footing with meat. The **foods** that grow in Provence – olives and garlic, asparagus and courgettes, white peaches, muscat grapes, melons and strawberries, cêpe and morille mushrooms, almonds and sweet chestnuts, basil and wild thyme, to name but a few – are an essential part of the hot, sensual environment. The **wines** too, from the dry, light rosés of the Côtes de Provence to the deep and delicate reds of the Côtes du Rhône *villages* and Châteauneuf-du-Pape, both complement and owe their brilliance to the intensity of sunshine. The great chefs, of which Provence has more than its fair share, buy everything they need, except for beef and butter, from local suppliers. Wandering through the food markets, you may well feel that, in this respect at least, the local version of Genesis is not far off the mark.

The People

Any number of cheap novels could be written with the characters who make the headlines in Provence and the Côte d'Azur: the St-Laurent-suited Marseille gangster residing in a seventeenth-century Aix mansion; the police chief who runs a prostitution racket; the mayor diverting public funds to his own expense account; Brigitte Bardot's St-Tropez neighbour who sues her for castrating his pet donkey; the shipping magnates and stars of TV soap operas on their ocean liners moored near Cannes; the neo-Fascist leader who wins a hefty percentage of the vote; the international tennis stars tax-exiled in Monte-Carlo; the royal family of Monaco.

Luckily these characters spend most of their largely ill-gotten gains avoiding any contact with ordinary people. As well as the rich and famous, the region attracts the artistic and reclusive, foreigners from northern Europe who can indulge in second homes, and nameless numbers who have come here and found themselves unable to imagine living anywhere else. In the big cities, Marseille in particular, there are large populations of immigrant origin. Their lives are a nightmare of racial harassment and discrimination and they have often lost all expectation of courtesy from whites. To use this as an excuse to shy away from courtesy or contact only intensifies the racism.

As for the **Provençaux** themselves, they bear little resemblance, fortunately, to their portrayal in the films *Jean de Florette* and *Manon des Sources*. Like peasant farmers anywhere in Europe, the older generation combines old-fashioned values – inevitably including male chauvinism – and a certain suspicion of outsiders with generous hospitality and an innate gregariousness. **Provençal** is still spoken in the more remote regions and crops up in many street and place names. The regional French accent is highly distinctive, even to a foreign ear. In the east, in the upper part of the Roya valley, the intonation is unmistakably Italian.

By **the coast** people no longer live off the land except where they have good terrain for vineyards. Selling off their hectares to developers has made sound financial sense even while they curse the consequences. Though most of the resentment of outsiders is directed at the second home owners, making a living out of tourism brings out the worst in everyone; chiefly for the fact that they have to earn a year's wage in three or four summer months.

Where to go

The main limitation on where you go is your means of **transport**. Large parts of inland Provence, where the landscapes never cease to take your breath away, are very difficult to explore other than by foot or with your own vehicle. By the same token, they are the least developed and unspoilt areas, where traditions are strongest, and facilities – save for hikers and campers – the most meagre. Even the **Grand Canyon du Verdon**, the region's unique geographical feature, involves tediously long bus-rides to reach. But this and the **Parc du Mercantour** in the high mountains in the northeast are the two most spectacular destinations in the whole province.

Of the **cities**, **Toulon** is the one to avoid. **Nice**, the so-called "Queen of the Riviera", which was ceded to France only a hundred years ago, combines everything that's best and worst in contemporary Provence and is perhaps the most immediately endearing of them all. **Marseille**, a synonym for vice and crime that tourists usually avoid, is a majestic metropolis where innovative art thrives and where, contrary to its reputation, you can have a perfectly relaxed, indulgent and entertaining stay. The star excrescences of the coast, **Cannes** and **Monte-Carlo**, have a twisted entertainment value. **Aix-en-Provence** is the mini-Paris of Provence, exquisitely pretty, refined and respectable. **Avignon** has the history of medieval Provence writ large and the best contemporary arts festival. For **Roman remains**, **Orange**, **Vaison-la-Romaine**, **Carpentras**, **Arles** and **Nîmes** are the places to visit.

You can follow **Napoléon's journey** in 1815 from Elba to Paris between Grasse and Sisteron. Or you can trace the **transhumance routes** through the mountains, happening on flocks of sheep accompanied by goats, donkeys and the shepherds. You can watch **wildlife**: flamingoes, bulls and white horses in the strange flatlands of the **Camargue**, or chamois, mouflons and marmots in the **Parc du Mercantour**. If **modern art** is your passion you must go to **St-Paul-de-Vence**, **St-Tropez** and **Hauts-de-Cagnes**; or **Nice** for Matisse and Chagall; **Biot** for Léger; **Antibes** and **Vallauris** for Picasso; and **Menton** and **Villefranche** for Cocteau.

When to go

Beware **the coast** at the height of summer. The heat and humidity can be overpowering and the crowds, the exhaust fumes and the costs overwhelming. For

swimming the best months are from June to mid-October, with May a little on the cool side, but only by summer standards. As for sunbathing, that can be done from **February through to October**. February is one of the best months for the Côte d'Azur – museums, hotels and restaurants are mostly open, the mimosa is in blossom, and the contrast with northern Europe's climate at its most delicious. The worst month is **November** when almost everything is shut and the weather turns cold and wet.

The same applies to **inland Provence**. Remember that the lower Alps are usually under **snow** from late **November to early April** (though recent winters have had snow in Nice followed by no falls on the lower ski-resorts). **October** can erupt in storms that quickly clear and in **May**, too, weather can be erratic. In **summer**, vegetation is at its most barren save high up in the mountains. Wild bilberries and raspberries, purple gentians and leaves turning red to gold are the rewards of autumn walks. **Springtime** brings such a profusion of wild flowers you hardly dare to walk. In March a thousand almond orchards blossom.

The only drawback with the off-seasons is the **Mistral** wind. This is a violent, cold, northern airstream that is sucked down the valley of the Rhône whenever there's a depression over the sea. It can last for days, wrecking every fantasy of carefree Mediterranean climes. **Winter** is its worst season but it rarely blows east of Toulon, so be prepared to move that way. And one last point: according to some current theorists, the south of France will be a desert in a hundred years. Unexpected changes to the normal **weather patterns** have already happened and it's no longer possible to predict the climate with the old certainty. Still, the chances of you shivering on Pampelonne beach at midday in July remain remote.

Average daytime temperatures

	Jan	Feb	Mar	Apr	May	Jun	Jul	Aug	Sep	Oct	Nov	Dec
Central Provence	12.2	11.9	14.2	18.5	20.8	26.6	28.1	28.4	25.2	22.1	16.8	14.1
Rhône Valley	7.4	6.7	10.8	15.8	17.3	25.6	27.6	27.6	23.5	16.5	10.4	7.8
Riviera/Côte d'Azur	12.2	11.9	14.2	18.5	20.8	26.6	28.1	28.4	25.2	22.2	16.8	14.1

Average sea temperatures

	May	Jun	Jul	Aug	Sep	Oct
Montpellier to Toulon	15	19	19	20	20	17
Ile du Levant to Menton	17	19	20	22	22	19

All temperatures are in **Centigrade**: to convert to **Fahrenheit** multiply by 9/5 and add 32. For a recorded **weather forecast** you can phone the Paris forecasting office at ☎45.55.91.09 (☎45.55.95.02 for specific inquiries).

PART ONE

THE BASICS

GETTING THERE FROM BRITAIN AND IRELAND

Getting to the south of France by car isn't difficult, though if you're starting from Ireland it is a long drive. Using an overnight Channel ferry and the autoroutes, you'd be hard pressed to make the trip in much less than 24 hours, although the *Shuttle* service through the Channel Tunnel can reduce the time by a couple of hours. If you are going to drive, far better to break your journey and arrive at your destination in daylight.

These days, **train travel** is a surprisingly swift (with *Eurostar* passenger trains cutting journey time to Paris), though not especially cheap, alternative. Going by **bus** or, of course, **hitching** is the most cost-effective means of getting there. If you shop around, though, **flying** may turn out to be the best bet, especially if your time is limited.

FLIGHTS

Flying to Provence or the Côte d'Azur is a real treat. For the last few hundred miles clear skies are assured, giving you breath-taking views of the Alps and the sea, and for most of the year there's the enveloping warmth when you get off the plane.

Nice and **Marseille** are the region's two airports, though unfortunately neither one is a particularly cheap destination. You're likely to find the best deals for Nice, which has the most charter traffic; Marseille caters mainly for business travellers, with flights often booked up weeks in advance. Flight times are around one hour 45 minutes from London, and there are quick and frequent bus links to the city centres. Alternative points of arrival include **Montpellier** and **Lyon**, and, slightly further afield, **Perpignan** and **Toulouse**. All have direct flights from London.

Flying from Britain to any of these airports, you have a choice between summer **charter** flights and year-round **scheduled** flights. Package holiday firms block-book charter flights, and sell the left-over seats cheaply to flight agents known as bucket shops. They have fixed dates for both outward and return flights and a maximum stay of one month. Scheduled flights are generally more expensive (though percentage reductions for children are bigger), and offer rather more flexibility.

Most regular travel agents can advise on both charter and scheduled flights, though you'll do well to contact some of the **specialist operators** detailed on p.4. Also worthwhile is a thorough check on the **classified adverts** in the Sunday newspapers and the Saturday travel sections of *The Guardian*, *The Independent* and *The Daily Telegraph*. If you want to fly from London, check the classifieds, too, in *Time Out* and *The Evening Standard*, or in the free travel magazine, *TNT*, found outside mainline train stations.

FLIGHTS FROM LONDON

There are always promotional and special fares on **scheduled flights** to **Nice**, making Apex fares (booked 2 weeks in advance, maximum one-month stay including a Saturday night), at around £250 return with most airlines, seem prohibitive. It's far better to keep a look out for **promotional fares** such as those offered by *Air France* which can go as low as £100 mid-week to £110 for a weekend return (stay one Saturday night, maximum one

> **FLIGHTS: HIGH AND LOW SEASON**
>
> **High season**
> June 1 to September 1
>
> **Low season**
> January to March
> September 2 to December 13

USEFUL ADDRESSES IN BRITAIN AND IRELAND

AIRLINES

Air France, 177 Piccadilly, London W1V 0LX (☎0181/742 6600).

Air UK, Stansted Airport, Stansted, Essex CM24 1QT (☎0345/666 777).

British Airways, 156 Regent St, London W1R 6LB (☎0181/897 4000).

British Midland, Donington Hall, Castle Donington, Derby DE74 2SB (☎0345/554 554).

RAIL AND BUS

British Rail International, 1 Victoria Station, London SW1V 1JY (☎0171/834 2345).

Eurolines, *National Express*, 164 Buckingham Palace Rd, London SW1W 9JP (all enquiries ☎0990/808080).

Eurostar, Waterloo Station, London SE1 8SE (reservations ☎0345/881881).

Eurotrain/Campus Travel, 52 Grosvenor Gardens SW1W 0AG (☎0171/730 3402; train tickets for under-26s only); and regional *Campus Travel* offices.

Le Shuttle, PO Box 300, Folkestone, Kent CT19 4QW (☎0990/353535).

SNCF (French Railways), 179 Piccadilly, London W1V 0BA (reservations ☎0345/300 003; train information ☎0891/515 477; premium rate 39–49p).

Wasteels, Victoria Station (by platform 2), London SW1V 1JZ (☎0171/834 7066). Train ticket specialists: youth/student fares, standard tickets and senior fares; also bus tickets and flights.

SPECIALIST AGENCIES FOR INDEPENDENT TRAVEL

Campus Travel, 52 Grosvenor Gardens, London SW1W 0AG (☎0171/730 3402); 541 Bristol Rd, Bournbrook, Selly Oak, Birmingham B29 6AU (☎0121/414 1848); 39 Queens Rd, Clifton, Bristol BS8 1QE (☎0117/929 2494); 5 Emmanuel St, Cambridge CB1 1NE (☎01223/324283); 53 Forest Rd, Edinburgh EH1 2QP (☎0131/668 3303); 105–106 St Aldates, Oxford OX1 1DD (☎01865/242067).
Branches at YHA Adventure shops and university campuses. Student/youth specialists.

Council Travel, 28a Poland St, London W1V 3DB (☎0171/287 3337).
Several offices around France.

Nouvelles Frontières, 11 Blenheim St, London W1Y 9LE (☎ 071/629 7772).
France's largest tour operator with over 200 agencies world-wide.

STA Travel, 86 Old Brompton Rd, London SW7 3LH and 117 Euston Rd, London NW1 2SX (☎0171/361 6161); 75 Deansgate, Manchester M3 2BW (☎061/834 0668); 88 Vicar Lane, Leeds LS1 7J (☎ 0113/244 9212); 25 Queens Rd, Bristol BS8 1QE (☎ 0117/929 4399); 38 Sidney St, Cambridge CB2 3HX (☎01223/36 6966); 36 George St, Oxford OX1 2OJ.
Global independent travel specialist.

South Coast Student Travel, 61 Ditchling Rd, Brighton, E Sussex BN1 4SD (☎01273/570226).
Plenty to offer non-students as well.

USEFUL ADDRESSES IN IRELAND

Aer Lingus, 42 Grafton St, Dublin (☎01/844 4747); 46–48 Castle St, Belfast B21 1HB (☎0645/737747).

British Airways, 60 Dawson St, Dublin 2 (free phone ☎0800/626747); 9 Fountain Centre, College St, Belfast BT1 6ET (☎0345/222111).

Budget Travel, 134 Lower Baggot St, Dublin 2 (☎01/661 1866).

French Holiday Centre, 3 Malboro St, Cork (☎021/252725).

USIT, 19/21 Aston Quay, O'Connell Bridge, Dublin 2 (☎01/679 6833); 10–11 Market Parade, Patrick St, Cork (☎021/270900); Fountain Centre, College St, Belfast BT1 6ET (☎01232/324073).

Note that addresses and telephone numbers may not be in the same location: some airlines and agents use a single telephone-sales number for several offices.

month) in off-peak times, with summer prices of around £200 for *Discover France* fares. Quite a saving when you consider that in summer, a scheduled *Air France* Apex ticket (maximum 3 months), would set you back £320 return.

For a more changeable ticket, the *Eurobudget* at £400 is open for one year – it's a particularly good deal for under-25s.

Air France have one flight daily from Heathrow to Nice and four weekly from Gatwick to Marseille (daily in summer).

British Airways have more frequent flights: direct to Nice from Heathrow (3 daily), Gatwick (1 daily) and Manchester (1 weekly), and Gatwick to Marseille (3 daily). Keep an eye out for their *World Offer* tickets – with return flights to Marseille from £180, and to Nice from £205.

British Midland fly twice daily from Heathrow to Nice; their lowest offered ticket is £100 midweek low season, £110 for weekend departures.

Air UK offer scheduled flights out of Stansted flying twice weekly to Nice, daily from March to the end of September; low-season tickets are available for £125 to £135 return, but again a standard ticket is around £250.

Charter flights to **Nice** are available from mid-May to September and start from around £145, though by phoning around bucket shops like the *Charter Flight Centre* (☎0171/931 0504), you might strike it lucky and get a cheaper last-minute deal. However, for July and August, it's best to book far in advance.

Full-time **students** or those **under 26** can take advantage of discounted flights from agents such as *Campus Travel* and *STA* (see p.4).

AIR AND RAIL

Air France have a deal with *SNCF*, the French state rail network, whereby you **fly direct to Paris** then take a **train on to Provence**. Departures are from any one of twelve UK or Irish airports. Using the ultra-fast *TGV* (see p.6) you can get from Paris to Marseille in just four hours forty minutes for around £200. To Nice and St-Raphaël prices are a little higher. For details contact *Air France Holidays* (see p.7). There are special rates for children.

Now that the *TGV* station at **Roissy Charles-de Gaulle Airport** is open, you can continue your journey by train to southeastern destinations without having to go via the centre of Paris.

Alternatively you can book a charter flight from **Paris to Nice** through the London office of *Nouvelles Frontières* (see p.4) along with either a flight or a cheap train ticket to Paris.

OTHER DEALS OUTSIDE LONDON

Scheduled direct flights from British regional airports are very expensive, and unless you can take advantage of the ***Air France* rail tickets** (see opposite), and **student/under-26 discounted scheduled flights** from Manchester to Nice (available from *Campus Travel*, with *BA* at £170 direct and *Air France* at £200 with a change in Paris), it usually pays to go to London and then fly on to France from there.

Regional **charters** do exist, but availability is a big problem and prices are unfavourable in relation to London flights, even taking into account the added cost of travelling to Gatwick or Stansted.

It's also worth considering a **package deal**, which can offer exceptionally cheap travel even if you go it alone on the actual holiday. See the box on p.7 for contacts.

FLIGHTS FROM IRELAND

You cannot fly direct to **Nice** and **Marseille** either from **Dublin** or **Belfast**, but must go via **London** or **Paris**. *Air France Holidays* (see p.7) have package deals including flights from Dublin and Belfast, and *USIT* can offer student flights to Nice from IR£230 in the summer and as low as IR£110 in winter. Again, though, the best deal is likely to be the *Air France* rail ticket.

Alternatives **via Britain** are unlikely to be attractive considering the additional time factor and the cost of a flight from Ireland to Britain. For up-to-date details on the situation, try contacting *USIT* (see p.4), who are specialists in independent and student/youth travel.

GETTING THERE BY TRAIN

You can buy train tickets from large travel agents to get you from **any station in Britain** to **any station in Provence**. Most routes will involve going through London and almost certainly Paris – where you have to change from the Gare du Nord to the Gare de Lyon. For the London–Paris leg you can either take the ***Eurostar*** service through the Channel Tunnel, a journey of three hours, or catch a train to one of the southern ferry ports and then cross the Channel by ferry/hovercraft. From Paris there's the choice of an ordinary train or the world's fastest, the *TGV* (*Train à Grande Vitesse*). The fast track goes as far as Valence and on to

Marseille (soon to open), with *TGVs* continuing at slower speeds along the coast to Nice.

The opening of the Channel Tunnel has led to competitive cut-rate deals on **train and ferry/hovercraft** fares via Calais, Boulogne or Dieppe. Getting from London Victoria to Paris this way works out slightly cheaper than using the Chunnel, but takes considerably longer (6hr by hovercraft, 7–8hr by ferry) and is obviously less convenient, though services are frequent (up to 20 a day in peak season) and tie in well with the trains. By train and ferry the best deals are on the conveniently scheduled (though slightly slower) night services. Students and anyone under 26 can buy heavily discounted *BIJ* tickets from *Eurotrain* outlets (like *Campus Travel*) and most student travel agents.

The **Channel Tunnel** has slashed travelling time by train from London Waterloo to Lille (2hr) and Paris Gare du Nord (3hr). There are up to eight *Eurostar* high-speed trains (the high-speed bit happens once you hit France, with trains chugging it through England) a day running from London Waterloo to Paris Gare du Nord (3hr), and six trains a day to Lille.

***Eurostar* tickets** for London–Lille return cost around £64 for a second-class promotional advance fare or £72 if booked two weeks in advance. Tickets for London–Paris return can cost anything from £69 for a promotional advance fare (second class) to £229 first class pay-as-you-arrive (first-class seats come with airline-style service, meals included). All the prices quoted depend on the time of week and day, and the season. Generally, an advance second-class return, booked at least 14 days in advance and including a Saturday night stay costs £87; a more flexible advance ticket is £95. Available thirty minutes before departure, a *Leisure* ticket provides a seat in second class and must include a Saturday night stay for £125; sit in first class and be fed for £185, with the same conditions attached. There are now direct *Eurostar* services from Scotland, the Midlands and the North of England. Bookings can be made through high-street travel agents, by calling *Eurostar* direct (see p.4), or through *SNCF* (French Railways; see p.4) in London.

The ***TGV*** is a very attractive option and little more expensive than ordinary trains. The cost of the compulsory supplement – because everyone has to be seated when you're doing 170mph – varies: Paris to Aix-en-Provence is an extra 38–95F. You can reserve either when you buy your ticket in Britain, or by phoning the Gare de Lyon (☎43.82.50.50) or at the station just before you leave.

If you're heading for **Gap or northeastern Provence** you can take the *TGV* to Valence or Grenoble and continue west or south by ordinary train. For the **coastal resorts**, change from the *TGV* onto the normal schedules at Marseille, Toulon, St-Raphaël, Cannes, Antibes or Nice. ***TGV* journey times from Paris** are: 2hr 30min to Valence, 3hr 30min to Avignon, 4hr 40min to Marseille, and 7hr to Nice.

Special fare options include thirty percent discounted ***BIJ*** tickets, available for anyone **under 26** from *Eurotrain, Wasteels,* or any student travel office, not taking into account the various discounts available if you book in advance.

There are thirty-percent reductions for those **over 60** if you hold a **British Rail Senior Card** and a **Rail Europe Senior Card** (from *Wasteels* or major travel agents). There are also discounts available with the various rail passes, detailed below.

RAIL PASSES

If you plan to use the rail network a great deal in Provence, or to visit other regions of France, you might do well to consider buying a *Eurodomino* or *Eurail* pass.

The ***Eurodomino*** pass, available from *SNCF* (see box on p.4) and some major travel agents, offers unlimited travel (including, with normal supplements, the *TGV*) throughout France for any three, five, or ten days during a period of one month. There are substantial reductions for those under 26, plus reductions on *Eurostar* and *Hoverspeed* Channel crossings. For three days, a pass costs £105 (adult) or £85 (youth); for five days, £135 (adult) or £110 (youth); for ten days, £205 (adult) or £175 (youth). If you have a *Senior Citizen's Railcard*, you can extend it by buying a *Rail Europe Senior Card* (see above) to cover most of western Europe and get thirty- to fifty-percent reductions when buying train tickets.

If your trip to France is part of a bigger trawl through Europe, look to buying a continent-wide pass like the **InterRail** (for those based in Britain and Ireland) or the **Eurail** (for North Americans and Antipodeans; see p.13 and p.17). Neither pass is valid on trains in Great Britain and Northern Ireland, but will help you get across to France more cheaply, with substantial discounts on *Eurostar* and on Channel ferries. Once you get to France, you will still have to pay seat reservation supplements if you wish to use the *TGV*.

An *InterRail* pass can cover the length and breadth of Europe if you buy an "All Zones Pass" (£277 for one month), but you can pick and choose from a combination of seven geographical zones. Any one zone costs £185 for fifteen days, any two zones £220 for one month, while three zones cost £246 for one months' travel. You need to be under 26 years of age to qualify and to have been resident in Europe for at least six months. Unfortunately, the *InterRail* "26 plus pass" excludes France.

Eurail passes are available to people of all ages, and do offer unlimited rail travel in France – plus sixteen other countries. Strictly speaking,

TOUR AND ACCOMMODATION OPERATORS IN THE UK

Any travel agent will be able to provide details of **packages** in France, though some of the following are available only direct to the public. As many include ferry crossings (occasionally flights) in the deal, they can be very good value especially for a family or large group. In addition to this selection, more complete lists are available from the **French Government Tourist Office**, 178 Piccadilly, London W1V 0AL (Mon–Fri 9am–5pm; *France Information Line* ☎0891/244 123 Mon–Fri 9am–10pm, Sat 9am–5pm). The same address is good for *Gîtes de France* (☎0171/493 3480), still one of the main sources of cottage rental.

Air France Holidays ☎0181/742 3377.
Flight and accommodation, fly-drive and air-and-rail packages. Flight plus a week in a hotel in Nice for two from £470.

The Alternative Travel Group ☎01865/251195.
"Walking through History" tours in Provence.

Belle France ☎01892/890885.
Walking tours in Haute Provence; emphasis on food and family hotels.

Canvas Holidays ☎01383/621000.
France specialists: great camping packages and lots of sites .

CEI French Centre ☎0171/734 7224.
French language courses year-round in Aix-en-Provence, Avignon, Cannes and Nice. Prices include tuition and accommodation: from £290 a week in Avignon to £1180 for four weeks in Cannes.

Club Cantabrica Holidays ☎01727/866177.
Specializing in the upmarket end of outdoor holidays: mobile homes, caravans and campsites. Also, air, bus or self-drive packages.

Cresta Holidays ☎0161/927 7000.
Flight-drive hotel or apartment packages to many destinations on the coast.

Dominique's Villas ☎0171/738 8772.
Upmarket agency with a diverse and tempting range of properties, mostly for large groups.

Drive France ☎0181/395 8888.
Gîtes, cottages and farmhouses for rent along the Rhône Valley and in the Vaucluse.

Eurocamp ☎01565/626262.
Family holiday specialist offers camping packages with a selection of sites in the south.

France Afloat ☎0171/704 0700.
Canal holidays throughout France, including the delta land of the Camargue. Cruisers from £530 per week in April to £930 in August.

Inntravel ☎01653/628811.
Upmarket intimate walking, cycling and horse-back riding holidays with expert local guides.

Keycamps ☎0181/395 4000.
Camping holidays and mobile homes. A two-week tent holiday on the Côte costs £390 for two adults and two children in high season.

La France des Villages/La France des Activités ☎01449/737664.
Off-the-beaten-track specialists with villas, farms and attractive chambres d'hôtes. Plus horse-riding and boating holidays.

Lagrange ☎0171/371 6111.
Apartments and houses at coastal resorts and at the foot of Mont Ventoux. From £170 a week for a studio in low season.

Martin Randall Travel ☎0181/742 3355.
Cultural tours led by specialists: from "Art on the Côte d'Azur" (one week £960); "The Romans in Provence" (6 days £850); to the Aix Musée Festival (one week £840). All prices include flights, three- to five-star hotels, half-board and admission charges.

NSS Riviera Holidays ☎01482/42240. *Chalets, mobile homes and cottages in and around St-Raphaël. Mainly self-drive.*

Susie Madron's Cycling for Softies ☎0161/248 8282.
Easy-going cycle holidays operator; starting point in St Remy de Provence. Seven-day tours with flight, accommodation, half-board, bike and back-up from around £850 per person.

Vacances en Campagne ☎01798/869433.
Self-catering specialist with a selection of apartments, cottages and large manor houses. High standards; not cheap, but good value.

non-European residents must purchase a *Eurail* pass before leaving home – but you can buy them in the UK if you've been here no more than six months. If you plan to be constantly on the go, you can purchase a *Eurail* pass for travel on consecutive days (£392 for 15 days, £510 for 21 days, £628 for 1 month, £864 for 2 months, £1100 for 3 months), or for a more leisurely pace, opt for a *Flexipass*, allowing a number of days travel in a two-month period (£274 for 5 days, £440 for 10 days, £582 for 15 days). If you're under 26, the *Eurail Youth Fare* gives you unlimited second-class travel (consecutive: £313 for 15 days, £456 for 1 month, £604 for 2 months; *Flexipass*: £201 for 5 days, £313 for 10 days, £425 for 15 days). Finally, there's the scaled-down version of the *Flexipass*, the *Europass*, which allows first-class train travel in France, Germany, Italy, Spain and Switzerland or three- and four-country combinations on any number of days from five to fifteen; prices range from £221 for a three-country pass to £523 for a five-country pass (5 days). The *Europass* youth pass, using second class, starts from £156 for four countries (5 days), ranging up to £379 for five countries (15 days).

For more detail on French train passes, some of which can be bought in London, see "Getting Around" on p.27.

GETTING THERE BY BUS

Travelling to Provence by bus saves around fifteen to twenty percent on rail fares. The journey, at around 23 hours, is tolerably comfortable, broken up by the ferry crossing, a couple of meal stops, and additional short halts for coffee.

The **route** is a direct run from London to Dover, ferry across to Calais, then down to **Nice** via Sisteron, Grasse, Cannes, Juan les Pins and Antibes; to **St-Raphaël** via Valence, Aix-en-Provence, Marseille, Toulon, Hyères and Fréjus.

All services are operated by *Eurolines* (☎0171/730 8235) and leave London's Victoria Coach Station three times a week, with an extra express service in summer. **Tickets** are available from any *National Express* bus station in Britain, and add-on fares are sold from any British destination. Sample return fares from London are £109 to Nice and £92 to Marseille.

BY CAR – AND LE SHUTTLE

The most convenient way of taking your car across to France is to drive down to Folkestone, load your car on the *Shuttle*, and be whisked through the Channel Tunnel in 35 minutes (plus 10min either side to load and unload), emerging at Sangatte, just outside Calais. The Channel Tunnel entrance is off the M20 at Junction 11A, just outside Folkestone. Because of the frequency of the service (24hr; every 30min 6am–midnight, then every 75min), you don't have to buy a ticket in advance. You're expected to sit inside your car in the carriages, although you can get out to stretch your legs. Though the *Shuttle* is a quick way to get to France, be warned that there have been instances of delays.

Tickets are available through *Le Shuttle's* **Customer Service Centre** (see p.4) or from your local travel agent. Fares, calculated per car, regardless of the number of passengers, are at their most expensive between April and July – when you should expect to pay around £147 for a five-day return ticket, or £133 each way for a standard ticket. There are also cheaper Apex prices at a twenty-percent discount, if you book sixty days in advance. Out of season, a five-day return is £70, a standard ticket £63 each way; day returns are available at £39.

If you don't want to drive far once you've reached France, you can take advantage of *SNCF's Motorail* (☎0171/203 7000), putting your car on the train in Calais or Paris. Prices, however, are prohibitive; in summer, Calais to Nice, for example, costs £518 return for car and driver, plus £101 for an additional adult and £50 for children between four and eleven. Since the fourteen-hour trip is overnight, you're also looking at £24 per person, no child reductions, for an obligatory couchette – breakfast is included. Outside of peak holiday seasons, you'll pay £402 for car and driver, with slightly higher add-ons of £112 per extra adult and £56 per child.

BY CAR – AND THE FERRIES

Though you can meander through Normandy, the Loire and the Massif Central to get to Provence, the most direct **driving routes** go south from Paris, which is most easily reached from the ports of Calais, Boulogne and Dunkerque. Dieppe is more expensive, and only an hour or so closer to Paris. Note that the **minimum age** for driving is 18. For more about driving in France, see p.28.

Any travel agent in the UK or France should be able to supply up-to-date **ferry schedules** and reserve space in advance (essential in peak

1996 FERRY DETAILS

Routes and Prices

	Operator	Crossing time	Frequency	One-way Fares Small car, 2 adults	Foot passenger
BRITTANY					
Portsmouth–St-Malo	*Brittany Ferries*	9hr	April to mid-Nov 1 daily; 2–3 weekly rest of year	£74–181	£21–44
Plymouth–Roscoff	*Brittany Ferries*	6hr	1–3 daily	£65–174	£19–41
NORMANDY					
S'thampton–Cherbourg	*Stena Sealink*	5–8 hr	1–2 daily	£74–188	£14–35
Portsmouth–Cherbourg	*P&O*	5–7hr	1–4 daily	£53–110	£19–32
Poole–Cherbourg	*Brittany Ferries*	4hr 15min	1–2 daily	£67–156	£18–39
Portsmouth–Caen	*Brittany Ferries*	6hr	2–3 daily	£70–155	£18–37
Portsmouth–Le Havre	*P&O*	6–7hr	2–3 daily	£70–150	£18–35
Newhaven–Dieppe (Catamaran)	*Stena Sealink*	2hr 15min	3–4 daily	£114–160	£26
Newhaven–Dieppe	*Stena Sealink*	4hr	2–4 daily	£66–136	£24
PAS-DE-CALAIS					
Folkestone–Boulogne (Catamaran)	*Hoverspeed*	55min	4–6 daily	£93–133	£22
Dover–Calais	*Stena Sealink*	1hr 30min	15–20 daily	£72–150	£26
Dover–Calais	*P&O*	1hr 15min	20–25 daily	£72–150	£25
Dover–Calais	*Sea France*	1hr 30min	10–15 daily	£110–155	£26
Dover–Calais (Hovercraft)	*Hoverspeed*	35min	9–14 daily	£124–181	£25
Ramsgate–Dunkerque	*Sally Line*	2hr 30min	5 daily all year	£63–147	£22
FROM IRELAND					
Cork–Roscoff	*Brittany Ferries*	14hr	March–Oct 1–2 weekly	IR£184–296	IR£50–74
Cork–Le Havre	*Irish Ferries*	22hr 30min	June–Aug 1 weekly	IR£220–285	IR£62–82
Rosslare–Cherbourg	*Irish Ferries*	17–18hr	1–3 weekly	IR£215–285	IR£57–82
Rosslare–Le Havre	*Irish Ferries*	21hr	2–3 weekly	IR£215–285	IR£57–82

Ferry operators in England and Ireland

Brittany Ferries
Portsmouth ☎0990/360360
Plymouth ☎0990/360360
Poole ☎0990/360360
Cork ☎0121/277801

Hoverspeed
Dover ☎01304/240241

Irish Ferries
Dublin 2 ☎016610511
Cork ☎021/504333
Rosslare ☎053/33158

P&O European Ferries
Dover ☎01304/212121
Portsmouth ☎01705/772244
Central reservations ☎0990/980980

Sally Line
Kent ☎01843/595522
London ☎0171/409 2240

Sea France
Kent 01304/204 202

Stena Sealink
Reservations: Kent ☎01233/647047
24-hour information ☎01891/500254

season). Or you can contact the ferry companies directly. Bear in mind that the Dover–Calais route has better ships than Dover–Boulogne, and that seasickness sufferers will find going by SeaCat very uncomfortable in rough conditions.

From **Ireland**, the best port to head for is Le Havre, which has excellent road links with Paris. Cherbourg is a long way west with more than 100km before you hit the highway to the capital.

GETTING THROUGH PARIS

It helps if you can time your journey so as not to arrive in Paris during the morning or evening rush hour, though this may be unavoidable.

Coming from Boulogne, Dunkerque or Calais, whether on the A26 and A1 *autoroutes* or on the N1, you'll hit the ringroad – the **boulevard périphérique** – at **Porte de la Chapelle**. Don't panic, but get onto this fearsome track, unless it is the rush hour (in which case you might as well head through the city with plenty of traffic-jam time to glance at the sights).

It doesn't really matter which way round the *périphérique* you go, though westwards is usually quicker. On a good afternoon you can be at the **Porte d'Orléans** in fifteen minutes. This is where you exit, following the **A6** *autoroute* signs to **Lyon** (there are no tolls for 40km).

You can avoid the *périphérique* **coming from the Normandy ports** on the A13 or N13. But you need to keep your wits about you as *autoroutes* cross, merge and divide after **Versailles**. Head towards Rungis and Orly until you see the signs for the **A6** and Lyon. If, inadvertently, you end up at the *périphérique* (at the Porte de St-Cloud most likely) turn right onto it and exit at Porte d'Orléans.

HEADING SOUTH

South from Paris, there are **two main routes**. Firstly, there's the **Autoroute du Soleil** (the **A6**, becoming the **A7** after Lyon) which runs all the way to Marseille, with the **Autoroute La Provençale** (the **A8**) continuing to Nice.

Alternatively, the **N7** takes a more westerly path to Lyon and then runs parallel to the highway down the Rhône Valley (outside Paris you leave the A6 at the first toll gate, signed to Nemours and Montargis). Chapter One of the *Guide* details routes from the Rhône valley into Provence.

The **distances** are about the same on either route: around 700km from Paris to Marseille. From Calais to Marseille is approximately 1100km. The N7 is much more relaxed (though not when all the world is on the road), and cheaper, since you pay no tolls; when traffic's thin you can make excellent time, and you get to see a great deal of French countryside. Following the *autoroutes*, beware that in total the **tolls** from Calais to Nice come to nearly £58.

The main **times to avoid** on the French roads are the last weekends in July and August, and the holiday weekend closest to August 15.

RIDE-SHARES AND HITCHING

If you want to cover the ground by car but want to avoid the very real dangers of hitching in France, and are prepared to pay something, it might be worth trying the **ride-share organization** *Allostop*. For a registration fee of 70F for one lift, they will put you in touch with a driver covering your route – to whom you then pay 20 centimes per kilometre. In Paris contact *Allostop* at 84 passage Brady, 10e (Mon–Fri 9am–7.30pm, Sat 9am–1pm & 2–6pm; ☎42.46.00.66).

If you are still determined to **hitch**, the route from Calais or Boulogne towards Paris is notoriously difficult. Getting lifts onwards to Provence is even harder. It has been done, but don't even consider it if you have only a short holiday – your time can too easily run out before you've had a chance to glimpse the sea. The best plan is to approach drivers on the ferry across from Britain. You might just get the promise of a lift before docking. Two **useful tips**: you'll almost certainly make better time heading straight to Paris and straight out again than trying to avoid it; and find out what *département* number your destination is. All car licence numbers in France end with these two figures and it means you can make extra efforts when you spot the right vehicle. Marseille is Bouches-du-Rhône (13), and the Côte is Var (83) and Alpes Maritime (06).

GETTING TO FRANCE FROM NORTH AMERICA

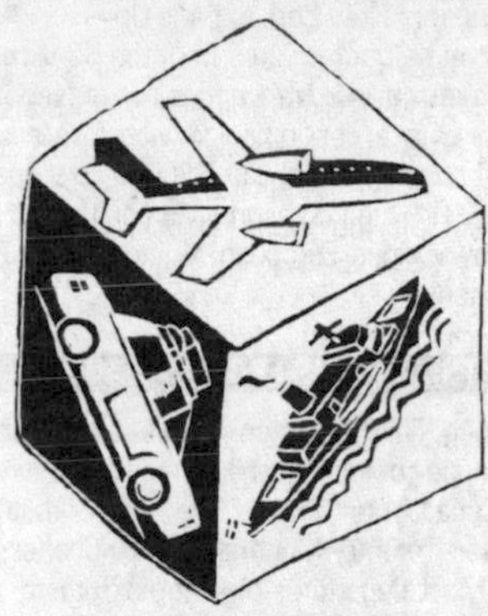

Getting to France from the USA or Canada is straightforward; there are direct flights from over thirty major US cities to Paris (the only trans-Atlantic gateway in France), with connections from all over the continent. Nearly a dozen different scheduled airlines operate flights, making Paris one of the cheapest destinations in Europe. In fact, only London can offer more discounted flights; and while a visit to England may appeal, the price difference is rarely sufficient to make a stopover in London a money-saving idea.

It's worth knowing that several outlets in the USA and Canada can do rail bookings and special passes for *SNCF French Railroads* (see p.14). Note that *Eurail* passes (see p.13) are also useful if France is part of a longer European trip, since you can use it to get from any part of Europe to France.

FLIGHTS

The cheapest fare on any scheduled flight is usually a non-refundable **APEX**, which normally entails booking at least 21 days in advance, travelling midweek, and staying for at least seven days (maximum stay 3 months). You also get penalized if you change your schedule.

Many airlines offer youth or student fares to **under-25s**; a passport or driving licence is sufficient proof of age, though these tickets are subject to availability and can have eccentric booking conditions. It's worth remembering that most cheap return fares involve spending at least one Saturday night away and that many will only give a percentage refund if you need to cancel or alter your journey, so make sure you check the restrictions carefully before buying a ticket. Apart from special offers, this is likely to be the best deal you'll get direct from an airline ticket counter.

The best guarantee of a cheap flight, however, is to contact a **travel agent** specializing in **discounted fares** (see p.13) or the travel sections of the *New York Times*, *Washington Post*, and *Los Angeles Times*. Restrictions on such tickets are often not all that stringent; you need not assume that youth or student fares are the best bargain, or worry if you're not eligible for them. The independent travel specialists ***STA Travel*** and ***Council Travel*** are two of the most reliable, but not surprisingly the French group ***Nouvelles Frontières*** has some good offers. These firms, together with several of the other larger agents, act as "**consolidators**" for particular airlines with which they maintain contracts to sell seats on specific terms, invariably below the airlines' own fares, though sometimes less conveniently.

Charter flights (a flight chartered by a tour operator from an airline to ferry tourists) are sold by most agents, and can be even cheaper for scheduled services. However, they tend to hedge you in with restricted dates and major financial penalties if you cancel. They're worth considering if you're very organized and know exactly what you plan to do.

If you're prepared to travel light at short notice and for a short duration it might be worth getting a **courier flight**. *Now Voyager* (☎212/431 1616) arranges courier flights to Europe from JFK, Newark and Houston. Tickets (from about US$400 round-trip) are issued on a first-come, first-served basis, and there's no guarantee that the Paris route will be available at the specific time you want.

Estimating the **cost of round-trip economy class fares** to Paris is tricky, especially as routes, carriers and the state of the market in general are changing all the time (see box on p.12).

FLIGHTS TO PARIS FROM THE US

Airlines are always running special deals, particularly from January to March when prices tend to be cut considerably. As an example, a low-season special fare out of New York to Paris is

FLIGHTS: HIGH AND LOW SEASON

High season
June 1 to September 15

Low season
January 1 to March 31
September 16 to December 13

around $330 midweek; the "normal" low-season price is $560 midweek.

The most comprehensive range of flights from the US is offered by ***Air France***, the French national carrier, which flies non-stop to Paris Charles de Gaulle airport from Anchorage, Boston, Chicago, Houston, Los Angeles, Miami, New York (JFK and Newark) and Washington DC – in most instances daily. The French airline, ***UTA*** operates three flights a week from San Francisco non-stop to Paris Charles de Gaulle.

The major American competitors are not much cheaper than *Air France*, and offer fewer non-stop routes. ***American*** and ***TWA*** have the biggest range of "direct" routes. *American* flies to Paris Orly non-stop from Chicago, Dallas, New York JFK and Raleigh-Durham, with a stop from LA (via Dallas), San Francisco (via Chicago) and San Diego (via JFK), and with good or guaranteed connections from fourteen cities in the south and west. *TWA* flies non-stop to Paris Charles de Gaulle from Boston, New York, St Louis and Washington DC, with one-stop flights from Chicago and LA and guaranteed connections (same flight number) from Atlanta, Kansas City, Portland, San Francisco and Seattle.

Delta and ***Continental*** both fly non-stop to Paris Orly. For airlines flying daily to Paris Charles de Gaulle, try ***Northwest*** and ***United***. Lastly, there are twice-weekly direct flights (often cheap) with ***PIA Pakistan International Airways*** from New York to Paris Orly.

You can be quoted fares from the US **directly intc Provence**: *Air France* flies out of New York to Paris, with a continuing service to Marseille (using *Air Inter* airline), for $660 in low season and $910 in high season. Montpellier is also served by various European airlines out of Paris and London.

SAMPLE ROUND-TRIP SCHEDULED FARES TO PARIS

Typical lowest discounted fares in low season, flying midweek.

Atlanta: $660
Boston: $520
Chicago: $648
Cincinnati: $660
Dallas: $730
Houston: $690
Los Angeles: $798
Miami: $650
New York: $540
Raleigh: $660
St Louis: $710
San Francisco: $760
Washington DC: $570

FLIGHTS TO PARIS FROM CANADA

The strong links between France and Québec's Francophone community ensure regular air services from Canada to Paris. The main route is Vancouver–Toronto–Montréal–Paris Charles de Gaulle. Most departures orginate in Toronto, with ***Air France*** flying almost daily to Charles de Gaulle, either non-stop or via Montréal foı about $600 in low season and $960 in high season. Again, you can fly direct to Marseille, with a stop in Paris for $855 in low season and $1100 in high season. The fares from Montréal are comparable. ***Air Canada*** and ***Canadian Airlines*** fly direct to Paris from Toronto and Montréal, again almost daily, and *Canadian Airlines* flies in from Vancouver twice weekly to guarantee the connection to Paris.

PACKAGE TOURS FROM THE US

Dozens of tour operators specialize in travel to France, and many can put together very **flexible deals**, sometimes amounting to no more than a flight plus car or train pass and accommodation; if you're planning to travel in moderate or luxury style, and especially if your trip is geared around special interests, such packages can work out cheaper than the same arrangements made on arrival.

Although phone numbers of tour operators are given in the box on p.13, you're better off making tour reservations through your local travel agent. An agent will make all the phone calls, sort out the details and arrange flights, insurance and the like – all at no extra cost.

FLYING VIA THE UK

Although **flying to London** has long been considered the cheapest way of reaching Europe, price differences these days are minimal enough for there to be little point travelling to France via London unless you've specifically chosen to visit the UK as well. Having said that, you may be able

AIRLINES AND TOUR OPERATORS IN THE USA AND CANADA

AIRLINES

Air Canada US toll-free number is ☎1-800/776 3000; ☎1-800/555 1212 for local toll-free number.

Air France ☎1-800/237 2747; in Canada ☎1-800/667 2747.

American Airlines ☎817/267 1151 or 1-800/433 7300.

British Airways ☎1-800/247 9297; in Canada ☎1-800/668 1059.

Canadian Airlines ☎1-800/426 7000; in Canada ☎1-800/665 1177.

Continental Airlines ☎1-800/231 0856.

Delta Airlines ☎1-800/241 4141; in Canada ☎1-800/555 1212 for local toll-free number.

Icelandair ☎1-800/223 5500.

KLM ☎1-800/374 7747; in Canada ☎1-800/361 5073.

Northwest Airlines ☎1-800/447 4747.

Sabena ☎1-800/955 2000.

Swissair ☎1-800/221 4750; in Canada ☎1-800/267 9477.

Tower Air ☎1-800/221 2500.

TWA ☎1-800/221 7702.

United Airlines ☎1-800/538 2929.

US Air ☎1-800/622 1015.

Virgin Atlantic Airways ☎1-800/862 8621.

NORTH AMERICAN TOUR OPERATORS

Abercrombie & Kent ☎1-800/323 7308.
Deluxe trekking, biking, canal, rail and skiing packages.

American Express ☎1-800/241 1700.
Packages and city breaks.

AESU Travel ☎1-800/638 7640.
Riviera packages for under-35s.

Backroads ☎1-800/462 2848.
Trendy bike tours.

Butterfield & Robinson ☎1-800/268 8415.
Trekking.

Contiki Tours ☎1-800/CONTIKI.
Vacations for under-35s.

Cosmos Tourama/Globus ☎1-800/338 7092.
Group tours and city breaks; Cosmos has the budget trips.

Daily-Thorp Travel ☎212/307 1555.
Specialist tours for the music festivals.

Euro-Bike Tours ☎1-800/321 6060.
Luxury bike tours.

Europe Train Tours ☎1-800/551 2085.

The French Experience ☎1-800/28 FRANCE.
Self-drive tours, apartment and cottage rental.

International Study Tours ☎1-800/833 2111.
Introductory sightseeing.

Mountain Travel-Sobek ☎1-800/227 2384.
Trekking specialist.

Saga International Holidays ☎1-800/343 0273.
Specializes in group travel for seniors.

Wilderness Travel ☎1-800/368 2794.
Trekking.

to pick up a flight to London at an advantageous rate: competition to fill seats in the trans-Atlantic skies is close to cut-throat these days.

In recent years, ***Virgin Atlantic*** has offered some of the best fares from New York, and has now added flights from Los Angeles, Miami, and Boston to its schedules (all into Gatwick). ***British Airways*** has entered the fray with a series of rival offers. In the summer, the savings are bound to be less, but shop around as there may yet be some European bargains. As well as JFK and Newark, *BA* has regular non-stop flights from Philadelphia, Boston, San Francisco, and Los Angeles – and from Detroit via Montréal.

TRAIN PASSES

Although there are a number of train passes available for travel within France, all of which are good value (details on p.27), a **Eurail Pass** makes most sense if you're planning to travel through other European countries as well. You can purchase *Eurail* passes from one of the agents listed overleaf.

A further alternative is to attempt to buy an *InterRail* Pass in Europe (see p.6) – most agents don't check residential qualifications, but once you're in Europe it'll be too late to buy a *Eurail* pass if you have problems. For more details on passes, see p.6.

DISCOUNT FLIGHT AGENTS AND CONSOLIDATORS IN THE USA AND CANADA

Air Brokers International ☎1-800/883 3273 or 415/397 1383.
Consolidator and specialist in RTW tickets.

Air Courier Association ☎303/278 8810.
Courier flight broker.

Airhitch ☎212/864 2000.
Standby-seat broker. For a set price, they guarantee to get you on a flight as close to your preferred destination as possible, within a week.

Council Travel ☎1-800/226 8624 or 212/661 1450; branches in many other US cities.
Nationwide US student/budget travel agency. A sister company, Council Charter ☎1-800/223 7402, *specializes in charter flights.*

Educational Travel Center ☎1-800/747 5551 or 608/256 5551.
Student/youth and consolidator fares.

Interworld Travel ☎305/443 4929.
Consolidator.

Moment's Notice ☎718/234 6295.
Discount travel club.

Nouvelles Frontières/New Frontiers ☎1-800/366 638; in Canada ☎514/526 8444; other branches in LA, San Francisco and Québec City.
French discount travel firm.

Now Voyager ☎212/431 1616.
Courier flight broker and consolidator.

STA Travel ☎1-800/777 0112; other branches in the Los Angeles, San Francisco and Boston areas.
Worldwide discount travel firm specializing in student/youth fares; also student IDs, travel insurance, car rental, rail passes, etc.

TFI Tours International ☎1-800/745 8000 or 212/736 1140; other offices in Las Vegas and Miami.
Consolidator.

Travel CUTS ☎416/979 2406; other branches all over Canada.
Organization specializing in student fares, IDs and other travel services.

Travelers Advantage ☎1-800/548 1116.
Full-service travel club.

Travac ☎1-800/872 8800 or 212/563 3303.
Consolidator and charter broker.

Travel Avenue ☎1-800/333 3335 or 312/876 6866.
Full-service travel agent that offers discounts in the form of rebates.

UniTravel ☎1-800/325 2222 or 314/569 2501.
Consolidator.

Worldtek Travel ☎1-800/243 1723 or 203/772 0470.
Discount travel agency.

Worldwide Discount Travel Club ☎305/534 2082.
Discount travel club dealing in packages and cruises only.

USEFUL RAIL ADDRESSES IN NORTH AMERICA

The **Eurail Pass** is the main discount rail deal available to Americans. For details contact *STA Travel* (see box above) or one of the addresses below.

BritRail Travel International, 1500 Broadway, New York, NY 10036 (☎1-800/677 8585).
UK passes, rail-drive and multi-country passes and Channel Tunnel tickets. Also sells ferry tickets across the Channel.

Canadian Reservations Centre, 2987 Dundas East, Suite 105, Mississauga, ON L4X 1M2 (☎1-800/361 7245).
Specializes in Eurail and other passes.

CIE Tours International, 108 Ridgedale Ave, Morristown, NJ 07962 (☎1-800/243 7687).
A prime source for booking rail travel in Europe.

Rail Europe, 226 Westchester Ave, White Plains, NY 10604 (☎1-800/438 7245).
Official Eurail pass agent in North America; also sells the widest range of European regional and individual country passes.

GETTING THERE FROM AUSTRALASIA

Although there are direct flights from Australia to Paris on *UTA*, it's generally easier and cheaper to fly to Britain and then make your way to France. *Qantas* doesn't fly to France at all, only using its connections with *Air France* in London. There are also alternative stopover points in Europe, often available at economical fares.

There are **no direct flights to Provence** from Australia or New Zealand. All routes require either a transfer or stopover in the carrier's hub cities. Alternatively pick up a cheap flight to London and then travel onto Provence by land or air. For cheap flights see "Getting There from Britain and Ireland" on p.3.

FLIGHTS FROM AUSTRALIA

From eastern cities to Provence in low season you can expect to pay around A$2250 and A$2900 in high season. From Darwin and Perth, low season costs A$2050 and high season is A$2700.

FLIGHTS: HIGH AND LOW SEASON

High season
May 16 to May 31
June 1 to August 31
December 1 to January 15

Low season
January 16 to end of February
October 1 to November 30

Some of the cheapest fares are with *Garuda* to Nice (via transfers in Amsterdam/Paris and Jakarta), which has several services a week from Adelaide, Sydney, Melbourne, Brisbane and Cairns; count on paying around A$1550 low season and A$2030 high season; from Perth and Darwin, it's slightly cheaper at A$1450/A$1930.

Aeroflot fly from Sydney to Marseille via Moscow once a week at A$1750/A$2120. *KLM* fly from Sydney to Nice and Marseille via Amsterdam for A$1780/A$2520. More expensive is *Air France-Qantas* with weekly flights from Sydney, Melbourne, Adelaide and Brisbane via transfers in Singapore and Paris at A$2050/A$2500.

Some airlines offer **fly-drive packages** and **free onward flights** to Provence; prices are about the same as the published fare. From Sydney, Melbourne, Brisbane, Adelaide and Perth: *Alitalia* flies to Rome three times a week (also from Cairns); *Singapore* to Paris or Rome several weekly; *Thai* to Rome or Paris three times a week (not from Adelaide); *JAL* to Paris or Rome from Cairns, Brisbane and Sydney only.

Contact a travel agent for the latest information on these limited special deals as they change constantly throughout the year.

FROM NEW ZEALAND

Flights to Provence from New Zealand are limited, with usual published fares at NZ$2400 in low season and NZ$3200 in high season. At the cheap end is *Garuda* flying to Nice twice weekly from Auckland via a stopover in Jakarta or Bali and a transfer in either Amsterdam or Paris for NZ$2110/NZ$2420. More expensive, but offering fly-drive and free onward travel to Provence are: *British Airways* to London several times weekly from Auckland; *Alitalia* to Rome several weekly from Auckland; *Cathay* to Paris once weekly or Rome twice weekly from Auckland; *Thai* to Paris or Rome three times weekly.

ROUND THE WORLD

Round the world routings that take in Paris use various combinations of airlines. For Provence, you'll need a combination that allows side trips. Six free stopovers are usually offered by participating airlines with additional stopovers around $100 each in Australia and New Zealand. Fares start from A$2400 for both Australia and New Zealand.

AIRLINES IN AUSTRALIA AND NEW ZEALAND

Aeroflot ☎02/9233 7911. No NZ office.

Air France ☎02/321 1000; in New Zealand ☎09/303 1229.

Air New Zealand ☎02/9223 4666; in New Zealand ☎09/357 3000.

Alitalia ☎02/9247 1308; in New Zealand ☎09/379 4457.

British Airways ☎02/9258 3300; in New Zealand ☎09/356 8690.

Cathay Pacific ☎02/931 5500; in New Zealand ☎09/379 0861.

Garuda ☎02/334 9900; in New Zealand ☎09/366 1855.

Japanese Airlines ☎02/9283 1111; in New Zealand ☎09/379 9906.

KLM ☎02/9231 6333; toll free 1-800/505 747. No NZ office.

Lufthansa/Lauda Air ☎02/367 3888; in New Zealand ☎09/303 1529.

Malaysian Airlines ☎02/364 3500; local call rate ☎13 2627; in New Zealand ☎09/373 2741.

Qantas ☎02/957 0111; in New Zealand ☎09/357 8900.

Royal Brunei Airlines ☎07/3221 7757. No NZ office.

Singapore Airlines ☎02/9236 0144; local call rate ☎13 1011; in New Zealand ☎09/379 3209.

Thai Airways ☎02/844 0999, toll free ☎1-800/422 020; in New Zealand ☎09/377 3886.

United Airlines ☎02/237 8888; in New Zealand ☎09/307 9500.

NOTE: *☎1-800 numbers are toll free, but only apply if dialled outside the city in the address.*

TRAVEL AGENTS

Australia

Accent on Travel ☎07/3832 1777.

Anywhere Travel ☎02/663 0411.

Brisbane Discount Travel ☎07/3229 9211.

European Travel Office ☎03/9329 8844.

Flight Centres ☎02/9241 2422; ☎03/650 2899; other branches nationwide.

France Accommodation ☎03/9877 6066.

France and Travel ☎03/9670 7253.

France Unlimited ☎03/9650 9892.

French and International Travel ☎02/299 8696.

French Bike Tours ☎03/9531 8787.

French Cottages and Travel ☎03/9859 4944.

French Travel Connection ☎02/956 5884.

Passport Travel ☎03/9824 7183.

STA Travel ☎02/9212 1255; ☎03/347 4711; toll free ☎1-800/637 444 ; other offices nationwide.

Topdeck Travel ☎08/8232 7222.

Tymtro Travel ☎02/9223 2211.

New Zealand

Budget Travel ☎09/309 4313; toll free ☎0800/808 040.

European Travel Office ☎09/525 3074.

Flight Centres ☎09/309 6171; ☎09/379 7145; ☎04/472 8101; branches countrywide.

STA Travel ☎09/366 6673; ☎04/385 0561; ☎03/379 9098; other offices nationwide.

Thomas Cook ☎09/379 3920.

OUTDOOR SPECIALISTS

Adventure World ☎02/956 7766; toll free ☎1-800/221 931; in New Zealand ☎02/524 5118.

Eurolynx in New Zealand ☎09/379 9716.

Exodus Expeditions toll free ☎1-800/800 724.

France Ski International ☎02/683 5185.

Snowscene ☎008/777 053.

Walkabout Gourmet Adventures ☎03/5159 5556.

Try either *Cathay Pacific-UA*'s "Globetrotter", priced at A$2350/NZ$3000, or *Air New Zealand-KLM-Northwest*'s "World Navigator" at A$2900/NZ$3500). *Qantas-BA*'s "Global Explorer" is A$2500/NZ$2400 in low season; A$3099/NZ$2999 in high season. *Thai Airways* combine with several carriers to provide a variety of routes worldwide for A$3000/NZ$3400. *Singapore-TWA*'s "Easyworld" fare, only available in Australia, allows unlimited stopovers worldwide and limited backtracking (flat rate A$3100).

For unlimited flexibility, *UA*, in conjunction with a variety of airlines, also offer an unrestricted RTW fare for around A$4500/NZ$4800.

AIR PASSES

Air passes, coupons and discounts on further flights within Europe vary with airlines, but the basic rules are that they must be prebooked with the main ticket, are valid for three months, and are available only with an international return fare with the one airline – for example, you have to fly to France with *British Airways* alone to be elegible for their airpass deals, costing around A$110 for each flight within France. *Air France* offer a **Euroflyer** for use in France and Europe at A$100/NZ$110 each coupon each flight.

Both airlines also arrange **fly-drive packages**; check with an agent for current deals as prices are very variable. *KLM*'s **Passport to Europe** uses coupons for single flights within Europe: three coupons for $410, up to six for $720; *Lufthansa* start at $380 for three coupons, with extra flights $110 each, to a maximum of nine.

TRAIN PASSES

There are a number of train passes available for travel within France (see p.27), which can be obtained through most travel agents or from ***CIT***, 123 Clarence St, Sydney (☎02/299 4754), which also has branches nationwide. There is no New Zealand office, so all enquires should go through the Australian offices.

However, the best value, if you are planning to travel through other European countries as well, is the *Eurail* pass (see p.6 for details). **Eurail** passes can be bought from A$730/NZ$820 (for 15 consecutive days) and *Eurail Flexipases* from A$510/NZ$570 (for 5 days in 2 months). *Eurail Youth Flexipasses* (for under-26s) are from A$455/NZ$510 (5 days in 2 months), and are available through *Thomas Cook*'s New Zealand (see p.16) and Australian offices, and most travel agents.

RED TAPE AND VISAS

Citizens of EU countries, Canada, New Zealand and the United States do not need visas to enter France, and can stay for up to three months.

All other passport holders (including British Travel Document holders) must obtain a visa before arrival in France. Obtaining a visa from your nearest French consulate is fairly routine, but check their hours before turning up, and leave plenty of time, since there are often queues. Australians can obtain a visa on the spot in London. Note that the British Visitor's Passport is no longer valid.

Three types of **visa** are currently issued: a transit visa, valid for two months; a short-stay (*court séjour*) visa, valid for ninety days after the date of issue and good for multiple entries; and a long-stay (*long séjour*) visa, which allows for multiple stays of ninety days over three years, but which is issued only after an examination of an individual's circumstances. Non-visa citizens who **stay longer than three months** are officially supposed to apply for a **Carte de Séjour**, for which you'll have to show proof of income at least equal to the minimum wage; EU passports are rarely stamped, so there is no evidence of how long you've been in the country. If your passport does get stamped, you can cross the border to Italy (a non-Schengen country) and re-enter for another ninety days legitimately.

Visa requirements for **Monaco** (an independent principality) are identical to those of France; there are no border controls between the two.

FRENCH EMBASSIES AND CONSULATES

Australia 492 St Kilda Rd, Melbourne, Vic 3001 (☎03/820 0921); 31 Market St, Sydney, NSW 2000 (☎02/261 5779); 6 Perth Ave, Yarralumla, Canberra, ACT 2600 (☎06/270 5111).

Canada *Embassy*: 2 Elysée, pl Bonaventure, Montréal, QUE H5A 1B1 (☎514/878 4381 to 87); *Consulates*: 1 pl Ville Marie, Bureau 22601, Montréal, QUE H3B 4S3 (☎514/878 4381); 1110 av des Laurentides, QUE G1S 3C3 (☎418/688 0430); 130 Bloor St W, Suite 400, Toronto, ONT M5S 1N5 (☎416/925 80441); 1201 736 Granville St, Vancouver, BC V6Z 1H9 (☎604/681 2301); 42 Sussex Drive, Ottawa, ON K1M 2C9 (☎613/789 1795).

Ireland 36 Ailesbury Rd, Dublin 4 (☎01/269 4777).

Netherlands Vijzelgracht 2, Amsterdam (☎20/ 624 8346).

New Zealand 1–3 Willeston St, PO Box 1695, Wellington (☎04/720 200).

Norway Drammensveien 69, 0224 Oslo 2 (☎02/ 41820).

Sweden Narvavägen 28, Stockholm 115–23 (☎08/63685).

UK *French Consulate General* (*Visas Section*): 6a Cromwell Pl, PO Box 67, London SW7 (☎0171/838 2050); 7–11 Randolph Cres, Edinburgh (☎0131/225 7954).

USA *Embassy*: 4101 Reservoir Rd NW, Washington, DC 20007 (☎202/944 6195); *Consulates*: 3 Commonwealth Ave, Boston MA 02116 (☎617/266 1680); 737 N Michigan Ave, Olympia Center, Suite 2020, Chicago, ILL 60611 (☎312/787 5359); 10990 Wilshire Bd, Suite 300, Los Angeles, CA 90024 (☎310/479 4426); 934 Fifth Ave, New York, NY 10021 (☎212/606 3621); 540 Bush St, San Francisco, CA 94108 (☎415/397 4330).

CUSTOMS

With the Single European Market you can bring in and take out most things as long as you have paid tax on them in an **EU country** and they are for personal consumption. Customs may be suspicious if they think you are going to resell goods. Limits still apply to drink and tobacco bought in duty-free shops: 200 cigarettes, 250g tobacco or 50 cigars; 1l of spirits or 2l fortified wine, or 2l sparkling wine and 2ls table wine; 60ml perfume and 250ml of toilet water.

COSTS, MONEY AND BANKS

The Côte d'Azur has a reputation for being excessively expensive and it certainly will be if you indulge in the quayside-cocktail-sipping, haute cuisine and nightclub-larking lifestyle that this coast notoriously caters for. Many, but by no means all, of the hilltop villages in Provence are equally geared up to the indulgences of the very rich. The major cities, including those on the coast, have budget options for accommodation and eating out that, as in the rest of France, are relatively low cost by northern European standards. However, prices do go up considerably in July and August, and the Côte d'Azur and Riviera are more expensive than the rest of the region.

For a comfortable existence, with a hotel room for two, a light restaurant lunch and a proper restaurant dinner plus moving around, café stops and museum visits, you need to **allow about 600–700F a day per person**.

However, if you are careful about watching the pennies, staying at a hostel (45–100F) or camping (25–60F a head) and being strong-willed about not sitting down in cafés, **you could manage on 180–250F**, including a cheap restaurant meal.

For two or more people **hotel accommodation** can be almost as cheap as the hostels, though a sensible average estimate for a double room would be around 300F. As for food, you can spend as much or as little as you like. There are large numbers of reasonable **restaurants** with three- or four-course menus for between 90F and 120F, with midday meals almost always cheaper than in the evening. **Picnic food**, obviously, is much less costly, especially when you buy in the markets and cheap supermarket chains. **Wine** and **beer** are both very cheap in supermarkets; buying wine from the barrel at village co-op cellars will give you the best value for money. The mark-up on wine in restaurants is high, though the house wine in cheaper establishments is still very good value. **Drinks** in cafés and bars are what really make a hole in your pocket – you have to accept that you're paying for somewhere to sit. Black coffee, draught lager and pastis are the cheapest drinks to order.

Transport need not be a large item of expenditure, unless you're planning to drive a lot in a gas-guzzling **car** using the highways. Petrol prices are around 6F a litre for leaded, around 5.7F for unleaded, and around 4F a litre for diesel; note that there are 3.8 litres to the US gallon. The French highways still have tolls, and these are particularly high in Provence.

French **trains** are good value (some sample approximate round-trip fares: Marseille–Nice 275F; Nice–Menton 48F), with many discounts available. **Buses** are cheaper, though prices vary enormously from one operator to another. **Bicycles** cost between 60F and 80F per day to rent.

Museums and **monuments** can make considerable dents in budgets. **Reduced admission** is often available for those over sixty, under eighteen, and for students under 26 for which you'll need the *ISIC* (International Student Identity Card). Several towns operate a global ticket for their museums and monuments. These are detailed in the *Guide*.

CURRENCY AND THE EXCHANGE RATE

French currency is the ***franc*** (abbreviated as F or sometimes FF), divided into 100 centimes. Francs come in notes of 500, 200, 100, 50 and 20F, and there are coins of 20, 10, 5, 2, and 1F, and 50, 20, 10 and 5 centimes. For as long as the French franc holds its strength the exchange rate for sterling, the US and Australian dollar is the most significant and unfortunate factor in the costs of holidays in France. At the time of writing the exchange rate has been hovering miserably around 7.3F to the pound, 5F to the US dollar, 3.7F to the Canadian dollar and 3.6F for the Australian dollar. The franc may well have to devalue which will benefit the pound most of all, then the Canadian dollar, the US dollar less so and the Australian dollar hardly at all.

CHANGING MONEY

Standard **banking hours** are 9.30am–noon and 2–4pm, and banks are closed Sunday and either Monday or, less usually, Saturday. **Rates of exchange** and **commissions** vary from place to place – a 30F charge for changing 200F is not uncommon; the *Banque Nationale de Paris* usually offers the best rates and takes the least commission. There are **money-exchange counters** at airports and the train stations of all big cities, and usually one or two in the town centre as well; these often keep much longer hours than the high-street banks. You'll also find automatic money **exchange machines** which take dollars and notes of all European currencies but give a very poor rate of exchange. It would be a sensible precaution to buy some French francs before leaving. For cash advances, see p.20.

TRAVELLERS' CHEQUES AND CREDIT CARDS

Obtaining **French franc travellers' cheques** can be worthwhile: they can often be used as cash, and French banks are obliged by law to give you the face value of the cheques when you change them, so commission is only paid on purchase.

It is worth getting a selection of denominations of travellers' cheques. Make sure you keep the purchase agreement and a record of cheque serial numbers safe and separate from the cheques themselves. In the event that cheques are lost or stolen, the issuing company will expect you to report the loss forthwith to their office in France; most companies claim to replace lost or stolen cheques within 24 hours.

CONTACT NUMBERS

In case of credit card loss:

American Express ☎47.77.72.00.

American Express travellers' cheques ☎05.90.86.00.

Barclaycard ☎47.62.75.00.

Diners' Club ☎47.62.75.00.

Eurocard ☎47.62.75.00.

Visa ☎47.62.75.00.

All the above numbers are in Paris – dial 16.1 first if phoning from Provence.

Credit cards are also widely accepted for goods and services: just watch for the window stickers. *Visa* is the most universally recognized; *American Express*, *Mastercard/Access* and *Eurocard* less so. It's always worth checking, however, that restaurants and hotels will accept your card; smaller ones often don't, and even train stations in small towns may refuse them. Be aware that French cards have a smart chip and machines may reject the magnetic strip of British, American or Australasian cards, even if they are valid. If your card is refused because of this, we suggest you say *"Les cartes britanniques/americaines/canadiennes/de Nouvelle Zealand ne sont pas cartes à puce, mais à piste magnetique. Ma carte est valable et je vous serais très reconnaissant(e) de demander la confirmation auprès de votre banque ou de votre centre de traitement."*

Credit cards can also be used to get **cash advances** from banks and from cash-dispensing machines where the appropriate sign is displayed. For *Visa* cards (*Carte Bleue*), you can use the same PIN number as in Britain and the US. For *Mastercard/Access*, you need to apply for a special European PIN number before you go. If your credit card is also a **direct debit card**, you can use that facility where the cash dispensers show the *Delta* or *Switch* signs. This is the best way of getting money, with no commission charged.

Europeans can use **Eurocheques**, backed up with a card, which can be used for paying shop and restaurant bills in the same way as an ordinary cheque at home. With a PIN number, you can also use them in cash machines which show the same symbol as on your card. Although there is only one percent commission on each cheque, you have to pay an annual fee for the service of around £10, and you must apply for a card in advance. On the positive side, you can specify the exact amount you want and use the cheques in some places where credit cards are not accepted (though you'll have to write out the sum in French). It takes up to six weeks for the money to be deducted from your account. Also worth considering are post office **International Giro Cheques**, which work in a similar way to ordinary bank cheques except that you can cash them at post offices, which are even more widespread and have longer opening hours than banks.

Before leaving home, check with your bank or credit card company the number to ring if your credit card is **lost or stolen**. For some cards, you have to ring a number in your home country. The numbers in France featured above will tell you British or US contact numbers to ring if necessary.

HEALTH AND INSURANCE

Citizens of all EU countries are entitled to take advantage of French health services under the same terms as residents, if they have the correct documentation. British citizens need form E111, available from post offices. North American and other non-EU citizens have to pay for most medical attention and are strongly advised to take out some form of travel insurance.

Under the French social security system, every hospital visit, doctor's consultation and prescribed medicine is charged. Although all employed French people are entitled to a refund of 75–80 percent of their medical expenses, this can still leave a hefty shortfall, especially after a stay in hospital (accident victims even have to pay for the ambulance that takes them there).

To find a **doctor**, stop at any *pharmacie* and ask for an address. Consultation fees for a visit should be around 75–85F and in any case you'll be given a *Feuille de Soins* (Statement of Treatment) for later documentation of insurance claims. Prescriptions should be taken to a *pharmacie* which is also equipped – and obliged – to give first aid (for a fee). The medicines you buy will have little stickers (*vignettes*) attached to them, which you must remove and stick to your *Feuille de Soins* together with the prescription itself. In serious emergencies, you will always be admitted to the **local hospital** (*Centre Hospitalier*), either under your own power or by ambulance.

As getting a refund entails a complicated bureaucratic procedure and in any case does not cover the full cost of treatment, it's always a better idea to take out ordinary **travel insurance**, which generally allows full reimbursement, less the first few pounds or dollars of every claim, and also covers the cost of repatriation.

If you're travelling in your own car you may want to have breakdown cover which includes **personal insurance**.

BRITISH COVER

Bank and credit cards (particularly *American Express*) often have certain levels of medical or other insurance included, especially if you use them to pay for your trip. This can be quite comprehensive, anticipating anything from lost or stolen baggage and missed connections to charter companies going bankrupt.

If you're going to ski, rock-climb or engage in any other high-risk activities, the premiums will be higher, but definitely worth it – the cost of a mountain rescue can run into hundreds of thousands of francs; check carefully that any insurance policy you are considering will cover you in case of an accident. Note also that very few insurers will arrange on-the-spot payments in the event of a major expense or loss; you will usually be reimbursed only after going home. In all case of loss or theft of goods, you will have to contact the local police to have a report made out so that your insurer can process the claim.

Most travel agents and tour operators will offer you insurance when you book your flight or holiday, and some will insist you take it. These policies are usually reasonable value, though as ever, you should check the small print. If you feel the cover is inadequate, or you want to compare prices, any travel agent, insurance broker or bank should be able to help. If you have a good "all risks" home insurance policy it may well cover your possessions against loss or theft even when overseas, and many private medical schemes also cover you when abroad – make sure you know the procedure and the helpline number.

In **the UK**, travel insurance schemes to cover medical expenses and theft or loss are sold by all travel agents and banks, from around £45 a month: *ISIS* policies, from *STA Travel* or branches of *Endsleigh Insurance*, are usually good value. *Columbus Travel Insurance* also does an annual multi-trip policy which offers twelve months' cover for £125.

The *RAC* and *AA* offer car breakdown cover, including towing costs, labour, dispatch of spare parts and repatriation of the vehicle, plus medical expenses and loss of luggage or money, from around £100 for a family for fifteen days. Whichever policy you opt for, read the small print to see what is covered before signing up, although most are broadly similar. It is common for money and credit cards to be covered only if stolen from your person. If you have any other insurance policies – house and contents insurance, for example – you'll find some of the optional extra cover in travel insurance only duplicates what you already have at home. Remember that claims can only be dealt with if a report is made to the local police within 24 hours and a copy of the report (*constat de vol*) sent with the claim; addresses of the Commissariat de Police are given in the main towns and cities.

NORTH AMERICAN COVER

Before buying an insurance policy, check that you're not already covered. **Canadians** are usually covered for medical mishaps overseas by their **provincial health plans**, although they are unlikely to pick up the full tab in the event of an accident. Holders of official **student and youth cards** (see p.23) are entitled to accident coverage and hospital in-patient benefits. **Students** will often find that their student health coverage extends during the vacations and for one term beyond the date of last enrollment. Bank and credit cards (particularly *American Express*) often provide certain levels of medical or other insurance, and travel insurance may also be included if you use a major credit or charge card to pay for your trip. **Homeowners' or renters'** insurance often covers theft or loss of documents, money and valuables while overseas, though conditions and maximum amounts vary from company to company.

After exhausting the possibilities above, you still might want to contact a specialist **travel insurance** company; your travel agent can usually recommend one, or see the box below. Policies are comprehensive (accidents, illnesses, delayed or lost luggage, cancelled flights, etc), but maximum payouts tend to be meagre. In particular, ask whether the policy pays medical costs up front or reimburses you later, and whether it provides for medical evacuation to your home country. For policies that include lost or stolen luggage, check exactly what is and isn't covered, and ensure the per-article limit will cover your most valuable possession.

TRAVEL INSURANCE COMPANIES AND AGENTS

Britain

AA, shops throughout Britain (☎0345/555577).

Columbus Travel Insurance, 17 Devonshire Square, London EC2M 4SQ (☎0171/375 0011).

Endsleigh, 97–107 Southampton Row, London WC1B 4AG (☎0171/436 4451).

RAC Freephone (☎0800/550055).

STA Travel, 86 Old Brompton Rd, London SW7 3LH (☎0171/937 9921).

North America

Access America, PO Box 90310, Richmond, VA 23230 (☎1-800/284 8300).

Carefree Travel Insurance, PO Box 310, 120 Mineola Blvd, Mineola, NY 11501 (☎1-800/323 3149).

Council Travel, 205 E 42nd St, New York, NY 10017 (☎800/743 1823).

Desjardins Travel Insurance, Canada only (☎1-800/463 7830).

International Student Insurance Service (**ISIS**) – sold by **STA Travel**, 48 E 11th St, New York, NY 10003 (☎1-800/777 0112).

Travel Assistance International, 1133 15th St NW, Suite 400, Washington, DC 20005 (☎1-800/821 2828).

Travel Cuts, 187 College St, Toronto, ON M5T 1P7 (☎416/979 2406).

Travel Guard, 1145 Clark St, Stevens Point, WI 54481 (☎1-800/826 1300).

Travel Insurance Services, 2930 Camino Diablo, Suite 300, Walnut Creek, CA 94596 (☎1-800/937 1387).

Australasia

AFTA, 144 Pacific Hwy, North Sydney (☎02/956 4800).

Cover More, Level 9, 32 Walker St, North Sydney (☎02/9202 8000; toll-free ☎1-800/251 881).

Ready Plan, 141–147 Walker St, Dandenong, Victoria (toll-free ☎1800/337 462); 10th Floor, 63 Albert St, Auckland (☎09/379 3208).

UTAG, 347 Kent St, Sydney (☎02/9819 6855; toll-free ☎1800/809 462).

Premiums vary, so shop around. The best deals are usually available through student/youth travel agencies – *ISIS* policies, for example, cost $48–69 for fifteen days (depending on coverage), $80–105 for a month, $149–207 for two months, or up to $510–700 for a year. If you're planning to do any "dangerous sports" (skiing, mountaineering, etc), figure on a surcharge of twenty to fifty percent.

Most North American travel policies apply only to items lost, stolen or damaged while in the custody of an identifiable, responsible third party – hotel porter, airline, luggage consignment, etc. Even in these cases you will have to contact the local police within a certain time limit to have a complete report made out so that your insurer can process the claim. Note also that very few insurers will arrange on-the-spot payments in the event of a major expense or loss; you will usually be reimbursed only after going home.

Full-time students in North America are entitled through the **International Student Identity Card** (**ISIC**) to up to $3000 in emergency medical coverage and $100 a day for sixty days in the hospital, plus there's a 24-hour hotline to call in the event of a medical, legal or financial emergency. The card, which costs US$16 for Americans and Can$15 for Canadians, is available from *Council Travel*, *STA* and *Travel Cuts* (see p.22 for addresses).

AUSTRALASIAN COVER

Travel insurance is put together by the airlines and travel agent groups (see box on p.16) in conjunction with insurance companies. They are all comparable in premium and coverage. Adventure sports are covered – except mountaineering with ropes, bungy jumping (some policies), unassisted diving without an Open Water licence; check policy first.

In **Australia**, *CIC Insurance*, offered by *Cover-More Insurance Services*, with some branches also in Victoria and Queensland, has some of the widest cover available and can be arranged through most travel agents. A typical insurance policy will cost: A$180/NZ$210 for one month, A$260/NZ$300 for two months and A$330/NZ$380 for three months.

As with all policies, make sure that you are covered for any activities you might be planning, especially if you are trekking or skiing.

DISABLED VISITORS

France has no special reputation for providing facilities for disabled travellers, and for people in wheelchairs the haphazard parking habits and stepped village streets are serious obstacles. In the major cities and coastal resorts, there are accessible hotels, and ramps or other forms of access are gradually being added to museums and other sites. Public toilets with disabled access are rare. *APF*, the French paraplegic organization, has an office in each *département* which will be the most reliable source of information on accommodation with disabled access.

Public transport is certainly not wheelchair-friendly, and although many train stations now have ramps to enable wheelchair-users to board and descend from carriages, at others it is still up to the guards to carry the chair. In Marseille there is a special office which operates a transport system (see p.187). At the time of writing, cars with hand controls are not available for rent in Provence.

As far as **airlines** go, *British Airways* has a better-than-average record for treatment of disabled passengers; from North America, *Virgin* and *Air Canada* come out tops in terms of disability awareness (and seating arrangements) and might be worth contacting first for any information they can provide.

PLANNING A HOLIDAY

There are **organized tours and holidays** specifically for people with disabilities – the contacts (overleaf) will be able to put you in touch with any specialists for trips to France. It's important to become an authority on where you must be self-reliant and where you may expect help, especially regarding transport and accommodation. It is also vital to be honest – with travel agencies, insurance companies and travel companions. Know your limitations and make sure others know them. If you do not use a wheelchair all the time but your walking capabilities are limited, remember that you are likely to need to cover greater distances while travelling (often over rougher terrain and in hotter temperatures) than you are used to. If you use a wheelchair, have it serviced before you go and carry a repair kit.

Read your travel **insurance** small print carefully to make sure that people with a pre-exisiting medical condition are not excluded. And use your travel agent to make your journey simpler: airline or bus companies can cope better if they are expecting you, with a wheelchair provided at airports and staff primed to help. A **medical certificate** of your fitness to travel, provided by your doctor, is also extremely useful; some airlines or insurance companies may insist on it. Make sure that you have extra supplies of drugs – carried with you if you fly – and a prescription including the generic name in case of emergency. Carry spares of any clothing or equipment that might be hard to find; if there's an association representing people with your disability, contact them early in the planning process.

CONTACTS FOR TRAVELLERS WITH DISABILITIES

France

APF (*Association des Paralysés de France*), HLM Les Serrets, Manosque (☎92.72.34.37); 11 allée Alphée Cartier, Marseille (☎91.08.08.28); 90 av du Général-Nogués, Toulon (☎94.62.97.75), 3 rue du Marquis-de-Calvières, Avignon (☎90.89.41.92).

Britain

Access Project, 39 Bradley Gardens, London W13 8HE.
Information service giving details of disabled facilities throughout the world.

Holiday Care Service, 2nd floor, Imperial Building, Victoria Rd, Horley, Surrey RH6 9HW (☎01293/774535).
Information on all aspects of travel.

RADAR, 12 City Forum, 250 City Rd, London EC1V 8AS (☎0171/250 3222; Minicom ☎0171/250 4119).
A good source of advice on holidays and travel.

Tripscope, The Courtyard, Evelyn Rd, London W4 5JL (☎0181/994 9294).
Phone-in travel information and advice service.

North America

Directions Unlimited, 720 N Bedford Rd, Bedford Hills, NY 10507 (☎1-800/533 5343).
Tour operator specializing in custom tours for people with disabilities.

Information Center for People with Disabilities, Fort Point Place, 27–43 Wormwood St, Boston, MA 02210 (☎617/727 5540; TDD ☎617/345 9743).
Clearing house for information, including travel.

Jewish Rehabilitation Hospital, 3205 Place Alton Goldbloom, Montréal, PQ H7V 1R2 (☎514/688 9550, ext 226).
Guidebooks and travel information.

Kéroul, 4545 ave Pierre de Coubertin, CP 1000, Station M, Montréal, PQ H1V 3R2 (☎514/252 3104).
Organization promoting and facilitating travel for mobility-impaired people. Annual membership $10.

Mobility International USA, PO Box 10767, Eugene, OR 97440 (Voice and TDD: ☎503/343 1284).
Information and referral services, access guides, tours and exchange programs. Annual membership $20 (includes quarterly newsletter).

Society for the Advancement of Travel for the Handicapped (SATH), 347 5th Ave, New York, NY 10016 (☎212/447 7284).
Non-profit travel-industry referral service that passes queries on to its members as appropriate; allow plenty of time for a response.

Travel Information Service, *Moss Rehabilitation Hospital*, 1200 West Tabor Rd, Philadelphia, PA 19141 (☎215/456 9600).
Telephone information and referral service.

Twin Peaks Press, Box 129, Vancouver, WA 98666; ☎206/694 2462 or 1-800/637 2256.
Publisher of the Directory of Travel Agencies for the Disabled *($19.95), listing more than 370 agencies worldwide;* Travel for the Disabled *($14.95); the* Directory of Accessible Van Rentals *and* Wheelchair Vagabond *($9.95), loaded with personal tips.*

Australasia

ACROD (*Australian Council for Rehabilitation of the Disabled*), PO Box 60, Curtin ACT 2605 (☎06/682 4333); 55 Charles St, Ryde (☎02/9809 4488).
A body that provides lists of travel agencies and tour operators for people with disabilities.

Disabled Persons Assembly, PO Box 10, 138 The Terrace, Wellington (☎04/472 2626).
Provides details of tour operators and travel agencies for people with disabilities.

INFORMATION AND MAPS

The French Government Tourist Office gives away maps and glossy brochures as well as lists of hotels and campsites for the Provence–Alpes–Côte d'Azur region and for the five *départements*: Alpes-de-Haute Provence, Alpes-Maritimes, Bouches-du-Rhône, Var and Vaucluse. Some of these, like the footpath maps, lists of festivals and so on, can be useful.

TOURIST OFFICES

In Provence itself you'll find a **tourist office** – usually an *Office du Tourisme* (*OT*) but sometimes a *Syndicat d'Initiative (SI)* – in practically every town and many villages (addresses and opening hours are detailed in the *Guide*). For the practical purposes of visitors, there is little difference between them: *SI*s have wider responsibilities for encouraging business, while *OT*s deal exclusively with tourism.

From these offices you can get specific local information, including listings of hotels and restaurants, leisure activities, car and bike rental, walks, laundries and countless other things. Always ask for the free town plan. In the Alps they display daily meteorological information and have contacts for walking and climbing guides and ski schools. In the big cities you can usually also pick up free *What's On* guides. In small villages where there is no *OT* or *SI*, the *mairie*, or town hall, will often offer a similar service.The regional or departmental tourist offices also offer useful practical information (for addresses see "Sports and Outdoor Activities" on p.52).

MAPS

In addition to the various free leaflets – and the maps in this guide – you'll probably need a reasonable **road map**. For most purposes, certainly for driving, the most convenient is the *IGN* red series no. 115 (scale 1:250,000) which charts the entire area or the larger *Michelin* 1:200,000 no. 245. In the same scale in *Michelin's* yellow series you need no. 84 for the coast and Alpes Maritimes and no. 81 for inland Provence.

For exploring a particular area, and for **walking or cycling**, the larger *IGN* maps – their green

FRENCH GOVERNMENT TOURIST OFFICES

Australia BNP Building 12th floor, 12 Castlereagh St, Sydney NSW 2000 (☎612/231 5244).

Canada 1981 av McGill College, Suite 490, Montréal, QUE H3A 2W9 (☎514/288 4264); 30 St Patrick St, Suite 700, Toronto ONT M5T 3A3 (☎416/593 6427).

Ireland 35 Lower Abbey St, Dublin 1 (☎1/703 4046).

Netherlands Prinsengr. 670, 1017 KX Amsterdam (☎020/627 33 18).

Norway Storgaten10A, 0155 Oslo 1 (☎22/42 33 87).

Sweden Normalmstorg 1 Av, S11146 Stockholm (☎08/679 79 75).

UK 178 Piccadilly, London W1V 0AL (☎0891/244 123).*

USA 610 Fifth Ave, Suite 222, New York, NY 10020-2452 (☎212/757 1125); 645 N Michigan Ave, Chicago, IL 60611-2836 (☎312/337 6301); 9454 Wilshire Blvd, Beverly Hills, CA 90212-2967 (☎213/271 7838; Cedar Maple Plaza, 2305 Cedar Springs Blvd, Dallas, TX 75201 (☎214/720 4010).

**In Britain, the FGTO has an information service, EuropAssistance, on a premium rate (Mon–Fri 9am–10pm, Sat 9am–5pm; 49p peak rate, 39p cheap rate). This is much easier to get through on; brochures will be sent free of charge, and specific queries are quickly referred to the relevant organization.*

(1:100,000 and 1:50,000) and blue (1:25,000) series – are invaluable. For even greater detail *IGN* also do a 1:10,000 series (10cm on the map for every 1km on the ground). These maps can be bought at almost all newsagents and bookshops, and from some tourist offices.

If you're driving to Provence the *Michelin* map no. 989 is the best for the **whole of France**. A useful free map, obtainable from French filling stations and traffic information kiosks, is the *Bison Futé*, showing alternative back routes to the congested main roads.

MAP OUTLETS

UK

London: *Daunt Books*, 83 Marylebone High St, W1 (☎0171/224 2295); *National Map Centre*, 22–24 Caxton St, SW1 (☎0171/222 4945); *Stanfords*, 12–14 Long Acre, WC2 (☎0171/836 1321); *The Travel Bookshop*, 13–15 Blenheim Crescent, London W11 2EE (☎0171/229 5260); *The Travellers Bookshop*, 25 Cecil Court, WC2 (☎0171/836 9132).

Edinburgh: *Thomas Nelson and Sons Ltd*, 51 York Place, EH1 3JD (☎0131/557 3011).

Glasgow: *John Smith and Sons*, 57–61 St Vincent St G2 5TB (☎0141/221 7472).

Note: Maps by ***mail or phone order*** *are available from* Stanfords *(☎0171/836 1321).*

North America

Chicago: *Rand McNally*, 444 N Michigan Ave, IL 60611 (☎312/321 1751).

Montréal: *Ulysses Travel Bookshop*, 4176 St-Denis (☎514/289 0993).

New York: *British Travel Bookshop*, 551 5th Ave, NY 10176 (☎1-800/448 3039 or 212/490 6688); *The Complete Traveler Bookstore*, 199 Madison Ave, NY 10016 (☎212/685 9007); *Rand McNally*, 150 E 52nd St, NY 10022 (☎212/758 7488); *Traveler's Bookstore*, 22 W 52nd St, NY 10019 (☎212/664 0995).

San Francisco: *Sierra Club Bookstore*, 730 Polk St, San Francisco, CA 94109 (☎415/923 5500); *The Complete Traveler Bookstore*, 3207 Filmore St, CA 92123 (☎415/923 1511); *Rand McNally*, 595 Market St, CA 94105 (☎415/777 3131).

Santa Barbara: *Map Link Inc*, 25 E Mason St, Santa Barbara, CA 93101 (☎805/965 4402); *Pacific Traveler Supply*, 529 State St, CA 93101 (☎805/963 4438; phone orders: ☎805/965 4402).

Seattle: *Elliot Bay Book Company*, 101 S Main St, WA 98104 (☎206/624 6600).

Toronto: *Open Air Books and Maps*, 25 Toronto St, M5R 2C1 (☎416/363 0719).

Vancouver: *World Wide Books and Maps*, 1247 Granville St, V6Z 1E4 (☎604/687 3320).

Washington DC: *Rand McNally*, 1201 Connecticut Ave NW, 20003 (☎202/223 6751).

Note: Maps by ***mail or phone order*** *are available from* Rand McNally*(☎1-800/333 0136 ext 2111).*

Australasia

Adelaide: *The Map Shop*, 16a Peel St, SA 5000 (☎08/8231 2033).

Auckland: *Speciality Maps*, 58 Albert St (☎09/307 2217).

Brisbane: *Hema*, 239 George St, Qld 4000 (☎07/221 4330).

Melbourne: *Bowyangs*, 372 Little Burke St, Vic 3000 (☎03/9670 4383).

Perth: *Perth Map Centre*, 891 Hay St, WA 6000 (☎09/322 5733).

Sydney: *Travel Bookshop*, 20 Bridge St, NSW 2000 (☎02/9241 3554).

GETTING AROUND

If you want to visit the main cities then travelling by train will be the most reliable and economical means. You can then use the bus network to radiate out from the towns, though this is much easier in western Provence than the less populated east. By far the best way of getting around, however, is with your own transport, preferably motorized as much of the terrain is daunting for all but the most super-fit and super-muscled cyclist. Approximate journey times and frequencies for public transport can be found in the "Travel Details" at the end of each chapter and local peculiarities are also pointed out in the text of the *Guide*.

TRAINS

The main **rail line** in Provence and the Côte d'Azur links all the major cities of the coast and the Rhône Valley, with Marseille as its hub. From here a second major line runs north along the Durance Valley to Manosque and Sisteron on its way to Gap. From Nice a line runs north through Tende to Turin. From Avignon trains head west into Languedoc and to Marseille via Cavaillon. Nice and Digne are linked by the *Chemin de Fer de Provence* (a narrow-gauge line), which is a brilliant ride in itself, and connects with the main rail network north of Digne by bus. *InterRail* passes only give you a fifty-percent reduction on this line – the French rail passes are fully valid.

The French national rail company, the **SNCF**, deserves its reputation for efficiency. Trains are fast, frequent and reliable, and the system is more or less idiot-proof. All but the smallest stations have an information desk and *consignes automatiques* – coin-operated lockers big enough to take a rucksack.

Fares are reasonable. The ultra-fast *TGVs* (*Trains à Grande Vitesse*), which will soon be running at full speed to Marseille, require a supplement at peak times and compulsory seat reservations costing around 20F. When buying tickets, whether from automatic machines or the counter service, note that *TGV* ticket prices vary according to demand so, for example, a later train may be cheaper.

All **tickets** – but not passes (see below) – must be date-stamped in the orange machines at station platform entrances, and it is an offence not to "*Compostez votre billet*". Train journeys may be broken any time for up to 24 hours.

Regional **rail maps** and complete **timetables** are on sale at tobacconist shops. Leaflet timetables for a particular line are available free at stations. *Autocar* at the top of a column means it's an *SNCF* bus service, on which rail tickets and passes are valid.

DISCOUNTS AND PASSES

Within France, the *SNCF* itself offers a whole range of **discounted fares** on standard rail prices on *Période Bleue* (blue period) and *Période Blanche* (white period) days. A leaflet showing the blue and white (discount) periods is given out at *Gares SNCF* (train stations). A quota of discounted seats is available on all *TGV* trains, irrespective of the "period".

In addition to these discounts, couples can have a free **Carte Couple**, entitling them to a 25-percent discount on *TGVs* or on other trains if they start their journey on a blue-period day. Over-60s can get the **Carte Vermeil**, which comes in two versions: the **Quatre Temps**, which costs 140F and covers four journeys, and the **Plein Temps**, which costs 265F for unlimited travel. Both are valid for one year and offer up to fifty percent off tickets on *TGVs* as well as other journeys starting in blue or white periods. The same percentage reductions are available for under-26s with a **Carissimo** pass, which costs 180F for four journeys and 205F for eight, and is valid for one year. This pass also entitles the cardholder to secure the same ticket reductions for up to three travelling companions also aged between 12 and 25. Under-16s can obtain the same advantages for themselves and up to four travelling companions of any age by purchasing a **Carte Kiwi** costing 285F for four journeys and 435F for unlimited travel. These train passes can be bought through most travel agents in France or from main *SNCF* stations and in Britain from *French Railways*, 179 Piccadilly, London W1V 0BA in person or by credit card from *The Rail Shop* on ☎0345/300 003. For Europe-wide train passes, see p.6.

For anyone planning to travel **from Britain** to Provence and the rest of France, the **Eurodomino** pass (see p.6) offers unlimited train travel through France for any three (£105), five (£135) or ten (£205) days within a calendar month (under-26s pay £85, £110 and £175 respectively). The pass also entitles you to substantial reductions on train/ferry links to France. The *Eurodomino* pass is available from accredited *British Rail* travel agents and the *International Rail Centre* at London Victoria (see p.4).

In addition to being able to take advantage of the French passes, those coming directly **from the US** can buy the **France Railpass**, covering any three days in one month for $125 (second class) or $180 (first class).

BUSES

Provence is not as badly served by buses as many regions in France, with good networks radiating out from Aix and Nice, plus inland services between the two and along the coast between Toulon and St-Raphaël which do not duplicate train routes. In the least touristy areas timetables tend to be geared to **school and market needs** which usually means getting up at the crack of dawn to catch them. You may need to time your visit for a particular day of the week and fix up accommodation in advance.

SNCF buses are useful for getting to places on the rail network where the trains no longer stop; they are included on rail timetables. The rest of the bus network is run by a plethora of **private companies** that rarely manage to coordinate their services. Although most towns have a **gare routière** (bus station) – usually near the *Gare SNCF* – it's not necessarily used by all the operators. Instead of wading through the reams of different timetables get the ticket office to help you or ask at the local tourist office.

DRIVING

Provence is superb driving country, whether on the coastal corniches or the zig-zagging mountain routes. Driving allows you to explore remote villages and the most dramatic landscapes which are otherwise inaccessible, and roads like the **Route Napoléon**, the **Corniche Sublime** and the **Grande Corniche** were built expressly to give breath-taking views.

With a full complement of passengers the costs need not be excessive and the added ease of camping with a car or motorbike to carry the gear can allow you to save on the price of accommodation. **Fuel** costs around 6F a litre for leaded, 5.7F for unleaded, and 4F a litre for diesel; prices are lower at supermarket chains such as *Intermarché*.

All the **highways** (*autoroutes*) in Provence have tolls except for the urban stretches, the A51 between Marseille and Aix, and the A53 from Marseille to Martigues. Some sample charges are: Aix to Nice 83F; Aix to Sisteron 40F; Aix to Toulon 34F. The toll for the spur into Monaco is particularly dear (19F from Nice).

Car rental costs upwards of £170/$120 a week. It is usually cheaper to arrange from Britain or the US before you leave – *Holiday Autos* offer competitive deals on car rental in France. You'll find the big firms – *Hertz, Avis, Europcar* and *Budget* – at airports and in most big cities, with addresses detailed throughout the *Guide*. Local firms can be cheaper but you need to check the small print and be sure of where the car can be returned to. It's normal to pay an indemnity of around 1000F against any damage to the car – they will take your credit-card number rather than cash. You should return the car with a full tank. Extras are often pressed on you, like medical cover, which you may already have from travel insurance. The cost of car rental includes the compulsory car insurance.

All the major car manufacturers have garage/service stations in France – you'll find them in the Yellow Pages (*Pages Jaunes*) of the phone book under *Garages d'automobiles*. For **breakdown services** look under *Dépannages*. If you have **an accident or break-in**, you should make a report to the local police (and keep a copy) in order to make an insurance claim.

In **mountainous areas** fuel stations are few and far between so it's wise to carry a can. Many of the high passes are closed from mid-October to May, June or even July. Notices give you good

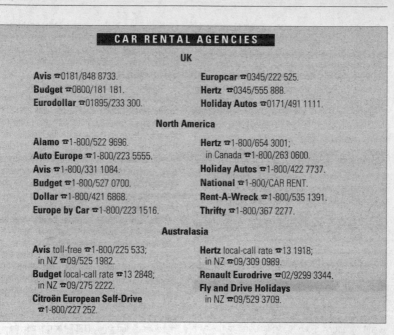

CAR RENTAL AGENCIES

UK

Avis ☎0181/848 8733.
Budget ☎0800/181 181.
Eurodollar ☎01895/233 300.
Europcar ☎0345/222 525.
Hertz ☎0345/555 888.
Holiday Autos ☎0171/491 1111.

North America

Alamo ☎1-800/522 9696.
Auto Europe ☎1-800/223 5555.
Avis ☎1-800/331 1084.
Budget ☎1-800/527 0700.
Dollar ☎1-800/421 6868.
Europe by Car ☎1-800/223 1516.
Hertz ☎1-800/654 3001; in Canada ☎1-800/263 0600.
Holiday Autos ☎1-800/422 7737.
National ☎1-800/CAR RENT.
Rent-A-Wreck ☎1-800/535 1391.
Thrifty ☎1-800/367 2277.

Australasia

Avis toll-free ☎1-800/225 533; in NZ ☎09/525 1982.
Budget local-call rate ☎13 2848; in NZ ☎09/275 2222.
Citroën European Self-Drive ☎1-800/227 252.
Hertz local-call rate ☎13 1918; in NZ ☎09/309 0989.
Renault Eurodrive ☎02/9299 3344.
Fly and Drive Holidays in NZ ☎09/529 3709.

warning. In **July and August** the traffic jams on the coastal roads can be horrendous, in particular between Hyères and Cannes, and Nice and Menton. For recorded information on **road conditions** call *Inter Service Route* on ☎91.78.78.78.

Car **parking** is usually free in towns between midday and 2pm; otherwise charges vary from 5F to 15F an hour.

And finally, if you smoke, never throw your cigarette-end out of the window. The undergrowth of Provence and the Côte d'Azur in summer is bone-dry kindling wood, and a single spark can start a raging **fire**.

RULES OF THE ROAD

British, EU and US **driving licences** are valid in France, though an *International Driver's Licence* makes life easier if you get a police officer unwilling to peruse a document in English. The vehicle's registration document (*carte grise*) and the insurance papers must be carried. If your car is right-hand drive, you must have your headlight dip adjusted to the right before you go – it's a legal requirement.

The law of *priorité à droite* – giving way to traffic coming from your right, even when it is coming from a minor road – is being phased out as it is a major cause of accidents. It still applies in built-up areas, so you still have to be vigilant in towns, keeping a look out along the roadside for the yellow diamond on a white background that gives you right of way – until you see the same sign with an oblique black slash, which indicates vehicles emerging from the right have right of way. "*STOP*" signs mean stop completely: "*CEDEZ LE PASSAGE*" means "Give Way".

Fines for driving violations are exacted on the spot, and only cash is accepted. Exceeding the speed limit by 1–30kmph can cost as much as 5000F. Speed limits are: 130kmph (80mph) on the tolled *autoroutes*; 110kmph (68mph) on two-lane highways; 90kmph (56mph) on other roads; and 60kmph (37mph) in towns.

HITCHING

Provence is one of the few areas in France where hitching is still fairly common, particularly along the coast in summer (see p.10). **Inland Provence** is less easy, though in the remote areas it's an accepted way for locals to get around.

In general, looking as clean, fresh, ordinary and respectable as possible makes a very big difference, as many a conversation with French drivers makes clear. Experience also suggests that hitching the less frequented **D-roads** paradoxically gets you to your destination more quickly. In **mountain areas** a rucksack and trekking gear often ensure lifts from fellow aficionados. When leaving a city study the map to find a train station on the road a few miles out and go there by rail.

Autoroutes are a special case; hitching on the highway itself is strictly illegal, but you can make excellent time going from one service station to another. If you get stuck at least there's food, drink and shelter. It helps to have *Michelin*'s *Guide des Autoroutes*, showing all the rest stops, service stations, tollbooths (*péages*), exits, etc. All you need apart from that is a smattering of French and not too much luggage. Remember to get out at the service station before your driver leaves the *autoroute*. The tollbooths are a second best (hitching there is legal), but ordinary approach roads are very difficult.

CYCLING

The French have a great respect for cycling – it's a national sport and passion. This shows in the warm reception given to cyclists and to the care and courtesy extended by French drivers (except in large cities where bikes are not normally used as a means of transport and on the corniche roads where everyone drives crazily fast). In Provence you'll see cyclists beetling up **mountains**, often overtaking heavy vehicles, but if you're not up to such strenuous pedalling the **Rhône Valley** is the only area that is consistently easy-going. The other things to bear in mind are the high summer **temperatures** and relentless frazzling sun. If you are willing to tackle inclines, however, cycling is a wonderfully sensual way to explore the region, and will get you fit very quickly.

Restaurants and hotels along the way are nearly always obliging about looking after your bike, even to the point of allowing it into your room. Most large towns have well-stocked retail and **repair shops**, where parts are normally cheaper than in Britain or the US. However, if you're using a foreign-made bike, it's a good idea to carry spare tyres, as French sizes are different. Inner tubes are not a problem, as they adapt to either size, though make sure you get the right valves.

The **train network** runs various schemes for cyclists, all of them covered by the free leaflet *Train et Vélo*, available from most stations. On *autorails* (when marked with a bicycle in the timetable) you can travel with a bike as free accompanied luggage. On *TGV*s and Corail coaches folding bikes or bikes with the wheels removed and packed in covers no bigger than 120 x 90cm (which you can buy at cycle shops) can be carried. Otherwise, you have to send your bike as registered luggage (135F parcelled up, 180F unparcelled; 15F for packaging). Although it may well arrive in less time, the *SNCF* won't guarantee delivery in under five days; and you do hear stories of bicycles disappearing altogether. *British Airways* and *Air France* both take bikes free. You may have to box them though, and you should contact the airlines first.

Bikes for rent – usually mountain bikes (*vélos touts terrains* commonly abbreviated

A CYCLING VOCABULARY

to adjust	*ajuster*	to deflate	*dégonfler*	rack	*le porte-bagages*
axle	*l'axe*	dérailleur	*le dérailleur*	to raise	*relever*
ball-bearing	*le roulement à billes*	frame	*le cadre*	to repair	*réparer*
battery	*la pile*	gears	*les vitesses*	saddle	*la selle*
bent	*tordu*	grease	*la graisse*	to screw	*visser*
bicycle	*le vélo*	handlebars	*le guidon*	spanner	*la clef (mécanique)*
bottom bracket	*le logement du pédalier*	to inflate	*gonfler*	spoke	*le rayon*
brake cable	*le cable*	inner tube	*la chambre à air*	to straighten	*rédresser*
brakes	*les freins*	loose	*dévissé*	stuck	*coincé*
broken	*cassé*	to lower	*baisser*	tight	*serré*
bulb	*l'ampoule*	mudguard	*le garde-boue*	toe clips	*les cale-pieds*
chain	*la chaîne*	pannier	*le pannier*	tyre	*le pneu*
cotter pin	*la clavette*	pedal	*le pédale*	wheel	*la roue*
		pump	*la pompe*		
		puncture	*la crevaison*		

to *VTTs*) – are often available from campsites, youth hostels and *gîtes d'étape*, as well as specialist cycle shops, some tourist offices and train stations. Costs are between 60F and 80F per day and around 240F a week. Deposits between 1000F and 2300F are required – you can give them credit card details rather than cash but make sure you get a proper receipt. The bikes are often not insured and you will be presented with the bill for its replacement if it's stolen or damaged so check whether you are covered for this by your travel insurance.

The best **maps** are the contoured *IGN* 1:10,000 series. In the UK, the *Cyclists Touring Club*, Cotterell House, 68 Meadrow, Surrey GU7 3HS (☎0483/417217), will suggest routes and supply advice for a small fee, and they run a particularly good insurance scheme.

MOPEDS AND SCOOTERS

Mopeds and **scooters** are relatively easy to find: everyone in France, from young kids to grandmas, rides one of these, and although they're not built for any kind of long-distance travel, they're ideal for shooting around town and nearby. Places that rent out bicycles will often also rent out mopeds; you can expect to pay 175F a day for a 50cc Suzuki, for example, or 220F for an 80cc motorbike. Crash helmets are compulsory only on machines over 125cc, but you'd be a fool not to wear one even on a moped.

WALKING

Provence has an extensive network of footpaths and some of the most rewarding trekking country, both in the mountains and in the coastal hinterland. There's the national network of **long distance footpaths**, known as *sentiers de grande randonnée* – **GR** for short – marked by horizantal red and white striped signs, of which numbers 4, 5, 6 and 9 plus various offshoots run through the region. The **national and regional parks** – the Camargue, the Lubéron and the Mercantour – have additional networks, and then there are the smaller paths and forest tracks, all usually well signed. Coastal paths exist but only in short stretches.

Each GR is described in a **Topo guide** (available in Britain from *Stanfords*, see p.26 and from bookshops and newsagents in Provence), which gives a detailed account of the route (in French), including maps, campsites, refuge huts, sources of provisions, etc. In addition, tourist offices can put you in touch with guides and organizations for **climbing and walking expeditions**.

Specialized walking maps are produced by *Didier Richard* on a 1:50,000 scale. These include *Alpes de Provence* (no. 1), *Mercantour* (no. 9), *Haute-Provence* (no. 19), *Au Pays d'Azur* (no. 26) and *Maures et Haut Pays Varois* (no. 25); they are available in most major bookshops in the region and from *Stanfords* in the UK (see p.26). For **French guide books** on walking, the best publishers are *Editions Edisud*. Many of the paths are mentioned in this guide, too, and some walks are detailed.

In July and August it's important to book a bed at the **mountain refuge huts** in advance. Phone numbers for many of the Alpine refuges are given in the *Guide*; you can also get lists from local tourist offices. Several are run by the *Club Alpin Français* which takes bookings from its office in Nice (☎93.62.59.99).

The warning to drivers about cigarette ends applies to walkers too. If you stub one out on the ground you must make sure that it is completely extinguished. Equally never light **fires**, however much you think a clearing is big enough for safety. You may find many paths and tracks have *defense d'entrée* signs in summer. These restrictions are to protect the forest from the risk of fire and should be respected – you can also be heavily fined if you're found on out-of-bounds paths.

ON THE WATER

You don't have to own a yacht to sail into the Côte d'Azur resorts. There are companies offering transport services from the *gare maritimes* (maritime ports) of many coastal towns, either out to islands or to neighbouring ports. Though not the cheapest way to get about, this can sometimes be the quickest when the summer traffic jams on the coastal roads are at their worst.

Trips down the Rhône are always slow and expensive. The boats tend to be of the Parisian *bateaux-mouches* variety – huge and ugly – and the deals often involve overpriced dinner-dance affairs. Inland, the **rivers of Provence** are harnessed to hydroelectric power stations and an extensive irrigation system. There are numerous barrages and water levels change at the flick of a switch (and with no warning). **Canoeing and rafting**, though possible in many stretches, should not, therefore, be undertaken without local guidance.

Details about boat trips and centres for canoeing and rafting are listed in the *Guide*.

ACCOMMODATION

Finding accommodation on the spot in the main cities of Provence and the Côte d'Azur is not a major problem except in July and August. At any time of year, though, booking a couple of nights in advance can be reassuring, saving the effort of trudging round and ensuring that you know what you'll be paying. Elsewhere, on the coast most of all, it's a different matter. The Côte d'Azur's summer season lasts from around mid-May to mid-September, and hotels, youth hostels and campsites are all stretched beyond their limits. The worst time of all is between July 15 and August 15 when the French take their holidays en masse. Your chances of finding anything then without advance booking become very slim indeed, though most tourist offices will do their best to help.

The problems are rather different **inland**, where the villages are often dominated by *résidences secondaires* (second homes) rather than hotels; those **hotels** that there are, and **bed and breakfast** in private houses (*chambres d'hôtes*), can get booked up well in advance. **Campsites**, however, are plentiful and rarely full once you're north of the Autoroute La Provençal.

Aside from the summer, the one bad month is **November** when almost all hoteliers take their holidays and the campsites are closed.

Phone numbers as well as addresses have been given in the *Guide* and the language section at the back should help you make a reservation, though many hoteliers and campsite managers, and almost all youth hostel managers, will speak some English.

HOTELS

Hotel **recommendations** are given in the text of the *Guide* for almost every town or village mentioned with a price range for each (see box below).

If you're travelling in peak season it's worth having as many addresses as possible. Local **accommodation lists** are available from tourist offices and lists for the Provence-Alpes-Côte d'Azur region and each individual *département* can be obtained before you leave from any French Government Tourist Office.

ACCOMMODATION PRICE CATEGORIES

All the hotels, youth hostels and guesthouses listed in this book have been price-graded according to the following scale, and although costs will rise slightly overall with the life of this edition, the relative comparisons should remain valid. Of the big cities, Marseille has the largest choice of cheap hotels; Avignon, Aix and Nice have a good choice of hostel-style accommodation. In the Côte d'Azur and Riviera resorts hotel prices often double in summer. If you are staying more than three days it's often possible to negotiate a lower price, particularly out of season. The prices quoted are for the cheapest available double room in high season, although remember that many of the cheap places will have more expensive rooms with en-suite facilities.

What you get for your money varies enormously between establishments. For under 250F the bed is likely to be old and floppy. There won't be soundproofing and probably no shower in the room though you may have your own toilet, bidet and washbasin. Over 250F the decor may not be anything to write home about, but rooms will have their own bath or shower and toilet, and perhaps even a TV and telephone and comfortable furniture. At more than 450F, you should expect a higher standard of fittings and something approaching luxury.

① Under 160F	② 160–220F	③ 220–300F	④ 300–400F
⑤ 400–500F	⑥ 500–600F	⑦ 600–700F	⑧ Over 700F

A very useful option, especially if it's late at night, is the **Formule 1 chain**, well signposted on the outskirts of several towns. Characterless motels, they provide box-like rooms for up to three people for 140F. With a *Visa*, *Mastercard*, *Eurocard* or *American Express* credit card, you can let yourself into a room at any hour of the day or night. Reservations can be made on ☎36.685 685 (premium call at 2,19F a minute). The hotels are not difficult to find as long as you're travelling by car, and a brochure with full details can be picked up at any one.

All French hotels are **graded** from **zero to four stars**. The price more or less corresponds to the number of stars, though the system is a little haphazard, often having more to do with ratios of bathrooms to guests than quality; ungraded and single-star hotels are often very good. At the cheapest level, what makes a difference in cost is whether a room contains a **shower**: if it does, the bill will be around 30–50F more. **Breakfast**, too, can add 25–80F per person to a bill – you will nearly always do better at a café but some hotels will insist on providing it. **Single rooms** are only marginally cheaper than doubles so sharing always cuts cost considerably. Most hotels willingly provide rooms with extra beds, for three or more people, at good discounts.

In high season many hotels demand ***demi-pension*** (half-board) which is not necessarily a bad deal, though it can get very boring eating in the same place all the time. Though it's illegal for hotels to insist on you taking meals when the cost is separate from the price of the room, many do and you may have little option but to agree. One plausible way out worth trying is to say you are *invité/e* (invited out).

Chambres d'hôtes

Chambres d'hôtes (bed and breakfasts in private houses) are fairly widespread, particularly in small villages. They vary in standard but are rarely an especially cheap option – usually costing the equivalent of a two-star hotel. However, if you're lucky, they may be good sources of traditional home-cooking. A selection are listed in the *Guide*; full lists are available from tourist offices and you can also find them detailed with *gîtes de France* and *gîtes d'étape* (see below) by *département* in leaflets available from French Government Tourist Offices and the larger tourist offices.

HOSTELS, GITES D'ETAPE AND REFUGES

At between 50F and 80F per night for a dormitory bed, **youth hostels** – *auberges de jeunesse* – are invaluable for single travellers on a budget. Some offer double rooms for around 100F, but it can be cheaper for couples, and certainly for groups of three or more people, to share a room in a hotel – particularly if you've had to pay a bus fare out to the edge of town to reach them. However, many hostels are beautifully sited, and they allow you to cut costs by preparing your own food in their kitchens, or eating in their cheap

YOUTH HOSTEL ASSOCIATIONS

Australia
Australian Youth Hostels Association, Level 3, 10 Mallett St, Camperdown, NSW (☎02/565 1325).

Canada
Hostelling International/Canadian Hostelling Association, Room 400, 205 Catherine St, Ottawa, ON K2P 1C3 (☎613/237 7884 or ☎1-800/663 5777).

England and Wales
Youth Hostel Association (*YHA*), Trevelyan House, 8 St Stephen's Hill, St Albans, Herts AL1 2DY (☎01727/855215); 14 Southampton St, London WC2 (☎0171/836 1036).

France
Fédération Unie des Auberges de Jeunesse, 27 rue Pajol, 75018 Paris (☎44.89.87.27).

Ireland
An Oige, 39 Mountjoy Square, Dublin 7 (☎01/830 4555); *Youth Hostel Association of Northern Ireland*, 22 Donegall Rd, Belfast BT12 5JN (☎01232/324 733).

New Zealand
Youth Hostels Association of New Zealand, PO Box 436, Christchurch 1 (☎03/379 9970).

Scotland
Scottish Youth Hostel Association, 7 Glebe Crescent, Stirling, FK8 2JA (☎01786/451181).

USA
Hostelling International-American Youth Hostels (*HI-AYH*), 733 15th St NW, Suite 840, PO Box 37613, Washington, DC 20005 (☎1-800/444 6111).

canteens. To stay at many of the hostels you must be a member of *Hostelling International* (*HI*), which currently costs £9/$25 for over-18s, £3/$10 for under-18s. Head offices are listed in the box on p.33. You can also join at *Fédération Unie des Auberges de Jeunesse* (*FUAJ*) hostels (100F for over-26s, 70F for under-26s) or buy a 19F "Welcome Stamp" which when you've collected six gives you international membership. If you don't have your own sleeping bag you'll have to pay around 16F for hire of bedding.

You'll find other hostels that do not belong to the *HI*, and in the main cities there are *foyers* or *résidences* – residential hostels for young workers and students – which often have age limits or are women only, and university accommodation, usually available only in July and August. Prices are rarely more than 100F for a single or double room and all are detailed in the *Guide*.

A third hostel-type alternative exists in the **countryside** throughout Provence, in the ***gîtes d'étape***. These are less formal than the youth hostels, often run by the local village or municipality (whose mayor will probably be in charge of the key), and provide bunk beds and primitive kitchen and washing facilities for around 40F. Designed primarily for people trekking or on bikes or horses, they are marked on the large-scale *IGN* walkers' maps and listed in the individual *GR Topo guides*, as well as in the *département* leaflets available from French Government Tourist Offices and local tourist offices.

In the mountains there are **refuge huts** on the main GR routes, open normally only in summer. They are extremely basic and not always very friendly places, and must be booked in advance in high summer (see "Walking" on p.31). Costs per night are around 90F for high mountain huts, 70F mid-mountain and 60F for those by a road. A list of refuge huts in the Alpes Maritimes *département* is available from the *Comité Départemental de Tourisme*, 55 promenade des Anglais, Nice (☎93.44.50.59) and for the Alpes de Haute Provence *département* from the *Comité Départemental de Tourisme*, 42 bd Victor-Hugo, Digne-les-Bains (☎92.31.57.29).

RENTED ACCOMMODATION: GITES DE FRANCE

If you are planning to stay a week or more in any one place it might be worth considering **renting a house**. You can do this by checking adverts from the innumerable **private and foreign owners** in British Sunday newspapers (the *Observer* and *Sunday Times*, mainly), or trying one of the many firms that market travel and accommodation packages (see the box on p.7 for a recommended selection).

The easiest and most reliable method, however, is to use the official French Government service, the **Gîtes de France**, based in Britain at 178 Piccadilly, London W1V 9DB (☎0171/493 3480), or in Australia, through *Explore Holidays*, PO Box 256, Carlingford, NSW 2118. Their guide contains properties all over France, listed by *département*. The houses vary in size and comfort, but all are basically acceptable holiday homes. There is a description of each one, and the computerized booking service means that you can instantly reserve one for any number of full weeks. Costs vary with sea-view houses on the Côte d'Azur and Riviera inevitably commanding very high prices. Inland you should be able to rent a comfortable house in the countryside with room for four to five people for around 2000F–2500F a week in July and August. *Gîtes Accessible à Tous*, also available from *Gîtes de France* (£7 plus postage) lists the *gîte* accommodation especially equipped for the disabled.

CAMPING

Most towns and villages have at least one **campsite** (notable exceptions being Marseille which has none, and Nice which has only one a long way out). Camping is extremely popular with the French and for those from the north of the country Provence is a favourite destination. The cheapest sites – at around 25F per person per night – are usually the **camping municipal**, run by the local municipality. They are always clean and have plenty of hot water, and often situated in prime positions. Some youth hostels also have space for tents.

On the **Côte d'Azur** campsites can cost three times regular prices for few (or no) extra facilities, and tend to be monstrously big. At full capacity in July and August they can be far too crowded for comfort. Most of the sites recommended in the guide are the smaller ones. Inland, ***camping à la ferme*** – on somebody's farm – is another (generally facility-less) possibility. Lists of sites are detailed in the French Tourist Board's *Accueil à la Campagne* booklet and are available from local tourist offices. You should make sure of what you'll be charged before you pitch up – it's easy to get stung the following morning.

Phone numbers for campsites are given in the text of the *Guide* so you can check ahead for space availability. We also give the French grading from one to four stars which indicates the sophistication of the facilities. As a rough estimate for a family of four with a car and caravan or tent, **prices** should be from 40F to 60F for one-star sites, 50F to 70F for two-star sites, 90F to 110F for three-star sites and 100F to 120F for four-star sites.

Camping rough (*camping sauvage*, as the French call it) is possible but you must ask permission from the owner of the land first. Farmers can be very nasty if you don't and their weapons include guns as well as dogs. In the remote areas of northeastern Provence, where it may not be clear who owns the land, you'll probably be OK but don't camp within the protected area of the Parc de Mercantour. Nor should you ever camp in the forests in summer. However careful you think you might be, it only takes one stray spark to start a galloping inferno, and both local people and police are vigilant.

Camping **on the beach** is standard practice only on certain stretches in the Camargue. Elsewhere you'll be vulnerable to theft and mugging; if the police arrive, arrests are not unknown.

If you're planning to do a lot of camping, an **international camping carnet** is a good investment, available from home motoring organizations, or from one of the following: in Britain, the *Camping and Caravan Club*, Greenfields House, Westwood Way, Coventry, CV4 8JH (☎01203/694995); *Family Campers and RVers* (*FCRV*), 4804 Transit Rd, Building 2, Depew, NY 14043 (☎1-800/245 9755) in the US; and in Canada, 51 W 22nd St, Hamilton, Ontario LC9 4N5 (☎1-800/245 9755).

The carnet serves as useful identification, covers you for third-party insurance when camping and is good for discounts at member sites. FCRV annual membership costs $20, and the carnet an additional $10.

FOOD AND DRINK

Food is as good a reason as any for going to Provence. The region has one of the great cuisines of France and some very fine wines in the Vaucluse, on the coast and at Châteauneuf-du-Pape.

For experiencing food and wine at their best, there's a phenomenal number of top gourmet **restaurants**, matched only in the rest of the country by Lyon and Paris. Many of these are cheap by British standards, their extravagance only relative to the prices of less elaborate but still gorgeously gluttonous meals you can have. Inevitably quality can suffer in some of the tourist hotspots, but if you take your time – treating the business of choosing a place as an interesting appetizer in itself – you should be able to eat consistently well without spending a fortune.

The **markets** of Provence (the best ones all detailed in the *Guide*) are a great sensual treat as well as lively social events. *Marchés paysans* are common where *paysans* (small-holders, the backbone of French farming) sell directly to the public.

Provence is also the homeland of **pastis**, the cooling aniseed-flavoured drink traditionally served with a bowl of olives before meals.

BREAKFAST AND SNACKS

A *croissant*, *pain au chocolat* (a choc-filled *croissant*) or a sandwich in a bar or café, with hot chocolate or coffee, is generally the best way to eat **breakfast** – at a fraction of the cost charged by most hotels. *Croissants* and sometimes hard-boiled eggs are displayed on bar counters until around 9.30 or 10am. If you stand – cheaper than sitting down – you just help yourself to these with your coffee, the waiter keeps an eye on how many you've eaten and bills you accordingly.

At **lunchtime** and sometimes in the evening, you may find cafés offering a plat du jour (chef's daily special) at between 40F and 70F or *formules*, a limited or no-choice menu. The *croque-monsieur* or *croque-madame* (variations on the toasted-cheese sandwich) is on sale at cafés, brasseries and many street stands, along with *frites, crêpes, galettes* (buckwheat pancakes), *gauffres* (waffles), *glaces* (ice creams) and all kinds of fresh sandwiches. For variety, there are Tunisian snacks like *brik à l'œuf* (a fried pastry with an egg inside), *merguez* (spicy North African sausage) and Middle Eastern *falafel* (deep-fried chickpea balls with salad). Local specialities include the Niçois *pan bagnat*, an oil-dripping bun stuffed with salad and fish, and *pissaladière*, an onion, black olives and anchovy flan.

Crêperies, serving filled pancakes from around 35F upwards, are very popular. But quality is very variable, as it is with the ubiquitous **pizzerias** *au feu du bois* (wood-fire baked).

For **picnics**, the local outdoor market or supermarket will provide you with almost everything you need from tomatoes and avocados to cheese and pâté. Cooked meat, prepared snacks, ready-made dishes and assorted salads can be bought at *charcuteries* (delicatessens), which you'll find everywhere – even in small villages, though the same things are cheaper at supermarket counters. You purchase by weight, or you can ask for *une tranche* (a slice), *une barquette* (a carton), or *une part* (a portion). You'll also find hot, whole spit-roasted chicken on every high street and at most markets.

Salons de thé, which open from mid-morning to late evening, serve brunches, salads, quiches, and the like, as well as gâteaux, ice cream and a wide selection of teas. They tend to be a good deal pricier than cafés or brasseries – you're paying for the posh surroundings. At ***pâtisseries***, along with the usual cakes, breads and pastries, you'll find *fougasse* or *fougassette*, a five-finger-shaped bread containing olives, anchovies, sausage or cheese, or flavoured with orange, lemon or rose water. *Chichi* (a light, scented doughnut) are sold from street stalls; the region's other classic sweet nibbler is nougat.

FULL-SCALE MEALS

There's no difference between **restaurants** (or *auberges* or *relais* as they sometimes call themselves) and **brasseries** in terms of quality or price range. The distinction is that brasseries, which resemble cafés, serve quicker meals at most hours of the day, while restaurants tend to stick to the traditional meal times of noon to 2pm and 7 to 9.30 or 10.30pm. After 9pm or so, restaurants often serve only à la carte meals – invariably more expensive than eating the set menu. In touristy areas in high season and for all the more upmarket places it's wise to make reservations – easily done on the same day. In small towns it may be impossible to get anything other than a bar sandwich after 10pm or even earlier; in major cities, town-centre brasseries will serve until 11pm or midnight and one or two may stay open all night.

When hunting, avoid places that are half empty at peak time, use your nose and regard long menus with suspicion. Don't forget that hotel restaurants are open to non-residents and often very good value. Since restaurants change hands frequently and have their ups and downs, it's also worth asking people you meet (locals not fellow tourists) for recommendations. This is the conversational equivalent of commenting on the weather in Britain and will usually elicit strong views and sound advice.

Prices and what you get for them are posted outside. Normally there is a choice between one or more **menus** where the number of courses has already been determined and the choice is limited. The *carte* (menu) has everything listed. *Service compris* or *s.c.* means the service charge is included. *Service non compris, s.n.c.* or *service en sus* means that it isn't and you need to calculate an additional fifteen percent. **Wine** (*vin*) or a drink (*boisson*) may be included, though rarely on menus under 90F. When ordering wine, ask for *un quart* (quarter-litre), *un demi-litre* (half-litre) or *une carafe* (a litre). You'll normally be given the house wine unless you specify otherwise; if you're worried about the cost ask for *vin ordinaire*. In the *Guide* the lowest price menu or the range of menus is given; where average à la carte prices are given it assumes you'll have three courses and half a bottle of wine.

PROVENCAL CUISINE

Intense sunshine combined with all-important irrigation make Provence one of the great food regions of France. Just about everything flourishes here but pride of place must go to the olive tree, introduced to Provence by the ancient Greeks two and a half thousand years ago, and perfectly suited to the warm, dry climate. Olives accompany the traditional Provençal aperitif of pastis; they appear in sauces and salads, on tarts and pizzas, and mixed with capers in *tapenade* paste spread on bread or biscuits. Olive oil is the starting point for almost all Provençal dishes. Spiced with chillies or Provençal herbs (wild thyme, basil, rosemary and tarragon) it is also poured over pizzas, sandwiches, and used to make vinaigrette and mayonnaise for all the varieties of salad, including the bitter leaves of the Niçois *mesclum*.

The ingredient most often mixed with olive oil is the other classic of Provençal cuisine, garlic. Whole markets are dedicated to strings of white and pale purple garlic. Two of the most famous concoctions of Provence are *pistou*, a paste of olive oil, parmesan cheese, garlic and basil, and *aïoli*, a garlic mayonnaise and the traditional Friday dish in which it's served with salt cod and vegetables.

Vegetables and fruit have double or triple seasons in Provence, often beginning while Northern France is still in the depths of winter. Ratatouille ingredients – tomatoes, peppers, aubergines, courgettes and onions – are the favourites, along with purple-tipped asparagus and baby potatoes. Courgette flowers fritters or stuffed with *pistou* is one of the most exquisite Provençal delicacies. As for fruits, the melons, white peaches, apricots, figs, cherries and Muscat grapes are unbeatable. Almond trees grow on the plateaux of central Provence (eaten when they are still green in summer) along with lavender, which gives Provençal honey its distinctive flavour.

Sheep, taken up to the mountains in the summer months, provide the staple meat, of which the best is *agneau de Sisteron*. But it is fish that features most on traditional menus. The fish soups of *bouillabaise*, famous in Marseille, and *bourride*, served with a chilli-flavoured mayonnaise known as *rouille*, are served all along the coast, as are whole sea bream, monkfish, sea bass or John Dory, covered with Provençal herbs and grilled over an open flame. Sea food, from spider crabs to clams, sea urchins to crayfish, crabs, lobster, mussels and oysters, are piled onto huge *plateaux de fruits de mer*, not necessarily representing Mediterranean harvests, more the luxury associated with this coast. October to April is the prime seafood season.

The one source of food unsuited to the dry heat of Provence is cattle, which is why olive oil rather than butter and cream dominate Provençal cuisine, and why the cheeses are invariably made from goats' or ewe's milk. Famous *chèvres* (goats' cheeses) are *Banon*, wrapped in chestnut leaves and marinated in brandy, the aromatic *Picadon* from the foothills of the Alps, *Poivre d'Ain*, pressed with wild savory, and *Lou Pevre* with a pepper coating.

Provençal cuisine is extremely healthy. A traditional meal should leave you feeling perfectly able to dance the night away, or, more prosaically, to pig yourself without fear of heart attack. Except of course for the famous chocolates, candied fruit and chestnuts, almond sweets and nougat, plus all the gluttonous ice-cream concoctions served with cocktails on the promenade cafés.

In the French sequence of **courses**, any salad (sometimes vegetables, too) comes separate from the main dish, and cheese precedes a dessert. You will be offered coffee, which is always extra (as much as 20F or more) to finish off the meal. You can specify if you like it strong (*serré*) or weak (*léger*).

At the bottom of the price range, **menus** revolve round standard dishes such as steak and fries (*steack frites*), chicken and fries (*poulet frites*), stews (*daubes* or a whole variety of other terms) and various concoctions involving innards such as *pieds et paquets* (feet and tripe of sheep). If you're simply not that hungry, just go for the plat du jour.

Going **à la carte** offers much greater choice and, in the better restaurants, access to the chef's specialities. You pay for it, of course, though a simple and perfectly legitimate ploy is to have just one course instead of the expected three or four. You can share dishes or just have several starters – a useful strategy for vegetarians. There's no minimum charge.

The French are much better disposed towards **children** in restaurants than other nationalities, not simply by offering reduced-price children's menus but in creating an atmosphere, even in otherwise fairly snooty establishments, that positively welcomes kids; some even have in-house

FOODS AND DISHES

Basic terms

Pain	Bread	*Sel*	Salt	*Couteau*	Knife
Beurre	Butter	*Sucre*	Sugar	*Cuillère*	Spoon
Céréale	Cereal	*Vinaigre*	Vinegar	*Cure-dent*	Toothpick
Lait	Milk	*Moutarde*	Mustard	*Table*	Table
Huile	Oil	*Bouteille*	Bottle	*L'addition*	Bill
Confiture	Jam	*Verre*	Glass	*Offert*	Free
Poivre	Pepper	*Fourchette*	Fork		

Snacks (*Casse-croûtes*)

Un sandwich/ une baguette...	**A sandwich...**
au jambon/fromage	with ham/cheese
au jambon beurre/ fromage beurre	with ham & butter/cheese & butter
au pâté (de campagne)	with pâté (country-style)
croque-monsieur	Grilled cheese and ham sandwich
croque-madame	Grilled cheese, ham or bacon and fried egg sandwich
Pan Bagnat	Bread roll with egg, olives, salad, tuna, anchovies and olive oil
Tartine	Buttered bread or open sandwich

And some terms

(Re)chauffé	(Re)heated
Cuit	Cooked
Cru	Raw
Emballé	Wrapped
A emporter	Takeaway
Fumé	Smoked
Salé	Salted/spicy
Sucré	Sweet

Oeufs	**Eggs**
au plat /sauté à la poêle	Fried eggs
à la coque	Boiled eggs
durs	Hard-boiled eggs
brouillés	Scrambled eggs
poché	Poached eggs

***Omelette** ...*	**Omelette** ...
nature/aux fines herbes	plain/with herbs
au fromage	with cheese

Soups (*soupes*) and starters (*hors d'œuvres*)

Bisque	Shellfish soup
Baudroie	Fish soup with vegetables, garlic and herbs
Bouillabaisse	Soup with five fish and other bits to dip
Bouillon	Broth or stock
Bourride	Thick fish soup with garlic, onions and tomatoes
Consommé	Clear soup
Pistou	Parmesan, basil and garlic paste or cream added to soup
Potage	Thick vegetable soup
Rouille	Red pepper, garlic and saffron mayonnaise served with fish soup
Velouté	Thick soup, usually fish or poultry

Starters

Assiette anglaise	Plate of cold meats
Crudités	Raw vegetables with dressings
Hors d'œuvres variés	Combination of the above plus smoked or marinated fish

Pasta (*pâtes*), pancakes (*crêpes*) and flans (*tartes*)

Pâtes fraîches	Fresh pasta	*Socca*	Thin chickpea flour pancake
Nouilles	Noodles	*Panisse*	Thick chickpea flour pancake
Raviolis	Pasta parcels of meat or chard, a Provençal, not Italian invention	*Pissaladière*	Tart of fried onions with anchovies and black olives
Crêpe au sucre/ aux oeufs	Pancake with sugar/eggs		

Fish (*poisson*), seafood (*fruits de mer*) and shellfish (*crustaces* or *coquillages*)...

Aiglefin	Small haddock or fresh cod	*Crabe*	Crab	*Maquereau*	Mackerel
Anchois	Anchovies	*Crevettes grises*	Shrimp	*Merlan*	Whiting
Amande de mer	Small sweet-tasting shell fish	*Crevettes roses*	Prawns	*Morue*	Salt cod
Anguilles	Eels	*Daurade*	Sea bream	*Moules (marinière)*	Mussels (with shallots in white wine sauce)
Araignée de mer	Spider fish	*Ecrevisse*	Freshwater crayfish	*Oursin*	Sea urchin
Baudroie	Monkfish or anglerfish	*Eperlan*	Smelt or whitebait	*Pageot*	Sea bream
Barbue	Brill	*Escargots*	Snails	*Palourdes*	Clams
Bigourneau	Periwinkle	*Favou(ille)*	Tiny crab	*Poissons de roche*	Fish from shore-line rocks
Brème	Bream	*Flétan*	Halibut	*Poulpe*	Octopus
Bulot	Whelk	*Friture*	Assorted fried fish	*Poutine*	Small river fish
Cabillaud	Cod	*Gambas*	King prawns	*Praires*	Small clams
Calmar	Squid	*Girelle*	Type of crab	*Raie*	Skate
Carrelet	Plaice	*Grenouilles (cuisses de)*	Frogs (legs)	*Rascasse*	Scorpion fish
Chapon de mer	Mediterranean fish (related to Scorpion fish)	*Grondin*	Red gurnard	*Rouget*	Red mullet
Claire	Type of oyster	*Hareng*	Herring	*Rouquier*	Mediterranean eel
Colin	Hake	*Homard*	Lobster	*St-Pierre*	John Dory
Congre	Conger eel	*Huîtres*	Oysters	*Saumon*	Salmon
Coques	Cockles	*Langouste*	Spiny lobster	*Sole*	Sole
Coquilles St-Jacques	Scallops	*Langoustines*	Saltwater crayfish (scampi)	*Telline*	Tiny clam
		Limande	Lemon sole	*Thon*	Tuna
		Lotte de mer	Monkfish	*Truite*	Trout
		Loup de mer	Sea bass	*Turbot*	Turbot
				Violet	Sea squirt

...and fish terms

Aïoli	Garlic mayonnaise/or the dish when served with salt cod and vegetables	*Darne*	Fillet or steak
Anchoïade	Anchovy paste or sauce	*En papillote*	Cooked in foil
Arête	Fish bone	*Estocaficada*	Stockfish stew with tomatoes, olives, peppers, garliic and onions
Assiette de pêcheur	Assorted fish	*La douzaine*	A dozen
Béarnaise	Sauce of egg yolks, white wine, shallots and vinegar	*Frit*	Fried
Beignets	Fritters	*Friture*	Deep-fried small fish
Bonne femme	With mushroom, parsley, potato and shallots	*Fumé*	Smoked
Brandade	Crushed cod with olive oil	*Fumet*	Fish stock
Colbert	Fried in egg with breadcrumbs	*Gelée*	Aspic
Croutons	Toasted bread, often rubbed with garlic, to dip or drop in fish soups	*Gigot de mer*	Baked fish pieces, usually monkfish
		Goujon	Several types of small fish, also deep-fried pieces of larger fish coated in breadcrumbs

...and fish terms (cont...)

Grillé	Grilled	*Pané*	Breaded
Hollandaise	Butter and vinegar sauce	*Poutargue*	Mullet roe paste
A la meunière	In a butter, lemon and parsley sauce	*Raïto*	Red wine, olive, caper, garlic and shallot sauce
Mousse/ mousseline	Mousse	*Quenelles*	Light dumplings
		Tourte	Tart or pie

Meat (*viande*) and poultry (*volaille*)

Agneau (de pré-salé)	Lamb (grazed on salt marshes)	*Jambon*	Ham
		Langue	Tongue
Andouille, andouillette	Tripe sausage	*Lapin, lapereau*	Rabbit, young rabbit
		Lard, lardons	Bacon, diced bacon
Bœuf	Beef	*Lièvre*	Hare
Bifteck	Steak	*Merguez*	Spicy, red sausage
Boudin blanc	Sausage of white meats	*Mouton*	Mutton
Boudin noir	Black pudding	*Museau de veau*	Calf's muzzle
Caille	Quail	*Oie*	Goose
Canard	Duck	*Os*	Bone
Caneton	Duckling	*Pintade*	Guinea fowl
Cervelle	Brains	*Porc, pieds de porc*	Pork, pig's trotters
Châteaubriand	Porterhouse steak	*Poulet*	Chicken
Cheval	Horse meat	*Poussin*	Baby chicken
Contrefilet	Sirloin roast	*Ris*	Sweetbreads
Coquelet	Cockerel	*Rognons*	Kidneys
Dinde, dindon, dindonneau	Turkey of different ages and genders	*Rognons blancs*	Testicles
		Sanglier	Wild boar
Entrecôte	Ribsteak	*Saucisson*	Dried sausage
Faux filet	Sirloin steak	*Steak*	Steak
Fricadelles	Meatballs	*Tête de veau*	Calf's head (in jelly)
Foie	Liver	*Toro*	Bull meat
Foie gras	Fattened (duck/ goose) liver	*Tournedos*	Thick slices of fillet
Gésier	Gizzard	*Travers de porc*	Spare ribs
Magret de canard	Duck breast	*Tripes*	Tripe
Gibier	Game	*Veau*	Veal
Graisse	Fat	*Venaison*	Venison

Meat and poultry terms – dishes . . .

Aïado	Roast shoulder of lamb, stuffed with garlic and other ingredients	*Coq au vin*	Chicken cooked until it falls off the bone with wine, onions, and mushrooms
Bœuf à la gardiane	Beef or bull meat stew with carrots, celery, onions, garlic and black olives, served with rice	*Gigot (d'agneau)*	Leg (of lamb)
		Grillade	Grilled meat
		Hâchis	Chopped meat or mince hamburger
Canard à l'orange	Roast duck with an orange-and-wine sauce	*Pieds et paquets*	Mutton or pork tripe and trotters
Canard périgourdin	Roast duck with prunes, *pâté de foie gras* and truffles	*Steak au poivre (vert/rouge)*	Steak in a black (green/red) peppercorn sauce
Cassoulet	A casserole of beans and meat	*Steak tartare*	Raw chopped beef, topped with a raw egg yolk
Choucroute	Pickled cabbage with peppercorns, sausages, bacon and salami		

. . . and terms

Blanquette, civet, daube, estouffade, hochepôt, navarin and *ragoût*	All are types of stew
Aile	Wing
Blanc	Breast or white meat
Broche	Spit-roasted
Brochette	Kebab
Carré	Best end of neck, chop or cutlet
Civit	Game stew
Confit	Meat preserve
Côte	Chop, cutlet or rib
Cou	Neck
Cuisse	Thigh or leg
Epaule	Shoulder
Mariné	Round piece
Médaillon	Marinated
Pavé	Thick slice
En croûte	In pastry
Farci	Stuffed
Au feu de bois	Cooked over wood fire
Au four	Baked
Garni	With vegetables
Grillé	Grilled
Marmite	Casserole
Mijoté	Stewed
Rôti	Roast
Sauté	Lightly cooked in butter

For steaks:

Bleu	Almost raw
Saignant	Rare
A point	Medium
Bien cuit	Well done
Très bien cuit	Very well cooked

Garnishes and sauces:

Americaine	White wine, Cognac and tomato
Arlésienne	With tomatoes, onions, aubergines, potatoes and rice
Au porto	In port
Auvergnat	With cabbage, sausage and bacon
Beurre blanc	Sauce of white wine and shallots, with butter
Bonne femme	With mushroom, bacon, potato and onions
Bordelaise	In a red wine, shallots and bone-marrow sauce
Boulangère	Baked with potatoes and onions
Bourgeoise	With carrots, onions, bacon, celery and braised lettuce
Chasseur	White wine, mushrooms and shallots
Chatêlaine	With artichoke hearts and chestnut purée
Diable	Strong mustard seasoning
Forestière	With bacon and mushroom
Fricassée	Rich, creamy sauce
Galantine	Cold dish of meat in aspic
Mornay	Cheese sauce
Pays d'Auge	Cream and cider
Piquante	Gherkins or capers, vinegar and shallots
Provençale	Tomatoes, garlic, olive oil and herbs
Véronique	Grapes, wine and cream

Vegetables (*légumes*), herbs (*herbes*) and spices (*épices*), etc

Ail	Garlic
Anis	Aniseed
Artichaut	Artichoke
Asperges	Asparagus
Avocat	Avocado
Basilic	Basil
Betterave	Beetroot
Blette/bette	Swiss chard
Cannelle	Cinnamon
Capre	Caper
Cardon	Cardoon, a beet related to artichoke
Carotte	Carrot
Céleri	Celery
Champignons: cèpes, chanterelles, girolles, morilles	Mushrooms of various kinds
Chou (rouge)	(Red) cabbage
Choufleur	Cauliflower
Ciboulettes	Chives
Concombre	Cucumber
Cornichon	Gherkin
Echalotes	Shallots
Endive	Chicory
Epinards	Spinach
Epis de maïs	Corn on the cob
Estragon	Tarragon
Fenouil	Fennel
Férigoule	Thyme (in Provençal)
Fèyes	Broad beans
Flageolet	White beans
Fleur de courgette	Courgette flower
Genièvre	Juniper
Gingembre	Ginger
Haricots	Beans
Verts	String (French)
Rouges	Kidney
Beurres	Butter
Blancs	White
Laitue	Lettuce
Laurier	Bay leaf
Lentilles	Lentils
Maïs	Corn
Marjoline	Marjoram
Menthe	Mint
Navet	Turnip
Oignon	Onion
Panais	Parsnip
Pélandron	Type of string bean
Persil	Parsley
Petits pois	Peas
Piment	Pimento
Pois chiches	Chick peas

Vegetables (*légumes*), herbs (*herbes*) and spices (*épices*), etc (cont...)

Pois mange-tout	Snow peas	*Radis*	Radishes	*Sauge*	Sage
Pignons	Pine nuts	*Raifort*	Horseradish	*Serpolet*	Wild thyme
Poireau	Leek	*Riz*	Rice	*Thym*	Thyme
Poivron (vert, rouge)	Sweet pepper (green, red)	*Romarin*	Rosemary	*Tomate*	Tomato
Pommes de terre	Potatoes	*Safran*	Saffron	*Truffes*	Truffles
		Sarrasin	Buckwheat		

Dishes and terms

Beignet	Fritter
Farci	Stuffed
Gratiné	Browned with cheese or butter
Jardinière	With mixed diced vegetables
A la parisienne	Sautéed in butter (potatoes); with white wine sauce, and shallots
A l'anglaise	Boiled
A la grecque	Cooked in oil and lemon
Râpeé(e)s	Grated or shredded
Pistou	Ground basil, olive oil, garlic and parmesan
Primeurs	Spring vegetables
Salade verte	Lettuce with vinaigrette
Gratin dauphinois	Potatoes baked in cream and garlic
Mesclum	Salad combining several different leaves
Pommes château, fondantes	Quartered potatoes sautéed in butter
Pommes lyonnaise	Fried onions and potatoes
Ratatouille	Mixture of aubergine, courgette, tomatoes and garlic
Rémoulade	Mustard mayonnaise, sometimes with anchovies and gherkins, also salad of grated cerleriac with mayonnaise
Parmentier	With potatoes
Sauté	Lightly fried in butter
A la vapeur	Steamed
Je suis végétarien(ne). Il y a quelques plats sans viande?	I'm a vegetarian. Are there any non-meat dishes?
Biologique	Organic
Primeurs	Early vegetables
Raclette	Toasted cheese served with potatoes, gherkins and onions
Salad niçoise	Salad of tomatoes, radishes, cucumber, hard-boiled eggs, anchovies, onion, artichokes, green peppers, beans, basil and garlic (rarely as comprehensive, even in Nice)
Duxelles	Fried mushrooms and shallots with cream
Fines herbes	Mixture of tarragon, parsely and chives
Frisé(e)	Curly
Gousse d'ail	Clove of garlic
Herbes de Provence	Mixture of bay leaf, thyme, rosemary and savory
Petits farcis	Stuffed tomatoes, aubergines, courgettes, peppers
Tapenade	Olive and caper paste
Tomates à la provençale	Tomatoes baked with breadcrumbs, garlic and parsely

Fruits (*fruits*), nuts (*noix*) and honey (*miel*)

Abricot	Apricot	*Fraises (de bois)*	Strawberries (wild)	*Noix*	Nuts
Acajou	Cashew nut	*Framboises*	Raspberries	*Noix*	Walnut
Amandes	Almonds	*Fruit de la passion*	Passion fruit	*Orange*	Orange
Ananas	Pineapple			*Pamplemousse*	Grapefruit
Banane	Banana	*Grenade*	Pomegranate	*Pastèque*	Watermelon
Brugnon, nectarine	Nectarine	*Groseilles*	Redcurrants	*Pêche (blanche)*	(White) peach
		Mangue	Mango	*Pistache*	Pistachio
Cacahouète	Peanut	*Marrons*	Chestnuts	*Poire*	Pear
Cassis	Blackcurrants	*Melon*	Melon	*Pomme*	Apple
Cérises	Cherries	*Miel de lavande*	Lavender honey	*Prune*	Plum
Citron	Lemon	*Mirabelles*	Small yellow plums	*Pruneau*	Prune
Citron vert	Lime			*Raisins*	Grapes
Dattes	Dates	*Myrtilles*	Bilberries	*Reine-Claude*	Greengage
Figues	Figs	*Noisette*	Hazelnut		

... and terms

Agrumes	Citrus fruits
Beignet	Fritter
Compôte	Stewed fruit, sometimes just the juice
Coulis	Sauce of puréed fruit
Crème de marrons	Chestnut purée
Flambé	Set aflame in alcohol
Fougasse	Bread flavoured with orange flower water or almonds, can also be savoury
Frappé	Iced

Desserts (*desserts* or *entremets*), pastries (*pâtisseries*) and confectionery (*confiserie*)

Bombe	A moulded ice-cream dessert
Brioche	Sweet, high-yeast breakfast roll
Calissons	Almond sweets
Charlotte	Custard and fruit in lining of almond fingers
Chichis	Doughnuts shaped in sticks
Clafoutis	Heavy custard and fruit tart
Crème Chantilly	Vanilla-flavoured and sweetened whipped cream
Crème fraîche	Sour cream
Crème pâtissière	Thick eggy pastry-filling
Crêpes suzettes	Thin pancakes with orange juice and liqueur
Fromage blanc	Cream cheese
Gaufre	Waffle
Glace	Ice cream
Île flottante/ œufs à la neige	Soft meringues floating on custard
Macarons	Macaroons
Madeleine	Small sponge cake
Marrons Mont Blanc	Chestnut purée and cream on a rum-soaked sponge cake
Mousse au chocolat	Chocolate mousse
Nougat	Nougat
Palmiers	Caramelized puff pastries
Parfait	Frozen mousse, sometimes ice cream
Petit Suisse	A smooth mixture of cream and curds
Petits fours	Bite-sized cakes/pastries
Poires Belle Hélène	Pears and ice cream in chocolate sauce
Tarte Tropezienne	Sponge cake filled with custard cream topped with nuts
Tiramisu	Marscapone cheese, chocolate and cream concoction
Truffes	Truffles
Yaourt, yogourt	Yoghurt

Terms:

Barquette	Small boat-shaped flan
Bavarois	Refers to the mould, could be a mousse or custard
Biscuit	A kind of cake
Chausson	Pastry turnover
Chocolate amer	Unsweetened chocolate
Coupe	A serving of ice cream
Crêpes	Pancakes
En feuilletage	In puff pastry
Fondant	Melting
Galettes	Buckwheat pancakes
Gênoise	Rich sponge cake
Pâte	Pastry or dough
Sablé	Shortbread biscuit
Savarin	A filled, ring-shaped cake
Tarte	Tart
Tartelette	Small tart

Cheese (*Fromage*)

The cheeses produced in Provence are all either *chèvre* (made from goat's milk) or *brebis* (made from sheep's milk). The most renowned are the *chèvres*, which include Banon, Picodon, Lou Pevre, Pelardon and Poivre d'Ain.

Le plateau de fromages is the cheesboard, and bread, but not butter, is served with it. Some useful phrases: *une petite tranche de celui-ci* (a small piece of this one); *je peux le gouter?* (may I taste it?).

Basics

Pain	Bread	*Huile*	Oil	*Vinaigre*	Vinegar	*Couteau*	Knife
Beurre	Butter	*Poivre*	Pepper	*Bouteille*	Bottle	*Cuillère*	Spoon
Oeufs	Eggs	*Sel*	Salt	*Verre*	Glass	*Table*	Table
Lait	Milk	*Sucre*	Sugar	*Fourchette*	Fork	*L'addition*	Check

And one final note: always call the waiter or waitress *Monsieur* or *Madame* (*Mademoiselle* if a young woman). **Never** use *garçon*, no matter what you've been taught at school.

games and toys for them to occupy themselves with. It is regarded as self-evident that large family groups should be able to eat out together.

A rather murkier area is that of **dogs** in the dining room; it can be quite a shock to realize that some of your fellow diners are attempting to keep dogs under control beneath their tables.

VEGETARIANS

On the whole, vegetarians can expect a somewhat lean time in Provence and the Côte d'Azur. A few towns have specifically vegetarian restaurants (which are detailed in the text), but elsewhere you'll have to hope you find a sympathetic restaurant (*crêperies* can be good standbys). Sometimes restaurants are willing to replace a meat dish on the *menu fixe* with an omelette; other times you'll have to pick your way through the *carte*. Remember the phrase *je suis végétarien(ne); il y a quelques plats sans viande?* (I'm a vegetarian; are there any non-meat dishes?).

Many vegetarians swallow a few principles and start eating fish and shellfish on holiday. **Vegans**, however, should probably forget about eating in restaurants and cook for themselves.

DRINKING

Wherever you can eat you can invariably drink and vice versa. Drinking is done at a leisurely pace whether it's as a prelude to food (*apéritif*), a sequel (*digestif*), or the accompaniment and **cafés** are the standard places to do it. Every bar or café displays the full **price list**, usually without the fifteen-percent service charge added, for drinks at the bar (*au comptoir*), sitting down (*la salle*), or sitting on the terrace (*la terrasse*) – all progressively more expensive. You pay when you leave and you can sit for hours over just one cup of coffee.

WINE

Wine is drunk at just about every meal or social occasion. Red is *rouge*, white *blanc*, or there's *rosé*. *Vin de table* or *vin ordinaire* – **table wine** – is generally drinkable and always cheap. ***A.O.C.*** (*Appellation d'Origine Contrôlée*) wines are another matter. Even buying direct from the vineyard you won't get a bottle of *Châteauneuf-du-Pape* for less than 60F, a *Gigondas* or *Vacqueras* for less than 45F or a *Bandol* for less than 35F. But there are plenty of *Côtes du Ventoux*, *Côtes du Lubéron* and *Côtes de Provence* wines that can be bought for 10–15F a bottle. Restaurant markups of *A.O.C.* wines can, however, be outrageous.

The basic **wine terms** are: *brut*, very dry; *sec*, dry; *demi-sec*, sweet; *doux*, very sweet; *mousseux*, sparkling; *méthode champenoise*, mature and sparkling. There are grape varieties as well but the complexities of the subject take up volumes. A glass of wine is simply *un rouge*, *un rosé* or *un blanc*. If it is an A.O.C. wine you may have the choice of *un ballon* (round glass) or a smaller glass (*un verre*). *Un pichet* (a pitcher) is normally a quarter-litre.

The best way to **buy bottles** of wine is directly from the producers (*vignerons*), either at vineyards, at *Maisons* or *Syndicats du Vin* (representing a group of wine-producers), or at *Coopératifs Vinicoles* (wine-producer co-ops). At all these places (for which you'll find details in the *Guide*) you can sample the wines first. It's best to make clear at the start how much you want to buy (if it's only one or two bottles) and you will not be popular if you drink several glasses and then leave

WINES OF PROVENCE

The most famous wine of the region is Châteauneuf-du-Pape, grown on the banks of the Rhône just north of Avignon. To the northwest, around the Dentelles, a clutch of villages have earned their own *appellations* within the Côtes du Rhône Villages region. They include the spicy and distinctive Gigondas and the sweet Muscat from Beaumes-de-Venise.

Further west, are the light, drinkable but not particularly special wines of the Côtes du Ventoux and Côtes du Lubéron.

Many of the vineyards in central Provence and along the coast were planted in World War I in order to supply, as speedily as possible, every French soldier with his ration of a litre a day. In the last 25 years, as the money to be made from property has soared, wine producers have had to up their quality in order for vineyards to compete with building as a profitable use of land. The Côtes de Provence *appellation* now has some excellent wines, in particular the rosés around the Massif des Maures.

The best of the coastal wines come from Bandol, with some gorgeous dusky reds; Cassis too has its own *appellation*; and around Nice the *Bellet* wines are worth discovering.

without making a purchase. The most economical option is to buy *en vrac*, which you can also do at some wine shops (*caves*), taking an easily obtainable plastic five- or ten-litre container (usually sold on the premises) and getting it filled straight from the barrel. In cities supermarkets are the best places to buy your wine.

SPIRITS

Stronger alcohol is drunk from 5am as a pre-work fortifier, and then at any time through the day according to circumstance, though the national reputation for drunkenness has lost much of its truth. Cognac or Armagnac **brandies** and the dozens of ***eaux de vie*** (brandy distilled from fruit) and **liqueurs** are made with the same perfectionism as is applied to the cultivation of vines. Among less familiar names, try *Poire William* (pear brandy), *marc* (a spirit distilled from grape pulp), or just point to the bottle with the most attractive colour. Local specialities in Alpine areas include herb liqueurs that go by various names, and *gentiane*, distilled from the flower. Measures are generous, but they don't come cheap: the same applies for imported spirits like whisky, always called *Scotch*.

The aniseed drink **pastis**, served with ice (*glaçons*) and water is a Provençal invention and one of the most popular **aperitifs** of the region. *Pastis 51*, *Ricard* and *Pernod* are all owned (along with several hundred other drinks) by Paul Ricard whose name adorns every other glass and ashtray in Provence.

Cocktails are served at most late-night bars, discos and music places, as well as at upmarket hotel bars.

BEERS AND SOFT DRINKS

The familiar light Belgian and German brands, plus French brands from Alsace, account for most of the **beer** you'll find in Provence. Draught beer (*à la pression*, usually *Kronenbourg*) is the cheapest drink you can have next to coffee, wine and pastis – ask for *un demi* (1/3 litre). For a wider choice of draught and bottled beer you need to go to the special beer-drinking establishments or English-style pubs found in most coastal cities.

On the **soft drink** front, you can buy cartons of unsweetened fruit juice in supermarkets, although in the cafés the bottled (sweetened) nectars such as apricot (*jus d'abricot*) and blackcurrant (*cassis*) still hold sway. You can also get fresh orange and lemon juice (*orange/citron pressé*) – at a price. Otherwise there's the standard canned lemonade, Coke (*coca*) and so forth.

Bottles of **spring water** (*eau minérale*) – either sparkling (*pétillante*) or still (*eau plate*) – are available everywhere, from the big brand names to the obscurest spa product. But there's not much wrong with the tap water (*l'eau du robinet*).

COFFEE AND TEA

Coffee is invariably espresso and very strong. *Un café* or *un express* is black; *une crème* is with milk; *un grand café* or *une grand crème* is a large cup. In the morning you could also ask for *un café au lait* – espresso in a large cup or bowl filled up with hot milk. *Un déca* is decaf, widely available.

Ordinary **tea** (*thé*) is *Lipton*'s nine times out of ten; to have milk with it, ask for *un peu de lait frais* (some fresh milk). After overeating, **herb teas** (*infusions* or *tisanes*), served in every café, can be soothing. The more common ones are *verveine* (verbena), *tilleul* (lime blossom), *menthe* (mint) and *camomile*. *Chocolat chaud* – **hot chocolate** – unlike tea, lives up to the high standards of French fare and can be had in any café.

COMMUNICATIONS: POST, PHONES AND MEDIA

French **post offices** – *postes* or *PTTs* – are generally open 9am–noon and 2–5pm (Mon–Fri) and 9am–noon on Saturday. However, don't depend on these hours: in the larger towns you'll find a main office open throughout the day (usually 8am–8pm), while in the villages, lunch hours and closing times can vary enormously.

You can **receive mail** at any post office; it should be addressed (preferably with the surname underlined and in capitals) **Poste Restante**, followed by the name of the town and its postcode, detailed in the *Guide* for all the main cities. To collect your mail you need a passport or other convincing ID and there may be a charge of around a couple of francs. You should ask for all your names to be checked, as filing systems are not brilliant.

Sending letters, the quickest international service is by *aérogramme*, sold at all post offices. You can buy ordinary stamps (*timbres*) at any *tabac* (tobacconist); note that postcards (*cartes postales*) go at a cheaper rate than letters (*lettres*) but are slower. If you're sending **parcels** abroad, try to check prices in various leaflets available: small *postes* don't often send foreign mail and may need reminding, for example, of the reductions for printed papers and books. **Faxes** can be sent from all main post offices and from many newsagents: the official French word is *télécopie*, but everyone understands *fax*.

PHONE CALLS

You can make domestic and international phone calls from any telephone box (or ***cabine***) and can receive calls where there's a blue logo of a ringing bell. Most call boxes only take **phone cards** (*télécartes*), obtainable from post offices, *PTT* boutiques, train stations and some *tabacs*; the cheapest card is 46F for 50 units. You can also use credit cards in many call boxes. Coin-only boxes, still common in cafés, bars and rural areas, take 50 centimes, 1F, 5F and 10F pieces; put the money in after lifting up the receiver and before dialling. You can keep adding more coins once you are connected. You can also make calls from **booths at main post offices**. You apply at the counter to be assigned a number and then dial. The disadvantage with these – odd considering the French obsession with technology – is that you can't tell how much you're spending. It's worth counting your units and checking – mistakes are sometimes made.

For **calls** within France – local or long distance – simply dial all eight digits of the number, except to Paris, when you should first dial ☎16/1. From October 1996 all French phone numbers will have ten digits: for Provence you will need to add 04 to the beginning of the existing number. The 16 for dialing between Paris and the provinces will then disappear.

Cheap rates operate between 10.30pm and 8am on weekdays and on weekends after noon on Saturday. A local six-minute call will cost around 50 centimes.

The major **international calling codes** are given in the box on p.47; remember to omit the initial 0 of the local area code from the subscriber's number. By far the cheapest means of making international calls is to use a **calling card**. Costs are going down all the time; curently the cheapest deals are from the British companies Interglobe, Mercury and World Telecom which need to be purchased in the UK. The American AT&T card is available in France. The cards are either pre-paid or charged to your credit card or on your phone bill if you are a customer. You dial a free number (make sure you have the relevant number for France with you), your account number and then the number you wish to call. The drawback is that the free number is often engaged and you have to dial a great many digits.

To avoid payment altogether, you can, of course, make a reverse-charge or **collect call** –

TELEPHONING

IDD CODES

From France dial ☎19 + IDD code + area code minus first 0 + subscriber number

Britain ☎44 Ireland ☎353 USA and Canada ☎1 Australia ☎61 New Zealand ☎64

From Britain to Provence: dial ☎00 33 + eight-digit number

From the USA and Canada to Provence: dial ☎011 33 + eight-digit number

From Australia to Provence: dial ☎011 33 + eight-digit number

From New Zealand to Provence: dial ☎044 33 + eight-digit number

From Provence to Paris: dial ☎16/1 + number

Note that all French numbers will be ten digit after October 1996; for Provence add 04.

TIME

France is one hour ahead of GMT, except for a short period during October, when it's the same. It is six hours ahead of Eastern Standard Time, and nine hours ahead of Pacific Standard Time. This also applies during daylight savings seasons from the end of March to the end of September.

USEFUL NUMBERS WITHIN FRANCE

Telegrams By phone: internal ☎36.55; external ☎05.33.44.11 (all languages).

Time ☎36.99.

International operator For Canada and US ☎19.13.11; for all other countries ☎19.13 followed by IDD number.

International directory assistance For Canada and US ☎19.13.12.11; for all other countries ☎19.13.12 followed by IDD number.

French operator ☎13.

French directory assistance ☎12.

known in French as "*téléphoner en PCV*". You can also do this through the operator in the UK, by dialling ☎19.00.44 and asking for a "reverse-charge call". To get an English-speaking *AT&T* operator for North America, dial ☎19.00.11.

Some British **mobile phones**, as long as they're digital, will work in Provence.

MINITEL

Phone subscribers in most French cities have a **minitel**, an on-line computer allowing access through the phone lines to all kinds of directories, databases, chat lines etc. You will also find them in post offices. Most organizations, from sports federations to government institutions to gay groups, have a code consisting of numbers and letters to call up information, leave messages, make reservations etc. You dial the number on the phone, wait for a fax-type tone, then type the letters on the keyboard, and finally, press *Connexion Fin* (the same key ends the connection). If you're at all computer literate and can understand basic keyboard terms in French (*retour* – return, *envoi* – enter, etc), you shouldn't find them hard to use. Be warned that most services cost more than phone rates.

THE MEDIA

Most **British newspapers** plus the *International Herald Tribune*, are on sale in the large cities and resorts the day after publication.

Of the national **French daily papers** *Le Monde* is the most intellectual and respected, with no concessions to entertainment (such as pictures) but a correctly styled French that is probably the easiest to understand. *Libération* is moderately left-wing, independent and more colloquial, with good, if choosy, coverage. *L'Humanité* is the Communist Party newspaper (*L'Humanité Dimanche* is the bulkier Sunday version), with a diminishing readership; *Le Figaro* is the main paper with right-wing sympathies.

Regional newspapers enjoy much higher circulation than the Paris nationals and, though not brilliant for news, are useful for listings. *Le Provençal* and the very tabloidish *Nice Matin* are the two big ones in Provence, followed by *Var-Matin* and *Le Dauphiné Vaucluse*. There's also *La Marseillaise* (available everywhere except the Alpes-Maritimes *département*) which originated as a Resistance paper during the war, and is firmly to the left. *Le Méridional*, in contrast, is a right-wing rag with strong sympathy for the Front National (Le Pen's fascist party).

National weeklies on the *Newsweek/Time* model include the wide-ranging and left-leaning *Nouvel Observateur* and its right-wing counterpart *L'Express*. The best and funniest investigative journalism is in the weekly satirical paper, *Le Canard Enchainé*. *Charlie Hebdo* is a sort of *Private Eye* or *Spy Magazine* equivalent. For really indepth analysis of national and international events and trends *Le Monde* publishes the **monthly** *Le Monde des Débats* and *Le Monde Diplomatique*.

The Riviera Reporter is a free **English-language magazine** with a mix of culture and politics, which you can pick up at any of the English bookshops on the Riviera. A newish French cultural magazine for the Alpes Maritimes and eastern Var is *Zig Z'Art*, available free from cultural venues and bookshops. Finally, *Macadam* is a magazine with culture, humour and social and political issues sold by the homeless who keep a percentage of the cover price (10F).

TV AND RADIO

French TV broadcasts six channels, three of them public, along with a good many more cable and satellite channels, which include *CNN* and the *BBC World Service*. The main French TV **news** is at 8pm on *TF1* and *Antenne 2*. *Arte*, the fifth channel, shows undubbed movies. Best French documentaries are on the cable channel *Planete*.

If you've got a **radio**, you can tune into English-language news on the *BBC World Service* between 6.195 and 12.095MHz shortwave at intervals throughout the day and night. The *Voice of America* transmits on 90.5, 98.8 and 102.4FM. For **news** in French, there are the state-run *France Inter* (88.10 MHz), *Europe 1* (FM 92.8) or round-the-clock news on *France Infos* (FM 105.5). **Local radio stations** include the English-language *Riviera Radio* (FM106.3 and 106.5) with news at 6–7am and 11am, and the *BBC World Service* overnight.

BUSINESS HOURS AND PUBLIC HOLIDAYS

Almost everything – shops, museums, tourist offices, most banks – closes for a couple of hours at midday. The basic working hours are 8am to noon and 2 to 6pm, with shops usually open till 7pm. In summer the midday break often extends to 3pm.

There is of course some variation. **Food shops** often don't reopen till halfway through the afternoon, closing just before dinner time between 7.30 and 8pm. Sunday and Monday are the standard closing days; in villages you may not even find a single *boulangerie* (bakery) open. The main thing to watch out for if you're picnic-shopping is getting it done in time before the French shut their doors for lunch. **Banks** close at 4pm and in small towns may be closed on Monday. Small hotels often close on Sunday or Monday, restaurants likewise.

Museums and monuments tend to open at around 10am and close between 5 and 6pm. Summer times may differ from winter times; if they do, both are indicated in the listings through the book. **Summer hours** usually extend from

PUBLIC HOLIDAYS

There are thirteen national holidays (*jours fériés*), when most shops and businesses, though not museums or restaurants, are closed.

January 1

Easter Sunday

Easter Monday

Ascension Day (40 days after Easter)

Whitsun (seventh Sunday after Easter, plus the Monday)

May 1 (May Day)

May 8 (Victory in Europe Day)

July 14 (Bastille Day)

August 15 (Assumption of the Virgin Mary)

November 1 (All Saints' Day)

November 11 (1918 Armistice Day)

Christmas Day

Monaco, in addition to the above, takes days off on January 27 (Fête de Ste-Dévote) and November 19 (Fête Nationale Monégasque).

mid-May or early June to mid-September, but they sometimes apply only during July and August, occasionally even from Palm Sunday to All Saints' Day. Don't forget **closing days** – usually Tuesday or Monday, sometimes both.

Churches and cathedrals are almost always open all day, with charges only for the crypt, treasuries or cloister and little fuss about how you're dressed. Where they are closed you may have to take a look during Mass on Sunday morning or during other services for which times are usually posted up on the door. In small towns and villages, however, getting the key is not difficult – ask anyone nearby or hunt out the priest, whose house is known as the *presbytère*.

CULTURE AND FESTIVALS

Every town of any size in Provence or on the Côte d'Azur has its summer festival season, commonly called *Les Estivales*, which, more often than not, is pure tourist hype, bearing little or no relation to local customs or history. In the Carmargue and the Crau, however, and throughout inland Provence, particularly in the remoter mountain areas, there are numerous small-scale fêtes which are genuine manifestations of traditional village life. The region continues to attract visual artists – and their customers – as it has done throughout the century. The other arts, though not so dominant, are well catered for in the long-established festivals and in the theatres, opera houses and concert venues of the major cities.

THE ARTS

Marseille is the great city for **all-round culture**, from classic theatre to experimental performance, major art retrospectives to contemporary photography, video and multi-media, opera to acid jazz, plus football, political demonstrations and street happenings.

Avignon and **Aix** are the next most innovative cities on the arts front. Like Marseille they have their own resident **theatre companies** and **orchestras**; the most renowned **drama**

SANTONS

Santons are painted pottery Christmas nativity figures, a speciality of Provence. Their uniqueness is in representing not just the holy family and shepherds but every nineteenth-century village character. So you'll have the olive-oil presser, the wine grower, the butcher, baker, soap maker and market gardener, women baking and carrying water, a gypsy band, plus the priest and mayor and even groups of *pétanque* players, all in immaculate detail. The figures are about 12cm high and their setting is a Provençal village with model houses, hillsides of pebbles and moss, twig vines and lime trees. In Aubagne, one of the main centres of *santon* art along with Aix and Marseille where they originated, scenes from Pagnol's novels are represented with *santons*.

You can visit *santonnier* workshops, see displays in museums or special exhibitions, attend the great *santon* fair in Marseille, or buy them from every craft and souvenir shop.

and dance festival in France takes place in Avignon with a large fringe component; and Aix has **dance**, **contemporary music** (including rock and jazz) festivals, and an excellent new cultural centre, the Cité du Livre. **Monaco**, like Nice, Avignon and Marseille, has its own **opera house** and attracts world-class musicians; it also hosts a **circus festival**. International **rock stars** play in Nice and Marseille; Juan-les-Pins has the best **jazz** festival, closely followed by Nice; Châteauvallon near Toulon is famous for **dance** and Orange for its **classical music festival** in the Roman theatre. **Classical concerts** are performed in many churches, often with free or very cheap admission; **Menton** has one of the most beautiful outdoor venues for its festival of chamber music.

Cinema is treated very seriously. The **Cannes film festival** has the highest status, both nationally and internationally; it is, though, very much a credentials-only event. Better to try the Festival of Cinema in **La Ciotat** where the techniques of film-making were originated by the Lumière brothers in 1895. On a day-to-day level, there are good cinemas throughout Provence and the Côte d'Azur where you can see undubbed **foreign films** (*version originale* or *v.o.* means it's in the original language and subtitled).

But of all the arts, it's **painting, sculpture** and **ceramics** that Provence is most famous for; as well as all the suberb art collections and exhibitions there are also numerous **art galleries** in the cities and coastal villages.

All the major cultural festivals are described in the *Guide* with details of where to get programme information and make bookings. You'll also find the addresses and phone numbers of many theatres, cinemas and cultural centres.

Marseille and Nice both have good weekly **listings magazines** available free from the tourist offices: *Taktik* which also covers Aix and the rest of the Bouches-du-Rhône, and *Le Farfelu* covering, rather more sketchily, the Alpes-Maritimes. *Scènes d'Azur*, if it survives, gives wider coverage of the Alpes Maritimes (available from cultural venues and bookshops). In addition, there's the commercial weekly listings mags *L'Officiel des Loisirs* (2F) and *Semaine des Spectacles* (5F) which both come out on Wednesday and cover the Bouches-du-Rhône, Var and Alpes-Maritimes. Otherwise the local papers, which have separate sections for the different areas, will be your best bet. The annual brochures *Musées Galeries d'Art Côte d'Azur* and *Itinéraire Officiel de l'Art*, available from most of the Riviera tourist offices, list all the art museums, galleries and the big art exhibitions.

TRADITIONAL FESTIVALS

For the average Provençal man, a game of *boules*, a football match on the television or several *petits verres* with mates on market day constitute the sum total of entertainment (women tend to stay inside and work, or sit together on sunny benches with their knitting and kids).

Special days celebrate **wine-making**, **transhumance** (the movement of sheep between their winter and summer pastures), **olive** and other **harvests** – chestnuts, lavender, jasmine, for example. Plus there are one or two annual **village festivals**, for which local pipe bands, children in traditional costumes and the church with all its medieval superstitious trappings process to various shrines. These days culminate with a beanfeast, much drinking and the sense of age-old community duly reaffirmed. Ever since the poet Frédéric Mistral and friends started the Provençal revival in the nineteenth century, these local traditions have been kept going, not as tourist attractions and not entirely as photo-opportunities for the mayor. Their original meanings may have lost relevance, but they're still a real part of contemporary village life, and fun. As an outsider, the events may just look quaint but watching people enjoy themselves can be a pleasure in itself and the festive spirit usually induces extra hospitality.

The Tarasque festival in **Tarascon** is a good one for kids. The gathering of the gypsies in **Les-Stes-Maries-de-la-Mer** is one of the strangest and most exciting: it attracts vast crowds and, these days, a heavy police presence. The **folklore festivals** of Arles and Nice have rather more commercial origins, but can be very enjoyable none the less.

Bonfires are lit and fireworks set off for **Bastille Day** and for the **Fête de St Jean** on June 24, three days from the summer solstice. **May Day** is also commonly celebrated. **Mardi Gras** – the last blow-out before Lent – is far less of an occasion than in other Catholic countries,

CALENDAR OF EVENTS

Dates change fom year to year so it's always worth checking with local tourist offices.

January

Circus Festival (sometimes held in Dec or Feb) – Monaco

Monte-Carlo Car Rally (end of month) – Monaco

Science Festival (last week) – Cavaillon

February

Classical Music Festival (end of Feb to March) – Cannes

Dance Festival (end of Feb to beginning of March) – Avignon

Lemon Festival (end of Feb to March) – Menton

Mardi Gras Carnival (week before Lent) – Nice

Mimosa Procession (third Sun) – Bormes

Olive Oil Festival (first Sun) – Nyons

March

Dance Festival – Cannes

April

Arts Festival (mid-April to mid-May) – Monaco

Fête des Gardians (bull and horse herdsmen; last Sun in month to May 1) – Arles

Ski Grand Prix – Isola 2000

Tennis Open – Nice

Tennis Open – Monaco

Wine Festival (25) – Châteauneuf-du-Pape

May

Arts Festival (end of month to mid-July) – Châteauvallon

Film Festival (second week) – Cannes

Formula 1 Grand Prix (Ascension weekend) – Monte-Carlo

Gypsy Festival (24–25) – Les-Stes-Maries-de-la-Mer

Processions (16–18 & June 15) – St-Tropez

Rose Festival (second weekend) – Grasse

Strip Cartoon Festival – Orange

June

Bottle procession (1) – Boulbon

Cinema Festival (mid-month) – La Ciotat

Classical Music Festival – Vence

Comedians Festival – Cannes

Contemporary Music Festival (mid-June to first week July) – Aix

Dance Festival – Châteauvallon

Dance, Music, Folklore and Theatre Festival (end of June and beginning of July) – Arles

Fête de St-Jean (24)

Jazz and Chamber Music Festival (last 2 weeks) – Aix

Music Festival (Whitsun) – Apt

Sacred Music Festival – Nice

Sculpture Symposium (second fortnight) – Digne

Tarasque Festival (last full weekend) – Tarascon.

Transhumance Festival (Whit Monday) – St-Rémy

Transhumance Festival (last weekend of month) – St-Etienne-de-Tinée

Triathalon (beginning of month) – Nice

July

Bastille Day (14)

Chorègies (operatic and choral music; mid-July to early Aug) – Orange

Dance Festival (mid-month) – Aix

Fête de St-Eloi (second Sun or penultimate Sun) – Graveson, Châteaurenard and Maillane

Firework Festival (to Aug) – Monaco

Folklore Festival – Nice

Food Festival (around third weekend) – Carpentras

Gypsy Festival (mid-month) – Arles

Jazz Festival (second fortnight) – Juan-les-Pins

Jazz Festival (first fortnight) – Nice

Jazz Festival (third week) – Salon

Music Nights in the Citadel (end of July and beginning Aug) – Sisteron

Music, Theatre and Dance Festival – Carpentras

Olive Festival (weekend before July 14) – Nyons

Opera and Music Festival (mid-July to mid-Aug) – Aix

Painting Festival – Cagnes-sur-Mer

Photography Show (second week) – Arles

Provençal Festival (end July to beginning Aug) – Avignon and neighbouring towns

Sorgue Festival of music, theatre and dance – L'Isle-sur-la-Sorgue and neighbouring villages

Theatre, Dance and Music Festival plus Fringe Festival (second week July to first week Aug) – Avignon

Theatre, Dance and Music Festival – Marseille

Theatre, Jazz and Classical Music Festival (last 2 weeks) – Gordes

CALENDAR OF EVENTS (CONT...)

Theatre, Music and Art Festival (mid-July to end Aug) – Apt

Theatre, Music and Art Festival (mid-July to end Aug) – Vaison

Venetian Festival (first Sat) – Martigues

Wine Festival (14) – Vacqueyras

August

Chamber Music Festival – Menton

Garlic Festival (end of month) – Poilenc

Graphic Arts (last week) – Lurs

Harvest Festival (15) – St-Rémy

Haute-Provence Festival (first fortnight; arts and crafts) – Forcalquier and neighbouring villages

Jasmin Festival (first Sun) – Grasse

Lavender Festival (end of month) – Digne

Square *Boules* championship – Cagnes-sur-Mer

September

Rice Harvest (mid-month) – Arles

Sheep Fair – Guillaumes

October

Sea procession and blessing (Sun nearest to 22) – Stes-Maries-de-la-Mer

November

Côtes du Rhône wine festival – Avignon

Santons Fair (last Sun to end of Dec) – Marseille

December

Provencal Midnight Mass (24) – Aix, Les Baux, Fontveille, Lucéram, St-Michel-de-Frigolet, St-Rémy, Ste-Baume, Séguret, Tarascon

Wine and Traditions Festival (first Sun) – Séguret

and where it is celebrated – in Nice and other Riviera towns – it's designed for commercial interests and municipal prestige.

Finally, at **Christmas**, Mass is celebrated in many Provençal churches, with real shepherds offering real sheep, and the crib scene enacted by parishioners in traditional garb. A thirteen-course non-meat supper is traditionally served on Christmas Eve.

You'll find details of the most popular events as well as many small, lower-key traditional festivities throughout the *Guide*.

SPORTS AND OUTDOOR ACTIVITIES

Football is the most popular spectator sport in Provence, with motor racing famous in Monaco and enthusiasm over cycle races as great as in the rest of France. The most typically Provençal competitive pastime is pétanque. Outdoor activities in the region include hang-gliding, skiing, all types of water sport, climbing and mountain trekking.

SPECTATOR SPORTS

On every town or village square in Provence, in every park, or sometimes in a specially built arena, you'll see ***pétanque***, the Provençal version of *boules*, being played. The principle is the same as bowls but the terrain is always rough, never grass, and the area much smaller. The metal ball is usually thrown upwards from a distance of 10m or a little more, to land and skid towards the marker (*cochonnet*). In Provence, uniquely, the players are allowed to move as they "point" (the first throw) or "aim" (the adversary's throw). There are café or village teams, endless championships, and, on the whole, it's very male dominated.

The spectator sport most passionately followed in Provence is *le foot* – **football**. The best team is Olympique de Marseille; but conviction for cheating in a European match soon followed by bankruptcy has put the team in the doldrums. A new ownership package will hopefully see it back in the First Division and the European Champions League. Monaco's team competes at the European level and Cannes is in the First Division. Eric Cantona is as popular in his home town of Marseille as he is in Manchester.

The **Tour de France** cycling race in July generally has a stage in Provence, with one or other of the highest mountain passes on the route. It's here in the lower Alps that you're likely to see the greatest number of shiny black backsides above bulging calf muscles speeding up the inclines without a waver. Cycling combined with running and swimming brings in the crowds for Nice's and Antibes' **triathalons**.

In and around the **Camargue**, the number-one sport is **bullfighting** (described in the *Guide* under "Arles"). Though not to everyone's taste it is at least a considerably less gruesome variety than that practised by the Spanish.

The famous **Formula One Grand Prix** takes place in Monaco and some of the remote inland routes are used for **rally-driving**. Monaco also hosts its international **Tennis Open** championships.

PARTICIPATORY SPORTS

Water sports on the **Côte d'Azur** are practised on the whole for the glamour factor (and for pleasure) rather than for competition. The waters and winds of the Mediterranean are far too temperate to exercise high-powered sailing or windsurfing skills. But for learning and just playing about in the body-heat water, it's potentially ideal. The problem, though, is congestion, and no one following the rules of the water. So beware the madcap jet skiers and power-boat racers. The other great drawback is inevitably the cost of hiring the equipment. Every resort has several outlets – for sailing, windsurfing, water-skiing, wet-biking, scuba-diving – so you can shop around for the best prices, but it will still take a major chunk out of your budget, and prices go up every year.

Air-borne sports, particularly **hang-gliding**, are extremely popular in Provence. Fayence is the main centre for **gliding** and St-André-les-Alpes one of many places with an excellent hang-gliding centre. *Baptêmes* (initiations) are not too expensive.

More and more green-, or rather health-conscious, French holiday-makers are taking to **trekking** in the mountains with most ski resorts now catering for summer activities, like pony-trekking, climbing and walking, in a big way. The rivers and artificial lakes of Provence also provide opportunities for **canoeing**, **rafting**, and more gently paddling about in **boats**, windsurfing and yachting. Details of helpful organizations and centres catering for these pursuits are given in the *Guide* and above under "Getting Around" (see p.27).

Horse-riding is catered for by numerous *Centres Equestres* throughout Provence, particularly in the Camargue. Addresses are given in the *Guide*; tourist offices will be able to supply more details. Normally what's offered is an accompanied ride in a group but there are some places where you can gallop off on your own.

Climbing has become very fashionable; the main areas are the Alps, the Dentelles and the Lubéron; and the national organization is the *Club Alpin Français* with offices in Nice (14 av Mirabeau; ☎93.62.59.99) and Avignon (7 rue St-Michel; ☎90.25.40.48).

Skiing – whether downhill, cross-country or mountaineering – is enthusiastically pursued in Provence, especially when it can be combined with a spot of water-skiing the same day. There are over a dozen ski-resorts within two hours'

INFORMATION ON SPORTS AND LEISURE ACTIVITIES

All the *Comités Départementals de Tourisme* (*CDT*s), the departmental tourist boards, produce helpful brochures on all leisure activities, with useful addresses of specialist organizations. The big city tourist offices are likely to have these, or you can go to the *CDT* office for moe detailed information. Addresses are:

Alpes-de-Haute-Provence: 42 bd Victor-Hugo, Digne (☎92.31.57.29).

Alpes Maritimes: 55 Promenade des Anglais, Nice (☎93.37.78.78).

Bouches-du-Rhône: 6 rue du Jeaune Anarcharsis, Marseille (☎91.54.92.66).

Var: 5 av Vauban, Toulon (☎94.09.00.69).

Vaucluse: Pl Campana, Avignon; (☎90.86.43.42).

drive of the coast, the three biggest being **Auron**, **Valberg** and **Isola 2000**, though recent weather changes have affected snowfalls in the lower Alps. It can be an expensive sport to pursue on your own and the Provence resorts are rarely covered by the international package operators, though some, like La Foux d'Allos, are much cheaper in terms of ski-lift charges than the higher resorts north of Provence. If a weekend's skiing takes your fancy local deals are available: the *Comités Départementals de Tourisme* in Digne or Nice (see box on p.53) or the *Club Alpin Français* (14 av Mirabeau, Nice; ☎93.62.59.99) will be the best sources of information, or you can phone the tourist offices at the resorts which you'll find in the *Guide*. All hotels and tourist offices in the Alps post up meteorological information; you can check the snow at different resorts on ☎42.66.64.28.

Finally, two highly promoted activities of the Côte d'Azur, one with a long history and potentially ruinous, the other newly fashionable and environmentally suspect, are **gambling** and **golf**. At least the former can be a spectator sport.

TROUBLE AND THE POLICE

Petty theft is endemic along the Côte d'Azur and pretty bad in the crowded hangouts of the big cities. It obviously makes sense to take the normal precautions: not flashing wads of notes or travellers' cheques around; carrying your bag or wallet securely; and never letting cameras and other valuables out of your sight. But the best security of all is having a good insurance policy and keeping a separate record of cheque numbers, credit-card numbers and the phone numbers for cancelling them (see p.20), and the relevant details of all your valuables.

Drivers face the greatest problems, most notoriously break-ins though having your vehicle stolen, particularly in Nice or Marseille, is not uncommon. It's always best to park overnight in guarded car parks; where that's not possible try to park in a busy street or in front of a police station. Never leave anything in the boot and remove your tapedeck if you can. It's not just foreign number plates that attract thieves; hired cars with non-local registration numbers are also favourite prey.

If you need to **report a theft**, go along to the local ***commissariat de police*** (addresses are given for all the main cities), and make sure you get the requisite piece of paper for a claim. The first thing they'll ask for is your passport, and vehicle documents if relevant. Although the police are not always as co-operative as they might be, it is their duty to assist you if, say, you've lost your passport or all your money.

If you have an **accident while driving**, officially you have to fill in and sign a *constat à l'aimable* (jointly agreed statement); car insurers should give you this with a policy, though in practice few seem to have heard of it. For non-criminal **driving violations** such as speeding,

EMERGENCIES

Ambulance ☎15

Police ☎17

Fire Service ☎18

Note: It's common for the fire brigade, les sapeurs pompiers, *to be called for medical problems; they all have paramedical training and equipment.*

the police can impose an on-the-spot fine. If you don't have the necessary cash you could find yourself passing several unpleasant hours at the police station.

By law you are supposed to carry ID with you at all times and the police have the right to stop and ask to see it.

COMMITTING CRIMES

Camping outside authorized sites can bring you into contact with the authorities, though it's more likely to be the landowner who tells you to move off. *Gendarmes* have been known to stalk the beaches, sweating in their uniforms, telling everyone to cover up their bottom halves and in Cannes there are on-the-spot fines for toplessness on the street, but there's no equivalent of the British public decency laws. **Topless sunbathing** is universally acceptable; nudity is in principle limited to specifically naturist beaches: best to follow the rule of when in Rome ...

More seriously, anyone caught smuggling or possessing **drugs**, even a few grammes of marijuana, is liable to find themself in jail and consulates will not be sympathetic. This is not to say that hard-drug consumption isn't a visible activity: there are scores of kids dealing in *poudre* (heroin) in Marseille and Nice and the authorities are unable to do much about it. As a rule, people are no more or less paranoid about marijuana busts than they are in the UK.

Generally, too, **treatment by the police** is little different from anywhere else – not something you'd go out of your way to experience. Should you be arrested on any charge, you have the right to contact your consulate (see "Listings" for Marseille, Nice or Monaco).

RACIAL AND SEXUAL HARASSMENT

The large industrial cities of Provence and the Côte d'Azur towns have the highest proportion of extreme right-wing voters in France. All three cities gained by the neo-fascist Front National in the municipal elections of 1995 were in the region: Orange, Toulon, Marignane. The mayor of Nice, though not in name National Front, is as close to the party as makes no difference. **Racist attitudes** in the populace and the police are rife. Being black, particularly if you are Arab or look as if you might be, makes your chances of avoiding unpleasantness very low. Hotels claiming to be booked up, police demanding your papers, and abuse from ordinary people is horribly frequent. In addition, even entering the country can be difficult. Changes in passport regulations have put an end to outright refusal to let some British holidaymakers in, but customs and immigration officers can still be obstructive and malicious. In North African-dominated areas of cities, identity checks by the police are very common and not pleasant. If you suffer a racial assault, you're likely to get a much more sympathetic hearing from your consulate than from the police. The national anti-racism organization, *Mouvement contre le Racisme et pour l'Amitié entre les Peuples (MRAP)*, has an office in Marseille at 17 rue du Refuge, ☎91.90.06.22.

Sexual harassment is generally no worse or more vicious than in the UK but it can be a problem making judgements about situations without the familiar linguistic and cultural signs. A "*Bonjour*" or "*Bonsoir*" on the street is usually a pick-up line. If you return the greeting, you've left yourself open to a persistent monologue and a difficult brush-off job. On the other hand, topless bathing doesn't usually invite bother and it's quite common, if you're on your own, to be offered a drink in a bar and not to be pestered even if you accept. Hitching is a risk, though some women do hitch alone in the more built-up areas of the Côte d'Azur.

If you need help, go to the police, although don't expect too much from them. The *mairie/hôtel de ville* (town hall) will have addresses of women's organizations (*Femmes Battues, Femmes en Détresse* or *SOS Femmes*), though this won't be much help outside business hours. The national **rape crisis** number, *SOS Viol*, is ☎05.05.95.95, but it's not 24 hour (Mon–Fri 10am–6pm) and may not have English speakers. Again your consulate may be the most sympathetic assistance available.

GAYS AND LESBIANS

France is more liberal on homosexuality than most other European countries. The legal age of consent is fifteen and in general, the French consider sexuality to be a private matter.

The dominance of extreme-right sympathies in many parts of Provence, however, means gays tend to be discreet – and lesbians almost always are. Marseille is the only place where gay and lesbian pride is celebrated, though Nice has a thriving gay club scene. As in many Mediterranean cultures, physical contact between women or men is seen as 'natural' but kissing in public may raise hackles. Addresses for clubs and bars are listed in the *Guide* – mainly in Marseille, Nice and Aix.

GAY CONTACTS AND INFORMATION

ARCL (*Archives, Recherches et Cultures Lesbiennes*), Post box (BP) 362, 75526, Paris Cedex 11; answerphone ☎48.05.25.89. Fri 6–8pm – hours may change. *ARCL* publish a yearly directory of lesbian and feminist addresses in France (available at the *Bibliothèque Marguerite Durand* in Paris) and a fairly regular bulletin. They also organize frequent meetings.

David & Jonathan, 92bis rue Picpus, Paris 12e; ☎43.42.09.49 (M° Michel-Bizot). 24-hr answerphone for gay Christians.

Maison des Femmes, 8 Cité Prost, off rue Chanzy, Paris 11e; ☎43.48.24.91 (M° Faidherbe-Chaligny). Mon 6–8pm, Wed 3–8pm, Fri 6–8pm; Fri café 8pm–midnight. Run by *Paris Féministe*, this is the home of the *Groupe des Lesbiennes Féministes* and the *Mouvement d'Information et d'Expression des Lesbiennes*. A cafeteria operates on Friday nights, and there are occasional events organized.

Minitel. 3615 GPS is the Minitel number to dial for information on groups, contacts, messages etc. The service was set up by *Gai Pied*. There are also any number of chat lines.

Gay media

Exit. Gay newspaper with useful addresses.

Fréquence Gaie, 98.2 FM. 24-hr gay and lesbian radio station with music, news, chat, information on groups and events, etc.

Illico. A monthly with lonely hearts and Minitel numbers.

Lesbia. The most widely available lesbian publication, available from most newsagents. Each monthly issue features a wide range of articles, listings, reviews, lonely hearts and contacts.

Spartacus International Gay Guide. Guidebook focusing mainly on gay travel in Europe.

Gay/lesbian travel contacts

Detour Guides, 1016 3rd Ave, Sacramento, CA 95818 (☎916/448-4120). Series covers London, Paris, Amsterdam and several American cities.

Different Drummer Tours, PO Box 528, Glen Ellyn, IL 60137 (☎1-800/645-1275). Scheduled and customized international tours.

Different Strokes Tours, 1841 Broadway, New York, NY 10023 (☎1-800/688-3301). Customized international tours.

International Gay Travel Association, PO Box 4974, Key West, FL 33041 (☎1-800/448-8550 or 305/292-0217). Trade group that can provide a list of gay-owned or gay-friendly travel agents, accommodation and other travel businesses.

Key Tours, 1 Kensington St, London W8 4EB (☎0171/ 229 6961). Gay tour operator.

Uranian Travel, 111 Kew Road, Richmond, Surrey TW9 2PN (☎0171/332 1022). Package holidays and hotel bookings.

WORK AND STUDY

Temporary agricultural work in Provence and the Côte d'Azur is hard to come by and, in summer, catering work or work in the tourist industry is a better bet. For longer-term employment, au-pair positions and English teaching are distinct possibilities if you take time to plan and make contact in advance.

If you're looking for something secure, it's important to plan well in advance. The best **general sources for all jobs in France** are the publications *Emplois d'été en France* (Vacation Work, 9 Park End St, Oxford, UK; ☎01865/241978), *Work Your Way Around the World* (Vacation Work, 1507 Dana Ave, Cincinnati, Ohio, USA) and *1000 Pistes de Jobs* (*L'Étudiant*, 27 rue du Chemin-Vert, 75011 Paris). *Working Holidays* (Central Bureau, Seymour Mews House, Seymour Mews, London W1H 9PE) is also useful. In Provence, the two main papers, *Nice Matin* and *Le Provençal* carry job ads.

By law all EU nationals are entitled to exactly the same pay, conditions and trade-union rights as French nationals. France has a **minimum wage** (the *SMIC*), currently around 35F an hour. Employers, however, are likely to pay lower wages to temporary foreign workers who don't have easy legal resources.

The **University of Aix and Marseille** has its science faculties in Marseille and arts faculties in Aix, very popular with American students. Nice also has a university.

TEMPORARY WORK

Grape-picking during the wine harvest in September is possible, though many vineyards are automated and others too small to take on outsiders. Youth hostels in wine-growing areas sometimes recruit grape-pickers or you could always try asking at the local *Agence Nationale de l'Emploi* (ANPE) whose address you'll find in the phone book.

Getting a temporary job as a deck-hand or skivvy **on a yacht** is also feasible, but you'll have to hang about the ports, and getting on board will be very much a matter of luck. Pay and conditions are likely to be abysmal – it's assumed that you're there for the glamorous ride and you'll certainly be made to work for it. Another casual option, if you speak some French, is **bar work** in the many clubs run by American, Dutch, English or Irish managers on the coast. Again it's a matter of being in the right place at the right time.

Temporary jobs in the **travel industry** revolve around courier work – supervising and working on bus tours or summer campsites. You'll need good French (and maybe even another language) and should write to as many tour operators as you can, preferably in early spring. Getting work as a courier on a campsite is slightly easier. It usually takes in putting up tents at the beginning of the season, taking them down again at the end, and general maintenance and trouble-shooting work in the months between. *Canvas Holidays* (☎01383/644000) or *Riviera Holidays* (01482 448905) in Britain are worth approaching, or the *Union Française des Centres de Vacances* (☎45.39.22.23) in Paris. Competition is fairly intense.

LONGER-TERM EMPLOYMENT

Teaching English is one of the easier ways of getting a job in France. It's best to apply from Britain; check the ads in the *Guardian's* "Education" section (every Tuesday), or in the weekly *Times Educational Supplement*. Late summer is usually the best time. You don't need fluent French to get a post, but a *TEFL* (*Teaching English as a Foreign Language*) qualification may well be required. If you apply from home, most schools will fix up the necessary papers for you. It's also quite feasible to find a teaching job when you're in France, but you may have to accept semiofficial status and no job security. For the addresses of schools, look under *Écoles de Langues* in the Professions directory of the local phone book. Offering **private lessons** (via university noticeboards or classified ads), you'll have lots of competition, and it's hard to reach the people who can afford it, but it's always worth a try. Marseille is probably the best city to try this as there are fewer English-speaking students around. Aix University is full of Americans, who tend to get most of what's available in that city and elsewhere, particularly on the coast, there are all the kids of the English and American residents to compete with.

Au pair work is usually arranged through one of a dozen agencies, all of which are listed in *Working Holidays*. In Britain, *The Lady* is *the* magazine for classified adverts for such jobs, arranged privately. As initial numbers to ring, try *Euroyouth* (☎01702/341434) in Britain, or *Accueil Familial des Jeunes Etrangers* (☎42.22.50.34) in Paris, or the *American Institute for Foreign Study* (☎203/869 9090) in the US, who can place female au pairs only; any of them will fill you in on the general terms and conditions (never very generous), and the state of the market. You shouldn't get paid less than 1000F a month (on top of board and lodging). It is wise to have an escape route (like a ticket home) in case you find the conditions intolerable – many people have had bad experiences. *Euroyouth* also runs a summer holiday scheme, placing people in French families for two to three weeks, where you get free board and lodging in exchange for English lessons.

CLAIMING BENEFIT

If you're an EU citizen – and you do the paperwork in advance – you can sign on for **unemployment benefit**. To do so, you must collect form E303 before leaving home, available in Britain from any DSS office. The procedure is first to get registered at an *ANPE* office (*Agence Nationale pour l'Emploi*), then take the form to your local *ASSEDIC* (benefits office) and give them an address, which can be a hostel or a hotel, for the money to be sent to. You sign once a month at the *ANPE* and receive benefit a month in arrears, in theory. In practice payments can be delayed in small towns for up to three months. After three months, you must anyway either leave the country or get a *carte de séjour*. EU pensioners can arrange for their pensions to be paid in France, but not, unfortunately, to receive French state pensions.

STUDYING IN FRANCE

It's relatively easy to be a **student** in France. Foreigners pay no more than French nationals (around 1300F a year) to enrol for a course, and the only problem then is to support yourself. Your *carte de séjour* and – if you're an EU citizen – social security will be assured, and you'll be eligible for subsidized accommodation, meals and all the student reductions. In general, French universities are much less formal than British ones and many people perfect their fluency in the language while studying. There are strict entry

STUDYING FOR NORTH AMERICANS

Note: most universities have semester abroad programmes to certain countries; the following are independent organizations that run programmes in France.

American Institute for Foreign Study, 102 Greenwich Ave, Greenwich, CT 06830 (☎1-800/727 2437).
Language study and cultural immersion for the summer or school year.

Council on International Educational Exchange (CIEE), 205 E 42nd St, New York, NY 10017 (☎1-800/641 2433).
The non-profit parent organization of Council Travel and Council Charter, CIEE runs summer, semester and academic-year programmes.

School for International Training, Kipling Rd, PO Box 676, Brattleboro, VT 05302 (☎802/257 7751).
Accredited college semesters abroad, comprising language and cultural studies, homestay and other academic work.

requirements, including an exam in French, for undergraduate degrees, not for post-graduate courses. For full **details and prospectuses**, contact the Cultural Service of any French embassy or consulate (see p.18).

Language schools all along the coast provide **intensive French courses** for foreigners; some are detailed in the *Guide*. The most popular is the summer Language and Civilization course at Aix. A complete list is given in the hand-out *"Cours de Français pour Etudiants Etrangers"*, also obtainable from embassy or consular cultural sections. Finally, it's worth noting that if you're a full-time student in France, you can get a **work permit** for the following summer as long as your visa is still valid.

DIRECTORY

ALARM CALLS ☎36.88 or with a digital phone dial ☎*55* then the time (for example 0715 for 7.15); the cost is 3.65F.

BEACHES are public property within 5m of the high-tide mark, so you can kick sand past private villas and hotel sunbeds. Under a different law, however, you can't camp. Getting to many beaches and parking a car often require entry through *terrain privé* (private land). In some instances, such "private beaches" charge a daily fee of 30 or 40F per car, but in return you may find facilities such as showers, plus beach bars and restaurants.

CAMERAS AND FILM Film is considerably cheaper in North America than France or Britain, so stock up if you're coming from there. If you're bringing a video camcorder, make sure any tapes you purchase in France are VHS. The normal French format, PAL, will only give black and white when played on VHS machines. Again, American videotape prices are way below French prices.

CHILDREN AND BABIES pose few travel problems. They're generally welcome everywhere, and in most bars and restaurants. **Hotels** charge by the room, with a small supplement for an additional bed or cot, and family-run places will usually babysit or offer a listening service while you eat or go out. Many **restaurants** have children's menus or will cook simpler food on request. You'll have no difficulty finding disposable nappies (*couches à jeter*), but nearly all baby foods have added sugar and salt, and French milk powders are very rich indeed. *SNCF* charge nothing on **trains and buses** for under-fours, and half-fare for four to eleven-year-olds (see p.7 for other reductions). Most local tourist offices have details of specific activities for children; along the coast there are a great number of classy funfairs, marinelands, zoos, go-karting tracks etc, all designed to extract the maximum amount of money off you. But almost every town has a municipal **children's playground** with a good selection of activities. Something to beware of – not that you can do much about it – is the difficulty of negotiating a child's **buggy** over the cobbles and steps of many of the hilltop villages.

CONTRACEPTIVES Contraception was only legalized in 1967 but condoms (*préservatifs* or *capotes*) have been available at all pharmacies ever since, as well as, now, from many clubs and street dispensers in larger cities. The Provence-Côte d'Azur is the French region with the highest number of people infected with **HIV** – just because you're on holiday, don't forget to practise safe sex. You can also get from pharmacies spermicidal cream and jelly (*dose contraceptive*), plus suppositories (*ovules, suppositoires*), and (with a prescription) the pill (*la pillule*), a diaphragm or IUD (*un sterilet*).

ELECTRICITY is 220V out of double, round-pin wall sockets.

FISHING You need to become a member of a fishing club to get rights – this is not difficult, and any tourist office will give you a local address.

FOREST FIRES Every summer forest fires in Provence and the Côte d'Azur hit the international headlines. Vast tracts become blazing infernos long before the sprayers from Nice or Marseille can reach the area. Loss of life is common and people's homes are frequently destroyed. So always take the utmost care. The emergency number for the fire service is ☎18.

LAUNDRY Laundries are common in French towns, and some are listed in the *Guide* – elsewhere look in the phone book under *Laveries Automatiques*. The alternative *blanchisserie* or *pressing* services are likely to be expensive, and hotels in particular charge very high rates. If you're doing your own washing in hotels, keep quantities small as most forbid doing any laundry in your room.

LEFT LUGGAGE There are lockers at all train stations and *consignes* for bigger items or longer periods.

SWIMMING POOLS Swimming pools or *piscines* are well signposted in most French towns and reasonably priced. Tourist offices have their addresses.

TIME France is one hour ahead of Britain throughout the year, except for a short period during October when it's the same. It is six hours ahead of Eastern Standard Time, nine hours ahead of Pacific Standard Time. This also applies during daylight-saving seasons, which are observed in France (as in most of Europe) from the end of March until the end of September.

TOILETS are usually to be found downstairs in bars, along with the phone, or there are the automatic concrete monsters on the streets costing 1F. Dirty, hole-in-the-ground, squatting loos are still common. The usual euphemism for toilet is "WC", always pronounced "vé-sé".

WATER The fountains in the squares of towns and villages of Provence are there to provide water. Unless a notice says *Eau non potable* – a very rare occurence – the water is drinkable and deliciously cool.

WEATHER Recorded information on weather conditions is available in each *département*.

Alpes-de-Haute-Provence ☎36.68.02.04.

Alpes Maritimes ☎36.68.02.06.

Bouches-du-Rhône ☎36.68.02.13.

Var ☎36.68.02.83.

Vaucluse ☎36.68.02.84.

PART TWO

THE GUIDE

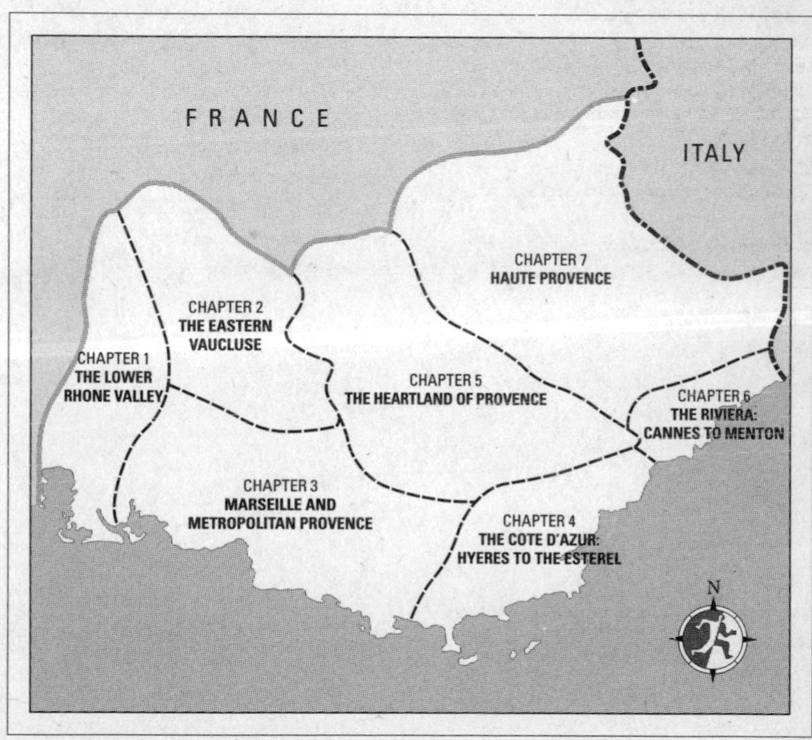
FRANCE
ITALY
CHAPTER 7
HAUTE PROVENCE
CHAPTER 2
THE EASTERN
VAUCLUSE
CHAPTER 1
THE LOWER
RHONE VALLEY
CHAPTER 5
THE HEARTLAND OF PROVENCE
CHAPTER 6
THE RIVIERA:
CANNES TO MENTON
CHAPTER 3
MARSEILLE AND
METROPOLITAN PROVENCE
CHAPTER 4
THE COTE D'AZUR:
HYERES TO THE ESTEREL
N

CHAPTER ONE

THE LOWER RHONE VALLEY

Long a frontier between France and Provence, the last stretch of the **Rhône Valley** has seen centuries of fortification on its banks, at **Beaucaire** and **Villeneuve-lès-Avignon** on the French side, at **Tarascon**, **Boulben** and **Barbentane** in Provence. Once the north–south route of ancient armies, medieval traders and modern rail and road, the valley, in parts, is now as industrialized as the least attractive parts of the north.

The river has also been a vital trading route, bringing wealth and fame to **Arles** at the mouth of its delta, though its waters now act as a dumping ground for the heavy industries along its banks. Arles, the centre of Roman *Provincia*, which stretched from the Pyrenees to the Alps, became the capital of Gaul towards the end of the Roman era. Its great amphitheatre, like the theatre in the Roman city of **Orange**, still seats thousands for summer entertainments. At **Glanum**, outside **St-Rémy-de-Provence**, are the overlaid remains of Greek and Roman towns and between Arles and St-Rémy the Roman's brilliant use of water power is in evidence in the **Barbegal** mill.

The prime city of this stretch, **Avignon**, focuses on medieval times when it belonged to the popes, a link that remained until the Revolution. One of France's major centres of art and architecture, Avignon has the best cultural event, a **festival of dramatric arts and dance** that has been going now for half a century.

After the relentless industrialization of the riverbanks all the way to Avignon, save for the famous vineyards of **Châteauneuf-du-Pape**, the **countryside** begins with the modest rural attractions of two plains, **La Petite Crau** and **La Crau**, enclosed by the River Durance and the Rhône, and separated by the abrupt ridge of the **Alpilles**. Here the villages and small towns have retained a nineteenth-century charm with customs and traditions revived by the great Provençal poet **Frédéric Mistral**, a native of La Petite Crau. This is also countryside that **Van Gogh** painted when he spent a year at Arles and then sought refuge in St-Rémy. Both towns pay tribute to his tragic brilliance.

Below Arles, where the Rhône divides, is the strange watery land of the **Camargue**, with a natural history and way of life quite distinct from surrounding regions. The wet expanses sustain flocks of flamingoes and a multitude of other

HOTEL ROOM PRICES

For a fuller explanation of these price codes, see the box on p.32 of *Basics*.

① Under 160F	② 160–220F	③ 220–300F	④ 300–400F
⑤ 400–500F	⑥ 500–600F	⑦ 600–700F	⑧ over 700F

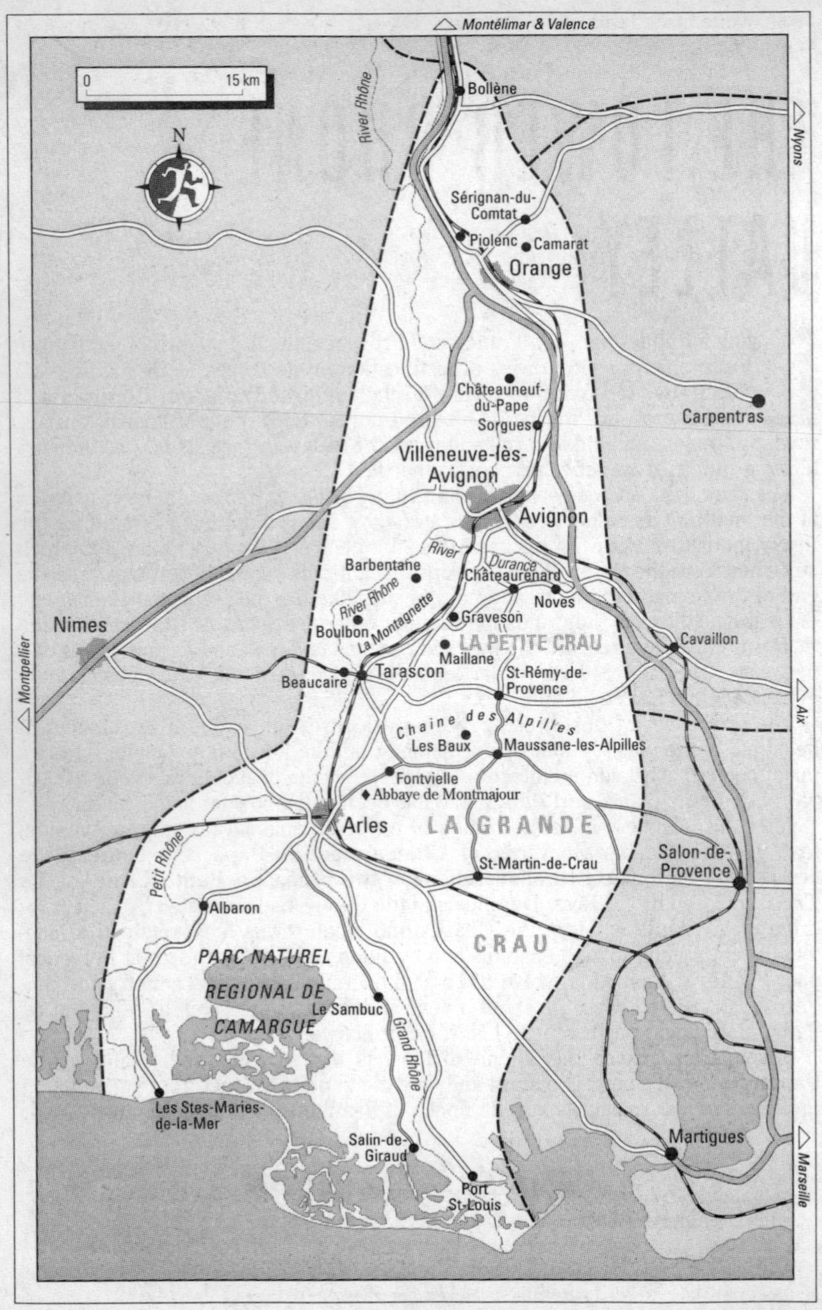

Montélimar & Valence
0
15 km
N
River Rhône
Bollène
Nyons
Sérignan-du-Comtat
Piolenc
Camarat
Orange
Châteauneuf-du-Pape
Sorgues
Carpentras
Villeneuve-lès-Avignon
Avignon
River Durance
Barbentane
Châteaurenard
Noves
River Rhône
La Montagnette
Graveson
Boulbon
LA PETITE CRAU
Maillane
Cavaillon
Nimes
Beaucaire
Tarascon
St-Rémy-de-Provence
Montpellier
Aix
Chaine des Alpilles
Les Baux
Maussane-les-Alpilles
Fontvielle
Abbaye de Montmajour
Arles
LA GRANDE
CRAU
Petit Rhône
St-Martin-de-Crau
Salon-de-Provence
Albaron
PARC NATUREL REGIONAL DE CAMARGUE
Le Sambuc
Grand Rhône
Les Stes-Maries-de-la-Mer
Salin-de-Giraud
Port St-Louis
Martigues
Marseille

birds, while black bulls and wild white horses graze on the edges of the marshes and lagoons. The Camargue also provides a sanctuary for unique social traditions. It is here, to **Les-Saintes-Maries-de-la-Mer**, that the **gypsies** gather every year from all over the Mediterranean to celebrate their patron saint, Sarah.

Orange

ORANGE was the former seat of the counts of Orange, a title created by Emperor Charlemagne in the eighth century, and passed to the Dutch crown of Nassau in the sixteenth century. Its most memorable member was the Protestant Prince William, who ascended the English throne with his consort Queen Mary in 1689; the Protestant Orange Order in Ireland was founded to support William's military campaign against his Catholic predessesor, James II, which ended with the Battle of the Boyne. The city today, however, is best known for its ancient sights and the spectacular **Roman theatre**, which hosts two important summer **music festivals**.

The quality of these festivals, however, has been put in jeopardy by Le Pen's *Front National* victory in the municipal elections of 1995. A huge debate is raging amongst French artists, with many of Arab or African origin arguing that it's now more important than ever for them to perform here, while others declare they will have nothing to do with events that increase the town hall's income and prestige. The **strip cartoon festival** in May, which used to bring in weird and wonderful characters, may also be affected.

Orange has never been the friendliest of towns, though its medieval street plan, Thursday market, fountained squares and houses with ancient porticos and courtyards are attractive enough. Aside from the theatre, the triumphal **Roman arch**, and **museum** with an unlikely Welsh connection, there's not much to detain you, and you may feel that, however distant, the parallels between Roman culture and today's neo-fascists are such that you can give the whole place a miss with a clear conscience. If you're happy to linger, however, there is a surprising treat in the old residence of the nineteenth-century scientist, the **Hamas** of **Jean-Henri Fabre**, close to Orange.

Arrival, information and accommodation

The **gare SNCF** is about 1500m east of the centre, at the end of av Frédéric-Mistral. The nearest bus stop is at the bottom of rue Jean-Reboul, the first left as you walk away from the station. Bus #2, direction *Nogent*, will take you to the *Théâtre Antique* and the next stop, *Gasparin*, to the **tourist office** on av Charles-de-Gaulle (April–Sept Mon–Sat 9am–7pm, Sun 9am–1pm; Oct–March Mon–Sat 9am–5pm; ☎90.34.70.88). The **gare routière** is close to the centre on place Pourtoules, just east of the theatre. There's undergound parking here if you're coming in **by car**.

You'll have no problem finding accommodation in Orange, except during the July Chorégies festival.

Hotels

Arcotel, 8 pl des Herbes (☎90.34.09.23). Overlooking the pretty pl des Herbes, it is small, appealing and good value. ③

L'Arène, pl de Langes (☎90.34.10.95). Spacious rooms and all mod cons. ⑤

Fréau, 3 rue Ancien-Collège (☎90.34.06.26). Central, simple and cheap, and immaculately kept by two elderly women. Advance bookings are advisable. Closed Aug. ②

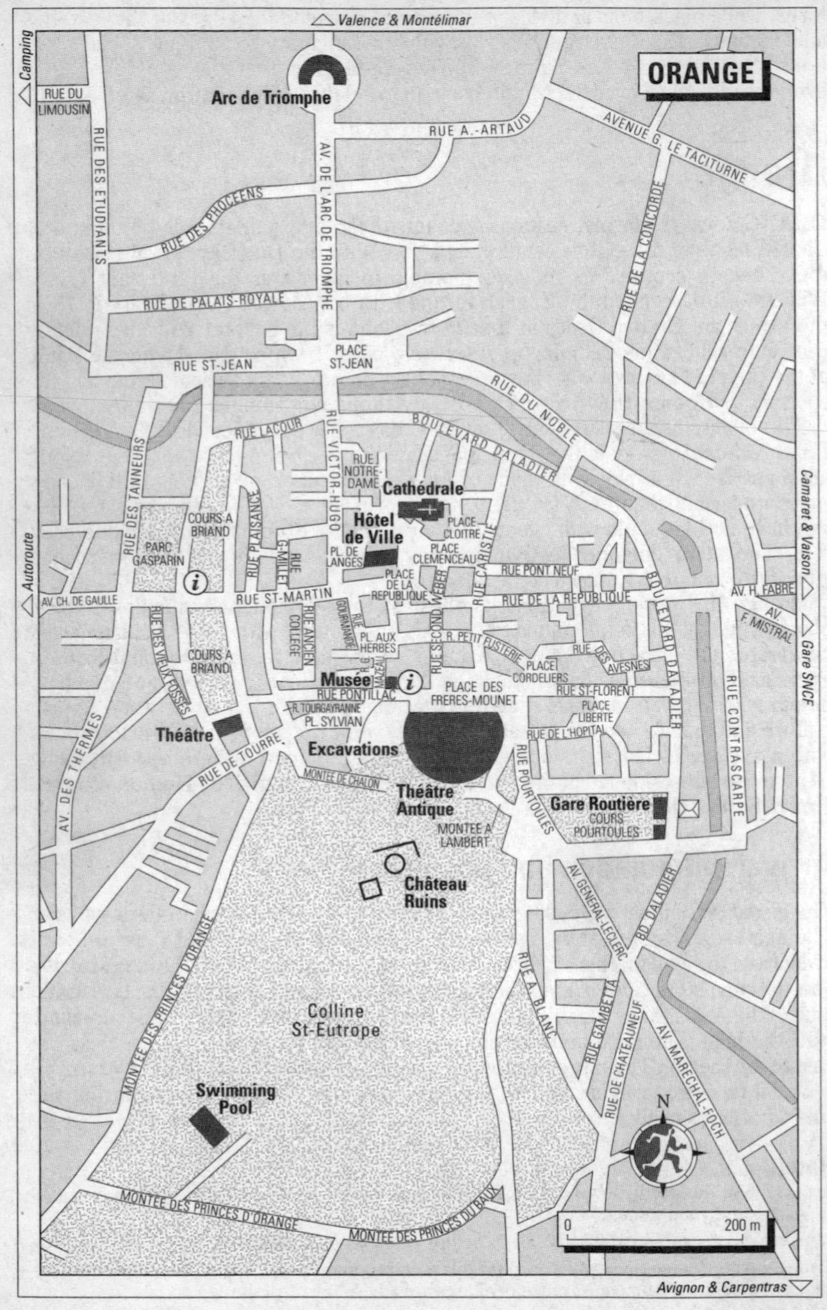
ORANGE
Valence & Montélimar
Camping
Autoroute
Camaret & Vaison
Gare SNCF
Avignon & Carpentras
Arc de Triomphe
Cathédrale
Hôtel de Ville
Musée
Théâtre
Excavations
Théâtre Antique
Château Ruins
Gare Routière
Colline St-Eutrope
Swimming Pool
PARC GASPARIN
COURS A BRIAND
PLACE ST-JEAN
PLACE CLOITRE
PLACE CLEMENCEAU
PLACE DE LA REPUBLIQUE
PL. DE LANGES
PL. AUX HERBES
PLACE DES FRERES-MOUNET
PLACE CORDELIERS
PLACE LIBERTE
PL. SYLVIAN
COURS POURTOULES
RUE DU LIMOUSIN
RUE DES ETUDIANTS
RUE DES PHOCEENS
AV. DE L'ARC DE TRIOMPHE
RUE A.-ARTAUD
AVENUE G. LE TACITURNE
RUE DE LA CONCORDE
RUE DE PALAIS-ROYALE
RUE ST-JEAN
RUE DU NOBLE
RUE LACOUR
BOULEVARD DALADIER
RUE VICTOR-HUGO
RUE NOTRE-DAME
RUE DES TANNEURS
RUE PLAISANCE
RUE G.-MILLET
RUE CARISTIE
RUE PONT NEUF
RUE DE LA REPUBLIQUE
AV. H. FABRE
AV. F. MISTRAL
AV. CH. DE GAULLE
RUE ST-MARTIN
RUE ANCIEN COLLEGE
RUE SECOND WEBER
R. PETIT FUSTERIE
RUE DES AVESNES
RUE DES VIEUX FOSSES
RUE PONTILLAC
RUE ST-FLORENT
R. TOURGAYRANNE
RUE DE L'HOPITAL
RUE CONTRASCARPE
AV. DES THERMES
RUE DE TOURRE
MONTEE DE CHALON
MONTEE A LAMBERT
RUE POURTOULES
AV. GENERAL-LECLERC
BD. DALADIER
RUE A. BLANC
RUE GAMBETTA
RUE DE CHATEAUNEUF
AV. MARECHAL-FOCH
MONTEE DES PRINCES D'ORANGE
MONTEE DES PRINCES DU BAUX
N
0
200 m

Le Glacier, 46 cours Aristide-Briand (☎90.34.02.01). One of the most comfortable of the town's hotels. ④

Louvre et Terminus, 89 av Frédéric-Mistral (☎90.34.10.08). Useful if you don't want to shift your luggage far from the train station. ⑤

Campsite

Le Jonquier, 1321 rue Alexis-Carrel (☎90.34.19.83). Three-star site to the northwest of the centre and equipped with tennis courts, pool and mini golf. Open mid-March to Oct.

The Town

Orange is not a very big town and can be easily covered on foot. Its old streets lie north of the enormous Roman theatre which, with the hill of St-Europe behind, are the dominating features.

The theatre

Days off in Orange circa 5 BC were entertainingly spent from dawn to dusk at the **Theatre**, where an audience of ten thousand could watch farce, clownish improvisations, song and dance, and occasionally, for the sake of a visiting dignitary, a bit of heavy Greek tragedy, usually in Latin. Today, although the action is limited to summer music, the theatre (April–Oct daily 9am–6.30pm; Nov–March 9am–noon & 1.30–5pm; 25F combined ticket with museum) is still the focus of the town, an awesome shell at the heart of the old medieval centre, which has survived periods as a fortification, slum and prison, before its careful reconstruction in the last century. In 1879 the first performance in 350 years was staged, initiating the Orange **Chorégies**, a festival of musical and dramatic arts (see box overleaf).

Said to be the best-preserved Roman theatre in existence, Orange's theatre is the only one with the stage wall still standing – and stand it does, across 103m to a height of 36m. The outer face, viewed from place des Frères-Mounets, resembles some monstrous prison wall, despite the ground-level archways leading into the backstage areas. Near the top you can see the blocks that held the poles of an awning which hung over the stage and the front rows. Those at the back were protected from the sun by the hill of St-Eutrope into which the seats are built. Rows were allocated strictly by rank, an inscription "*EQ Gradus III*" (third row for knights) is visible near the orchestra pit. The enormous **stage** could accommodate vast numbers of performers, and the acoustics, thanks to the complex projections of the stage wall, allowed a full audience to hear every word. Though missing most of its original decoration, the inner side of the stage wall is an extremely impressive sight. Columned niches, now empty of their statues, run the length of the wall; below them an over-life-size statue of Augustus, raising his arm in imperious fashion, looks down centre stage.

If the spectators got bored with the performance they could slip out of the west door to a complex in a semicircle cut into the rock. According to some archeologists, this contained baths, a stage for combats and a gymnasium equipped with three 180-metre running tracks alongside the wall of rue Pontillac, parts of which still stand. Others say it was the forum, or even a circus. There are widely differing views on how the excavations should be interpreted, though all agree that the massive capital was part of a temple.

The best view of the theatre in its entirety, and for which you don't have to pay, is from **St-Eutrope hill**. You can follow a path up the hill either from the top of

FESTIVALS

Since 1986 Orange has hosted a **Festival BD** (*Bandes-Dessinées* or cartoon strips) in May. The cours Aristide Briand is filled with stalls and there are exhibitions, talks, films, and displays of thousands of comic books in the library, museum and municipal and Roman theatres. Details from Sabords 8·1 (☎90.51.19.95).

In July Orange is packed with opera fanatics for the **Chorégies** or choral festival performed in the Roman theatre. Regrettably it has turned away from productions of the spoken classics which actors such as Sarah Bernhardt performed here at the turn of the century, but if you're interested, and prepared to make a reservation well in advance, details can be had from the *Bureau des Chorégies*, place Silvain, 84107 Orange (☎90.34.24.24). Ticket prices range from 80F to 880F. The theatre is also used for jazz, film, folk and rock concerts during the **Nuits d'Eté du Théâtre Antique** in June. Prices range from 100F to 350F; details from the *Centre Culturel Mosaïque*, place Silvain (☎90.34.63.00). Tickets for both festivals can be bought from *FNAC* shops in all the big French cities.

cours Aristide-Briand, montée P. de Chalons, or from cours Pourtoules, montée Albert Lambert, until you are looking directly down onto the stage. The **ruins** around your feet are those of the short-lived seventeenth-century **castle** of the princes of Orange. Louis XIV had it destroyed and the principality annexed to France, a small setback for William of Orange of the Netherlands who was to become king of England, Wales and Ireland.

The museum and Arc de Triomphe

Orange's **Musée Municipal** is across the road from the theatre entrance (April–Oct Mon–Sat 9am–7pm, Sun 10am–6pm; Nov–March Mon–Sat 9am–noon & 1.30–5pm, Sun 9am–noon & 2–5.30pm; 25F combined ticket with the theatre). Its various documents concerning the Orange dynasty include a suitably austere portrait of the very first Orangeman, William (Guillaume) the Taciturn, grandfather to William III. The museum also has an interesting – for classical historians at least – property register and land survey of the city in 77 AD, and various bits and pieces from the theatre are also on display. In the best traditions of provincial town museums there's also an extremely unlikely collection of works by one Frank Brangwyn, a Welsh painter who learnt his craft with William Morris and whose commissioned designs for the House of Lords were rejected as being better suited to a nightclub. The pictures here are stark portrayals of British workers early this century.

If you've arrived by road from the north you will have passed the town's second major monument, the **Arc de Triomphe** whose intricate friezing and relief gloat over imperial victories against the Gauls. Classicists rave about it as one of the largest, best-preserved and oldest triple-bayed Roman arches in existence. However, its position in the middle of a main road makes looking at pictures of it a more attractive option than studying the real thing.

Eating and drinking

Eating out in Orange is unlikely to prove an exceptional experience but there's no shortage of choice. *La Fringale*, 10 rue de Tourre (closed Wed & Sat midday, & Sun midday out of season; open till 11pm) is a fast-food resto with cheap *frites* and plats du jour to eat in or take away. At *Le Yaca*, 24 place Silvain (closed Tues evening & Wed) there's a generous choice of efficiently served dishes for under 100F in an old vaulted chamber. Next door, *L'Aigo Boulido* (☎90.34.18.19) stays open after festival performances and has a 70F menu; and *Le Galois,* opposite, does midday salads for under 50F. Probably the best meal in Orange is to be had at *Trimalcion*, 12 rue Petite Fusterie (closed Sun & Mon evening out of season; ☎90.34.09.96) with fish specialities and flambéed foie gras and menus from 98F to 180F.

For **drinking**, head for place de la République in the centre, where you'll find *Les Négociants*, the *Commerce* and the less expensive *Café de l'Univers* with photos of old Orange on the walls. These places are busy when the shops are open but not very lively at night. On the other side of cours Aristide-Briand, the *Café des Thermes*, 29 rue des Vieux-Fossés, has a good selection of beers, pool and a youngish clientele, and is a better bet for evening entertainment.

Around Orange

If you have your own transport, it's an enjoyable drive to the village of **SERIGNAN-DU-COMTAT**, 8km northeast of Orange; otherwise, there are three buses a day from both Orange and Avignon. Along the way are beautiful views of the smooth lower slopes of Mont Ventoux, and if you take the minor roads (D975, then D43) you pass the tiny wine-producing village of **CAMARAT**, guarded by a round-towered gateway topped with a campanile. Camarat's one claim to fame was a black Virgin Mary holding Jesus on her lap rather than to her breast. In 1736 the bishop of Orange ordered the "indecent" statue to be burnt.

Sérignan is no bigger than Camarat, and would be unexceptional were it not for **Jean-Henri Fabre** (1823–1915), whose statue stands beside the red-shuttered buildings of the Mairie. A remarkable self-taught scientist who spent the last 36 years of his life here, Fabre is famous primarily for his insect studies; he also composed poetry, wrote songs and painted his specimens with artistic brilliance as well as scientific accuracy. As a boy his family's poverty constantly interrupted his education, but with the help of scholarships and, later, with pure, stubborn self-discipline, he attained diplomas in mathematics and all three sciences. In his forties, with seven children to support, he was forced to resign from his teaching post at Avignon because parents and priests thought his lectures on the fertilization of flowering plants to be licentious if not downright pornographic. His friend John Stuart Mill eventually bailed him out with a loan, allowing him to settle in Orange. Darwin was also a friend with whom he had lengthy correspondence, though Fabre was too religious to be an evolutionist.

Fabre's house, which he named the **Harmas** (Latin for fallow land) is on the edge of the village on the N976 from Orange (Oct–March Mon & Wed–Sat 9–11.30am & 2–4pm; April–Sept till 6pm; 15F). You can see his study with various specimens of insects and other invertebrates and his complete classification of the herbs of France and Corsica. Unlike so many vaunted workplaces of the famous dead, this room gives a strong sense of a person in love with the world he researched, an impression that is confirmed by the selection on the ground floor of Fabre's extraordinary **water-colours** of the fungi of the Vaucluse. The stunning colours and almost hallucinogenic detail make these pictures more like holograms than plastic art. After visiting the house you're free to wander round the **garden** where over a thousand species grow in wild disorder, exactly as Fabre wanted it.

Sérignan has a very smart **hotel-restaurant**, *L'Hostellerie du Vieux Château*, set in large grounds on rte de Sainte-Cécile-les-Vignes (☎90.70.05.58; ⑧) and a lovely little **restaurant**, *La Roselière*, 4 rue du Renoyer (closed Wed & Thurs midday), offering a menu at around 100F out of season, otherwise around 150F.

Six kilometres to the north of Orange, just before **POILENC**, is the well-advertised **Cirque Alexis-Gruss**. Be warned that not only is its little circus museum very tatty and uninspiring, but animals panting for water are kept in tiny enclosures. Poilenc is the place to go on the last weekend in August for its traditional **garlic festival**.

Towards Avignon: Châteauneuf-du-Pape

The stretch of the Rhône approaching Avignon is a pretty sight at sunset, when the pollutants in the air assure vivid reds and pinks. At other times the banks are an all-too-visible tangle of pipeways, ducts and chimneys from assorted industries. Due east of Orange, across the river, sprawls the Marcoule Atomic Energy Centre, where nuclear power is used in the creation of industrial and medical components as well as electricity. The river water cooling its reactors has already done similar circuits several times over in the journey down from Lyon. It's used more appropriately in the hydroelectric power stations at Caderousse and Avignon. There is, however, one place amid this landscape that exerts a strong pull to outsiders. This is **CHATEAUNEUF-DU-PAPE**, a large village on the backroad from Orange to Avignon (10km from Orange; 4 buses daily).

Châteauneuf-du-Pape takes its name from the ruins of the fourteenth-century Avignon popes' summer château, but neither this nor the medieval streets around **place du Portail**, the hub of the village, give Châteauneuf its appeal. It is the local **vineyards** that produce the magic, with grapes warmed at night by the large pebbles that cover the ground and soak up the sun's heat by day. Their rich ruby red wine is one of the most renowned in France, but the white, too, is exquisite.

Wine tasting

The *appellation Châteauneuf-du-Pape* does not, alas, come cheap, nor is there a centre where you can taste a good selection from the scores of *domaines*. If you're intent on buying, check the lists from the **tourist office** on place du Portail (July & Aug Mon–Sat 9am–8pm, Sun 10am–5pm; rest of year Mon–Sat 9am–12.30pm & 2–6pm; ☎90.83.71.08) and the *Fédération des Syndicats de Producteurs* at 12 av Louis-Pasteur. You could ask for the addresses of the previous April 25 competition when the village celebrates Saint Marc, patron saint of wine-growers, with a procession from the church and a tasting by professionals to determine the best wines from the last vintage. Otherwise, you can visit an *Association de Vignerons* such as *Prestige et Tradition*, 3 rue de la République (daily 8am–noon & 2–6pm), *Reflets*, 2 chemin du Bois de la Ville (Mon–Fri 8am–noon & 2–6pm), or *La Vinothèque*, 9 rue de la République (daily 9am–7pm), who group together several producers.

For a casual introduction, the best bet is the *Cave Père Anselme* on av Bienheureux-Pierre-de-Luxembourg, which has a **Musée des Outils de Vignerons** (daily 9am–noon & 2–6pm; free admission), plus free tasting of its own and other Rhône wines.

If you can coincide with the first weekend of August you'll find free *dégustation* stalls throughout the village, as well as parades, dances, equestrian contests, folkloric floats and so forth, all to celebrate the reddening of the grapes in the **Fête de la Véraison**. As well as wine, a good deal of grape liqueur (*marc*) finds its way down people's throats.

Practicalities

Getting too drunk to leave Châteauneuf is not advisable unless you're prepared to pay dearly for your excesses. The options are confined to three **hotels**: *La Garbure*, 3 rue Joseph-Ducos (closed Wed and last 3 weeks in Aug; ☎90.83.75.08; ③), which has only five rooms; the four-star *Hostellerie du Château des Fines Roches*, rte d'Avignon (closed Sun evening and Mon out of season; ☎90.83.70.23; ⑧) with seven rooms, and *La Mère Germaine*, av Cdt-Lemaitre (closed Jan–March; ☎90.83.70.72; ④) close to place de Portail and also with just seven rooms. There are two **chambres d'hôtes**, though equally likely to be booked up: chez Mme Melchor, *La Font du Pape* (☎90.83.73.97; ③) and chez Mme Dexheimer, *Clos Bimard*, rte de Roquemaure (March–Oct; ☎90.83.73.16; ②), and a two-star **campsite**, *Islon St-Luc* (☎90.83.76.77), about 2km down chemin de la Calade, south from place Portail.

You can **eat** well for around 100F at the brasserie *La Mule du Pape* at 2 rue de la République, which also has a gastronomic restaurant on the first floor (both closed Mon; ☎90.83.79.22). If you're going to blow money here, *La Mère Germaine* (see hotels above; closed Mon and Sun evening out of season) is the place to do it, with a panoramic view over the vineyards, all the best local wines and exquisite cooking. A menu under 200F is served for weekday lunches. For cakes, chocolates and ice creams, be tempted by *Delices Papales*, 2 rue Joseph-Ducros.

The **bus stop** is at the bottom of av des Bousquets which leads up to place Jean-Moulin, rue de la République and place Portail.

Avignon

AVIGNON, great city of the popes and for centuries one of the major artistic centres of France, can be very daunting. The monuments and museums, that tourist conscience says you've got to do, are huge; it's always crowded in summer and can be stiflingly hot. But it is an immaculately preserved medieval town with endless impressively decorated buildings, ancient churches, chapels and convents, and more places to eat and drink than you could cover in a month. During the **Festival d'Avignon** in July and the beginning of August it is *the* place to be.

The Avignon "intra muros" that people visit is only a small corner of a large industrial city whose suburbs merge with the neighbouring towns alongside the *Autoroute du Soleil* 8km east. The Rhône is full of effluents and currents that make swimming unthinkable, but there is cultivated open countryside close at hand on the **Ile de la Barthelasse**, and the much less crowded town of **Villeneuve-Lès-Avignon** on the opposite bank in Languedoc.

The papal city: some history

Avignon's monuments, and most of its history, are bound up almost entirely with the fourteenth century, when the city became the residence of the popes. **Pope Clement V**, taking refuge from anarchic feuding in Rome and northern Italy, first moved the papal headquarters here in 1309, a temporary act that turned out to

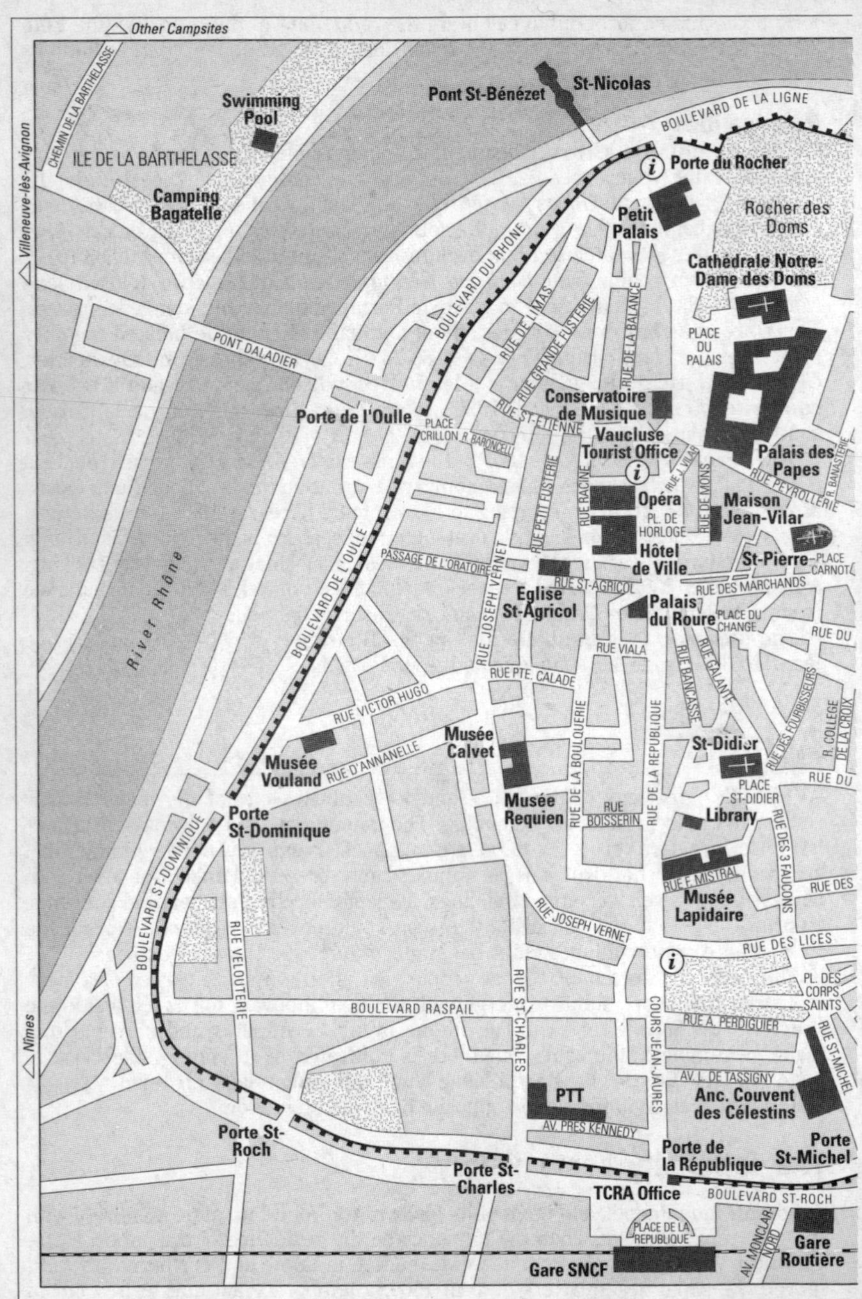
Other Campsites
Villeneuve-lès-Avignon
Nîmes
Swimming Pool
ILE DE LA BARTHELASSE
Camping Bagatelle
CHEMIN DE LA BARTHELASSE
Pont St-Bénézet
St-Nicolas
BOULEVARD DE LA LIGNE
Porte du Rocher
Petit Palais
Rocher des Doms
Cathédrale Notre-Dame des Doms
PLACE DU PALAIS
Palais des Papes
PONT DALADIER
River Rhône
BOULEVARD DU RHONE
RUE DE LIMAS
RUE GRANDE FUSTERIE
RUE DE LA BALANCE
Conservatoire de Musique
Porte de l'Oulle
PLACE CRILLON
R. BARONCELLI
RUE ST-ETIENNE
Vaucluse Tourist Office
RUE J. VILAR
RUE DE MONS
RUE PEYROLLERIE
R. BANASTERIE
RUE RACINE
RUE PETIT FUSTERIE
Opéra
PL. DE HORLOGE
Maison Jean-Vilar
Hôtel de Ville
St-Pierre
PLACE CARNOT
PASSAGE DE L'ORATOIRE
BOULEVARD DE L'OULLE
RUE JOSEPH VERNET
RUE ST-AGRICOL
Eglise St-Agricol
Palais du Roure
RUE DES MARCHANDS
PLACE DU CHANGE
RUE DU
RUE VIALA
RUE BANCASSE
RUE GALANTE
RUE PTE. CALADE
RUE VICTOR HUGO
RUE DES FOURBISSEURS
R. COLLEGE DE LA CROIX
Musée Calvet
Musée Vouland
RUE D'ANNANELLE
RUE DE LA BOULQUERIE
RUE DE LA REPUBLIQUE
St-Didier
PLACE ST-DIDIER
Musée Requien
RUE BOISSERIN
Library
RUE DES 3 FAUCONS
Porte St-Dominique
BOULEVARD ST-DOMINIQUE
RUE VELOUTERIE
RUE F. MISTRAL
Musée Lapidaire
RUE DES
RUE JOSEPH VERNET
RUE DES LICES
PL. DES CORPS SAINTS
BOULEVARD RASPAIL
RUE ST-CHARLES
COURS JEAN-JAURES
RUE A. PERDIGUIER
RUE ST-MICHEL
AV. L. DE TASSIGNY
PTT
Anc. Couvent des Célestins
AV. PRES KENNEDY
Porte St-Roch
Porte St-Charles
Porte de la République
Porte St-Michel
TCRA Office
BOULEVARD ST-ROCH
PLACE DE LA REPUBLIQUE
AV. MONCLAR NORD
Gare SNCF
Gare Routière

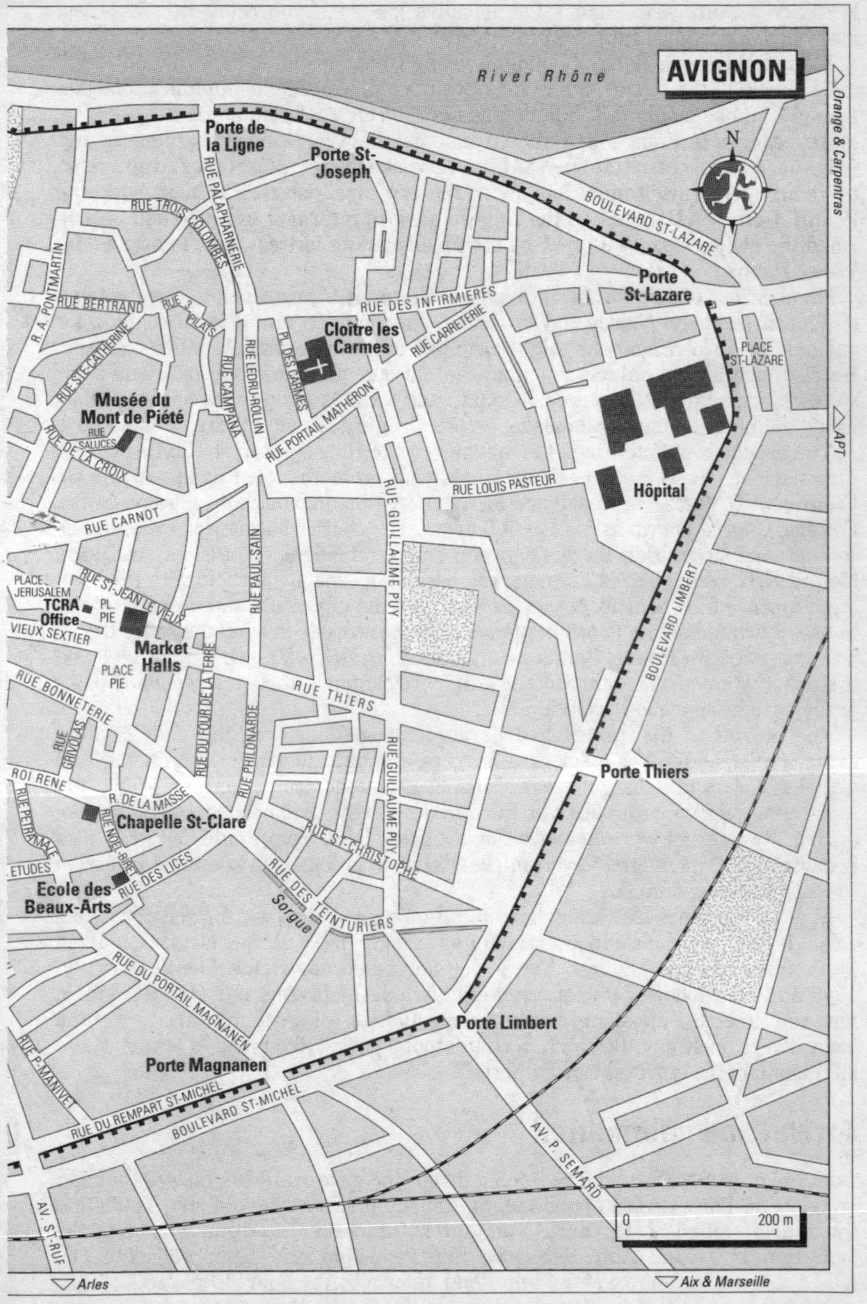
AVIGNON
River Rhône
Orange & Carpentras
APT
Arles
Aix & Marseille
N
0
200 m
Porte de la Ligne
Porte St-Joseph
Porte St-Lazare
Cloître les Carmes
Musée du Mont de Piété
Hôpital
TCRA Office
Market Halls
Porte Thiers
Chapelle St-Clare
Ecole des Beaux-Arts
Porte Limbert
Porte Magnanen
BOULEVARD ST-LAZARE
PLACE ST-LAZARE
RUE TROIS COLOMBES
RUE PALAPHARNERIE
R. A. PONTMARTIN
RUE BERTRAND
RUE 3 PILATS
RUE DES INFIRMIERES
RUE CARRETERIE
PL. DES CARMES
RUE LEDRU-ROLLIN
RUE CAMPANA
RUE STE-CATHERINE
RUE SALUCES
RUE DE LA CROIX
RUE PORTAIL MATHERON
RUE LOUIS PASTEUR
RUE GUILLAUME PUY
RUE CARNOT
RUE PAUL-SAIN
PLACE JERUSALEM
RUE ST-JEAN LE VIEUX
PL. PIE
VIEUX SEXTIER
PLACE PIE
RUE BONNETERIE
RUE DU FOUR DE LA TERRE
RUE THIERS
BOULEVARD LIMBERT
RUE GRIVOLAS
RUE PHILONARDE
ROI RENE
R. DE LA MASSE
RUE PETRAMALE
RUE NOEL-BIRET
ETUDES
RUE DES LICES
RUE ST-CHRISTOPHE
RUE DES TEINTURIERS
Sorgue
RUE DU PORTAIL MAGNANEN
RUE P-MANIVET
RUE DU REMPART ST-MICHEL
BOULEVARD ST-MICHEL
AV. P. SEMARD
AV. ST-RUF

last over seventy years, and a few decades longer, if you count the city's last flurry in defence of its antipope pretenders.

Though the town, unlike the neighbouring Châteauneuf-du-Pape, did not originally belong to the papacy, it had the advantage of excellent communications and a good Catholic landlord. Clement was not entirely confident about his security, however, even in France, and shifted his base between Vienne, Carpentras and Avignon. His successor, **Jean XXII**, had previously been bishop of Avignon, so he re-installed himself quite happily in the episcopal palace. The next Supreme Pontiff, **Benoît XII**, accepted the impossibility of returning to Rome and demolished the bishop's palace to replace it with an austere fortress, now known as the **Vieux Palais**.

Number four of the nine Avignon popes, **Clement VI**, managed to buy the town off Queen Jeanne of Naples and Provence, apparently in return for absolution for any possible involvement she might have had in the assassination of her husband. He also built a **new palace** adjoining the old one, a much more luxurious affair showing distinctly worldly tastes. The fifth and sixth Avignon popes further embellished and fortified the papal palace, before **Gregory XI**, after years of diplomacy, and an appeal from Catherine of Siena, moved the Holy See back to Rome in 1377. This did not please the French cardinals who promptly voted in the **Antipope Clement VII** to take up residence in Avignon, thus initiating the division in the Catholic Church known as the Great Schism. The courier business in excommunications and more worldly threats between Rome and Avignon flourished. **Antipope Benoît XIII**, who replaced Clement VII, became justifiably paranoid with the shifting alliances of the Schism. It was he who built the **city walls** and ordered all the houses surrounding the *Palais des Papes* to be destroyed, creating the space that is now the **place du Palais**. Benoît was hounded out by the French king in 1403 and thereafter Avignon had to be content with mere cardinals, though it remained papal property right up to the Revolution.

The **period of the popes** had its attractions. Along with the Holy Fathers came a vast entourage of clerks, lawyers, doctors, flatterers, merchants and wheeler-dealers of Italian, French, Catalan, Languedocian or German origin, not to mention pilgrims from all over Europe. Jews were given sanction, and so too, during the Schism, were heretics fleeing papal bulls from Rome. The city also became a catchment area for criminals, either to practise, or to escape justice in the neighbouring domains.

Most of the popes also knew how to put on a good show for the religious festivals. Visiting monarchs and ambassadors were greeted with spectacular candle-lit processions and banquetings. Every vice flourished, the **Black Death** struck in 1348 and was followed by intermittent periods of plague and famine, and in between times the appalling overcrowding took its toll. Avignon was, to say the least, a very lively city. Petrarch, a contemporary, described it as "a sewer where all the filth of the universe has gathered".

Arrival and information

Both the **gare SNCF**, on bd St-Rochand, and the **gare routière**, on av Montclar, are close to Porte de la République, on the south side of the old city. You'll find the **tourist office** at 41 cours Jean-Jaurès (Mon–Fri 9am–1pm & 2–6pm, Sat 9am–1pm & 2–5pm; April–Sept also Sun 9am–1pm & 2–5pm; ☎90.82.65.11), which also has an annexe at the other end of town by the Pont St-Bénézet.

If you're **driving**, it's best to park on either side of Pont Daladier outside the walls on the west side of the city as, once stuck in the narrow one-way system, driving in the city becomes very tiresome. The city's two main bus termini with *TCRA* offices for route maps and tickets (6.50F each or 36F for ten) are by Porte de la République (stops *Poste, Cité Administrative, Gare routière* and *Gare*) and place Pie, where you'd put the compass point to draw Avignon's walls. From *Cité Administrative* all buses go to place de l'Horloge.

Accommodation

Even outside festival time, finding a **room** in Avignon can be a problem: cheap hotels fill fast so it's a good idea to book in advance. It's worth remembering, too, that Villeneuve-lès-Avignon is only just across the river and may have rooms when its big neighbour is full. If in doubt, *VaucluseTourisme Hébergements* (Mon–Fri 9am–6pm, Sat 10am–5pm; ☎90.82.05.81), located in the main tourist office in summer and in place Campana in winter, can provide comprehensive information on accommodation in Avignon and the region as well as booking rooms for a small fee. All **campsites** are located on the Ile de la Barthelasse between Avignon and Villeneuve-lès-Avignon, an idyllic spot; take bus #10 from Poste to Porte de l'Oulle opposite Pont Daladier and then walk or take bus #20 onto the island. During the festival a temporary site is set up behind the Bagatelle with minimal facilities. Look out, also, for the odd **farmhouse** advertising rooms.

Hotels

Hôtel de l'Angleterre, 29 bd Raspail (☎90.86.34.31). Located in the southeast corner of the old city, this is an old and traditional hotel with some very reasonably priced rooms, well away from night-time noise. ④

La Cité des Papes, 1 rue J-Vilar (☎90.86.22.45). Between pl de l'Horloge and pl du Palais with the best views naturally going with the most expensive rooms, but comfort assured in all. ③–⑧

La Ferme, chemin du Bois, Ile de la Barthelasse (☎90.82.57.53). A sixteenth-century farm on the island in the Rhône (signed right off Pont Daladier as you cross over from Avignon), with well-equipped and pleasant rooms and greenery all around. ④

Garlande, 20 rue Galante (☎90.85.08.85). Delightful address right in the centre of the city on a narrow street. Well known so book in advance. ④

Ibis, 42 bd St-Roch (☎90.85.38.38). Within the train station complex, part of a chain and noisy, but with great views if you get a room facing the city. ④

Innova, 100 rue Joseph-Vernet (☎90.82.54.10). Small, friendly, and well worth booking. ③

Le Magnan, 63 rue Portail-Magnanen (☎90.86.36.51). Just inside the walls by Porte Magnanen a short way east from the station. Quiet, and with a very pleasant shaded garden. ④

Mignon, 12 rue Joseph-Vernet (☎90.82.17.30). Good value and stylish. ③

Hôtel de Mons, 5 rue de Mons (☎90.82.57.16). A thirteenth-century chapel imaginatively converted and very central. All the rooms are odd shapes and you breakfast beneath a vaulted ceiling. ④

Splendid, 17 rue Agricole-Perdiquier (☎90.86.14.46). Near pl des Corps-Saints, this is cheap but not very cheerful. ③

St-Roch, 9 rue Paul-Mérindol (☎90.82.18.63). Spacious, clean and quiet. ④

Hostels and foyers

Hameau Champfleury, 33 av Eisenhower (☎90.85.35.02). Individual rooms for around 150F including breakfast. Southeast of the *gare SNCF*; bus #1 or #2 to Champfleury stop. Mid-June to mid-Sept. ①

Pavillon Bleu Bagatelle, chemin de la Barthelasse, Ile de la Barthelasse (☎90.86.30.39). Rooms for 4 to 8 people, for under 80F, including breakfast. Bus #10 from Poste to Porte de l'Oulle, then bus #20 to *Bagatelle* stop. Open all year. ①

Residence La Madeleine, 4 impasse des Abeilles, 25 av Monclar-Nord (☎90.85.20.63). Studios with kitchenette for 2 people around 180F; for 3 or 4 people 220F. Turn right out of the station and first right, away from the old town. June–Sept. ②

Squash Club Hébergement, 32 bd Limbert (☎90.85.27.78). Three dormitories and an obsession with squash; under 50F a night. Bus #2 or #10, to the east along the city walls from the *gare SNCF*; stop *Thiers*. Closed Christmas holidays. ①

Campsites

Camping Bagatelle (☎90.86.30.39). A 3-star campsite alongside the Auberge Bagatelle; the closest to the city centre; *Bagatelle* stop. Open all year.

Camping Municipal Pont St-Bénézet (☎90.82.63.500). A 4-star site about 3km from the centre overlooking Pont St-Bénézet; *Bénézet* stop. Open March–Oct.

Les Deux Rhônes, chemin de Bellegarde, Ile de la Barthelasse (☎90.85.49.70). Around 4km from the city, but cheaper and smaller than the other two; *Traille* stop. Open June–Sept.

Parc des Libertés, Ile de la Barthelasse (☎90.85.17.73). The cheapest of the four. Open mid-April to mid-Sept.

The City

Avignon's **walls** still form a complete loop around the city. They appear far too low to be a serious defence, but half the full height is buried since it was impossible to excavate the moat during the nineteenth-century restoration work. All the gates and towers, however, were successfully repaired and there's a strong sense of being in an enclosed space quite separate from the modern spread of the city.

Running inside the wall gate, cours Jean-Jaurès becomes **rue de la République**, the main axis of the old town, leading straight up to **place de l'Horloge,** the central square. Beyond that is **place du Palais**, the **Rocher des Doms** park and the **Porte du Rocher** overlooking the Rhône by the Pont d'Avignon, or Pont St-Bénézet as it's officially known. Avignon's major monuments occupy a compact quarter inside the northern loop of the walls. The **Palais des Papes**, northeast of the square and home of the medieval popes, is obviously the city's major sight, but there are cardinals' and secular palaces dotted about the centre and, as you'd expect, a fair smattering of churches (most with very limited opening hours). The best of the **city's museums** are the **Petit Palais** and the **Musée Calvet**, and, for a break from the monumental, there are the pedestrian streets west of the papal palace towards place des Carmes, and to the southeast of the centre, the atmospheric **rue des Teinturiers**.

Around place du Palais

Serious sight-seeing is bound to start off here, a huge cobbled square with all the major monuments close at hand: the **Palais des Papes**, the **Cathedral**, the **Petit Palais**, the **Rocher des Doms park** and **Pont St-Bénézet**. Another dominant building on place du Palais is the beautiful seventeenth-century **Hôtel des Monnaies**, the old mint, now the music conservatory, with a facade of griffons, cherubs, eagles and swathes of fruit. To the west of the square is the redeveloped Quartier de la Balance, now teeming with souvenir shops, but once home to the gypsies in the nineteenth century.

Palais des Papes

The **Palais des Papes**, rising high above place du Palais on the east side (Nov–March daily 9am–12.45pm & 2–6pm; rest of year 9am–7pm, staying open till 8pm Aug 20 to Sept 30; last ticket 45min before closure; guided tours in English 43F, unguided visits 32F; 10F exhibition supplement mid-May to Sept; May 13 to June 25 & Aug 13 to Sept 30 Fri & Sat evening visits 9pm, 60F; exhibition and concert programme available from ticket office), is a monster of a building, doing to the vertical what Versailles does to the horizontal. If you want to get a dramatic neck-cricking angle on its towering height, follow rue Peyrolerie around the south end of the Palais.

Inside, so little remains of the original decoration and furnishings that you can be deceived into thinking that all the popes and their retinues were as pious and austere as the last official occupant, Benoît XII. The denuded interior certainly gives sparse indication of the corruption and decadence of fat, feuding cardinals and their mistresses, the thronging purveyors of jewels, velvet and furs, the musicians, chefs and painters competing for patronage, the riotous banquets and corridor schemings.

The visit begins in the **Consistoire** of the **Vieux Palais**, where sovereigns and ambassadors were received and the cardinals' council held. The flooring and the frescoes covering all the walls were destroyed by fire in 1413, with the only decoration now comprising fragments of frescoes moved from the cathedral and a nineteenth-century line-up of the popes, in which all nine look remarkably similar because the artist used the same model for each portrait.

If it's medieval artistry you're after, however, go to the **Chapelle St-Jean**, off the Consistoire, and the **Chapelle St-Martial** on the floor above. Both were decorated by a Sienese artist, Matteo Giovanetti, and commissioned by Clement VI, who demanded the maximum amount of blue, the most expensive pigment, derived from lapis lazuli. The frescoes have suffered at the hands of soldiers, who tried to chip off all the heads in one piece to sell when the palace was a barracks in the nineteenth century. But this allows you to see something of the technique, the outline drawn on the stone then covered up bit by bit with the plaster on which the paint was applied. The **kitchen** on this floor also gives an idea of medieval times, and a hint of the scale of papal gluttony: the square walls transform into an octagonal chimney-piece for a vast central cooking fire. Major feasts were held in **Le Grand Tinel** which was also part of the conclave in which the cardinals were locked up in order to elect a new pope. You can see very clearly in the masonry the arches that were unblocked to give the cardinals the added space of the rooms to the south and west in which to conspire and scheme in isolation from the world.

In the **Palais Neuf**, Clement VI's **bedroom** and **study** are further evidence of this pope's secular concerns, with wonderful food-oriented murals and painted ceilings. Beautifully restored, they illustrate in detail fishing, falconry, hunting and other courtly pursuits. However, austerity resumes in the cathedral-like proportions of the **Grande Chapelle**, or *Chapelle Clementine*, and in the **Grande Audience**, its twin in terms of volume, on the floor below.

When you've completed the circuit, which includes a heady walk along the roof terraces, you can watch a glossy but informative film on the history of the palace (English headphones available). During evening visits or concerts the illuminations give it a proper Gothic atmosphere.

THE FESTIVAL D'AVIGNON

Unlike most provincial festivals of international renown, the **Festival d'Avignon** is dominated by theatre rather than classical music, though there is plenty of that, as well as lectures and exhibitions, and of course, dance. 1995 saw theatrical interpretations of Homer, Primo Levi, Shakespeare, Beckett, Molière and Dostoyevsky with directors and companies as diverse as Ariane Mnouchkine and Footsbarn, plus new dance by Maguy Marin, André Preljocaj, Lucinda Childs and Pina Bausch. Each year a non-European country or region is invited to bring the best of its performing arts, traditional, modern and avant-garde, to the festival. In 1995 it was India, with *The Madwoman of Chaillot* in Punjabi, an episode of the Mahabharata and contemporary combinations of poetry and dance among the offerings. These were all part of the mainstream "*in*" festival as opposed to the "*Festival Off*", or the fringe.

The Festival d'Avignon and the Festival Off take place every year for three weeks from the second week in July. 1996 will be the fiftieth year and is likely to be spectacular. The main festival uses all of the city's great buildings as stages, the best of all being the Cour d'Honneur of the Palais des Papes. The programme with details of how to book is available from the second week in May from the *Bureau du Festival d'Avignon*, 8 bis rue de Mons (☎90.82.67.08) or from the tourist office. Ticket prices are very reasonable (between 120F and 180F) and go on sale from the second week in June. As well as phone sales (11am–7pm; ☎90.14.14.14), they can be bought from FNAC shops in all major French cities. During the festival, tickets are available until 3pm for the same day's performances.

The *Festival Off* takes place in eighty different venues and on the streets from 10am to midnight. The programme is available from the end of June from *Avignon Public Off*, BP5, 75521 Paris Cedex 11 (☎1.48.05.20.97). During the festival the office is in the Conservatoire de Musique on place du Palais. Ticket prices range from 50F to 80F and a *Carte Public Adhérent* for 65F gives you 30F off all shows.

During festival time everything stays open late and everything gets booked up. There are up to two hundred thousand visitors and getting around or doing anything normal becomes virtually impossible.

The cathedral, Petit Palais and Pont St-Bénézet

The **Cathédrale Notre-Dame-des-Doms** (daily 7.30am–7.30pm) directly north of the Palais des Papes might once have been a luminous Romanesque structure, but the interior has had a bad attack of Baroque. In addition, nineteenth-century maniacs mounted an enormous gilded Virgin on the belfry, which would look silly enough anywhere, but, when dwarfed by the fifty-metre towers of the popes' palace, is absurd.

For something a little more relaxing, take a rewarding stroll in the **Rocher des Doms park**, just behind the cathedral. As well as ducks and swans and views over the river to Villeneuve and beyond, it has a sundial in which your shadow tells the time. The **Petit Palais** (Jan–June & Sept–Dec Mon & Wed–Sun 9.30am–noon & 2–6pm; July & Aug Mon–Sun 10am–6pm; 20F; Oct–March free on Sun), west of the park and below the Dom rock also has treats, though the scale of the collections in this episcopal palace is dauntingly extreme. There are almost a thousand paintings and sculptures, the most important part of the collection being Italian works from the thirteenth to fifteenth centuries. It's easy to get stuck, with more than a dozen rooms still to go, on the mastery of colour and facial expressions of a Simone Martini or Fabriano; or to pass out from a surfeit of *Madonna and Childs* before you've reached Botticelli's masterpiece on the subject or the Niçois painter, Louis Bréa's

Assumption of the Virgin. Anyone intrigued by labyrinths can look out for a *Theseus and the Minotaur*, the labyrinth in the foreground is identical to the one on the floor of Chartres cathedral, and is thought by some to have mysterious powers of healing.

To the west of the park and north of the Petit Palais, and well signed, is the half span of **Pont St-Bénézet** (April–Sept daily 9am–6.30pm; rest of year Tues–Sun 9am–1pm & 2–5pm; 10F or 28F combined ticket with Musée en Images). Repairing the bridge from the ravages of the Rhône was finally abandoned in 1660, three and a half centuries after it was built, and only four of the original 22 arches remain. It can be walked, danced or sat upon, but if you take small children, beware the precipitous, barely protected drops on either side. The bridge is also known as the Pont d'Avignon from the famous song. One theory has it that the lyrics say "*Sous le pont*" (under the bridge), rather than "*Sur le pont*" (on the bridge), and refer to the thief and trickster clientele of a tavern on the Ile de la Barthelasse (which the bridge once crossed) dancing with glee at the arrival of more potential victims.

To the right of the entrance to the bridge is the **Musée en Images** (April–Sept 9am–7pm; Oct to mid-Nov & Feb–March Tues–Sun 9am–5pm; 24F or 28F combined ticket with bridge), a twenty-minute slide show telling the history of the city (English tapes available). It's a bit pricey and predictable but a pleasantly lazy way of seeing some of the glories of the city's art and architecture.

Around place de l'Horloge

The café-lined **place de l'Horloge**, frenetically busy most of the time, is the site of the city's imposing nineteenth-century **Hôtel de Ville** and its Gothic **clock tower**, and the **Opéra**. Around the *place*, on rues de Mons, Molière and Corneille, famous faces appear in windows painted on the buildings, and of those who recorded their impressions of the city, it was the sound of over a hundred bells ringing that stirred them most. Of a Sunday morning, traffic lulls permitting, you can still hear a myriad different peels from churches, convents and chapels in close proximity, not quite as numerous after the centuries, but nearly. Many ecclesiastical buildings were knocked down during the Revolution and in the years up to 1815, when a minority of Avignonnais were still fighting against union with France. It was a bloody time: in 1791 a supporter of the new order was murdered in church; in response sixty counter-revolutionaries were buried alive in the ice-house of the papal palace.

The restored fourteenth-century **Eglise St-Agricol**, just behind the Hôtel de Ville, is one of Avignon's best Gothic edifices, with a beautifully carved fifteenth-century facade, and, inside, a Renaissance altarpiece of Provençal origin, and paintings by Nicolas Mignard and Pierre Parrocel (Wed 10am–noon, Sat 4–6pm, Sun 8–10pm). To the east of Eglise St-Agricol, just behind rue St-Agricol on rue Collège du Roure is the elegant fifteenth-century **Palais du Roure**, a centre of Provençal culture, whose gateway and courtyard are definitely worth a look; there may well be temporary art exhibitions, and if you want a rambling tour through the attics to see Provençal costumes, publications and presses, photographs of the Carmargue in the 1900s and an old stage coach, you need to turn up at 3pm on Tuesday (or make an appointment ☎90.80.80.88; free).

To the west of place de l'Horloge are the most desirable Avignon addresses, both now and three hundred years ago. High, heavy facades dripping with cupids, eagles, dragons, fruit and foliage range along **rue Petite-Fusterie** and **rue Joseph-Vernet**, where you'll find the most expensive shops selling chocolate, haute couture and baubles, with restaurants and art galleries to match.

THE FESTIVAL PROVENCAL

The Palais du Roure is the main Avignon venue for the **Festival Provençal**, which for over two decades has been celebrating the Provençal language and traditions in poetry, theatre, dance and song. It takes place during July and the beginning of August, with events in several Vaucluse cities. Details from the Palais du Roure on ☎90.80.80.88.

On the east side of the *place* on rue de Mons, the seventeenth-century Hôtel de Crochans is home to the **Maison Jean Vilar** (Tues–Fri 9am–noon & 2–6pm, Sat 10am–5pm; free), named after the great theatre director who set up the Week of Dramatic Art in 1947 which became the festival the following year. It houses festival memorabilia, an excellent library dedicated to the performing arts, and a collection of videos of everything from Stanislavski to last year's street theatre. These are sometimes shown in the foyer, or at special screenings, but you can also arrange your own viewing, with one day's notice – the catalogue is at the main desk. The Maison also puts on temporary exhibitions, workshops and public lectures with renowned theatre people.

The Banasterie and Carmes quartiers

The **quartier de la Banasterie** behind the Palais des Papes is almost solid seventeenth and eighteenth century. The heavy wooden doors with highly sculptured lintels bear the nameplates of lawyers, psychiatrists and dietary consultants. It's worth poking your nose into the courtyard of the Hôtel de Fonseca, built in 1600 at 17 rue Ste-Catherine to admire its mullioned windows and old well. Between Banasterie and place des Carmes are a tangle of tiny streets guaranteed to get you lost. Pedestrians have priority over cars on many of them, and there are plenty of tempting café or restaurant stops. At 6 rue Saluces, you'll find the peculiar **Musée du Mont de Piété** (Mon–Fri 8.30–11.30am & 1.30–5.30pm; free), an ex-pawnbrokers shop and now the town's archives, which has a small display of papal bulls and painted silk dessicators for determining the dry weight of what was the city's chief commodity.

The Carmelite convent of the **Eglise St-Symphorien** once spread over the whole of place des Carmes, right down to the bell tower on rue Carreterie which was built in the 1370s with the bell cage added in the sixteenth century. In the church (Mon–Fri 8–9am & 6.30–7.30pm, Sat 5–7pm, Sun 8.45am–noon) is a stunning painting of *St Eloi* by Nicolas Mignard. The cloisters have become a theatre for Avignon's oldest permanent company, the *Théâtre des Carmes*, run by André Benedetto.

Further up rue Carreterie, at no. 155, you'll find *Shakespeare*, Avignon's English bookshop which also serves as a tea room, meeting place and venue for readings and performances (Tues–Sat 11am–7pm; sometimes open on Fri evenings and Sun afternoons).

From St-Pierre to St-Didier

To the south of rue Banasterie on place St-Pierre is one of the most spectacular of Avignon's churches, the Renaissance **Eglise St-Pierre** (Fri 2.30–5.30pm, Sat 9–11am, Sun 8.30–11.30am). When closed you can still admire its greatest artwork, the doors, carved in 1551. In the Annunciation scene on the right-hand side, Mary looks as if she's saying "Who the hell are you?" to Gabriel, who points to the dove as his credentials.

The **Musée Aubanel** on place St-Pierre is dedicated to Provençal literature and to printing, a significant activity in the city prior to the Revolution since the French censors had no jurisdiction here. It's open by appointment only (☎90.82.95.54; free).

South of St-Pierre is the main pedestrian precinct centering around **place du Change**. **Rue des Marchands** and **rue du Vieux-Sextier** have their complement of chapels and late medieval mansions, in particular the **Hôtel des Rascas** on the corner of rues des Marchands and Fourbisseurs, and the **Hôtel de Belli** on the corner of rues Fourbisseurs and Vieux-Sextier. The Jewish quarter, where during the time of the popes Jews had to wear yellow caps and were locked in every night, was around rue du Vieux-Sextier and place Jérusalem (where there's a synagogue). To the east is **place Pie**, site of the hideous modern **market halls** and an open flower market.

To the south, more Renaissance art is on show in the **Eglise St-Didier** (Mon–Sat 9am–noon & 2–7pm, Sun 10am–noon), chiefly the altarpiece in which the realism of Mary's pain has prompted the somewhat uncomfortable name of *Notre-Dame du Spasme*. There are also some fourteenth-century frescoes in the left-hand chapel.

Southwest: some museums

The excellent **Musée Calvet** (Mon & Wed–Sun 10am–noon & 2–6pm; free), 65 rue Joseph-Vernet, and the impressive eighteenth-century palace housing it are undergoing gradual restoration and transformation with new galleries opening up bit by bit. In the summer of 1995 you could see Brugel's *La Kermesse*, a fine collection of sixteenth-century portraits, a Vasarely tapestry, Rodin's bust of Victor Hugo and a small selection of moderns, including Vlaminck's *Sur le Zinc* and Bonnard's *Jour d'Hiver*. Hopefully the eclecticism of the full collection – from an Egyptian mummy of a five-year-old boy to intricate wrought-iron work, taking in along the way Renaissance armchairs, Géricault adventure-tableaux, Utrillos, Laurençons and Dufys, Dutch still-lifes, Gallo-Roman pots and sixteenth-century clocks – will soon be on show again.

The remaining crop of museums is considerably less compelling. Next door to the Musée Calvet is the **Musée Requien** (Tues–Sat 9am–noon & 2–6pm; free). The subject is natural history and its sole advantage is in being free and having clean toilets. With little more to recommend it is the **Musée Lapidaire**, a museum of Roman and Gallo-Roman stones, housed in the Baroque chapel at 27 rue de la République (Mon & Wed–Sun 10am–noon & 2–6pm; free Nov–April, summer 6F). Finally, at the **Musée Vouland** at the end of rue Victor-Hugo near Porte St-Dominique (June–Sept Tues–Sat 9am–noon & 2–6pm; Oct–May Tues–Sat 2–6pm only; 20F) you can feast your eyes on the fittings, fixtures and furnishings that French aristocrats indulged in both before and after the Revolution. There's some brilliant Moustiers faïence, exquisite marquetry and Louis XV ink-pots with silver rats holding the lids.

Southeast: to rue des Teinturiers

Between the noisy rue de la République and place St-Didier, on rue Labourer is the impressive fourteenth-century former cardinal's residence, now the municipal library, the **Mediathèque Ceccano** (Mon 1–6pm, Tues–Sat 10am–6pm). As well as quiet gardens to read in, there are also beautifully painted ceilings, and occasional exhibitions.

Through the park by the tourist office (where there's an old British red phone box) you come to **place des Corps-Saints**, a lively area of cafés and restaurants whose tables fill the *place*.

Just to the north rue des Lices runs eastwards, past the Ecole des Beaux Arts, after which rue Noel-Biret leads north up to the end of rue du Roi-Réné where you'll find the **Chapelle St-Claire.** This is where, during the Good Friday service in 1327, the poet Petrarch first saw and fell in love with Laura, a fact recorded in a note on the pages of the poet's copy of Virgil.

Continuing along rue des Lices, you come to **rue des Teinturiers**, the most atmospheric street in Avignon. Its name refers to the eighteenth- and nineteenth-century business of calico printing. The cloth was washed in the Sorgue which still runs alongside the street turning the wheels of long-gone mills. It's also an excellent street for restaurant-browsing, though the water tends to get a bit smelly as you reach the ramparts.

Eating and entertainment

Good-value midday **meals** are two a penny in Avignon and eating well in the evening needn't break the bank. The large terraced café-brasseries on place de l'Horloge, rue de la République, place du Change and place des Corps-Saints will all serve quick basic meals. Rue des Teinturiers and the Banasterie and Carmes *quartiers* are good for menu browsing if you're budgeting, and the streets between place de Crillon and place du Palais if you're not.

Restaurants and cafés

Le Belgocargo, 10 pl des Châtaignes (☎90.85.72.99). Belgian restaurant specializing in *moules, frites* and beer; midday menu with drink for under 50F. Closed Sun & Mon evening out of season.

Brunel, 46 rue Balance (☎90.85.24.83). Superb regional dishes; menus from 200F. Closed Sun & Mon, and mid-July to mid-Aug.

Le Carnot, corner of rue Carnot and rue de la Croix. Young, noisy café with bar football etc.

Les Célestins, pl des Corps-Saints. Café-bar with a young, fairly trendy clientele.

Christian Etienne, 10 rue Mons (☎90.86.16.50). One of Avignon's best restaurants in a fourteenth-century mansion. Exotic combinations such as fennel sorbet with a saffron sauce and some great fish dishes. From 300F but with a midday "Déjeuner provençal" for 160F. Closed Sat midday and Sun; last orders 9.30pm.

La Cintra, 44 cours Jean-Jaurès. Dependable brasserie with a menu under 80F. Daily till midnight.

Côté Jardin, 7 rue des Trois-Carreaux (☎90.82.26.70). Tiny attractive resto and very good value. Booking advisable. Around 100F.

L'Entrée des Artistes, 1 pl des Carmes (☎90.82.46.90). Small, friendly bistro serving traditional French dishes; 115F menu. Closed Sat midday, Sun & first 2 weeks Sept.

Les Félibres, 14 rue Limas (☎90.27.39.05). Bookshop-cum-*salon-de-thé* serving traditional plats du jours and good *pâtisseries*. Open Mon–Sat noon–6.30pm.

La Ferme, chemin du Bois, Ile de la Barthelasse (☎90.82.57.53) A traditional farmhouse with well-prepared simple dishes from 100F. Closed Sat midday, & Mon out of season.

La Fourchette, 17 rue Racine (☎90.85.20.93). A fixed menu at the bottom of the range (around 140F) offers you marinated sardines, vegetable terrine, stuffed tomatoes and excellent meat and fish stews. Closed Sat and Sun and last 2 weeks in Aug; last orders 9.30pm.

Grand Café du Commerce, 21 rue St-Jean-de-Vieux. Pleasant café for all tastes.

Hiély-Lucullus, 5 rue de la République (☎90.86.17.07). Avignon's top gastronomic palace, serving beautiful Provençal cuisine – gratin of mussels and spinach, stuffed rabbit, sole in red pepper sauce, lamb grilled in rosemary, scallop salad, a huge selection of goats' cheese and orgasmic puddings. The Rhône wines are the very best, and add a good whack to what will be an already groaning bill. At lunchtime, except Sun, there's a 140F menu, wine included. Closed Mon, Tues midday out of season and the last 2 weeks of June; last orders 9.15pm.

La Maison du Traiteur, pl des Corps-Saints. Cheap sandwiches and snacks to take away or eat at tables on the *place*.

Le Petit Bédon, 70 rue Joseph-Vernet (☎90.82.33.98). According to fellow chefs the "pot-belly" does the best meal for under 250F to be had in the city. Closed Mon evening and Sun and last 2 weeks in Aug; last orders 10.30pm.

Shakespeare, 155 rue Carreterie. English bookshop and *salon de thé*. Closed Sun, Mon and evenings.

La Tache d'Encre, 22 rue des Teinturiers (☎90.85.46.03). The food isn't brilliant (under 100F) but the musicians – jazz, rock, *chansons*, African or salsa – usually are. Congenial atmosphere, with live music Fri and Sat nights, occasionally weekdays, too; booking advisable. Closed midday Sat & Sun.

Tapas Bodega, 10 rue Galante (☎90.82.56.84). Spanish music, sometimes live. Tapas at 10F each. Daily 11.45am–1am.

Tapas Tabarca, 3 pl des Corps-Saints. Tapas bar; around 15F a dish.

Les Trois Clefs, 26 rue des Trois-Faucons (☎90.86.51.53). Inventive dishes based around seasonally fresh vegetables, game and fish. The hare in *tapenade* and the *sandre au jus de ratatouille* are recommended. Menu including wine for 140F. Closed Sun; last orders 9.30pm.

Venaissin, 16 pl de l'Horloge (☎90.86.20.99). In the height of summer you'd be very lucky to get a table here. It's the only cheap brasserie on pl de l'Horloge that serves more than just *steack-frites*. Two menus under 100F.

Wooloo Mooloo, 16 bis rue des Teinturiers (☎90.85.28.44). An old printshop with all the presses still there. Dishes from around the world; good selection of teas; under 100F. Occasional theme nights with music.

Markets, chocolates, cakes and ice creams

The city's main **food market** is in the covered halls on place Pie every Tuesday to Sunday. Between portes St-Michel and Magnanen on rue rempart St-Michel there's a **weekend market** selling food and general goods. Place des Carmes has a **flower market** on Saturday morning and a **flea market** on Sunday morning; and an **antique market** takes place on Saturday morning on place Crillon where antiquarians have their expensive shops. On the first Saturday of the month, and every Saturday from July 1 to August 5 cours Jean-Jaurès has a **book and record market**.

The best **pâtissier** in Avignon is *Mallard*, 32 rue des Marchands (Mon–Sat 8.30am–7.15pm). For ace **ice creams** and sorbets made on the premises, try *Remy Brousse* at 35 rue St-Agricol; and *Puyricard* **chocolates** can be bought at 33 rue Joseph-Vernet. For the passionately sweet-toothed, there's *Le Restaurant des Desserts*, 11–13 rue de la Balance (closed Mon & Sun evening; ☎90.82.32.10) that serves nothing but desserts.

Nightlife and entertainment

There's a fair amount of **nightlife and cultural events** in Avignon, particularly café-théâtre, though a lot of the city's energy is saved up for the festival. For more information, try at the tourist office which hands out a free bi-monthly calendar, called *Rendez-Vous* and also stocks the monthly rock fanzine *Rock in Town*. You can also pick up an English language publication, *Langue Provençal Journal*, at the English bookshop on the second floor of 23 rue de la République.

Live music and discos

Le 5/5, 1 rempart St-Roch (☎90.82.61.32). Mainstream disco for the young and local. Thurs–Sat from 11pm.

L'Affiche, 25 rue Carnot (☎90.27.02.44). Bar restaurant with live jazz, jazz-rock and jazz-fusion Fri and Sat nights.

AJMI Jazz Club, c/o La Manutention, rue Escalier Ste Anne (☎90.86.08.61). Hosts major acts and some adventurous new groups. Thurs is Jazz night.

Le Bistroquet, Quartier du Mouton, Ile de la Barthelasse (☎90.82.25.83). Rock bar with live gigs except in June. Open Tues–Sat 7pm–3.30am.

L'Esclave Bar, 12 rue du Limas. Gay bar and disco, open 10pm–5am; shows Wed & Sun; drinks from 40F.

Pub Z, corner of rue Bonneterie and rue Artaud. Rock bar all black and white in honour of the zebra. Open till 1.30am; closed Sun & first 3 weeks Aug.

Les Sources, 24 bd St-Michel, by Porte Magnanen (☎90.86.32.76). Food, theatre, jazz nights, flamenco and rock – not all at the same time!

La Tache d'Encre, 22 rue des Teinturiers (☎90.85.46.03). Live music Fri and Sat nights, occasionally weekdays, too; booking advisable. The jazz, rock, *chansons*, African or salsa are usually brilliant. Closed midday Sat & Sun. Under 100F.

Tapas Bodega, 10 rue Galante (☎90.82.56.84). Spanish music, sometimes live. Tapas at 10F each. Daily 11.45am–1am.

Theatre and cinema

Théâtre du Balcon, 38 rue Guillaume-Puy (☎90.85.00.80). A venue that has put on African music, twentieth-century classics and contemporary theatre.

Le Cercle, 15 rue Galante (☎90.86.44.83). The former Utopia cinema is used for a variety of events, such as "Les Rendez-Vous Galante" where people perform, recite and tell stories.

Théâtre du Chêne Noir, 8 bis rue Ste-Catherine (☎90.82.40.57). May have mime, a musical or Molière on offer.

Opéra, pl de l'Horloge (☎90.82.23.44). Classical opera and ballet.

Péniche Dolphin Blues, Port de Plaisance, Quai de la Ligne (☎90.82.46.96). One-person shows and café-théâtre in a barge moored below the city walls near Porte de la Ligne.

Utopia, 5 rue Figuière & 4 rue Escalier Ste Anne (☎90.82.65.36). Cinema showing avant-garde, obscure or old-time favourites, always in the original language. The tourist office has programmes.

Listings

Airport Aéroport Avignon-Caumont (☎90.81.51.15). Internal French flights only.

Bike rental *Dopieralski*, 80 rue Guillaume-Puy (☎90.86.32.49); *Masson Richard*, pl Pie (☎90.82.32.92); *Vélomania*, 1 rue de l'Amelier (☎90.82.06.98).

Boat trips *Le Mireio*, allée de l'Oulle (☎90.85.62.25). Offers trips upstream towards Châteauneuf-du-Pape and downstream to the Camargue – all year round, two-week advance booking recommended; *Le Cygne*, quai de la Ligne, 300m upstream from Pont Bénézet (☎66.59.35.62), does trips to Beaucaire and Tarascon, Aigues-Mortes and Arles.

Bookshops *Shakespeare*, 155 rue Carreterie (Tues–Sat 11am–7pm); *English Bookshop*, 23 rue de la République. *FNAC*, 14 rue de la République.

Bus Information and tickets: Urban Tourelle de la République (☎90.82.68.19) and place Pie (☎90.85.44.93). Long distance, 5 av Montclar (☎90.82.07.35).

Car parks Guarded parking (24hr) at 16 bd Saint-Roch, near the train station and at 1 rue P-Mérindol; there's also free, unguarded parking by Porte d'Oulle.

Car rental *Budget*, 89 rte de Montfavet (☎90.87.03.00). Located on bd St-Ruf are *Eurorent* at no. 3 (☎90.86.06.61), *AAC* at no. 15 (☎90.85.69.11), and *Europcar* at no. 27 (☎90.82.49.85).

Currency exchange *Chaix Conseil*, 43 cours Jean-Jaurès (April–Oct daily 10am–10pm; closed Nov–March); 24-hr automatic exchange at *Société Lyonnaise de Banque*, 13 rue République and at *Caixa Bank*, 64 rue Joseph-Vernet.

Emergencies Doctor/ambulance ☎15 or *SOS Médecins* (☎90.82.65.00); Hospital, *Centre Hospitalier H-Duffaut*, 305 rue Raoul-Follereau (☎90.80.33.33).

Laundry 24 rue Lanterne; 27 rue Portail Magnanen; 66 pl des Corps Saints; and 9 rue Chapeau-Rouge.

Pharmacy For a night pharmacy, call police at bd St-Roch on ☎90.80.51.00 for addresses.

Police Municipale 10 pl Pie (☎90.82.94.26).

Post office *PTT*, cours Président-Kennedy (Mon–Fri 8am–7pm, Sat 8am–noon).

Swimming pool *Piscine de la Barthelasse* on the Ile de la Barthelasse; also near the bridge facing the city (May–Sept 10am–7pm; 24F/20F). Do not attempt to swim in the Rhône.

Taxis Place Pie (☎90.82.20.20).

Trains Information ☎90.82.50.50; reservations ☎90.82.56.29.

Women *Vaucluse Information Femmes*, 9 rue Carnot (9am–noon & 2–6pm; closed Fri; ☎90.88.41.00).

Villeneuve-Lès-Avignon

VILLENEUVE-LES-AVIGNON rises up a rocky escarpment above the west bank of the river, looking down upon its older neighbour from behind far more convincing fortifications. In the thirteenth and fourteenth centuries, when its citadel and bridge defences were built, the Rhône at Avignon was the French border, not just with the papal enclave but with the county of Provence, whose allegiances shifted between the many different rivals of the king of France. Despite that, and the French king's habit of claiming land, and therefore taxes, in areas of Avignon that the river flooded, Villeneuve operated largely as a suburb to Avignon, with palatial residences constructed by the cardinals and a great monastery founded by Pope Innocent VI.

To this day Villeneuve is, strictly speaking, part of Languedoc not Provence, and would score better in the hierarchy of towns to visit were it further from Avignon whose monuments it can almost match for colossal scale and impressiveness. In summer at least it benefits, providing venues for the Festival, as well as accommodation overspill; it's certainly worth a day, whatever time of year you visit.

Arrival, information and accommodation

From Avignon's *gare SNCF*, the half-hourly Villeneuve–Les Angles #10 bus (rather than the Les Angles–Villeneuve bus #10) runs direct to place Charles-David (*Bellevue* stop) in Villeneuve in under ten minutes, or five if you catch it from Porte d'Oulle. After 8pm you'll have to take a taxi or walk; it's only 3km. Also on the *place* you'll find the **tourist office** (Mon–Fri 9.30am–noon & 2–5/7pm, Sat 9.30am–noon; ☎90.25.61.55; annexe in summer at entrance to La Chartreuse), which will help you find a room.

Finding pleasant **accommodation** in Avignon should not be too much of a problem, although note that it can get very busy during the festival period.

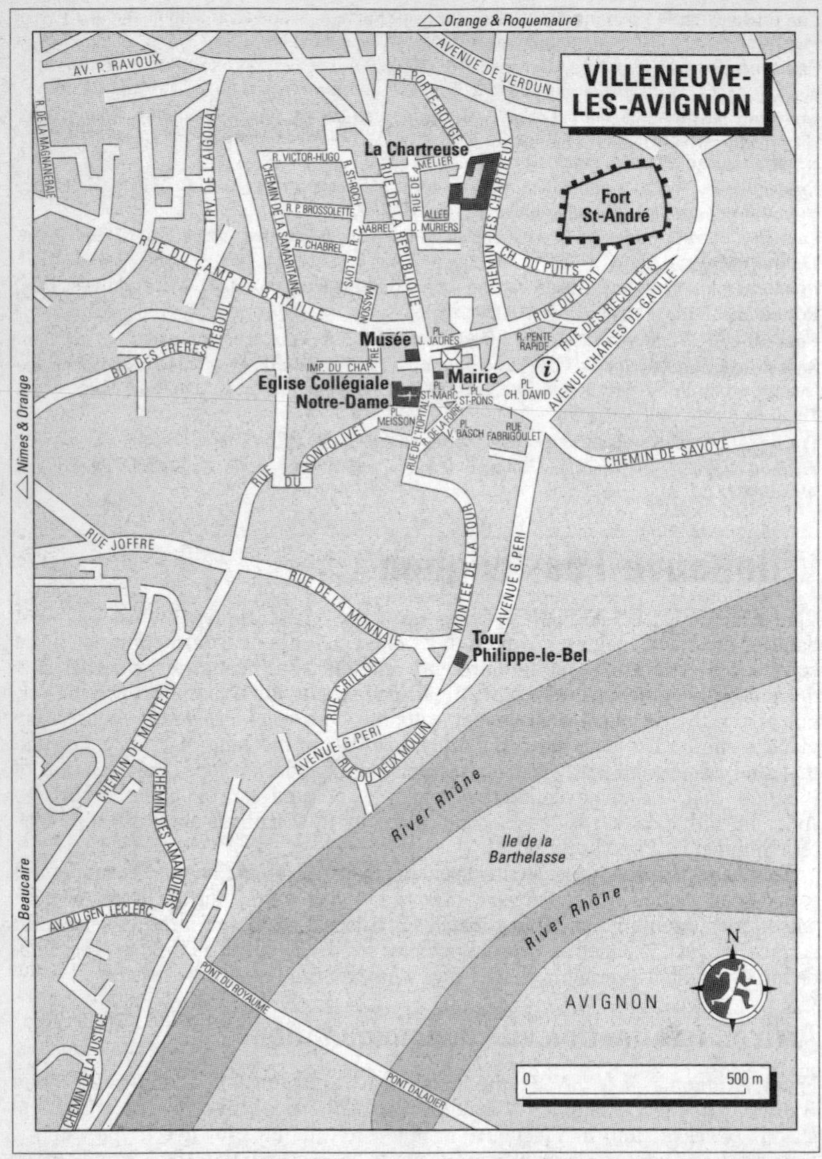

Hotels

L'Atelier, 5 rue de la Foire (☎90.25.01.84). A sixteenth-century house with huge open fireplaces and a walled garden. Very good value. ④

Beauséjour, 61 bd Gabriel-Péri (☎90.25.20.56). Overlooking the river near the Pont du Royaume. The rooms on the road side are a bit noisy: close to the bridge into Avignon. ③

Les Cèdres, 39 bd Pasteur (☎90.25.43.92). A Louis XIV mansion with pool and restaurant. ⑤

Central, 15 rue de la République (☎90.25.44.12). A bargain in the heart of Villeneuve. Closed mid-Aug to mid-Sept. ②

Jardins de la Livrée, 4 bis rue Camp de Bataille (☎90.26.05.05). Bed & Breakfast, plus excellent value midday and evening meals; very friendly hosts and clean, comfortable rooms. The only drawback is the noise – all night – of passing trains. No credit cards. ④

Le Prieuré, 7 pl du Chapitre (☎90.25.18.20). Indisputably the first choice, if money is no object and you fancy being surrounded by tapestries, finely carved doors, old oak ceilings and other baronial trappings. Also, the restaurant has a very good reputation. ⑧

Hostels and foyers

Résidence P. L. Loisil, av Pierre-Sémard (☎90.25.07.92), to the left at the top of rue de la République. Beds for 66F a night in rooms for three to four people (cheap meals available). It also has 24 rooms equipped for the disabled. ①

YMCA hostel, 7 bis chemin de la Justice (☎90.25.46.20). Beautifully situated overlooking the river by Pont du Royaume, with balconied rooms for two to six people, and an open-air swimming pool. Around 80–100F including breakfast; full or half board obligatory for stays of more than one night. Bus stop *Pont d'Avignon* on the Les Angles–Villeneuve bus, or *Général-Leclerc* on the Villeneuve–Les Angles bus. ①

Campsite and self-catering

Camping municipal de la Laune, chemin St-Honoré (☎90.25.76.06) off the D980, near the sports stadium and swimming pools. Pleasant three-star site with plenty of shade; disabled facilities. Bookings can also be made through the tourist office (☎90.25.61.33). Open April–Sept.

Les Logis St-Eloi, 14 pl de l'Oratoire (☎90.25.40.36). A complex of studio apartments with kitchenettes situated in sixteenth- and seventeenth-century buildings. ③–⑤.

The Town

Villeneuve clusters around rue de la République which runs north from the Collègiale Notre-Dame church on pl St-Marc. The Fort St-André lies on a rise to the east.

For a good overview of Villeneuve – and Avignon – make your way to the **Tour Philippe-le-Bel** at the bottom of montée de la Tour (bus stop *Philippe-le-Bel*). This tower was built to guard the French end of Pont St-Bénézet, and a climb to the top (April–Sept Mon & Wed–Sun 10am–12.30pm & 3–7pm; Oct–March 10am–noon & 2–5.30pm; closed Feb) rewards with stunning views.

Even more indicative of French distrust of its neighbours is the enormous **Fort St-André**, whose bulbous, double-towered gateway and vast white walls loom over the town (July & Aug daily 9.30am–7.30pm; April, June & Sept 9.30am–12.30pm & 2–6.30pm; Oct–March 10am–noon & 2–5pm). Inside, refreshingly, there's not a hint of a postcard stall or souvenir shop, just tumbled-down houses and the former abbey, with its gardens of olive trees, ruined chapels, lily ponds and dovecots. Its cliff-face terrace is the classic spot for artists to aim their

VILLENEUVE'S MUSEUMS AND MONUMENTS

A *Passeport pour l'Art* (45F) gives you entry to the Fort St-André, Tour Philippe-le-Bel, La Chartreuse du Val de Bénédiction, Collègiale Notre-Dame and its cloister and the Musée Pierre-de-Luxembourg. The *passeport* is available from all of the above and from the tourist office.

brushes, or photographers their cameras, over Avignon. You can reach the approach to the fortress, montée du Fort, from place Jean-Jaurès on rue de la République, or by the "rapid slope" of rue Pente-Rapide, a cobbled street of tiny houses leading off rue des Recollets on the north side of place Charles-David.

Almost at the top of rue de la République, on the right, allée des Muriers leads from place des Chartreux to the entrance of **La Chartreuse du Val de Bénédiction** (April–Sept 9am–6.30pm; Oct–March 9.30am–5.30pm), one of the largest Charterhouses in France and founded by Innocent VI, the sixth of the Avignon popes, whose sharp profile is outlined on his tomb in the church. The buildings, which were sold off after the Revolution and gradually restored this century, are totally unembellished. With the exception of the Giovanetti frescoes in the chapel beside the refectory, all the paintings and treasures of the monastery have been dispersed, leaving you with a strong impression of the austerity of the strict practices of the Carthusian order. The only communication allowed was one hour of conversation a week plus the rather less congenial public confessions. Monks left the enclosure for one three-hour walk per week; within, their time was spent as much on manual labour as on prayer, and their diet was strictly vegetarian.

You are free to wander round unguided, through the three cloisters, the church, chapels, cells and communal spaces; there's little to see but plenty of atmosphere to be absorbed. It is one of the best venues in the Festival d'Avignon, and so is the fourteenth-century **Eglise Collègiale Notre-Dame** and its cloister on place St-Marc close to the Mairie (April–Sept Mon & Wed–Sun 10am–12.30pm & 3–7pm; Oct–March 10am–noon & 2–5.30pm; closed Feb). It's decorated with paintings of the Avignon School and with caring cupids tending Christ's hands and feet on the altar. However, Notre-Dame's most important treasure, a rare fourteenth-century smiling *Madonna and Child* made from a single tusk of ivory, allegedly carved by a convert from Islam, is now housed, along with many of the paintings from the Chartreuse, in the **Musée Pierre-de-Luxembourg** just to the north along rue de la République (April–Sept Mon & Wed–Sun 10am–12.30pm & 3–7pm; Oct–March 10am–noon & 2–5.30pm; closed Feb). The spacious layout includes a single room, with comfortable seats and ample documentation, given over to the most stunning painting in the collection, *Le Couronnement de la Vierge*, painted in 1453 by Enguerrand Quarton as the altarpiece for the church in the Chartreuse. With fiercely contrasting red, orange, gold, white and blue, the statuesque and symmetrical central figures of the coronation form a powerful and unambiguous subject. To either side of them, in true medieval style, the social hierarchy is defined, using a greater variety of form and colour. Along the bottom of the painting the scale of detail leaps several frames, with flames engulfing sinners, devils and their assistant beasts carrying away victims, walled towns with pin-size figures, and in the distance Mont St-Victoire and the cliffs of Estaque. No other painting in the collection matches Quarton's work and many are too obviously public relations pieces for their patrons, placing the pope, lord or bishop in question beside the Madonna or Christ. Philippe de Champaigne's *La Visitation* is an exception in showing the motion of a living moment.

Eating and drinking

Villeneuve's centre has a good choice of **eating** places, both for reasonable run-of-the-mill meals and for gourmet blow-outs in beautiful surroundings. Just up to the right as you approach place St-Marc from place Charles-David *Cave St-Marc* is a good place for **wine buying** (9.30am–12.15pm & 3.30–7.15pm; closed Wed & Sun). A food, clothes and bric-à-brac **market** is held on Thursday morning on place Charles-David.

Restaurants and cafés

Aubertin, 1 rue de l'Hôpital (☎90.25.94.84). A sumptuous restaurant, serving a midday menu (150F; à la carte 300F upwards) in the shade of the old arcades by the Collègiale Notre-Dame. Closed Sun evening, & Mon out of season.

La Banaste, 28 rue de la République (☎90.25.64.20). Good-value Provençal fare but better to eat within rather than on the noisy roadside; menus from around 90F. Closed Tues out of season.

Bar-Tabac de la Mairie, pl St-Marc. Completely ordinary locals' café, hence its charm.

La Calèche, 35 rue de la République (☎90.25.02.54). Traditional dishes; menus start around 85F; closed Sun, & Thurs out of season.

La Magnaneraie, 37 rue Camp de Bataille, off rue de la Magnanerie (☎90.25.11.11). Very posh and very good with a menu for 170F; courgette flowers stuffed with cream of mushrooms and a *gâteau d'agneau* are the specialities; à la carte over 400F.

La Mamma Lucia, pl V-Basch (☎90.25.00.71). Italian specialities with pavement tables to watch the world go by. Menus from 80F. Closed Wed and Tues evening out of season.

La Petite Crau and La Montagnette

A short way downstream from Avignon, the Rhône reaches its confluence with the Durance. Between the two rivers and the Chaine des Alpilles to the south is an area that was once a watery wasteland, part swampy marsh, part submerged. The rocky outcrop of **La Montagnette**, running parallel to the Rhône for 10km, and the hill at **Châteaurenard** were the only extensive bits of solid ground. However, the plain, known as **La Petite Crau**, steadily irrigated since Roman times, is today a richly cultivated area, with cherries and peaches as its main crops. The plain is criss-crossed with water channels, while row upon row of cypresses and poplars form windbreaks for the fruit trees. Villages in the area are few and far between, built on the scattered bases of rock, and many retain their medieval elements of fortified walls and churches and tangled narrow streets.

If you have your own **transport**, La Petite Crau and La Montagnette can easily be day trips out from Avignon, Tarascon or St-Rémy. By **bus**, it's more problematic, as links between the villages do exist but they're sporadic. Buses from Avignon to Châteaurenard are frequent, and some of these go on to Noves. Graveson is served by the twice-daily SNCF Arles bus, and Boulbon and Barbentane by the Tarascon service. No **trains** stop at the stations.

Accommodation

This is an exceptionally good area for cheap, unpretentious **hotels** where your fellow guests are more likely to be French than foreign.

Campsites are equally good value, especially *campings à la ferme* for which you can get details from the **Mairies** at Barbentane (☎90.95.50.39) and Maillane (☎90.95.74.06), and the **tourist offices** at Graveson (☎90.95.71.05) and Châteaurenard (☎90.94.23.27).

Châteaurenard and Noves

The main activity at **CHATEAURENARD**, the metropolis of La Petite Crau, is a massive wholesale market for the fruit and vegetables grown this side of the river. The ordinary market takes place on Sunday and will fill the central streets. Dominating the town's physical features are the two remaining towers of its Romanesque and Gothic medieval **castle** (daily 10.30am–12.30pm & 3–6.30pm; Sept–June closed Fri & Sat am; 5F), described by Frédéric Mistral as "twin horns on the forehead of a hill". If you're passing through, take the time to climb the castle's **Tour du Griffon** to look across La Petite Crau to the Alpilles and La Montagnette. In a recess within the castle is engraved a 700-year-old Troubadour poem, in Provençal, praising the beauty of the new building erected "by such a wise king".

For cheap and basic **accommodation** in Châteaurenard you could try *Le Central*, 27 cours Carnot (☎90.94.10.90; ③), *Les Glycines*, 14 av Victor-Hugo (☎90.94.10.66; ②–③) or *Le Rustic*, place Victoire (☎90.94.13.36; ①). *La Roquette* **campsite** on av J-Mermoz in Châteaurenard (closed Nov–March; ☎90.94.27.02) is small with very reasonable tarifs.

La Buvette des Tours, just below the castle, serves cheap salads, grills and pizzas on summer evenings (Thurs–Sun). Otherwise, the *Brasserie des Producteurs*, 4 rue R-Ginoux (Mon–Sat; ☎90.94.04.61; menu from 70F) has reasonable food.

Five kilometres east of Châteaurenard, the little village of **NOVES** is typical of the area, with a fourteenth-century gateway and a house reputed to have been lived in by Laura, the subject of Petrarch's besotted sonnets.

Outside Noves on the Châteaurenard road the *Auberge de Noves* (☎90.94.19.21; ⑧) is a seriously expensive hotel-restaurant in a beautiful farmhouse with exquisite furnishings and impeccable service. Nove's **campsite** *Le Pilon d'Agel* (closed Oct–March; ☎90.95.16.23) has a pool, disabled facilities and horses to rent.

Mistral and La Montagnette

The poet whose connections with La Petite Crau are indisputable is Frédéric Mistral, who was born in **MAILLANE** in 1830 and buried there in 1914. Primarily responsible for the turn-of-the-century revival of all things Provençal, he won the Nobel Prize for Literature, a feat no other writer of a minority language has ever achieved. The house that he built and lived in from 1876 till the end of his life has been preserved intact as the **Museon Mistral**, 11 rue Lamartine (Tues–Sun 9–11.30am & 2/2.30–6pm; 10F), along with his office, bedroom and dining room as they were when he died.

The Petite Crau plain was Mistral's "sacred triangle", and its customs and legends were very often his primary source of inspiration. Black Madonnas and various saints feted in these villages were, and often still are, bestowed with the power to bring rain or cure diseases. In his memoirs Mistral describes the procession of Saint Anthime from **Graveson** to **LA MONTAGNETTE**, where on reaching the church, the people spread out a feast on the perfumed grass and knocked back bottles of local wine for the rest of the day. If it hadn't rained by the time they got home, they punished the saint by dipping him three times in a ditch.

The church where this pious drinking took place belonged to the ancient abbey of **St-Michel-de-Frigolet**, founded a thousand years ago in a sheltered hollow amongst the rocks of La Montagnette, halfway between Graveson and Boulbon.

The name derives from *ferigoulo*, Provençal for thyme, which grows profusely in these hills, hence the perfumed grass of the feast. The thyme is also used to make a liqueur, *Le Frigolet*, which can be bought at the end of a guided tour of the abbey (Mon–Fri 2.30pm; Sun & hols 4pm; free). Mistral went to school in these buildings before they returned to ecclesiastical use in the mid-nineteenth century. The highlight of the visit is the series of fourteen paintings on the *Mysteries of the Virgin Mary* by Mignard in the main church, but you may find the cloisters (free access – ask at the shop by the entrance) more spiritually inspiring.

The valleys cutting through the scrubbed white rock of La Montagnette are shaded by olive, almond and apricot trees, oaks and pines. The heights never extend above 200m, and the smell of thyme is omnipresent; easy and exhilarating walking country.

If you're looking for somewhere **to stay**, try the quiet and comfortable *Le Mas des Amandiers*, just outside Graveson village on the road to Avignon (closed Nov–March; ☎90.95.81.76; ④) which has an open-air pool.

Boulbon and Barbentane

One footpath from St-Michel-de-Frigolet takes you over the ridge and, after 5km or so, down to **BOULBON**. As a strategic site overlooking the Rhône, Boulbon was heavily fortified in the Middle Ages, and today the ruins of its enormous fortress, built half within and half above a rocky escarpment, are like some picture-book crusader castle. The village also has its bibulous tradition, though this one is popular, one would imagine, with only half the villagers. On the first day of June the men gather with a bottle of wine apiece and process to St-Marcellin chapel in the cemetery, one of Boulbon's six Romanesque places of worship. At the end of the service the wine is blessed, the bottles are lifted first in homage to the *Seigneur* and then to the lips. But some of the wine must remain undrunk, to be corked and preserved as an antidote to illness and misfortune.

Eight kilometres from Boulbon, at the northern edge of La Montagnette in **BARBENTANE**, the fourteenth-century **Tour Angelic** keeps watch on the confluence of the Rhône and Durance. The town has two medieval gateways and a beautifully arcaded Renaissance building, the **Maison des Chevaliers**, plus a much more recent **Château** (guided tours 10am–noon & 2–6pm; April–June & Oct closed Tues; Nov–March closed Mon–Sat; 30F), designed for grandeur rather than defence. This is a seventeenth-century ducal residence with gorgeous grey and white Tuscan marble floors, and all the vases, painted ceilings, chandeliers and delicate antique furniture that you would expect of a house still owned by generations of the same family of aristocrats. The Italianate gardens are the best part.

Barbentane's **hotels** range from the rudimentary comfort of *Les Négociants*, 15 cours J-B-Rey (☎90.95.52.45; ②) to *Castel Mouisson*, Quartier Castel Mouisson

THE FETE DE SAINT-ELOI

Boulbon celebrates the **Fête de Saint-Eloi** on the last Sunday of August. This involves chariots drawn by teams of horses in Saracen harness doing the rounds of the village, and much drinking by all the villagers. Elsewhere, notably in Graveson, Châteaurenard and Maillane, this saint, whose role is protector of beasts of burden, is feted on the penultimate Sunday of July.

MARKETS

If you're in La Petite Crau on a Friday, the **Marché Paysan** in Graveson, place du Marché (mid May to Oct 4–8pm) is not to be missed with *paysans* from the Grande and Petite Crau, the Carmargue and from across the Durance selling their goats' cheeses, honey and jams, rice, olives and olive oil, flowers and aromatic plants as well as fruit and veg picked the same morning.

The ordinary morning markets here are on Friday in Graveson, Thursday in Maillane and Noves, Sunday in Châteaurenard, Wednesday in Barbentane and Tuesday in **ROGNONAS**, the village just across the Durance from Avignon.

(closed mid-Oct to mid-March; ☎90.95.51.17; ③) with good facilities and a pleasant garden and pool.

Two **restaurants** are worth going out of your way for: the *Auberge de Noves* (see under 'Châteaurenard and Noves' on p.90) where you can dine on such delicacies as oysters cooked in Châteauneuf-du-Pape and duck en croûte with herbs and acacia honey (weekday menu 200F; 250F menu with wine, otherwise over 450F); and *L'Oustalet Maianen* in Maillane (closed Mon, Sun evening & mid-Oct to March; ☎90.95.76.17), with a brilliant-value midweek menu for under 100F, and a gorgeous four-course for 135F.

St-Rémy-de-Provence and Les Baux

The scenery of La Petite Crau changes abruptly with the eruption of the **Chaine des Alpilles**, whose peaks look like the surf of a wave about to engulf the plain. At the northern base of the Alpilles nestles **St-Rémy-de-Provence**, a dreamy place where Van Gogh sought psychiatric help and painted some of his most lyrical works. It's ideally situated for exploration of the hills (or La Petite Crau), and easy to get to by bus. A short way south of St-Rémy are the remains of the ancient city of **Glanum**, and along the ridge of the Alpilles is the medieval stronghold of **Les Baux**, a place supremely dedicated to expensive tourism; both are difficult to get to by public transport.

St-Rémy-de-Provence

ST-REMY is a beautiful place, as unspoilt as the villages around, and its old town (*Vieille Ville*) is contained within a circle of boulevards no more than half a kilometre in diameter. Outside this ring, the modern town is sparingly laid out so, for once, you don't have to plug your way through dense developments before you reach the heart of the city. Outside the old town, all the attractions lie to the south towards Glanum: the **Roman arch**, the hospital of **St-Paul-de-Mausole** and the **Mas de la Pyramide** farmhouse in the old Roman quarries.

Arrival, information and accommodation

Arriving by **bus** you'll be dropped at **place de la République**, the main square abutting the *Vieille Ville* to the west. The **tourist office** (Oct–May Mon–Sat 9am–noon & 2–6pm; June–Sept Mon–Sat 9am–noon & 3–7pm, Sun 9am–noon; ☎90.92.05.22), just south of the centre on place Jean-Jaurès, between av Pasteur and av Durand-Maillane reached by following bd Marceau until it becomes av Durand-Maillane, provides excellent free guides on **cycling** and **walking** routes in and around the Alpilles and has addresses for renting **horses** and for **gliding** at a club that claims to hold the world record for the longest flight. If you want to **rent a bicycle**, **tandem** or **car**, go to *Florelia,* 35 av de la Libération, the road to Cavaillon (☎90.92.10.88). If you prefer to get around by **taxi**, call ☎90.92.48.20, 90.92.33.47, 90.92.25.71 or 90.92.46.92. If you're desperate for news of home, the *Maison de la Presse* opposite *La Brasserie des Alpilles* stocks some **English-language newspapers** and paperbacks.

The town has a fairly wide choice of **accommodation**, though real bargains are quite hard to come by. You may prefer to use one of the three campsites close by.

HOTELS

Hôtel des Antiques, 15 av Pasteur (☎90.92.03.02). A nineteenth-century mansion close to the tourist office with huge grounds, pools and wonderfully aristocratic furnishings in the dining room and salons. Closed Nov–March. ⑥

Les Arts–La Palette, above the *Café des Arts* at 30 bd Victor-Hugo (☎90.92.08.50). An excellent location and very friendly. Closed Wed & Feb. ④

Canto Cigalo, chemin de Canto Cigalo (☎90.92.14.28). By the canal to the southeast of the old town; quiet and comfortable. ④

Le Castellet des Alpilles, 6 pl Mireille (☎90.92.07.21). South of the old town, past the tourist office; small and friendly, and some rooms with great views. Closed Mon, and Tues midday; half-board compulsory in season. ⑤

Grand Hôtel de Provence, 36 bd Victor-Hugo (☎90.92.06.27). On the eastern edge of the old town with a large garden; pleasant enough for the price. Closed Oct to mid-March. ③

Mexican Café, 4 rue du 8 Mai 1945 (☎90.92.17.66). A newish hotel and restaurant in the middle of town with just 5 rooms. ③

Nostradamus, 3 av Taillandier (☎90.92.13.23). Studios for 2 to the north of the old town by the municipal pool. Not wildly atmospheric but cheap. ③

Villa Glanum, 46 av Vincent-van-Gogh (☎90.92.03.59). Next door to the archeological site; pleasant, not too overpriced and has a swimming pool. Most rooms with disabled facilities. Half-board compulsory; closed mid-Nov to Dec. ④

Ville Verte, av Fauconnet/pl de la République (☎90.92.06.14). Central with a garden and pool and 7 rooms with disabled facilities. It also organizes walking, climbing and cycling trips. ④

CAMPSITES

Le Mas de Nicolas, av Théodore-Aubanel (☎90.92.27.05). A four-star municipal site with pool, 2km along the rte de Mollèges to the northeast. Closed Nov–Feb.

Monplaisir, chemin Monplaisir (☎90.92.22.70 or 90.92.12.91). To the north, 1km along the route de Maillane. Two-star and much the cheapest. Closed Nov–Feb.

Pegomas, rte de Noves (☎90.92.01.21). One kilometre east on the road to Cavaillon. Three-star with pool. Closed Nov–Feb.

The Vieille Ville

To explore the **Vieille Ville** take any of the streets leading off the boulevards which encircle it and start wandering up alleyways and through immaculate leafy squares. **Rue Parage** off bd Gambetta is particularly appealing with its central drain now a channelled stream of clear water. Several ancient stately residences line its route as the street meanders up to the fountained **place Favier**, where you'll find St-Rémy's two main museums.

For an introduction to the region, the **Musée des Alpilles** is a good first visit. Housed in the *Hôtel Mistral de Mondragon*, a Renaissance mansion with a romantic interior courtyard (daily 10am–noon & 2–5pm, till 8pm in Aug; closed Jan–March; 14F or 34F combined ticket for the Musée Archéologique and Glanum), the museum features interesting displays on folklore, festivities and traditional crafts, plus intriguing local landscapes, some creepy portraits by Marshall Pétain's first wife, and souvenirs of local boy Nostradamus.

The collection in the neighbouring **Musée Archéologique** housed in the fifteenth-century *Hôtel de Sade* on rue du Parage (guided visits several times daily 10am–4pm/5pm/6.30pm; closed Jan–March; 14F or on combined ticket), comes from the archeological digs at the Greco-Roman town of Glanum (see overleaf), for which the combined ticket is also valid. Its primary function is for categorization and the hour's tour may be a bit much for the non-committed, but there are some stunning pieces, in particular the well-coiffeured heads of two women, possibly Livia and Octavia, wife and sister of Augustus.

From place Favier you can follow the central rue Carnot or cross over into rue Millaud and then into **rue Hoche** where a fountain topped by a bust marks the house where Nostradamus was born on December 14, 1503. Only the facade of the house is contemporary with the futuristic savant, and it's not open to visits. Between rue Hoche and rue Millaud opposite place de la République, on av de la Résistance, you'll come across the town's main church, the **Collégiale St-Martin**, a Neoclassical lump of a building whose only interest is its much renowned organ, painted in a surreal lime-green (recitals every Sat from June to Sept at 5.30pm).

Back in the centre of the old town, off rue Carnot at 8 rue L-Estrine is the eighteenth-century **Hôtel d'Estrine**, home to the **Centre d'Art Présence Van Gogh**, which hosts contemporary art exhibitions and has a permanent exhibition of Van Gogh reproductions and extracts from letters plus an audio-visual presentation of the painter on a different theme each year (Tues–Sun 10.30am–12.30pm & 2.30–6.30pm; 20F for exhibitions, otherwise free). A wide selection of Van Gogh books, prints and post cards is available from the shop.

For those in search of culture, visit one of the many **art galleries** scattered throughout St-Rémy: *Le Grand Magasin*, 24 rue de la Commune (daily 10am–12.30pm & 2.30–7.30pm; closed Mon out of season) combines contemporary works of art with jewellery, accessories and household objects of a stylish and original nature; *Lézard'Ailleurs*, 12 bd Gambetta (variable opening hours), is an antique shop and often hosts contemporary art exhibitions.

South of the Vieille Ville

Outside the old town enclosure, a short way south of the tourist office on rue Jean-de-Nostredame, is the beautiful Romanesque **chapel of Notre-Dame-de-Pitié**, which exhibits the art of the Greek painter, Mario Prassinos (1916–85) who settled in the village of Eygalières, near St-Rémy (April–June, Sept & Oct 2.30–6.30pm, July & Aug 10.30am–noon & 3.30–7.30pm; 15F). Tree forms, a favourite motif of his work, become a powerful graphic language in the series of oil paintings created for the chapel, *Les Peintures du Supplice*, provoked by Prassinos' horror of torture.

If you keep heading south, following av Vincent-van-Gogh, you'll come to **Les Antiques**, a triumphal arch celebrating the Roman conquest of Marseille and a mausoleum thought to commemorate two grandsons of Augustus. Save for a

ST-REMY'S FETES

The best time to visit St-Rémy is for the **Fête de Transhumance**, on Whit-Monday, when a two-thousand-strong flock of sheep, accompanied by goats, rams and donkeys, does a tour of the town before being packed off to the Alps for the summer; or for the **Carreto Ramado**, on August 15, a harvest thanksgiving procession in which the religious or secular symbolism of the floats reveals the political colour of the various village councils. A pagan rather than workers' **Mayday** is celebrated with donkey-drawn floral floats on which people play fifes and tambourines. On July 14, August 15 and the fourth Sunday in September, the intrepid local youth attempt to set loose six **bulls** that are herded round the town by their mounted chaperons.

certain amount of weather erosion, the mausoleum is perfectly intact. The arch is less so, but both display intricate patterning and the unaesthetic proportional sense of the Romans (free access). The Antiques would have been a familiar sight to one whose aesthetic sense was always on the side of the angels. In 1889 **Vincent van Gogh**, then living in Arles, requested that he be put away for several months. The hospital chosen by his friends was in the old monastery **St-Paul-de-Mausole**, a hundred yards or so east of the Antiques, which remains a psychiatric clinic today. Although the regime was more prison than hospital, Van Gogh was allowed to wander out around the Alpilles and painted prolifically during his twelve-month stay. The *Champs d'Oliviers, Le Faucher, Le Champ Clôturé* and *La Promenade du Soir* are amongst the 150 canvases of this period. The church and cloisters can be visited from 9am to noon and 2 to 6pm (no charge; take av Edgar-Leroy or allée St-Paul from av Vincent-van-Gogh, go past the main entrance of the clinic and into the gateway on the left at the end of the wall).

Not far from the hospital and to the right you'll see signs for the **Mas de la Pyramide** (daily 9am–noon & 2–5/6pm; worth waiting by the gate if there's no immediate answer to the bell; 9F), an old troglodyte farm in the Roman quarries for Glanum with a field of lavander and cherry orchard surrounded by cavernous openings into the rock filled with ancient farm equipment and rusting bicycles. Standing in the centre of the lavender field is a twenty-metre slice of rock – the pyramid that gives the farm its name – revealing the depth of the ancient quarrying works. The farmhouse is part medieval, part Gallo-Roman and has some fascinating pictures of the owner's family who have lived here for generations.

Eating and entertainment

At all times of the year, you'll find plenty of **brasseries** and **restaurants** in and around old St-Rémy. *Le Jardin de Frédéric*, 8 bd Gambetta (closed Wed; ☎90.92.27.67), has a 120F midday menu, and usually some interesting dishes on offer. There are a few good options on rue Carnot (leading from bd Victor-Hugo east through the old town to bd Marceau) including *La Gousée d'Ail* at no. 25 (closed Wed; ☎90.92.16.87) where veggies can feast on pasta with pestou and almonds; *Le Gaulois* at no. 57 (☎90.92.11.53) which, though not brilliant, is at least generous with a menu under 100F; and *La Maison Jaune* at no. 15 (closed Mon & Sun pm; ☎90.92.56.14) with polenta and pigeon roasted in Baux wines on the 250F menu, and grilled aubergines and *bourride de lotte* on the 100F lunchtime menu. *Lou Planet* at 7 place Favier is a scenic spot to dine on crêpes and *Le Bistrot des Alpilles,* 15 bd Mirabeau (Mon–Sat; open till midnight; ☎90.92.09.17) is the popular brasserie for *gigot d'agneau* and *tarte citrone* (70F midday menu, evening 160F).

For **café lounging** head for the *Café des Arts,* 30 bd Victor-Hugo (open till 12.30am; closed Feb) where the works of local painters are exhibited. Next door is the *Librarie des Arts,* a good bookshop with lovely picture books on the region. If you're after **picnic fare**, do your shopping at the Wednesday morning **market** on the pedestrian streets of the old town or at the Saturday market in place de la Mairie. The *boulangerie* at 5 rue Carnot sells the special *épis de St Rémy,* which are spiky baguettes. In season you'll see and smell great bunches of basil and marjoram which are grown in abundance around St-Rémy; aromatic oils are another speciality of the town, which are produced and sold *Chez Florame* at 34 bd Mirabeau (Mon–Sat 10am–noon & 3–6pm).

Films at the *Ciné Palace* on av Fauconnet are sometimes screened in the original language (Wed & Fri–Sun; programme from the tourist office), but if you fancy something a little more lively, try the two **discos**, *La Haute Galine,* quartier de la Galine (☎90.92.00.03) and *La Forge,* av de la Libération (☎90.92.31.52), which can be fun, or the *Café Latin* on rue Roger Salengro (running north from place de la République), which sometimes has live music.

Glanum

One of the most impressive ancient settlements in France, **GLANUM**, 500m south of Les Antiques was dug out from the alluvial deposits at the foot of the Alpilles (April–Sept daily 9am–7pm; Oct–March daily 9am–noon & 2–5pm; 26F or 34F combined ticket with Musée des Alpilles and Musée Archéologique). The site was originally a Neolithic homestead until the Gallo-Greeks, probably from Massalia (Marseille), built a city here between the second and first centuries BC. The Gallo-Romans constructed yet another town here from the end of the first century BC to the third century AD.

Glanum can be very difficult to get to grips with. Not only were the later buildings moulded on to the earlier ones, but the fashion at the time of Christ was for a Hellenistic style. You can distinguish the Greek levels from the Roman most easily by the stones: the earlier civilization used massive hewn rocks while the Romans preferred smaller, more accurately shaped stones. The leaflet at the admission desk is helpful, as are the attendants if your French is good enough.

As the site narrows in the ravine at the southern end you find a Grecian edifice around a **spring**, the feature that made this location so desirable. Steps lead down to a pool, with a slab above for the libations of those too sick to descend. An inscription records that Agrippa was responsible for restoring it in 27 BC and for dedicating it to Valetudo, the Roman goddess of health. But **altars** to Hercules are still in evidence, while up the hill to the west are traces left by prehistoric people whose life depended on this spring. The Gallo-Romans directed the water through canals to heat houses and, of course, to the **baths** that lie near the entrance to the site. There are superb sculptures on the Roman **Temples Geminées** (twin temples), as well as fragments of mosaics, fountains of both periods, and first-storey walls and columns.

Les Baux

At the top of the Alpilles ridge, 10km southwest of St-Rémy, lies the distinctly unreal fortified village of **LES BAUX**. Unreal partly because the ruins of the eleventh-century citadel are hard to distinguish from the edge of the plateau whose rock is both foundation and part of the structure. And unreal too, because this *Ville Morte* (Dead City) and a vast area of the plateau around it are accessible only via a turnstile from the living village below, which remains a too-perfect collection of sixteenth- and seventeenth-century churches, chapels and mansions.

Once upon a time Les Baux lived off the power and widespread possessions in Provence of its medieval lords, who owed allegiance to none. When the dynasty died out at the end of the fourteenth century, the town, which had once numbered six thousand inhabitants, passed to the counts of Provence and then to the kings of France, who in 1632, razed the feudal citadel to the ground and fined the population into penury. From that date until the nineteenth century both citadel and village were inhabited almost exclusively by bats and crows, until the discovery of bauxite (the aluminium ore takes its name from Les Baux) in the neighbouring hills, which gradually brought back some life to the village. But it was the discovery in more recent times that large amounts of money can be made from ancient wealth that has transformed the place. Today the population stays steady at around four hundred, while the number of visitors exceeds 1.5 million a year.

The village

The lived-in village has a great many beautiful buildings, which include those housing its half-a-dozen or so museums. One of the best museums is the **Musée Yves Brayer** in the Hôtel des Porcelets (summer daily 10am–noon & 2–5/5.30/6.30pm; winter closed Wed; 20F), showing the paintings of the twentieth-century figurative artist whose work also adorns the seventeenth-century **Chapelle des Pénitents Blancs**. Other contemporary Provençal artists' works are displayed in the **Musée d'Art Contemporain**, housed in the sixteenth-century Hôtel de Manville (summer daily 9am–8pm; winter 9am–noon & 2–5pm; 20F). The museum of the **Fondation Louis Jou** in the fifteenth-century Hôtel Jean de Brion (April–Sept daily 10am–1pm & 2–7pm; 15F) contains the presses, wood lettering blocks and hand-printed books of a master typographer whose workshop opposite is still used for manual printing (products on sale in the boutique) and for Apple Macintosh DTP courses which must leave Louis Jou turning in his grave. The **Musée des Santons** in the old Hôtel de Ville (daily 8am–8pm; 10F) displays traditional Provençal Christmas crib figures, while pick of the bunch is the **Musée de l'Olivier** in the Romaneque Chapelle St-Blaise (March–Nov daily 8am–7.30pm; summer till 9pm; 30F combined ticket with the citadel), featuring slide shows of paintings of olive trees and their artistic treatment by Van Gogh, Gauguin and Cézanne.

At the southern extremity of the village, the **Musée d'Histoire des Baux** in the vaulted space of Tour de Brau (daily 8/9am–5.30/7.30pm; combined ticket for museum, citadel & Musée de l'Olivier 30F) has a collection of archeological remains and models to illustrate the history from medieval splendour to Bauxite works. The museum is the entry point for the **Citadelle de la Ville Morte**, the main reason for coming to Les Baux. The most impressive ruins are those of the feudal castle demolished on Richelieu's orders; there's also the partially restored **Chapelle Castrale** and the **Tour Sarrasine**, the cemetery, ruined houses half carved out of the rocky escarpment, and some spectacular views, the best of which is out across the Grande Crau from beside the statue of the Provençal poet Charloun Riev at the southern edge of the plateau.

Practicalities

The **tourist office** is at the beginning of Grande Rue (April–Nov daily 9.30am–12.30pm & 2.30–6.30pm; ☎90.54.34.39). You have to park – and pay – before entering the village, and as you'll soon discover, nothing in Les Baux comes cheap, least of all **accommodation**. There is just one cheapish option, the *Hostellerie de la Reine Jeanne* (☎90.54.32.06; ④) by the entrance to the village, which has very friendly staff and good **food** with menus starting from 100F. If you're feeling rich and want to treat yourself, try the beautiful hotel-restaurant run by an Englishman and his French wife, *Le Mas d'Aigre* (☎90.54.33.54; ⑥), just below Les Baux to the east on the D27a, which has a fabulous garden with views up to the ruined castle, exquisite rooms and a semi-troglodyte restaurant where impeccable food is served. All the ingredients are fresh, and everything, including the bread, is made on the premises; main menus start from 300F but there's a *menu régional* for around 200F and a remarkably good-value lunch-time menu (open to non-residents) for around 100F, wine and coffee included. It is possible to get crêpes, pizzas and other **snacks** without breaking the bank in Les Baux, but the atmosphere of the place makes you feel as if you're being ripped off anyway.

The Val d'Enfer

Within walking distance from Les Baux, along the D27 leading northwards, is the valley of quarried and eroded rocks that has been named the **Val d'Enfer** (Valley of Hell). Dante, it is thought, came here while staying at Arles, and took his inspiration for the nine circles of the Inferno. Jean Cocteau used the old bauxite quarries and the contorted rocks for his film *Le Testament d'Orphée*, which also has scenes in Les Baux itself.

More recently, the very same quarries have been turned into an audiovisual experience under the title of the **Cathédrale des Images** (signposted to the right downhill from Les Baux's car park; mid-March to mid-Nov 10am–7pm; continuous projection; 35F). You are englobed by images projected all over the floor, the ceilings and the walls of these vast rectangular caverns, and by music that resonates strangely in the captured space. The content of the show, which changes yearly, does not really matter. It is just an extraordinary sensation, wandering on and through these changing shapes and colours. As an inventive use for an erstwhile worksite it can't be bettered.

Tarascon and Beaucaire

To the south of La Montagnette, the castles of **Beaucaire** and **Tarascon** face each other across the Rhône, the former in Languedoc on the west bank, the latter on the Provence side. Although the castles are regarded as classics, neither of the towns set below them is wildly alluring (Beaucaire probably just has the edge). Tarascon has one of the most famous Provençal carnivals, based on an amphibious monster known as the *Tarasque*, and is home to the **Souleïado** textile company. Near Beaucaire a reconstructed **Roman winery** has been put

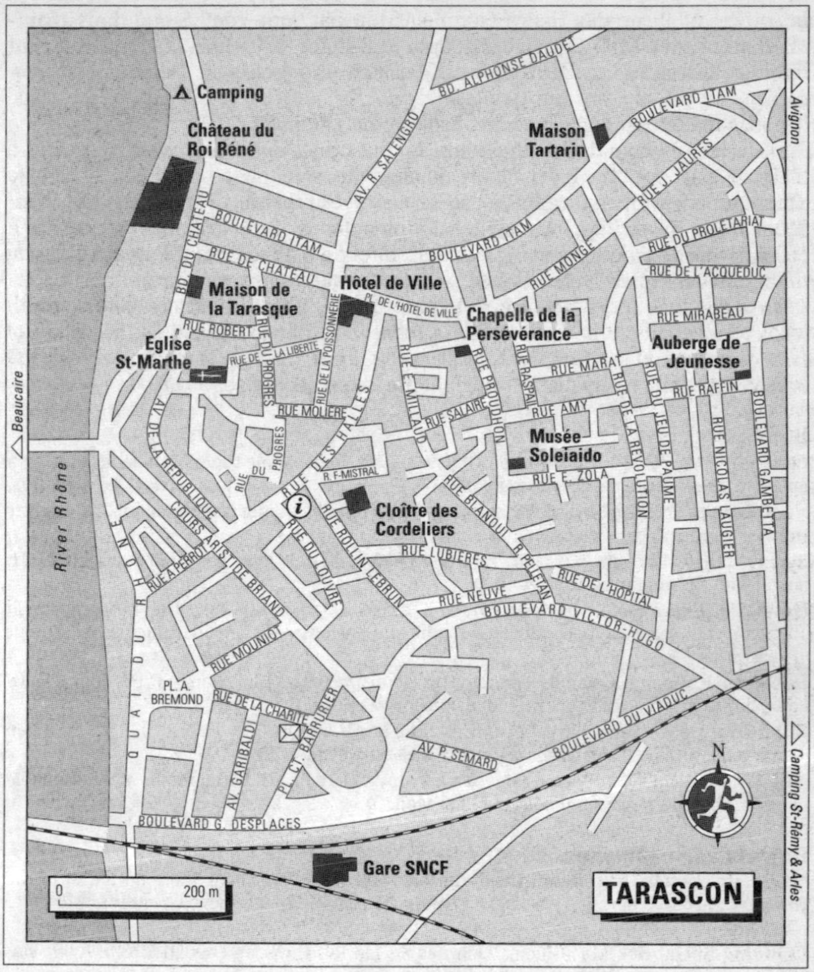

back to work. They're useful bases, too, for excursions into Languedoc with Nîmes and the Pont du Gard close at hand.

Arrival, information and accommodation

Both towns are served by Tarascon's **train station** and have good **bus links** with Avignon, Arles, St-Rémy and Nîmes. The **gare SNCF** is south of Tarascon's centre on bd Gustave-Desplaces (☎90.91.04.82). **Buses** from other towns leave from and arrive at the *Café des Fleurs* stop, in front of the station. Beyond the car park across the boulevard, cours Aristide-Briand leads to the road bridge across the Rhône, with the castle just upstream, and, to your right off the *cours*, the **tour-**

ist office at 59 rue des Halles (summer Mon–Sat 9am–7pm, Sun & hols 10am–12.30pm; winter Mon–Sat 9am–12.30pm & 2–6pm; ☎90.91.03.52). You can **rent bikes** in Tarascon at *MBK*, 1 rue E-Pelletan and **boats** in Beaucaire at very reasonable prices from the *Capitainerie du Port* on the south side of the canal opposite the tourist office on cours Sadi Carnot (☎66.58.68.67).

Beaucaire is bounded to the south by the Canal du Rhône which provides a pleasure port for the town before joining the river just below the bridge to Tarascon. The **tourist office** is at 24 cours Gambetta, overlooking the canal 300m from the bridge (Mon–Sat 9.30am–noon & 2–5.30/6pm; ☎66.59.26.57). Heading north from here along rue de l'Hôtel de Ville or rue R-Pascal takes you to the central **Eglise Notre-Dame**, with the castle a short way further north.

Tarascon has more **accommodation** to offer than Beaucaire, and a youth hostel, but it should be easy to find a room in either town, and as the centre of Beaucaire is just a kilometre's walk away from that of Tarascon, across the bridge, it doesn't really matter which of the two you choose.

Hotels

Les Echevins, 26 bd Itam, Tarascon (☎90.91.01.70). Reasonable rooms in a handsome town house. Closed weekends out of season. ③

Napoléon, pl Frédéric-Mistral, Beaucaire (☎66.59.17.57). An inexpensive option by the river with very low-priced single rooms. ③

Le Provençal, 12 cours A-Briand, Tarascon (☎90.91.11.41). Very basic but beats the youth hostel with a room for three at 140F. ①

Hôtel de Provence, 7 bd Victor-Hugo, Tarascon (☎90.91.06.43). The best choice in Tarascon with spacious air-conditioned rooms and balconies for breakfasting. Closed Fri out of season. ⑤

Hôtel du Rhône, pl Colonel-Bérrurier, Tarascon (☎90.91.03.35). Some of the rooms have had a lick of paint recently but no complaints for the price. ②.

Robinson, rte de Remoulins, Beaucaire; 2km north on D986 (☎66.59.21.32). In the open countryside with pool and tennis court, and a warm welcome. ④

Hôtel Saint-Jean, 24 bd Victor-Hugo, Tarascon (☎90.91.13.87). Large rooms and reasonable comfort. Closed Fri & Sun midday out of season. ③

Hostels and campsites

HI youth hostel, 31 bd Gambetta, Tarascon (☎90.91.04.08). About 500m northeast of the *gare SNCF*. Has 65 dormitory beds, and **bikes** for rental; 11pm curfew. Open from March to mid-Dec.

Camping St-Gabriel, Mas Ginoux, Quartier St-Gabriel, Tarascon (☎90.91.19.83). A two-star site 5km southeast of town off the Arles road.

Camping Tartarin, rte de Vallabrègues (☎90.91.01.46). A two-star site right beside the river in Tarascon, just north of the castle.

Le Rhodanien, rue du Champ de Foire, Beaucaire (☎66.59.25.50). A three-star site centrally located on the riverbank. Open April–Oct.

Tarascon

The **Château du Roi Réné** (Easter–Sept daily 9am–7pm; Oct–Easter 9am–noon & 2–5pm; closed hols; guided visits every hour; 26F) is the obvious first place to head for, a vast impregnable mass of stone, beautifully restored to its determinedly defensive fifteenth-century pose. Its towers facing the enemy across the river are square, those at the back round, and nowhere on the exterior is there any

THE TARASQUE AND TARTARIN

The **Tarasque** is said to have been tamed by Saint Martha after a long history of clambering out of the Rhône, gobbling people and destroying the ditches and dams of the Camargue with its long crocodile-like tail. On **the last full weekend of June** it storms the streets of Tarascon in the fashion of a Chinese dragon, 6m long with glaring eyes and shark-size teeth, the tail swishing back and forth to the screaming delight of all the kids. The monster represents paganism, but it also serves as a reminder of natural catastrophe, in particular floods, kept at bay in this region by the never totally dependable drainage ditches and walls.

Another legend, of an entirely different and much more recent origin, plays its part in the life of the town. The character from Tarascon called **Tartarin** is a mid-nineteenth-century literary creation, the work of Alphonse Daudet who came from this part of Provence. For a long time the writer dared not set foot in the city, thanks to the garrulous, bragging caricature of a Provençal petty bourgeois he had invented. Tartarin makes out he is the great adventurer, scaling Mont Blanc, hunting leopards in Algeria, bringing back exotic trees for his garden at 55 bis bd Itam. The address is real, and is dedicated to the fictional character: **Maison de Tartarin** (Mon–Sat 10am–noon & 2.30–5/7pm; 8F) with a waxwork figure waiting gun in hand in the hall. During the Tarasque procession, a local man, chosen for his suitably fat-bellied figure, strolls through the town as Tartarin.

hint of softness. Inside, however, is another matter. The castle was a residence of King Réné of Provence, and of his father who initiated the building, and was designed with all the luxury that the period permitted. The mullioned windows and vaulted ceilings of the royal apartments and the spiral staircase that overlook the **cour d'honneur** all have graceful Gothic lines and in the **Salle des Festins** on the ground floor and the **Salle des Fêtes** on the first floor the wooden ceilings are painted with monsters and other medieval motifs. Tapestries of a later date (François I) hang in the king's chambers and in several rooms graffiti dating from the fifteenth to the twentieth centuries testify to the castle's long use as a prison. There's an inscription by an eighteenth-century English prisoner in the **Salon du Roi**, and in the **Salles des Gallères** are carvings of boats, some dating from the crusades, done by prisoners awaiting judgement. In the **Salle des Gardes** the base of one vault column shows a man reading a book, sculpted at a time when such an activity was truly novel.

The visit ends with the climb up to the **roof**, from which revolutionaries and counter-revolutionaries were thrown in the 1790s. It's likely to be a bad experience for anyone with vertigo, and sometimes, depending on the winds, unpleasant for everyone due to the fumes from Tarascon's paper mill just downstream from the town. You can clearly see the polluting culprit, and, to the west, the far less substantial but still dramatic castle of Beaucaire.

The **Collégiale Royale Sainte-Marthe** (free entry), which stands across from the castle, has the saint who saved the town from the Tarasque monster, lying in stone on her tomb in the crypt and appearing in the paintings by Nicholas Mignard and Vien that decorate the Gothic interior. There are also works by Pierre Parrocel and Van Loo.

It's apparent from a wander round **the town** that the castle creams off most of the budget for old building restoration but it can be quite a pleasant change not to be surrounded by immaculate historic heritage. The streets of Renaissance *hôtels* interspersed with older houses with Gothic decoration, the classical town hall and medieval arcades along rue des Halles are all very subdued, with just the shutters adding a soft diversity of colour. Only during the Tuesday morning **market** does the town really come to life.

In the centre of the town, on place Frédéric-Mistral off rue Rollin-Lebrun, the sixteenth-century **Cloître des Cordeliers** (Mon & Wed–Sun 10am–noon & 2.30–5.30/7pm; 5F) has had its three aisles in light cream stone beautifully restored. It's used for exhibitions, sometimes of contemporary paintings, often by young artists. Other exhibitions are organized alongside a permanent collection of crib figures in the **Chapelle de la Persévérance** (Mon–Sat 10am–noon & 2–6pm; 10F) at 8 rue Proudhon, part of an erstwhile "refuge" for putting away women and girls suspected of living "bad lives". Further down rue Proudhon, at no. 39, is the **Musée Souleïdo** (summer Mon–Sat 10am–6pm; winter Mon–Fri 8am–noon & 1.30–5.30pm, 4.30pm on Fri; by appointment only on ☎90.91.08.80), which belongs to the family business which revived a 200-year-old traditional Tarascon activity and now has shops all over Provence selling the distinctive brightly coloured and eye-dancing patterned printed fabrics. The museum is lovely, with all the eighteenth-century wood-blocks from which many of the patterns still come, and tastefully displayed products including a table-setting dedicated to the bulls of the Carmargue.

Beaucaire

A statue of a bull standing at the head of the Canal du Rhône greets you as you arrive in **BEAUCAIRE** from Tarascon. To the north, between the castle and the river, is a bullring, plus a theatre, on the site of the old *champs de foire*. The fair held here, founded in 1217, was one of the largest in medieval Europe, attracting traders from both sides and both ends of the Mediterranean as well as merchants from the north along the Rhône. The fairs reached their heyday in the eighteenth century but died in the nineteenth century with the onset of rail freight.

The facades of the classical mansions and arcades around **place** and **rue de la République** and **place Clemenceau** that speak of former fortunes are gradually being restored. The Mansart-designed **Hôtel de Ville** and the much more modern market halls on place Clemenceau are very attractive, as is the seventeenth-century house at 23 rue de la République. Between the two is the eighteenth-century church of **Notre-Dame-des-Pommiers** with a frieze from its Romanesque predecessor embedded in the eastern wall, visible from rue Charlier.

To reach the **Château Royale de Beaucaire**, which is also having extensive works, follow the ramparts north of the bridge and then cut into town on rue Victor-Hugo, cross place de la République and follow rue de la République until you reach place du Château. Every afternoon a falconry display with medieval costumes and music is staged here (July & Aug daily 3–6pm; Sept–June Wed 2–5pm; 40F). It's great for kids, and the birds perform very well, but it's a shame that this has replaced the free ramble around the ruins, including the climb to the top of the tower that allowed you to appreciate the great advantage it had over Tarascon, whose castle lies far below. Only the gardens are open (April–Sept Mon & Wed–Sun 9.30–11.30am & 2.15–6.45pm; Oct–March 10.15am–noon & 2–5.15pm; closed hols; free); go in the morning if you want peace and quiet. Also in the gardens, the **Musée Auguste-Jacquet** (same hours as the castle grounds;

10F) has a small but interesting collection of Roman remains, mostly from a mausoleum, and documents relating to the medieval fair.

The castle was destroyed on Richelieu's orders when the town gave support to one of the cardinal's rivals, the duc de Montmorency. However, one irregular-sided tower still stands intact with the battlements and machicolations typical of thirteenth-century military strategy and, despite Richelieu's efforts, most of the walls overlooking the river have survived, as has the monumental staircase linking the upper and lower sections of the castle and a Romanesque chapel.

A much more enlivening Roman find is the winery with its original oak trunk press and amphorae containers at **La Mas des Tourelles** (April–Oct daily 2–7pm; rest of year Sat only 2–6pm; 25F, includes a tasting), 4km along the road to Bellegarde. The wine-maker and archeologist proprietor has put the Roman cellars to work again, using precise classical methods and recipes. Some of these are rather strange; apparently the Romans liked fortifying their wine with honey or seasoning it with fenugreek, dried iris bulbs, quince and pigs' blood.

Eating and drinking in Tarascon and Beaucaire

Eating cheaply in Tarascon and Beaucaire is not a problem, but eating well is another matter. The one good **restaurant** is at Tarascon's *Hôtel St-Jean* (see hotels on p.100) with Provençal dishes often featuring green or pink peppercorns and a very generous menu under 100F. The *Hôtel Terminus* by the station on place Col-Berrurier (closed Wed & Sat midday; ☎90.91.18.95) offers a wide selection of starters and main dishes on a 75F menu though the food's nothing to write home about. Beaucaire's quai Gal-de-Gaulle on the north side of the canal, is where you'll find the best concentration of restaurants and cafés though none are very special.

Markets and festivals in Tarascon and Beaucaire

Market days are Tuesday in Tarascon, along rue des Halles, and Thursday and Sunday in Beaucaire in the covered halls, place Clemenceau and cours Gambetta. On the first Friday of the month Beaucaire has a bric-à-brac market on cours Gambetta.

Both towns are very quiet most evenings; *El Souleïado* bar on rue des Halles in Tarascon is one of the few bars to stay open after 10pm, but things cheer up at festival time. Tarascon's end-of-June **Tarasque festival** (see box on p.101) involves public balls, bull and equestrian events and a firework and music finale. Beaucaire has its summer **Estivales**, a week of bull fighting, medieval processions, music, fireworks and so forth around July 21, plus its own Rhône monster legend, the **Drac** feted on the first weekend in June and followed by a jazz concert.

La Grande Crau

La Grande Crau (or just plain La Crau) stretches between the Alpilles and the Rhône delta, and east to Salon, and was once, a very long time ago, the bed of the Rhône and the Durance. Legend has a different explanation for the rounded pebbles that cover so much of this expanse. Hercules, they say, was having trouble taking on local Ligurians and the Mistral wind both at once, so he called on Zeus for aid. This arrived in the form of a pebblestone storm, water off a duck's back to the classical hero. The name Crau does in fact derive from a Greek word for "stony" that Homer uses, but that is not surprising since no doubt some of the ancient Greek settlers at Arles were literate.

Much of the area, like La Petite Crau, is irrigated and planted with fruit trees protected by windbreaks of cypresses and poplars. But other parts are still a stony desert in summer when the grass between the pebbles shrivels up. As winter approaches sections of the old Roman Via Aurelia are used as drove roads for sheep leaving their summer pastures in the mountains to overwinter here. At this time of year there are only the winds to contend with; in summer it is unbearably hot and shadeless.

Towards Arles: Chapelle St-Gabriel, Barbegal and Montmajour Abbey

In more amenable countryside, between the western end of the Alpilles and Arles, are some interesting stop-offs. The first is the extremely old **Chapelle St-Gabriel**, just 5km from Tarascon on the D33 to Les Baux, immediately after the junction with the main Avignon–Arles road. It's built on the site of a Gallo-Roman settlement, with a very appealling facade, possible sculpted by the same artists responsible for St-Tromphime's tympanum in Arles, and although Tarascon's tourist office has the keys, there's not that much to see inside. Between Chapelle St-Gabriel and a ruined medieval tower the GR6 footpath heads up towards the Alpilles ridge and Les Baux. For a ten-kilometre round walk you could follow the GR6 until you hit a small road, turn left down to **St-Etienne-du-Gres** and left again along the D32.

South of **FONTVIEILLE**, a popular pilgrimage for the French as the place where the writer Alphonse Daudet used to stay, the road past the small literary museum, *Moulin de Daudet*, leads south to the crossroads with the D82 where the remains of two Roman aqueducts are visible. Continuing south a left turning, signed to *Meunerie Romain*, brings you to the dramatic excavation of the **Barbegal mill**, a sixteen-wheel system powered by water from one of the aqueducts, constructed in 3 or 4 BC which may well have produced up to three tonnes of flour a day.

The road from Fontvieille to Arles takes you past the Romanesque ruins of the **Abbaye de Montmajour** (5-min bus ride from Arles; April–Sept daily 9am–7pm; Oct–March 9am–noon & 2–5pm; 27F), an unkempt, cobwebby ruin. Take heed when you climb the 124 steps of the fortified watchtower, as you will undoubtedly be surprised by dozens of pigeons flapping about when you arrive. The view of the Crau, the Rhône and the Alpilles is stunning, and below, in the **cloisters**, an excellent stone menagerie of beasts and devils enlivens the bases of the vaulting. Just 200m from the abbey, in the direction of Fontvieille, the eleventh-century funerary chapel of **Ste-Croix** with its perfect proportions and frieze of palm fronds stands amid tombs cut out of the rock in a farmyard.

Arles

ARLES, on the east bank of the Rhône, is a major town on the tourist circuit, its fame sealed by the extraordinarily well-preserved Roman arena, **Les Arènes**, at the city's heart, and backed by an impressive variety of other stones and monuments, both Roman and medieval. Roman Arles provided grain for most of the western empire and was one of the major ports for trade and shipbuilding; under

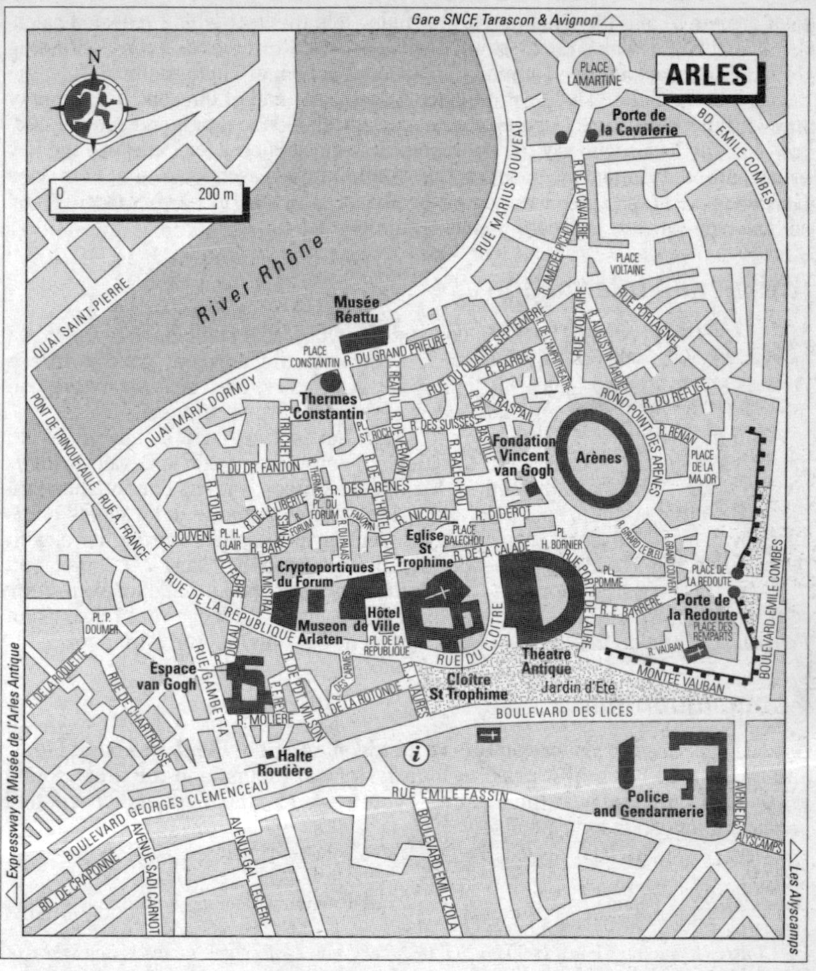

Constantine, it became the capital of Gaul, Britain and Spain. After the Roman Empire crumbled the city, along with Aix, refound its fortunes as the main base of the counts of Provence before unification with France. For centuries it was Marseille's only rival, profiting from the inland trade route up the Rhône whenever France's enemies were blocking the port of Marseille. Arles began to decline when the railline put an end to this advantage, and it was an inward-looking depressed town that **Van Gogh** came to in the late nineteenth century. It was a prolific though lonely and unhappy period for the artist, ending with his self-mutilation and asylum in St-Rémy-de-Provence. The **Fondation Vincent Van Gogh** pays tribute to him through the works of modern artists.

Today, Arles is a staid and conservative place, whatever the political colour of its mayors, but it comes to life for the **Saturday market** that brings everyone from the Carmargue and the Crau into town. It also fills the year with a crowded calendar of festivals, of which the most worthwhile are the **Rencontres Internationales de la Photographie** based around the National School of Photography in July, the dance, music, folklore and theatre **Festiv'Arles** at the end of June and beginning of July, and the **Mosaïque Gitanes** with gypsy and flamenco dance and song in mid-July. For the locals who say the photographic festival is only for Parisians, the key events are the annual opening of the bullfighting season with the **Fête des Gardiens** on May 1, the crowning of the **Reine d'Arles**, once every three years, and the **rice harvest** festivities in mid-September.

Arrival and information

The **gare SNCF** (☎90.82.50.50) is conveniently located a few blocks to the north of the Arènes. Most **buses** also arrive here at the adjacent **gare routière** (☎90.49.38.01), though some, including all local buses, use the *halte-routière* on the north side of bd Georges-Clemenceau, just east of rue Gambetta.

From the station, av Talabot leads to **place Lamartine**, right by one of the old gateways of the city, **Porte de la Cavalerie**. From here rue de la Cavalerie takes you up to the Arènes and the centre. **Rue Jean-Jaurès**, with its continuation **rue Hôtel-de-Ville**, is the main axis of old Arles. At the southern end it meets bd G-Clemenceau and **bd des Lices**, the promenading and market thoroughfare, with the **tourist office** directly opposite (April–Sept Mon–Sat 9am–7/7.30pm, Sun 9am–1pm; Oct–March Mon–Sat 9am–6pm, Sun 10am–noon; holidays 9am–7pm; ☎90.18.41.20), which has an annexe in the *gare SNCF*. You can rent **bikes** from *Peugeot* at 15 rue du Pont or *Dall'Oppio* (March–Oct only) on rue Portagnel.

Accommodation

Arles is well used to visitors and there's little shortage of **hotel rooms** at either end of the scale. The best place to look for cheap rooms is in the area around Porte de la Cavalerie near the station. If you get stuck, the tourist office will find you accommodation for a small fee.

Hotels

Calendal, 22 pl Pomme (☎90.96.11.89). Generous rooms overlooking a garden in a quiet square near the Arènes. Closed Jan & Feb. ③

Le Cloître, 16 rue du Cloître (☎90.96.29.50). A cosy hotel with some rooms giving views of St-Trophime. Closed mid-Nov to Feb. ④

Constantin, 59 bd de Craponne, off bd Clemenceau (☎90.96.04.05). Pleasant, well kept and comfortable, with prices kept down by the proximity of the Nîmes highway (some traffic noise) and its location some distance from the centre. ③

Diderot, 5 rue Diderot (☎90.96.10.30). A lot nicer than most of its similarly priced neighbours. Closed Jan 8 to March 25 & Nov 20 to Dec 5. ③

Le Forum, 10 pl du Forum (☎90.93.48.95). Spacious rooms in an old house at the ancient heart of the city, with a swimming pool in the garden. A bit noisy and hot but very welcoming. Closed Dec 20 to Jan 21. ⑥

Gaugin, 5 pl Voltaire (☎90.96.14.35). Comfortable, cheap and well run. Advisable to book. ②

Lamartine, 1 rue Marius-Jouveau (☎90.96.13.83). A gloomy but adequate hotel. ②

Mireille, 2 pl St-Pierre (☎90.93.70.74). On the other side of the river with the more expensive and very luxurious rooms overlooking a swimming pool. Closed mid-Nov to Feb. ⑦

Hôtel de la Muette, 15 rue des Suisses (☎90.96.15.39). Very pleasant and welcoming. ③

Musée, 11 rue du Grand-Prieuré (☎90.93.88.88). Quiet location opposite the Musée Réattu, small rooms but with charm. ④

Grand Hôtel Nord Pinus, 14 pl du Forum (☎90.93.44.44). Favoured by the *vedettes* of the bullring and decorated with their trophies, and, unfortunately, with stuffed bulls' heads. But one of the most luxurious options. ⑧

Hostel and campsites

HI youth hostel, 20 av Maréchal-Foch (☎90.96.18.25). Nearly 2km from centre; take bus #8 from pl Lamartine, direction *Fourchon*, stop *Fournier*. Not brilliant facilities, but 2am curfew. Reception 7.30–10am and 5pm–midnight. Open Feb to mid-Jan. ①

La Bienheureuse, 7km out on the N453 at Raphèles-les-Arles, with regular buses from Arles (☎90.98.35.64). Two-star, best of Arles' half-dozen campsites, the restaurant here is furnished with pieces similar to those displayed in the Musée Arlaten, and full of pictures of popular Arlesian traditions.

Camping City, 67 rte de Crau (☎90.93.08.86). Two-star site close to town on the Crau bus route. Open all year.

The City

The centre of Arles fits into a neat triangle between bd E-Combes to the east, bds Clemenceau and des Lices to the south, and the Rhône to the west. The **Musée de l'Arles Antique** is south of the expressway, not far from the end of bd Clemenceau; **Les Alyscamps** is down across the train lines to the south. But these apart, all the **Roman and medieval monuments** are within easy walking distance in this very compact city centre. The main square, with the cathedral and town hall, is **place de la République**; the hub of popular life is **place du Forum**.

MUSEUMS AND MONUMENTS

For years contemporary Arles has given priority to maintaining its **monuments**, and to building the huge Musée de l'Arles Antique outside the centre which opened in early 1995. Meanwhile the town's debts rose to alarmingly high levels and unemployment shot above fifteen percent, and in May 1995 the administration changed from right to left, leaving the rearrangement of the town centre's museums in some disarray. The tourist office has as little clue as anyone else as to what is going on, so be prepared for variable opening hours, closures and unexpected changes. The Musée Arlaten may extend into the former Musée d'Art Chrétien above the Cryptoportiques; the future use of Ste-Anne's church, formerly the Musée d'Art Païen, and the galleries above Cloître St-Trophime, formerly the Musée Nécropole, are uncertain; if and when the Thermes de Constantin will have a proper museum treatment remains to be seen.

A **global ticket** (55F from the Musée Réattu or the tourist office) should in principle be available, covering the Arènes, Théâtre Antique, Cloître St-Trophime, Cryptoportiques, Les Alyscamps, Thermes de Constantin and the Musée Réattu.

Musée de l'Arles Antique and the Cirque Romaine

Since Arles is so dominated by its ancient past, the new **Musée de l'Arles Antique** (Mon & Wed–Sun April–Sept 9am–8pm, Oct–March 10am–6pm; 35F), on the spit of land between the Rhône and the Canal de Rhône just west of the city centre, is no bad place to start. The triangular building, designed by Peruvian architect Henri Ciriani, is positioned on the axis of the **Cirque Romaine**, an enormous race-track currently being excavated, that stretched from the museum 450m to the town side of the expressway. Built in the middle of the second century, the track was 101m wide and allowed an audience of 20,000 to watch the chariot races. You can look down into the digs crossed by av de la 1er Division Française Libre, the road in front of the museum, but the models inside the museum will give you a much better idea of Roman Arles' third major entertainment venue.

The museum is a treat, open plan, flooded with natural light and immensely spacious. It covers the prehistory of the area and then takes you through the centuries of Roman rule from Julius Caesar's legionaire base and the development during the reign of Augustus, through to the Christian era from the fourth century when Arles was Emperor Constantine's capital of Gaul, to the fifth century, the height of the city's importance as a trading centre when Emperor Honorius could say "the town's position, its communications and its crowd of visitors is such that there is no place in the world better suited to spreading, in every sense, the products of the earth".

The exhibits are arranged chronologically as well as thematically, so, for example, there are sections on medicine, on the use of water power (with more details on the Barbegal mill), on industry and agriculture. Fabulous mosaics are laid out with walkways above; and there are numerous sarcophagi with intricate sculpting depicting everything from music and lovers, to gladiators and Christian miracles.

Around place de la République

An obelisk of Egyptian granite that may once have stood in the middle of the Cirque Romaine was placed in the centre of **place de la République** to glorify Louis XIV who fancied himself as a latter-day Augustus. But it pales into insignificance before the doorway of the **Cathédrale St-Trophime**, one of the most famous bits of twelfth-century Provençal stone carving in existence. It depicts the Last Judgement, trumpeted by angels playing with the enthusiasm of jazz musicians while the damned are led naked and in chains down to hell and the blessed, all female and draped in long robes, process upwards.

The cathedral itself was started in the Dark Ages on the spot where, in 597 AD Saint Augustine was consecrated as the first bishop of the English. It was largely completed by the twelfth century. A font in the north aisle and an altar illustrating the crossing of the Red Sea in the north transept were both originally Gallo-Roman sarcophagi. The high nave is decorated with d'Aubusson tapestries, in which the one depicting Mary Magdalene bathing Christ's feet has a cat jumping from one oil container to another chased by a dog being ridden by a child. You'll find more Romanesque and Gothic stone carving, this time with New Testament scenes enlivened with other myths such as Saint Martha leading away the tamed Tarasque, in the extraordinarily beautiful **cloisters**, accessible from place de la République to the right of the cathedral (April–Sept daily 9am–7pm; Oct–March daily 10am–4.30pm; 15F or 20F during exhibitions).

Across place de la République from the cathedral stands the palatial seventeenth-century **Hôtel de Ville**, inspired by Versailles. You can walk through its vast entrance hall with its flattened vaulted roof, designed to avoid putting extra stress on the **Cryptoporticus** below. This is a huge, dark, dank and wonderfully spooky horse-shoe shaped underground gallery, built by the Romans, possibly as a food store, possibly as a barracks for public slaves, but certainly to provide sturdy foundations for the forum above. Access is currently from rue Balze (April–Sept daily 9am–7pm; Oct–March daily 10am–4.30pm; 12F).

In case you feel that life stopped in Arles, if not after the Romans, then at least after the Middle Ages, head for the **Musée Arlaten** on rue de la République (daily 9am–noon & 2–5/6/7.30pm; Oct–June closed Mon; 15F), set up in 1896 by Frédéric Mistral with his Nobel Prize money. In the room dedicated to the poet, a cringing notice instructs you to piously salute the great man's cradle. That apart, the collections of costumes, documents, tools, pictures and paraphernalia of Provençal life are alternatively tedious and intriguing. The evolution of Arlesian dress is charted in great detail for all social classes from the eighteenth century to World War I and includes a scene of a dressmaking shop. Two other life-size scenes portray a visit to a mother and new-born child, and a bourgeois Christmas dinner, not to be looked at if you're hungry. The room devoted to Provençal mythology, including a Tarasque from the Tarascon procession, is entertaining if not very enlightening. If the museum has been extended it will provide access to the Cryptoporticus.

Down rue du Président-Wilson from the Musée Arlaten and right into rue P.F-Rey brings you to the **Espace Van Gogh**, the former Hôtel-Dieu where Van Gogh was treated. It now houses a *mediathèque* and university departments, with arty shops and a *salon de thé* in the arcades. The flowerbeds in the courtyard are a re-creation of the hospital garden based on Van Gogh's painting and the descriptions of the plants that he wrote in letters to his sister.

Around the Arènes

The amphitheatre, known as the **Arènes** (April–Sept daily 9am–7pm; Oct–March daily 10am–4.30pm; 15F), in the southeast corner of the city, is the most impressive of the Roman monuments, dating from the end of the first century. To give an idea of its size, it used to shelter over two hundred dwellings and three churches, built into the two tiers of arches that form its oval surround. This medieval *quartier* was cleared in 1830 and the Arènes was once more used for entertainment. Today, though not the largest Roman amphitheatre in existence and missing its third storey and most of the internal stairways and galleries, it is a very dramatic structure and a stunning venue for performances. It still seats 20,000 spectators.

The **Théâtre Antique** (April–Sept daily 9am–7pm; daily Oct–March 10am–4.30pm; 15F), just south of the Arènes, comes to life in July during the dance and theatre festival and for the *Fête du Costume*, in which local folk groups parade in traditional dress. A resurrected Roman, however, would be appalled at the state of this entertainment venue, with only one pair of columns standing, all the statuary removed and the sides of the stage littered with broken bits of stone. It was built a hundred years earlier than the Arènes and quarried for stones to build churches not long after the Roman Empire collapsed, then became part of the city's fortifications, with one of the theatre wings being turned into the **Tour Roland** whose height gives you an idea of where the top seats would have been. A convent and houses were then built over the area and it was only excavated at the turn of the century. Below the theatre the pleasant **Jardins d'Eté** lead down to bd des Lices.

The quiet and attractive southeast corner of the city between bd Emile-Combes and the Arènes and theatre has vestiges of the ramparts built over the Roman walls down montée Vauban and in the gardens running alongside the boulevard past the old Roman gateway, the **Porte de la Redoute**. Just by the gate you can see where the aqueduct from Barbegal brought water into the city.

Facing the Arènes from the west, at 26 Rond-Point des Arènes, the Palais de Luppé houses the **Fondation Vincent Van Gogh** (daily 10am–12.30pm & 2–

7pm; 30F) which exhibits works by contemporary artists inspired by Van Gogh. Francis Bacon was the first to contribute with a painting based on Van Gogh's *The Painter on the Road to Tarascon* that was destroyed during World War II. Roy Lichtenstein repaints *The Sower*; Hockney, Christo, César and Jasper Johns pay their hommage as well as musicians, poets, photographers and the fashion designer Christian Lacroix who grew up in Arles. The collection is sometimes on tour when it is replaced by an exhibition on one of the contributors.

If you take rue des Arènes from the Rond-Point to place du Forum you pass, at no. 16, the **Ecole Nationale de la Photographie** where there is usually a small exhibition in the foyer that you can look at for free.

Place du Forum to the river and Van Gogh

On **place du Forum**, still the centre of life in Arles today, you can see the pillars of an ancient archway and the first two steps of a monumental stairway that gave access to the Roman forum, now embedded in the corner of the *Nord-Pinus* hotel. The statue in the middle of the *place* is of Frédéric Mistral.

Heading south towards the river you reach the **Thermes de Constantin** (April–Sept daily 9am–noon & 2–7pm; Oct–March daily 10am–noon & 2–4.30pm; 12F), the considerable ruins of what may well have been the biggest Roman baths in Provence. You can see the heating system below a thick Roman concrete floor and the divisions between the different areas but there's nothing to help you imagine the original. The most striking feature, an apse in alternating brick and stonework, which sheltered one of the baths, is best viewed from outside on place Constantin.

To the right, along rue du Grand Prieuré, is the entrance to the **Musée Réattu** (April–Sept daily 9am–noon & 2–7pm; Oct–March daily 10am–noon & 2–4.30pm; 15F) where you can return to the twentieth century, assuming that you ignore the rigid eighteenth-century classicism of works by the museum's founder and his contemporaries. Of the moderns, Picasso is the best represented with the sculpture *Woman with Violin* and 57 ink and crayon sketches from between December 1970 and February 1971 which he donated to the museum. Amongst the split faces, clowns and hilarious Tarasque, is a beautifully simple portrait of Picasso's mother. Zadkine's study in bronze for the two Van Gogh brothers, Mario Prassinos' black and white studies of the Alpilles, Cesar's *Compression 1973* and works by contemporary artists are dotted about the landings, corridors and courtyard niches of this very beautiful fifteenth-century priory, and there are very good temporary exhibitions.

If you walk to the back of the building, you'll see its gargoyles jutting over the river. There are lanterns along the river wall (and wonderful sunsets), though much of the river front and its bars and bistros, where weary workers once drank and danced away their woes, was destroyed during World War II.

Another casualty of the bombing was the "Yellow House" where **Van Gogh** lived before entering the hospital at St-Rémy. It stood on place Lamartine opposite the café, now a supermarket, which he painted as the *Café de Nuit*. Van Gogh had arrived by train in February 1888 to be greeted by snow and a bitter Mistral wind. But he started painting straight away, and in this period produced such celebrated canvases as *The Sunflowers*, *Van Gogh's Chair*, *The Red Vines* and *The Sower*. He used to wander along the river bank wearing candles on his hat, watching the light of night-time; *The Starry Night* is the Rhône at Arles.

Van Gogh was desperate for Gauguin to join him, though at the same time worried about his friend's dominating influence. From the daily letters he wrote to his brother Théo, it was clear that the artist found few kindred souls in Arles. Gauguin did eventually come and moved in with Van Gogh. The events of the night of December 23, when Vincent cut off his ear after rushing after Gauguin brandishing a razor blade, were recorded by the older artist fifteen years later. No one knows the exact provocation. Van Gogh was packed off to the *Hôtel-Dieu* hospital where he had the fortune to be treated by a young and sympathetic doctor, Félix Rey. Van Gogh painted Rey's portrait while in the *Hôtel-Dieu* and the hospital itself, in which the inmates are clearly suffering, not from violent frenzy, but from inexpressible unhappiness.

Les Alyscamps

The Romans had their burial ground, **Les Alyscamps** (April–Sept daily 9am–7pm; Oct–March daily 10am–4.30pm; 12F), southeast of the centre and it was used by the well-to-do Arlesians well into the Middle Ages. Now only one alleyway, foreshortened by a rail line, is preserved; to reach it follow av des Alyscamps from bd des Lices. Sarcophagi still line the shaded walk, whose tree trunks are azure blue in Van Gogh's rendering. Some of the tombs have an axe engraved on them which is thought to have played the same function as a notice saying "Burglar alarm fitted". There are numerous tragedy masks, too, though any with special decoration have long since been moved to serve as municipal gifts, as happened often in the seventeenth century, or to reside in the museums. But there is still magic to this walk which ends at the church of **St-Honorat** where more sarcophagi are stored.

Eating, drinking and entertainment

Arles has a good number of excellent-quality and cheap **restaurants**. If you're looking for quick meals, or just want to watch the world go by, there's a wide choice of **brasseries** on the main boulevards, of which the most appealing is *La Grande Brasserie Arlésienne*, 14 bd des Lices (closed Tues).

For **all-night** eating, *Le Grand Bastière* out of Arles on the road to Stes-Maries-de-la-Mer, serves grills cooked on a huge fireplace from 9pm to 5 or 6am. It's 4.5km from the expressway on the left just after the turning to Gagaron and doesn't look like a restaurant (you'll know you're in the right place if you see beat-up old American cars in the drive). There's no need to book.

Saturday is the big day of the week in Arles for the **market** that extends the length of bd Georges-Clemenceau, bd des Lices and bd Emile-Combes and many of the adjoining streets. The atmosphere is festive with all the brasseries full of friends having their weekly get-together, and stunning displays of local produce, in particular the cheeses and olives. A smaller food market takes place every Wednesday on bd E-Combes and bric-à-brac stalls spread down bd des Lices the first Wednesday of the month.

For all-round **entertainment**, go to *Le Méjan-Actes Sud* on quai Marx-Dormoy (☎90.96.30.35), which offers **classical concerts** and **films**, along with meals and a bookshop.

Cafés, bars and ice cream

The Art Gallery, pl Constantin. A new contemporary art gallery and *salon de thé*, run by a Welshman and Frenchman, is being installed in the fifteenth-century Hôtel de l'Hoste (closed Sun).

Fonfon, at the bottom of bd des Lices, towards the expressway. The best ice-creams in Arles.

Le Café La Nuit, pl du Forum. Immaculately re-created café à la Van Gogh; open late.

Bar Le Paris, pl du Forum. Young and noisy, its waiters greeted by each new arrival with kisses on both cheeks. The best of the pl du Forum bars.

The Shop around the Corner, 45 rue du 4 septembre. A small and aimiable *salon de thé* selling cakes, ice creams, drinks and plats du jour for under 50F all day except Sun.

Restaurants

L'Affenage, 4 rue Molière (☎90.96.07.67). A choice of over 25 different starters and Provençal specialities with generous portions in the stables of an eighteenth-century coach house. Menus from 90F to130F. Closed Sun.

Hostellerie des Arènes, 62 rue du Réfuge (☎90.96.13.05). The service may be a bit abrupt but the food is real French family cooking. Good pizzas and two menus under 100F. Closed Tues.

Le Grillon, corner of rond-Point des Arènes & rue Girard-le-Bleu (☎90.96.70.97). Pleasant cheapie overlooking the Arènes with menus from 79F. Closed Wed.

La Gueule de Loup, 39 rue des Arènes (☎90.96.44.56). Cosy restaurant serving traditional dishes with one menu under 100F.

Lou Marquès & Le Cloître, Hôtel Jules Cesar, bd des Lices (☎90.93.43.20). Lou Marquès is the top gourmet palace in the top grand hotel. The specialities, which include *baudroie* (monkfish), *langoustine* salad and Carmague rice cake are all served with the utmost pomposity. A midday menu for 150F, otherwise from 200F; à la carte over 350F. Closed Nov & Dec. The other restaurant in the hotel, *Le Cloître*, is a lot cheaper; midday menu at around 100F. Closed Nov & Dec.

Le Médieval, 9 rue Truchet (☎90.96.65.77). A star-value four-course menu at 125F in an old abbey building. Closed Wed out of season.

L'Olivier, 1 bis rue Réattu (☎90.49.64.88). Small, elegant and very agreeable restaurant serving wine by the glass and with a delicious 135F menu (the cheapest).

La Paillote, 28 rue Dr Fanton (☎90.96.33.15). Excellent quality at very low prices and a chance to try the local speciality of bull steak. Closed Thurs midday and all day out of season.

Poisson Banane, 6 rue Forum (☎90.96.02.58). Serves the Caribbean speciality of fish and banana and other fruit and meat mixtures with a menu under 100F before 9pm. Open evenings only to 12.30am; closed Wed except in July.

Le Tambourin, 65 rue Amédée-Pichot (☎90.96.13.32). Fish and seafood in a pleasant atmosphere. Menus under 100F. Closed Mon.

Le Vaccarès, 9 rue Favorin (☎90.96.06.17). Overlooks pl du Forum and serves both new and old dishes in a light, inventive fashion. The lamb with *tapenade* and the fish *à la poutargue* (pressed in millet roe) are exceptional; menus from 135F, à la carte over 300F. Closed Mon and Sun evening.

Listings

Car parks *Parking des Lices* off bd des Lices.

Car rental *Europcar* (☎90.93.23.24); *Eurorent* (☎90.93.50.14) and *Hertz* (☎90.96.75.23), all on bd Victor-Hugo. *Avis* (☎90.96.82.42) on av Talabot.

Currency exchange 22 bis rue des Arènes; several banks on pl de la République.

Emergencies ☎15; *Centre Hospitalier J-Imbert*, quartier Fourchon (☎90.49.29.29).

Pharmacy Phone gendarmerie on ☎90.96.02.04 for address.

Police On bd des Lices opposite the Jardins d'Eté (☎90.18.45.00).

Post office *PTT*, 5 bd des Lices, 13200 Arles.

Swimming pool Stade Municipal off av Maréchal-Foch (June to mid-Sept, closed Mon).

Taxis ☎90.96.90.03; 90.49.69.59; 90.93.31.16.

BULLFIGHTING IN ARLES AND THE CAMARGUE

Bullfighting in Arles and the Camargue is not the Spanish-style *mise-à-mort*, and it's usually the bullfighters, or *razeteurs*, who get hurt, not the beast. The sport remains a passion with the populace, who treat the champion *razeteurs* like football stars, while the bulls are feted and adored, and before retirement are given a final tour around the arena while people weep and throw flowers.

The **shows** involve various feats of daring and, being much closer to the scene, you will feel more involved than with other dangerous sports. The most common show is where the bull has a cocade at the base of its horns and ribbons tied between them. Using blunt razor-combs (a recent regulation), the *razeteurs* have to cut the ribbons and get the cocades. The drama and grace of the spectacle is the stylish way the men leap over the barrier away from the bull. For some shows involving horsemen arrows are shot at the bull though these don't go in deep enough to make the animal bleed.

All this may leave you feeling cold, or sick, but it's your best way of taking part in local life, and of experiencing the Roman arena in Arles, whatever your feelings are about the parallels with Roman barbarity. It may help to know that no betting goes on, but people just add to the prize money as the game progresses. The tourist office, local papers and publicity around the arena will give you the details; be sure to check shows are not *mise-à-mort*.

The Camargue

The Camargue is one of those geographically enclosed areas that are separate and unique in every sense. Its ever-shifting boundaries, the **Petit Rhône**, the **Grand Rhône** and **the sea**, are invisible until you come upon them; its horizons infinite because land, lagoon and sea share the same horizontal plain. And both animal and human life have traits peculiar to this drained and ditched and now protected delta land.

The region is home to the **bulls** and the **white horses** that the Camargue *gardians* or herdsmen ride. Neither animal is truly wild though both run in semi-liberty. In recent times new strains of bull have been introduced because numbers were getting perilously low. The Camargue horse remains a distinct breed, of origin unknown, that is born dark brown or black, and turns white around its fourth year. It is never stabled, surviving the humid heat of summer and the wind-racked winter cold outdoors. The **gardians** likewise are a hardy community. Their traditional homes, or *cabanes*, are thatched and windowless one-storey structures, with bulls' horns over the doors to ward off evil spirits. They still conform, to some extent, to the popular cowboy myth, and play a major role in guarding Carmarguais traditions. Throughout the summer, with spectacles involving bulls and horses in every village arena, they're kept busy and the work carries local glamour. Winter is a good deal harder, and fewer and fewer Carmarguais property owners can afford the extravagant use of land that bull-rearing requires.

The two towns of the Camargue are as distant and as different as they could possibly be. **Les-Stes-Maries-de-la-Mer** is the area's overcrowded resort, famous for its gypsy gathering, while **Salin-de-Giraud** is linked to the industrial complex around the Golfe de Fos. Such villages as there are hardly qualify as more than hamlets. The rest of the habitations are farmhouses or *mas*, set well back from the handful of roads, and not within easy walking distance of their neighbours.

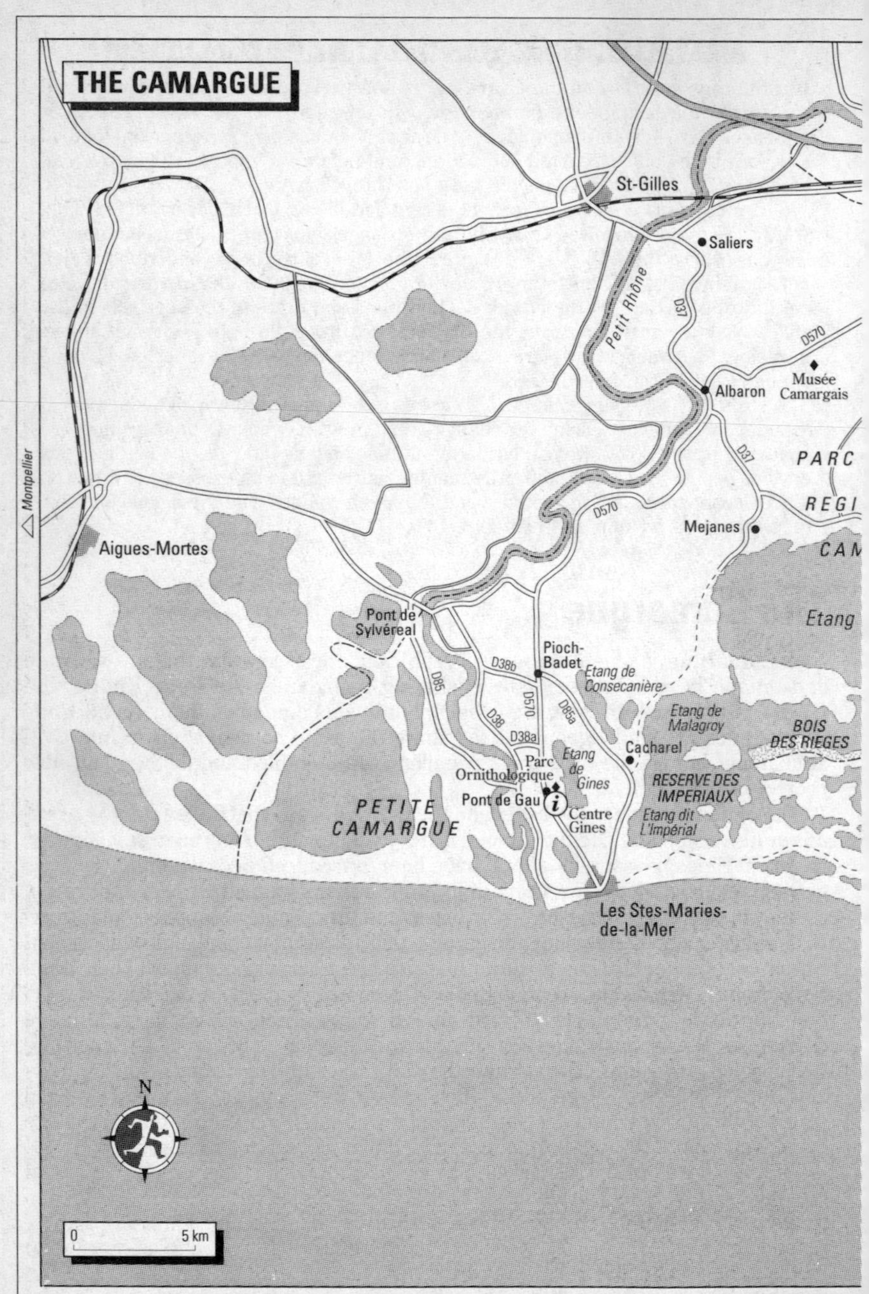
THE CAMARGUE
St-Gilles
Saliers
Petit Rhône
D37
D570
Musée
Camargais
Albaron
D37
PARC
REGI
CAM
Montpellier
D570
Mejanes
Aigues-Mortes
Etang
Pont de
Sylvéreal
Pioch-
Badet
D38b
Etang de
Consecanière
D85
D570
D85a
Etang de
Malagroy
BOIS
DES RIEGES
D38
D38a
Cacharel
Parc
Ornithologique
Etang
de
Gines
RESERVE DES
IMPERIAUX
Pont de Gau
Centre
Gines
Etang dit
L'Impérial
PETITE
CAMARGUE
Les Stes-Maries-
de-la-Mer
N
0
5 km

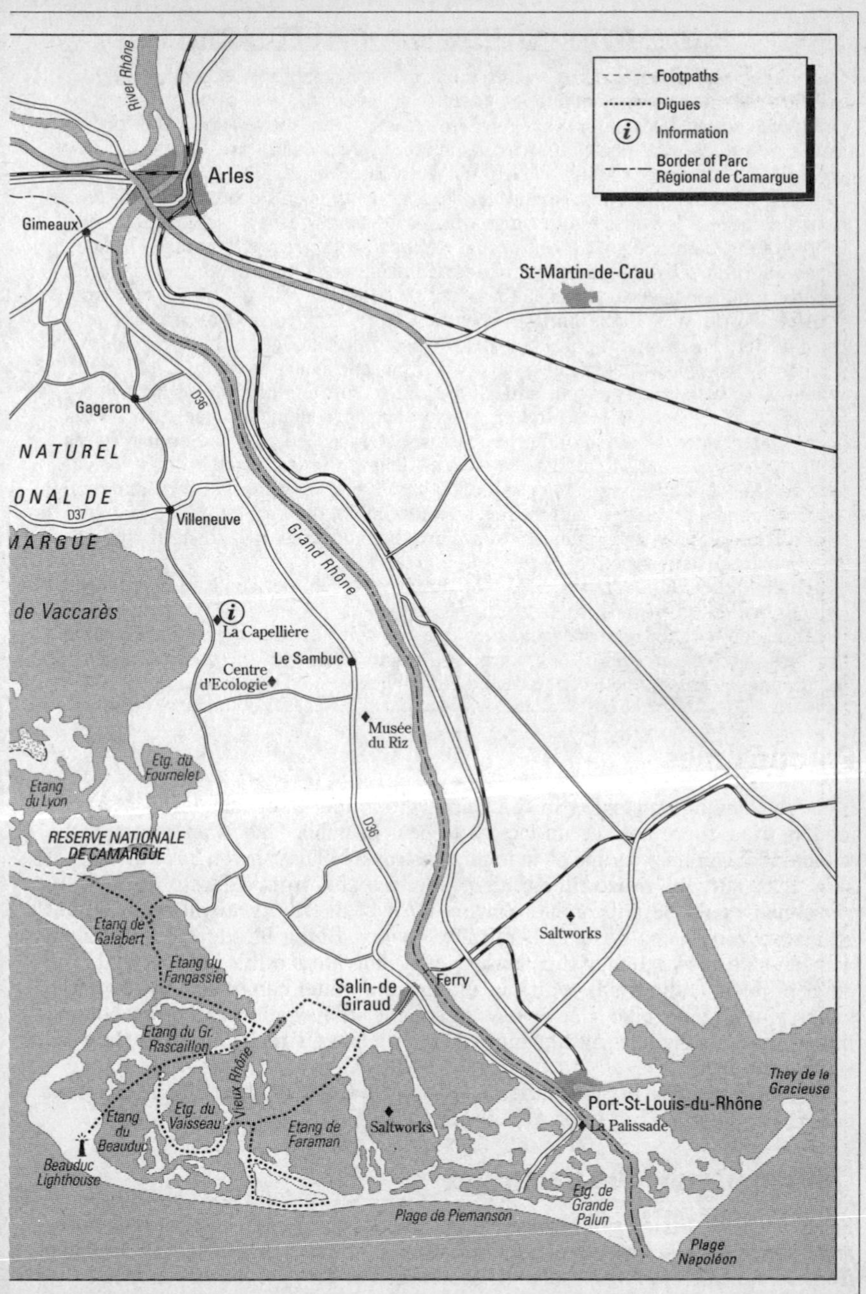

Footpaths
Digues
Information
Border of Parc Régional de Camargue
River Rhône
Arles
Gimeaux
St-Martin-de-Crau
Gageron
D36
NATUREL
ONAL DE
MARGUE
D37
Villeneuve
Grand Rhône
de Vaccarès
La Capellière
Le Sambuc
Centre d'Ecologie
Musée du Riz
Etg. du Fournelet
Etang du Lyon
RESERVE NATIONALE DE CAMARGUE
D36
Saltworks
Etang de Galabert
Etang du Fangassier
Ferry
Salin-de Giraud
Etang du Gr. Rascaillon
Vieux Rhône
They de la Gracieuse
Port-St-Louis-du-Rhône
Etang du Beauduc
Etg. du Vaisseau
Etang de Faraman
Saltworks
La Palissade
Beauduc Lighthouse
Etg. de Grande Palun
Plage de Piemanson
Plage Napoléon

WILDLIFE, AGRICULTURE AND INDUSTRY

The bulls and horses are just one element in the Camargue's exceptionally rich **wildlife**, which includes flamingoes, marsh- and seabirds, waterfowl and birds of prey; wild boars, beavers and badgers; tree frogs, water snakes and pond turtles; and a rich **flora** of reeds, wild irises, tamarisk, wild rosemary and famous juniper trees, which grow to a height of 6m, and form the *Bois des Rièges* on the islands between the *Etang du Vaccarès* and the sea, part of the central **National Reserve** to which access is restricted to those with professional research credentials. The whole of the Camargue is a *Parc Naturel Régional*, with great efforts made to keep an equilibrium between tourism, agriculture, industry and hunting on the one hand, and the indigenous ecosystems on the other.

After World War II the northern marshes were drained and re-irrigated with fresh water. The main crop planted was rice, so successfully that by the 1960s the Camargue was providing three-quarters of all French consumption of the grain. Vines were also reintroduced, and in the nineteenth century they survived the disease that devastated every other wine-producing region because their stems were under water. There are other crops – wheat, rapeseed and fruit orchards – as well as trees in isolated clumps. To the east, along the last stretch of the Grand Rhône, the chief business is the production of salt, first organized in the Camargue by the Romans in the first century AD, and now one of the biggest saltworks in the world. The salt pans and pyramids cannot help but add an extra-terrestrial aspect to the Camargue landscape.

Though the Etang du Vaccarès, the Réserve des Impériaux and the central islands are out of bounds, there are paths and sea dykes from which their inhabitants can be watched, and special nature trails (detailed overleaf). The ideal months for bird-watching are the mating period of April to June, with the greatest number of flamingoes present between April and September.

Practicalities

If you're planning on **staying in the Camargue** rather than using Arles as a base for day trips, there are certain factors to bear in mind. One is an aspect of the wildlife that can be so brutal as to totally destroy a holiday: if you have the sort of skin that attracts **mosquitoes**, then the months from March through to November could be unbearable. Staying right beside the sea will be okay, but otherwise you'll need serious chemical weaponry. Biting flies are also prevalent and can take away much of the pleasure of cycling around this hill-less land. The other problem is the winds, which in autumn and winter can be strong enough to knock you off your bike. Conversely, in summer the weather can be so hot and humid that the slightest movement is an effort. There's really no **ideal time** for visiting the area.

The **tourist office** in Stes-Maries is at 5 av Van Gogh (daily summer 9am–1pm & 3–7pm; winter 9.30am–noon & 2.30–6pm; ☎90.97.71.15).

Getting around the Camargue

Fairly frequent **buses** run between Arles and Stes-Maries, fewer between Arles and Salin and there's no direct service between the two. Timetables are available from *Les Cars de Camargue* at 24 bd Clemenceau or the *gare routière* in Arles.

For **drivers and cyclists** the main thing to be wary of is taking your car or bike along the dykes. Maps and road signs show which routes are closed to vehicles and which are accessible only at low tide, but they don't warn you about the surface you'll be driving along. The other problem is **theft** from cars. There are well-organized gangs of thieves with a particular penchant, as locals will testify, for British licence plates.

You can **rent bikes** at Stes-Maries at *Camargue Vélos*, 27 av Frédéric-Mistral (☎90.97.94.55), *Brun Sports*, place Mireille (☎90.97.81.83), *Le Vélociste*, pl des Remparts (☎90.97.83.26), and at *Le Vélo Saintois* on rte de Cacharel (☎90.97.86.44). The other means of transport to consider is **riding**. There are around thirty farms that rent out horses, by the hour, half-day or whole day.

For transport as an end in itself, there's the **paddle steamer** *Le Tiki III* which leaves from the mouth of the Petit Rhône, off the route d'Aigues-Mortes 2.5km west of Stes-Maries (☎90.97.81.68), and operates trips up-river from mid-March to mid-November. The *Soleil*, a much less pretty vessel but designed for very shallow water, leaves from the port in Stes-Maries and follows the shoreline to the Petit Rhône (April–Sept; 1hr-30min trips; ☎90.97.85.89). Other boats offer fishing expeditions – get details from the **tourist office** which can also provide addresses.

Accommodation

From April to October **rooms** in Stes-Maries should be booked in advance, and for the gypsy festival, several months before. Prices go up considerably during the summer and at any time of the year are more expensive than at Arles. There are some cheaper rooms in Salin, Le Sambuc and Albaron. A number of outlying *mas* (farmhouses) rent out rooms, usually quite expensively; if you have some form of transport, they can be idyllic locations from which to tour the region.

The only two **campsites** are close to Stes-Maries, both huge and expensive. **Camping on the beach** is not officially tolerated, but even at Stes-Maries people sleeping beneath the stars rarely get told to move on. The fifteen-kilometre seaside **Plage d'Arles**, also known as Plage de Piémançon, south of Salin-de-Giraud, is a favoured venue for *camping sauvage* in summer. As many as a thousand camper-vans, caravans and tents pitch up and vans selling provisions visit daily. The eastern end of the beach is naturist, and in all there are 8km of firm sand from which to choose your spot.

Hotels

La Brise de Mer, 31 av G-Leroy, Stes-Maries (☎90.97.80.21). Overlooking the sea, with a moderately priced restaurant. Obligatory half-board in July & Aug. ⑤

La Camargue, 58 bd de la Camargue, Salin-de-Giraud (☎42.86.82.82). A little bit brighter than *Les Saladelles*. Closed mid-Nov to mid-Jan. ③

Camille, 13 av de la Plage, Stes-Maries (☎90.97.80.26). Characterless cheapie but with a sea view. Closed Jan to April & Nov to Dec 25. ②

L'Estable Chez Kiki, 13 rte de Cacharel, Stes-Maries (☎90.97.83.27). Nothing very special but serviceable and not expensive. Closed Nov–March. ③

Le Flamant Rose, in Albaron between Arles and Stes-Maries (☎90.97.10.18). Acceptable hotel-restaurant with some bargain rooms. Closed March. ④

Longo Maï, Le Sambuc (☎90.97.21.91). On the main road by the central crossroads and not a great deal of character, but comfortable and with horses and bikes for rent. ③

Lou Santuari, rte de l'Eglise, Le Sambuc (☎90.97.21.71). Small, very charming, family-run hotel, 600m from the main road. ③

Mangio Fango, rte d'Arles, Stes-Maries (☎90.97.80.56). About 600m from Stes-Maries, overlooking the Etang des Launes with pool and patios. ⑥

Hostellerie du Mas de Cacharel, rte de Cacharel, Stes-Maries, 4km north on D85a (☎90.97.95.44). Select and expensive rooms in one of the oldest Camargue farms, with horses to ride. Closed Dec to Feb. ⑤

Mas des Rièges, rte de Cacharel, Stes-Maries (☎90.97.85.07). Down a track signed off the D85a close to Stes-Maries. An upmarket hotel in an old farmhouse, with swimming pool and garden. Closed Dec–Feb. ⑤

Le Mediterranée, 4 rue Frédéric-Mistral, Stes-Maries (☎90.97.82.09). Centrally located, with some of the cheapest rooms in town. Closed Dec to Feb. ③

Hôtel de la Plage, 95 bd de la République, Stes-Maries (☎90.97.85.09). Not on the sea as the name would suggest, but centrally located. Closed Jan. ④

Le Sauvageon, petite rte du Bac, Stes-Maries (☎90.97.89.43). Pretty little auberge in its own garden 9km north on the D38b linking the D38 and D570. ③

Les Saladelles, 4 rue des Arènes, Salin-de-Giraud (☎42.86.83.87). Old-fashioned cheapie. ③

Les Vagues, 12 av T-Aubunal, Stes-Maries (☎90.97.84.40). A low-priced option overlooking the sea on the rte d'Aigues-Mortes. ③

Hostel, campsites and chambre d'hôtes

HI hostel, on the Arles–Stes-Maries bus route, 10km north of Stes-Maries in the hamlet of Pioch-Badet (☎90.97.51.72). Open all year; horse rides organized and bikes for rent.

Camping La Brise, rue Marcel-Carrière on the east side of the village (☎90.47.84.67). On Arles-Stes-Maries bus route, stop *La Brise*. Three-star campsite open all year.

Camping Le Clos du Rhône, at the mouth of the Petit Rhône, 2km west of the village on the rte d'Aigues-Mortes (☎90.97.85.99). Only 2 of the Arles-Stes-Maries buses continue to here (*Clos du Rhône*). Four-star campsite open mid-June to mid-Sept.

Mas de Pioch, Pioch-Badet (☎90.97.55.51). Chambre d'hôte c/o Mme Cavallini; pool and large rooms; excellent value but needs booking well in advance. Easter–Sept. ③

The Musée Carmarguais, nature trails and information centres

Soon to be up and running, an interactive multi-media presentation of the Carmargue, created by Alain Giaccone, was motivated to combat the misunderstanding of what the Parc Naturel Régional is, evidenced by the number of people who ask directions to the entrance (check with Stes-Maries' or Arles' tourist office).

Otherwise, the **Musée Carmarguais** (April–Sept daily 9.15am–5.45/6.45pm; Oct–March Mon & Wed–Sun 10am–4.45pm; 25F), on the way to Stes-Maries from Arles halfway between Gimeaux and Albaron, gives a straightforward introduction to the area. It documents the history, traditions and livelihoods of the Camarguais people in the old sheep barn of a working farm. The displays are excellent and you can also follow a 3.5-kilometre trail through the farm land.

There are three main **trails** around the prohibited central area of the Carmargue. You can skirt the Réserve des Impériaux along a drovers path, the *draille de Méjanes*, between Cacharel, 4km north of Ste-Maries, and the D37 just north of Méjanes. Another trail, with one of the best observation points for **flamingoes**, follows the dyke between the Etangs du Fangassier and Galabert, starting 5km west of Salin-de-Giraud. Between these two is the *Digue à la Mer* running just back from the beach of Stes-Maries' bay. Cars are not permitted on these stretches, nor are you allowed on the sand dunes: you'll see a great many no entry signs and these should definitely be respected.

At Pont de Gau, on the western side of the Camargue, 4km short of Les-Stes-Maries, the **Centre Ginès/François Huë** is one of the Parc Naturel Régional de Carmargue's information centres (9am–12.30pm & 2–5/6pm; closed Fri). It has videos, slides and exhibitions on the local environment, its eco-systems and fragility, and is the place to go for detailed maps of paths and dykes. Just down the road is the **Parc Ornithologique** (9am–sunset; closed Dec–Jan) with some of the less easily spotted birds kept in aviaries, plus trails across a thirty-acre marsh and a longer walk, all with ample signs and information.

On the other side of the Carmargue, the main nature trail is at **La Capelière** (9am–noon & 2–5pm; closed Sun am; free) on the D36b on the eastern edge of the Etang de Vaccarès. There are exhibitions on Carmargue wildlife, information on the best means of seeing it, plus initiation trails and hides.

Further south, 7km beyond Salin-de-Giraud just off the D36d beside the Grand Rhône, **La Palissade** (mid-June to Aug daily 9am–5pm; rest of year Mon–Fri 9am–5pm; 15F) concentrates on the fauna and flora of its neighbouring lagoons, with a small and rather boring exhibition but a good nine-kilometre trail past duck and flamingo nesting grounds, and a shorter 1500-metre path. The bank of solar panels is to ensure continuous electricity during power cuts.

A short way past Le Sambuc on the way to Salin, the Domaine Petit Manusclat has a small **museum** dedicated to **rice** with waxwork scenes, tools and other dusty paraphernalia (Mon–Sat 10am–noon & 2–6pm; 15F) plus a shop where you can buy the local rice and rice cakes.

Les Stes-Maries-de-la-Mer

LES-STES-MARIES-DE-LA-MER is the town most people head for in the Camargue, and is best known for its annual festival on May 24 and 25, when gypsies converge on the town to ask favours from their patron saint Sarah. It is swamped by people throughout the summer and is becoming grossly overdeveloped, exploiting its monopoly as the only Carmargue resort by catering for every leisure activity to excess. Apart from peace and quiet you're not going to want for anything here. There are miles of beaches; a new pleasure port with boat trips to the lagoons; horses to ride; water sports; and the arenas for bullfights, cavalcades and other entertainment (events are posted on a board outside). The tourist office will happily weigh you down with details.

Though grossly commercialized, Stes-Maries is still an extremely pretty town with its streets of white houses and the grey-gold Romanesque **church** with its strange outline of battlements and watchtower. Inside, at the back of the crypt is the tinselled and sequined statue of Sarah (see box overleaf) always surrounded by candles and abandoned crutches and calipers. The church itself has beautifully pure lines and fabulous acoustics, and during the time of the Saracen raids it provided shelter for all the villagers and even has its own fresh water well. Between April and mid-November the church tower is open, affording the best view possible over the Camargue.

The local **Musée Baroncelli** (9am–noon & 2–5/6pm; closed Wed and Oct; 15F), on rue Victor-Hugo, is named after the man who, in 1935, was responsible,

THE LEGEND OF SARAH – AND THE GYPSY FESTIVALS

Sarah was the servant of Mary Jacobé, Jesus's aunt, and Mary Salomé, mother of two of the apostles, who, along with Mary Magdalene and various other New Testament characters, were driven out of Palestine by the Jews and put on a boat without sails and oars – or so the story goes.

The boat subsequently drifted effortlessly to the island in the mouth of the Rhône where the Egyptian god Ra was worshipped. Here Mary Jacobé, Mary Salomé and Sarah, who was herself Egyptian, settled to carry out conversion work while the others headed off for other parts of Provence. In 1448 their relics were "discovered" in the fortress **church** of Stes-Maries on the erstwhile island, around the time that the Romanies were migrating into western Europe from the Balkans and from Spain. It's thought the two strands may have been reunited in Provence.

Whatever the explanation, the gypsies have been making their **pilgrimage** to Stes-Maries since the sixteenth century. It's a time for weddings and baptisms as well as music, dancing and fervent religion. On May 24, after mass, the shrines of the saints are lowered from the high chapel to an altar where the faithful stretch out their arms to touch them. Then the statue of Black Sarah is carried by the gypsies to the sea. On the following day the statues of Mary Jacobé and Mary Salomé, sitting in a wooden boat, follow the same route, accompanied by the mounted *gardians* in full Camargue cowboy dress, Arlesians in traditional costume, and all and sundry present. The sea, the Camargue, the pilgrims and the gypsies are blessed by the bishop from a fishing boat, before the procession returns to the church with much bell ringing, guitar playing, tambourines and singing. Another ceremony in the afternoon sees the shrines lifted back up to their chapel.

In recent years the authorities have thought the event was getting out of hand and there's now a heavy police presence and the all-night candle-lit vigil in the church has been banned. There is a certain amount of hostility between some townspeople and the *gitans* though the municipality has actively countered the racism. It's a wonderful event to be part of, but inevitably makes finding accommodation in the town impossible. Another pilgrimage takes place on the Sunday closest to October 22, dedicated solely to Mary Jacobé and Mary Salomé and without the participation of the gypsies.

along with various *gardians*, for initiating the gypsies' procession down to the sea with Sarah. This was motivated by a desire to give a special place in the pilgrimage to the Romanies. The museum covers this event, other Carmarguais traditions and the region's fauna and flora.

Eating and drinking

On summer evenings every other bar and restaurant has flamenco-guitarists playing on the *terrasses* while the streets are full of buskers with a crazy variety of instruments. The atmosphere can be carnival or tackily artificial, depending on your mood.

As you might expect, few of the **restaurants** in Stes-Maries are bargains, though there are any number to choose from, and out of season the quality improves, and the prices come down. The specialities of the Camargue include *tellines*, tiny shiny shellfish served with garlic mayonnaise; *boeuf gardian*, bull's meat; eels from the Vaccarès; rice, asparagus and wild duck from the district; and *poutargue des Stes-Maries*, a mullet roe dish. The town **market** takes place on place des Gitans every Monday and Friday.

Les Alizés, 36 bis av T-Aubanel (☎90.97.71.33). Local specialities including bull sausage and Vaccarès eels. A view over the port. Two menus under 100F.

L'Impérial, 1 pl des Impériaux (☎90.97.81.84). Good fish dishes with interesting sauces. Menus from 110F. Closed Tues out of season & Nov–March.

Le Kahlua, 1 rue Jean Roche (☎90.97.98.56). Tapas, grills and cheap wine on the *terrasse* overlooking pl des Gitans. Open till 1am.

Les Montilles, 9 rue du Capitaine-Fouque (☎90.97.73.83). Cheap menus, sometimes including a delicious duck mousse.

Salin-de-Giraud and around

In total contrast to Stes-Maries, **SALIN-DE-GIRAUD** is an industrial village, based on the saltworks company and its related chemical factory, with workers' houses built on a strict grid pattern during the Second Empire.

If you want to take a look at the lunar landscape of the **salt piles**, there's a viewing point with information panels just south of Salin off the D36d. The Salin saltworks are the world's highest-capacity salt-harvesting site, covering an area of 110 square kilometres and producing 800,000 tonnes a year for domestic use and export. Across the Grand Rhône (there's a ferry at Salin) and downstream you can see **Port-St-Louis**, where the rice and salt of the Camargue are loaded onto ships, and where, surprisingly, a small fishing fleet still operates.

In summer three of the Arles–Salin buses continue on to the long sandy **Plage d'Arles** which stretches westwards from the mouth of the Grand Rhône. Due west of Salin a tortuous route of dyke-top tracks takes you to the **Pointe de Beauduc**, a wide spit of sand facing Stes-Maries across the bay. Amidst the shacks and caravans you'll find *Chez Juju* and *Chez Marc et Mireille*, two fish **restaurants** where you can try freshly scooped *tellines*. It's a bit like barbecueing on the beach, and not cheap, but it's the best Carmarguais dining experience.

Back in Salin the centre of life is one of the two **bars**, the *Bar des Sports*, next to the *Saladelles* hotel, where *belote* (a card game) championships are held and where the local fan club for Marseille's football team is based. Original paintings by local artists are on the walls, there's a model ship crystallized in salt, pinball, bar football and arcade games, and a normally gregarious clientele. On Friday evenings in July and August, entertainment shifts to the *arènes* between the main road and the river.

travel details

Trains

Of the **ordinary trains** on the main line between Paris and the Côte d'Azur at least 9 daily stop at Orange, all of them at Avignon (15–20min from Orange) and at least 18 at Arles (10–15min from Avignon). The main line from Marseille to the Spanish border stops at Arles (15–25min).

TGV

Avignon to: Marseille (8 daily; 55min); Montpellier (6 daily; 1hr); Paris (10 daily; 3hr 55min).

Ordinary trains

Arles to: Narbonne (3 daily; 2hr); Nîmes (frequent; 30min); Tarascon (frequent; 10min).

Avignon to: Tarascon (frequent; 10min); Toulouse (4 daily; 4hr 10min).

Buses

Arles to: Les Baux (4 daily; 30min); Salin (4–5 daily; 1hr), stopping at Le Sambuc (35min); Salon (6 daily; 1hr 5min), stopping at Raphèle (5min); Stes-Maries (5 daily; 1hr), stopping at Albaron (25min); St-Rémy (1 daily; 35min).

Avignon to: Arles (frequent; 1hr 10min); Beaucaire (frequent; 45min), some of them stopping at Barbentane (20min), Boulbon (30min) and Graveson (15min); Camaret (1 daily; 45min); Châteaurenard (hourly; 20min); Les Baux (2 daily; 55min); Manosque (2 daily; 2hr 30min); Marseille (5 daily; 2hr 5min), also stopping at Aix (1hr 40min); Montélimar (2 daily; 2hr 35min); St-Rémy (8 daily; 40min), a few of which stop at Noves (15min); Tarascon (frequent; 40min).

Orange to: Avignon (hourly; 45min–1hr 10min); stopping at Châteauneuf-du-Pape (4 daily); Sérignan (5 daily; 20min).

Tarascon to: Arles (3 daily; 20min); St-Rémy (3 daily; 20min).

CHAPTER TWO

THE EASTERN VAUCLUSE

As an area with a distinct identity the **Vaucluse département** dates only from the Revolution. It was created to tidy up all the bits and pieces, the papal territory of the Comtat Venaisson that became part of France in 1791, the principality of Orange won by Louis XIV in 1713, plus parts of Provence that didn't fit happily into the initial three *départements* drawn up in 1791. It's still a bit untidy with the **Papal Enclave** surrounded by the Drôme département, but that apart, it has the natural boundaries of the Rhône, **Mont Ventoux**, the limit of the **Vaucluse plateau** and the **River Durance**. The Rhône Valley is covered in *The Lower Rhône Valley*; this chapter deals with everything Vauclusian to the east.

In ancient times **Vaison-la-Romaine**, **Cavaillon**, **Carpentras** and **Apt** were part of the imperial Roman belt while the outlying villages were still tribal strongholds. During the Wars of Religion Carpentras was strongly papal, whereas the southern Lubéron supported the new religion. To this day there is very little unifying character to the area, save that its people have always been Provençal, whether ruled by Rome, Holland or France.

The main urban centres, Cavaillon, Carpentras and Apt, are basically market towns, with life centred on the seasons of the best fruit and vegetables in Provence. Of far greater appeal are the villages and countryside. The jagged rocky teeth of the **Dentelles**, the panorama from the windswept heights of Mont Ventoux and the great green surge of the **Lubéron** give three complete landscape contrasts. Then there are the multi-hued ochre mines of **Rustrel** and **Roussillon**, and the **River Sorgue** with its many channels and mysterious source at **Fontaine-de-Vaucluse**.

The **villages** are just as diverse: the dedicated **wine-producing communities** of the Dentelles; the chic **medieval hilltop habitats** surrounding Apt; the abandoned villages at **Buoux** and **Oppède-le-Vieux**; **Gordes**, home of **Victor Vasarely's** seminal art; romantic Fontaine; and **Cucuron**, which is strongly Provençal in character. The purest architecture in all Provence is present in two of the great trio of twelfth-century **Cistercian monasteries**, **Sénanque** and **Silvacane**.

The Enclave des Papes and Nyons

As an alternative to heading down the Rhône Valley into Provence, you can head east between Montelimar and Donzère into the **Enclave des Papes** and on through Nyons south towards Mont Ventoux or east towards Sisteron.

HOTEL ROOM PRICES

For a fuller explanation of these price codes, see the box on p.32 of *Basics*.

① Under 160F	② 160–220F	③ 220–300F	④ 300–400F
⑤ 400–500F	⑥ 500–600F	⑦ 600–700F	⑧ over 700F

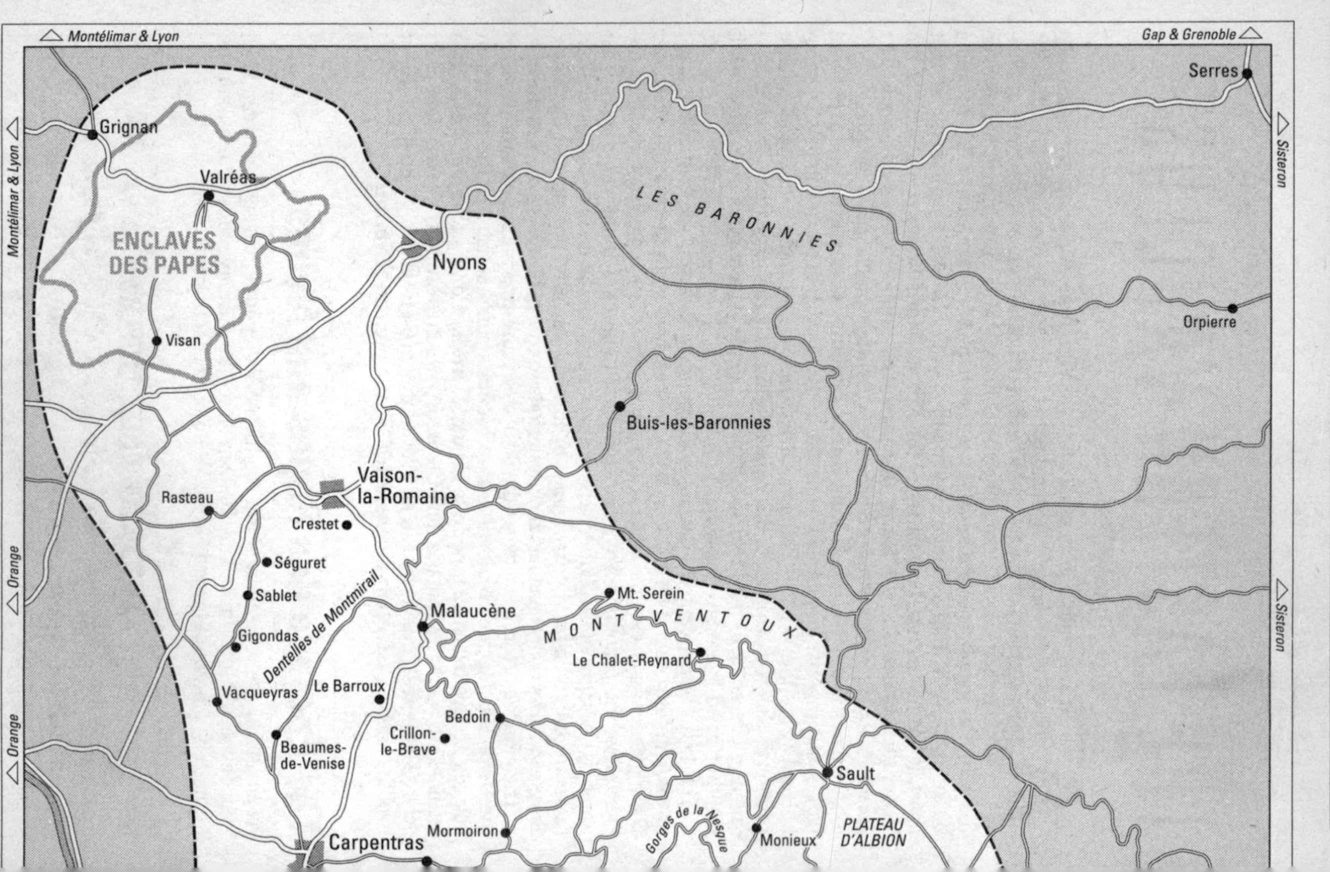
Montélimar & Lyon
Gap & Grenoble
Serres
Grignan
Montélimar & Lyon
Sisteron
Valréas
LES BARONNIES
ENCLAVES DES PAPES
Nyons
Orpierre
Visan
Buis-les-Baronnies
Vaison-la-Romaine
Rasteau
Crestet
Orange
Séguret
Sablet
Mt. Serein
Sisteron
Malaucène
Dentelles de Montmirail
Gigondas
MONT VENTOUX
Le Chalet-Reynard
Vacqueyras
Le Barroux
Bedoin
Crillon-le-Brave
Beaumes-de-Venise
Orange
Sault
Gorges de la Nesque
Mormoiron
Monieux
PLATEAU D'ALBION
Carpentras

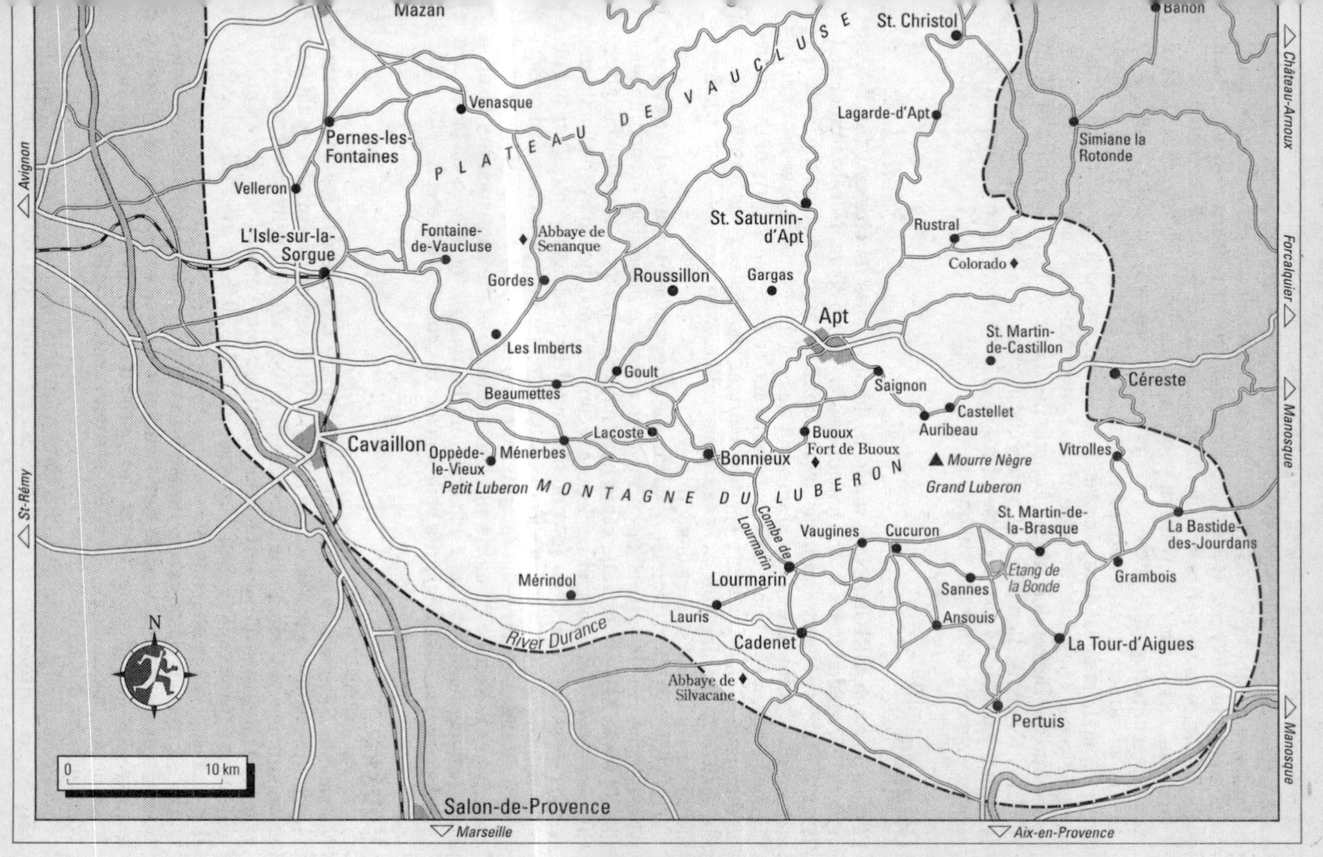
Mazan
St. Christol
Banon
Château-Arnoux
Venasque
Lagarde-d'Apt
Pernes-les-Fontaines
PLATEAU DE VAUCLUSE
Simiane la Rotonde
Avignon
Velleron
St. Saturnin-d'Apt
Rustral
L'Isle-sur-la-Sorgue
Fontaine-de-Vaucluse
Abbaye de Senanque
Colorado
Forcalquier
Gordes
Roussillon
Gargas
Apt
St. Martin-de-Castillon
Les Imberts
Goult
Céreste
Beaumettes
Saignon
Manosque
Castellet
Auribeau
Lacoste
Buoux
Cavaillon
Oppède-le-Vieux
Ménerbes
Bonnieux
Fort de Buoux
Mourre Nègre
Vitrolles
Petit Luberon
MONTAGNE DU LUBERON
Grand Luberon
St-Rémy
Combe de Lourmarin
St. Martin-de-la-Brasque
Vaugines
Cucuron
La Bastide-des-Jourdans
Etang de la Bonde
Mérindol
Lourmarin
Sannes
Grambois
Lauris
Ansouis
N
River Durance
Cadenet
La Tour-d'Aigues
Abbaye de Silvacane
Pertuis
Manosque
0
10 km
Salon-de-Provence
Marseille
Aix-en-Provence

The Enclave des Papes, centred around **Valréas**, is not part of the Drôme *département* that surrounds it, but part of Vaucluse, an anomaly dating back to 1317 when the land was bought by Pope Jean XXII as part of his policy of expanding the papal states around his Holy See at Avignon. When the Vaucluse *département* was drawn up the Enclave was allowed to keep its old links and hence is part of Provence.

Grignan, just outside the western edge of the enclave, and Valréas both have luxurious **châteaux**, and there are **vineyards** everywhere, often edged with roses as an attractive early warning system for aphid attack. East of the enclave, the pretty undulating landscape comes to an abrupt end with the arc of mountains around **Nyons**. These are the edge of the **Lower Alps** that curve southeast from Nyons into the **Baronnies range**, forming the border of Provence north of Mont Ventoux. Nyons is therefore not a Provençal city but it feels like one and is a delightful place, not least because of its solid protection against northern and eastern winds, including the Mistral.

Grignan

Passing through **GRIGNAN**, it would be hard to miss its **château** (April–Oct daily hourly guided tours 9.30–11.30am & 2.30–5.30/6.30pm; Nov–March closed Tues; 25F). It is not only enormous, taking up all the high ground of the town, but incongruous against the heavy towers and walls of the town's St-Saveur's church, the medieval houses below the southern facade and the older parts of the castle on the north. Though eleventh century in origin, the château was transformed in the sixteenth century into a Renaissance palace, with tiers of huge windows facing the south and statues lining the roof.

The château's most famous resident was the writer **Madame de Sévigné**, whose letters are historians' favourite source for the life of the French nobility during Louis XIV's reign. She came here for long periods to visit her daughter, the countess of Grignan, and her letters record the good life led by the family and friends: how they dined on fowl pre-flavoured by feeding the birds on thyme, marjoram and other herbs, on succulent doves, exquisite figs, melons and muscat grapes. At the same time she complained of the bitter cold whenever the Mistral blew. You can see the comforts and craftsmanship of the contemporary furnishings, plus eighteenth-century additions, in the tour of the *salons*, galleries and grand stairways, Mme Sévigné's bedroom and the count's apartments.

Valréas

Madame de Sévigné's granddaughter lived in the Château de Simiane, a mainly eighteenth-century mansion whose arcades, windows and balustrades would look more at home in Paris, though the pan-tiled roofs are distinctly Provençal. It is now the **Hôtel-de-Ville** of **VALREAS**, and hosts contemporary art shows in July and August (Mon & Wed–Sun 9am–noon & 2.30–5.30/6.30; free; 15F for exhibitions and special opening hours).

The other example of *ancien régime* ornamentation in the town is the painted wooden ceiling of the **Chapelle des Pénitents Blancs** on place Pie (July & Aug twice-weekly guided tours: ask at the tourist office for details). It stands to the west of the much more subdued eleventh-century **Eglise Notre-Dame-de-Nazareth**, famous for its organ.

Just outside the town, in a warehouse on the road to Orange, there's the **Musée du Cartonnage et de l'Imprimerie** (April–Sept Wed–Sun 10am–noon

& 3–6pm; Oct–March Wed–Sat 10am–noon & 2–5pm; 10F), a rather intriguing museum of packaging.

Valréas is pleasant enough to wander round, though you won't find much going on unless you're there on June 23 and 24, for the night-time procession and show of the *Nuit de Petit St-Jean*, or the first Sunday in August, for the *Fête des Vins de l'Enclave*. The most interesting diversions lie in buying local **wines**. As well as the *Côte du Rhône appellation* there's also *Valréas Villages* and *Visan Villages*, distinctive enclave wines, with flavours of violet, red fruits and pepper, credited with persuading the pope to buy this area in the first place. The **Caves Coopérative** is at the Caveau St-Jean, av de l'Enclave des Papes; you can also visit the private cellars (full list from the tourist office).

Practicalities

The **tourist office** is on place Aristide-Briand (Mon–Sat 9am–noon & 2.30–5.30pm; ☎90.35.04.71). If you're planning to **stay**, the best options are the *Grand Hôtel*, 28 av Gén-de-Gaulle (☎90.35.00.26; ③–④) on the outskirts of town, or the more moderate *Camargue*, 49 cours Jean-Jaurès (☎90.35.01.51; ②–③), both with reasonable restaurants. There's also a two-star **campsite**, *Camping de la Couronne*, by the river on the rte du Pègue (March–Oct; ☎90.35.03.78).

A good **place to eat** is *La Ferme Champ-Rond*, chemin des Anthelmes (closed Mon & Sun evening; ☎90.37.31.68), off rte de St-Pierre to the southeast, with fresh local food and not too expensive. In town, *L'Etrier*, 2 cours Tivoli (closed Tues evening, plus Wed evening out of season; ☎90.35.04.94) has menus starting from around 60F going up to the *menu gastronomique* for around 300F. You can sample the **local wines** at the beautiful turn-of-the-century *Café de la Paix* on rue de l'Hôtel-de-Ville. The **market** is held on Wednesday on place Cardinal-Maury and cours du Berteuil on the eastern side of town, with local truffles figuring prominently between November and March.

Around the Enclave: food and accommodation

Just outside the village of **GRILLON**, 4km from Grignan on the Valréas road, the **hotel-restaurant** *Auberge des Papes*, rte de Grignan (mid-April to Sept; ☎90.37.43.67; ④–⑤) offers quiet, comfortable rooms and meals based around truffles (restaurant closed Tues out of season; menus from 100F).

In **VISAN**, on the southern edge of the Enclave, the hotel-restaurant *Le Midi*, av des Alliés (☎90.41.90.05; ②–④) is very reasonable and serves good local dishes from around 120F (closed Tues). There's also a two-star campsite, *Camping de l'Hérein* , rte de Bouchet (☎90.41.95.99).

Nyons

After Grignan and Valréas, **NYONS**, on the River Aigues, seems a real metropolis, though its population is well under ten thousand. It is an extremely attractive place, perfect for lazing about in cafés or strolling through its medieval centre and riverside aromatic gardens. If Nyons is on your way into Provence you can begin to appreciate the essentials of its cooking here: olives and olive oil, garlic, wild mushrooms, and endless varieties of fruit and vegetables, with seasons quite different to the north. If Nyons is on your way out, then this is the place to do the final shopping.

Arrival and accommodation

Nyons is not on any train line but has regular bus links with Montélimar and Avignon. Buses arrive at **place Buffaven** on the edge of the old town, just northeast of the large central square, **place de la Libération**, where you'll find the **tourist office** (summer Mon–Sat 10am–noon & 3–6pm, Sun 10am–noon; winter Mon–Sat 10am–noon & 2–5pm; ☎75.26.10.35).

Nyons' remote position makes it easy to find **rooms** and there are plenty of bargains. The municipal **campsite** is extremely central, too.

Hotels

La Caravelle, 8 rue des Antignans (☎75.26.07.44). Small hotel, looking out over a garden to the river; about 700m from the town centre. ④

Lou Caleu, pl de la République (☎75.26.08.20). Friendly, cheap and dead central. ①–②

Les Oliviers, 2 rue A-Escoffier (☎75.26.11.44). Small, pleasant bargain hotel with a garden on the edge of the old town to the north. ①–③

Le Petit Nice, 4 av Paul Laurens (☎75.26.09.46). Very cheap rooms just to the west of pl de la Libération. ①–②

La Picholine, promenade de la Perrière (☎75.26.06.21). Up in the hills to the north of the town; quiet, secluded and comfortable with a swimming pool and good restaurant. ④

Campsites

Camping des Clos, 1km along the road to Gap (☎75.26.29.90). Four-star with pool. Open all year.

Camping Municipal, promenade de la Digue (☎75.26.22.39). Three-star next to the municipal swimming pool between the river and pl de la Libération. April–Oct.

The Town

You can sit for hours on the pavement terraces of **place de la Libération**'s cafés and brasseries, watching people pass amid a background of fountains, plane trees, palms and curly wrought-iron lampposts, and taking in the views beyond of steep wooded slopes that never block out the sun. On Thursdays the *place* and its neighbour to the northeast, place Buffaven, are taken over by a huge and wonderful **market**. A smaller one happens on Monday and in July and August there's a market on Sunday morning in the old town.

East of place de la Libération, the arcaded **place du Dr-Bourdongle** leads into a web of streets, covered passages and stairways running up to the **quartier des Forts**, so named for the now-ruined feudal castle, the fourteenth-century **Château Delpinal**, of which three towers remain, and the extraordinary **Tour Randonne**, a nineteenth-century chapel, with a neo-Gothic pyramid supporting a statue of the Madonna, sitting delicately on the heavy crenellated base of a thirteenth-century keep.

Towards the river, which is crossed by a single-spanned Romanesque bridge, the Pont Roman, there are pleasantly untouristy streets, scattered with bars, restaurants and some highly unusual **shops**, like the *Galerie du Pontias* at 20 rue des Bas Bourgs, selling the sort of traditional crafts normally seen only in folklore museums. Just beside the bridge, at 4 av de la Digue are **Les Vieux Moulins** (Sept–June Tues–Sat 10am–noon & 2.30–6pm; July & Aug daily 10am–noon & 2.30–6pm; 20F), an old artisanal complex of two eighteenth- and nineteenth-century oil presses, an eighteenth-century soapworks, and a traditional Provençal kitchen.

OLIVE PRODUCE

Olives are the product for which Nyons is famous. Black eating olives are a speciality, as is *tapenade* (a paste of olives, capers and herbs), but the biggest business is making olive oil, a process you can watch between December and February. Among firms that welcome visitors are *J Ramade*, av P-Laurens (just before place Oliver-de-Serres on the left), who have a video explaining all the subtleties, and *Moulin à Huile Autrand-Dozol*, on av de la Digue by the Pont Roman. The tourist office can provide more addresses, and there's also a **museum** on the subject on rue des Tilleuls (Tues–Sat 3–6pm; 10F).

At the **Coopérative Agricole du Nyonsais** on place Oliver-de-Serres you can buy all the olive products including *tapenade* under the brandmark *Nyonsolive*, as well as nut or chile oils, wines and honey (Mon–Sat 8am–noon & 2–6pm, Sun 9.30am–noon & 2.30–6pm). The **Coopérative Fruitière** is on the same square, its business being the refrigeration and packing of apricots and cherries. A small shop on the right-hand side of the building retails the summer fruits.

West along the river (about 500m) is the small but sensual **Jardin des Arômes** (open daylight hours; free), a garden of aromatic plants from which essential oils are made.

Eating and drinking

The best bet for a **meal**, with a brilliant view and cheap *steack frites*, is the *Bar du Pont*, overlooking the old Pont Roman from the old town. At the hotel-restaurant *Les Alpes*, 9 rue des Déportés, you can eat paella and couscous (☎75.26.04.99; also has a few rooms; ②). On the same street, there's a choice of Tex-Mex at *Tequila Sunrise* or pizzas at *L'Alicoque*. Very good classic Provençal food and wines can be had at *Le Petit Caveau*, 9 rue Victor-Hugo (closed Sun evening, Mon out of season; ☎75.26.20.21; one menu under 100F, à la carte 250F upwards). Otherwise you have all the place de la Libération brasseries to choose from.

Vaison-La-Romaine

VAISON-LA-ROMAINE lies between Nyons and Orange to the north of the Dentelles. The best approach is from the southeast along the Malaucène road. The first glimpse of the town is of a ruined twelfth-century castle outlined against the sky. As you get closer you see the storeys of old pale stone houses and towers beneath it, and the eighteenth-century town laid around its Roman predecessor. The two are linked by a Roman bridge, spanning the River Ouvèze in a single arch. The population of Vaison only finally settled on both sides of the river late this century. The original Celtic Voconces, like the late medieval Vaisonnais, chose the high ground, for identical defensive reasons. Their eighteenth-century descendants moved back to the right bank, leaving the citadel to wait for twentieth-century romantics to bring it back into fashion.

The older generation in Vaison recall the days when shops were little more than front rooms and you would interrupt the cooking or other household chores when you went in to be served. They talk of a barber who played the violin and would always finish the final bars before getting out the soap and towels. These days the population of the town and its tourist visitors can keep several dozen bars, hotels and restaurants busy, as well as numerous souvenir and sports shops.

Vaison hit the headlines in 1992 when the River Ouvèze burst its banks, killing thirty people, and destroying riverside houses, the modern roadbridge, and an entire industrial quarter. Though the town has recovered remarkably, its character has changed. It seems much more commercialized, and less friendly, perhaps because of the mass of ghoulish "tourists" who flocked to the town to see the damage.

It still, however, has the strong attractions of its medieval **Haute Ville** with a ruined cliff-top castle, the **Pont Romain** that held out against the floods, a cloistered former cathedral and the exceptional excavated remains of two **Roman districts**. Just south of Vaison there are sculptures in natural settings to be discovered at the **Crestet Centre d'Art**.

Arrival, information and accommodation

Buses to and from Carpentras, Orange and Avignon stop at the **Gare routière** on av des Choralies near the junction with av Victor-Hugo east of the town centre on the north side of the river. Heading down av Victor-Hugo you'll come to the main square, **place de Montfort**, from which it's a short walk further down to **Grande Rue** which leads left down to the **Pont Romain** and right, becoming av Général-de-Gaulle, to **place du Chanoine Sautel**. Here you'll find the **tourist office** (Mon–Fri 9.30am–noon & 2–5.45pm, Sat & Sun 10am–noon & 2–5.45pm; ☎90.36.02.11) between the two Roman archeological sites.

There's not a great choice of **hotels** and few bargains. The brilliant riverside **campsite** has been closed since the floods but there is still a very central site.

Hotels

Le Beffroi, rue de l'Evêché in the *haute ville* (☎90.36.04.71). Stylish lodgings in a sixteenth-century residence; the rooms are furnished to befit the building and are not outrageously expensive. Closed mid-Nov to mid-Dec & mid-Feb to mid-March. ⑤–⑦

Le Burrhus, pl Montfort (☎90.36.00.11). The cheapest rooms in town and noisy at weekends as it's above all the terraced cafés. ②–③

Hôtel des Lis, cours Henri-Fabre (☎90.36.00.11). Right in the centre, with some very large rooms. ③–⑥

Le Logis du Château, Les Hauts de Vaison (☎90.36.09.98). Along montée du Château south of the river and to the west of the *Haute Ville*; spacious rooms with lovely views. ④

Hostel and campsite

Camping du Théâtre Romain, chemin du Brusquet, off av des Choralies, quartier des Arts (☎90.28.78.66). Small three-star with good facilities; open mid-March to Oct.

Centre Culturel à Coeur Joie, Le Moulin de César, rte de St-Marcellin (☎90.36.00.78). Just 1km east of town down av Geoffroy from the Pont Roman, with basic but adequate rooms for 2 to 4 people. ①

The Town

Of all the distinctive epochs, it is the style and luxuries of the **Roman** population that are the most intriguing. The two excavated Roman residential districts in Vaison lie to either side of av Général-de-Gaulle: the **Fouilles Puymin** to the east and the **Fouilles de la Villasse** to the west (daily 9/9.30am–12.30pm & 2–5.45/6.45pm; ticket for both plus the Puymin museum and the cathedral cloisters 35F).

The Puymin *fouilles* (excavations) contain the theatre, several mansions and houses thought to be for rent, a colonnade known as the *portique de Pompée* and the museum for all the items discovered. The Villasse *fouilles* reveal a street with pavements and gutters with the layout of a row of arcaded shops running parallel, more patrician houses (some with mosaics still intact), a basilica and the baths. The houses require a certain amount of imagination, but the street plan of La Villasse, the colonnade with its statues in every niche, and the theatre, which still seats seven thousand people during the July festival, make it easy to visualize a comfortable, well-serviced town of the Roman ruling class.

Most of the detail and decoration of the buildings is displayed in the **museum** (daily 10am–1pm & 2.30–5.30/6.15pm) in the Puymin district. Tiny fragments of painted plaster have been jigsawed together with convincing reconstructions of how whole painted walls would have looked. There are mirrors of silvered bronze, lead water pipes, taps shaped as griffins' feet, dolphin door knobs, weights and measures, plus household and building implements. The busts and statues are particularly impressive: a silver head of one of the Villasse villas' owners; the Emperor Domitian, under whose reign the conquest of Britain was completed, carrying a shield of Minerva and the Gorgon's head; Hadrian looking sexier from behind than in front.

Tickets can be bought at the Puymin entrance just by the tourist office or in the cloisters of the former **Cathédrale Notre-Dame**, west down chemin Couradou which runs along the south side of La Villasse. The apse of the cathedral, which was badly flooded, is a confusing overlay of sixth-, tenth- and thirteenth-century construction, some of it using pieces quarried from the Roman ruins. The **cloisters** are fairly typical of early medieval workmanship, pretty enough but not wildly exciting. The only surprising feature is the large inscription visible on the north wall of the cathedral, a convoluted instruction to the monks to bring peace upon the house by loving the monastic rule and following God's grace.

The Pont Romain and the Haute Ville

The **Pont Romain** has had to have extensive repair works since its battering in the 1992 flood but it says a lot for Roman engineering that it fared better than the modern road bridge. Its new casings need weathering to return it to its former picturesqueness, but the grace of its high arch remains.

From the bridge rue du Pont climbs upwards towards place des Poids and the fourteenth-century gateway to the medieval **Haute Ville**. More steep zigzags take you past the Gothic gate and overhanging portcullis of the belfry and into the heart of this sedately quiet, uncommercialized and rich *quartier*. There are fountains and flowers in all the squares, and right at the top, from the twelfth- to fifteenth-century **Castle**, you'll have a great view of Mont Ventoux. In summer the *haute ville* livens up every Tuesday when Vaison's **market** spreads up here.

Eating and drinking

The restaurant to head for in Vaison is *Le Bateleur* at 1 place Théodore-Aubanel, downstream from the Pont Romain on the north bank (closed Mon, Sun evening & Oct; ☎90.36.28.04; 125F menu, à la carte around 200F). The lamb stuffed with almonds and the rascasse soufflé are highly recommended. *L'Auberge de la Bartavelle*, 12 place Sus-Auze (closed Mon; ☎90.36.02.16) has specialities from southwest France, for around 100–200F. Homemade bread and savoury tarts are to be had at *La Gloriette et Pomponette*, 22 Grande Rue (closed Sun, & Thurs out of season; ☎90.28.77.74) as well as traditional menus for around 110F. There are more menus to consider on cours Taulignan and place de la Poste, and a pleasant *crêperie*, the *Van Gogh* on rue Troque-Ponce.

In the haute ville the restaurant of *Le Beffroi* (see "Hotels" on p.130) has a surprisingly cheap menu, and the food is very acceptable though served with stiff formality. At the far end of rue de l'Evêché on place du Vieux-Marché, *La Fête en Provence* (closed Wed, & Thurs midday out of season; ☎90.36.36.43) has good game dishes on the 150F menu and a decent menu under 100F. Otherwise there's a *crêperie* and pizzeria on place des Poids.

Standard **brasserie fare** is available on place de Montfort, the obvious **drinking** place to gravitate towards. If you want to be in a more "local" ambience try *Vasio Bar* on cours Taulignan. The *Maison des Vins* in the same building as the tourist office has all the wines from the Dentelles villages and Ventoux.

Le Crestet and the Centre d'Art

South of Vaison, 3.5km down the Malaucène road, a turning to the right leads up to **LE CRESTET**, a tiny hilltop village with a private château at the top and a little snack bar, *Le Panorama* (summer daily till 9pm; in winter Sat & Sun only) from where you can admire a fantastic view. It includes the ruined château of Entrechaux, the Barronnies range and Mont Ventoux. From the village, signs direct you the short distance to the **Crestet Centre d'Art** from where you can discover sculptures placed within the surrounding forest of oak, pine and honeysuckle. You can go at any time and there's no charge; nor will the Centre provide you with a map though there is one on the wall at the entrance. Go behind the building leaving it on your right and then turn sharp left within 20m; the path then makes a clockwise loop – if you reach a dirt road you've gone too far. None of the sculptures are titled or signed and most are off the main path. Some are formed from the trees themselves, others are startling metal structures like a mobile and a meccano cage. One of the first ones you're likely to come across is Parvine Curie's *La Grande Tête*, concrete cubes positioned so that Vaison's ruined château is directly behind.

South of Le Crestet, signed off the D76 to the Vasion–Malaucène road, is a lovely **hotel** in the middle of nowhere, *Le Mas de Magali* (☎90.36.39.91; ③–④) run by a Dutch couple with a pool and *terrasse* looking eastwards to the mountains.

The Dentelles

The jagged hilly backdrop of the **DENTELLES DE MONTMIRAIL** is best appreciated in contrast to the level fields, orchards and vineyards lying to their south and west. The name *Dentelles* refers to lace; the pinnacles that slant, converge, stand parallel or veer away from each other were thought to resemble the contorted pins on a lace-making board, though the word's alternative connection with "teeth" (*dents*) is equally appropriate. For geologists the Dentelles are Jurassic limestone folds, forced upright and then eroded by the wind and rain.

The range runs southwest to northeast between **Carpentras** and Vaison. On the western and southern slopes lie the **wine-producing villages** of **Gigondas**, **Beaumes-de-Venise**, **Sablet**, **Séguret**, **Vacqueyras** and, across the River Ouzère, **Rasteau**. Several carry the distinction of having their own individual *appellation contrôlée*, within the *Côtes du Rhône* or *Côtes du Rhône Villages* areas. In other words their wines are exceptional and they are well feted. If you're in the region over the July 14 holiday head straight for Vacqueyras for the bacchanalian **Fêtes des Vins**. At any time of the year a more sober introduction to the subject is on offer at Rasteau's museum.

Besides *dégustations* and bottle buying, you can go for long **walks** in the Dentelles, happening upon mysterious ruins or photogenic panoramas of Mont Ventoux and the Rhône Valley. The pinnacles are also favourite scaling faces for apprentice **rock-climbers**: the Col de Cayron is one of the favourite pinnacles to climb with all the gear; the Dent du Turc needs only decent shoes and a head for heights to give a thrill.

The wines and villages

GIGONDAS has the most reputed **wine** in the Dentelles. It is almost always red, quite strong, has a back taste of spice or nuts and is best aged at least four or five years. Sampling the varieties could not be easier since the **Syndicat des Vins** runs a *caveau des vignerons* (closed Wed) in place de la Mairie where you can taste and ask advice about the produce from forty different *domaines*. The bottles cost exactly the same as at the vineyard, and you can buy *en vrac* (by crate), a real bargain for this quality of wine. The Gigondas **tourist office** in place du Portail (Mon–Fri 9.30am–noon & 2–6pm, Sat 9.30am–noon; ☎90.65.85.46) can provide lists of particular *domaines* or *caves* grouping several *vignerons* for the other villages.

If the art and science of wine and the whole business of wine-tasting is a mystery to you, then take a visit to **RASTEAU** and the **Musée du Vigneron** (April–Oct Mon & Wed–Sun 9.30am–12.30pm & 1.30–6pm; Nov–March Mon–Fri 1.30–5.30pm, Sat & Sun 9.30am–12.30pm and 1.30–6pm; 15F). The museum is on the D975 between Rasteau and **Roaix** and belongs to the *Domaine de Beaurenard* which also has vineyards in Châteauneuf-du-Pape. Along with a fairly predictable collection of bottles and nineteenth-century implements, there's a half-hour video on the whole Côtes du Rhône area. The charts and panels are rather harder work, but instructive on geology, soil, vine types, fossils, parasites, wine-growing throughout the world, wine and the stars, and wine and health, with a piece by Salvador Dalí on *Châteauneuf-du-Pape*. A *dégustation* is offered and there's no obligation to buy.

The most distinctive wine, and elixir for those who like it sweet, is *Beaumes-de-Venise muscat*. Pale amber in colour and with a hint of roses and lemon following the muscat flavour, it can usually convince the very driest palates of its virtue. The place to buy it is at **BEAUMES-DE-VENISE**, in the *Cave des Vignerons* (Mon–Sat 8.30am–noon & 2–6pm), a huge low building on the D7 overlooked by the Romanesque bell-tower of Notre-Dame D'Aubune. The *cave* also sells red, rosé and white *Côtes du Rhône Villages*, and the light *Côtes du Ventoux*. The **church** in Beaumes reflects the key concern of the area in the trailing vines and classical wine containers sculpted over the door. The tourist office, near the church, can again provide lists of *domaines* or *caves* for the area.

SABLET is the largest of the villages, and the least obviously chic. One road spirals up the dome on which the oldest houses are built. It's quiet with very little commerce. **VACQUEYRAS**' only claim to fame, apart from its **wine festival**, is as the birthplaces of a troubadour poet **Raimbaud**, who wrote love poems to one Beatrice in Provençal and died in the Crusades in 1207. You'll see plenty of signs for wine producers to visit around the village.

There is a fair amount of cosmetic hype about the star Dentelles village, **SEGURET**, but for all that it is alluring. Among its many medieval charms is a one-handed clock on the belfry, and, on Christmas Eve, in place of the standard Provençal crib, is a living re-enactment of the Nativity in which people play the parts their grandparents and great-grandparents played before them. The **Fête des Vins et Festival Provençal Bravade** in the last two weeks of August is a relatively recent publicity creation incorporating processions for the Virgin Mary and the patron saint of wine-growers as well as games and guns.

Séguret is good for walks and cycling. There's a cyclable path to Vaison, the *Chemin de la Montagne*, or you can follow the GR4 to the minimal remains of the **Prébayon nunnery**, abandoned in 962 AD, when the Trignon broke its banks. A bridge across the stream and dense vegetation add the appropriate Gothic touch.

Practicalities

Although it's possible to get to the villages by public transport from Vaison or Carpentras, having your own vehicle is definitely an advantage. You can **rent bikes** at *Loca-Sport*, place du Village in Sablet (☎90.46.96.17), and at the *Gite d'Etape des Dentelles* in Gigondas (☎90.65.80.85) which is also the place to go for **walking and climbing information**. *Edisud* publish a good guide, *Randonnées au Ventoux et dans les Dentelles* by I & H Agresti.

There's a fair scattering of **hotels and hostels** in the area but booking ahead is a good idea. In Gigondas *Les Florets*, 2km from the village towards the Dentelles (☎90.65.85.01; half-board obligatory in season; ④–⑤) has great charm and an excellent Provençal restaurant (closed Wed; menus from 100F), as does the very upmarket *Hôtellerie de Montmirail* which you reach via Vacqueyras (☎90.65.84.01; menus from 150F; ⑥–⑦). For quiet, old-fashioned hotels in Beaumes try the *Auberge St-Roch*, av Jules–Ferry (closed Mon & mid-Aug to mid-Sept; ☎90.62.94.29; ②), and *Le Relais des Dentelles* (closed Mon; ☎90.62.95.27; ②), past the old village and over the river. Séguret has two very posh hotels, *Domaine de Cabasse,* rte de Sablet (closed Jan–March; ☎90.46.94.01; ④–⑦), and *La Table du Comtat* in the village (☎90.46.91.49; ⑥–⑦), both with very few rooms and good restaurants. There's also a youth hostel/*gîte d'étape,* the *Maison Internationale de Rencontre,* rte de Sablet, 500m from the Séguret village on the Vaison road (closed mid-Nov to March; ☎90.65.93.31; ①). In Rasteau *Belle Rive* (closed mid-Nov to April; ☎90.46.10.20; ⑤) is a quiet hotel with a fine view from the *terrasse,* and good food including a rosemary-flavoured *crème brûlée.* The *Centre Départemental d'Animation et d'Accueil,* rte du Stade (☎90.46.15.48; ①), offers dormitory accommodation plus three two-bed rooms, with full pension for under 180F, a bargain.

There are **campsites** in Sablet, *Le Panoramic* (April–Oct; ☎90.46.96.27) Beaumes, *Municipal Roquefiguier* (April–Oct; ☎90.62.95.07) and Vacqueyras, *Municipal les Quierades* (April–Aug; ☎90.65.84.24).

Besides the hotel-restaurants mentioned above, places to stop for a **drink or eat** are few and far between once you leave the villages. In Sablet the *Café des*

Sports near the summit of the village feeds you for under 100F with no fooling around with menus. In Séguret *Le Mesclum,* rue des Poternes (closed Mon & Oct–Easter; ☎90.46.93.43), is quite expensive but renowned for the fresh local ingredients in its dishes. *L'Oustalet* in Gigondas, place du Portail (closed Mon evening & Tues; ☎90.65.85.30), has a pleasant shaded terrace and reasonably priced food or you can eat at a farmhouse, the *Auberge du Grand Bourjassot* just outside the village (June–Sept; closed Wed; booking necessary; ☎90.65.88.80).

Le Barroux

On the east side of the Dentelles, on the Vaison–Malaucène road, the very untouristy **LE BARROUX** is a perfect *village perché* with a twelfth- to eighteenth-century **château** at the top that was restored just before World War II, burnt by the Nazis and restored again from 1960 to 1990 (Easter–All Saints Day daily 2.30–6pm; 20F).

Les Géraniums on place de la Croix (☎90.62.41.08; ②–③), in Le Barroux, is a very peaceful, comfortable and unpretentious **hotel** in the heart of the village with views of the Dentelles; its *terrasse* restaurant serves very decent food with menus from 80F.

Mont Ventoux and east

From the Rhône, Lubéron and Durance, the summit of **MONT VENTOUX** repeatedly appears on the horizon. White with snow, black with storm-cloud shadow or reflecting myriad shades of blue, the barren pebbles of the final 300m are like a colour weather vane for all of western Provence. From a distance it looks distinctly alluring, a suitable site for what was the first recorded notion of landscape in European thought. The fourteenth-century Italian poet Petrarch climbed the heights simply for the experience; the local guides he chartered for the two-and-a-half-day hike before there were any tracks on the slopes, considered him completely crazy.

Meteorological information is gathered, along with TV transmissions and *Mirage* fighter jet movements, from masts and dishes at the top. The tower directing the conglomeration of receptors is in consequence no beauty, its chief design characteristic being to withstand winds from every direction, including the northern Mistral that can accelerate to 250km per hour across Ventoux. Wind, rain, snow and fearsome sub-zero temperatures are the dominant natural accompaniments to this tarmacked mountaintop.

The deforestation dates from Roman times, and by the nineteenth century it had got so bad that the entire mountain appeared shaved. Oaks, pines, box wood, fir and beech have since been replanted and the owls and eagles have returned but the greenery is unlikely ever to reach the summit again. The road that slides up the 1900m and down again with such consummate, if convoluted ease was built for the purposes of testing prototype cars, an activity that continued up till the mid-Seventies. Mont Ventoux is also a sporadic highlight of the Tour de France, hence its appeal in summer for passionately committed cyclists. Around the treeline is a memorial to the great British cyclist Tommy Simpson, who died here from heart failure, on one of the hottest days ever recorded in the race; his last words – "Put me back on the bloody bike".

But the chief human endeavour here marks the surface of the road with giant rows of graffiti of cosmopolitan individuals' names, local wines, the *CGT*, and, predictably for this part of the world, *FN* and *Le Pen*. Despite the unpromising environment, rest assured that from the summit, you have one of the most wonderful **panoramas**, not just in France, but in the whole of Europe. Between **November and May** all the road graffiti is covered up with only the tops of the black and yellow poles beside the road sticking up above the snow. People ascending Mont Ventoux will be on **skis**, leaving base either at Mont Serein on the north face or from the smaller southern station of Le Chalet-Reynard.

Practicalities

If you want to make the **ascent on foot** the best path to take is from **Les Colombets** or **Les Fébriers**, hamlets off the D974 east of **BEDOIN** whose **tourist office** on Espace M.L-Gravier (Easter–Aug Mon–Sat 9am–noon & 2–7pm, Sun 9am–noon; Sept–Easter Mon–Fri 9am–noon & 2–6.30pm, Sat 9am–noon; ☎90.65.63.95), can give details. They also organize a **night-time ascent**, every Friday in July and August, leaving around 10pm to camp near the summit and wake to watch the sun rise. *Egobike* (☎90.65.66.18), opposite the Bédoin tourist office, rents out **bikes** if you want to join the superfit cyclists in braving the gusts and horribly long steep inclines. For a scarier but less tiring view of the mountain, *Ciel Mont Ventoux* in Malaucène, av de Verdun (☎90.65.13.11), organizes hang-gliding sessions. In **Mont Serein** the *Chalet d'Accueil Mt-Serein* (☎90.63.42.02) can provide info on **ski-rental**, runs and lifts.

Bédoin has several **campsites**, including the two-star *Camping Pastoury* on the Malaucène road (mid-March to Oct; ☎90.65.60.79) and over a dozen **gîtes ruraux** for anyone considering spending a week or more in the area.

Le Chalet-Reynard on the south face has a small **restaurant**, *Le Chalet-Reynard* (☎90.61.84.55; menus from 80F), always full of walkers in the summer and skiers in the winter. At Malaucène, the **hotel** (☎90.65.20.35; ①) above the *Gim'Son bar* on cours Isnards is a good old-fashioned family *pension*, a bit noisy but a great bargain with rooms for three at 150F. At the other end of the scale, the *Hostellerie de Crillon le Brave*, place de l'Eglise (☎90.65.61.61; ⑧) in **Crillon-le-Brave** just west of Bédoin, offers exquisitely tasteful luxury with rates starting at 750F.

The Nesque Gorge

Coming to Ventoux from the southwest, the more scenic route is the **D942** from Carpentras to **Sault**, an approach that runs through the **NESQUE GORGE**. The Nesque itself is dry most of the year and invisible from most of the road whose engineering is more impressive than the geological fault above which it clings. It's a barren area with just one landmark located on the southern side before the belvedere where the gorge turns northeast again towards **MONIEUX**. The 200-metre-high **Rocher du Cire** is coated in wax from numerous hives that wild bees have made, and supposedly provided the men of Monieux with the reputation-enhancing exploit of abseiling down it to gather honey. This may well be a macho myth, certainly no one does it now. Nor do many people live in Monieux though there is a cheap **gîte d'étape**, the *Ferme St-Hubert* (Fri, Sat & Sun only; ☎90.64.04.51; ①), and a little restaurant, *Les Lavandes* (closed Mon out of season; ☎90.64.05.08; around 120F).

The Plateau d'Albion

At **SAULT**, 6km northeast of Monieux, the steep forested rocks give way to fields of lavender, cereals and grazing sheep. Wild products of the woods, lactaire and grisel mushrooms, truffles and game, as well as honey and other lavander products are bought and sold at the Wednesday **market** day in this small, unpretentious town, autumn being the best time for these local specialities. It also has major **fairs** on the Wednesday before Palm Sunday, St John's Feastday (June 23), August 16 and November 25. If you miss the market, *La Maison de Producteurs* on rue de la République can sell you all the goodies.

In the **PLATEAU D'ALBION**, which lies between Sault and **St-Christol**, Mount Ventoux is no longer visible. A ring of hills guards this treeless, undulating plain in which the chalky ground is riven by fissures, subterranean caverns and tunnels. Habitation is almost nonexistent and it's a shock when the narrow, badly surfaced and traffic-less D30 suddenly becomes a three-lane, superbly smooth highway which continues through St-Christol and down to **Lagarde d'Apt**. Part of the reason for this change is the enormous **airforce base** with its massive hangars and tall rectangular khaki-coloured blocks just north of St-Christol. Inside the base's gate are two six-metre-high models of missiles with *Force Aérienne Stratégique* written down their sides. This is the other reason for the special highway, for France's eighteen land-based **nuclear missiles**, with a range of 400km, are sited in this plain. In 1995 President Chirac said St-Christol's base would close, though not before the year 2000 by which time the missiles will be past their "use-by" date. Disarmament, however, is clearly not on the cards. Chirac's statement coincided with his announcement that nuclear testing in the Pacific would be resumed. The Plateau d'Albion may be host in the twenty-first century to a newer generation of these horrors.

Carpentras

With a population approaching thirty thousand, **CARPENTRAS** is a substantial town for this part of the world. It is also a very old one, its known history commencing in 5 BC when it was capital to a Celtic tribe. The Greeks who founded Marseille came to Carpentras to buy honey, wheat, goats and skins. For a brief period in the fourteenth century the town became the papal headquarters and gave protection to Jews expelled from France. For all its ancient remains, however, Carpentras seems incapable of working up an atmosphere to imbue the present with its past. Today, the best reasons for coming to Carpentras are the **Friday market** and **festival time**, last fortnight in July (see boxes on pp.139 and 141), and it also serves as a good base for excursions into the Dentelles, Mont Ventoux, the Nesque Gorge and the towns and villages south towards Cavaillon and Apt.

Arrival, information and accommodation

Buses arrive either on av Victor-Hugo or on place Terradou from where it's a short walk to av Georges-Clemenceau and right to av Victor-Hugo and place Aristide-Briand. The **train station** is freight only, serving the vast wholesale fruit and vegetable market a couple of kilometres to the south. The **tourist office** is at 170 allée Jean-Jaurès (July & Aug daily 9am–7pm; Sept–June Mon–Fri 9am–

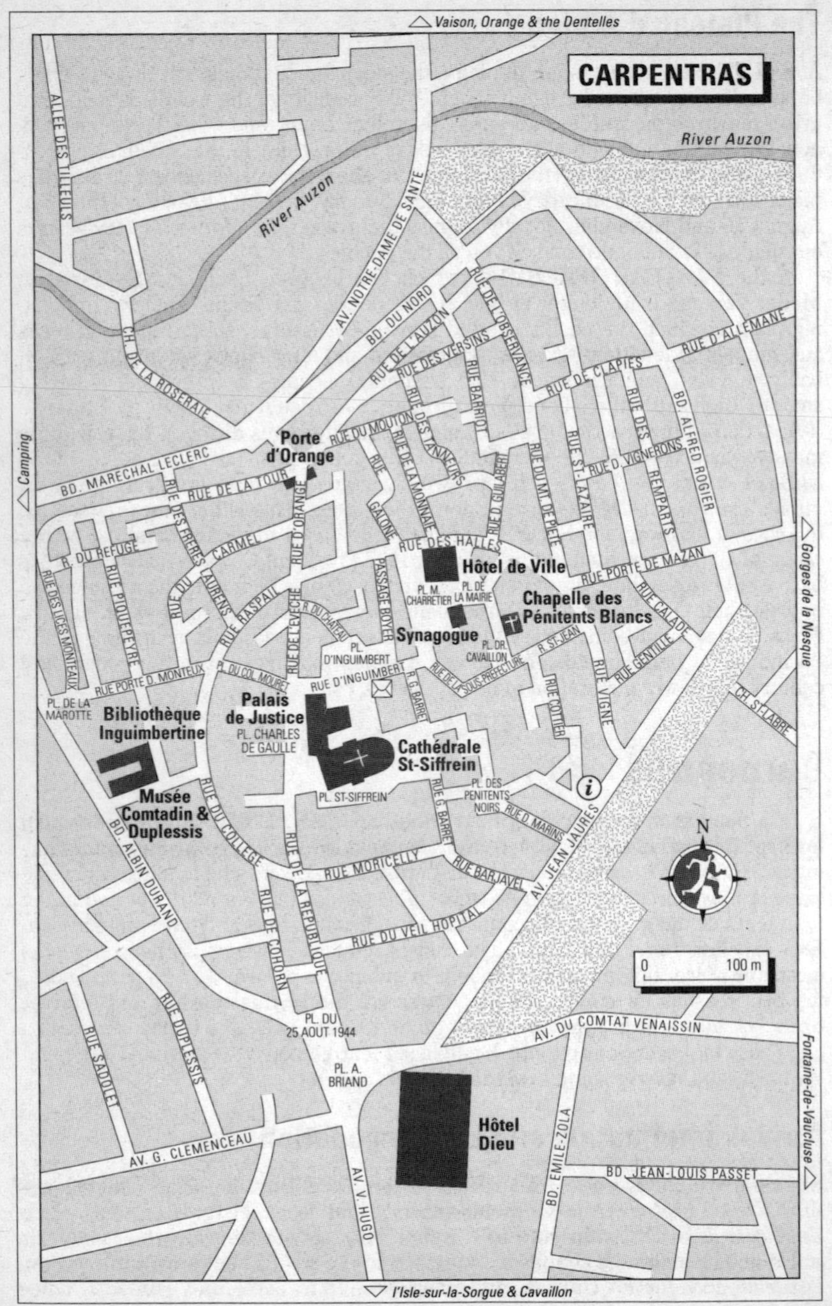
CARPENTRAS
Vaison, Orange & the Dentelles
River Auzon
Camping
Gorges de la Nesque
Fontaine-de-Vaucluse
l'Isle-sur-la-Sorgue & Cavaillon
Porte d'Orange
Hôtel de Ville
Chapelle des Pénitents Blancs
Synagogue
Palais de Justice
Bibliothèque Inguimbertine
Musée Comtadin & Duplessis
Cathédrale St-Siffrein
Hôtel Dieu
ALLEE DES TILLEULS
AV. NOTRE-DAME DE SANTE
BD. DU NORD
CH. DE LA ROSERAIE
BD. MARECHAL LECLERC
RUE DE L'AUZON
RUE DES VERSINS
RUE DE L'OBSERVANCE
RUE BARRIOT
RUE DE CLAPIES
RUE D'ALLEMANE
RUE DES VIGNERONS
BD. ALFRED ROGIER
RUE D. VIGNERONS
RUE DES REMPARTS
RUE DU MOUTON
RUE DES TANNEURS
RUE DE LA MONNAIE
RUE D. GUILABERT
RUE DU MT. DE PIETE
RUE ST-LAZAIRE
RUE DE LA TOUR
RUE DES FRERES LAURENS
RUE D'ORANGE
RUE GALONE
RUE DES HALLES
RUE PORTE DE MAZAN
R. DU REFUGE
RUE DU CARMEL
RUE RASPAIL
PASSAGE BOYER
PL. M. CHARRETIER
PL. DE LA MAIRIE
RUE CALADE
RUE DES LICES MONTEAUX
RUE PIQUEPEYRE
R. DU CHATEAU
RUE DE L'EVECHE
PL. D'INGUIMBERT
PL. DR. CAVAILLON
R. ST-JEAN
RUE GENTILLE
RUE VIGNE
CH. ST-LABRE
RUE PORTE D. MONTEUX
PL. DU COL. MOURET
RUE D'INGUIMBERT
R. G. BARRET
RUE DE LA SOUS PREFECTURE
RUE COTTIER
PL. DE LA MAROTTE
PL. CHARLES DE GAULLE
PL. ST-SIFFREIN
RUE DU COLLEGE
RUE G. BARRET
PL. DES PENITENTS NOIRS
RUE D. MARINS
AV. JEAN JAURES
BD. ALBIN DURAND
RUE MORICELLY
RUE BARJAVEL
RUE DE LA REPUBLIQUE
RUE DE COHORN
RUE DU VEIL HOPITAL
RUE DUPLESSIS
RUE SADOLET
PL. DU 25 AOUT 1944
PL. A. BRIAND
AV. DU COMTAT VENAISSIN
AV. G. CLEMENCEAU
AV. V. HUGO
BD. EMILE-ZOLA
BD. JEAN-LOUIS PASSET
N
0
100 m

THE CARPENTRAS FRIDAY MARKET

Friday is the major **market** day in Carpentras. Edibles are spread all round the town, flowers and plants down av Jean-Jaurès and antiques and bric-à-brac on rue Porte-de-Monteux and place Colonel-Mouret. From November 27, date of the annual St-Siffrein fair, to the beginning of March, place du 24 Août 1944 is given over every Friday morning to truffles, the rooted not the chocolate kind. In April you'll find strawberries, and throughout the year all the fruit and veg that sprout so early in the lowlands of the Vaucluse. Outside market days, **food shopping** is best done in and around rue des Halles and there are great jams and chocolates to be had at 28 rue de la Sous-Préfecture.

12.30pm & 2–6.30pm, closes 6pm on Sat; ☎90.63.00.78), halfway along av Jean-Jaurès which runs northeast from place Aristide-Briand. The town proper is small enough to cover easily on foot but if you need a **bike** try *Terzo Sports* on av Mistral (☎90.67.31.56) or *Euro Moto* on av Comtat Venaissin (☎90.63.24.59).

Carpentras' **hotels** all congregate on the circle of boulevards; there are plenty of bargains but don't expect quiet. On bd Albin-Durand try *Le Théâtre* at no. 7 (☎90.63.02.90; ①–②) or *Le Cours* at no. 65 (☎90.63.10.07; ①–③) with some better rooms, which are both pauper options. Equally basic and with just twelve doubles, *La Lavande*, 282 bd A-Rogier (☎90.63.13.49; ①–②), is usually full. For something much more pleasant, *Le Fiacre*, 153 rue Vigne (☎90.63.03.15; ②–⑤) close to the tourist office, is a good-value hotel in an old townhouse with a garden, and *Safari Hotel*, 1 av JH-Fabre (☎90.63.35.35; ④–⑤), though lacking character has good amenities, including a pool and tennis courts.

The nearest **campsite** is the two-star *Camping Le Brégoux,* chemin du Vas, just outside the village of **Aubignan**, 5km north on the D7 towards Beaumes-de-Venise (open mid-March to Oct; ☎90.62.62.50).

The Town

A birds' eye view of Carpentras shows clearly the perimeter line of the town in the Dark Ages (rues Vigne, des Halles, Raspail, du Collège and Moricelly), enclosed in the ring of boulevards that follow the line of the medieval town wall. Of this only the massive, crenellated **Porte d'Orange** and the odd rampart on rue des Ramparts and rue des Lices-Monteux remain.

At the heart of town on place Gal-de-Gaulle, the **Palais de Justice** was built as an episcopal palace to indulge the dreams, or more likely the realized desires, of a seventeenth-century cardinal of Carpentras. Nicolas Mignard was commissioned to fresco the walls with sexual scenes of satyrs and nymphs but a later incumbent had all the erotic details effaced. Tours of the building (summer only, times variable, ask at tourist office) are less interesting as a consequence.

The *palais* is attached to the fifteenth-century **Cathédrale St-Siffrein** behind which, almost hidden in the corner, stands a **Roman arch**, inscribed with happy imperial scenes of prisoners in chains. Fifteen hundred years after the cathedral's erection, Jews, coerced, bribed or otherwise persuaded, entered the building in chains to be unshackled as converted Christians. The door they passed through, the **Porte Juive**, is on the southern side and bears the strange symbolism of rats encircling and devouring a globe. Apart from this the cathedral is dull, as is the space around it; there are not enough café tables to cover the breadth of place

Général-de-Gaulle and the plane trees, lanterns and black swan fountains of place d'Inguimbert are ruined by a slot-meter toilet. Running between place d'Inguimbert and rue des Halles, however, the **Passage Boyer** is a high and beautiful glazed shopping arcade. It was built by the unemployed in the short-lived scheme to generate jobs after the revolution of 1848.

Following rue d'Inguimbert eastwards brings you to the area of the ancient **Jewish ghetto** and a slightly livelier part of the modern town. The original **synagogue** on place de la Juiverie was built in the days when the Jews had to pay movement taxes every time they left or entered the ghetto, and when their rights to be in Carpentras at all depended on papal whim. In 1741 when the present synagogue was constructed on the old foundations, Bishop d'Inguimbert refused to allow it to be as high as the **Chapelle des Pénitents Blancs** on rue Bidault. The rabbi's response was to paint the ceiling blue with stars "for then I'll have all the skies". This, along with its low hanging chandeliers, the purification baths (for women after menstruation as well as brides) and the bread ovens, can all be visited (Mon–Fri 10am–noon & 3–5pm, till 4pm Friday; closed Jewish feast days; free).

Just beyond place Aristide-Briand, the town's main pole of activity, is the huge eighteenth-century **Hôtel-Dieu** building, which still functions as a hospital though you can visit its original opulent **pharmacy** (Mon, Wed & Thurs 9–11.30am; 8F). As well as gorgeously decorated vials and boxes containing cat's foot extract, Saturn salt, deer antler shavings and dragon blood, the painted lower cupboards tell a very "Age of Reason" moral tale of wild and happy monkeys ending up as tame and dutiful labourers.

You could take a look at the local history museum, the **Musée Comtadin** on bd Albert-Durand (Mon & Wed–Sun 10am–noon & 2–4/6pm; 2F combined ticket with Musée Duplessis) but it's hard to get excited by the collection of keys, guns, *santons*, seals, ex-votos, papal bulls, bells and bonnets (though the sheep bells with different pitches are quite nice). Dimly lit pictures provoke little curiosity and yet they do merit some, in particular the portraits of famous Carpentrassiens including that of François-Vincent Raspail, after whom so many French streets are named. Born just after the Revolution and condemned to death during the White Terror, Raspail was a committed republican all his life, criticising every brand of nineteenth-century conservatism and dedicating much of his work as a doctor to making medicine available to the poor. One of his fellow radical Vaucluse *députés* in the 1876 parliament, Alfred Nacquet, who proposed divorce rights for women, also hangs in these musty rooms. A painting by Denis Bonnet of medieval Carpentras features a non-existent hill to show the separate Jewish area within the city walls.

Above the Musée Comtadin is the **Musée Duplessis** (same hours and ticket), named after a mediocre eighteenth-century painter from Carpentras whose wealth and influence had much to do with the people he painted. Besides these, the collection includes Roman bits, an Egyptian tablet with a Pharaonic scene captioned in Aramaic, and some very wonderful Renaissance miniatures. In the same mansion, on the left as you enter the courtyard, is the **Bibliothèque Inguimbertine**, where several hundred thousand volumes on the history of Provence, Books of Hours, musical scores and early manuscripts are available for consultation (Mon 2–6.30pm, Tues–Fri 9.30am–6.30pm, Sat 9.30am–noon; closed July).

Contemporary art is displayed in changing exhibitions at the nearby **Chapelle du Collège** on rue du Collège (daily 10am–12.30pm & 2–6pm).

CARPENTRAS FESTIVALS

Music, theatre and dance events are put on during the last fortnight in July for the **Estivales**. Details can be had from the *Bureau du Festival*, La Charité, 77 rue Cottier (☎90.63.46.35).

On August 15, Vaucluse food is celebrated in the **Festival des Saveurs Provençales**, a day of gourmandize in which the minutiae of old-fashioned food production is debated and feted, with prizes given and plenty of tastings.

Eating, drinking and entertainment

As far as **eating** in Carpentras goes, *Le Marijo* at 73 rue Raspail (closed Fri evening & Sun; ☎90.60.42.65) is excellent with menus under 130F. For a cheaper option, try *Le Trapier* (☎90.63.24.11) on the pretty place Galonne off rue des Halles, with menus under 80F. *Le Vert Galant*, 12 rue Clapies (closed Sat midday & Sun; ☎90.67.15.50), serves more sophisticated fare, with a weekday lunchtime menu for around 100F, otherwise from 170F. You'll find crêpes at *Les III Rois* on rue Calade, a side street off rue Porte-de-Mazan. Take-away Thai, Chinese and Vietnamese food is available from *La Perle d'Asie* on place du Théâtre and quick pizzas from *La Garrigue*, 90 rue Cottier (daily till 11pm).

For **drinking** the *Pub Peter Polo* on the corner of place A-Briand attracts a trendy crowd. There are several more *café-brasseries* on the *place* and during the truffle season, the buyers, middlemen and *truffiers* do great business in the bar of the *Univers* hotel (over the last few years truffles have become harder to find and prices have quadrupled). The cafés on place Charles-de-Gaulle, including *Le Siècle*, all close by 7.30pm, but you can stay up late listening to good British rock, playing dice and chatting with non-trendy types at *Le Petit Montmartre*, 40 rue David-Guillabert. Alternatively there's a piano bar, *Pub St-Croc* (closed last week in June) on the corner of rue Juiverie and place Maurice-Charretier.

Pernes-Les-Fontaines, Venasque and southwards

Halfway between Carpentras and **L'Isle-sur-la-Sorgue** is the exquisite small town of **PERNES-LES-FONTAINES**, while 9km to its east, just before the roads start to wind over the Plateau de Vaucluse towards APT, is the equally pretty village of **VENASQUE**, with some worthwhile gastonomic stops. Between Pernes and Venasque the **D57** heads south, giving immense views westwards over the Rhône valley. After passing the **Château de Saumane** where the Marquis de Sade spent some of his childhood, it meets the aqueduct carrying the canal de Carpentras, just west of **Fontaine-de-Vaucluse**.

Venasque

VENASQUE is perfectly contained on a spur of rock, with three round towers and a curtain wall at its highest end, and, at the lowest point, a church with a sixth-century baptistry, built on the site of a Roman temple which may have been dedicated to Venus. Like most model Provençal villages it swings between a sleepy winter state and a tourist honey pot role in summer, with just a brief intermediate interlude in May and June when a daily market concentrates exclusively on cherries.

Beyond its situation, Venasque's attractions are **gastronomic**. *Haute cuisine*, with all the ingredients fresh from the market, is to be had at the *Auberge de la Fontaine* on place de la Fontaine (closed Wed; ☎90.66.02.96; 200F upwards). You'll need to book for the main restaurant but on the ground floor *Le Bistro* serves much cheaper and less sophisticated dishes but of the same high quality. The *auberge* also has five very expensive suites (⑧). The hotel-restaurant, *Les Ramparts* (closed Wed & Jan–March; ☎90.66.02.79; ③–④), at the top of the main street, rue Haute, also has a good restaurant, with an excellent fish dish with citrus fruits, *dorade des agrumes*, usually on the menu; around 120F. The only other **hotel** is *La Garrigue*, rte de L'Appiè (closed mid-Oct to Easter; ☎90.66.03.40; ④–⑤). For details of other **accommodation** possibilities such as **chambres d'hôtes**, ask at the **tourist office** on Grande Rue (mid-March to Oct Mon–Thurs 10am–12.30pm & 2–6pm, Fri 2–6pm; July to Aug 7 10am–12.30pm & 3–7pm; ☎90.66.11.66).

Pernes-les-Fontaines

PERNES has a similar atmosphere to Venasque. Though a proper town, not a single building puts a foot wrong in the display of the picturesque. The fountains of its name (36 in all), the ramparts, gateways, castle, towers, covered market hall, Renaissance streets and half a dozen chapels all blend into a single complex structure. The passages between its squares feel more like corridors between rooms.

Approaching from La Roques or Venasque you pass the **fontaine de la Lune** on your left. From such moony waters explanations were contrived of the debauchery that went on around **Porte St-Gilles** opposite, in terms, inevitably, of women's sexual folly. Through this gateway rue Raspail crosses to Porte Notre-Dame with the **cormorant fountain** and seventeenth-century **market hall** in front. The Nesque flows under the *Porte* and alongside the quai de Verdon, where the Saturday **market** is held, to the place du Comtat Venaisson, home to the **tourist office** (Mon–Sat 9am–noon & 1–6.30pm; ☎90.61.31.04).

The town's great medieval artwork is the **frescoes** in the **Tour Ferrande**. The frescoes are from the same era as the Bayeux tapestry and share its style, though not the consequence of the historical tale they tell. The colours and the detail are impressive, but the problem is access to them: you need to phone the tourist office to get a guided tour.

Practicalities

An afternoon's wander may well be enough to sample Pernes-les-Fontaines' charms but, if you find yourself seduced, some **hotel** possibilities include *La Margelle*, place Aristide-Briand on the boulevard ring to the south of the village (☎90.61.30.36; ②), with a rambling back garden and cheap menus; or, just outside the town on the Carpentras road, *Prato-Plage* (☎90.61.31.72; ②–③) with a restaurant on the edge of an artificial lake. The municipal **campsite** is in the quartier Coucourelles (open April–Sept; ☎90.61.31.67) and campervans can park overnight (except on Fri) on quai de Verdon.

On place L-Giraud *La Fontaine aux Saveurs* (☎90.61.68.73) sells local products, including wine and truffles, and serves, at all hours, a truffle salad for around 50F and a truffle menu for under 180F. *Le Sourire*, on place Aristide-Briand, does excellent woodfire **pizzas** at a very reasonable price.

L'Isle-sur-la-Sorgue

L'ISLE-SUR-LA-SORGUE, not to be confused with **Sorgues** on the Rhône, lies 23km east of Avignon, halfway between Carpentras and **Cavaillon**. The town is embraced and permeated by a stretched-out hand of water, the five branches of the River Sorgue, which were once full of otters and beavers, eels, trout and crayfish, and their currents turned the power wheels of a medieval cloth industry. Tanneries, dyeing works, and, in the eighteenth century, silk production, all water-run, ensured, along with the river's living riches, considerable prosperity for "the Island".

Those times are largely past. An epidemic killed off all the crayfish a hundred years ago and the eels and aquatic animals have long since gone, while the huge blackened wheels turn now only as mementoes, the buildings where their energy was once harnessed standing empty, plants growing from the crumbling brick-work. But in summer fishing punts continue to crowd the streams and L'Isle is a cheerful place, particularly for its well-known Sunday **antiques market**. L'Isle is also a useful base when the much more touristy **Fontaine-de-Vaucluse** is full up.

Arrival, information and accommodation

Trains from Avignon and Cavaillon arrive at the **gare SNCF**, southwest of the town centre, and **buses** arrive by place Gambetta. The **tourist office** is in the former granary on place de l'Eglise (Sun & Mon 9.30am–1pm & 3–7pm, Tues–Sat 9am–7pm; ☎90.38.04.78). **Bikes** can be rented from *MBK Comtat* on place Gambetta (☎90.38.07.54).

L'Isle-sur-la-Sorgue is not a great tourist destination, so **rooms** tend to be fairly cheap – but watch out for water-loving midges. *Au Vieux Isle*, 15 rue Danton (☎90.38.00.46; ①), in one of the narrow alleyways of the old town, is pretty basic but with a pool table, bar football and occasional concerts. More cheap rooms, over-looking the widest branch of the river, can be found at *Le Bassin*, av Charles-de-Gaulle (☎90.38.00.46; ②). Moving a bit more upmarket, *Le Pescador* in Partages-des-Eaux 1.5km upstream of the town (follow signs to Carpentras and turn right immediately after crossing the main branch of the river; closed Nov–March; ☎90.38.09.69; ③) is in an idyllic spot at the point where the waters divide. Or you can stay in an eighteenth-century coach house out in the countryside, the *Mas de Cure Bourse*, chemin de la Serre (☎90.38.16.58; ④–⑤), a few kilometres southwest of town signed left off the D25 to Caumont, the continuation of av de l'Egalité. The rooms are decorated in Provençal style and the restaurant is very good.

The municipal three-star **campsite**, *La Sorguette*, 41 Les Grandes Sorgues (open mid-March to Oct; ☎90.38.05.71), is by the river on the Apt road.

The Town

L'Isle-sur-la-Sorgue's claim to be the Venice of Provence is somewhat over the top. An afternoon's wander around the town will probably suffice, but you can head upstream for a pleasant waterside drink or dance at Partage-des-Eaux and go canoe-ing on the river.

The central **place de l'Eglise** and **place de la Liberté** have the greatest evidence of past prosperity, most glaringly in the Baroque seventeenth-century **church** (Tues–Sat 10am–noon & 3–6pm), glutted with paintings and frescoes in the erotic drapery style and by far the richest religious edifice for miles around. Each column in the nave supports a sculpted Virtue: whips and turtle-doves are Chastity's props, a unicorn accompanies Virginity, and medallions and inscriptions carry the adornment down to the floor. Above the west door, angels, Christ, the Supreme Being and Mary veer heavenwards in gilded relief like flying ducks. Only the ceiling is bare. Heading north of the place de l'Eglise, you'll come to the eighteenth-century **Hôtel Donadeï de Campredon** at 20 rue du Docteur-Tallet (Tues–Sun 9.30am–12.30pm & 2–6pm; 25F), which hosts temporary exhibitions of modern sculpture.

The **Hôpital** on quai des Lices at the western edge of the old town is in the much more restrained style of the eighteenth century. Its monumental staircase carries de Sade's arms, and its chapel, fountained garden and pharmacy can all be visited (apply to the *gardien* at the main gate; daily 10.30–11.30am & 2.30–4/5pm; free). The pharmacy, though not as impressive as the one at Carpentras, has beautiful Moustiers porcelain vases and painted boxes containing such things as calcium extracted from crayfish eyes (a remedy for syphilis) and an epileptic cure that killed with an overdose of a single drop.

Every year the Isle fishermen retain their medieval guild tradition of crowning a kng of the Sorgue, whose job is to oversee the rights of catch and sale. The **Festival de la Sorgue** at the end of July sees all of them out in traditional gear and two teams battling from boats in an ancient jousting tournament. On the **spring equinox** the people of **VELLERON**, 5km downstream, process down to the river and launch a fleet of tiny luminous rafts to celebrate the start of spring. If you want to get on the river yourself *Canoë Evasion* signed right off the D25 towards Fontaine-de-Vaucluse organizes **canoe trips** and has **bikes** for rental.

The Sunday market of **antiques** and secondhand stuff centres on the Village des Antiquaires on av de l'Egalité spilling out onto the boulevards. Interesting bric-à-brac is also for sale at *La Petite Curieuse*, 23 impasse de la République, off the main shopping street of rue de la République.

Eating and drinking

In the old days the **local specialities** were *écrevisse* (crayfish) *en coquille* and an omelette flavoured with a certain Sorgue weed. Nowadays grilled trout is the standard meal, to be had at *Le Bassin* hotel (see p.143 under "Arrival, information and accommodation"; reasonable four-course menu around 130F). For something more special, try *La Prévoté*, 4 rue JJ-Rousseau (Tues–Sun; ☎90.38.57.29; weekday lunchtime menu around 130F, otherwise 200F upwards) behind the church. In Partage-des-Eaux the *Pescador* hotel (see p.143; closed Mon except in July & Aug; menu from 100F) has good fish dishes, or you can eat and dance at *La Guinguette* next door (☎90.38.10.61; menu around 100F). The *Mas de Cure Bourse* (see p.143 under "Arrival, information and accommodation") is also reputed for its food, with dependably fresh ingredients.

Café de l'Industrie on quai de la Charité by place E Char has excellent coffee and plats du jour for 60F, and there's the busy brasserie, *Café de la Sorgue*, on quai Jean-Jaurès. Good cakes and ice creams can be had at the *salon de thé La Petite Théière* at 30 av de la République.

Thursday is **market** day but the best place to buy food is at Velleron where producers sell their goods direct at a busy *marché paysan* (summer Mon–Sat 6–8pm; winter Tues, Fri & Sat only 4.30–6pm). For inexpensive wine, *Le Caveau de la Tour de l'Isle* at 12 rue de la République is the place to go (closed Sun pm & Mon).

On place de l'Eglise you can **drink** at the downmarket *Bar Le César* with its faded mirrors or at the swish fin-de-siècle *Café de France.*

Fontaine-de-Vaucluse

The splitting streams of L'Isle-sur-la-Sorgue have their source only 6km to the east in a mysterious tapering fissure deeper than the sheer 230-metre cliffs that barricade its opening at the top of a gorge above **FONTAINE-DE-VAUCLUSE**. Fascination with the **source**, one of the most powerful natural springs in the world, coupled with the beauty of the ancient riverside village where the fourteenth-century poet Petrarch pined for his Laura, has lead to an excess of visitors – well over a million a year – and museums for them to visit. But despite the crowds, Fontaine is still a supremely romantic place.

The source and the village

The waters of the Sorgue sometimes appear in spectacular fashion, bursting down the gorge (in March and April normally), at other times seeping stealthily through subterranean channels to meet the riverbed further down. The best time to admire them is in the early morning before the crowds arrive.

If you're intrigued by the source, and understand French, visit the **Norbert-Casteret Musée de Spéléologie** (June–Aug daily 10am–noon & 2–6.30pm; Feb–May & Sept–Oct closed Mon & Tues; closed Nov–Jan; 28F) in the underground commercial centre alongside chemin de la Fontaine. It's run by volunteers eager to communicate their passion for crawling about in the bowels of the earth. If such activity is on a par for you with spider or rat fraternizing, all the more reason to follow this tour through mock-up caves and passages. The museum winds up with a collection of underworld concretions gathered by Casteret, one of France's most renowned cavers, ranging from huge jewellery-like crystals to pieces resembling fibre optics. Displays also document the intriguing history of the exploration of the spring, from the first 23-metre descent in 1878 to the robotic camera that reached the bottom a few years ago, its blurry pictures apparently showing a horizontal passage disappearing into the rock. It's thought that water seeping through a vast plateau of chalk (stretching as far north as Banon) hits an impermeable base that slopes down to Fontaine.

However the water arrives, it has long been put to use to turn the wheels of manufacturing. The first paper mill was built at Fontaine in 1522, and the last, of 1862 vintage, ceased operations in 1968. The medieval method of pulping rags to paper has been re-created at the far end of the complex, the **Moulin à papier Vallis Clausa** (daily 9am–12.30pm & 2–6/8pm; Sun opens 10.30am; free). Flowers are added to the pulp and the resulting paper is printed with all manner of drawings, poems and prose from Churchill's "Blood, Sweat and Tears" speech to the legend of how God created Provence, on sale in the vast Vallis Clausa shop. There are other quality craft shops in the complex, including one selling household objects carved in olive wood, and an exhibition of *santons*.

Up above on chemin de la Fontaine is the impressive and intense **Musée de la Résistance** (July & Aug Mon & Wed–Sun 10am–7pm; Sept to mid-Oct & mid-April to June 10am–noon & 2–6pm; Whitsun 10am–noon & 1–5pm; Easter 10am–noon & 2–6pm; mid-Oct to Dec Sat & Sun only 10am–noon & 1–5pm; March to mid-April Sat & Sun only 10am–noon & 2–6pm; 10F). The museum acknowledges the extent to which the war period still perturbs the collective memory of the French. It makes it very clear that Marshall Pétain's anti-semitic laws were not instructions from Berlin but argues that a great many French people must have opposed them since three-quarters of the French Jewish population escaped deportation. The re-created classroom and other displays of daily life bring home the authoritarian, anti-intellectual and patriarchal nature of France's fascist regime, its insistence on work, family and *patrie*, and the military cult of Pétain. A section is dedicated to the artists who refused to collaborate, another to the German Resistance. The overriding purpose of the museum is not to judge or apologize, but to remind people of the humanity of resistance.

In total, and grotesque, contrast, the **Musée de la Justice et l'Injustice** a few doors down displays torture equipment and the methods of carrying out the death penalty based around the collection of the official French executioner in occupied Algeria from 1949 to 1953. There are appropriate statements by sociologists, but nothing to suggest that the horrors it evokes did not stop in the 1950s (daily 1–7pm; 20F).

Across the river, through an alleyway just past the bridge, is the comforting **Musée de Pétrarque** (mid-April to mid-Oct Wed–Sun 9.30am–noon & 2–6.30pm; winter weekends only; 15F) with beautiful old books dating back to the fifteenth-century and pictures of Petrarch, his beloved Laura and of Fontaine where he passed sixteen years of his unrequited passion. The museum also hosts temporary art exhibitions.

Practicalities

Buses from L'Isle-sur-la-Sorgue drop you by the car park just before the church. The **tourist office** is on chemin de la Fontaine (summer Mon–Sat 9am–6/7.30pm; winter 10am–6pm; ☎90.20.32.22) which leads off to the left up to the source.

Rooms in Fontaine are likely to be fully booked in summer, so if you want to count on a bed, phone ahead, or try in L'Isle which should be more promising. Fontaine's **place de la Colonne** is particularly pleasant with hotel balconies, terraced restaurants and cafés overhanging the river. The cheapest and most beautifully situated **hotel** is the *Hostellerie Le-Château* (☎90.20.31.54; ④) with a restaurant (closed Tues evening & Wed) serving fresh trout on a menu for around 100F. On the road back to L'Isle, about 3km from Fontaine and on the right, are two hotels worth trying: the very good value *L'Ermitage Vallis Clausa* (☎90.20.32.20; ②–③) and the smaller, less attractive *Font de Lauro* (☎90.20.31.49; ②–③) down a track just past the other. The *HI* **youth hostel**, about 1km from the village on chemin de la Vignasse (closed Dec–Jan; reception 8–10am & 5–11pm; ☎90.20.31.65; ①), is very pleasant and rents out **bikes**. *Les Pres* **campsite** (open all year; ☎90.20.32.38) is 500m downstream from the village with tennis courts and swimming pool.

The **restaurant** of *L'Ermitage Vallis Clausa* (see above) has better food than anything you're likely to be served in Fontaine, though for scenic *terrasses, Pétrarque & Laure* (☎90.20.31.48) is hard to beat. If you arrive early, the *boulangerie Le Moulin de la Fontaine* near the church does breakfasts, and a few doors down there's a *crêperie*. There is a **market** on Tuesday.

On the north side of the river, above the aqueduct, is a little hut called *Pêche de la Truite* where you can rent rods and lines. Just upstream *Kayak Vert* (☎90.20.35.44) rents **canoes** for a half-hour or hour's paddling, or for a pretty effortless eight-kilometre ride down to L'Isle-sur-la-Sorgue (where the canoes can be handed over).

Cavaillon

Any approach to **CAVAILLON** will take you through fields of fruit and vegetables, watered by the Durance and Coulon rivers. Market gardening is the major business of the city and to the French, Cavaillon, its Roman origins notwithstanding, is known simply as a melon town. The **melon** in question is the *Charentais*, a small pale green ball with dark green stripes and brilliant orange flesh, in season from May to September. Together with asparagus and early spring vegetables, they are sold every weekday morning at one of the largest wholesale markets in Europe.

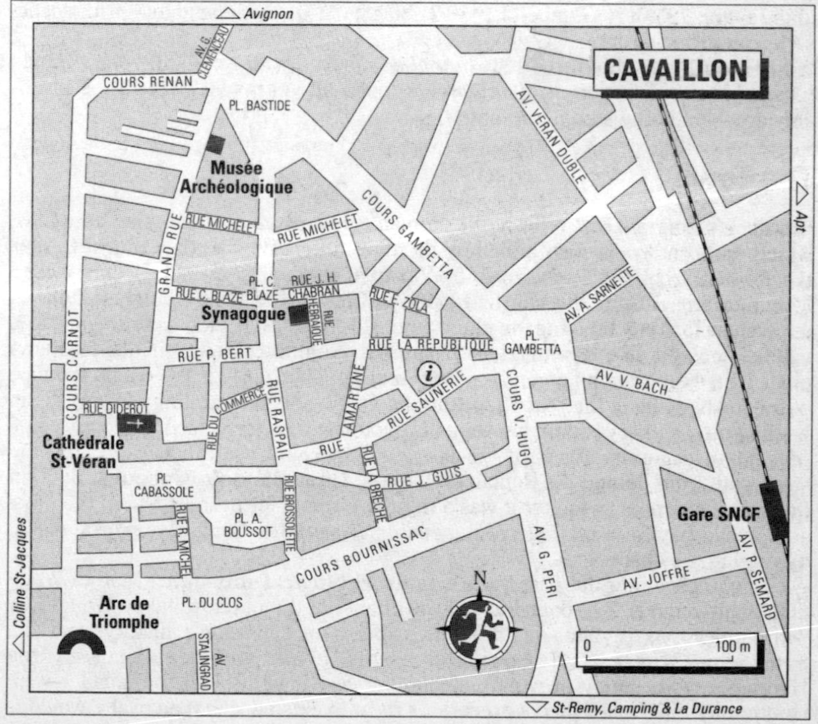

In the last week of January Cavaillon hosts a **science festival**, bringing together serious boffins, journalists, artists and celebrities with events free and open to all. Otherwise, there are a couple of events combining commercialism with festivities that could cheer up a visit: the *Foire St-Véran* in the second week in November and the *Fête de St-Gilles* in the first week of September. It must be said, however, that this doesn't make Cavaillon very interesting for much of the year, although it's certainly a useful stopover, with train and bus connections to Avignon, Salon, Aix and Carpentras, as well as to the Lubéron to the east.

Arrival, information and accommodation

The **gare SNCF** (☎90.71.04.40) and the **gare routière** (☎90.78.32.39) are on the east side of town, with bd Paul-Doumer, opposite the *gare routière*, leading to place Gambetta. From here, rue Saunerie, with the **tourist office** at no. 79 (daily 9am–12.30pm & 1.30–6.30pm, closed Sun in winter; ☎90.71.32.01), leads into the town centre, a series of curving, narrow shopping streets. **Bikes** can be rented from *Cycles Rieu*, 25 av Mal-Joffre (☎90.71.45.55).

In the centre of town, the most attractive budget **hotel** is *Le Parc*, 183 place F-Tourel (☎90.71.57.78; ①–③), followed by *Le Grenouillet*, 133 av Berthelot (closed Dec–March; ☎90.78.08.08; ①–②), which is very agreeable for the price. *Le Christel*, digue des Grands Jardins, quartier Boscodomini (☎90.71.07.79; ④–⑤), is a modern, luxurious hotel overlooking the Durance, with pool and tennis courts, and *Toppin*, 70 cours Gambetta (☎90.71.30.42; ③–④), is dependable, with rustic-style comfortable rooms.

For **camping**, the three-star *Camping de la Durance*, digue des Grands Jardins, in the direction of the *autoroute* (open all year; ☎90.71.11.78), is invariably crowded in the summer months.

The Town

Cavaillon's sole ancient relic is the Roman **triumphal arch** on place du Clos, which on Mondays is surrounded by the more interesting weekly **market**. After the Roman arch, the **Cathédrale St-Véran** (10am–noon & 2/3–4/6pm, closed Mon morning & Sun), due north of place du Clos, is Cavaillon's chief monument, an archaic-looking building on the south side of which God appears above a sundial looking like a winged and battered Neptune. Inside, in the St-Véran chapel, an exuberant nineteenth-century marble altar glorifies the edible produce of the town, while in the rear chapel on the north side is a painting of Saint Véran hauling off a slithery reptile known as Couloubre, who terrorized the locality in 6 AD. For a panoramic view of the surrounding countryside you can climb the steep path from behind the Roman arch to the **Chapelle Saint-Jacques**. Built on the site of a temple to Jupiter it was a regular outpost for hermits whom the peasants would pay to warn them of impending storms (or Couloubre appearances) by ringing the chapel bell.

For glimpses into the past there's an **archeological museum** (Mon & Wed–Sun 10am–noon & 2–5/6pm; 20F) in the chapel of the old hospital on Grand Rue with projections of films on different aspects of Cavaillon's history, and the **Synagogue/Musée Juif Comtadin** (same hours and admission) in rue Hebraïque with plenty of ritual objects, but few insights into the small Jewish community that established a precarious right to existence in medieval Cavaillon.

Eating and drinking

For a **melon feast**, *Prevot*, 353 av de Verdon (closed Mon & Sun afternoon; ☎90.71.32.43) on the outskirts of town heading for the *autoroute* and St-Rémy, does a "*menu melon*" from June to September: lobster with petals of melon, fillet of beef on dried melon and iced melon with nougat and Beaumes-de-Venise Muscat for 350F. Cavaillon's best **restaurant** is *Alain Nicolet*, 3km southeast of town on the road to Pertuis at **Cheval Blanc** (July & Aug daily; Sept–June Tues–Sun; last orders 9.30pm; ☎90.78.01.56), which has immaculate, traditional Provençal cooking and home-made sorbets; 250F upwards with a cheaper weekday lunchtime menu. For less of a blow-out, you could try *La Faim de Loup*, 129 av Mal-Joffre (☎90.78.31.68; around 110F), which does a great leek tart; *Le Grillon*, 50 cours Victor-Hugo (Mon & Wed–Sun; ☎90.71.33.87; from 80F), for tagines, coucous, pastillas plus Provençal specialities and excellent Algerian wines, or charcoal grills at *Le Pantagruel*, 5 place de Cabassole (☎90.76.11.30; menus from 75F).

For a stylish place to **drink** there's *Le Fin de Siècle*, 46 place du Clos (closed Aug–Sept, & Wed), with appropriate mirrors, heavy gold cornices and fantasy pictures, and upstairs an excellent-value restaurant (Mon & Wed–Sun; ☎90.71.12.27) with menus from 100F.

Gordes

GORDES, 6km north of the main Avignon–APT road, and the same distance east of Fontaine-de-Vaucluse (but only as the crow flies), seems to have a publicity machine working overtime to ensure its prominence in the picturesque Provençal hilltop village circuits. A one-show "festival", a local radio broadcast, a snail race or a gathering of bottle-top collectors will give rise to posters plastered over the entire region in which only the place name figures in oversize capitals. Numerous film directors, media personalities, musicians and painters have added a Gordes address to their main Paris residence, and the place is full of expensive restaurants, cafés and art and artisanal shops.

All of which suggests you should probably avoid it like the plague. But there are good reasons for its popularity with the rich and famous. Its picture postcard pose of ancient stone turning gold in the setting sun as you climb the winding roads towards it, is spectacular. In addition its castle holds a collection of works by former resident **Victor Vasarely**, and there's a superb array of ancient drystone architecture in the nearby **Village des Bories.** Gordes is also close to the **Abbaye de Sénanque** and to a couple of museums dedicated to glass and to olive oil. There's also a **festival** in the last two weeks of July when Gordes is awash with theatrical performances, jazz and classical music concerts.

The village

In the past, near-vertical staircases hewn into the rock gave the only access to the summit where the church and houses surround a twelfth- to sixteenth-century **castle**, with few aesthetic concessions to the business of fortification. At the turn of the century most of Gordes' villagers had abandoned the old defensive site and the place was in ruins. Redeemed by being a centre of resistance during World

War II, Gordes was discovered by various artists, including Chagall and the Hungarian scientist of art and design, **Victor Vasarely**.

Vasarely undertook the restoration of Gordes castle and in 1970 opened his **Didactic Museum** (Sept–June Mon & Wed–Sun 10am–noon & 2–6pm; July–Aug daily; 25F) within its Renaissance interior. The most immediately accessible works are the gorgeous tapestries of cubes turning into spheres, colours chasing their way through squares, circles and diamonds, and black and white creations such as the *Zebras* where their forms are created solely by their stripes. There is also an immense number of drawings, paintings and sketches, displayed in sliding showcases. A series entitled *Périod Fausses Routes* reveals Vasarely struggling towards abstract geometric forms, another the post-1948 beginnings of his *alphabet plastique*. His rigorous self-imposed training can be seen in the studies of movement, of colour, of space, texture, light and shadow, all involving real forms but in which only the chosen element is dominant. It's a huge collection (and currently being rearranged, possibly to include some of the works from the troubled Fondation Vasarely in Aix) and a great monument to a cultural vision that has become very unfashionable in recent years, in Vasarely's words: "Creation was, is and will be collective; without Leonardo da Vinci there would have been no Cézanne, without Cézanne there would have been no Mondrian and so forth. In short, the aim of any human work – whether its gestation be conscious or unconscious – cannot be other than social."

Practicalities

There are infrequent **buses** covering the 16km from Cavaillon to Gordes; they drop you at place du Château. **Bikes** can be rented at the Elf station at Les Imberts on the D2 halfway between Gordes and the Avignon–Apt road.

Gordes **tourist office** in the Salle des Gardes of the castle (daily 9am–noon & 2–6pm; ☎90.72.02.75) is helpful and has lists of *chambres d'hôtes* and details of whatever's on. It also displays an extraordinary model of the village made out of matchsticks. Finding **rooms** is particularly difficult during the summer **festival**. One very reasonably priced **hotel** is *Le Provençal* on place du Château in the village (☎90.72.10.01; ②–③) with just seven rooms. *Les Romarins*, overlooking the village on the rte de Sénanque (☎90.72.12.13; ⑤–⑦), and *La Gacholle*, rte des Murs (closed mid-Nov to mid-March; ☎90.72.01.36; ⑥–⑧), are both old country houses with traditionally styled comfortable rooms; *La Gacholle*'s views over the Lubéron are unbeatable. The most luxurious option is *Domaine de l'Enclos* (☎90.72.08.22; ⑤–⑧) set in a terraced garden with spacious rooms on the rte de Senanque. Halfway between Gordes and Murs on the D15 there's a very pleasant two-star **campsite**, *Camping des Sources* (closed Nov–March; ☎90.72.12.48; early booking advisable).

The obvious **eating** place is the *Comptoir du Victuailler*, place du Château (closed Tues evening and Wed out of season; ☎90.72.01.31), always full of Parisians in summer and with a 100F lunchtime menu in July and August, otherwise 150F upwards. The restaurant at *La Gacholle* hotel (see above) is pleasant but pricey (menus from 160F); *Tante Yvonne* (closed Sun evening & Wed out of season; ☎90.72.02.54) on place du Château is a bit less expensive (menus from 135F and 2 rooms; ③). **Market** day is Tuesday.

In the vicinity of Gordes are two excellent restaurants. *Le Bistrot à Michel* on Grande Rue in **Cabrières d'Avignon**, on the winding road to Fontaine (closed Tues, and Mon except in July & Aug; last orders 9.15pm; ☎90.76.82.08), is a favourite with the second-home-owning Parisians and serves up exquisitely simple food in a dining room decorated with Pagnol film posters or in the garden (Mon–Sat midday menu around 100F; à la carte 250F upwards). At *Le Mas Tourteron* in **Les Imberts**, chemin de St-Blaise (Tues–Sun; ☎90.72.00.16) you can eat gorgeous Provençal specialities in a shaded garden (Mon–Sat midday menu 130F, otherwise from 280F) or much cheaper quick lunches in *Le Petit Comptoir* bistro in the same establishment.

Around Gordes

To the east of Gordes, 3.5km signed off the D2 to Cavaillon, is a rural agglomeration that is worlds away from Vasarely's "architectural integrations". Yet some of what he calls "constants of human genius", the basic units of geometry and structure, are without doubt incorporated in the **Village des Bories** (daily 9am–sunset; 25F). In this walled enclosure, houses, barns, bread ovens, wine stores and workshops all have the monotone surface of dry-stone walls with almost identically sized slabs. The shapes of the buildings, however, are a different matter: curving pyramids and cones, some rounded at the top, some truncated and the base almost rectangular or square. Cleverly designed, rain runs off their exteriors and the temperature inside remains constant whatever the season. It is their outlines that make you think they must be prehistoric, and neolithic rings and a hatchet have been found on the site, but most of these buildings in fact date from the eighteenth century and were lived in until about one-hundred years ago. Some may well have been adapted from or rebuilt over earlier constructions, and there are extraordinary likenesses with a seventh- or eighth-century oratory in Ireland, and with huts and dwellings as far apart as the Orkneys and South Africa.

Abbaye de Sénanque

The **Abbaye de Sénanque** (March–Oct Mon–Sat 10am–noon & 2–6pm; Nov–Feb 2–5/6pm; 18F), predating both the *bories* and the castle, has been reinhabited and returned to its former use. It is one of a trio of twelfth-century monasteries established by the Cistercian order in Provence and stands alone, 4km north of Gordes, amid fields of lavender in a hollow of the hills, its weathered stone sighing with age and immutability.

The interior is huge, silent and cold. In 1969 the monks departed, retaining the title deeds, and Sénanque became a "Cultural Encounter Centre", favouring all the world's major religions. A hundred years earlier the Sénanque monks had resuscitated the old Benedictine monastery on St-Honorat (see p.323) and it is from there that they recently returned to follow the austere regime of work and prayer at Sénanque again.

From the *Abbaye* the loop back to Gordes from Sénanque via the D177 and D15 reveals the northern Lubéron in all its glory.

Les Bouilladoires

The area around Gordes was famous for its olive oil before severe frosts killed off many of the trees. A still-functioning Gallo-Roman press made from a single slice of oak 2m in diameter, as well as ancient oil lamps, jars and soap-making equipment, can be seen at the **Moulin des Bouillons** (Mon & Wed–Sun Feb–Nov 10am–noon & 2–5/7 pm; 30F) in **LES BOUILLADOIRES**, on the D148 just west of St-Pantaléon, 3.5km south of Gordes, and well signed from every junction. The Gordes bus from Coustellet, on the main Avignon–Apt road, stops just outside.

The ticket for the Moulin also gives you access to the **Musée du Vitrail Frédérique Duran** (same hours) signalled by a huge and rather gross sculpture by Duran and housed in a semi-submerged bunker next door to the Moulin. Duran's contemporary stained-glass creations are extremely garish but if you want to learn about the long history of stained glass, you can, though perhaps the most attractive items are the gorgeous, strutting fowl and hedges of rosemary in the gardens around the two museums.

The Petit Lubéron

The great fold of rock of the **LUBERON** runs for fifty-odd kilometres between the Coulon and the Durance valleys from **Manosque** to Cavaillon. It is divided by the **Combe de Loumarin**, the only way to cross the mountain for 20km on either side, into the **Grand Lubéron** to the east and the **PETIT LUBERON** to the west. Though many forestry tracks cross the ridge, they are barred to cars (and too rough for bikes), and where the ridge isn't forested it opens into table-top pastures where sheep graze in summer. The northern slopes have Alpine rather than Mediterranean leanings: the trees are oak, beech and maple; cowslips and buttercups announce the summer. But it is still very hot and there are plenty of **vines** on the lower slopes.

The Lubéron has long been popular as rich escape country for Parisians, Germans, the Dutch and the British, well before the unbelievable success of the arch evocation of yuppiedom, *A Year in Provence*, made the media dub this "Peter Mayle country". *Résidences secondaires* are everywhere and ruins, like **de Sade**'s **château** in Lacoste and the **Abbaye de St-Hilaire** near Bonnieux, are being restored by their private owners. The villages, especially **Lacoste**, are almost too immaculate but the appeal of the countryside is undeniable.

WALKING AND CYCLING IN THE LUBERON

There are **footpaths** up to the Petit Lubéron ridge from the string of little *villages perchés* along the northern foothills; one of the loveliest areas for walking is the Massif des Cèdres above the D3 between **Ménerbes** and **Lacoste**. The main GR6 leaves the D2 between Cavaillon and Gordes at **Robion**, passes through the atmospheric ruined village of **Oppède-le-Vieux** and crosses over the top to follow the southern slopes eastwards. Where it turns south the GR97 climbs back up to the ridge and down again at **Lourmarin**. There are any number of walking guides available: local tourist offices, bookshops and the *Maison du Parc* in Apt (see p.157) will have good selections.

The Coulon Valley is good cycling country, with a cycle track following the small roads between Cavaillon and Apt. These two towns are the best places to rent bikes though *Les Roues du Lubéron,* rte de Lacoste, Mernerbes (☎90.72.37.45), which organizes cycle trips, also rents them out. Public transport is not dependable at all, in this land of Merc convertibles.

The villages

OPPEDE-LE-VIEUX, above the vines on the steeper slopes of the Petit Lubéron, is relatively free as yet of Parisian film actors, designers and the like.

There's only one café, the *Bar des Poulinets*, and a quirky shop on the road alongside with stones and fossils, oddments made from lavender, *santons*, postcards and good books on the locality. The square in front of the ramparts suggests, with its Renaissance gateway, a monumental town within. But behind the line of restored sixteenth-century houses there are only ruins which go up and up until you reach the remains of the medieval **castle**.

The *Oppèdois* used to have the reputation of being a bunch of crazies living among these ruins. There is certainly a madness to the place but the lunacy is the ease with which you can break your neck: there are no fences or warning signs, steps break off above gaping holes, paths lead straight to precipitous edges and at the highest point of the castle you can sit on a foot-wide ledge with a drop of ten or more metres below you. Be warned for yourself but particularly if you have children of clambering age.

Moving eastwards from Oppède-le-Vieux, **MENERBES** is the next hilltop village. Shaped like a ship, its best site, on the prow as it were, is given over to the dead. From this cemetery you look down onto an odd jigsaw of fortified buildings and mansions, old and new. In the other direction houses with exquisitely tended terraces and gardens, and shuttered up outside holiday time, ascend to a mammoth wall that completely bars the way. It's the citadel and now another *résidence secondaire*. Ménerbes has suffered from its association with Peter Mayle, though as his books have been translated into more and more languages, the hordes of British Mayle followers have been followed by other nationalities, currently the Japanese. The author himself has long since left Provence.

Outside Ménerbes, left off the D103 towards **BEAUMETTES**, the wine producing *Domaine de la Citadelle* has a **museum of corkscrews** (Mon–Sat 10am–noon & 2–6.30pm, Sun 10am–noon & 3–6pm; 20F), dating back to the seventeenth century. The fascinating collection includes a Cézar compression, a corkscrew combined with pistol and dagger, others with erotic themes and many with beautifully sculpted and engraved handles. You can also visit the wine cellars where you'll be offered a complimentary tasting. Between Ménerbes and Lacoste, on the D109, you can admire the seventeeth-century cloisters, exquisite Renaissance stairway and ancient dovecots of the **Abbaye de St-Hilaire** (daily 10am–noon & 2–5pm; 18F).

LACOSTE and its **château** are visible from all the neighbouring villages. If daylight views have enticed you, you should see it at moonlight while a wind rocks the hanging lanterns on the narrow cobbled approaches to the château whose most famous owner was the Marquis de Sade. This was his retreat when the reaction to his writings got too hot, but in 1778, after seven years here, he was locked up in the Bastille and the castle destroyed soon after. Some people say the current owner, who has been repairing the building for over three decades, is looking for hidden treasure. It's not open for visits except in groups by appointment (☎90.75.80.39).

From the *terrasse* by the old church on the heights of the steep village of **BONNIEUX** you can see Gordes, Roussillon and neighbouring Lacoste, 5km away. Halfway down the village, on rue de la République, there's the **Musée de la Boulangerie** (June–Sept Mon & Wed–Sun 10am–noon & 3–6.30pm; April–May & Oct–Dec Sat, Sun & hols only, same hours; closed Jan & Feb; 10F) of traditional bread-making and on av des Tilleuls the **Eglise Neuve** exhibiting four fifteenth-century wood paintings (summer only 3–6.30pm; free).

From Bonnieux the D149 joins the Apt–Avignon road just after the triple-arched **Pont Julien** over the Coulon which dates back to the time when Apt was

THE WARS OF RELIGION IN THE LUBERON

During five days in April 1545 a great swathe of the Petit Lubéron between Lourmarin and Mérindol was burnt and put to the sword. Three thousand people were massacred and six hundred sent to the galleys. Their crime was having Protestant tendencies in the years leading up to the devastating Wars of Religion. Despite the complicity of King Henri II, the ensuing scandal forced him to order an enquiry which then absolved all those responsible: the Catholic aristocrats from Aix.

Lourmarin (see p.160) itself suffered minor damage but the castle in **MERINDOL** was violently dismantled, together with every house. Mérindol's remains, on the hill above the subsequent village on the south side of the Petit Lubéron, are a visible monument to those events. The south face of the Petit Lubéron is to this day sparsely populated.

the Roman base of Apta Julia. Before you reach the bridge you'll see signs for the **Château La Canorgue**, a good place to try the light and very palatable *Côtes de Lubéron* wines (Mon–Sat 9am–noon & 3–7pm).

Practicalities

There are not many **hotels** in these parts, nor are they cheap. Basing yourself at Cavaillon or Apt may be the most sensible option. One exception is the very pleasant *Café de France* in **Lacoste** (☎90.75.82.25; ③), with eight rooms. Just outside Ménerbes, on rte des Baumettes, the *Hostellerie Le Roy Soleil* (☎90.72.25.61; ⑥–⑧) is quiet and very agreeable while at **Bonnieux** there's the *César* (☎90.75.80.18; ④) on place de la Liberté at the top of the village and the *Hostellerie du Prieuré* (☎90.75.80.78; ④–⑦) in the centre of the village, but neither is very exceptional. **Chambres d'hôtes** include *M et Mme Bal* in Oppède-le-Vieux (☎90.76.93.52; ③) and *La Bouquière* in Bonnieux, quartier St-Pierre (☎90.75.87.17; ④), both of which need to be booked months in advance.

The top **restaurant** is *Le Simiane* on rue Sous-barri in Lacoste which changes its menu daily to offer all the regional specialities (closed Wed & Thurs lunchtime; ☎90.75.83.31; menu 150F, à la carte 250F). The *Café de France* (see above) in the same village provides copious helpings at midday of omelettes and fries, lamb and fries, and *salade niçoise*, for under 80F. In Bonnieux *Le Fournil*, overlooking the fountain of place Carnot (winter closed Mon & Tues midday; ☎90.75.83.62; menus from 120F), serves lovely Provençal dishes laced with olive oil and garlic. There's a Friday **market** in Bonnieux and one on Tuesday in Lacoste.

Apt and neighbouring villages

The sole town in the Lubéron is **APT**, not much of a place for sightseeing, nor greatly renowned for the charm and friendliness of its people. Its large confectionary factory spews mucky froth into a concrete-channelled River Coulon and in early spring, when mimosa is blossoming down on the coast, the temperature around Apt can drop to well below freezing. It's nevertheless a useful base with excellent shops and a very lively Saturday **market**. From mid-July through August a **festival**, *Les Tréteaux de Nuit*, provides a choice of shows with concerts, plays, *café-théâtre* and exhibitions.

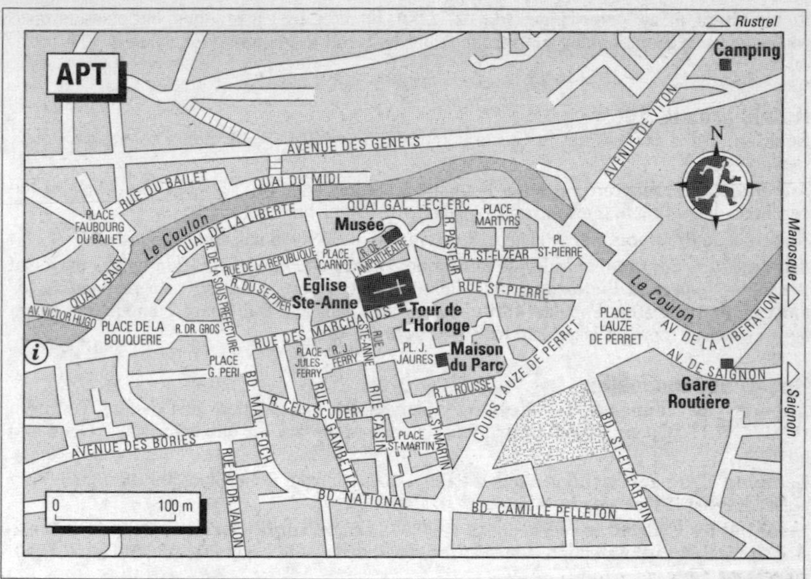

Apt is a good central point for touring the area: the villages of **Rustrel** and **Roussillon** to the north, with their **ochre mines**, and to the south, the hilltop villages of **Saignon** and **Buoux** with its fascinating **abandoned village**, are all within a ten-kilometre radius of Apt.

Arrival, information and accommodation

Arriving by **bus** (Apt's gare SNCF is freight only) you'll be dropped either at the main **place de la Bouquerie** or at the **gare routière** on av de la Libération at the eastern end of the town (☎90.74.20.21). The **tourist office** is at 2 av Philippe-de-Girard (Mon–Sat 8.30am–noon & 2–6/7pm; ☎90.74.03.18), just up to your left as you face the river from place de la Bouquerie. Arriving by **car**, you may have to try the quays for parking space but place de la Bouquerie is still the focal point to head for. You can **rent bikes** from *Guy Agnel,* 27 quai Général-Leclerc (☎90.7417.16), or *Garage Maretto* a few doors down.

There's a reasonable choice of **accommodation** in and around Apt; hotels in the town are less likely to be booked up than in the more scenic hilltop villages.

Hotels in Apt

L'Aptois, 6–8 cours Lauze-de-Perret (☎90.74.02.02). In the old town, at the end of place de la Bouquerie, this has some cheap rooms and a streamlined modern exterior belying the dog-sick decor within. ②–④

Auberge du Lubéron, 17 quai Léon-Sagy (☎90.74.12.50). Directly across the river, this is probably the most desirable, though not the most expensive, hotel in town. ③–⑤

Le Palais, 12 pl Gabriel-Péri (☎90.04.89.32). The lowest-priced rooms to be had, bang in the centre above a rather uninspired pizzeria. Closed Mon. ①–②

Relais de Roquefure, Le Chêne, 6km from Apt on the N100 towards Avignon (☎90.04.88.88). Good value with horse and cycle outings organized. ③–④

Victor-Hugo, 67 av Victor-Hugo (☎90.04.74.60). Flanked by gas stations, but pleasant once you're inside a room looking out on the courtyard, and extremely good value for the price. ②–③

Hotels around Apt

Résidence des Ocres, rte de Gordes, Roussillon (☎90.05.60.50). Some rooms with good views. ③–④

Auberge du Presbytère, pl de la Fontaine, Saignon (☎90.74.11.50). In the centre of the perched village 4km to the southeast of Apt; some rooms have ace views. ③–④

Auberge de Rustreou, 3 pl de la Fête, Rustrel (☎90.04.90.90). Small and welcoming. ③–④

Auberge des Seguins, quartier de la Combe, Buoux (☎90.74.16.37). Run by the mayor of Buoux, an expert on the history and wildlife of the Lubéron and the man responsible for most of the footpaths. Popular with climbers and walkers. Half-board compulsory. Dorm beds as well as rooms. Closed mid-Nov to March. ①–③

Hostel and campsites

Auberge de Jeunesse Le Regain, 2.5km north of Saignon just before Auribeau (☎90.74.39.34). Open mid-Feb to mid-Jan; no card necessary for one-night stays. Good info on walks. ①

Camping L'Arc en Ciel, 2km along the D104 to Goult from Roussillon (☎90.05.73.96). Very pleasant 2-star in pine woods. Mid-March to Oct.

Camping les Cèdres, av de Viton, Apt (☎90.74.14.61). Campers for once are treated to a 2-star site within easy walking distance of the town, across the bridge from pl St-Pierre. Open all year round.

Camping le Lubéron, rte de Saignon, Apt (☎90.04.85.40). Two-star with swimming pool, restaurant and disabled facilities. Easter–Oct.

The Town

Saturday is the day to come to Apt when cars are barred from the town centre to allow artisans and cultivators from the surrounding countryside to set up stalls. As well as featuring every imaginable Provençal edible, including 200-year-old species of vegetables grown by one trader (see under "Saignon" p.159), the **market** is accompanied by barrel organ, jazz musicians, stand-up comics, aged hippies and notorious local "characters". Everyone from successful Parisian artists with summer studios here, military types from the St-Christol base, serious ecologists, rich foreigners and local Aptois will be found milling around the central **rue des Marchands** for this weekly social commerce.

The great local speciality of fruits – crystallized, pickled, preserved in alcohol or turned into jam – features at the market but during the rest of the week you can go to *La Bonbonnière* on the corner of rue de la Sous-Préfecture and rue de la République for every sort of sweet and chocolate and the Provençal speciality *tourron*, an almond paste flavoured with coffee, pistachio, pine kernels or cherries. If you're really keen on sticky sweets you can ring *Apt Union*, the confectionary factory in quartier Salignan, 2km from Apt on the Avignon road (☎90.74.65.64) for a tour or just visit the shop which sells all the possible fruit concoctions (Mon–Sat 9am–noon & 2–6pm).

Other **shops** worth looking at are *Tamisier* on rue du Docteur-Gros selling kitchenware and the traditional fly-proof open boxes for storing cheese and sausage; *Station Peintre* on place de la Bouquerie with artists' materials at very good prices; *Jean Faucon*'s ceramics at 12 av de la Libération; and the *Librarie de l'Ouvert* , 88 rue des Marchands, with some English books for sale.

While window-shopping along rue des Marchands you can admire the **bell tower** spanning the street and may want to take a quick look around the town's few sites. The former **Cathedralé de Ste Anne** has several relics and ancient objects (Mon–Sat 10am–noon & 4.30–6pm, Sun 11am–noon; guided tour of the treasures July to mid-Sept 11am & 5pm); while the **musée archéologique** at 4 rue de l'Amphithéâtre (June–Sept Mon & Wed–Sat 10am–noon & 2–5pm, Sun 2–5pm; Oct–May Mon & Wed–Sun 2–5pm; 10F) is not wildly exciting either, with the minimal remains of a Roman theatre in the basement. Temporary exhibitions of contemporary art are sometimes held in the **Chapelle de Recollets** at 17 rue Louis-Rousset, organized by *Artifices*, 47 rue de la République (☎90.04.62.29), which groups together some of the best artists based in the Lubéron and arranges visits to studios.

Eating and drinking

If you haven't stuffed yourself with chocolates and candied fruit, you can **eat** a cheap and extremely palatable four-course meal at *Le Brémondy* on place St-Pierre (Mon–Sat; ☎90.04.70.39), or there's *La Calèche*, 4 rue Cély, similarly priced but not quite as friendly. Of the hotels (see p.156 above) the *Victor-Hugo* does plats du jour for under 50F and at the *Auberge du Lubéron* you can eat very well with a superb choice of desserts (closed Mon & Sun evening; menus from 130F). Pricey Argentinian specialities and much cheaper pizzas are available at *Argentin*, 12 quai Général-Leclerc (☎90.74.53.09), with live music weekend nights. In the industrial zone on the Avignon road opposite the turning to Gargas, the tropically decorated restaurant, *Le Père OK* has jazz, blues or theatre on Saturday nights (☎90.04.63.58; from 100F). Further out on the Avignon road, at Le Chêne, there's extremely good food and a chance to try all the local goats'

PARC NATUREL REGIONAL DU LUBERON

The **Parc Naturel Régional du Lubéron** is administered by the *Maison du Parc* in Apt at 1 place Jean-Jaurès. It's a centre of activity with laudable aims – nature conservation and the provision of environmentally friendly tourist facilities – though many people have misgivings about the practicalities of the project.

Any glance at a map will show the area covered by the park to be shot through with holes, *communes* where the local mayor has chosen to opt out. This makes a bit of a mockery of the park's key purpose of protecting the environment. Cynics, probably rightly, say that these mayors own large tracts of land which they do not want the park to interfere with.

The park has in fact very few powers and even less money and mostly has to be content with giving technical and architectural advice that doesn't have to be followed. Certain attempts to assist small local producers have, according to the park's critics, back-fired badly.

Be that as it may, the **Maison du Parc** (Mon–Sat 8.30am–noon & 1.30–6/7pm) is the place to go for anyone wanting information about the fauna and flora of the Lubéron, footpaths, cycle routes, pony-trekking, *gîtes* and campsites. You can watch a video about plant and animal life and buy recordings of Lubéron birdsongs.

The centre also houses a small **Musée de la Paléontologie** (10F) which is specifically designed to amuse children and is fun. A submarine-type "time capsule" door leads down to push-button displays that include magnified views of insect fossils and their modern descendants.

cheeses plus a lavander *crème brûlée* at *Bernard Mathys* (closed Tues & Wed; ☎90.04.84.64; menus from 160F).

A smaller food **market** takes place in Apt on Tuesday and good **wine** *en vrac* can be bought from the *Château de Mille's* exclusive shop opposite the Argentinian restaurant on quai Général-Leclerc.

Around Apt

Though Apt makes a useful base for a number of day trips, **local buses** run rarely more than once a day and not often at useful hours. For **cyclists**, as well as the Cavaillon–Apt track, there's one that runs eastwards 10km alongside the N100 to **Saint-Martin-de-Castillon** (eventually to extend to **Forcalquier**; route maps from the tourist office or the *Maison du Parc* in Apt) from where you could head north towards Rustrel. For **walkers** the GR92 climbs from Apt through **Saignon** to the **Sommet du Mourre Nègre**, the highest point of the Lubéron, with shorter paths from Auribeau or Castellet.

Roussillon and Rustrel

Perching precariously above the soft-rock cliffs, the buildings of **ROUSSILLON** radiate all the different shades of the seventeen ochre tints once quarried here. During the war Samuel Beckett came here to escape from occupied Paris. Apparently he loathed it so much that on returning to the capital he had a nervous breakdown. There are no reminders of his visit and today the activities of the village reflect the variety of luxury that every other pretty Provençal village promotes and profits from. A spiralling tour past potteries, antique shops and restaurants up to the summit viewing table may or may not be worth the effort. But if your interest is in seeing the **ochre quarries** themselves, a well-signed footpath leads from the car park on place de la Poste where you'll also find the **tourist office** (Easter–Nov Mon–Sat 10am–noon & 2.30–7pm, Sun 2.30–7pm; Dec–Easter daily 2–6pm; ☎90.05.60.25) and a *Centre Social et Culturel* with occasional art exhibitions. A museum dedicated to the ochre quarries is planned. For **meals**, *La Treille*, 1 rue du Four (☎90.05.64.27), serves a mixture of North African, Turkish and Scandinavian specialities with one menu under 100F, or you can get a crêpe at *La Gourmandine* on place l'Abbé-Avon.

There are other quarries in the neighbouring village of **Gargas**, some now used for mushroom cultivation, and more near **RUSTREL** known as the **Rustrel Colerado**, which are the most dramatic. They're signed off the D22 towards Gignac, just before you reach Rustrel from Apt, and in summer cars will have to pay a 12F parking fee. Having passed the remains of old settling tanks that look like unearthed foundations and a small ruined building, you can either take the second left signed in blue or follow the yellow signs up the main track. The blue route is quite hard to follow particularly when the stream sees no difference in the creamy ochre sand of the path and its own course, but persevere and you will end up in an amphitheatre of coffee, vanilla and strawberry ice cream whipped into pinnacles and curving walls. If you continue with the blue trail climbing up above a little waterfall, you can turn left then left again onto a wider path with blue and yellow signs. This soon brings you to the gods' seats over the quarry. Continue and you'll end up on the yellow route leading back to the settling tanks.

OCHRE QUARRYING

Ochre quarrying has been practised in the Vaucluse since prehistoric times, producing the natural dye that gives a range of colours, unfaded by sunlight, from pale yellow to a blood red. By the nineteenth century the business was considerable. First overloaded donkeys, then horses hauling trucks, and by the 1880s trains, carried the dust to Marseille to be shipped round the world. In 1929 forty thousand tonnes of ochre were exported from the region. Twenty years later it was down to 11,500 tonnes, and in 1958 production finally stopped for lack of markets, competition from synthetic dyes and the fact that the foundations of Roussillon were being undermined.

Rustrel is a very sweet little village with far fewer *résidences secondaires* than Roussillon. Its **bar-restaurant** *Les Platanes* (closed Mon out of season; ☎90.04.93.99) is convivial, with good beers and a basement for live music most Saturday nights (meals around 140F).

Saignon

SAIGNON is only 4km from Apt but already high enough up the Lubéron to have an eagle's eye view of the town. The village itself, from below, appears as an immense fort with natural turrets of rock; on closer inspection it turns out to be a mix of crumbling farmhouses and perfectly restored summer residences with Dutch and British Volvos parked outside. The gardener, Monsieur Danneyrolles, whose ancient, organically grown species of vegetables are on sale in Apt's markets, lives here at La Molière; if you ring him on ☎90.74.44.68, he may show you round his fabulous **garden**.

Buoux

The fortified abandoned hilltop village known as the **Fort de Buoux**, 10km south of Apt, stands on the southern edge of a canyon, forged by the once powerful River Aiguebrun at the start of its passage through the Lubéron. Numerous relics of prehistoric life have been found in the Buoux valley and in the earliest Christian days anchorite monks survived against all odds in tiny caves and niches in the vertical cliff face. The remains of old Buoux, including water cisterns, storage cellars with thick stone lids, arrow-slitted ramparts, the lower half of a Romanesque chapel and a pretty much intact keep, span centuries. To reach the fort follow the road signed off the D113 to the end where there's a gateway, through which a ten- to fifteen-minute walk brings you to the entrance (daily 8am till sunset; 10F).

The village was demolished by command of Richelieu in the 1660s for being a centre of Protestantism, but the paranoia that must have been common in earlier eras is only too easy to imagine as you climb upwards through the ruins. Danger is an equally real experience for many of the modern visitors, though for them it's through choice. Approaching the fort, you'll almost certainly see **climbers** dangling across the cliff face. Most of them will be denizens of the corporate or municipal holiday homes that cluster round the road into the valley or of the *Auberge des Seguins* (see p.156).

Returning to the junction with the D113, going left takes you past the slender Romanesque tower of the former *Prieuré de St-Symphorien* and onto the Loumarin road, while going right brings you to the present-day village of **BUOUX** (the "x", by the way, is pronounced). The *Auberge de la Loube* restaurant (closed Wed evening out of season & Thurs; ☎90.74.19.58), just outside the village, has a considerable local reputation: some say it's pretentious and overpriced, others say it's *géniale* and delicious. Its summer midday menu for around 100F of three starters and three puds is a bit of both.

From Buoux, or indeed from Apt, the road to the Combe de Lubéron has fabulous westward views, and in the gorge itself you can stop off by the river, though in summer it's only a trickle.

From the Lubéron to the Durance

The **southern slopes of the Lubéron** come into the climatic sphere of the Mediterranean. They are filled with the smell of pines and wild thyme, the yellow and gold of honeysuckle and immortelle, and the quick movements and stillnesses of sun-basking reptiles. Unlike the humid northern face, here it is hot and grown dry. The lower slopes are taken up by vines, grown both for wine and the grapes, and cherry orchards. Where the land levels out, 12km or so back from the Durance, the ground is highly fertile and all the classic crops of Provence are grown. The smaller holdings, divided more aesthetically and greenly by organic windbreaks, specialize in one or other of the ingredients for ratatouille. Because of the importance of agriculture – **Cucuron** is famous for melons, **Lauris** for asparagus and **Pertuis** for potatoes – the villages here are still very Provençal in character, with far fewer Parisians and other foreigners than the northern Lubéron.

The beautiful villages of **Lourmarin**, **Vaugines** and **Cucuron** sit amidst vineyards and the unspoilt countryside of the Grand Lubéron foothills; **La Tour d'Aigues** has an elegant ruined château; **Ansouis** an inhabited aristocratic castle; **Cadenet** has a certain charm; and **Pertuis** has the best transport links and accommodation possibilities in the area. Across the Durance is the ancient **Silvacane Abbey**.

Lourmarin

LOURMARIN stands at the bottom of a *combe*, its Renaissance **Château** guarding with nonchalant ease a small rise to the west. A fortress once defended this strategic vantage point but the current edifice dates from the sixteenth century when comfort was beginning to outplay defence, hence the generous windows.

Since 1929 the château has belonged to the University of Aix, who use it to give summer sabbaticals to artists and intellectuals of various scientific and philosophical persuasions. Those that do more than just think usually leave behind a creation, and you can see these works on the guided **tour** (45min; July–Sept daily 10.30am–noon & 2.30–6.30pm; Oct–June daily 2.30–5.30pm; daily 30F), as well as the vast rooms with intricate wooden ceilings, massive fireplaces and beautifully tiled floors where these favoured cultural workers socialize. In July and August **concerts** are held in the château every Saturday evening, and throughout the summer **exhibitions** of all sorts are staged (contact the tourist office for more information). The most famous literary figure associated with Lourmarin is the writer Albert Camus, who spent the last years of his life here and is buried in the cemetery.

Practicalities

Lourmarin's **tourist office** is at 9 av Philippe-de-Girard (April to mid-Oct Mon–Sat 10.30am–12.30pm & 4–6pm; ☎90.68.10.77). There are any number of **restaurants** around the fountained squares of the village. The expensive but excellent *La Fenière* on rue du Grand-Pré (☎90.68.11.79; menus from 190F) can be trusted to use absolutely fresh ingredients in seriously gourmet combinations but not necessarily to be open (closed Mon & Sun evening, Tues midday except in July and Aug, and the first week of March, July and Oct). Good *paysan* dishes for a lot less can be had at *La Récréation,* 15 rue Philippe-de-Giraud (closed Tues evening & Wed; ☎90.68.23.73), with one menu around 100F. For places **to stay** there's the wonderfully situated *Hostellerie Le Paradou* on the D943 at the start of the *combe* (☎90.68.04.05; ③) and back towards Lourmarin, *Le Four à Chaux*, a *gîte* with dormitory beds and a few rooms (☎90.68.24.28; ①). There's a three-star **campsite**, *Les Hautes Prairies*, on rte de Vaugines (March–Dec; ☎90.68.02.89), with a pool, bar and restaurant. **Bikes** can be rented at *Freestyle* on rue du Temple (☎90.68.10.31).

East to Vaugines, Cucuron, Ansouis and La Tour d'Aigues

East from Lourmarin, if you take the minor road, the D56, the first place you come to is **VAUGINES**, a gorgeous little village with a nice old-fashioned café, *Café de la Fontaine*, opposite the *mairie*, and a **hotel** with great views, the *Hostellerie du Lubéron* (☎90.77.27.19; ④). Vaugines is the meeting point of the GR97 from the Petit Lubéron and the GR9 which crosses the Grand Lubéron to Buoux in one direction and in the other loops above Curcuron and skirts the Mourre-Nègre summit before running along the eastern end of the ridge.

The neighbouring village of **CUCURON** is a bit larger and almost as fetching, with some of its ancient ramparts and gateways still standing and a belltower with a delicate campinale on the central place de l'Horloge. Recently Cucuron was taken over by the film industry for the shooting of Rappeneau's *The Horseman on the Roof* based on a Giono novel and the most expensive French film to date. However, its main business is olive oil and it has a sixteenth-century mill in a hollow of the rock face on rue Moulin à l'Huile that is still used to press olives. At the top of the rock a **park** surrounds the site of the former citadelle. At the other end of the village is the **Eglise Notre-Dame de Beaulieu** which contains a sixteenth-century painting on wood amongst its art treasures. Between the end of May and the middle of August a huge felled poplar leans against the church, a bizarre tradition dating back to 1720 when Cucuron was spared the Plague. On rue de l'Eglise, a short way from the church is a small **museum** (10am–noon & 3–6pm; closed Tues morning; free) on local traditions and early history plus a collection of daguerreotypes.

On the north side of the village, by the reservoir bordered by plane trees, you'll find the **hotel-restaurant** *L'Etang* (☎90.77.21.25; ③) which serves very pleasant food (menus from 115F). There are two **campsites**: *Lou Badareu* at La Rasparine, to the southeast of the village towards La Tour d'Aigues (mid-March to Nov; ☎90.77.21.46) next to a rather expensive *gîte d'étape*, and *Le Moulin à Vent* on chemin de Gastoule off the D182 to Villelaure (April–Sept; ☎90.77.25.77). A Tuesday **market** is held on place de l'Etang.

Halfway between Cucuron and **Pertuis**, the perched village of **ANSOUIS** has a **château** lived in since the twelfth-century by the same family. The mother of the current ducal resident wrote a best-seller called *Bon Sang Ne Peut Mentir* (Good Blood Cannot Lie), but don't let that put you off visiting this superb castle with its remarkably rich furnishings from Flemish tapestries and silver chandeliers to kitchen pots and pans (May–Oct daily 2.30–6pm; Nov–April closed Tues; 30F). In the village below, the **Musée Extraordinaire** (daily 2–5.30/6.30pm; 20F) is dedicated to underwater life and has some extremely kitsch touches. The village **market** is held on Thursday.

The seventeenth-century **Château de Sannes**, just south of the D27 before the Bonde lake (where you can **swim**) between Cucuron and **La Motte-d'Aigues**, produces Côte de Lubéron wines *au naturel*, in other words with no fertilizers, pesticides or additives, as it would have been done when the eighteenth-century château was first inhabited (daily 8am–noon & 2–7pm). If you don't fancy this somewhat snooty set-up, you could try the *Vins Coopératives* in La Motte d'Aigues or in **Grambois**. For picnic food, **St-Martin-de-la-Brasque** has a smallholders' **market** every Sunday between May and October as well as a rather surprising *trompe l'oeil* mural of Roman ruins.

Heading for Pertuis from Grambois takes you through **LA TOUR D'AIGUES** where a vast shell of a **château** dominates the centre of the village. The castle was half destroyed during the Revolution but has preserved the most finely detailed Renaissance decoration based on classical designs including Grecian helmets, angels, bows and arrows and Olympic torches, on the gateway arch. You can admire most of the ruins' glories from the outside but there's also a **Musée de Faïence**, a **Musée de l'Histoire du Pays d'Aigues**, covering every academic aspect of this region's development from prehistoric times to the present, plus temporary exhibitions and a video on the southern Lubéron to be seen inside (July & Aug daily 10am–1pm & 3.30–6.30pm; Sept–June 9.30–11.30am & 3–6pm, closed Tues pm and Sat & Sun am; 25F). There's a shaded **café** on the other side of the main road from the castle and one **hotel**, *Les Fenouillets* (☎90.77.48.22; ④).

Pertuis

The one sizeable place this side of the Durance is **PERTUIS**, which hasn't a great deal to offer except for places to stay. Like so many Vaucluse towns, it does, however, come to life on **market** day, Friday in this case. At the beginning of May the **festival** of street theatre and strip cartoons can be fun, too.

Practicalities

SNCF **buses** from Meyrargues station arrive at the **gare routière** on place Garcin, within easy walking distance of the centre: leave the square on the opposite side from the bus station and turn left up rue Henri-Silvy. At **place Parmentier** you'll find flowers for sale on Friday and the main clothes shopping street, rue Colbert, leading up to **place Jean-Jaurès** which with **place du 4-Septembre** and **place Mirabeau** just to the north, constitute the hub of the town. The **tourist office** is on place Mirabeau (Mon–Sat 9am–noon & 2–6pm; ☎90.79.15.56) in the old keep that is all that remains of Pertuis' castle. The narrow streets of the *Vieille Ville* to the north are for the most part ungentrified, low lit and lifeless.

Of the **places to stay**, at the top end of the scale the *Sévan*, av de Verdon on the way out towards Manosque (☎90.79.19.30; ⑤–⑥), belongs to a chain and looks hideous but the rooms and the swimming pools are rather nice. In the centre, the *Hôtel du Cours*, place Jean-Jaurès (☎90.79.00.68; ③), and *Hôtel Cornare*, 24 rue de la Tour (☎90.79.14.34; ③–④), are small and friendly. On place Garcin, *L'Aubarestiero* (☎90.79.14.74; ②–③) is very quiet at night, only disturbed on Wednesday and Saturday mornings when vegetable stalls are set up in the square. The three-star municipal **campsite** *Les Pinèdes*, av Pierre-Augier (☎90.79.10.98), has excellent facilities. For getting away from Pertuis **bikes** can be rented at *Cycles Genin*, 73 rue Giraud (☎90.79.49.43).

You'll find plenty of **brasseries** and **restaurants** on the main squares and streets, but nothing wildly special. Opposite the hôtel de ville on rue Voltaire the *bar-tabac*, *Hunycl*, is a pleasant place to hang out.

Cadenet

The main road heading south from Lourmarin detours round **CADENET**, a place where people go about everyday business without much concern for sun-struck northerners. If you feel like stopping make sure you go to the central place du Tambour d'Arcole to see the statue of the manic drummer-boy, hair and coat tails flying as he runs. André Etienne is so commemorated for his inspired one-man diversion that confused the Austrians and allowed Napoléon's army to cross the River Durance in 1796.

Practicalities

The **tourist office** on place du Tambour d'Arcole (Mon & Wed–Sun 9.30am–noon & 3–6.30pm; ☎90.68.38.21) will also rent out **bikes** to those who want to explore the area. There's an excellent four-star **campsite** by a lake, the *Val de Durance* (closed Oct–March; ☎90.68.37.75), and a **restaurant** *Steffani*, 35 rue Gambetta (closed Tues pm & Wed; ☎90.68.07.14), which offers a midday week-day menu with wine for under 80F. **Market** day is Monday.

Silvacane Abbey

On the other side of the Durance from Cadenet stands the **Abbaye de Silvacane**, built by the same order and in the same period as the abbeys of Sénanque and Le Thoronet, although the "wood of rushes", from which the name Silvacane derives, had already been cleared by Benedictine monks before the Cistercians arrived in 1144. As at the other two great monasteries, the architecture of Silvacane reflects precisely the no-nonsense no-superfluity rule of Saint Benedict (Benoît) in which manual work, intellectual work and worship comprised the three equal elements of the day. These Cistercian monasteries were always built away from villages but in situations where water was available and the land could be cultivated, a vital precept of the regime.

There really is very little difference between the buildings that remain and how they would have appeared seven hundred years ago, with the exception of the refectory, rebuilt in 1423 and given Gothic ornamentation that the earlier monks would never have tolerated. The windows in the church would never have had stained glass either; and the only heated room was the *salle des monies* where the work of copying manuscripts was carried out. The daily reading of "the Rule" and public confession by the monks took place in the *salle capitulaire* and the *parloir* was the only area where conversation was allowed. You can still visit the stark pale-stoned splendour of the church and its compact surrounding buildings and cloisters (April–Sept daily 9am–7pm; rest of year Mon & Wed–Sun 9am–noon & 2–5pm; closed hols; admission 25F).

travel details

Trains

Cavaillon to: Avignon (5–9 daily; 25min); L'Isle-sur-la-Sorgue (7–9 daily; 7min); Marseille (change at Miramas 5 daily; 1–2hr).

L'Isle-sur-la-Sorgue to: Avignon (6–8 daily; 15–25min); Cavaillon (7–9 daily; 7min); Marseille (change at Miramas 5 daily; 1hr 7min–2hr 7min).

Meyrargues to: Aix (3 daily; 20min); Marseille (3 daily; 50min); Sisteron (3 daily; 1hr).

Buses

Apt to: Aix (2 daily; 2hr 20min); Avignon (4 daily; 1hr–1hr 55min); Bonnieux (2 daily; 20min); Cadenet (2 daily; 45min); Carpentras (3 weekly school term; 1hr 5min); Digne (2 daily; 3hr 10min); Lourmarin (2 daily; 30min); Pertuis (2 daily; 1hr 5min); Roussillon (2 daily; 20min); Rustrel (3 weekly; 35min); Sault (3 weekly; 1hr).

Carpentras to: Aix (3 daily; 1hr 50min); Apt (3 weekly school term; 1hr 5min); Avignon (frequent; 45min); Beaumes-de-Venise (2 daily; 15min); Bédoin (2–3 daily; 40min); Cavaillon (4 daily; 35–45min); Gigondas (3 daily; 40min); L'Isle-sur-la-Sorgue (3 daily; 15–30min); Malaucène (2 daily; 25min); Marseille (4 daily; 2hr 15min); Orange (4 daily; 25min); Pernes-les-Fontaines (3 daily; 5min); Sablet (2 daily; 45min); Sault (1 daily; 1hr 30min); Vacqueyras (2 daily; 25min); Vaison (2 daily; 45min); Venasque (2 daily; 25min).

Cavaillon to: Aix (3 daily; 1hr 10min); Apt (2 daily; 45min); Avignon (frequent; 45min); Bonnieux (3 weekly; 55min); Carpentras (4 daily; 35–45min); Gordes (2 daily; 45min); Lacoste (3 weekly; 35min); L'Isle-sur-la-Sorgue (4 daily; 15min); Oppède-le-Vieux (3 weekly; 20min); Pernes-les-Fontaines (3 daily; 30min).

L'Isle-sur-la-Sorgue to: Avignon (3 daily; 25–40min); Carpentras (3 daily; 15–30min); Cavaillon (4 daily; 15min); Fontaine-de-Vaucluse (3–4 daily; 5min).

Nyons to: Avignon (1 daily; 1hr 40min); Gap (1 daily; 2hr 55min); Grignan (2 daily; 40min); Vaison (3 daily; 30min); Valréas (2 daily; 20min).

Pertuis to: Aix (6 daily; 30min); Ansouis (1 daily; 10min); Apt (2 daily; 1hr 5min); Cucuron (1 daily; 20min); Meyrargues (3 daily; 16min); La Tour d'Aigues (3 daily; 10min).

Vaison to: Avignon (1 daily; 1hr 15min); Camaret (4 daily; 35min); Nyons (3 daily; 30min); Orange (3 daily; 55min); Rasteau (1–2 daily; 15min); Séguret (4 daily; 15min); Sablet (4 daily; 20min).

Valréas to: Avignon (3 daily; 1hr 30min); Grignan (2 daily; 20min); Nyons (2 daily; 20min); Orange (3 daily; 45min).

CHAPTER THREE

MARSEILLE AND METROPOLITAN PROVENCE

Encompassing **Marseille**, **Aix** and **Toulon**, **"Metropolitan Provence"** is by far the most populated and industrial part of the region, and indeed of southern France. It's cosmopolitan, culturally dynamic and wields considerable political and economic influence, not least for the way it dramatizes the severe consequences of dated industries and recession. But the area also has vast tracts of deserted mountainous countryside and a shoreline of high cliffs, deep jagged inlets and sand beaches with stretches still untouched by the holiday industry.

The two great poles of attraction are the contrasting cities of **Marseille** and **Aix-en-Provence**. Marseille, a vital commerical port for more than two millennia and France's second largest city, is, for all its notorious reputation, a wonderful place with a distinctive, unconventional character that never ceases to surprise. The charms of Aix, with one of the most perfect old town centres in all of France, are much more commonly sung. It glories in the medieval period of independent Provence and the riches of its seventeenth- and eighteenth-century growth.

The first foreigners to settle in Provence, the ancient **Greeks** from Phocaea and their less amiable successors from **Rome**, left evidence of their sophistication around the **Etang de Berre**, at **Les Lecques**, and most of all at Marseille. Museums in Marseille and Aix guard reminders of the indigenous peoples of Provence whose civilization the Romans destroyed.

Military connections are strong here. **Salon-de-Provence** trains French airforce pilots and **Toulon** is home to the French navy's Mediterranean fleet. Until very recently the planes for the one and the ships for the other, plus the freighters for Marseille, were all built at **Istres**, **La Seyne** and **La Ciotat**.

But between the battleships of Toulon and the petrochemical industries and tanker terminals around the Etang de Berre there are still great **seaside attractions**: the pine-covered rocks of the **Estaque**; the *calanques* (rocky inlets) between Marseille and **Cassis**; the sand beaches of La Ciotat bay and the coastal path to **Bandol**; and the heights from which to view the coast, close-up on the **route de Crêtes** or **Cap Sicié**, and at a distance from **Le Gros Cerveau** and **Mont Caume**.

HOTEL ROOM PRICES

For a fuller explanation of these price codes, see the box on p.32 of *Basics*.

① Under 160F	② 160–220F	③ 220–300F	④ 300–400F
⑤ 400–500F	⑥ 500–600F	⑦ 600–700F	⑧ over 700F

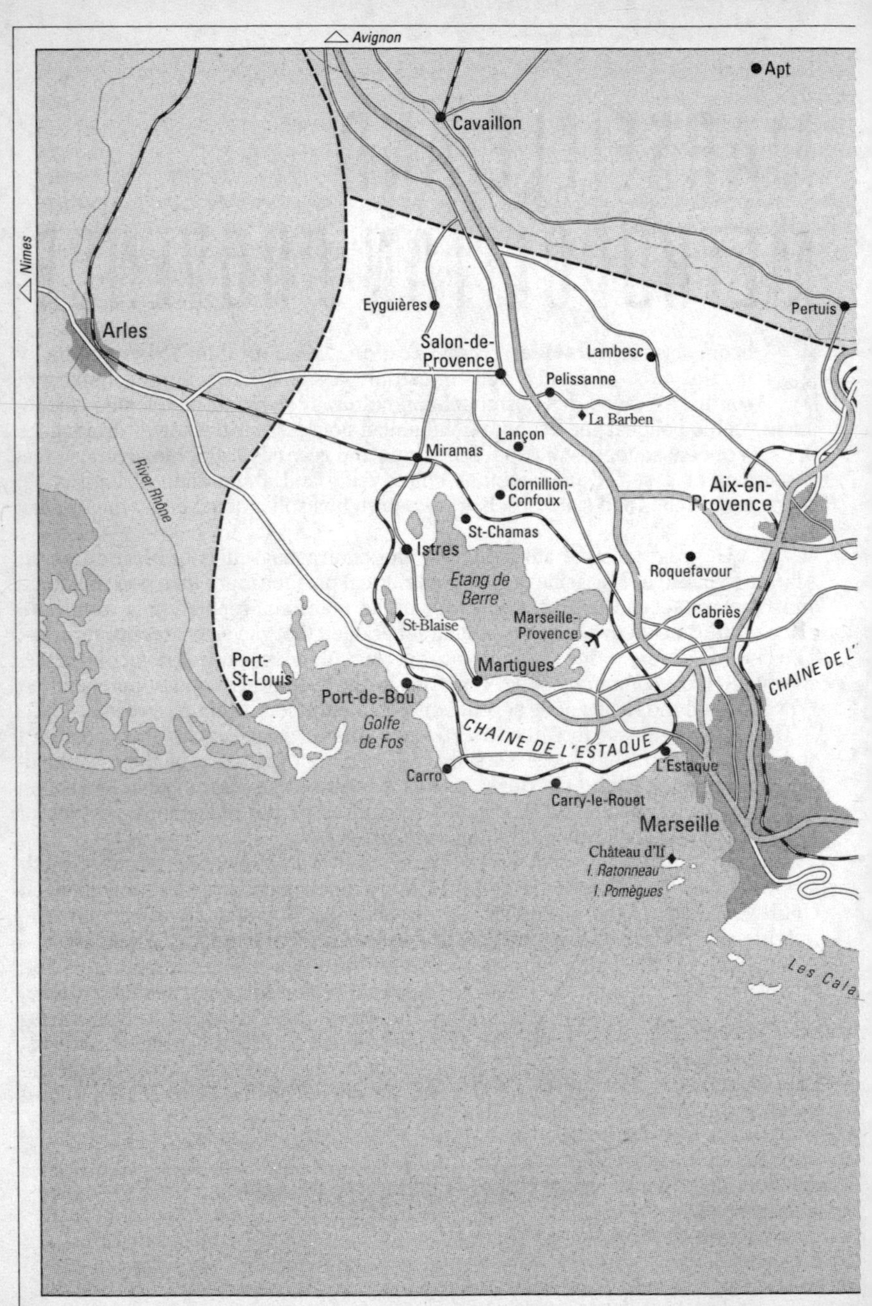
Avignon
Apt
Cavaillon
Nimes
Eyguières
Pertuis
Arles
Salon-de-Provence
Lambesc
Pelissanne
La Barben
Lançon
Miramas
River Rhône
Cornillion-Confoux
Aix-en-Provence
St-Chamas
Istres
Roquefavour
Etang de Berre
St-Blaise
Marseille-Provence
Cabriès
Port-St-Louis
Martigues
CHAINE DE L'
Port-de-Bou
Golfe de Fos
CHAINE DE L'ESTAQUE
L'Estaque
Carro
Carry-le-Rouet
Marseille
Château d'If
I. Ratonneau
I. Pomègues
Les Cala

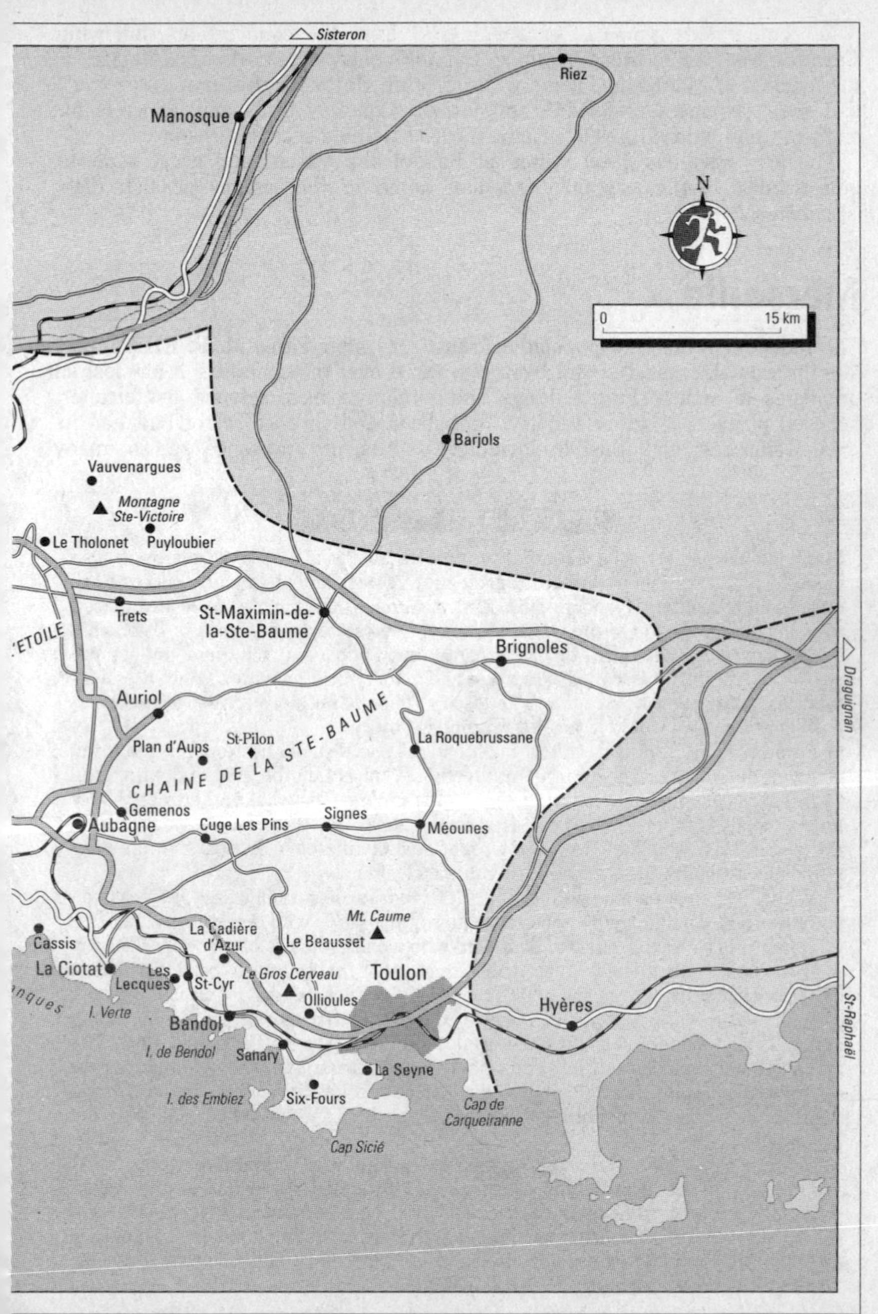
Sisteron
Riez
Manosque
N
0
15 km
Barjols
Vauvenargues
Montagne Ste-Victoire
Le Tholonet
Puyloubier
Trets
St-Maximin-de-la-Ste-Baume
ETOILE
Brignoles
Draguignan
Auriol
St-Pilon
Plan d'Aups
CHAINE DE LA STE-BAUME
La Roquebrussane
Gemenos
Aubagne
Cuge Les Pins
Signes
Méounes
Mt. Caume
La Cadière d'Azur
Le Beausset
Cassis
La Ciotat
Les Lecques
St-Cyr
Le Gros Cerveau
Toulon
Ollioules
Hyères
St-Raphaël
I. Verte
Bandol
I. de Bendol
Sanary
La Seyne
I. des Embiez
Six-Fours
Cap de Carqueiranne
Cap Sicié

For countryside, you can escape **inland** from the conurbations, following **Cézanne** from Aix to **Mont-Victoire**, **Pagnol's** characters north of **Aubagne**, or the legends of Mary Magdalene to the **Chaîne de la Ste-Baume.** Here you'll find great expanses of hillside and forest, with only birds and squirrels for company, and little villages like **Signes**, where nothing seems to change.

The area also has great **wines** at Bandol and Cassis, and great **seafood** gourmandise, particularly in Marseille, home of the famous sea-fish dish, *bouillabaisse*.

Marseille

The most renowned and populated French city after Paris, **MARSEILLE** has, like the capital, prospered and been ransacked over the centuries. It has lost its privileges to sundry French kings and foreign armies, refound its fortunes, suffered plagues, religious bigotry, republican and royalist Terror and had its own Commune and Bastille-storming. It was the presence of so many

POWER AND POLITICS

Marseille has all the social, economic and **political ills** of France writ large. It also has to contend with its notoriety for protection rackets and shoot-outs, **corruption**, drug-money laundering and prostitution. It's impossible not to notice the glazed eyes of young kids and of the women lounging on cars by street corners. That said, however, to some extent the city's dangerous reputation is unfair. Shoot-outs by the *milieu*, as the mafia is called, are rare, and underworld activities flourish just as much in the other towns of the Côte d'Azur. There's no more reason to feel paranoid here than you would in any big European city.

From 1989 to 1995 Marseille's independent socialist mayor Robert Vigouroux concentrated on prestige cultural improvements (or not, in the case of the dreadful Musée de la Mode, said to have been a "little gift" for his wife) and attracted very little new investment to the city. The switch to a right-wing mayor, Jean-Claude Gaudin, in 1995 is unlikely to make a great deal of difference, but prior to the elections the city centre benefited from a general clean-up.

Marseille's most famous politician is **Bernard Tapie**, a millionaire businessman with the common touch who entered politics in the 1980s with the express intention of seeing off Le Pen's *Front National*, and who won the hearts of the Marseillais by making their football team great again. Charges of fraud and tax evasion failed to dent his popularity, and in the 1994 European elections, he gained around seventy percent of the vote. But he has now been declared bankrupt and is appealing against a jail sentence for OM cheating to win the European League in 1993. The team, whose finances went haywire under Tapie's ownership, has been taken over by a town hall and private business consortium and has had to stay in the second division for a year as punishment. A come-back by Tapie is unlikely, though not impossible.

There is significant grassroots support for Le Pen, who scored most votes in the first round of the presidential elections of 1995, and the white middle class constantly complain that their city centre has been taken over by North Africans. Racism is rife, as is poverty, bad housing and rising unemployment, particularly amongst the young. It's a socially explosive mixture, but, again, one that Marseille shares with almost every other European city.

Revolutionaries from Marseille marching their way from the Rhine to Paris in 1792 which gave the name to the Hymn of the Army of the Rhine that became the national anthem, "La Marseillaise".

Today, it can't be denied that Marseille is a deprived city, that it is not particularly beautiful architecturally and that it has acres of grim and decrepit 1960s housing estates. Yet the same is true of many cities that nevertheless maintain a glamorous reputation – something this one has never bothered to aspire to. That perhaps is the key to its charm.

Work, not image has been Marseille's key identity. It has been a trading city for over two and a half thousand years, ever since ancient Greeks from Ionia discovered shelter in the Lacydon inlet, today the *Vieux Port*, and came to an agreement with the local Ligurian tribe. The story goes that the locals, noticing the exotic cargo of the strangers' boats, sent them off to the king's castle where the princess's wedding preparations were in full swing. The Ligurian royal custom at the time was that the king's daughter could choose her husband from among her father's guests. As the leader of the Greek party walked through the castle gate, he was handed a drink by a woman and discovered that she was the princess and that he was the bridegroom. The king gave the couple the hill on the north side of the Lacydon and Massalia came into being. And there ends, more or less, Marseille's association with romance.

Which is not to say Marseille cannot be romantic. It has a powerful magnetism as a true Mediterranean city, surrounded by mountains and graced with hidden corners that have the unexpected air of fishing villages. It has its triumph and glory architecture too, and the cosmopolitan atmosphere of a major port. But perhaps the most appealing quality is the down-to-earth nature of its inhabitants. Gregarious, generous, endlessly talkative and unconcerned if their style seems provocatively vulgar to the snobs of Aix or the Côte d'Azur, their animation makes this one of the most delightful European cities to visit. What's more, it is not a tourist city. Your status is no different from that of the people departing and arriving on the ships, those on business or fans of the city's mercurial football team, Olympique de Marseille or OM as it is universally called.

Arrival and information

Arriving by **car**, you'll descend into Marseille from the surrounding heights of one of three mountain ranges. From any direction the views encompass the barricade of high-rise concrete on the lower slopes, the vast roadstead with docks stretching miles north from the central **Vieux Port** and Marseille's classic landmark, the **Basilique de Notre-Dame-de-la-Garde** perched on a high rock south of the *Vieux Port*. The highways terminate here: follow the *Vieux Port* signs.

The city's **airport**, the Aéroport de Marseille-Provence (☎42.78.21.00), is 20km northwest of the city centre; a shuttle bus runs every twenty minutes from 5.30am to 9.50pm to the **gare SNCF St-Charles** (40F), on the northern edge of the *1er arrondissement* on esplanade St-Charles (☎91.08.50.50) with the **gare routière** (☎91.08.16.40) alongside on place Victor-Hugo. From esplanade St-Charles, a monumental staircase leads down to bd d'Athènes and thence to **La Canebière**, Marseille's main street which begins at the head of the **Vieux Port** (about a 15-min walk to the right from bd d'Athènes). The main **tourist office** is at 4 La Canebière (June–Aug daily 8.30am–8pm; Sept–May Mon–Sat 9am–7pm, Sun 10am–5pm; ☎91.54.91.11).

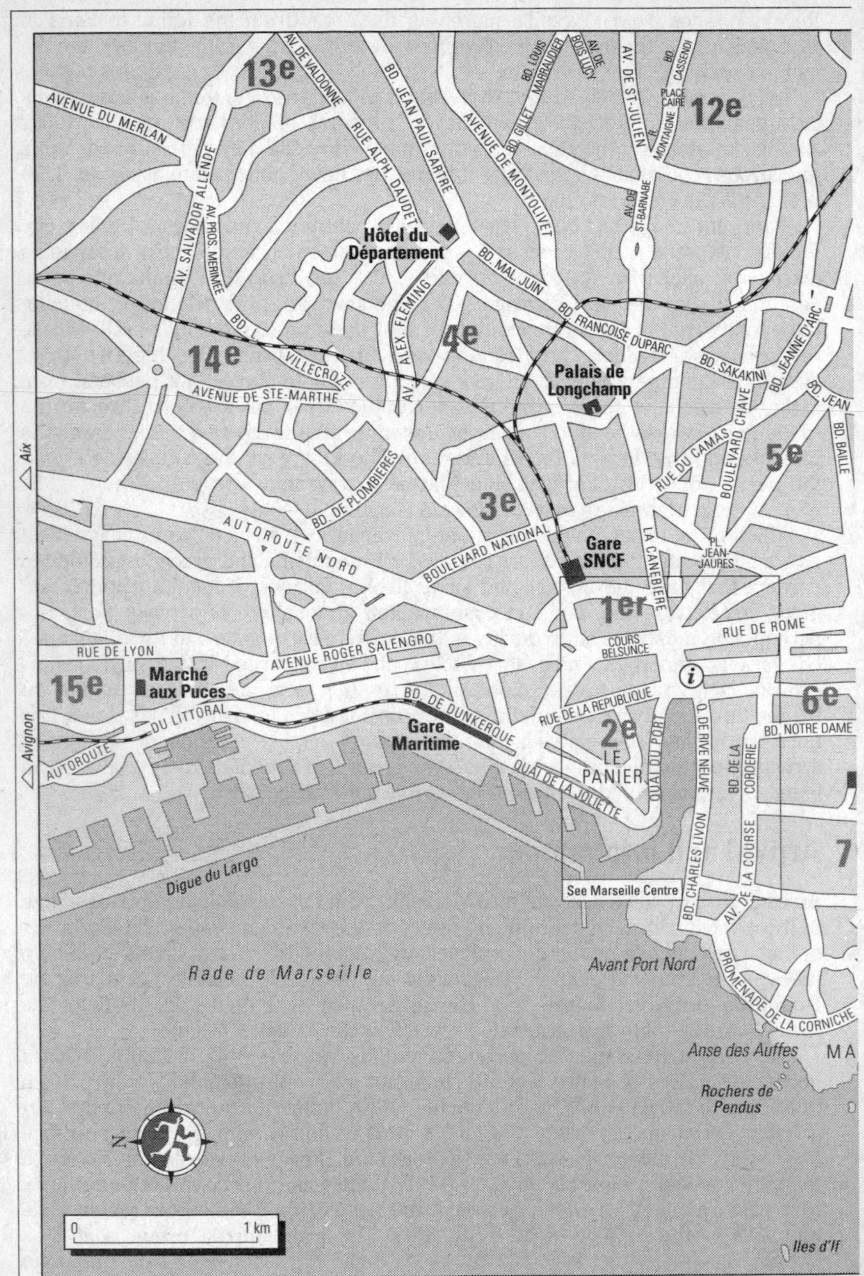
13e
12e
14e
4e
3e
5e
1er
2e
6e
15e
Hôtel du Département
Palais de Longchamp
Gare SNCF
Marché aux Puces
Gare Maritime
LE PANIER
AVENUE DU MERLAN
AV. DE VALDONNE
BD. JEAN PAUL SARTRE
RUE ALPH. DAUDET
AVENUE DE MONTOLIVET
BD. LOUIS MARRAUDIER
AV. DE BOIS LUCY
BD. GILLET
AV. DE ST-JULIEN
BD. CASSENDI
PLACE CAIRE
R. MONTAIGNE
AV. DE ST-BARNABE
AV. SALVADOR ALLENDE
AV. PROS. MERIMEE
BD. MAL JUIN
BD. FRANCOISE DUPARC
BD. SAKAKINI
BD. JEANNE D'ARC
BD. JEAN
BD. BAILLE
AV. ALEX. FLEMING
VILLECROZE
AVENUE DE STE-MARTHE
BD. DE PLOMBIERES
RUE DU CAMAS
BOULEVARD CHAVE
AUTOROUTE NORD
BOULEVARD NATIONAL
LA CANEBIERE
PL. JEAN-JAURES
RUE DE ROME
COURS BELSUNCE
RUE DE LYON
AVENUE ROGER SALENGRO
BD. DE DUNKERQUE
AUTOROUTE DU LITTORAL
RUE DE LA REPUBLIQUE
QUAI DU PORT
Q. DE RIVE NEUVE
BD. NOTRE DAME
BD. DE LA CORDERIE
QUAI DE LA JOLIETTE
BD. CHARLES LIVON
AV. DE LA COURSE
See Marseille Centre
Digue du Largo
Rade de Marseille
Avant Port Nord
PROMENADE DE LA CORNICHE
Anse des Auffes
Rochers de Pendus
Iles d'If
Aix
Avignon
N
0
1 km

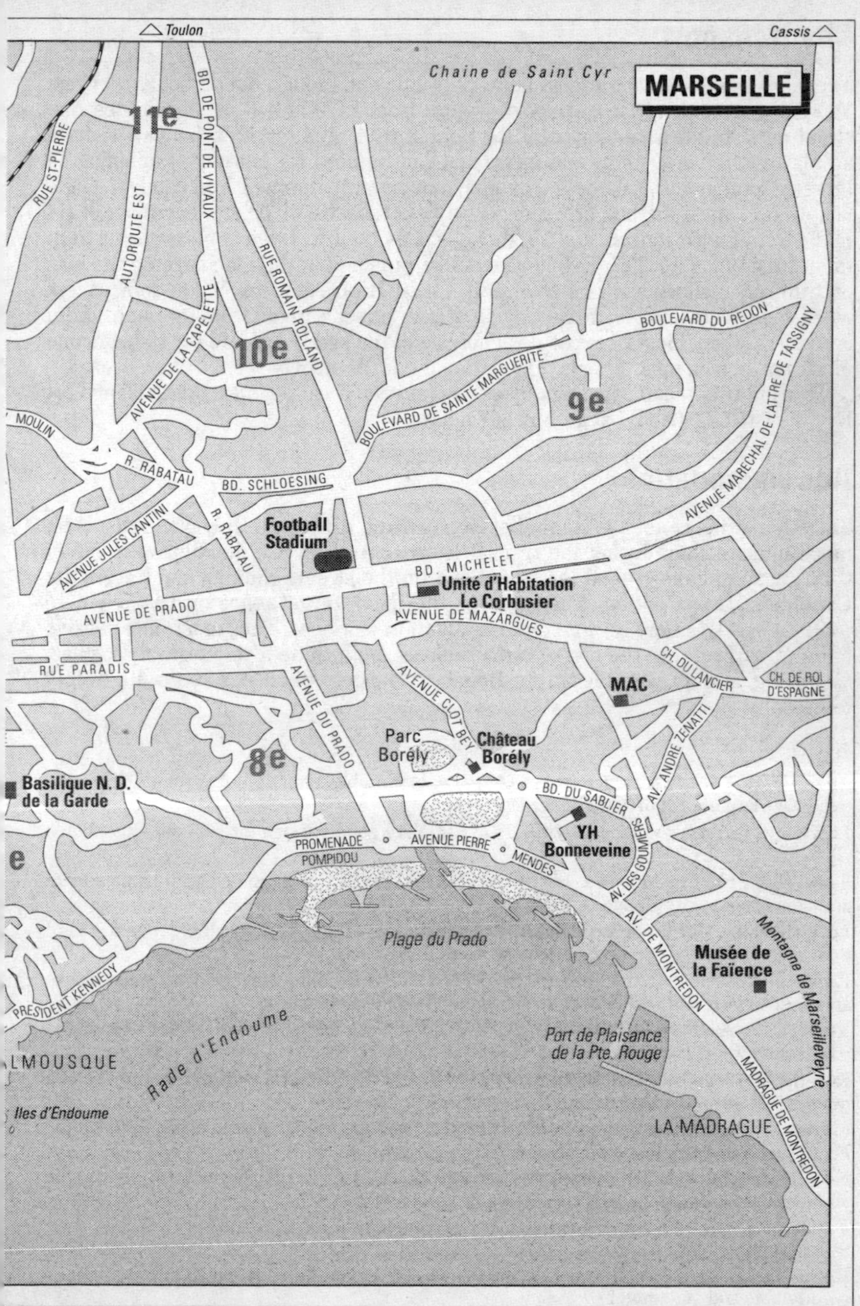

Toulon
Cassis
MARSEILLE
Chaine de Saint Cyr
11e
10e
9e
8e
e
RUE ST-PIERRE
AUTOROUTE EST
BD. DE PONT DE VIVAUX
RUE ROMAIN ROLLAND
AVENUE DE LA CAPELETTE
BOULEVARD DE SAINTE MARGUERITE
BOULEVARD DU REDON
AVENUE MARECHAL DE LATTRE DE TASSIGNY
MOULIN
R. RABATAU
BD. SCHLOESING
AVENUE JULES CANTINI
Football Stadium
BD. MICHELET
Unité d'Habitation Le Corbusier
AVENUE DE PRADO
AVENUE DE MAZARGUES
RUE PARADIS
CH. DU LANCIER
CH. DE ROI D'ESPAGNE
MAC
AVENUE DU PRADO
AVENUE CLOT BEY
Parc Borély
Château Borély
AV. ANDRE ZENATTI
Basilique N. D. de la Garde
BD. DU SABLIER
YH Bonneveine
PROMENADE POMPIDOU
AVENUE PIERRE MENDES
AV. DES GOUMIERS
AV. DE MONTREDON
Plage du Prado
Musée de la Faïence
Montagne de Marseilleveyre
PRESIDENT KENNEDY
Rade d'Endoume
Port de Plaisance de la Pte. Rouge
LMOUSQUE
Iles d'Endoume
LA MADRAGUE
MADRAGUE DE MONTREDON

City transport

The city's **bus, tram** and **métro** network is efficient, though not particularly cheap. You can get a plan of the **transport system** from *RTM* at 6–8 rue des Fabres, one street north of the Canebière near the Bourse (the city's stock exchange). **Tickets** are flat rate for bus, trams and métro and can be used for journeys combining all three as long as they take less than one hour seventy minutes. You can buy single tickets (8F) from the bus driver or métro ticket offices, or tickets in *carnets* of six (41F) from métro stations and *RTM* kiosks; a 24-hour travel ticket is available from the tourist office for 20F. Tickets need to be punched in the machines on the bus, on tramway platforms or at métro gates. The métro runs from 5am to 9pm, except when the OM football team are playing. **Night buses** run out from the centre from 9pm to 12.30am, most from rue des Fabres and the parallel rue de Bir Hakeim, one block north: pick up a "Flubus" guide from the *RTM* office.

Touring **bikes** and mountain bikes can be rented from *Green Bike*, 135 av Clot Bey, 8e (☎91.72.42.63), at around 90F a day.

Accommodation

Since Marseille is not a great tourist city, **finding a room** in July or August is no more difficult than during the rest of the year. **Hotels** are plentiful with lots of very cheap options around the Opéra and on the streets running south from the Canebière. If you get stuck for a room, the main tourist office on La Canebière (☎91.54.91.11) offers a free accommodation service. The most inexpensive options, as ever, are the city's **youth hostels**, both quite a way from the centre. **Camping** is only possible at the Bois-Luzy hostel which has room for twenty tents only.

Hotels

Alizé, 35 quai des Belges, 1er (☎91.33.66.97). Comfortable, soundproofed rooms, the more expensive looking out onto the *Vieux Port*. ④

Le Béarn, 63 rue Sylvabelle, 6e (☎91.37.75.83). Very good bargain for pleasant, quiet hotel, close to the centre. ②

Caravelle, 5 rue Guy-Mocquet, 1er (☎91.48.44.99). Friendly, quiet and close to La Canebière and cours Julien, just off bd Garibaldi. ②

Le Corbusier, Cité Radieuse, 280 bd Michelet, 8e (☎91.77.18.15). Stylish hotel on the third floor of the architect's prototype high rise; book in advance. ④

Edmond-Rostand, 31 rue Dragon, 6e (☎91.37.74.95). Helpful management, great charm and atmosphere, and well known, so you should book in advance. ②

Esterel, 124 rue Paradis, 6e (☎91.37.13.90). A hotel in a good, animated location with all the mod cons. ④

Lutétia, 38 allées Léon-Gambetta, 1er (☎91.50.81.78). Very central with pleasant rooms in a quiet street. ③–④

Manon, 36 bd Louis Salvator, 6e (☎91.48.67.01). Pleasant, though a little noisy, between the Préfecture and cours Julien. ①

New Hotel Astoria, 10 bd Garibaldi, 1er (☎91.33.33.50). A *belle époque* town house with sound-proofed, air-conditioned rooms just off La Canebière. ④

Pavillon, 27 rue Pavillon, 1er (☎91.33.76.90). In a central location and very friendly, apart from a yapping black poodle. ①

Relais St-Charles, 5 bd Gustave Desplaces, 1er (☎91.64.11.17). Just north of the station, a comfortable and quiet hotel. ③

Le Richelieu, 52 Corniche Kennedy, 7e (☎91.31.01.92). One of the more affordable of the Corniche hotels overlooking the plage des Catalans. ③

Le St Ferréol's Hôtel, 19 rue Pisançon, cnr rue St-Ferréol, 1er (☎91.33.12.21). Pretty decor, marble baths with jacuzzis, in a central pedestrianized area. ④–⑤

Tonic Hotel, 42 quai des Belges, 1er (☎91.55.67.46). Newly done-up and now the smartest of the *Vieux Port* hotels. Jacuzzi and steam bath in every room, from 560F for port view. ④–⑥

Youth hostels, foyers and chambre d'hôtes

HI youth hostel, 76 av de Bois-Luzy, 12e (☎91.49.06.18). Bus #8 direction St-Julien from Centre Bourse, stop Bois Luzy. Cheap, clean youth hostel in a former château a long way out from the centre. Camping also available. Curfew 11pm. Reception 7–10am & 5–10.30pm. Open all year. ②

HI youth hostel, 47 av J-Vidal, impasse du Dr-Bonfils, 8e (☎91.73.21.81). Métro Rond-Point du Prado, then bus #44 direction Roy d'Espagne, stop *Place Bonnefoi*. Not so cheap or secure as the Bois Luzy hostel, but the lack of curfew and proximity to the beach make up for it. Reception 7.30–9.30am & 5–11pm; open mid-Jan to mid-Dec. ②

Résidence Darius Milhaud, 100 traverse Charles Susini, 13e (☎91.61.44.39). Métro La Rose then bus #3 to Susini–Marie-Louise. Individual studios for 80F per night, a long way north. Open July & Aug.

M & Mme Schaufelberger, 2 rue St-Laurent, 2e (☎91.90.29.02). Métro Vieux Port. *Chambre d'hôtes* on the fourteenth floor of a high rise in Le Panier with great views from the balcony; separate entrance and bathroom; English spoken. ③

The City

Marseille is divided into sixteen *arrondissements* which spiral out from the focal point of the city, the **Vieux Port**. Due north lies **Le Panier**, the *Vieille Ville* and site of the original Greek settlement of Massalia. **La Canebière**, the wide boulevard leading from quai des Belges at the head of the *Vieux Port*, is the central east–west axis of the town, with the **Centre Bourse** and the little streets of **quartier Belsunce** bordering it to the north and the main shopping streets lying to the south. The main north–south axis is **rue d'Aix** becoming **cours Belsunce** then **rue de Rome, av du Prado** and **bd Michelet**. The lively, youngish quarter around **place Jean-Jaurès** and the trendy **cours Julien** lie to the east of rue de Rome. On the headland west of the *Vieux Port* are the villagey *quartiers* of **Les Catalans** and **Malmousque** from where the **Corniche** heads south past the city's most favoured residential districts towards the main beaches and expensive promenade bars and restaurants of the **Plage du Prado**.

The Vieux Port

The **Vieux Port** is, more or less, the ancient harbour basin, and the original inlet that the ancient Greeks sailed into. Historic resonances, however, are not exactly deafening on first encounter, drowned as they are by the stalling or speeding lanes of traffic. Yet the quayside cafés indulge the sedentary pleasures of observing street life; the morning **fish market** on the quai des Belges provides some natural Marseillais theatre; and the mass of cafés and seafood restaurants on the **pedestrianized streets** between the southern quay and cours Estienne d'Orves ensure that the *Vieux Port* remains the life centre of the city.

Two fortresses guard the harbour entrance. **St-Jean**, on the northern side, dates from the Middle Ages when Marseille was an independent republic, and is now only open when hosting exhibitions. Its enlargement of 1660, and the

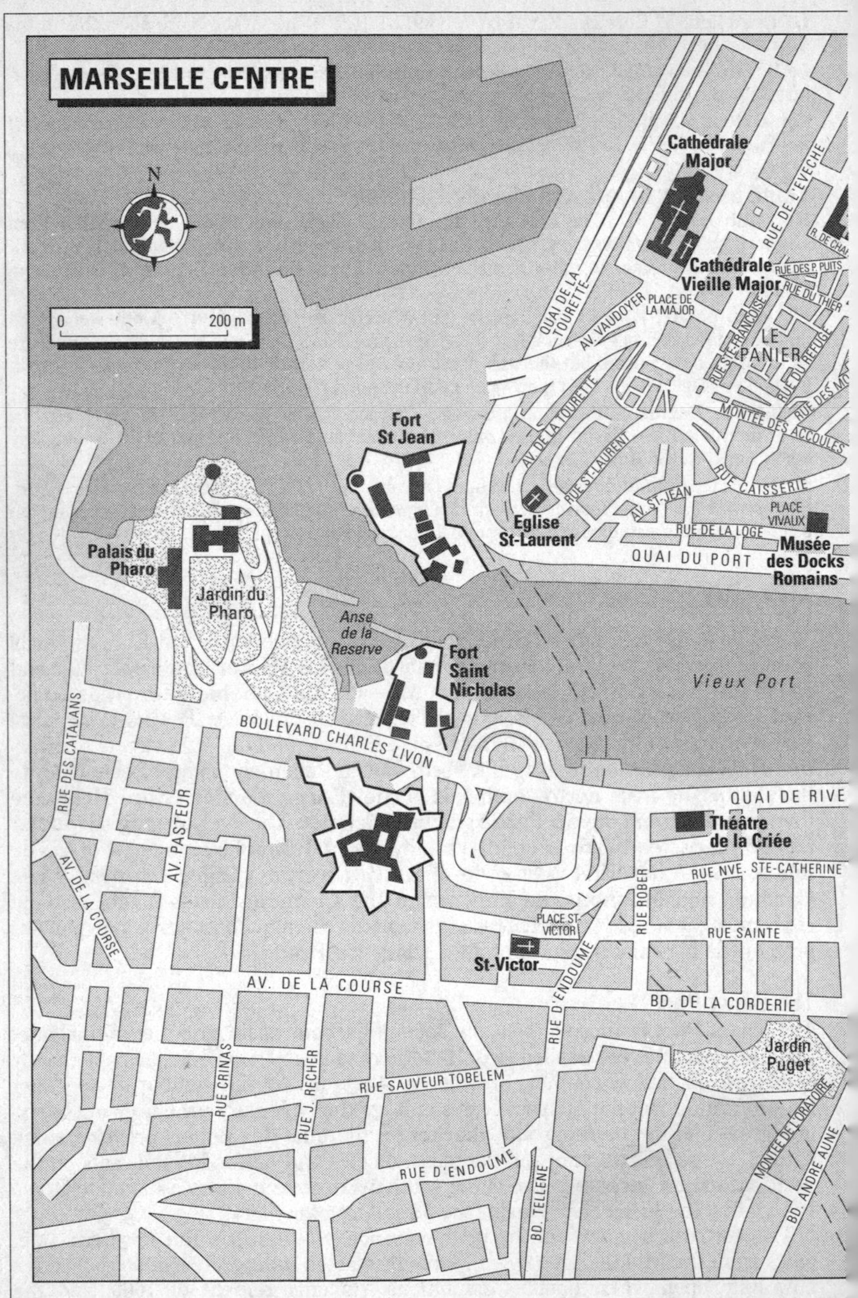
MARSEILLE CENTRE
N
0
200 m
Cathédrale
Major
Cathédrale
Vieille Major
PLACE DE
LA MAJOR
LE
PANIER
QUAI DE LA
TOURETTE
AV. VAUDOYER
RUE DE L'EVECHE
RUE DES P. PUITS
RUE DU THIER
RUE STE FRANÇOISE
RUE DU REFUGE
MONTEE DES ACCOULES
RUE CAISSERIE
AV. DE LA TOURETTE
RUE ST-LAURENT
AV. ST-JEAN
RUE DE LA LOGE
PLACE
VIVAUX
Fort
St Jean
Eglise
St-Laurent
QUAI DU PORT
Musée
des Docks
Romains
Palais du
Pharo
Jardin du
Pharo
Anse
de la
Reserve
Fort
Saint
Nicholas
Vieux Port
BOULEVARD CHARLES LIVON
QUAI DE RIVE
Théâtre
de la Criée
RUE DES CATALANS
AV. PASTEUR
AV. DE LA COURSE
RUE NVE. STE-CATHERINE
RUE ROBER
PLACE ST-
VICTOR
RUE SAINTE
St-Victor
RUE D'ENDOUME
AV. DE LA COURSE
BD. DE LA CORDERIE
Jardin
Puget
RUE CRINAS
RUE J. RECHER
RUE SAUVEUR TOBELEM
RUE D'ENDOUME
BD. TELLENE
MONTEE DE L'ORATOIRE
BD. ANDRE AUNE

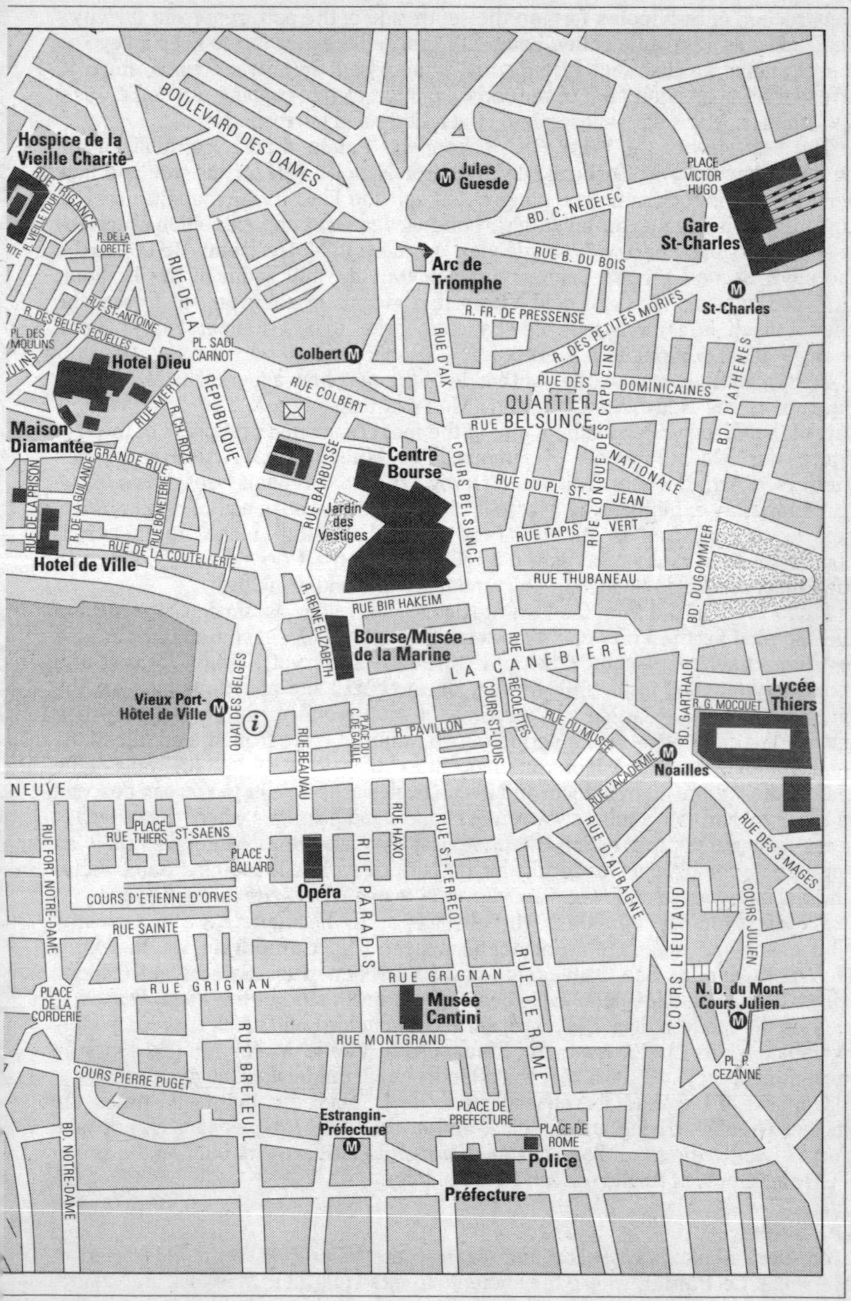

Hospice de la Vieille Charité
BOULEVARD DES DAMES
Jules Guesde
PLACE VICTOR HUGO
BD. C. NEDELEC
Gare St-Charles
RUE B. DU BOIS
Arc de Triomphe
St-Charles
R. FR. DE PRESSENSE
R. DES PETITES MORIES
RUE TRIGANCE
R. DE LA LORETTE
RUE DE LA REPUBLIQUE
RUE ST-ANTOINE
R. DES BELLES ECUELLES
PL. DES MOULINS
PL. SADI CARNOT
Colbert
Hotel Dieu
RUE MERY
R. CH. ROZE
RUE COLBERT
RUE D'AIX
RUE DES DOMINICAINES
QUARTIER BELSUNCE
BD. D'ATHENES
RUE LONGUE DES CAPUCINS
Maison Diamantée
GRANDE RUE
RUE DE LA PRISON
R. DE LA GUILANDE
RUE BONETERIE
RUE BARBUSSE
Centre Bourse
COURS BELSUNCE
NATIONALE
RUE DU PL. ST-JEAN
Jardin des Vestiges
RUE TAPIS VERT
RUE DE LA COUTELLERIE
Hotel de Ville
RUE THUBANEAU
BD. DUGOMMIER
R. REINE ELIZABETH
RUE BIR HAKEIM
Bourse/Musée de la Marine
RUE RECOLETTES
LA CANEBIERE
QUAI DES BELGES
Vieux Port-Hôtel de Ville
COURS ST-LOUIS
BD. GARTHALDI
R. G. MOCQUET
Lycée Thiers
RUE BEAUVAU
PLACE DU C. DE GAULLE
R. PAVILLON
RUE DU MUSEE
RUE L'ACADEMIE
Noailles
NEUVE
RUE FORT NOTRE-DAME
RUE THIERS
PLACE ST-SAENS
PLACE J. BALLARD
RUE HAXO
RUE ST-FERREOL
RUE PARADIS
RUE D'AUBAGNE
RUE DES 3 MAGES
Opéra
COURS D'ETIENNE D'ORVES
COURS LIEUTAUD
COURS JULIEN
RUE SAINTE
RUE GRIGNAN
PLACE DE LA CORDERIE
Musée Cantini
RUE DE ROME
N. D. du Mont Cours Julien
RUE MONTGRAND
RUE BRETEUIL
COURS PIERRE PUGET
PL. P. CEZANNE
BD. NOTRE-DAME
PLACE DE PREFECTURE
Estrangin-Préfecture
PLACE DE ROME
Police
Préfecture

construction of **St-Nicolas** fort, on the south side of the port, represent the city's final defeat as a separate entity. Louis XIV ordered the new fort to keep an eye on the city after he had sent in an army, suppressed the city's council, fined it, arrested all opposition and, in an early example of rate-capping, set ludicrously low limits on Marseille's subsequent expenditure and borrowing.

The best view of the *Vieux Port* is from the **Palais du Pharo**, built on the headland beyond Fort St-Nicolas by Emperor Napoléon III for his wife and now used for major rock concerts, congresses and the like. Its surrounding park is currently being dug up for an underground *mediathèque* and exhibition space but is still accessible. For a wider-angle view, head up to **Notre-Dame-de-la-Garde**, the city's Second Empire landmark which tops the hill south of the harbour. Crowned by a monumental gold Virgin that gleams to ships far out to sea, the church itself is a monstrous neo-Byzantine riot (daily summer 7am–7.30pm; winter 7.30am–5.30pm; free; bus #60).

Two small museums on the south side of the port may appeal. The **Musée du Santon**, 47 rue Neuve Ste-Catherine (Mon–Sat 9am–noon & 2.30–7pm; free), is part of the Carbonnel workshop, one of the most renowned producers of the crib figures for which Provence is famous. The **Maison de l'Artisanat et des Métiers d'Art**, 21 cours Estienne d'Orves (Tues–Sat 1–6pm; free), hosts excellent temporary exhibitions on Marseillais themes: from soap and olive oil production to the cultures of the different nationalities that make up the city's population. Two doors away is the intellectual haunt of *Les Arcenaulx*, a restaurant, *salon-de-thé* and bookshop (see under "Eating and drinking").

A short way inland from the Fort St-Nicolas, above the Bassin de Carénage and the slip road for the *Vieux Port*'s tunnel, is Marseille's oldest church, the **Abbaye St-Victor** (daily 8am–noon & 2–6pm; 10F entry for crypt). Originally part of a monastery founded in the fifth century on the burial site of various martyrs, the church was built, enlarged and fortified – a vital requirement given its position outside the city walls – over a period of two hundred years from the middle of the tenth century. It certainly looks and feels more like a fortress with the walls of the choir almost three metres thick, and it's no ecclesiastical beauty. You can descend to the crypt and catacombs, a warren of chapels and passages where the weight of stone and age, not to mention the photographs of skeletons exhumed, create an appropriate atmosphere to recall the horrors of early Christianity; Saint Victor himself, a Roman soldier, was slowly ground to death between two millstones.

Present Christian worship in the city has as its headquarters a less gloomy edifice but one of minimum aesthetic appeal. The **Cathédrale de la Major** (summer Mon & Sun 9am–noon & 2.30–5.30pm, Tues–Sat 8.30am–6.30pm; winter Tues–Sun 9am–noon & 2–5pm) on the north side of the *Vieux Port* overlooking the modern docks, is a striped neo-Byzantine solid block that completely overshadows its predecessor, the Romanesque **Vieille Major** (guided tours by appointment only, ☎91.90.53.57) that stands, much diminished, alongside.

Opposite the cathedrals, on esplanade de la Touret, a mural illustrates the ancient Greeks arriving at Marseille, and at the end of the esplanade, opposite Fort St-Jean, is the small Romanesque **Church of St-Laurent**, built on the site of a Greek Temple of Apollo (closed to the public).

Le Panier

From the cathedrals eastward, and down to the *Vieux Port*, is the oldest part of Marseille, **Le Panier**, where the ancient Greeks built their Massalia, and where, up until World War II, tiny streets, steep steps and houses of every era irregularly connected, formed a *Vieille Ville* typical of this coast. In 1943, however, Marseille was under **German occupation** and the quarter represented everything the Nazis feared and hated, an uncontrollable warren providing shelter for *"untermensch"* of every sort, including Resistance leaders, Communists and Jews. They gave the twenty thousand inhabitants one day's notice to leave. While the curé of St-Laurent pealed the bells in protest, squads of SS cleared the area and packed the people, including the curé, off to Fréjus, where concentration camp victims were selected. Out of seven hundred children, only sixty-eight returned. Dynamite was laid, carefully sparing the three old buildings that appealed to the Fascist aesthetic. Everything else, from the waterside to rue Caisserie and Grande Rue, was blown sky high.

After World War II, archeologists reaped some benefits from this destruction in the discovery of the remains of a warehouse on the first-century AD Roman docks. You can see vast food-storage jars for oil, grain and spices in their original positions, and part of the original jetty along with models, mock-ups and a video to complete the picture at the **Musée des Docks Romains** on place Vivaux (summer Tues–Sun 11am–6pm; winter Tues–Sun 10am–5pm; 10F).

The quarter preserves some of its old identity at the top of the slope, but the quayside area is postwar quick-and-cheap-build concrete. The landmark buildings that the Nazis spared are the seventeenth-century **Hôtel de Ville** on the quay, the half-Gothic, half-Renaissance **Hôtel de Cabre** on the corner of rue Bonneterie and Grande Rue and the **Maison Diamantée** of 1620, so called for the pointed shape of its facade stonework, on rue de la Prison. Neighbouring building works have disturbed the Maison Diamantée's foundations so it may be closed for repairs. Check though, as it houses the **Musée de Vieux Marseille** (summer Tues–Sun 11am–6pm; winter 10am–5pm; 15F), a wonderful hotch-potch of mementos celebrating old Marseille. One of the largest exhibits is a scaled model of the central area across La Canebière, made to commemorate the insurrection of June 1848. The model shows miniature dead bodies, people falling and shooting, plus all the streets that disappeared soon afterwards when the **Palais de Bourse** was built, specifically to erase *quartiers* that the authorities could not trust. There are also moving photographs of Le Panier prior to the Germans' similar, though more drastic, action, including a model of the transporter bridge across the *Vieux Port* that went with the dynamite. Another section covers the plague: antidote recipes, doctors' bizarre costumes and implements for purifying letters.

At the junction of rue de la Prison and rue Caisserie, the steps of Montée des Accoules lead up and across to **place de Lenche**, site of the Greek *agora*, a few blocks south of the cathedrals and a good café stop. The former Jesuit college, **Préau des Accoules**, at 29 Montée des Accoules, puts on exhibitions specially designed for children (summer Wed 2–6pm; winter Wed 1–5pm; free).

What's left of old Le Panier is above here, though the fifteen windmills of place des Moulins disappeared in the nineteenth century, and if you climb rue du Réfuge you'll find yourself in a modern demolition clearing. The exposed inner walls of old tenement buildings have superb state-of-the-art **murals** of TV screens and loud speakers, in violent contrast to the refined cultural centre at the far end of the clearing. This is the **Hospice de la Vieille Charité**, a seventeenth-century workhouse with a gorgeous Baroque chapel surrounded by columned arcades in pink stone. Only the tiny grilled exterior windows recall its original use. Local people say it was *"beaucoup plus jolie"* when a hundred families, all with at least ten children, lived in the hospice before it was dolled up. They scoff at the gentrification of Le Panier and jokingly ask how the bourgeois are going to get to the hospice without passing through this working-class and immigrant quarter.

But come they do, though only for the temporary exhibitions – usually brilliant – and evening concerts. The rest of the time the hospice is extraordinarily deserted, despite its two museums, café and excellent bookshop. The **Musée d'Archéologie Méditerranéenne** (Tues–Sun 10am–5pm; 15F, 25F for both museums) contains some very beautiful fourth- and fifth-century BC pottery and glass, an Egyptian collection with mummies and their accompanying boxes for internal organs plus a mummified crocodile. It also displays fascinating finds from a Celto-Légurian settlement between Marseille and Aix at Roquepertuse, including a double-headed statue. Less appealing is the **Musée des Arts Africains, Océaniens et Amérindiens** (Tues–Sun 10am–5pm; 15F, 25F for both museums), which is dark and spooky with a horrible collection of dried heads, and tediously long panels of text.

La Canebière and around

La Canebière, the famed broad boulevard that runs for about a kilometre down to the port, is the undisputed hub of the town, its name taken from the hemp (*canabé*) that once grew here and provided the raw materials for the town's thriving rope-making trade. Fashioned originally with the Champs-Elysées in mind, La Canebière is more a patchwork affair of hotels, cafés and shops, and, at the port end, two eminently missable museums: the **Musée de la Marine et de l'Economie** (Mon & Wed–Sun 10am–noon & 2–6pm; 15F), housed on the ground floor of the Neoclassical stock exchange, is filled with intricate models and paintings of ships on the high seas; while the **Musée de la Mode**, a bit further up at no. 11 (Mon–Sat noon–7pm; 25F), is only worth a visit if there are several exhibitions on, though there's no guarantee they'll be exciting. Better to head down to the basement and flip through books on design and fashion for free.

Behind the stock exchange is the **Centre Bourse** shopping centre and the **Jardin des Vestiges**, where the ancient port extended, curving northwards from the present quai des Belges. Excavations have revealed a stretch of the Greek port and bits of the city wall with the base of three square towers and a gateway, dated to the second or third century BC. Complementing the *Vestiges*, the beautifully lit and spaced **Musée d'Histoire de Marseille** inside the Centre Bourse (summer Tues–Sun 11am–6pm; winter Tues–Sun 10am–5pm; 15F), shows the main finds of Marseillaise excavations, of which the most dramatic is a third-century AD wreck of a Roman trading vessel. There's models of the city, reconstructed boats, everyday items like shoes and baskets, and a beautiful Roman mosaic of a dolphin, plus a great deal of information on text panels and a video about the Roman, Greek and pre-Greek settlements. Laws that were posted up in Greek Massalia are cited, forbidding women to drink wine and allowing would-be suicides to take hemlock if the 600-strong "parliament" agreed. One criticism: the "pyramid of power" diagram fails to point out the absence of women and slaves from Greek democracy.

While you're in the Centre Bourse, you could check out the free debates and arts events hosted by *FNAC* bookshop (Mon–Sat 10am–7pm; monthly programme available from the first floor).

Cours Belsunce/rue d'Aix, site of the mid-June to mid-July **garlic market**, runs west from the Canebière to **Porte d'Aix**, Marseille's *Arc de Triomphe*. This was part of the city's grandiose mid-nineteenth-century expansion which included the Cathédrale de la Major and the new Joliette docks, paid for with the profits of military enterprise, most significantly the conquest of Algeria in 1830. Today it's one of the North African male community's meeting places, where news and gossip is shared without the expense of cups of coffee.

Between cours Belsunce and rue d'Aix, bd d'Athènes and St Charles, the **quartier Belsunce** is very much an Arab district, though not exclusively so with many of the city's artists' studios and cheap apartments, lived in by all sorts. As well as hundreds of tiny shops selling North African food, music, household goods and clothes, trading takes place, on flattened cardboard boxes on the streets, of hi-fis, suits and jeans from France and Germany, and spices, cloth and metalware from across the Mediterranean. It's a huge and dynamic market without any French middlemen, hence the fear and anger it arouses in some quarters.

At the top end of bd d'Athènes, a monumental stairway leads up to **Gare St-Charles**. It was laid out in the 1920s with Art Deco railings, lamps and mammoth statues and has steps wide enough for people to sit and chat, play cards or lie drunk without constituting an obstruction.

More Arab trading, on a smaller scale, takes place just south of La Canebière around the lively **Marché des Capucines** (Mon–Sat 8am–7pm) by the former *Gare de l'Est*, now the **Galerie des Transports**, a museum dedicated to the city's public tranport (Wed–Sat 10am–5pm; free). The streets around here are fairly seedy, with plenty of insalubrious hotels and, come nightfall, prostitutes on every corner who, somehow typically for Marseille, tend to be quite exceptional in their friendliness to other women passing by.

The prime shopping quarter of Marseille, and a continuation of the red-light district, is encompassed by three streets running south from La Canebière: rue de Rome, rue Paradis and rue St-Ferréol which terminates at the pseudo-Renaissance Préfecture, where demonstrations in the city traditionally converge. Side streets like rue du Pavillon are full of tempting café and *pâtissier* stops: this is a good area for a midday meal.

Between rue St-Ferréol and rue de Rome, on rue Grignan, is the city's most important art museum, the **Musée Cantini** (summer Tues–Sun 11am–6pm; winter Tues–Sun 10am–7pm; 10F, 15F for exhibitions). The paintings and sculptures here date from the end of the nineteenth century up to the 1950s. The Fauvists and Surrealists are well represented along with works by Matisse, Léger, Picasso, Ernst, Le Corbusier, Miró and Giacometti. Only a proportion of the permanent collection is displayed at any one time, and even less during the many excellent temporary exhibitions.

The **daily market** known as **La Plaine** on place Jean-Jaurès is best on Saturday with a typically Marseille mix of food, underwear, cloth and bargain Italian shoes. The streets between place Julien and cours Julien are full of bars and music shops, and the *cours* itself, with pools, fountains, and restaurant tables, is one of the most pleasant places to idle in the city. *Madame Zaza of Marseille*, an original and affordable Marseillaise couturier, has her shop at no. 73; there are bookshops and art galleries to browse in, and a Sunday stamp market, with antiques and junk every second Sunday in summer months.

Northeast of La Canebière

The **Palais de Longchamp**, 2km east of the port (bus #80 and #41 or métro Longchamp-Cinq-Avenues), went up in 1869, the year when the opening of the Suez Canal gave a crucial advantage to the Mediterranean ports, bringing a new boom for

MARSEILLE'S COMMUNE

Within the space of four years from its completion in 1867, the Marseille **Préfecture** had flown the imperial flag, the red flag and the tricolour. The red flag was flying in 1871, during Marseille's Commune. The counter-revolutionary forces advanced from Aubagne, encountering little resistance, and took the heights of Notre-Dame-de-la-Garde from where they directed their cannons down onto the Préfecture. The defeat was swifter but no less bloody than the fate of the Parisian Communards. One of the Marseillaise leaders, Gaston Crémieux, a young idealistic bourgeois with great charisma, escaped the initial carnage but was subsequently caught. Despite clemency pleas from all quarters of the city, Thiers, president of the newly formed Third Republic and a native of Marseille, would not relent and Crémieux was shot by a firing squad near the Pharo Palace in November 1871.

Marseillais trade. It was built as the grandiose conclusion of an aqueduct at Roquefavour (no longer in use) bringing water from the Durance to the city. Water is still pumped into the centre of the colonnade connecting the two palatial wings of the building. Below, an enormous statue looks as if it's honouring some great feminist victory: three well-muscled women stand above four bulls wallowing passively in a pool from which a cascade drops the four or five storeys to ground level.

The palace's north wing is the city's **Musée des Beaux-Arts** (summer Tues–Sun 11am–6pm; winter Tues–Sun 10am–5pm; 15F), a hot and slightly stuffy place, but with a fair share of delights. Most unusual, and a very pleasant visual treat, are three paintings by Françoise Duparc (1726–76), whose first name has consistently found itself masculinized to François in both French and English catalogues. The nineteenth-century satirist from Marseille, Honoré Daumier, who served six months for his suitably vicious caricatures of Louis Philippe's government, has a whole room dedicated to his cartoons. Plans for the city, sculptures, and the famous profile of Louis XIV by the Marseille-born Pierre Puget are on display along with graphic contemporary canvases of the plague that decimated the city in 1720. The other wing of the palace is taken up with the **Musée d'Histoire Naturelle** – mouldy stuffed animals and lots and lots of fossils.

Just before you reach the palace is the **Musée Grobet-Labadi** (summer Tues–Sun 11am–6pm; winter Tues–Sun 10am–5pm; 15F), 140 bd Longchamp, a typical late nineteenth-century bourgeois townhouse filled with exquisite objects, but not wildly interesting. Northwest of the palace at the end of bd Mal-Juin stands the brand new **Hôtel du Département** (Metro St-Just). Deliberately set away from the centre of town in the run-down St-Just-Chartreux *quartier*, the new seat of local government for the Bouches-du-Rhône *département* is the biggest public building to be erected in the French provinces this century. It was designed by the English architect William Alsop, who used his hallmark ovoid glass tube shapes above and alongside vast rectangular blocks of blue steel and glass. In front of it, like a vast turtle's back, is the **Dôme**, a venue for shows and exhibitions. The hotel's great glass foyer is accessible during working hours and the tourist office can arrange architectural tours.

South: the Cité Radieuse, MAC, Parcs Chanot and Borély

Av du Prado, the continuation of rue de Rome, is an eight-lane highway, with impressive fountains and one of the biggest **daily markets** between métros Castellane and Perrier. At the Rond-Point du Prado, the avenue turns west to meet the corniche road at the statue of Michaelangelo's *David*.

Bd Michelet continues southwards alongside **Parc Chanot**, the city's biggest sports complex with Olympique de Marseille's ground. Despite OM's current relegation, their reputation for occasional brilliance is not in question and Marseille matches are always sold out.

Beyond Parc Chanot, set back just west of the boulevard, is a mould-breaking piece of architecture, Le Corbusier's **Cité Radieuse**, designed in 1946 and completed in 1952. A seventeen-storey housing complex on stilts, the *Cité* only fails to amaze now because so many apartment buildings the world over have imitated, inadequately more often than not, Le Corbusier's revolutionary model. There are 23 different layouts for the apartments, to suit single people and varying sized families, the larger ones with an upstairs and downstairs and balconies on both sides of the building with unhindered views of mountains and sea. One floor has shops, restaurants, a nursery and a post office. There's a hotel (see p.172) and, at the top, sports and recreational facilities amid sculptural and ceramic decoration. The whole complex is surrounded by lawns: a "vertical garden city" Le Corbusier called it, and a "*unité d'habitation*" in which each element, and most crucially the individual tenant, has autonomy within the collective space. Many of the original tenants are still in residence. To reach the *Cité* take the métro to Rd-Pt du Prado, then bus #21 to *Le Corbusier*.

Further south, at 69 av d'Haïfa, (bus #23 or #45 from métro Rd-Pt-du Prado, stop *Haïfa* or *Marie-Louise*), is the contemporary art museum, **MAC** (summer Tues–Sun 11am–6pm; winter Tues–Sun 10am–5pm; 15F). The permanent collection, displayed in perfect, pure-white surroundings, is the continuation of the Cantini collection, with works from the 1960s to the present. The artists include the Marseillais César and Ben, along with Buren, Christo, Klein, Niki de St-Phalle, Tinguely and Warhol. There's also the Cinémac (☎91.25.01.07), a cinema showing feature films, shorts and videos on different themes each month.

Between av d'Haïfa and the sea, just off av Prado is **Parc Borély**, with ponds, palm trees, a rose garden, botanical gardens (Mon–Fri 10am–5.30pm, Sat 1–5.30pm; free) and no restrictions about walking or picnicking on the grass. It was originally the grounds of the **Château Borély**, an eighteenth-century mansion which the town hall keeps promising to turn into a decorative arts museum. Next to the park is the race course with its old, elegant stands on the promenade by the Plage du Prado.

The Corniche and south to Les Goudes

The most popular stretch of sand close to the city centre is the small **plage des Catalans**, a few blocks south of the Palais du Pharo. This marks the beginning of Marseille's **Corniche av J-F-Kennedy**, initiated and partly built after the 1848 revolution, giving work to eight thousand unemployed. Despite its inland bypass of the Malmousque peninsula it's a corniche as good as any on the Riviera, with *belle époque* villas on the slopes above, the Iles d'Endoume and the Château d'If in the distance, cliffs below and high bridge piers for the road to cross the inlets of La Fausse-Monnaie and Les Auffes where the Monument aux Morts de l'Armée d'Orient frames its statue against the setting sun.

Prior to 1948, Malmousque and the **Vallon des Auffes** were inaccessible from the town unless you followed the "customs mens' path" over the rocks or took a boat. There was nothing on Malmousque, but the Vallon des Auffes had a fresh water source and a small community of fishermen and rope-makers. Amazingly it is not much different today, with fishing boats pulled up around the rocks, tiny jumbled houses and restaurants to serve the catch. Only one road, rue du Vallon-des-Auffes, leads out; otherwise it's the long flights of steps up to the corniche.

Malmousque is now a very desirable residential district, favoured by the champagne-socialist set, with Marseille's most expensive hotel-restaurant, *Le Petit Nice*, at one end and a military barracks at the other. Between the *terrain militaire* and the Anse de la Fausse-Monnaie there's a **coastal path** you can follow with views along the coast to Cap Croisette and out to the offshore islands. It's linked by steps to tiny bays and beaches: perfect for secluded swimming when the Mistral isn't whipping up the waves.

Behind the **Fausse-Monnaie** inlet, a path leads to an open-air theatre, set in a wilderness of trees and flowers unimaginable in any city other than Marseille. There's more greenery, of a formal nature, a short way further down the Corniche in the **Jardin Valmer** (bus stop *Corniche-J-Martin*) and you can explore the tiny streets that lead up into this prime district of mansions with high-walled gardens.

The Corniche J-F Kennedy ends at the Plage du Prado, the city's main sand beaches backed by a wide strip of lawns and the ugly Espace Borély complex of shops and restaurants. The promenade continues, however, with a glittering array, particularly at night, of restaurants, clubs and cafés all the way to Montredon. Marseille's newest museum, the **Musée de la Faïence** (summer Tues–Sun 11am–6pm; winter Tues–Sun 10am–5pm; 10F), is at 157 av de Montredon, in the nineteenth-century Château Pastré, set in a huge park that extends to the foot of the Montagne de Marseilleveyre (bus #19 from métro Rd-Pt du Prado, stop *Montredon-Chancel*). The eighteenth- and nineteenth-century ceramics, many of them produced in Marseille, are pretty enough, but the most stunning part of this small collection are the modern and contemporary pieces.

From Montredon to Les Goudes, where the gleaming white, beautifully desolate hills finally meet the sea and the coast road ends, there are easily accessible *calanques* (rocky inlets) that face the setting sun, ideal for evening swims and supper picnics. If you prefer to walk, the GR98 to Cassis starts from the top of av de la Grotte-Roland, off av de Montredon a short way beyond the Pastré park. It splits into the 98a which follows the ridge inland and 98b which descends to the sea at Callelongue, the last outpost of Les Goudes. *La Grotte* bar here is where walkers gather. A map of the paths is available from the tourist office: ask for their leaflet on the Calanques.

The Islands

> *Blacker than the sea, blacker than the sky, rose like a phantom the giant of granite, whose projecting crags seemed like arms extended to seize their prey.*

So the **Château d'If** appears to Edmond Dantès, hero of Alexandre Dumas' *The Count of Monte Cristo*, having made his watery escape after five years of incarceration as the innocent victim of treachery. In reality most prisoners of this island fortress died before they reached the end of their sentences – unless they were nobles living in the less fetid upper-storey cells, like one de Niozelles who was given six years for failing to take his hat off in the presence of Louis XIV, and Mirabeau who had run up massive debts with shops in Aix. More often, the crimes were political. After the revocation of the Edict of Nantes in 1685, thousands of Marseillais Protestants who refused to accept the new law were sent to the galleys and their leaders entombed in the Château d'If. Revolutionaries of 1848 drew their last breath here.

There's nothing else to the Ile d'If apart from the castle. Dumas fans will love it, others may raise an eyebrow at the cell marked "Dantès" in the same fashion as non-fictional inmates' names. But it's a (horribly) well-preserved sixteenth-century edifice and the views back towards Marseille are the best.

Boats leave from the quai des Belges at 6.45am and every hour from 9am to noon and 2 to 5pm, plus one at 6.30pm with slight seasonal variations. The château's opening hours fit the boat timetable and the journey takes fifteen minutes and costs around 40F. At rather more expense (60F) you can do a round trip taking in the other two islands of the **Frioul archipelago**, **Pomègues** and **Ratonneau**, which are joined by a causeway enclosing a yachting harbour. In days gone by these islands were used as a quarantine station, most ineffectually in the early 1720s when a ship carrying the plague was given the go-ahead to dock in the city, resulting in the decimation of half the population.

The **Iles d'Endoume**, the islands off Malmousque, with their abandoned monastery, can't be visited.

Eating and drinking

The Marseillais eat just as well, if not better, than the ancient aristos and skin-stretched stars of the Riviera. Fish and seafood are the main ingredients, and the superstar of dishes is the city's own expensive invention, **bouillabaisse**, a saffron- and garlic-flavoured fish soup with bits of fish, croutons and *rouille* to throw in and conflicting theories about which fish should be included and where and how they must be caught. The other city speciality is the less exotic *pieds et paquets*, mutton or lamb belly and trotters.

The best, and most expensive, **restaurants** are close to the Corniche, while for international choice cours Julien is the best place to head for. The pedestrian precinct behind the south quay of the *Vieux Port* is more upmarket and fishy, with plenty more restaurants between the Opéra and La Canebière. Cheap snacks are to be had in Le Panier as well as some good old-time bistros, and from the stands along cours Belsunce you can buy fries and sandwiches stuffed with meat dishes for under 15F.

As Marseille is a Mediterranean city, people tend to stay up late in summer. Around the *Vieux Port*, from place Jean-Jaurès to cours Julien, and the Plage du Prado are the areas where there are always lots of people around and **cafés** and **restos** open well into the night. Be warned that many restaurants take very long summer breaks.

Restaurants, cafés and bars

L'Abri Cotier, 1 bd des Baigneurs, 8e (☎91.72.27.29). Lovely restaurant overlooking the sea in Montredon. Around 150F. May–Sept daily; Oct to mid-Dec, March & April Wed–Sun noon only.

Chez Angèle, 50 rue Caisserie, 2e (☎91.90.63.35). Packed Le Panier local, with a bargain *menu fixe* for basic French food. Closed Sat evening, Sun & Aug.

Les Arcenaulx, 25 cours d'Estienne-d'Orves, 1er (☎91.54.77.06). Superb food for 250F to 300F a head in this intellectual haunt, which is also a bookshop. Cheap midday menus on weekdays. Last orders 11.30pm. Mon–Sat.

L'Art et les Thés, Centre de la Vieille Charité, 2er. The cultural centre's tea room. Mon & Wed–Sun noon–7pm.

L'Assiette Marine, 142 av Mendez-France, 8e (☎91.71.04.04). Serves fresh pasta in lobster sauce, aubergine and lamb with truffles, and other exquisite dishes, just north of the Plage du Prado. Menus at 135F and 300F.

Auberge "In", 25 rue du Chevalier-Roze, 2e (☎91.90.51.59). In a health-food shop on the edge of Le Panier. Vegetarian *menu fixe* served lunchtimes and early evenings. Mon–Sat.

Le Byblos Prado, 61 promenade de la Plage, 8e (☎91.22.80.66). Lebanese mezzes and wine from 150F. Closed Sun evening.

Le Cadratin, 17 rue St-Saëns, 1er. Friendly and cheap bar with Sixties music playing on the jukebox and a great mix of people, both foreign and local.

Pizzaria des Catalans, 3 rue des Catalans, 7e (☎91.52.37.82). Excellent pizzas just above the beach. Midday only Oct–April.

La Coupole, 5 rue Haxo, 1er. Elegant brasserie serving a midday plat du jour with a glass of wine for 100F. Seafood salads are a temptation. Daily 7am–midnight.

Dar Djerba, 15 cours Julien, 6e. Excellent Tunisian restaurant with beautiful tiling – ignore the stuffed camel's head. Around 150F.

L'Epuisette, Vallon des Auffes, 7e (☎91.52.17.82). Now that the renowned *Chez Fonfon* has changed hands, this is the place to eat the Auffes catch. From 200F. Closed Sun evening.

Chez Etienne, 43 rue Lorette, 2e. Another old-fashioned Le Panier bistro; hectic, cramped and crowded. Full meal 150–250F but you can just have a pizza. No bookings. Tues–Sat.

La Garbure, 9 cours Julien, 6e (☎91.47.18.01). Rich specialities from southwest France, including Bresse chicken. Around 150F. Closed Sat midday, Sun & mid-July to mid-Aug.

Chez Jimmy, rue Ste Françoise, 1er. Unnamed Le Panier snack bar opposite the *Bar des 13 Coins* serving very cheap sandwiches of meatballs, stuffed tomatoes, and chips.

La Kaena, 2 rue de la République, 2er. Popular Moroccan resto, with grills and couscous from 60F. Closed Mon midday & Sun.

Bar de la Marine, 15 quai Rive Neuve, 1er. A favourite bar for *Vieux Port* lounging and inspiration for Pagnol's celebrated Marseille trilogy. Mon–Sat.

Les Mets de Provence, 18 quai Rive-Neuve, 7e (☎91.33.35.38). A Marseille institution with authentic Provençal cooking and very reasonable midday menus. Closed Mon evening & Sun.

Chez Michel, 6 rue des Catalans, 7e (☎91.52.30.63). There's no debate about the *bouillabaisse* ingredients here. A basket of five fishes, including the elusive and most expensive one, the racasse, is presented to the customer before the soup is made. Quite simply the place to eat this dish. Expect to pay 250F for the *bouillabaisse* alone.

Chez Neale, 36 cours Julien, 6e. Salads, cakes and English breakfast served all day from 10am; brunch at weekends. Under 100F. Closed Mon evening and Sun.

Le Panier des Arts, 3 rue du Petit-Puits, 2e (☎91.56.02.32). Reasonably priced Provençal specialities, to a backgound of classical music, close to the Vieille Charité.

Café Parisien, 1 pl Sadi-Carnot, 2e. Very beautiful old-fashioned café, where people play cards and chess. Occasional painting exhibitions.

La Patalain, 49 rue Sainte, 1er (☎91.55.02.78). The head chef is a woman who excels at local specialities, in particular *pieds et paquets*. Menus from 190F. Closed Sat midday, Sun & mid-July to end-Aug.

Bar Le Petit Nice, 26 pl Jean-Jaurès, 1er. The place to head for on Sat morning during the market.

Bar de la Samaritaine, 2 quai du Port, 2e. The sunniest port-side bar with comfy terrace chairs.

Brasserie des Templiers, 21 rue Reine Elizabeth, 1er. Next to the Centre Bourse with quick eats and good beers.

Tom Pouce, 2 rue des Convalescents, 1er. Very cheap, studenty Tunisian resto in the quartier Belsunce.

Markets

The city's copious **street markets** provide a feast of fruit and veg, olives, cheeses, sausages and spit-roast chickens – everything you'd need for a picnic except for wine, which is most economically bought at supermarkets. The markets are also good for cheap clothes, particularly shoes. La Plaine and av du Prado are the biggest; the Capucins the oldest. On Sunday afternoons, when all else is closed, there's the **Marché du Soleil** and a few food stalls along rue Longue des Capucins (métro Noailles).

Marseille's Sunday morning **flea market** is a brilliant spectacle, and good for serious haggling. There's a relaxed atmosphere, plenty of cafés, and everything and anything for sale, including very cheap fruit and veg.

The markets

Quai des Belges, Vieux Port, 1er; métro Vieux Port. Fish sold straight off the boats; daily 8am–1pm.

Capucins, pl des Capucins, 1er; métro Noailles. Food Mon–Sat; with more fish, fruit and veg in the Halles Delacroix on rue Halles-Delacroix towards rue de Rome; 8am–7pm.

Place Carli, 1er; métro Nouailles. Antiquarian books and records. Daily 10am–5pm.

Cours Julien, 6e; métro N.-D.-du-Mont–Cours Julien. Food Mon–Sat; stamps Sun; antiquarian books second Sat of month; bric-à-brac second Sun of month.

Allées de Meilhan, La Canebière, 1e; métro Réformés. Flowers Tues & Sat; 8am–1pm.

La Plaine, pl Jean-Jaurès, 5e; métro N.-D.-du-Mont-Cours Julien. Food daily; general goods Tues, Thurs & Sat; organic produce Fri; 8am–1pm.

Prado, av du Prado, 6e; métro Castellane and Perrier. Food and general goods daily; flowers Fri; 8am–1pm.

Marché aux Puces, av du Cap-Pinède, 15e; bus #35, stop *Cap-Pinède* or #70, or bus #36, stop Lyon from métro Bougainville. Food Wed–Sun; antiques Fri–Sun; bric-à-brac Sat; flea market Sun; 8am–7pm.

Marché du Soleil, rue du Bon-Pasteur, 1er; métro Colbert/Jules Guesde. Food served daily 8am–7pm.

Specialist shops

Le Carthage, 8 rue d'Aubagne, 1er. Best Tunisian *pâtisseries* and Turkish delight.

Castelmuro, 31 rue paradis, 1er & 137 rue Jean-Mermoz, 8e. One of the best and upmarket *charcuterie*, chocolate and *pâtisserie* shop.

La Chaise Longue, 33 rue de Paradis, 1er. Stylish coffee cups and other household accessories.

Fuéri-Lamy, 21 rue Paradis, 1er. English books. Tues–Sun.

Librarie des Editions Parenthèse, 72 cours Julien, 6e. Books on architecture, art, cinema, photography and music.

Maupetit, 140 Canebière, 1er. Good general French bookshop.

La Passerelle, 26 rue des Trois-Mages, 1er. Café, travel agency and comic shop. Mon–Sat noon–midnight.

Nightlife and entertainment

Marseille's **nightlife** has something for everyone, with plenty of live rock and jazz, nightclubs and discos, as well as the more choice pastimes of theatre-, opera- and concert-going. Theatre is particularly innovative and lively in Marseille. The *Virgin Megastore* at 75 rue St-Ferréol is the best place to go for **tickets and information** on gigs, concerts, theatre, free films and whatever cultural events are going on. They also stock a wide selection of English books and run a café on the top floor, open, like the rest of the store, seven days a week until midnight. Other places to head for info are the book and record shop *FNAC* on the top floor of the Centre Bourse (Mon–Sat 10am–7pm), *La Passerelle* (see "Specialist shops" above), and the New Age music shop *Tripsichord* next door. At any of these places, you can pick up a copy of *Taktik*, Marseille's independent free weekly listings paper, which comes out on a Wednesday.

In an old abandoned abattoir just north of the Marché des Puces (bus #25/26 stop *Abattoirs*) various alternative theatre groups, bands and artists hang out and perform. It's not easy to find out details other than by paying a visit.

Live music

La Cave à Jazz, 24 quai de Rive-Neuve, 7e. Jazz club and a place for rock, fashion, theatre and dance.

Cité de la Musique, 4 rue Bernard du Bois, 1er (☎91.39.28.28). Jazz cellar and auditorium.

Le Degust Rock, 12 pl Jean-Jaurès, 5e. Small, rough, noisy and fun with rap, ragga muffin, rock and blues.

Maison de l'Etranger, 9 av Général Leclerc, 3e (☎91.28.24.01). A club not far from the *gare SNCF* St-Charles, which puts on regular world music gigs, especially Raï.

La Maison Hantée, 10 rue Vian, 6e (☎91.92.09.40). Country music, r'n'b and rock. Tues–Sun.

May Be Blues, rue Poggioli, 6e (☎91.42.41.00). Relaxed blues/jazz club. No entry charge, though drinks go up once the music starts. Wed–Sun 8pm–2am.

Au Moulin, 47 bd Perrin, 13e (☎91.06.33.94) métro St-Just. An obscure venue in the northwest of the city specializing in weird and wonderful European bands.

Pelle Mêle, 8 pl aux Huiles, 1er (☎91.53.85.26). Jazz bistro and piano bar. Mon–Sat 5pm–2am.

Le Stendhal, 92 rue Jean-de-Bernady, 1er (☎91.84.74.80). Wide selection of malt whiskies and beers, including Courage. Live music Tues & Thurs. Red and black interior, after Stendhal's novel.

Nightclubs

New Cancan, 20 rue Sénac, 1er (☎91.47.50.18). Gay club with high camp and transvestite shows.

Le New Orleans, 1 quai de Rive Neuve, 1er (☎91.54.71.09). Dancing from jazz be-bop to current chart toppers.

Le Pourquoi Pas, 1 rue Fortia, 1er (☎91.33.50.54). Offers Caribbean music and punch to get drunk on.

Rose Bonbon, 7 rue Venture, 1er, just off rue Paradis (☎91.67.99.15). As good a place as any if you're determined to bop.

Trolleybus, 24 quai de Rive-Neuve, 7e (☎91.54.30.45). Piano bar and disco in a series of vaulted rooms; mainly popular rock. Thurs–Sun.

Film, opera, theatre and concerts

Ballet National de Marseille, 20 bd Gabès, 8e (☎91.71.03.03). Roland Petit's famous dance company's home base.

Bastide de la Magalone, 245 bd Michelet, 9e (☎91.39.28.28). Classical music concerts.

Chocolat Théâtre, 59 cours Julien, 6e (☎91.42.19.29). Theatre-restaurant-exhibition space with shows ranging from male striptease to avant-garde improvisations.

Cinéma Paris, 31 rue Pavillon, 1er (☎91.33.15.59). The only cinema in Marseille which regularly shows VO (*version originale* – undubbed) films.

Théâtre de la Criée, 30 quai de Rive-Neuve, 7e (☎91.54.74.54). Home of the *Théâtre National de Marseille* and Marseille's best theatre.

Espace Julien, 33 cours Julien, 6e (☎91.47.09.64). A mixed-bag arts centre, with theatre, jazz, dance and exhibitions.

Théâtre de Marionettes Massalia, 41, rue Jobin, 3e (☎91.62.39.51). Lively puppet theatre with constantly changing programme of adult (evening) and children's (matinee) shows.

Théâtre du Merlan, av Raimu, 14e (☎91.98.24.35). Set amid horrific high-rise housing in the north of the city, this cultural centre is remarkable for having a police commissariat on the ground floor. Occasional shows in English.

Opéra, 1 pl Reyer, 1er (☎91.55.00.70). Symphony concerts and operas.

Listings

Airlines *Air France*, 14 La Canebière, 1er (☎91.39.39.39); *Air Inter*, 8 rue des Fabres, 1er (☎91.39.36.36); *British Airways* (☎91.90.77.10) and *TWA* (☎91.91.66.44), both 41 La Canebière, 1er.

Airport information Aéroport de Marseille-Provence ☎42.78.21.00.

Car parks Cours d'Estienne-d'Orves, 1er; cours Julien, 1er; allées Léon-Gambetta, 1er; pl Monthyon, 6e; Centre Bourse, 1er; Gare St-Charles, 1er; pl Félix-Baret, 6e; pl Gal-de-Gaulle, 1er.

Car rental *Budget*, 232 av du Prado, 8e (☎91.71.75.00); *Citer*, 96 bd Rabatau, 8e (☎91.83.05.05); *Europcar*, 7 bd Maurice-Bourdet, 1er (☎91.90.11.00); *Thrifty*, 6 bd Voltaire, 1er (☎91.05.92.18).

Consulates *Canada*, 24 av du Prado, 6e (☎91.37.19.37); *Great Britain*, 24 av du Prado, 6e (☎91.53.43.32); *USA*, 12 bd Paul-Peytral, 6e (☎91.54.92.00); *Ireland*, 148 rue Sainte, 1er (☎91.54.92.29).

Currency exchange *Comptoir de Change Méditerranéen*, Gare St-Charles (daily 8am–6pm); *Comptoir Marseillais de Bourse*, 22 La Canebière (Mon–Sat 8.30am–7pm).

Disabled information *Office Municipal pour Handicappés*, 128 av du Prado, 8e (☎91.81.58.80) has information on disabled access and facilities, and operates a transport service (call ☎91.78.21.67 a day ahead).

Emergencies ☎15; *SOS Médecins* (☎91.52.91.52); 24-hr casualty departments: *La Conception*, 144 rue St-Pierre, 5e (☎91.38.36.52); *SOS Voyageurs*, Gare St-Charles, 3e (☎91.62.12.80) – English spoken, will try to help with any crisis.

Ferries *SNCM*, 61 bd des Dames (☎91.56.32.00), runs ferries to Corsica, Tunisia and Algeria.

Gay and lesbian information *Collectif Gai et Lesbien Marseille Provence*, Maison des Associations, 93 La Canebière (Thurs only 7–11pm; ☎91.92.38.48).

Lost property 10 rue de la Cathédrale, 2e (☎91.90.99.37).

Pharmacy Gare St-Charles (Mon–Fri 7am–10pm, Sat 7am–8pm).

Police Commissariat Centrale, 2 rue Antoine Becker, 2e (daily 8am–noon & 2–6pm; ☎91.39.80.00).

Post office *PTT*, 1 pl de l'Hôtel-des-Postes, 1er.

Taxis ☎91.02.20.20; ☎91.49.91.00; English speaking ☎91.97.12.12.

Women's centre *CODIF*, 81 rue Senac, 1er (☎91.47.14.05), runs a library and information centre.

L'Estaque and westwards

Marseille's docks and its northern coastal sprawl finally end at **L'ESTAQUE**, an erstwhile fishing village much loved by painters in the last century, and easy to get to by train (10min on Miramas train). It was no rural paradise even in 1867 as a gouache by Cézanne of the factory chimneys of L'Estaque shows (given to Madame Zola and now exhibited in his studio in Aix). Yet it still has fishing boats moored alongside yachts, and the new artificial beaches to the west ensure that L'Estaque remains a popular escape from the city. For a good fish dinner try *La*

Reserve, at 226 chemin de Riau (Mon–Sat; ☎91.46.11.19). If you just want a snack, *chichis* (long, scented doughnut-like things) from the *Chichis Fruguis* kiosk on the promenade are delicious.

Between L'Estaque and **CARRY-LE-ROUET**, the hills of the Chaine de l'Estaque come right down to the coast, a gorgeous wilderness of white rock, pines and brilliant yellow scented broom. The shore is studded with *calanques* where the water is exceptionally clean and you can look across the roadstead of Marseille to the islands and the entrance of the *Vieux Port*. The train tunnels its way above the shore while the main road, the N568, then D5, takes an inland route through **La Rove** and **Ensues-la-Redonne**, with smaller roads looping down to the fishing villages and summer holiday homes of **Niolon**, **MEJEAN** and **La-Redonne**. At Méjean simple meals of grilled fish and *petites fritures* are served overlooking the tiny port at *Le Mange Tout* (summer daily; ☎42.45.91.68).

The charm of this stretch of coast ends abruptly at Carry-le-Rouet which merges into its western neighbour **SAUSSET-LES-PINS** without any break in the seaside houses and apartment buildings. The only reason to stop would be to spend well over 300F on a **meal** at *L'Escale* on the promenade of Carry's port where the *gâteau de poissons* is said to be divine (closed Mon evening & Sun; ☎42.45.00.47). If you're **camping**, however, you could head further west to **TAMARIS**, a tiny village with several campsites including *Lou Cigalon*, Corniche des Tamaris (☎42.49.61.71), and *Les Tamaris*, Calanque des Tamaris (☎42.80.72.11), both open from April to September. Beyond Tamaris there are long sandy beaches around the pleasantly downmarket resort of **CARRO** and once you're round the corner, sumptious seaside sunsets are assured from the heavy dose of particles hovering above the vast petrochemical port of Fos.

Around the Etang de Berre

The shores of the 22-kilometre-long and 15km-kilometre-wide **Etang de Berre**, northwest of L'Estaque, are not the most obvious holiday destination. The lagoon is heavily polluted, especially around the southern edges near Marseille's airport, and the sources are only too visible: oil refineries, petrochemical plants and tankers heading in and out of the Caronte Canal linking the lagoon with the vast industrial complex and port on the Golfe de Fos.

There are, however, some unexpected pockets: the ancient remains at **St Blaise**, the perched villages of **Miramas-le-Vieux** and **Cornillon-Confoux**, and, despite its close proximity to Europe's largest oil refinery, the town of **Martigues**.

Martigues

MARTIGUES straddles both sides of the Caronte Canal and the island in the middle, at the southwest corner of the Etang de Berre. In the sixteenth century when the union of three separate villages, Jonquières to the south, Ferrières to the north and the island, known simply as l'Ile, created Martigues (and the French flag or so they claim), there were many more canals than the three today. But Martigues has joined the long list of places with waterways to be dubbed the "Venice" of the region, and it deserves the compliment, however fatuous the comparison.

In the centre of the Ile, beside the sumptuous facade of the **Eglise de la Madeleine**, a low bridge spans the **Canal St-Sébastien** where fishing boats moor and houses in ochre, pink and blue look straight down onto the water. This appealing spot is known as the **Miroir aux Oiseaux** and was painted by Corot, Ziem and others at the turn of the century, some of whose works, including Ziem's *Vieux Port de Marseille*, can be seen in the **Musée Ziem** on bd du Juillet in Ferrières (July & Aug Mon & Wed–Sun 10am–noon & 2.30–6.30pm; rest of the year Wed–Sun 2.30–6.30pm; 10F).

Behind the idle strolling quaysides of the Ile's canal, new housing has been designed on a pre-modern, acute-angled layout. From **quai Toulmond** the white, green, and mirror boxes of new municipal offices across the water and the towering highway bridge above the Caronte Canal match the masts and bright hulls of the pleasure boats tied up along the quay.

A nineteenth-century swing bridge alongside a more delapidated modern road bridge joins the Ile to **Ferrières**, whose tiny streets of shops and bars spread back from the focal point of place Jean-Jaurès. To the south, the tanker passage of the Canal Galiffet is spanned by a drawbridge taking you into **Jonquières**, the third and most lively of Martigues' centres, with the best concentration of bars and restaurants lining the main axis of cours du 4 Septembre and esplanade des Belges.

Practicalities

Buses from Marseille stop at the station bar on quai Tessé just to the right of the bridge. From the **gare SNCF** take bus #3, direction *Ferrières*, to the centre. The **tourist office** is in Ferrières, just to the left of the road bridge on quai P-Doumer (July & Aug Mon–Sat 9am–7pm, Sun 10am–noon; Sept–June Mon–Fri 8.30am–noon & 2–6.30pm, Sat 9am–noon & 2–6.30pm; ☎42.80.30.72).

If you want to stay, the best **hotel** is the *St-Roch*, allée P-Signac, off av Georges Braque, Ferrières (☎42.80.19.73; ⑤), while *Le Provençal*, 35 bd du 14 Juillet, Ferrières (☎42.80.49.16; ③), is noisy but a lot cheaper.

On July and August evenings (except during the folklore festival towards the end of July) a custom known as the *Sardinades* involves thousands of plates of grilled sardines being sold along the quays. Aside from these, the **food** to look out for is *poutargue*, a paste made from salted mullet, and *melets*, seasoned fish fry fermented in olive oil. Three **restaurants** to try, all on the Ile, are *Berjac*, 19 quai Toulmond (☎42.80.36.80; from 200F); *Le Miroir*, quai Brescon (☎42.80.50.45; around 100F); or *Chez Marraine*, 6 rue des Cordonniers (closed Mon & Sun evening; ☎42.49.37.48; from 90F), where the fish soup is especially good.

St-Blaise, St-Mître-les-Remparts and Istres

Halfway between Martigues and **Istres** lies the walled village of **ST-MITRE-LES-REMPARTS** with its two original gateways. From the church at the culmination of the corkscrew nest of streets you can see westwards over the Etang du Pourra and Etang d'Engenier towards the Fos complex.

From the main road the D51 leads away from St-Mître village up to St-Blaise, where you'll reach a hill between two more lagoons, the Etang de Citis and Etang de Lavalduc, where the twelfth-century **Chapelle St-Blaise** stands beside a thirteenth-century wall and the **Oppidum St-Blaise** archeological site (Mon & Wed–Sun 9am–noon & 2–5/6pm; 20F). The ancient inhabitants of this well-defended site left their mark throughout eight distinct periods, from 7 BC to the fourteenth century. If the site is closed you can still walk around it, see the extraordinary surviving Greek ramparts through the fence, watch red squirrels and butterflies, sit among the red flowers that grow in the sand by the edge of the Lavalduc lagoon and generally enjoy the woods and water, which can sometimes appear blood red because of the algae encouraged by a high salt content.

The **Musée Archéologique**, place du Puits Neuf, at **ISTRES**, houses an impressive collection of Greek amphores gathered from wrecks in the Golfe de Fos, many with their hand-painted destinations still visible (Mon & Wed–Fri 2–6/7pm, Sat 10am–noon & 2–6/7pm; 10F). The museum also contains a unique bronze ship's figurehead of a boar. Also in the attractive *Vieille Ville* of this town, whose main business has been the construction of military jets, is a **Centre d'Art Contemporain** (Mon–Sat 1–7pm; 15F) which mounts prestigious exhibitions of contemporary art (take rue Justin Beaucaire to rue Alphonse-Daudet from place du Puits Neufs). Close by, place Hôtel-de-Ville has several pleasant **cafés**, while the best **restaurant**, *Le Saint-Martin* (closed Tues evening & Wed; ☎42.56.07.12; around 200F), is over to the east by the Des Heures Claires pleasure port on the Etang de Berre. Should you want to stay, there's a pleasantly situated **hotel**, *Le Castellan*, place Ste-Catherine (☎42.55.13.09; ③), north of the *Vieille Ville* by the park overlooking the Etang de l'Olivier. The **tourist office**, at 30 allées Jean-Jaurès (Mon–Fri 9am–noon & 2–6pm, Sat 9am–noon & 3–6pm; ☎42.55.51.15), is by the eighteenth-century archway at the northwest corner of the *Vieille Ville*.

Miramas and Cornillon-Confoux

The town of **MIRAMAS**, halfway between Istres and **Salon-de-Provence**, was a nineteenth-century creation tied to the expanding rail network. By the 1930s it had failed to develop any identity beyond its rail connections to the heavy industries of the coast, and was known simply as Miramas-Gare. Today it is still a major rail junction between Arles and Avignon, and Marseille, but it's not worth leaving the station to explore.

To its south, on the Etang de Berre, **ST-CHAMAS** has portside workers' houses, separated from the rest of the town by a viaduct between two high rocks, laid out on in a grid of terraces reminiscent of a north of England town.

Between these two unlikely neighbours, **MIRAMAS-LE-VIEUX** perches on its hill, a typical Provençal village. Narrow cobbled streets lead up past the pretty public gardens below place de la Marie to the immaculately restored medieval St-Vincent church and its tiny predecessor, still standing in the churchyard. Then on to place du Château and its well-kept castle ruins, the venue for musical soirées at the beginning of July. There are pottery shops and ice-cream vendors, and for all the efforts made, it remains attractive precisely for its lack of tourist crowds.

Though not on the lagoon itself, the neighbouring rock-perched village of **CORNILLON-CONFOUX**, 7km east of Miramas-le-Vieux, gives even better views taking in the Alpilles, the Lubéron and sometimes even Mont Ventoux as well as the Etang de Berre. Walking alongside the ramparts around the prow of the village, the streets behind silent save for the odd artisan chipping or potting away, gives the cinematographic impression of a landscape waiting for the final credits to roll.

If you stay on the main Aix road from St-Chamas, you'll see, just after the turning to Cornillon-Confoux, the **Pont Flavion,** a Roman triumphal arch topped with two lions spanning the Touloubre.

Salon-de-Provence

From the *autoroute du Soleil* the northern exit to **SALON-DE-PROVENCE** takes you past a memorial to **Jean Moulin**, the Resistance leader who was parachuted into the nearby Alpilles range in order to co-ordinate the different *maquis* groupings in Vichy France. He was eventually caught on June 21, 1943, tortured, deported and murdered by the Nazis. The bronze sculpture, by Marcel Courbier, is of a lithe figure landing from the sky like some latterday Greek god, very beautiful though somewhat perplexing if you're not aware of the invisible parachute.

In modern-day Salon, learning to fly Mirage jets is one of the principal activities, and, during some periods, they scream overhead day and night. The clien-

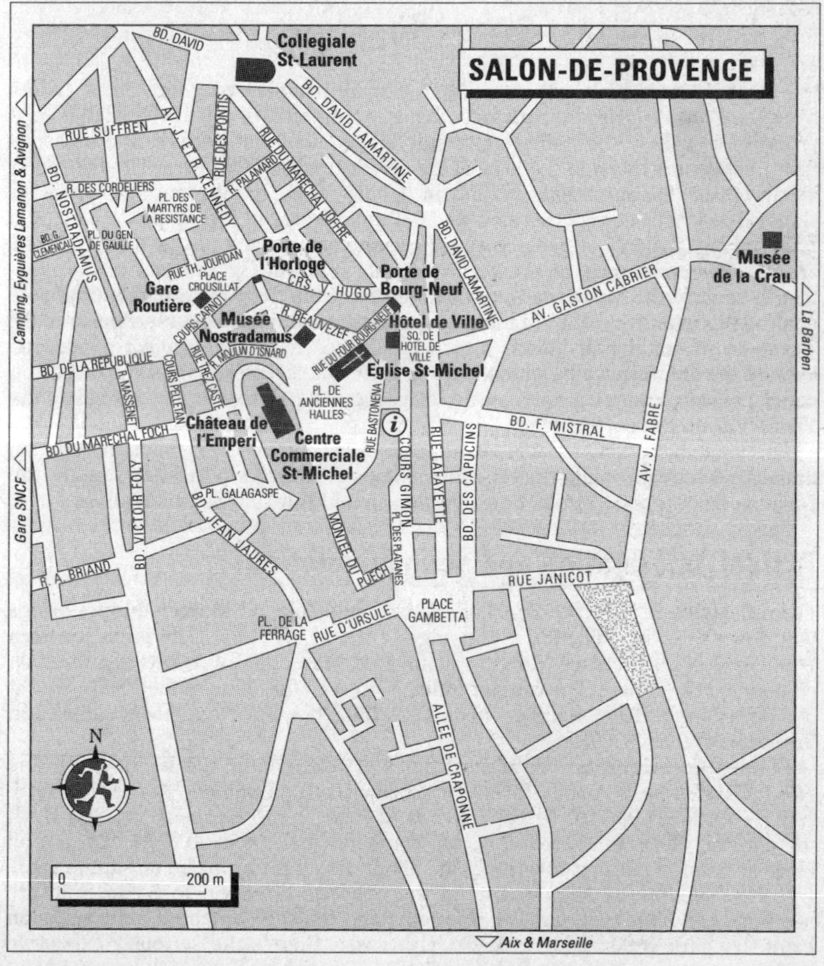

SALON AND THE CRAU

Salon lies at the eastern edge of Provence's most arid region, the **Crau**. In the face of perennial droughts, medieval Salon still managed to have successful tanneries, a saffron crop and flocks of sheep reputed for the quality of their mutton. In the mid-sixteenth century life dramatically changed when one Adam de Craponne engineered a canal from the River Durance through the gap in the hills at Lamanon and across the Crau to the Etang de Berre, and today, the area west of Salon is criss-crossed with canals. A contemporary account describes the people of Salon greeting the arrival of the waters with "applause, astonishment and joyful incredulity". The project was financed by Salon's foremost famous resident, Michel de Nostradamus. The **Musée de Salon et de la Crau** (Mon–Fri 9.30/10am–noon & 2/2.30–6pm, closed Sat & Sun am; 10F), a short way east of the town on the D17 towards Pélissanne, presents the wildlife of the Crau, in stuffed form, and details the oil- and soap-making industries of the town.

tele of the town's bars and restaurants usually includes blue-uniformed cadets from the *Ecole de l'Air* at the **airforce base** to the south of the town. Salon is very proud of its role in the nation's strategic forces, not least because the base has given a welcome boost to the local economy for the last fifty years. The tail-end of an aeroplane incongruously resting in a hole in the public gardens on place Général-de-Gaulle commemorates the 1987 anniversary of the school.

In the past, Salon's prosperity was due to the small black **olives** that produced an oil, *olivo selourenco*, of great gastronomic renown. By the end of the nineteenth century the *Salonaise* were making soap from their oil, a highly profitable commodity manufactured in the most appalling conditions in subterranean mills. Those to whom the dividends accrued built spacious *belle époque* residences outside the old town walls, which today are the hotels, cafés, banks and offices on cours Pelletan, cours Carnot, cours Victor-Hugo and cours Gimon, encircling the *Vieille Ville* to the north and east.

The famous predictions of **Nostradamus** were composed in Salon, though his museum is less appealing than the mementoes of **Napoléon** in Salon's castle, the Château de l'Emperi. A good time to visit is in mid-July for the **jazz festival**.

Arrival, information and accommodation

From the **gare SNCF** (☎90.56.04.05) on av Emile-Zola, bd Maréchal-Joffre brings you down to cours Pelletan, at the edge of the *Vieille Ville*. The **gare routière** (☎90.56.50.98) is on place Morgan, ajoining bd Maréchal-Joffre between the train station and the centre. The **tourist office** is on the other side of the *Vieille Ville* at 56 cours Gimon (Mon–Sat 9am–noon & 2–6.30/7pm, Sun 9am–noon; closed Sun in winter; ☎90.56.27.60).

Finding **accommodation**, at most times of year, should not be too hard. The *Hôtel d'Angleterre*, 98 cours Carnot (☎90.56.01.10; ③); *Vendôme*, 34 rue Maréchal-Joffre (☎90.56.01.96; ③); *Grand Hôtel de la Poste*, 1 rue Kennedy (☎90.56.01.94; ②) and the *Hôtel de Provence*, 45 bd Maréchal-Foch (☎90.56.27.04; ①), are all close at hand, if nothing to write home about. If you prefer to be out in the country, the *Domaine de Roquerousse*, in the opposite direction to Salon from the northern *autoroute* exit, has twenty rooms and ten self-contained units set in an extensive park (☎90.59.50.11; ③–⑤). Otherwise, there's the seriously expensive

Hostellerie de L'Abbaye de Sainte-Croix, 3km from Salon on the D16, route du Val-de-Cuech (☎90.56.24.55; ⑥–⑧), an ancient abbey in beautiful surroundings.

The canal-bank three-star **campsite**, inevitably named *Camping Nostradamus*, about halfway to **Eyguières** on the D17 and Arles bus route (rte d'Eyguières) also has some dormitory accommodation (March–Oct; ☎90.56.08.36), and studios for around 200F.

The Town

Place Crousillat, between cours Carnot and Victor-Hugo, centres on a vast mushroom of moss concealing a three-statued fountain. Opposite is the **Porte de L'Horloge**, the principal gateway to the **Vieille Ville** and a serious bit of seventeenth-century construction, with its Grecian columns, coats of arms, gargoyles and wrought-iron campanile. As you walk through the arch, you can see, at the top of rue de l'Horloge, a giant, gaunt figure against a pale blue background. This is a **mural of Nostradamus**, and arguably the best sight in the *Vieille Ville*.

The **Maison de Nostradamus** (summer daily 9.30am–noon & 2–6.30pm; winter daily 9am–noon & 2–6pm; 25F or 45F with the Musée Grevin) is on the street now named after him. He arrived in Salon in 1547, already famous for his aromatic plague cure, administered in Aix and Lyon, and married a rich widow. After some fairly long Italian travels, he returned to Salon and settled down to study the stars, the weather, cosmetics and the future of the world. Translations in numerous languages of his *Centuries*, the famous predictions, are displayed in the house along with pictures of events supposedly confirming them. There are more waxwork tableaux and audiovisuals meant to fill you with wonder, but nothing very earth-shattering – the most interesting is the 1979 sculpture by François Bouché in the courtyard.

Nostradamus died in Salon and his tomb is in the Gothic **Collégiale St-Laurent**, at the top of rue du Maréchal-Joffre. It's in the chapel to the left of the one opposite the south door; unfortunately the stolen portrait by his son has never been recovered.

In the mid-Sixties the town council decided that the *Vieille Ville* was falling apart and initiated a programme of demolition and rebuilding, completed in the late 1980s, amid proud mayoral slogans of "*Salon Renaissance, la Vitalité du Centre*". The effect, however, of having moved out the old inhabitants – save those in sixteenth-century houses with the money to renovate – has been to create a distressingly yuppiefied enclave, full of new apartments and office space. Flights of gleaming steps run down the castle rock to place des Centuries, a wide open space of little obvious purpose, overlooked by the *Centre Commerciale St-Michel* which houses the **Musée Grevin de la Provence** (summer daily 9.30am–noon & 2–6.30pm; winter daily 9am–noon & 2–6pm; 30F or 45F with Maison de Nostradamus), a dire series of waxwork scenes with taped commentaries.

The **Eglise St-Michel**, with its twelfth-century tympanum and two belfries, on rue du Bourg-Neuf, squats oddly in the midst of this architectural model of a town centre. Cafés with high-tech chairs and shops selling windsurfing gear have rather greater pulling power than the naive representation of Saint Michael battling with two serpents above the church's west door. Some streets, such as **rue Moulin-d'Isnard**, are more consistently ancient but what is lacking throughout is precisely what was supposed to be introduced by all the upheaval of the 1980s, a bit of life.

Château de l'Emperi and Napoléon

Given the lack of life, you might as well concentrate on the dead in the **Château de l'Emperi**, the centrepiece of the *Vieille Ville*. This is a massive structure, a proper medieval fortress to suit the worldliness of its proprietors, the archbishops of Arles. It now houses, equally appropriately, a **museum of French military history** (Mon & Wed–Sun 10am–noon & 2.30–6/6.30pm; 15F) from the time of Louis XIV to World War I.

Despite case after case of weapons and uniforms, the sections devoted to the Revolution and **Napoléon** are fascinating. There are National Convention decrees changing all the insignia of the armed forces' buttons to *République Française*; the requisition order for all shoes with double soles; a watercolour of the women citizens' militia; notices proclaiming war with the king of England. Then for Napoléon there's his hat with cockade, his handkerchief, a piece of his hair, his bed at St Helena in 1819, a table of victories between 1792 and June 1815, letters and pictures (as well as guns and horses) from his campaigns: Egypt, Italy, Austria, Prussia, Russia ... You can't escape the cult of the personality with Napoléon, he combines too many myths: rags to riches, the ever-victorious general with the common touch, the passionate lover, the odds-defying adventurer. What is more often forgotten is that he was also the leader of Europe's most progressive nation at that date.

Eating and drinking

The best choice of Salon's **restaurants** is *La Salle à Manger*, 6 rue Maréchal-Joffre (closed Mon & Sun evening; ☎90.56.28.01), with wonderful Italianate decor and lovely Provençal food at very reasonable prices (weekday menus under 100F) – it's very popular so book ahead. Otherwise, *La Brocherie des Cordeliers*, 20 rue d'Hozier (☎90.56.53.42; closed Sun midday & Mon), in a former thirteenth-century chapel, has menus under 100F and excellent *magret de canard*. For late-night eats, *La Boulangerie*, 13 rue Portalet (☎90.56.46.73; around 100F), is open daily from 7pm till dawn (Wed–Sun in winter) and for a cheap and filling couscous there's the *Restaurant Bleu*, 32 rue Palamard (☎90.56.51.93). The *Hostellerie de L'Abbaye de Ste-Croix* (see p.193) and *Le Mas du Soleil*, 38 chemin St-Côme (☎90.56.06.53), are the two top-notch gourmet restaurants, the latter slightly more affordable with two menus under 200F.

The place for **café lounging** is around the mossy fountain on place Crousillat, where you'll find *Bar de la Fontaine*, *Nostradamus* and the *Café des Arts*. On rue A-Moutin, opposite the hôtel de ville, there's a piano bar, *Le Grenier d'Abondance*. The *Vieille Ville* also has plenty of cafés, brasseries and bars but locals tend to gravitate to the boulevards.

Salon's famous olive oil and other produce can be bought at the Wednesday **market** on place Morgan or the Sunday market on place Gal-de-Gaulle.

Around Salon

Ten kilometres north of Salon, the main road and highway pass through a narrow gap in the hills by **LAMANON**, a village which was never much more than a stop-over on the *transhumance* routes (still followed by the Crau shepherds every June), though it does have a château with a vast plane tree outside its wrought-iron gate. Above the village, hidden amongst rocks and trees on the *Montagne du*

Défens, is a strange troglodyte village, the **GROTTES DE CALES**, which was inhabited from Neolithic times until the nineteenth century. Stairs lead down into natural and constructed grottoes with hooks and gutters carved into the rock; at the centre is a sacrificial temple. Access is free: follow the road going up to the right of the church which turns into a path, from which the Grottes are signed to the right.

EYGUIERES, just west of Lamanon, is one of those Provençal small towns endowed with everything from Romanesque churches, old fountains and wash-houses, to a ruined medieval castle, the remains of a Roman aqueduct, an eighteenth-century oil press and a Gallo-Grecian necropolis on the hill above. Less predictably, you may also see **llamas** grazing along with goats and horses. Llama milk is not the local speciality (that's omelettes with alfalfa), but llamas are excellent at keeping trim forest firebreaks. Goats are equally good but are forbidden, by a still existing Napoleonic law, from running loose in the forests.

Bears, elephants, big cats, hippos and a host of other non-native mammals and birds are kept for more conventional purposes at the **Château de la Barben** (daily 10am–6pm; closed weekdays in winter between noon & 1.30pm; 50F/25F), 12km east of Salon, beyond **Pelissanne**. This is no bad place to take young children, with plenty of entertainment like miniature train rides, as well as the standard zoo delights. The château was lived in for a while by Napoléon's sister, Pauline Borghese, and her apartments are still decorated in imperial style, while the rest retains a seventeenth-century luxury.

From **Lançon-de-Provence** to the south of Salon beyond the airforce base, to **Lambesc** due west of the town and on to the River Durance, you'll see plenty of signs inviting you to to taste the excellent Côteaux d'Aix-en-Provence **wines**. Some names to look out for are *Les Vignerons du Roy Réné, Château Calissane, Château de Caseneuve, Château Pontet-Bagatelle* and *Domaine de la Crémade*.

Aix-en-Provence

AIX-EN-PROVENCE would be the dominant city of central Provence were it not for the great metropolis of Marseille just 25km away. Historically, culturally and socially, however, the cities are moons apart and the tendency is to have a strong preference for one or other.

Aix is complacently conservative, and a stunningly beautiful town, its riches based on land owning and the liberal professions. Successful financiers, company directors and gangsters in Marseille all live in Aix; people dress immaculately; hundreds of foreign students, particularly Americans, come to study here; and there's a certain snobbishness, almost of Parisian proportions, in the air.

Aix began as Aquae Sextiae, a Roman settlement based around its hot springs of sodium-free water which are still used for cures in a thermal establishment on the site of the Roman baths in the northwest corner of the *Vieille Ville*. From the twelfth century until the Revolution Aix was the capital of Provence. In its days as an independent fiefdom, its most mythically beloved ruler, King Réné of Anjou, held a brilliant court renowned for its popular festivities and patronage of the arts. Réné introduced the muscat grape to the region, and today he stands in stone in picture-book medieval fashion, a bunch of grapes in his left hand, looking down the majestic seventeenth-century replacement to the old southern fortifications, the cours Mirabeau.

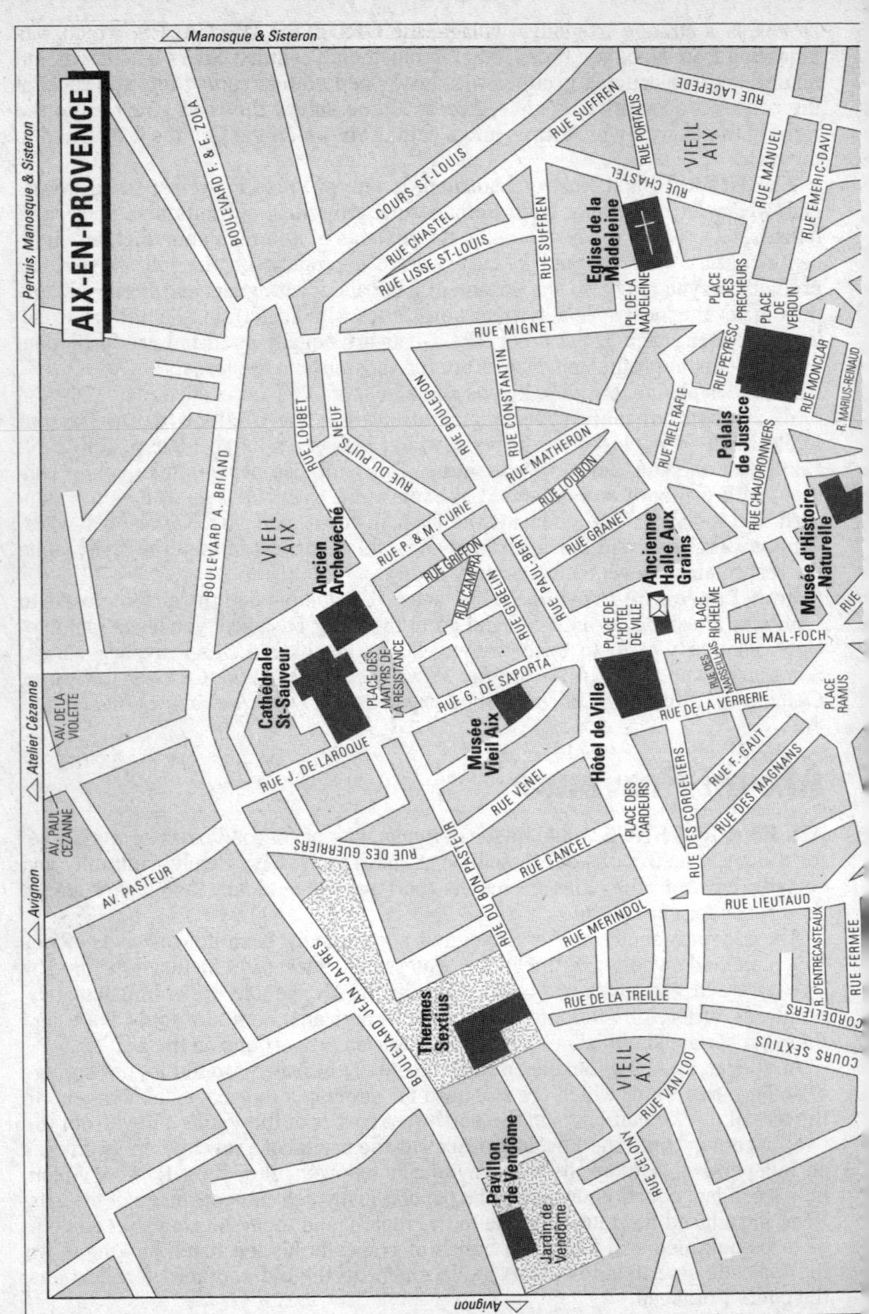
AIX-EN-PROVENCE
Manosque & Sisteron
Pertuis, Manosque & Sisteron
Atelier Cézanne
Avignon
VIEIL AIX
Eglise de la Madeleine
Palais de Justice
Musée d'Histoire Naturelle
Ancienne Halle Aux Grains
Hôtel de Ville
Ancien Archevêché
Cathédrale St-Sauveur
Musée Vieil Aix
Thermes Sextius
Pavillon de Vendôme
Jardin de Vendôme
BOULEVARD F. & E. ZOLA
COURS ST-LOUIS
RUE SUFFREN
RUE PORTALIS
RUE LACEPEDE
RUE CHASTEL
RUE LISSE ST-LOUIS
RUE MANUEL
RUE EMERIC-DAVID
PL. DE LA MADELEINE
PLACE DES PRECHEURS
PLACE DE VERDUN
RUE MIGNET
RUE PEYRESC
RUE MONCLAR
R. MARIUS-REINAUD
RUE LOUBET
NEUF
RUE DU PUITS
RUE BOULEGON
RUE CONSTANTIN
RUE MATHERON
RUE LOUBON
RUE RIFLE RAFLE
RUE CHAUDRONNIERS
BOULEVARD A. BRIAND
RUE P. & M. CURIE
RUE GRIFFON
RUE CAMPRA
RUE GIBELIN
RUE PAUL-BERT
RUE GRANET
PLACE DE L'HOTEL DE VILLE
PLACE RICHELME
RUE MAL-FOCH
RUE DES MARSEILLAIS
PLACE RAMUS
PLACE DES MATYRS DE LA RESISTANCE
RUE G. DE SAPORTA
RUE DE LA VERRERIE
AV. DE LA VIOLETTE
RUE J. DE LAROQUE
RUE VENEL
RUE DES CORDELIERS
RUE F.-GAUT
RUE DES MAGNANS
AV. PAUL CEZANNE
PLACE DES CARDEURS
RUE DES GUERRIERS
AV. PASTEUR
RUE DU BON PASTEUR
RUE CANCEL
RUE LIEUTAUD
RUE MERINDOL
R. D'ENTRECASTEAUX
RUE FERMEE
RUE DE LA TREILLE
CORDELIERS
COURS SEXTIUS
BOULEVARD JEAN JAURES
RUE VAN LOO
RUE CELONY

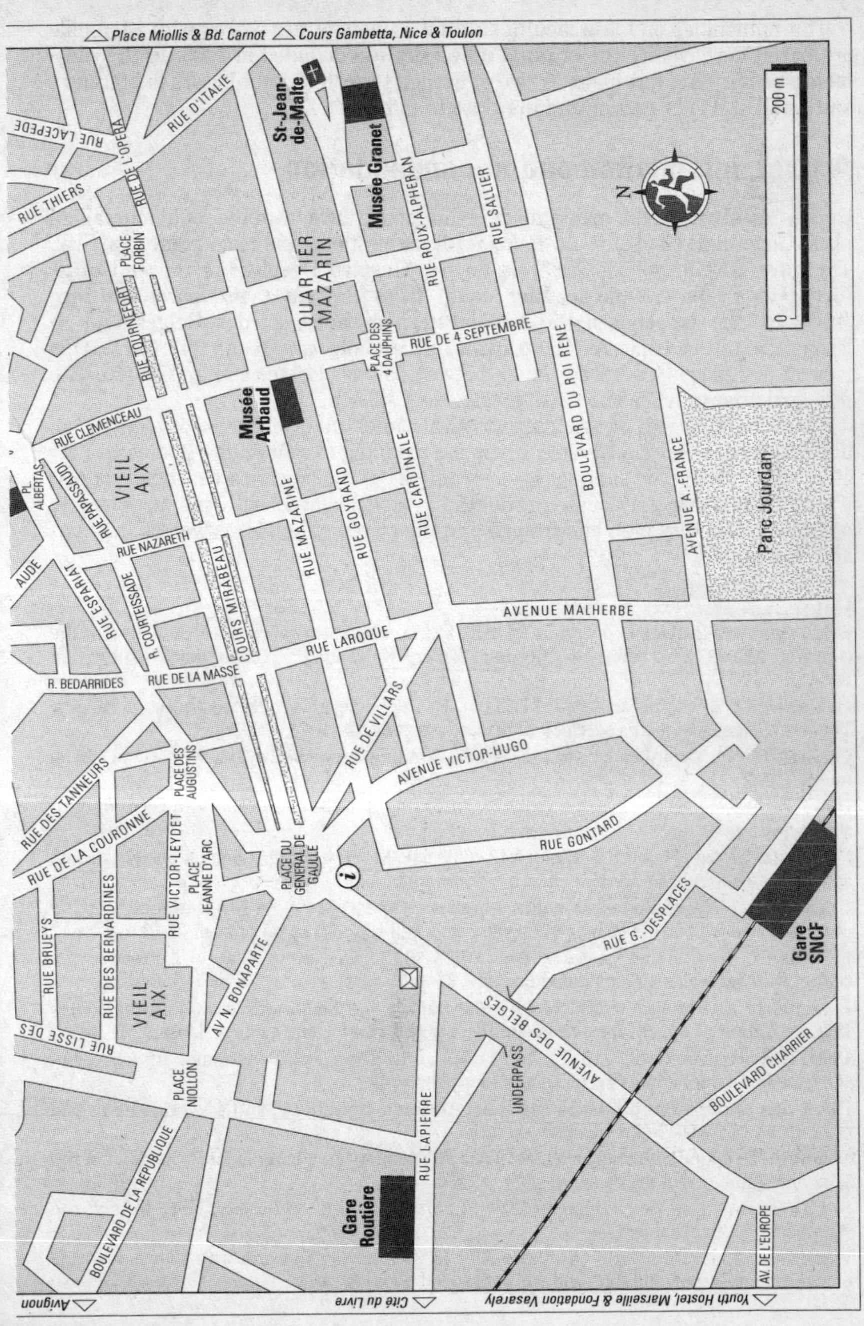

Place Miollis & Bd. Carnot
Cours Gambetta, Nice & Toulon
Youth Hostel, Marseille & Fondation Vasarely
Cité du Livre
Avignon
St-Jean-de-Malte
Musée Granet
Musée Arbaud
QUARTIER MAZARIN
VIEIL AIX
Parc Jourdan
Gare SNCF
Gare Routière
RUE LACEPEDE
RUE D'ITALIE
RUE THIERS
RUE DE L'OPERA
PLACE FORBIN
RUE ROUX-ALPHERAN
RUE SALLIER
PLACE DES 4 DAUPHINS
RUE DE 4 SEPTEMBRE
BOULEVARD DU ROI RENE
AVENUE A.-FRANCE
AVENUE MALHERBE
RUE CARDINALE
RUE GOYRAND
RUE MAZARINE
RUE TOURNEFORT
RUE CLEMENCEAU
PL. ALBERTAS
RUE PAPASSAUDI
RUE NAZARETH
AUDE
RUE ESPARIAT
R. COURTEISSADE
COURS MIRABEAU
RUE LAROQUE
RUE DE LA MASSE
R. BEDARRIDES
RUE DE VILLARS
AVENUE VICTOR-HUGO
RUE GONTARD
RUE DES TANNEURS
PLACE DES AUGUSTINS
RUE DE LA COURONNE
RUE VICTOR-LEYDET
PLACE JEANNE D'ARC
PLACE DU GENERAL DE GAULLE
RUE G.-DESPLACES
RUE BRUEYS
RUE DES BERNARDINES
VIEIL AIX
RUE LISSE DES
AV. N. BONAPARTE
AVENUE DES BELGES
UNDERPASS
BOULEVARD CHARRIER
PLACE NIOLLON
BOULEVARD DE LA REPUBLIQUE
RUE LAPIERRE
AV. DE L'EUROPE
N
0
200 m

The humanities and arts faculties of the university Aix shares with Marseille are based here, where the original university was founded in 1409. In the nineteenth century Aix was home to two of France's greatest contributors to literature and painting, Paul Cézanne and his close friend Emile Zolá.

Arrival, information and accommodation

Cours Mirabeau is the main thoroughfare of the town, with the multi-fountained place Général-de-Gaulle, or *La Rotonde*, at its west end, the main point of arrival. The **gare SNCF** (☎36.35.35.35) is on rue Gustavo Desplace at the end of av Victor-Hugo, the avenue leading south from the *place*; the **gare routière** (☎42.27.17.91) is between the two western avenues, av des Belges and av Bonaparte, on rue Lapierre. The **tourist office** (daily 9am–10pm; ☎42.16.11.61) is located at 2 place Général-de-Gaulle between av des Belges and av V-Hugo. The principal **post office** is also close by at 2 rue Lapierre.

From mid-July to mid-August (festival time) your chances of getting an unbooked **room** are pretty slim. If you are planning to visit during that period (or at any time during the summer if you want one of the city's scarce, cheap rooms) it's worth **reserving** a couple of months in advance at least. Rents and rates in central Aix are very high and reflected in the prices of hotels, as well as in shops and restaurants.

Hotels

Hôtel des Arts-Sully, 69 bd Carnot (☎42.33.11.77). The cheapest rooms to be found in the centre of Aix are a bit noisy, but the hotel is very welcoming. You can't book, so turn up early. ②

La Caravelle, 29 bd Roi-Réné (☎42.21.53.05). By the boulevards to the southeast of the city. The more expensive rooms overlook courtyard gardens. ③–⑤

Casino, 38 rue Victor-Leydet (☎42.26.06.88). Nothing very special, but with some cheap rooms. ②–④

Hôtel de France, 63 rue Espariat (☎42.27.90.15). Right in the centre and with very comfortable rooms. ③–④

Hôtel du Globe, 74 cours Sextius (☎42.26.03.58). Modern comfort behind ancient facade and likely to have clients from the nearby *Thermes*. ⑤

Grand Hôtel Nègre-Coste, 33 cours Mirabeau (☎42.27.74.22). A handsome eighteenth-century house with an old-fashioned elevator and well-sound-proofed rooms. ④–⑦

Le Manoir, 8 rue d'Entrecasteaux (☎42.26.27.20). Tucked away in a quiet street in the centre, with agreeable air-conditioned rooms. ④–⑥

Pasteur, 14 av Pasteur (☎42.21.11.76). Just outside the boulevards encircling the *Vieille Ville*, with some of the cheapest rooms in the city and an excellent-value restaurant. ①–③

Paul, 10 av Pasteur (☎42.23.23.89). Next door to the *Pasteur* and a bit more attractive, but still excellent value. Rooms for three and four people. ③

Hôtel des Quatre-Dauphins, 54 rue Roux-Alphéran (☎42.38.16.39). Old-world charm and compulsory breakfast in the quartier Mazarin. ⑥

Splendid, 69 cours Mirabeau (☎42.38.19.53). A bit noisy but a bargain for its position at the Roi Réné statue end of the cours. ③–④

St-Christophe, 2 av Victor-Hugo (☎42.26.01.24). Convenient and classy, close to both the station and cours Mirabeau. ④–⑤

Vigouroux, 27 rue Cardinale (☎42.38.26.42). In the *quartier* Mazarin with rooms available only during university holidays and with advanced booking. ③

Youth hostels, campsites and foyers

HI youth hostel, 3 av Marcel-Pagnol (☎42.20.15.99); 2km from the centre – take bus #8 or #12, direction Jas de Bouffan, stop *Vasarely*. Reception is open 7.30–10am & 5.30–10pm; restaurant April–Oct; no cooking facilities. Closed Dec 20 to Feb 1. ①

Airotel Camping Chanteclerc, rte de Nice, Val St-André (☎42.26.12.98); 3km from the centre on bus #3. Expensive, but facilities are excellent. Open all year.

Camping Arc-en-Ciel, rte de Nice, Pont des Trois Sautets (☎42.26.14.28); 3km southeast of town on bus #3. Not particularly cheap, but has very good facilities. Open March–Oct.

CROUS, Cité Universitaire des Gazelles, 38 av Jules-Ferry (☎42.26.47.00). Take bus #5, direction Gambetta, stop *Pierre-Puget*. This student organization can sometimes find cheap rooms on campus during July and August.

Foyer Hotel Sonacotra, 16 av du Petit-Barthélémy (☎42.64.20.87) and **Foyer La Providence**, 15 rue du Bon-Pasteur (☎42.23.33.98; young women only) are both worth a ring if you're desperate, though they are intended solely for the city's students.

The City

The old city of Aix, clearly defined by its ring of boulevards and the majestic cours Mirabeau, is in its entirity the great monument here, far more compelling than any one single building or museum within it. With so many streets alive with people, so many tempting restaurants, cafés and shops, plus the best markets in Provence, it's easy to pass several days wandering around without needing any itinerary or destination. Beyond Vieil Aix, there are a few museums in the Mazarin quartier south of cours Mirabeau, and further out, the threatened Vaserely foundation and Cézanne's studio. The Cité du Livre cultural complex is part of a major redevelopment all across the west side of Vieil Aix which will eventually include the new *TGV* train station.

Vieil Aix

As a preliminary introduction to *Aixois* life, a café-stopping stroll beneath the gigantic plane trees that shade **cours Mirabeau**, the main hub of Vieil Aix, is mandatory. The north side is one long line of cafés; the south side banks and offices, all lodging in seventeenth- to eighteenth-century mansions. These have a uniform hue of weathered stone, with ornate wrought-iron balconies and Baroque decorations, at their heaviest in the tired old muscle-men holding up the porch of the *Hôtel d'Espargnet* at no. 38.

Opposite the hotel is Aix's most famous café, *Les Deux Garçons*, with a reputation since World War II of serving intellectuals, artisticos and hangers on. The interior is all mirrors with darkening gilt panels and reading lights that might have come off the old Orient Express. The other cafés have a shifting hierarchy for being seen in. All are pricey, though very tempting with cocktails, ice creams, and wicker armchairs from which to watch the milling street.

To explore the heart of Aix, wander north from cours Mirabeau and then anywhere within the ring of cours and boulevards. The layout of **Vieil Aix** is not designed to assist your sense of direction but it hardly matters when there's a fountained square to rest at every 50m and a continuous architectural backdrop of treats from the sixteenth and seventeenth centuries.

In the midst of all the noisy market trade (see box overleaf) the major buildings may still catch your eye. The **Palais de Justice** is a Neoclassical construction on the site of the old counts of Provence's palace. Count Mirabeau, the

THE MARKET SQUARES

On **Saturdays** the whole of the centre of Vieil Aix is taken up with **markets**. Right in the middle, on **place Richelme**, you'll find fruit and vegetables: purple, white and copper onions; huge sprigs of undried herbs; the orange flowers from young courgettes; and, according to season, different forest mushrooms or red fruits in mouth-watering displays. Fish stalls spread down rue des Marseillais and, behind the post office, **place de l'Hôtel-de-Ville** is filled with lilies, roses and carnations. Across rue Méjanes to the east you can buy clothes – new, mass produced, hand-made or jumble – from stalls in rues Peyresc, Rifle-Rafle, Bouteilles, Chaudronniers and Monclar. Beyond the Palais de Justice, **place de Verdun** hosts its flea market with bric-à-brac and anything from real rabbit hats to plastic earrings, while the neighbouring **place des Prêcheurs** and **place de la Madeleine** display every edible from the region. Over to the west rue des Cordeliers is lined with more clothes stalls.

Moving at anything other than a snail's pace, let alone trying to admire achitectural rather than edible and perfumed details, is completely impossible. The same thing happens on Tuesdays and Thursdays, though with a slight diminuation.

aristocrat turned champion of the Third Estate, who accused the *Etats de Provence,* meeting in Aix for the last time in 1789, of having no right to represent the people, is honoured here by a statue and allegorical monument, as well as by cours Mirabeau. The **Eglise de la Madeleine** (closed Sun afternoon) is decorated with paintings by Van Loo, born in Aix in 1684, and by Rubens, as well as a three-panel medieval *Annunciation* in which Gabriel's wings are owl feathers and a monkey sits with its head just below the deity's ray of light.

On place Richelme a delicate though fairly massive foot hangs over the architrave of the old corn exchange, now the **post office**. It belongs to the goddess Cybele dallying with the masculine River Rhône. Just to the north, the **Hôtel de Ville** displays perfect classical proportions and embroidery in wrought iron above the door. Alongside stands a **clock tower** which you can use to tell the season as well as the hour of day.

The cathedral and neighbouring museums

Rue Gaston-de-Saporta takes you up from place de l'Hôtel-de-Ville to the **Cathédrale St-Sauveur**, a conglomerate of fifth- to sixteenth-century building works, full of medieval art treasures. The early sixteenth-century tapestries on the walls of the nave hung in England's Canterbury Cathedral until they were sold by the Puritans and picked up in Paris for next to nothing by an Aix church official. On the south wall of the central nave is a painting commissioned by King René in 1475, *Le Buisson Ardent.* The two side panels showing the king and his second wife are usually closed over the main picture. A notice in the south nave gives the times (Tues & Sun excluded) when the sacristan will open the picture and talk about it, at length, and very interestingly if you can follow his enthusiastic monologue (in French only).

The painting focuses on Mary and babe sitting in the burning bush with castles, possibly Tarascon and Avignon, in the receding distance, and Moses surprised by an angel in the foreground. All the details – the Virgin's mirror, the trunks of the bush, Moses removing his slipper, the angel's medallion, the dog's collar, the snail in the bottom right-hand corner, the thimble-sized face reflected in the spiral of Saint Maurice's armour in the left-hand panel – are steeped in theological significance.

While you're still hunting for the snail the sacristan closes the painting up again and unlocks the panels covering the west doors: four Old Testament prophets and twelve sibyls – wise women of antiquity who supposedly prophesied Christ's birth, death and resurrection – beautifully sculpted by a Toulon carpenter in 1510. But the best sculpture of all is in stone, in the Romanesque **cloisters**, fashioned some 430 years earlier (access through the cathedral).

A short way down from the cathedral, at 24 rue Gaston de Saporta, the art gallery **La Galerie du Festival** has a permanent small collection of original prints and sketches by Cézanne, Renoir, Pissaro and others. Further down, through place des Martyrs-de-la-Résistance, is the former bishop's palace, the **Ancien Archevêché**, the setting, each July, for part of the grandiose music festival, and housing the **Musée des Tapisseries** (Mon & Wed–Sun 9.30am–noon & 2/2.30–5/6pm; 13F). The tapestries are all rather wonderful: musicians, dancers and animals in a 1689 series of *Grotesques* in which the reds have faded the least; nine scenes from the life of Don Quixote, woven in the 1740s, including one with the somewhat club-footed cat being divested of its armour by various *demoiselles*; and four *Jeux Russiens* (Russian Games) of a few decades later with superb miscellaneous detail to them. There's also a contemporary section with one exhibition a year, for which the definition of tapestry is broadened to include textiles made of rope, raffia or feathers.

The **Musée du Vieil Aix** at 17 rue Gaston-de-Saporta (Tues–Sun 10am–noon & 2/2.30–5/6pm; 15F) could be worth a glance while you're in this part of town. It has a set of marionettes that were a vital part of the old *Fête-Dieu* religious procession, and a huge collection of *Santons*. Among the other odds and ends are paintings on velvet and a portrait of an Englishman receiving honorary citizenship for charitable works, nothing wildly entertaining.

Place d'Albertas and around

On summer evenings concerts are held in the elegant, cobbled eighteenth-century **place d'Albertas** off rue Espariat, which has a distinctly Parisian style. Aix's classiest couturier shops cluster in this area: Yves St-Laurent and Kenzo on rue Espariat, Chrisian Lacroix and others on rue Marius-Reinaud and rue Aude.

At 6 rue Espariat, a seventeenth-century mansion houses the **Musée de l'Histoire Naturelle** (daily 10am–noon & 2–6pm; closed Sun morning; 15F). The cherubs and garlands decorating the ceilings are slightly at odds with the stuffed birds and beetles, ammonites and dinosaur eggs below; this is a rainy day – or sunstroke – refuge.

Quartier Mazarin

South of cours Mirabeau, the **Quartier Mazarin** was built in five years in the mid-seventeenth century by the archbishop brother of the cardinal who ran France when Louis XIV was a baby. It's a very dignified district, with no wiggly streets, and very quiet.

Before you reach the beautiful four-dolphin fountain, the **Musée Paul Arbaud**, at 2a rue du 4-Septembre, is a dark, musty old house, to which you are reluctantly granted admission after ringing the bell (Mon–Sat 2–5pm; 15F). Its renowned collection is of Marseillais and Moustiers ceramics but there are more interesting items tucked away in the claustrophobic rooms of leather-bound books, silk wallpaper and painted and panelled ceilings. The best is a portrait by Pierre Puget of his mother who looks quizzical, half-disapproving, half-admiring and loving. There are also portraits of Mirabeau and family and royalist trinkets such as nobles' rings that were offered as bail for Louis XVI while he was imprisoned in Paris.

A couple of blocks away on place St-Jean-de-Malte in the former priory of the Knights of Malta, is the most substantial of Aix's museums, the **Musée Granet** (Mon & Wed–Sun 10am–noon & 2–6pm; 30F) covering art and archeology. It exhibits the ever-growing finds from the *Oppidum d'Entremont*, a Celtic-Ligurian township 3km north of Aix, which flourished for about a hundred years, along with the remains of the Romans who routed them in 124 BC. The display makes you marvel at the level of advancement of the earlier people, though an exquisite marble kneeling warrior from Persia placed alongside the Entremont sculptures of the same date allows a wider context from which to judge.

The museum's paintings are a mixed bag: Italian, Dutch, French, mostly seventeenth to nineteenth century, not very well hung or lit. François Granet (1775–1849), whose collection initiated the museum, was an Aixois painter; his portrait by Ingres hangs here but his own works are better represented in the *Musée Paul Arbaud*. The portraits of Diane de Poiters by Jean Capassin and Marie Mancini by Nicolas Mignard are an interesting contrast and there is also a self-portrait by Rembrandt. But the rows upon rows of eighteenth- and early nineteenth-century French paintings, including the massive *Jupiter and Thetis* by Ingres, are abysmal and make it only too clear why the country needed two revolutions. You finally reach one wall dedicated to the most famous Aixois painter, **Paul Cézanne**, who studied on the ground floor of the building, which at that date was the art school. Two of his student drawings are here as well as a handful of minor canvases such as *Bathsheba*, *The Bathers* and *Portrait of a Woman*.

Beyond Vieil Aix: artists and books

Cézanne used many studios in and around Aix but at the turn of the century, four years before his death, he had a house built for the purpose at what is now 9 av Paul-Cézanne, overlooking Aix from the north. It was here that he painted the *Grandes Baigneuses*, the *Jardinier Vallier* and some of his greatest still-lifes. The **Atélier Paul Cézanne** (Mon & Wed–Sun 10am–noon & 2/2.30–5/6pm; admission 14F) is exactly as it was at the time of his death in 1906: coat, hat, wine glass and easel, the objects he liked to paint, his pipe, a few letters and drawings . . . everything save the man himself, who would probably have been horrified at the thought of it being public. To get to the *atélier*, take bus #1, stop *terminus Beisson* or Coutheron/Puyricard bus, stop *Cézanne*.

Cézanne was born in Vieil Aix at 28 rue de l'Opéra, but grew up in a house to the west of the city on the slopes of the hill known as Jas de Bouffon now dominated by the **Vasarely Foundation**, at 1 av Marcel-Pagnol, a building in black and white geometric shapes created by the Hungarian-born artist himself in 1976 (bus #8 or #12, stop *Fondation Vasarely*). The seven hexagonal spaces of the ground floor are each hung with colour-wonder, dimension-doubling tapestries and paintings, while upstairs sliding showcases reveal hundreds of drawings, designs, collages and paintings related to all Vasarely's favourite themes, most importantly, the collective and social nature of art. The Foundation was set up for professional bodies and individuals involved with building, but unfortunately sleaze set in and the most recent director is serving a prison sentence for selling off works and pocketing the cash. The Foundation is now closed as a result and no one knows if or when it will reopen. You can check at the tourist office or by phoning the Foundation on ☎42.20.01.09.

Collective cultural life is the basis of the **Cité du Livre** in the old matchmaking factory at 8–10 rue des Allumettes, a short way south of the *gare routière* (open Tues, Thurs & Fri noon–6pm, Wed & Sat 10am–6pm; free). It includes libraries, a cinema, theatre space, a *videothèque d'art lyrique* (where you can watch just about any French opera performance) and any number of exhibitions. But best of all are the two entrances at the ends of the conglomerate of buildings: giant books leaning together as if on a shelf. They are a wonderful example of French imaginative design flair and the whole complex testifies to a continuing determination to keep culture safe from the free play of market forces by creating beauty in public places. It would have made Vasareley very happy.

Eating and drinking

Aix is stuffed full of **restaurants** of every price and ethnic origin. Place des Cardeurs, just northwest of the Hôtel de Ville, is nothing but restaurant, brasserie and café tables, while rue de la Verrerie, running south from place Hôtel de Ville, and place Ramus have an immense variety of Indian, Chinese and North African restaurants. Rue des Tanneurs is a good street for low-budgets. The **café-brasseries** on cours Mirabeau are also tempting, and in between them you'll find cheaper snackeries and peddlars of delicious fresh fruit juice.

Cafés and restaurants

L'Aligote, 6 pl des Cardeurs (☎42.63.00.26). Specialities from southwest France from 150F.

De l'Archevêché, pl des Martyrs-de-la-Résistance. Good midday pasta, tapas and salads for under 80F.

Les Bacchanales, 10 rue Couronne (☎42.27.21.06). Salmon with cèpes, rabbit with marjoram; inventive cooking with menus from 75F. Open till 1am in summer.

Le Basilic Gourmand, 6 rue du Griffon (☎42.96.08.58). Classic Provençal food on an 80F midday menu, accompanied by exhibitions of paintings.

Le Bistrot Latin, 18 rue Couronne (☎42.38.22.88). Escargot and black olive sauce, profiteroles and honey, and garlic rabbit are three of the top dishes here. Midday menu 89F, evening from 118F. Closed Mon midday and Sun evening.

La Bodéga, cnr rues de la Treille/Muletiers (☎42.96.54.00). Spanish resto serving paella Valencienne for around 150F on Fri & Sat only. Closed Sun.

Le Clos de la Violette, 10 av Violette (☎42.23.30.71). Aix's most renowned restaurant with dishes that might not sound very seductive, like stuffed lamb's feet and *pieds et paquets*, but are in fact gastronomic delights. More obviously alluring are the puddings: a clafoutis of greengages and pistachios with peach sauce and a tart of melting dark chocolate. 185F menu midday, otherwise menus from 300F and à la carte from 450F. Closed Mon midday and Sun.

Les Deux Garçons, 53 cours Mirabeau. The erstwhile haunt of Camus is done up in faded 1900s style and still attracts a motley assortment of literati. Good brasserie food, but not cheap. Service till midnight.

Café Le Grillon, 49 cours Mirabeau. One of the biggest and best brasseries on the cours.

L'Hacienda, cnr rue Mérindol/pl des Cardeurs (☎42.27.00.35). Outdoor tables and a 60F midday menu including wine, with delicious hacienda beef à la carte.

Le Jasmin, 6 rue de la Fonderie (☎42.38.05.89). Iranian food for around 100F. Closed Sat & Sun evenings.

Kéops, 28 rue de la Verrerie (☎42.96.59.05). Egyptian cuisine featuring falafel, stuffed pigeon and gorgeous milk-based desserts. From 120F.

Pizzaria Malta, 28 pl des Tanneurs (☎42.26.15.43). Nice atmosphere and cheap plonk to accompany the pizzas or pasta.

Le Montmartre, cnr of rues Verrerie and Marseillais (☎42.96.28.82). Varied dishes and good choice on cheap fixed menus.

Bar Tabac du Palais, cnr rue Manuel and pl des Prêcheurs. Small, pleasant bar from which to view the market.

Café de Paris, 41 cours Mirabeau. A classic expensive café on the cours.

Pizza Chez Jo/Bar des Augustins, pl des Augustins. Cheap pizzas and traditional plats du jour; usually packed, but you won't have to wait long for a table.

Le Platanos, 13 rue Rifle-Rafle (☎42.21.33.19). Very cheap and popular Greek resto with menus under 100F.

Tay Lai, 16 bis rue Marseillais (☎42.23.53.79). Popular and reasonably priced Vietnamese restaurant.

Nightlife and entertainment

Surprisingly, Aix does not have the variety of theatre and dance that you can find in Marseille, but there are some good **pubs** with **live music**, excellent **jazz** venues, and **classical concerts** given in the city's churches. If you fancy a trip to the cinema, then try *La Mazarin*, 6 rue Laroque (☎42.26.99.85), an independent cinema with most foreign films in VO (*version originale*).

A selection of concerts and other mainstream cultural events are listed in *Le Mois à Aix*, available free from the tourist office; the best place for bookings and for more info is at *FNAC* book and record shop. The best time for Aix nightlife is during the summer **festivals** (see below) when much of the entertainment happens in the street.

Blue Note, 10 rue de la Fonderie (☎42.38.06.23). American bar-restaurant with live jazz, blues, folk and country music Tues and Thurs nights.

Bugsy, 25 rue de la Verrerie (☎42.38.25.22). Pub with billiards and rock videos. Daily 6pm–2am.

La Chimère, montée d'Avignon, quartier des Platrières (☎42.23.36.28). Gay bar and disco on the northern ring road towards Sisteron; open nightly 10.30pm–5am.

Cité du Livre, 8–10 rue des Allumettes (☎42.25.98.65). Concerts, plays, dance, poetry readings and films.

La Fontaine d'Argent, 5 rue de La Fontaine-d'Argent (☎42.38.43.80). Café-théâtre with a diverse programme including dance.

AIX FESTIVALS

During the **annual music festivals** – *Aix en Musique* (rock, jazz, experimental and classical; mid-June to first week in July) and the *Festival International d'Art Lyrique et de Musique* (opera and classical concerts; last 2 weeks of July) – the alternative scene of street theatre, rock concerts and impromptu gatherings, turns the whole of Vieil Aix into one long party. Tickets for the international festival's mainstream events range from 80F to 890F and can be bought at the festival office at the entrance of the Palais de l'Ancien Archevêché in Vieil Aix (Mon–Sat 9am–1pm & 2–7pm; ☎42.17.34.34). Tickets for the *Festival International Danse* (classical to contemporary; 2 weeks in mid-July) for which several public rehearsals and performances are free, are available from the Espace Forbin, 3 place John-Rewald off cours Gambetta (☎42.63.06.75).

Hot Brass, chemin de la Plaine-des-Verguetiers, rte d'Eguilles-Célony (☎42.21.05.57). The best jazz club in Aix, with afternoon tea dances on Sunday from 3 to 8.30pm. Mon–Sat 10.30pm onwards; 100F entry and first drink.

London Taverne, 9 rue des Bretons (☎42.38.59.58). Pub with live jazz and rock.

Le Richelme, 24 rue de la Verrerie (☎42.23.49.29). Mainstream disco from 9pm daily.

Le Scat Club, 11 rue de la Verrerie (☎42.23.00.23). All kinds of jazz, rock, funk – the best live music venue in Vieil Aix; reasonable prices. Daily from 10pm.

Théâtre de la Fonderie, 14 cours St-Louis (☎42.63.10.11). New plays and dance.

Shopping

Aix's **markets** provide the greatest shopping pleasures but there are some good specialists.

For English-language books try *Paradox Bookstore*, 6 av Anatole-France, and *Les Bouquinists Obscurs*, 2 rue Boulégon, which, apart from selling an obscure selection of English books and comic books, also has secondhand tapes and records. More music is sold at *Compact Club*, 12 rue Gaston de Saporta. If you're looking for French language books, *Vents du Sud*, on place du Petit-Marché, is the best. *Santons*, the Provençal creche figures, are produced and sold at *Fouque*, 63 cours Gambetta.

Some of the best shops around, however, are those specializing in food. If you like your **bread** fresh and warm, the *Boulangerie-Pâtissier* on rue Tournefort, is always open, day and night, including Christmas, and sells pizzas, pastries and other snacks as well as bread. *Chez Poulain*, corner of rue des Tanneurs and rue Espariat, also sells brilliant bread and cakes. There is a fantastic selection of **cheeses** at *Gerard Paul* on rue Marseillais. Should you want to try *appellation contrôlée Coteaux d'Aix-en-Provence* **wines** to go with a picnic lunch, contact the *Maison des Agricultures*, 22 av Henri-Pontier (☎42.23.57.14), for information; they can also advise you on where you can buy **olive oil**. On the last weekend in July, the Coteaux d'Aix wines are celebrated with a fair on cours Mirabeau.

Chocolates and sweets are sold at *Puyricard* chocs at 7 rue Rifle-Rafle; *calissons*, Aix's speciality almond sweets, from *Du Roi Réné*, 7 rue Papassaudi.

Listings

Bike rental *Troc Vélo*, 62 rue Boulégon (Mon–Sat 9am–noon & 3–7pm). You can leave your passport rather than a deposit.

Car rental *ADA Discount*, 114 cours Sextius (☎42.96.20.14); *Avis*, 11 rue Gambetta (☎42.21.64.16); *Budget*, 16 av des Belges (☎42.38.37.36); *Europcar*, 55 bd de la République (☎42.27.83.00).

Currency exchange *American Express*, 15 cours Mirabeau; *Change d'Or*, 22 rue Thiers. Automatic machines at most banks.

Emergencies ☎15; *Centre Hospitalier*, chemin de Tamaris (☎42.33.50.00); *SOS Médecins* (☎42.26.24.00).

Laundry 60 rue Boulégon; rue de la Fonderie; 28 rue des Bernardines; 4 rue de la Treille.

Pharmacy For a late-night pharmacy, ring the *gendarmerie* on ☎42.26.31.96.

Police Av de l'Europe (☎42.93.97.00).

Post office *PTT*, 2 rue Lapierre, 13100 Aix.

Taxis ☎42.26.29.30, 42.27.62.12 or 42.21.61.61.

Women Contacts and information from *CIDF Information Femmes*, 24 rue Mignet (☎42.20.69.82).

Around Aix

If Aix begins to pall, there is gorgeous countryside to be explored around the city, east most of all, to Cézanne's favourite local subject, the **Mont Ste-Victoire**, and west where he also often painted, along the **Arc River**. Around are the diverse pulls of **Pyricard** wine and chocolates, the ancient sites at **Oppidum d'Entremont** and a strange artist's château in Vauvenargues.

Mont Ste-Victoire and Cézanne

Mont Ste-Victoire, 8km from Aix, is shaped like a rough pyramid whose apex has been pulled off centre. Above the tree line the limestone rock reflects every going light, turning blue, grey, pink or orange. In 1989 a terrible forest fire raged across the southern slopes. Replanting began in 1992 but it will be some years before the ring of dark green woods contrasting with the orange-brown of cultivated soil returns.

In his last period **Cézanne** painted and drew Ste-Victoire more than fifty times. As part of his childhood landscape it came to embody the incarnation of life within nature, and two of his greatest canvases, *La Montagne Sainte-Victoire* (1904) and *Le Paysage d'Aix* (1905), show clearly his divergence from the Impressionists. They are not plays of light in the beholders' eyes or brain but intricately colour-sculpted representations of solid physical nature. Because of Cézanne's insistence on the external reality of his natural subjects, seeing for yourself the views that he painted, always in the open, is a fascinating exercise. The best guide for this is a slim book available at the studio or in Aix bookshops, *Itinéraires de Cézanne*, by M.R. Bourges, the curator of Cézanne's studio.

You may, however, be more interested in **climbing Mont Ste-Victoire**. The southern face has a sheer 500-metre drop, but from the north the walk takes two hours and requires nothing more than determination. The path, the GR9 or the *Chemin des Venturiers*, leaves the D10 just before Vauvenargues, after a parking bay to either side of a brown gate with white posts. Once you've reached the top of the ridge at 945m, marked by a chapel and a monumental cross that doesn't figure in any of Cézanne's pictures, you can follow the path east to the summit, and descend southwards to **Puyloubier** (about 15km from the cross).

Vauvenargues

Leaving Aix via bd des Poilus the D10 road to **VAUVENARGUES** passes the lake and barrage of Bimont from where you can walk to **Le Tholonet**, which lies west of Ste-Victoire. If you want to drive, the sixty-kilometre circuit round the mountain is pretty wonderful. At Vauvenargues, a perfect, weather-beaten, red-shuttered fourteenth-century **Château**, bought by Picasso in 1958, stands just outside the village with nothing between it and the slopes of the mountain. **Picasso** lived there till his death in 1973, and is buried in the gardens, his grave adorned with his sculpture *Woman with a Vase*. The château, unfortunately, can't be visited but if the village appeals you can **stay** at a *chambre d'hôtes*, c/o Jacqueline Chery, *La Jacquière*, chemin des Mattes (May–Sept; ☎42.24.92.31; ③), or at a small hotel, *Au Moulin de Provence*, rue des Maquisards (☎42.66.01.79; ③), with a view over Mont Ste-Victoire and Picasso's château.

Le Tholonet

The D17 south of Ste-Victoire skirts the edge of woods leading up to the defensive face of the mountain. There are two parking places with confusing maps of paths. Heading upwards you soon get views of Ste-Victoire, from this angle looking like a wave with surf about to break. Modern aqueducts pass overhead, the responsibility of the *Société du Canal de Provence* who have their headquarters in the Italianate seventeenth-century **château** in **LE THOLONET**. The grounds are used for open-air concerts during the Aix music festival, but the château is otherwise closed.

On the east side of the village, by an old windmill, is a bronze relief of Cézanne on a stele. Above the village, on rte de largesse Campagne Régis, is a wonderful **restaurant**, *La Petite Auberge* (closed Mon & Sun evening; ☎42.66.84.24; menu around 100F). For those with lots of cash to blow, the **hotel-restaurant** *Relais Sainte-Victoire* in Beaurecueil (Tues–Sat; ☎42.66.94.98; ⑤–⑧), is the place to dine – meals from 200F – and retire.

There are **buses** from Aix to Le Tholonet and on to **Beaurecueil**, where the *Paradou* stop is in easy reach of the woods.

Oppidum d'Entremont

Three kilometres north of Aix is the archeological site of the **Oppidum d'Entremont**, once the chief settlement of one of the strongest confederations of indigenous people in Provence. Built in the second century BC, it was divided into two parts: the upper town, where it's assumed the leading fighters lived; and the lower town, for artisans and traders. Protected by curtain walls and towers, within which streets were laid out on a grid pattern, the site lay on an important trade crossroads from Marseille to the Durance Valley and from Fréjus to the Rhône. It was the Marseille merchants who finally persuaded the Romans to dispose of this irritant to their expanding business (see under "Musée Granet" on p.202).

The plateau on which this Celtic-Ligurian stronghold was built is as interesting for its view over Aix as for the ancient layout marked by truncated walls but denuded of all other objects. Take av Pasteur out of Aix centre; it's to your right after 2.5km just before you cross the N296, or bus #14 to *Puyricard* from av Pasteur, stop *Entremont*. Alternatively, a special bus leaves every half-hour from the Crédit Agricole on cours Sextius.

Puyricard

Continuing on the *Puyricard* bus to the *Chocolaterie* stop, or along the D14, you'll find **L'Usine de Puyricard** on your right, just before you reach the village. Creative base and factory of the best chocolates in France, the methods used are traditional and artisanal; the ingredients are the best-quality butter, cream, nuts and liqueurs without a trace of any preservatives or artificial colouring. You can buy *Puyricard* chocolates in Aix, and all the main Provençal cities, but you might as well drop in here if you're passing. The smell and the sight of all the arrayed varieties are overwhelmingly wonderful for any dedicated chocolate eater and though around 280F a kilo might sound exorbitant, a small box won't break the bank.

PUYRICARD itself is a pleasant enough little village with a twelfth-century church and a **campsite**, *Le Félibrige*, off the RN7 to Puyricard at La Calade (April–Sept; ☎42.92.12.11), which, though 5km from Aix, is more appealing than the campsites within the city suburbs, and also rents out **bikes**. If you want to sample some *Coteaux d'Aix-en-Provence* **wine**, the *Domaine de St-Julien-les-Vignes* (on the tiny road 3km northwest of Puyricard by the Canal de Verdon – marked on the map as *St-Julien ferme*) is open for individual buyers from 1 to 7pm daily. Further north, near the banks of the Durance, the northern limit of the *appellation*, the **Château de Fonscolombe** in Le Puy Sainte-Réperarde (☎42.61.89.62; phone first), produces excellent wine: in 1994 they won Aix's prize for the best red.

West and south of Aix

The **Arc River**, which runs south of Aix, and inspired Cézanne's *Grande Baigneuse*, can be followed westwards to the **Aquaduc de Roquefavour**. An alternative route to Roquefavour is along the **D64** from Jas de Bouffan, which is good bicycling terrain and offers several wine *dégustation* stops.

The valley at **ROQUEFAVOUR** steepens as you approach the three-tiered aqueduct, built to take Durance water to Marseille. Within 150m is a **hotel**, the *Arquier* (☎42.24.20.45; ③), with some cheap rooms and a terrace restaurant. Further downstream, by the junction of the D10 and D65, is the site of the **Oppidum de Roquepertuse** whose finds are displayed in Marseille's history museum.

CABRIES, 13km south of Aix off the road to Marseille, is a totally untouristy *village perché*, with a **château** built in the Dark Ages for the counts of Provence and lived in several centuries later by the artist **Edgar Mélik**, who bought it in 1934. He used to play the role of a supernaturally endowed count, filling the château with wolf-like dogs, playing his blood-red piano all night long, and painting demonic figures on the walls. The château, with Mélik's works plus temporary exhibitions of other artists, can be visited from 10am to noon and 2 to 6/7pm (closed Sun morning and Tues).

Inland from Marseille

Marseille's suburbs extend relentlessly east along the highway and N8 corridor north of the Chine de St-Cyr. You reach **Aubagne** before you realize you've left Marseille, even though the landscape is now dominated by mountains on all sides. The range to the east is the **Chaîne de la Ste-Baume**, a sparsely populated region of rich forests.

Further inland, on the eastward rail, main road and highway route from Aix, lie **St-Maximin-de-la-Ste-Baume**, which claims the relics of Mary Magdalene, and **Brignoles**, a small industrial town with a lot to recommend it as an inland base.

Aubagne

With a triangle of *autoroutes* around it, **AUBAGNE** is an easy place to pass by. It's the headquarters of the French Foreign Legion and not a wildly attractive place, but it does have some saving graces. Its second claim to fame is as the birthplace of writer and film-maker Marcel Pagnol and the setting for his tales. This makes Aubagne significant for the French, though the international success in the 1980s of Claude Berri's films of Pagnol's *Jean de Florette* and *Manon des Sources* have widened the appeal. In *Jean de Florette* an outsider inherits a property on the arid slopes of Garlaban, north of Aubagne. The local peasants who have blocked its spring watch him die from the struggle of fetching water, delighted that his new scientific methods won't upset their market share.

The soil around Aubagne is very good for flowers, fruit and vegetables (as long as you have water) and also makes excellent pottery; hence the town's further renown, for *santons* and ceramics, and the only School of Ceramics in Provence.

The Town

On Tuesday, Thursday, Saturday or Sunday, you can take your pick of the edible produce from the **market** stalls on cours Voltaire. From mid-July to the end of August, and in December, a huge daily **market of ceramics** and *santons* takes place on the central street of cours Maréchal Foch. At any time of the year you can visit potters' workshops in the *Vieille Ville* to the east of the *cours*: rue F-Mistral beyond the hôtel de ville is a good street to try.

The most impressive display of *santons* is *Le Petit Monde de Marcel Pagnol* (mid-Feb to mid-Nov Tues–Sun 9am–noon & 2–6pm; free) in a diorama on Esplanade de Gaulle opposite the **tourist office** (same hours; ☎42.03.49.98). On a model of the local district, complete with windmills, farms and villages, the finely detailed little figures play out their parts. It might sound twee, but it isn't because Pagnol's characters are no angels. From December to February, a Christmas crib with figures representing all the traditional trades and occupations replaces Pagnol's world. For real Pagnol fans, the tourist office supplies a map of all the places in the stories, but even if you've never heard of him, the walks up Garlaban and beyond are very pleasant.

The Chaîne de la Ste-Baume

The **Chaîne de la Ste-Baume** is the highest range in this part of Provence, and one of the least spoilt areas in the region. Once you're up on the plateau north of the *chaîne*, it's wonderful territory for walks and for bicycling, the woods, flowers and wildlife of the northern face showing a profusion rare in these hot latitudes. All of the area north to St-Maximin, south to **Signes**, west to **Gémenos** and east to **La Roquebrussanne** is protected. You are not allowed to camp in the woods or light fires, and a still extant royal edict forbids the picking of orchids.

For details of the numerous **footpaths**, including the **GR9**, **GR98** and **GR99**, the best guide is Gorgeon-Luchesi's *Randonnées pédestres dans la Ste-Baume*, published by *Edisud* and available in local tourist offices.

Into the range: Gémenos to Plan-d'Aups

GEMENOS, 3km east of Aubagne, has a beautiful seventeenth-century château as its **Hôtel de Ville** and is a tempting place to stop. There's a good **restaurant**, *Le Baron Brisse*, 48 chemin Jouques (closed Sun, Mon, end of July & beginning of Aug; ☎42.32.00.60; from 140F) and a luxury **hotel**, the *Relais de la Magdeleine*, on the N396 (mid-March to Nov; ☎42.32.20.16; meals from 250F; ⑥), a lovely vine-covered eighteenth-century manor house set in a park designed by Le Nôtre.

From Gémenos the D2 follows the narrow valley of St-Pons, past an open-air municipal theatre cut into the rock and the **Parc de St-Pons** with beech, hornbean, ash and maple trees around the ruins of a thirteenth-century abbey, before beginning the zig-zagging ascent to the Espigoulier pass. If you're on foot a path beyond the park soon links to the GR98 which climbs directly up the Ste-Baume and then follows the ridge with breath-taking views.

The mountainside on the way up is often scarred by fire but the ever-opening and closing views are magic. At **PLAN-D'AUPS** the dramatic climb levels out to a forested plateau running parallel to the ridge of Ste-Baume, which cuts across the sky like a massively fortified wall. A small **hotel**, *Lou Pèbre d'Ai* (☎42.04.50.42; ③) in the quartier Sainte-Madeleine, offers the only **restaurant** in this village of scattered buildings and one tiny Romanesque church. **Tourist information** is available from the *mairie* (office hours; ☎42.04.50.10).

Four kilometres on from Plan d'Aups is the starting point for a **pilgrimage** based on Provençal mythology, or simply a walk up to the peaks. The myth takes over from the sea-voyage arrival in Stes-Maries-de-la-Mer of Mary Magdalene, Mary Salomé, Mary Jacobé and St-Maximin (see p.120). **Mary Magdalene**, for some unexplained reason completely at odds with the mission of spreading the gospel, gets transported by angels to a cave just below the summit of Ste-Baume. There she spends 33 years, with occasional angel-powered outings up to the summit, before being flown to St-Maximin-de-la-Ste-Baume (see opposite) to die.

The **paths** up from the *Hôtellerie* (the pilgrimage centre beside the road) are dotted with oratories, calvaries and crosses. The *grotte* itself is suitably sombre, while the **St-Pilon summit** makes you wish for some of Mary's winged pilots.

East to La Roquebrussane and Mazaugues

The road east from Plan-d'Aups crosses the range, through miles of unspoiled forest (open to the public), to **LA ROQUEBRUSSANE**, where winged pilots can be arranged, after a fashion, in the form of **gliders**, quartier Le Riolet (☎94.86.97.52). Otherwise, La Roquebrussane has a large Saturday food **market**.

Around the village of **MAZAUGUES**, en route from the *Hôtellerie* to La Roquebrussane, you pass huge, nineteenth-century covered stone wells, built to hold ice which could then be transported on early summer nights down to Marseille or Toulon. The industry gave livelihoods to many an inhabitant of the Ste-Baume, in those pre-refrigerator and ozone-intact days. From Mazaugues the GR99 takes you, after an initial steep climb, on a gentle three- to four-hour walk down to **Signes** (it also links halfway with the GR98 from Ste-Baume).

Méounes-les-Montrieux

Looping back on the road to follow the southern face of the range, you pass through **MEOUNES-LES-MONTRIEUX**, with a couple of **hotels** including the small *Hôtel de France* on place de l'Eglise (☎94.33.98.02; ③), and three **campsites** of which the best is *Camping Club Gavaudan* (☎94.48.95.34), 1.5km from the village at the Château de Gavauden. The *Auberge de la Source* **restaurant** on the rte de Brignoles (☎94.33.98.08; from 150F) serves trout from its own pond in a beautiful garden.

Signes

From Méounes you can follow the lovely Gapeau stream which has its source just before **SIGNES**. This is yet another appealing little village, a place where palm trees and white roses grow around the war memorial, where the clock tower and fountains are at least five hundred years old, and where the people make their living from wine, olives, cereals and market gardening, or, in the case of two small enterprises, biscuits and nougat. At *Lou Goustetto* on the main road as you leave the village westwards, you can sample biscuits in a multitude of completely un-artifical flavours that include Provençal herbs and nuts, lemon, cinnamon, cocoa and honey. They are hard and unsweetened and excellent to munch as you climb the Ste-Baume. The other delicious edible comes from *Nougat Fouque*, 2 rue Louis-Lumière, a honey overdose that manages not to stick to your teeth.

The village has a tourist office of sorts in the Mairie (☎94.90.88.03) on place du Marché where the Thursday **market** takes place, and there's a **campsite**, *des Promenades*, 2km along the road to Méounes (open all year; ☎94.90.88.12). There are two or three small **hotels**, best of them the *Auberge Espereguins* (☎94.90.87.35; ③) on the rte de Méones, some *gîtes d'étape* (contact the *mairie*), and a solid local **restaurant**, *Le Chaudron* at 6 rue Bourgade.

There's more beautiful and deserted countryside west of Signes along the D2, which is perfect for easy cycling.

The OK Corral funfair and go-karting

For a break with old Provence, or compensation for kids, there's an **amusement park**, really more of a big funfair than a proper theme park, called *OK Corral*, located on the N8 towards Aubagne between the junction with the D2 and **Cuges-les-Pins** (June–Aug & school holidays daily 10.30am–6.30pm; April–May & Sept Wed, Sat & Sun; Oct Sun only; 75F/65F).

If the kicks aren't enough, there is also the chance to try **go-karting** on the *ATC* circuit, 3km past Cuges-les-Pins, before Col d'Ange on the junction of the N8 and the D1.

St-Maximin-de-la-Ste-Baume

From Aix the main N7 road and the *Autoroute La Provençale* take an eastwards path through low-lying, rather non-descript countryside though with enticing views of hills to north and south. If you want to head south on minor roads into the Chaîne de la St-Baume turn off at **TRETS**, where there's a good **market** on Wednesday and a **restaurant**, *Le Clos Gourmand*, 13 bd de la République (closed Mon & Sun evening; ☎42.39.81.03; menus from 100F), serving simple but satisfying fish dishes accompanied by cheapish local wines.

But if you keep heading east, on the N7 from Aix, or, if you're heading north from Ste-Baume through Nans-les-Pins, the first place of any interest is **ST-MAXIMIN-DE-LA-STE-BAUME**. Here, in 1279, the count of Provence claimed to have found the crypt with the relics of Mary Magdalene and Saint Maximin hidden by local people during a Saracen raid. The count started the construction of a **basilica** and **monastery** on place de l'Hôtel-de-Ville, which finally took their present shape in the fifteenth century, and have since seen lavish decoration of stone, wood, gold, silk and oil paint added, particularly during the reign of Louis XIV, one of many French kings to make the pilgrimage to the *grotte* and the crypt.

There is therefore plenty to look at in the basilica (summer daily 8am–7pm; winter daily 8–11.45am & 2–6pm), from the beautifully detailed wood panelling in the choir and the paintings on the nave walls, to the wondefully sculptured fourth-century sarcophagi and the utterly grotesque skull encased in a glass helmet framed by a gold neck and hair in the crypt. The building itself is a heavy Gothic affair, unusual for Provence, but the cloisters and chapterhouse of the monastery (April–Oct Mon–Fri 10–11.45am & 2–4.45/5.45pm; Sun 2–6.45; Nov–March closed Sat & Sun; 15F) are much more delicate, and are used for classical concerts (for details: ☎94.78.01.93).

To the south of the church a covered passageway leads into the arcaded rue Colbert, a former Jewish ghetto. All the medieval streets of St-Maximin with their uniform tiled roofs at anything but uniform heights have considerable charm, and there's a reasonable choice of restaurants, and shops selling the produce of local artisans.

Practicalities

The **tourist office** is in the Hôtel de Ville next to the basilica (office hours; ☎94.78.00.09). If you walk west along rue Général-de-Gaulle from the basilica you'll find a **hotel**, *Plaisance*, at 2 place Malherbe (☎94.78.16.74; ④), in a grand town house with spacious rooms. For a less appealing but cheaper option follow av Albert 1er past the *gare routière* to *Le Relais*, rte d'Aix (☎94.78.01.79; ②). The local three-star **campsite**, *Provençal* (April to mid-Oct; ☎94.78.16.97), is 3km out along the chemin de Mazaugues, the Marseille road. **Cafés** and **brasseries** congregate on place Malherbe, the present-day hub of St-Maximin. *Chez Nous*, 3–5 bd Jean-Jaurès (☎94.78.02.57), is the place to go for authentic, local sustenance.

Ten kilometres north, in the tiny quiet hilltop village of **ST ESTEVE** surrounded by vines on the road to **Barjols**, is *A la Fortune du Pot* (☎94.80.90.83; ②), a **chambre d'hôtes** serving excellent food.

Brignoles

BRIGNOLES, 16km east of St-Maximin, is a good base for a night or two's stay. It's a larger town, which for years made a living from its quarries, providing bauxite for the aluminium works in Marseille and Gardanne. Their near exhaustion and foreign competition has meant major redundancies, but the place still has plenty of life in its centre, alongside an untarted up medieval quarter full of quiet shaded squares and old facades with faded painted ads and flowering window boxes.

At the southern end of the old quarter is a thirteenth-century summer residence of the counts of Provence, now adapted as the **Musée du Pays Brignolais** (April–Sept Wed–Sat 9am–noon & 2.30–6pm, Sun 10am–noon & 3–5pm; Oct–March Wed–Sat 10am–noon & 2.30–5pm, Sun 9am–noon & 3–6pm; 10F). This museum dips into every aspect of local life that the town is proud of: from one of the oldest palaeo-Christian sarcophagi ever found to a reinforced concrete boat made by the inventor of concrete in 1840. There's a statue of a saint whose navel has been visibly deepened by the hopeful hands of misguided infertile women, a reconstruction of a bauxite mine, an automated crèche, a kitchen and the chapel of the palace.

Rue des Lanciers, with fine old houses where the rich Brignolais used to live, leads up from place des Comtes-de-Provence to **St-Sauveur**, a twelth-century church in which, on the left-hand side, you can see the remains of an older church. Behind St-Sauveur the stepped street of rue Saint-Esprit runs down to rue Cavaillon and place Carami, the café-lined central square of the modern town.

Just outside Brignoles, on the N7 towards Nice, there's a theme park, the **Parc Mini-France** (second week of March to mid-Oct daily 10am–dusk; July & Aug last admission midnight; 30F/20F), of definite appeal to children and quite fun for adults too. The two-hectare park is a landscaped model of France, bordered by lakes for the seas and with the top eighty tourist sites reconstructed in minature.

Practicalities

Buses stop at place des Augustines close to the **tourist office** (Mon–Fri 9am–noon & 2–6pm, Sat 9am–noon; ☎94.69.01.78) on place St-Louis, a short way north of place Carami and the main street, rue Jules-Ferry. **Hotels** in Brignoles are very good value: try *Le Carami*, 11 place Carami (☎94.69.11.08; ②), *Le Provence*, place du Palais de Justice (☎94.69.01.18; ②), or the slightly more upmarket *Le Paris*, 29 av Dréo (☎94.69.01.00; ③). In addition, there's a *Formule I* in the Ratan industrial quarter signed off the N7 to the west of town (☎94.69.45.05; ①). The three-star municipal **campsite** is 1km down the rte de Nice (☎94.69.20.10).

There's also a profusion of **eating and drinking** stops, none of which are very expensive. On place Carami you can get meals or snacks at *Le Central* bar-brasserie and the *Café de l'Univers*, and ice creams and cakes at *Treand*. *Le Pourquoi Pas* on rue Cavaillon (☎94.59.11.09; evenings only) serves pizzas and couscous, and does takeaway. *Le Bistroquet*, at 5 rue St-Esprits (☎94.59.07.05), is a good family-run place serving filling French fare prepared with great care. *Crep Show* (☎94.69.03.25), at the far end of rue Lice-de-Signon from the tourist office, is a restaurant with disco, live music and café-théâtre on weekend nights.

Alternatively, for summer **evening entertainment**, you could check out the **open-air theatre** in an olive grove 3km south of town on the rte de Camps-la-Source (☎94.80.81.38) which puts on classical concerts, jazz, theatre and variety acts from late June to late-August.

Back to the coast: Cassis

It's hard to imagine the little fishing port of **CASSIS** as a busy industrial harbour in the mid-nineteenth century trading with Spain, Italy and Algeria. Its fortunes had declined by the time Dérain, Dufy and other Fauvist artists started visiting at the turn of the century. In the 1920s Virginia Woolf stayed while working on *To the Lighthouse* and later Winston Churchill used to come to paint. These days it's packed out every summer, with electric guitarists busking round the port, and even a smell of chip fat lingering in the air. But a lot of people still rate Cassis the best resort this side of St-Tropez, its inhabitants most of all.

Arrival, information and accommodation

Buses from Marseille arrive at place Montmorin between the port and the beach, but the **gare SNCF** is 3km out of town with no bus connection. The **tourist**

office (Mon–Sat 10am–noon & 2.30–6pm; ☎42.01.71.17) is on place Baragnon just south of av Victor-Hugo, the main street leading to the port. Head down the D1 then left along the D559 and right on av A-Favier or Traverse St-Marc, but don't go all the way down on the off chance of finding a reasonably priced **room**; you won't, and if you're **camping** or **hostelling** you'll have to walk back up the steep one-kilometre climb to the D559. **Bikes** can be rented from *Roue Libre* (☎42.01.06.24) on quai St-Pierre.

Hotels

Le Clos de Arômes, 10 rue Paul-Mouton (☎42.01.71.84). Charming, quiet hotel with a lovely garden. April–Oct. ⑤

Le Golfe, quai Calendal (☎42.01.00.21). In the middle of all the bustle, overlooking the port. ④

Le Grand Jardin, 2 rue P-Eydin (☎42.01.70.10). Close to the port and not bad for the price. ④

Joli Bois, rte de la Ginesete (☎42.01.02.68). Just off the main road to Marseille, 3km from Cassis. A bargain but it only has 10 rooms, so again, it's best to book ahead. *Demi-pension* obligatory in season. ②

Laurence, 8 rue de l'Arène (☎42.01.88.78). Close to the port and market and the cheapest rooms in town. ③

Les Roches Blanches, av des Clanques (☎42.01.09.30). Perfect position overlooking the bay from the west with terraces and a pine wood leading down to the water. ⑧

Hostel and campsite

Les Cigales (☎42.01.07.34). Campsite just off the D559 from Marseille before av de la Marne turns down into Cassis, 1km from the port. Mid-March to mid-Nov.

HI youth hostel, *La Fontasse* (☎42.01.02.72). Gorgeously scenic, isolated in the hills above the *calanques* west of Cassis and inaccessible except on foot. From the D559 (bus stop *Les Calanques*), a road leads down towards the Col de la Gardiole, and when it becomes a track, take the left fork, and after another 2km you'll find the hostel. Rain water, beds and electricity are the only mod cons, but if you want to explore this wild uninhabited stretch of limestone heights, the people running it will advise you enthusiastically. To get to Cassis you can descend to the *calanques* and walk along the coast (about 1hr). Reception 8–10am & 5–11pm; open all year. ①

The Town

The white cliffs hemming it in and the value of its vineyards on the slopes above have spared Cassis relentless sprawl; instead the modern development is all a bit toytown. Portside posing and drinking aside, there's not much to do except sunbathe and look up at the ruins of the town's medieval **Castle**. It was built in 1381 by the counts of Les Baux and refurbished this century by Monsieur Michelin, the authoritarian boss of the family tyres and guides firm, whose granddaughter is now the proprietor.

Cassis has a small **museum** (summer Wed, Thurs & Sat 3.30–6.30pm; winter 2.30–5.30pm; free) in the eighteenth-century presbytery on rue Xavier d'Authier just behind the tourist office. It's got a bit of everything: nineteenth-century paintings and photographs of Cassis and Marseille, old furniture and costumes, Roman amphores, and an anglophile curator who will give you an enthusiastic guided tour.

The favoured lazy pastime, though, is to take a **boat trip to the calanques**, the long, narrow, deep fjord-like inlets that have cut into the limestone cliffs.

Several companies operate from the port, but check if they let you off or just tour in and out, and be prepared for rough seas (prices range from around 45F to 80F). If you're feeling energetic, you can take the well-marked **footpath** from the rte des Calanques behind the western beach; it's about a ninety-minute walk to the furthest and best inlet, **En Vau**, where you can climb down rocks to the shore. Intrepid pine trees find root-holds, and sunbathers find ledges on the chaotic white cliffs. The water is deep blue and swimming between the vertical cliffs is an experience not to be missed.

You can also walk to **Cap Canaille** below the cliffs on the east side of the town (the path leaves av du Revestel).

Eating and drinking

Sea urchins accompanied by Cassis wine are the speciality in Cassis. **Restaurant** tables are in abundance along the portside on quai des Baux, quai Calandal and quai Barthélemy; prices vary but the best bet is to follow your nose, and seek out the most enticing fish smells. The authentic Provençal ratatouille and freshly caught fish at *Chez Gilbert*, 19 quai Baux (closed Tues evening & Wed out of season; ☎42.01.71.36; 110F menu), are hard to beat. *Nino*, on quai Barthélemy (closed Mon & Sun evening out of season; ☎42.01.74.32; menus from 130F), serves pasta, *bouillabaise* and wonderful grilled fish. *Le Romano*, 15 quai Barthélemy (☎42.01.08.16), has a delicious fricassée of scallops and langoustines; menus from 120F. The most beautiful and gourmet restaurant is *La Presqu'île*, on rte des Calanques in the quartier de Port-Miou, overlooking both the *calanques* and the bay of Cassis and offering exquisite fish dishes and traditional Provençal fare (closed Mon & Sun evening except in July & Aug; ☎42.01.03.77; menus from 250F; booking essential). For **drinking**, as well as *plateau des fruits de mer*, the *Bar Canaille*, on the corner of quai Calandal and quai des Baux, has the best *terrasse* under the shade of a plane tree.

Cassis **wines**, from grapes grown on the slopes above the D559, are very special. Mistral described the white as "shining like a limpid diamond, tasting of the rosemary, heather and myrtle that covers our hills". If you arrive by train you can stop off at two **vineyards** on your way down the D1: the *Domaine des Quatres Vents* (☎42.01.01.12) and *Clos d'Albizzi* (☎42.01.11.43). There are more along the D41 which loops east from the station, and along the D559 towards La Ciotat; the tourist office can supply a full list. For **picnic food** to go with the wine, the Wednesday and Friday **market** is held around rue de l'Arène south of the port.

The Corniche des Crêtes

If you have a car or motorbike, the **Corniche des Crêtes** road between Cassis and La Ciotat (the D41a) is definitely a ride not to be missed. From Cassis the chemin St-Joseph turns off av de Provence, climbs at a maximum gradient to the *Pas de la Colle*, then follows the inland slopes of the Montagnes de la Canaille. Much of the landscape is often blackened by fire but every so often the road loops round a break in the chain to give you 390-metre-drop views over the sea. You can walk it as well: the path, beginning from *Pas de la Colle*, takes a precipitous straighter line passing the road at each outer loop, and takes about three and a half hours in all.

THE COSQUER CAVE

In 1991, **Henri Cosquer**, a diver from Cassis, discovered paintings and engravings of animals, painted handprints and finger tracings in a cave between Marseille and Cassis, whose sole entrance is a long, sloping tunnel which starts 37m under the sea. The cave would have been accessible from dry land no later than the end of the last ice age and carbon dating has shown that the oldest work of art here was created around 27,000 years ago. Over a hundred animals have been identified, including seals, auks, horses, ibex, bisons, chamois, red deer and a giant deer only known from fossils. Fish are also featured along with sea creatures that might be jellyfish. Most of the finger tracings are done in charcoal and have fingertips missing, possibly to convey a sign language by bending fingers.

Though the cave is unlikely ever to be made accessible to the public, Marseille's tourist office has run an exhibition on the cave two years running and may do so again.

La Ciotat

The shipbuilding town of **LA CIOTAT** is notable for its politics, having elected a communist mayor at the head of a united left list in 1995. She will certainly be trying hard to get the shipyards open again, something that is being seriously considered at the regional level. They closed in 1989 and the recession meant that no redevelopment was possible. You might not associate the building of 300,000-ton oil and gas tankers with the pleasures of a Mediterranean resort, but it is one of the surprising charms of La Ciotat that the **Vieux Port**, below a golden stone *Vieille Ville*, shelters the dramatic massive cranes and derricks of the shipyards as well as the fishing fleet and the odd yacht or two. It would be an enormous boost to the town if the changing shifts at the docks were once again to be an integral part of the same quayside scene as the pavement cafés and restaurants, and fishermen mending their nets.

In 1895 **Auguste and Louis Lumière** filmed the first ever moving pictures in La Ciotat and in 1904 went on to develop the first colour photographs. The town celebrates its relatively unknown status as the cradle of cinema with an annual **film festival** and with a few mementoes around the town.

La Ciotat is not a town for keyed-up museum or monument motivation. It's a relaxing place with excellent beaches to loaf on and little glamour glitter.

Arrival, information and accommodation

The **gare SNCF** (☎42.83.08.63) is 5km from the town centre but a bus meets every train and gets you to the *Vieux Port* in 20–35 minutes. The *Vieille Ville* and port look out across the Baie de la Ciotat, whose inner curve provides the beaches and resort-style life of La Ciotat's beachside extension, **La Ciotat Plage.** The **gare routière** (☎42.08.90.90) is at the end of bd Anatole-France by the *Vieux Port* right beside the **tourist office** (daily 10am–noon & 2–6pm; ☎42.08.61.32). **Bikes** can be rented from *Cycle Lleba* on av F-Mistral (☎42.83.60.30) or *Cyclazur* on av F-Gassion (☎42.08.90.74).

Hotels are cheap by Côte d'Azur standards, but if you want to go camping, La Ciotat has nine **campsites**, three of them by the sea.

Hotels

Beaurivage, 1 bd Beaurivage (☎42.83.09.68). The more expensive rooms have sea views. ②

Bellevue, 3 bd Guérin (☎42.71.86.01). Small, peeling hotel overlooking the port. ②

Best Western Miramar, 3 bd Beaurivage (☎42.83.09.54). The best hotel, set amid pines by the sea. Half-board compulsory in summer. ⑤

La Marine, 1 av F-Gassion (☎42.08.35.11). Just above the *Vieille Ville*; modern but very pleasant with little balconies. ②

Hôtel de la Rotonde, 44 bd de la République (☎42.08.67.50). Near the old port and good value. ③

Camping

Belle-Plage, 14 av de Fontsainte (☎42.83.14.72); bus #4, direction *gare SNCF*, stop *Fontsainte*. Three-star site, by the sea, but a little further east. April–Sept.

St-Jean, 30 av St-Jean (☎42.83.13.01); bus #4, direction *gare SNCF*, stop *St-Jean Village*. Three-star site by the sea and closest to the centre. End March to Sept.

The Town

The resplendently ornate nineteenth-century former *mairie* at the end of quai Ganteaume now houses the **Musée Ciotaden** (June–Sept Mon, Wed & Fri–Sun 4–7pm; Oct–May 3–6pm; 15F), charting the history of the town back to its foundation by the ancient Greeks of Marseille when local ship-building began. Further down the quay is the seventeenth-century church, **Notre-Dame-de l'Assomption**, with its Baroque facade and a striking early seventeenth-century painting by André Gaudion of the *Descent of the Cross* alongside modern works of art.

To the east along the seafront, on the corner of bd A-France and bd Jean-Jaurès, is the **Eden Cinema**, the world's oldest movie house. Further on, at plage Lumière, is a solid 1950s monument to Auguste and Louis Lumière who screened the world's first films (see box overleaf) in the château owned by their father (no longer standing), at the top end of allée Lumière. The brothers appear again in a mural on the covered market halls which house the modern cinema, visible as you walk up rue Regnier from bd Guérin north of the port.

The streets of the *Vieille Ville*, apart from rue Polius, are uneventful and a bit run down. If you feel the need to do something you can take a **boat trip** from quai de Gaulle out to the tiny offshore **Ile Verte**, where a small restaurant, the *Relais des Pêcheurs*, serves pizzas, grills and baked fish. The companies for the Ile Verte (15-min crossing) are *Vedette Voltigeur* (☎42.83.11.44) and *Vedette Mont Cristil* (☎42.71.53.32); for the *calanques* of Cassis and Marseille, from quai Ganteaume, *Vedette Provence* (☎42.08.63.55). At **Port St-Jean** in La Ciotat Plage you'll find **windsurfing**, **water-skiing** and **sailing** outfits.

Alternatively, you could explore the contorted rocks beyond the shipyards that the city's founders named "the eagle's beak" and which are now protected as the **Parc du Mugel** (daily April–Sept 9am–12.40pm & 2–7pm; Oct–Nov & Jan–March 10am–noon & 2–6pm). A path leads up from the entrance through overgrown vegetation and past scooped vertical hollows to a narrow terrace overlooking the sea. The cliff face looks like the habitat of some gravity-defying, burrowing beast rather than the erosions of wind and sea. To get there, take bus #3, direction *La Garde*, stop *Mugel*.

If you continue on bus #3 to Figuerolles you can reach the **Anse de Figuerolles** *calanque* down the avenue of the same name, and its neighbour, the

FILM IN LA CIOTAT

La Ciotat's train station has a commemorative plaque to the film *L'Arrivée d'un train en gare de La Ciotat*, which was one of a dozen or so films, including *Le déjeuner de bébé* and the comedy *L'Arroseur arrosé*, shown in the Château Lumière in September 1895. The audience jumped out of their seats as the image of the steam train hurted towards them. Three months later the reels were taken to Paris for the capital to witness cinema for the first time.

The town's **Festival du Cinéma** is a public and affordable event which takes place mid-June, usually revolving around a particular theme or genre. The venues include the Eden Cinema and the Chapelle des Penitents Bleus. A full programme for the festival, and films, theatre and music throughout the summer, is obtainable from the tourist office.

Gameau. Both have pebbly beaches and a completely different dominant colour from the *calanques* of Cassis.

Eating, drinking and entertainment

La Ciotat's **restaurants** are not gastronomically renowned, though *Coquillages Franquin*, at 13 bd Anatole-France (☎42.83.59.50), serves perfectly respectable fish dishes despite its unfortunate location by a petrol station. There are plenty of **cafés** and **brasseries** on the quays: *Le Louveteau* and *L'Escalet* have very cheap fixed menus; *Le Goéland* has omelettes and Breton crêpes; and there's an ample selection of **beers** at the *Bar Continental*. *La Fresque*, 18 rue des Combattants in the *Vieille Ville* (☎42.08.00.60), has decent fare and the *Bar à Tin* and *L'Entracte Bar* overlooking the **Cinema Lumière** and the Tuesday **market** on place E-Gras are pleasant places to drink. Also on place E-Gras, the *Atelier Convergences* gives jazz concerts every Friday evening.

In La Ciotat Plage *L'Orchidée*, the restaurant of *Best Western Miramar* (see "Hotels" on p.217) has a very good reputation and is not too expensive; in summer the hotel also serves snacks and quicker meals at its *La Palmeraie* brasserie. For further menu-browsing continue along bd Beaurivage.

There's also a Sunday **market** on the quays. The main shopping street is rue des Poilus running back from the port. *Lou Pecadou*, a fishmongers at no. 20, sells paella and other fish dishes from huge iron pans, and if you've run out of reading matter, *Wiesgrill* newsagents at no. 23 has a selection of second-hand English thrillers.

Les Lecques and St-Cyr

Across La Ciotat bay are the fine sand beaches and unremarkable family resort of **LES LECQUES**, an offshoot from the *Vieille Ville* of **ST-CYR-SUR-MER** behind. Sea lounging or careering down the double water shoot of the **Aqualand leisure centre**, by the roundabout where the road from the *autoroute* comes into St-Cyr (June–Sept 10am–6pm; 80F/65F), are the chief attractions and you can do a double take at the gilded copy of the Statue of Liberty.

The one reminder of the far past here dates back to Caesar and Pompey's contest for the control of Marseille. The decisive naval battle, which Caesar won, took place near a town called **Taureontum**, which may be under the sea or between Les Lecques and the fishing village of La Madrague but could equally well be nowhere near. What there are for sure, on the rte de la Madrague at the east end of the bay, are the remains of two **Roman villas**, dated first century AD, with three extant mosaics, patches of frescoes and numerous beautiful Greek and Roman vases and other household paraphernalia. The villas form the **Musée de Taureontum** (June–Sept Mon & Wed–Sun 3–7pm; Oct–May Sat & Sun only 2–5pm; 5F).

St-Cyr's **vineyards** belong to the excellent Bandol *appellation*. One of the best reds comes from the *Château des Baumelles*, a seventeenth-century manor house just out of St-Cyr to the right off the Bandol road (☎94.26.46.59 for an appointment). The *Domaine de Cagueloup* on the D66 towards La Cadière d'Azur (☎94.26.15.70) has open *dégustations* Monday to Friday from 8am to noon and 2 to 7pm: try the 1989 or 1992 red. St-Cyr has a food **market** on Sunday.

To find somewhere secluded to picnic you could explore the **coastal path**, which runs from La Madrague at the east end of Les Lecques' beach down to the Pointe du Déffend without passing a single house, and then on to Bandol (3hr 30min). To the east of Pointe du Déffend, on the calanque de Port-d'Alon, there's a gorgeous fish **restaurant**, *La Calanque* (☎94.26.20.08; menus from 150F).

Practicalities

The **tourist office** for Les Lecques and St-Cyr is on place de l'Appel du 19 juin, off av du Port (June to mid-Sept Mon–Sat 9am–7pm, Sun 10am–1pm & 3–7pm; mid-Sept to May Mon–Sat 9am–noon & 2–6pm; ☎94.26.13.46).

For **hotels**, the very small *Beau Séjour*, 34 av des Lecques (☎94.26.31.90; ②–④) offers some of the cheapest rooms to be found, or there's the comfortable *Grand Hôtel*, 24 av du Port, with a large garden leading down to the sea (April–Oct; ☎94.26.23.01; ④–⑥). Les Lecques has a large three-star **campsite**, *Les Baumelles*, on the beach right in the centre of the resort (March–Oct; ☎94.26.21.27). For a wide choice of **restaurants** try av du Port along the seafront.

Bandol

Halfway between La Ciotat and Toulon, **BANDOL** is a smallish, classy resort, rightly proud of its wines. Vineyards have kept much of its hinterland free of new building but the approaches to the town are a rash of cupboard houses, the hill above the centre is sliced by bands of condominiums, and bulldozers lurk at the ready by the patches of undeveloped land that forest fires have cleared. Bandol has some very cheap accommodation on offer, as well as all the usual expensive accoutrements of casino, discotheques, cocktail bars and water sports, and it's a good coastal base this side of Toulon. Exploring the coast, the wines and the hinterland are the main attractions, along with the **Ile de Bendor**, an offshore island, which, suitably enough, houses France's largest exposition of wines, spirits and alcohols.

The Ile de Bendor

Boats leave for the **Ile de Bendor** from quai de l'Hôtel-de-Ville on the port. The crossing takes about seven minutes (32 crossings: June–Sept daily 7am–1am; 2am crossing in July & Aug; Oct–May daily every half-hour 8am–8.30pm).

Bendor was an uninhabited rocky island when it was bought by the rags-to-riches *pastis* man **Paul Ricard** in the 1950s, and today, the atmosphere is peculiar: unlikely statues; an uneasy discrepancy between the people and the place; a 1950s architectural style that has been severely stamped on most of its buildings, and, consequently, a feeling that the whole set-up is fictional.

From March to the end of June, and from September to mid-November the island is taken over by business conferences and receptions. For the rest of the year activities revolve around the diving school, **Club Nautique** and **Fondation Paul Ricard**. The *Fondation* teaches dance and drawing, gives new artists a chance to show and sell their works, and hosts monthly exhibitions in the **Espace Culturel Paul Ricard** (Mon & Wed–Sun 10am–noon & 2.15–6pm). The *Club Nautique* organizes yacht races and windsurfing championships, and runs a sailing and windsurfing school.

The only other entertainment is the **Exposition Universelle des Vins et Spiritueux** (Easter–Sept 10.15am–noon & 2–6pm; closed Wed; free). Decorated with murals by art-school students, the cavernous hall has a comprehensive display of French wines and liquors and a slowly expanding selection of liquid intoxicants from the world over. The curator likes to claim that throughout the ages no culture has ever failed to produce alcohol, even eskimos for whom fermentation can't be easy. She has yet to gather all her proof but the collection does include an evil bottle of Chinese spirit in which a large gecko floats.

The mainland

Back on the mainland the thing to do is hunt out drink that isn't yet a museum piece, in particular Bandol's own *appellation* produced in the area encompassing St-Cyr (see p.219), **La Cadière-d'Azur**, **Le Castellet**, **Le Beausset**, **Evenos**, **Sanary**, **Six-fours** and the edge of **Ollioules**. It's the best of the *Côtes de Provence* wines with the reds the most reputed, maturing for over ten years on a good harvest, and bouquets sliding between pepper, cinnamon, vanilla and black cherries; the rosé is equally wonderful.

Back from the port on allées Vivien you'll find the **Maison des Vins du Bandol** (☎94.29.45.03), which sells its own selection of wines and will give you lists of *propriétaires* to visit. For cheese, sausages and the like to go with the wine, there's a daily **market** in front of the church a few blocks back from quai de l'Hôtel-de-Ville, which spreads onto the quayside on Tuesdays.

Bandol's most scenic sandy **beach** is around the **Anse de Renecros**, an almost circular inlet just over the hill west of the port (access from bd Louis-Lumière). Better still are the coves and beaches along the coastal path to Les Lecques which you reach via av du Maréchal-Foch on the western side of the Anse de Renecros (signed in yellow). There's good bicycling too in the countryside north of Bandol: you could head for the perched medieval village of **La Cadière d'Azur** (take the road above the station, left on the D559 then right) and on to the more touristy **Le Castellet**, then down to **Le Vieux Beausset**, south of Le Beausset, where the Romanesque **Chapelle Notre-Dame** (Tues–Thurs 10am–6.30pm, Sat & Sun 2–6pm; free) gives a suberb 360° view.

Practicalities

Arriving by **train**, turn left out of av de la Gare down av du 11 novembre and you'll reach the town centre above the port. The **tourist office** is on allées Vivien by the quayside (Mon–Sat 9am–noon & 2–6.30pm; ☎94.29.41.35). You can rent **bikes** at *Holiday Bikes* on rte de Marseille (☎94.32.21.89), west down av Loste on the other side of the rail lines from the station, or at *Hookipa Sport*, 3 rue Pierre-Toesca.

The three **hotels** on the **island** are priced for big company expense accounts; the *Soukana* (☎94.32.51.51; ⑤) at the far end of the island is a bit better but you'd still have to book months in advance. On the mainland the choice of cheap hotels includes the *Commerce*, 5 rue des Tonneliers (April–Oct; ☎94.29.52.19; ①); *Roses Mousses*, rue des Ecoles (closed Feb & Nov; ☎94.29.45.14; ②); *Bourgogne*, rue Marçon (☎94.29.41.16; ③); and *Brise*, bd Victor-Hugo (closed Nov; ☎94.29.41.70; ②). Moving upmarket, but still good value, are the *Coin d'Azur*, 23 rue Raimu (☎94.29.40.93 ⑤), a particularly nicely run hotel looking onto the Anse de Renecros, and the very pleasant *Golf Hôtel*, right on Renecros beach (☎94.29.45.83; ⑤). Bandol's top hotel, *Ile Rousse*, 17 bd Louis-Lumière (☎94.29.46.86; ⑤), has a terrace leading down to the sea from the west of the port and vast light rooms.

The *Club Nautique* on the Ile de Bendor provides very cheap **HI youth hostel accommodation** in five-bed dormitories (no membership necessary but book ahead; ☎94.29.52.91). If you're **camping**, try the three-star *Vallongue* (Easter to end Sept; ☎94.29.49.55), 2km out of town on the rte de Marseille.

If you prefer to be in a **village**, see if you can get one of the six rooms at the *Castel Lumière* in **LE CASTELLET**, 1 rue Portail (☎94.32.62.20; ④), which also has an excellent restaurant (closed Mon, some weekday lunchtimes & Sun evening; menus from 130F).

In the centre of Bandol, you'll find plenty of **restaurants** in rue de la République and allée Jean-Moulin, running parallel to the portside promenade. The *Auberge du Port*, 9 allée Jean-Moulin (☎94.29.42.63), has nice fish dishes, with menus from 105F and à la carte over 300F. The restaurant at the *Ile Rousse* (see above) is the place for seafood soup and a *crème brûlée* flavoured with lavender; menus from 150F; à la carte from 250F. Similarly priced, and arguably as good is *Le Clocher*, 1 rue de la Paroisse (closed Wed out of season & Sun midday; ☎94.32.47.65).

Le Bourbon Street Café at 2 bd Victor-Hugo is a tapas **bar** with occasional live music, while for something a little more sophisticated, *Poupoune* and *L'Escale* on quai Charles de Gaulle above the beach are obvious places for cocktail sipping.

The Cap Sicié peninsula and Ollioules

From the west, Toulon can be approached through the congested neck of the **Cap Sicié peninsula**, or, on the Aubagne road, through the twisting **gorge d'Ollioules**.

Ollioules and the heights of **Le Gros Cerveau** and **Mont Caume** above it, on either side of the gorge, are certainly worth visiting. The eastern side of the Cap Sicié peninsula merges with Toulon's former ship-building suburb of **La Seyne-sur-Mer**, while at the southern end a semi-wilderness of high cliffs and forest reigns. On the peninsula's western side Six-Fours-les-Plage sprawls between Bandol's neighbour **Sanary-sur-Mer** and **Le Brusc** on the western tip where you can get boats to another Ricard-owned island, **Ile des Embiez**.

The Cap Sicié peninsula: Sanary-Sur-Mer

The little fishing harbour of **SANARY-SUR-MER**, 7.5km east from Bandol, with its palm trees, nineteenth-century church spire and fountains with statues representing agriculture and fishery, retains quite a bit of charm despite the urban conglomoration it's now immersed in. If you want to stay, the *Centre Azur*, av du Nid (under-26 only; ☎94.74.18.87; ①), may have some rooms or there's the *Hôtel de la Tour*, quai Général-de-Gaulle (☎94.74.10.10; ④), with a perfect location overlooking the port. For a low-priced delicious fish meal you need to head 1km west from the port along av Gallieni and av de Portissol to *Le Cabanon* (☎94.74.13.89) on the Plage de Portissol. Back in the centre, the more expensive *Relais de la Poste*, place Poste (closed Mon evening and Sun; ☎94.74.22.20), has interesting dishes with fresh ingredients.

From Sanary the D559 and D63 head towards Toulon through **Six-Fours-les-Plages** which seems to be nothing but sprawling, hoarding-polluted suburbs. A small road off the D63, to the north, however, takes you up to **Notre-Dame de la Pépiole**, a stunning fifth- to sixth-century chapel in the midst of pines, cypresses and olive trees.

The southeast reaches of the peninsula are not exactly wilderness, but the sturdy sentinel of **Notre Dame de Mai** (once a primitive lighthouse, now a place of pilgrimage on September 14 every year) provides a reason to hike for an hour or two up the pretty backroads here. The best is the one that starts 2km east along the D16 from its junction with the D559. Signs indicate the chapel, just beyond an Elf station. It's 4km to the end, and top, worth it for heady views in every direction and 350-metre drops to the sea. At dusk when the wind is up you could be miles removed from any civilization. Even on a calm day, exploring the cliffs can give the same sensation, and should be done with a certain amount of caution. There are easy alternatives back down again, east around the headland to **La Seyne** or west to **Le Brusc** where you can reward yourself with a generous fish dinner at *Le St-Pierre*, 47 rue de la Citadelle (closed Tues evening & Wed out of season; ☎94.34.02.52; menu around 100F on weekdays).

Ile des Embiez

Paul Ricard's second privately owned island, in fact a small archipelego, turns out to be as dubious in conception as Bendor. The **Ile des Embiez** greets visitors with mock classical goddesses on pillars around the large **pleasure port** and scattered Greco-Roman picnic tables. The **Fondation Océanographique Ricard** (July & Aug daily 10am–12.30pm & 1–6.30pm; Sept–June daily 10am–noon & 1–5.45pm; Nov–March closed Wed am; 15F) has aquaria and exhibitions on underwater matter, there are pony and go-kart rides for the under-twelves and in summer a miniature road-train does the circuit of the island, all great fun for pre-teens. Away from the paying attractions, much of the island has been laid waste by various "works". In spring the more or less untramelled south-facing cliffs are a riot of yellow flowers but the rest of the year they're covered in dull scrub and, with the exception of a few pocket-handkerchief-sized beaches of fine gravel and crystal water, there's not much to induce a lengthy stay.

There's no problem about getting fed but **accommodation**, apart from a small youth hostel (no membership needed but book well in advance; ☎94.74.93.90; ①), is limited to one de luxe hotel and rented villas.

There are frequent **ferry crossings** daily from Le Brusc from 7am to 12.45am July to September and 7am to 8.30pm the rest of the year, (journey time 12min).

You can also reach the island from Sanary port from April to September (25min).

Cap Sicié campsites

Campsites are dotted around all over the Cap Sicié peninsula. Some to try are the three-star *Les Mimosas* (year-round; ☎94.94.73.15) on the D63 between Les Playes and Millone; the four-star *Les Girelles*, chemin Beaucours (Easter–Oct; ☎94.74.13.18) not too far from the sea in Sanary; the two-star *Janas* (June to mid-Sept; ☎94.74.80.76) on the edge of the forest in the southern part of Cap Sicié off the D16; and the four-star *Les Pins*, bd du Bord de Mer (Easter–Sept; ☎94.94.06.89) in Fabrégas on the last bit of build-up between La Seyne and the headland.

Ollioules

OLLIOULES derives its name from "olive" and it's one of those Provençal small towns that despite ruined medieval castle, arcaded streets, fountains and Romanesque church still manages to have an economy not totally dependent on tourism. Much of this rests on its floral wholesale and export market, the biggest in France, though open to the public only during the biannual September *Horti Azur* show and the *Foire aux Plantes* in May on the central place Jean-Jaurès. Small-scale artisans are also much in evidence, earning their keep making barrels, pots, nougat or reeds for musical instruments, as well as wine and olive oil. And on the cultural front, the *commune* contains the **Théâtre National de la Danse et de l'Image** in the château of Châteauvallon (off the D92 towards north Toulon), home base of Angelin Preljocaj's brilliant troupe, the *Ballet National Contemporain de Toulon*, with an impressive calendar of arts events as well as hosting an **international dance festival** every July (details from the centre ☎94.24.11.76 and from Ollioules or Toulon tourist offices).

Practicalities

The **gare SNCF** for Ollioules and Sanary is halfway between the two towns with regular buses to each. Or you can take a bus from Toulon's *gare SNCF*. The **tourist office**, on 16 rue Nationale (☎94.63.11.74), is open Monday to Saturday from 9am to noon; at other times try the *mairie* just across place Jean-Jaurès.

Very cheap **rooms** can be had at *L'Escale* hotel-bar-restaurant, 1 rue Hoche (☎94.63.21.07; ①), or *Au Bon Coin* hotel-crêperie, 11 rue Marceau (☎94.63.22.26; ①), both run by friendly couples and both just above place Jean-Jaurès. For **meals**, excellent fish and grilled meat is served (rather slowly) at *La Cave* on place Trototbas and *L'Estable Fleurie* on rte de la Seyne is distinguished by its seafood dishes. Omelettes and the like can be had from the *Bar-Tabac de la Mairie* on place Jean-Jaurès. If you're lucky you'll find the mobile pizza van, with wood-fired oven, parked in its regular spot on the *place*. A **market** takes place on place Jean-Jaurès Thursday mornings, and for some very special *Bandol A.O.C.* wine head for the *Domaine de Terrebrune*, 724 chemin de la Tourelle, signed off the rte du Gros Cerveau (Mon–Sat 9am–noon & 2–7pm, Sun 2–7pm), which produces a wonderful deep and dusky red **wine** and has an expensive but very good Provençal restaurant, with menus from 200F (closed Mon evening & Sun out of season; ☎94.74.01.30).

Mont Caume and Le Gros Cerveau

Though less dramatic in their inclines than the Cap Sicié cliffs, the mountain ranges to the north of the peninsula give the best panorama of this complex coast. **Mont Caume** to the east is by far the highest point in the locality. Access at the top is restricted by the military but you can get a view northwards across acres of forest to the Chaîne de la Ste-Baume and the distinctively sharp drop of the Montagne de la Loube by La Roquebrussanne.

The road between Mont Caume and the gorges takes in the village **LE BROUSSAN**, where a *bar-tabac*-newsagent-breadshop fulfils all immediate local needs, and **EVENOS**, where people still insist on living perched up in the winds around a ruined castle.

West of the gorges, the **Gros Cerveau** ridge reveals the islands of Embiez and Bendor, the Toulon roadstead, Cap Sicié and La Ciotat's shipbuilding yards. From an abandoned military barracks you can look down northwards onto the strange rock forms. Walks are limitless though watch out, in the hunting season, for *chasse gardée* signs.

Toulon

Viewed from the distant heights of Mont Caume or Notre-Dame-du-Mai, it's clear why **TOULON** had to be a major port. The heart-shaped *Petite Rade* gives over fifteen kilometres of shoreline around Toulon and its suburb **La Seyne-sur-Mer** to the west. Facing the city, about three kilometres out to sea, is **St-Mandrier**, a virtual island, connected to the Cap Sicié peninsula by the isthmus of Les Sablettes and protecting the *Grande Rade* both northwards and eastwards.

Toulon was half-destroyed in World War II and its rebuilt whole is dominated by the military and associated industries. The arsenal that Louis XIV created is one of the major employers of southeast France and the port is home to the French Navy's Mediterranean fleet. The shipbuilding yards of La Seyne have, however, been axed, closing the book on a centuries-old and at times notorious industry. Up until the eighteenth century, slaves and convicts were still powering the king's galleys, and following the Revolution, convicts were sent to Toulon with iron collars round their necks for sentences of hard labour. Victor Hugo's character, Jean Valjean, in *Les Misérables* "was released in October 1815, after being imprisoned in 1796 for having broken a window-pane and stolen a loaf of bread". After 1854 convicts were deported to the colonies in whose conquest ships from Toulon played a major part.

Today, French nationals of non-European origin face the threat of second-class treatment in housing and provision of local services from the town hall, controlled since May 1995 by the *Front National* whose main policy plank they describe as "preference for the French". It was a victory that shocked France – and Toulon for that matter – with the city being the most significant electoral gain for the extreme-right party to date.

Toulon has never been a particularly pleasant city and it's not likely to improve under its new masters. Its museums are dull; major gentrification works on the *Vieille Ville* are likely to be suspended after running up massive debts (plus financial scandals) under the previous administration; highway traffic crawls through the centre; it has all the paranoia of a big city with few of the charms; it's claustrophobic, ugly – in short, a place to avoid.

If you do get stuck in Toulon, there are at least cheap accommodation, good markets and cheap shops and restaurants, and you can escape the city centre by heading up **Mont Faron** or taking a boat across the roadstead to **La Seyne** or **St-Mandrier**.

Arrival, information and accommodation

The **gare SNCF** and **gare routière** are on place Albert-1er. Turning left and down bd de Tessé three blocks brings you to place Mazarin, with av Colbert running to the right, where you'll find the **tourist office** at 8 av Colbert (daily 10am–noon & 2–5.30pm; ☎94.22.08.22), with information on the surrounding area and further afield. A **bus map** is available from the RMTT kiosk on place de la Liberté, one block west from av Colbert. To reach the seaside suburb of Le Mourillon, take bus #3 or #13 from the centre.

One of the cheapest **hotels** in Toulon is the *Hôtel des Allées*, 18 allées Amiral Courbet (☎94.91.10.02; ②), where English is spoken and you can find rooms for up to four people; other inexpensive central options are the *Little Palace*, 6–8 rue Berthelot (☎94.92.26.62; ②), and *La Molière*, 12 rue Molière (☎94.92.78.35; ②) in the *Vieille Ville* by the theatre. In Le Mourillon, east of the centre, *La Corniche*, 17 Littoral Frédéric-Mistral (☎94.41.35.12; ③), has some very pleasant rooms, half of them with views over the sea. There's also a **hostel**, *Foyer de la Jeunesse*, 12 place d'Armes (☎94.22.62.00; ①), just west of the *Vieille Ville*, ten minutes' walk from the *gare SNCF*, with meals for 25F.

The Town

The **Vieille Ville**, crammed in between bd de Strasbourg and quai de Stalingrad on the old port, is pleasant enough during the day. It has a fine scattering of fountains, more often than not of dolphins, a decent selection of shops, particularly for clothes, and an excellent **market** (Thurs–Sun) around rue Landrin and cours Lafayette, as well as a covered fish market on place de la Poissonnerie. Big chunks of the *Vieille Ville* have disappeared with the construction of a gleaming new lycée and shopping centre, and place Victor Hugo around the theatre is all cleaned up and full of café tables, but towards the quays you'll still find every other door leads to a cheap restaurant, bar, jazz dive, nightclub or sex shop. As night falls, men outnumber women ten to one on the streets – and most of the women are working. This is less true in the **Mourillon quartier** to the east where trendy nightlife glitters down the Littoral Frédéric-Mistral and the beaches face the open sea.

The vast expanse of the **Arsenal** lies to the west of the *Vieille Ville*, with its former grandiose eighteenth-century gateway on place Monsenergue leading to the **Musée Naval/de la Marine** (Mon & Wed–Sun 10am–noon & 1.30–6pm; 25F) which displays figureheads, statues of admirals, an extensive collection of model ships and an enormous fresco showing the old arsenal before it was burnt by the British (see "Around the roadstead" p.228). To the north, across the formal gardens of **place d'Armes** and up the main boulevard, the **Musée d'Art**, 113 bd Maréchal-Leclerc (daily 1–7pm; free), is very disappointing (unless there's a special exhibition on), with all the best paintings held in reserve and never on

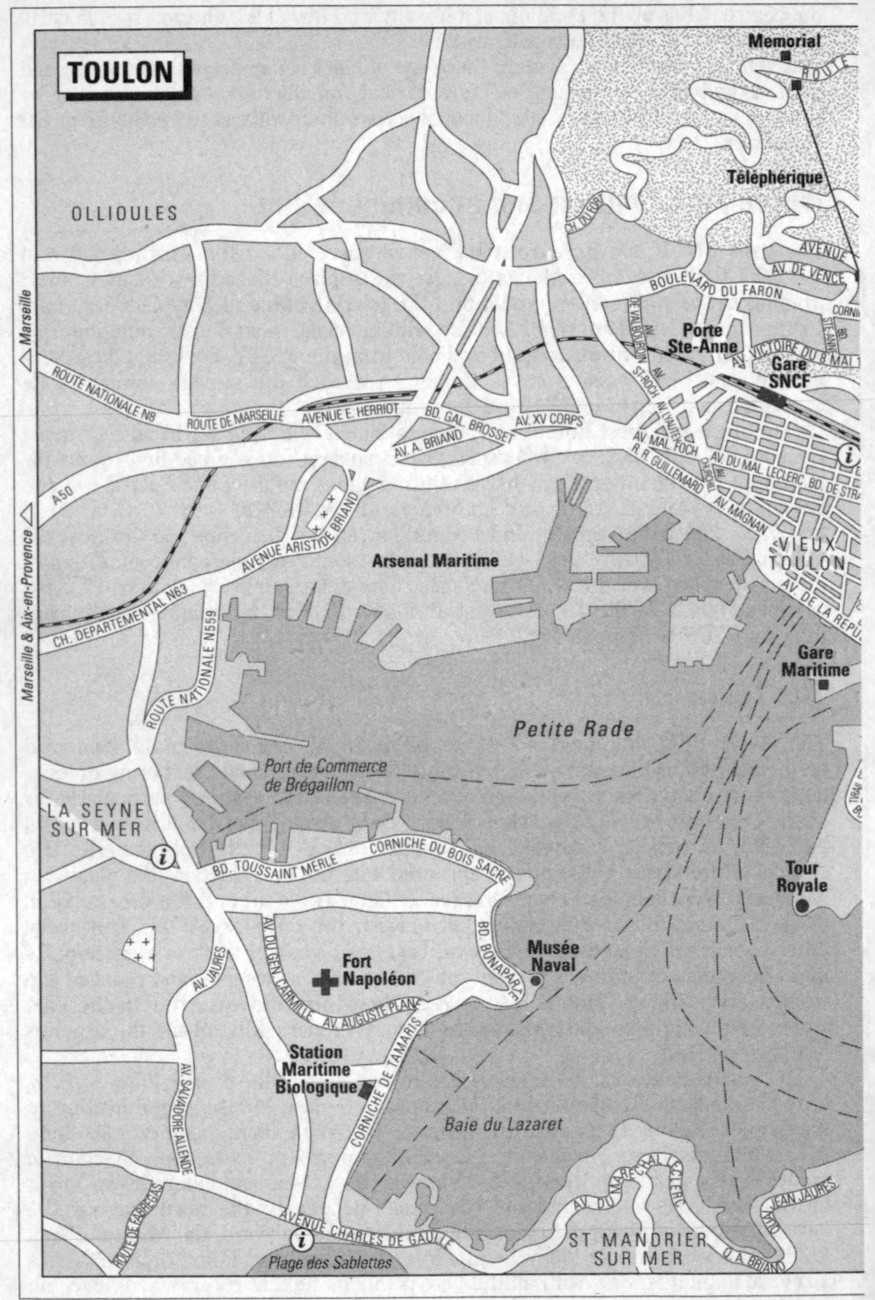

TOULON
OLLIOULES
Memorial
ROUTE
Téléphérique
AVENUE
AV. DE VENCE
BOULEVARD DU FARON
Porte Ste-Anne
Gare SNCF
AV. VICTOIRE DU 8 MAI
ROUTE NATIONALE N8
ROUTE DE MARSEILLE
AVENUE E. HERRIOT
BD. GAL. BROSSET
AV. XV CORPS
AV. A. BRIAND
AV. MAL. FOCH
R. R. GUILLEMARD
AV. DU MAL. LECLERC
BD. DE STRASBOURG
AV. MAGNAN
VIEUX TOULON
AV. DE LA RÉPUBLIQUE
A50
AVENUE ARISTIDE BRIAND
Arsenal Maritime
CH. DEPARTEMENTAL N63
ROUTE NATIONALE N559
Gare Maritime
Petite Rade
Port de Commerce de Brégaillon
LA SEYNE SUR MER
BD. TOUSSAINT MERLE
CORNICHE DU BOIS SACRÉ
Tour Royale
BD. BONAPARTE
Musée Naval
Fort Napoléon
AV. DU GEN. CARMILLE
AV. AUGUSTE PLANE
AV. JAURÈS
Station Maritime Biologique
CORNICHE DE TAMARIS
AV. SALVADORE ALLENDE
Baie du Lazaret
AV. DU MARÉCHAL LECLERC
QUAI JEAN JAURÈS
ST MANDRIER SUR MER
Q. A. BRIAND
AVENUE CHARLES DE GAULLE
ROUTE DE FABREGAS
Plage des Sablettes
Marseille
Marseille & Aix-en-Provence

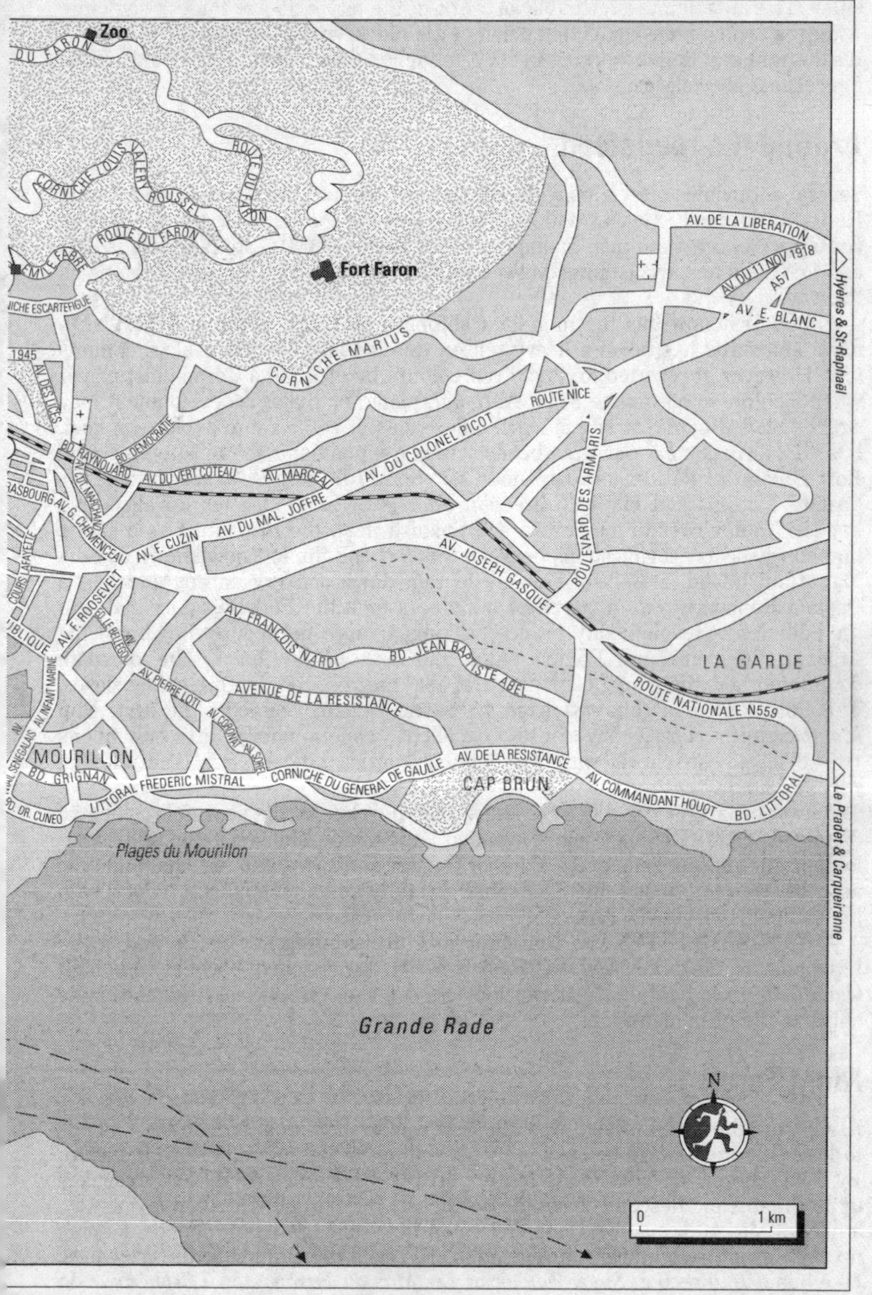
Zoo
DU FARON
CORNICHE LOUIS VALERY ROUSSEL
ROUTE DU FARON
ROUTE DU FARON
Fort Faron
EMILE FABRE
CORNICHE ESCARTEFIGUE
1945
AV. DES LICES
CORNICHE MARIUS
BD. DEMOCRATIE
BD. RAYNOUARD
AV. DU VERT COTEAU
AV. MARCEAU
AV. DU COLONEL PICOT
ROUTE NICE
AV. DE LA LIBERATION
AV. DU 11 NOV 1918
A57
AV. E. BLANC
Hyères & St-Raphaël
STRASBOURG
AV. G. CHEMENCEAU
AV. F. CUZIN
AV. DU MAL. JOFFRE
AV. JOSEPH GASQUET
BOULEVARD DES ARMARIS
COURS LAFAYETTE
AV. F. ROOSEVELT
AV. FRANCOIS NARDI
BD. JEAN BAPTISTE ABEL
LA GARDE
ROUTE NATIONALE N559
AV. INFANT MARINE
AV. PIERRE LOTI
AVENUE DE LA RESISTANCE
AV. CORONAT
AV. SOREL
MOURILLON
BD. GRIGNAN
LITTORAL FREDERIC MISTRAL
CORNICHE DU GENERAL DE GAULLE
AV. DE LA RESISTANCE
CAP BRUN
AV. COMMANDANT HOUOT
BD. LITTORAL
Le Pradet & Carqueiranne
BD. DR. CUNEO
Plages du Mourillon
Grande Rade
N
0
1 km

show. The most impressive public artwork in the city is Pierre Puget's sculpture **Atlantes**, which holds up all that is left of the old town hall on quai de Stalingrad. It's thought that Puget, working in 1657, modelled these immensely strong, tragic figures on galley slaves.

Around the roadstead

Several companies offer trips with commentary around the **Grande and Petite Rade**, but a much cheaper option, sparing you the guide, is to take the **public transport boats** from quai Stalingrad to La Seyne (#8M) , St-Mandrier (#28M) and Les Sablettes, the isthmus between them (#18M; which stops at Tamaris on the way).

Although it now has the merchant shipping port, the loss of **LA SEYNE's** naval shipyards has taken a heavy toll on this industrial working-class community. However, it reverted to its old red colours by electing a Communist mayor when Toulon voted for the *Front National*; plans for major redevelopment may well be stalled by the strong political differences. If you want to explore on land, bus #83, direction *Les Sablettes*, heads across the peninsula to the **Musée Naval Fort Balaguier** (Wed–Sun 10am–noon & 2–6pm; 10F; stop *Balaguier*, or take the boat to Tamaris and bus #83 direction *Fabrégas*). In 1793, after Royalists had handed Toulon over to the British and Spanish fleet, the British set up a line of immensely secure fortifications between this fort and the fort now known as **Fort Napoléon** inland. Despite the ability to rain down artillery on any attacker, a Captain Bonaparte with a bunch of volunteers took the Fort Balaguier and sent the enemies of revolutionary France packing, though not before they burnt the Arsenal, the remaining French ships and part of the town. The museum commemorates the young Napoléon and also has a section on the galley slaves. The Fort Napoléon (bus #81 from La Seyne's centre, direction *Le Mai*, stop *Montplaisant*, occasionally hosts excellent contemporary art exhibitions (☎94.87.83.43 or check with La Seyne's tourist office, place Ledru-Rollin; ☎94.94.73.09).

Between Balaguier and Les Sablettes, the shoreline of the peaceful residential district of **TAMARIS** has rickety wooden jetties and fishing huts on stilts overlooking the mussel beds of the Baie du Lazaret and a beautiful oriental building, now the Marine Biology Institute, constructed by a nineteenth-century local who had made his fortune in Turkey.

At **LES SABLETTES** you can lounge on the south-facing beach, and at the little port of **SAINT-MANDRIER-SUR-MER**, sandwiched between the high walls of *terrain militaire*, you can look across the harbour, past all the battle ships, to the grim metropolis.

Mont Faron

Aside from the harbour boat trips, the best way to pass an afternoon in Toulon is to leave the town 542m below you by ascending to the summit of **Mont Faron**. By road, chemin du Fort-Rouge to the northwest becomes rte du Faron, snakes up to the top and descends from the northeast, 18km in all. The road is one-way, a narrow slip of tarmac with no barriers on the cliff-edge hairpin bends, looping up and down through luscious vegetation. To reach the summit as the crow flies, take bus #40, direction *Super Toulon* or *Les Mas du Faron*, stop *Téléphérique* on bd Amiral-Vence where a **funicular** operates in summer (9am–7/8pm; 34F return). It's a bit pricey but a treat.

At the top there's a **memorial museum** to the Allied landings in Provence of August 1944 (daily 9.30am–12.15pm & 2.30–6.30pm; June closed Mon; 25F) with screenings of original newsreel footage. In the surrounding park are two restaurants, and a little further up to the right, a **zoo** specializing in big cats. Beyond the zoo you can walk up the hillside to an abandoned fort and revel in the cleanness of the air, the smell of the flowers and the distance from the city below.

Eating and drinking

Toulon's best rewards are mainly in **eating**. There are plenty of brasseries, cafés and restaurants along the quayside, some selling just sandwiches, while others offer seafood-based fixed menus for under 100F. Good couscous for around 100F is to be had *Chez Mimi*, 83 av de la République (☎94.28.79.60); Toulon's oldest restaurant, *Au Sourd*, 10 rue Molière, in the *Vieille Ville* (closed Mon, Sun & Aug; ☎94.92.28.52), specializes in fish dishes including *bouillabaisse*, with a good menu at 140F and à la carte at around 300F. North of bd Strasbourg, the *Pizzaria Luigi*, 40 rue Picot (closed midday Sat & Sun; ☎94.92.89.14), serves pizzas and delicious raviolis until midnight. The Littorial Frédéric-Mistral in Le Mourillon is choc-a-bloc with restaurants. Try *Le Bistrot de la Corniche* at no. 1 (closed Sun evening and Tues out of season; ☎94.32.09.09) which serves good-value *plateaux de fruits de mer* and Bandol wines, with menus from 100F.

East towards Hyères

Beyond Le Mourillon to the east, Toulon merges with **LE PRADET** where old houses with lovely gardens are shaded by pines above the cliffs leading to the Pointe de Carquieranne. A path follows the coast all the way round the headland to **Carquieranne** and steep steps lead down to beaches which are crowded during the day but lovely in the evening as they catch the sun setting over Toulon's harbour. At Plage de la Garonne (bus #23 or #39 to *Pradet Place*, then #91A/B to *La Garonne*) the beachside restaurant *El Plein Sud* serves grilled fish and cheap wine as night falls in summer.

Past Pointe de Carquieranne, between Pointe du Beau Rouge and the D559, a small road crosses the side of a hill guarded by two old forts with views of the Presqu'île de Giens and the Ile de Porquerolles (see *The Cote D'Azur: Hyères to the Esterel*). If you're cycling from Toulon to Hyères there's a proper track running beside the D559.

travel details

Trains

Aix to: Briançon (1–2 daily; 3hr 30min); Château-Arnoux–St Auban (3–4 daily; 1hr 5min–1hr 30min); Marseille (frequent; 30–35min); Manosque (3–4 daily; 40min); Meyrargues (3 daily; 15min); Sisteron (3–4 daily; 1hr 15min–1hr 40min).

Marseille to: Aix (frequent; 30–35min); Arles (10–12 daily; 45min); Aubagne (every 30min; 15–20min); Avignon (frequent; 50min–1hr); Bandol (every 30min; 40–45min); Cannes (frequent; 1hr 5min); Carry-le-Rouet (6–8 daily; 25–30min); Cassis (every 30min; 20–25min); Cavaillon (3–4 daily; 45min–1hr 15min); Hyères (2 daily; 1hr

25min); Istres (6–8 daily; 1hr–1hr 5min); La Ciotat (every 30min; 25–30min); La Couronne (6–8 daily; 35–40min); La Redonne-Ensués (6–8 daily; 20–25min); La Seyne–Six Fours (every 40min; 55min–1hr); Les Arcs-Draguignan (every hour; 1hr 25min–2hr 15min); L'Estaque (10–14 daily; 15min); Lyon (8 daily; 2hr 35min); Martigues (6–8 daily; 40–45min); Miramas (frequent; 25min–1hr 10min); Nice (frequent; 2hr 45min–3hr 15min); Niolon (5–8 daily; 20min); Ollioules–Sanary (every 40min; 45–50min); Paris (8 daily; 4hr 40min–7 hr 35min); St-Chamas (4 daily; 45min); St Cyr-Les-Lecques (every 30min; 35–40min); St-Raphaël (frequent; 1hr 45min); Salon (3–4 daily; 25–50min); Sausset-les-Pins (6–8 daily; 30–35min); Tarascon (5-6 daily; 1hr 5min); Toulon (frequent; 1hr–1hr 5min).

Miramas to: Arles (8–12 daily; 20min); Avignon (9–11 daily; 40min–1hr); Marseille (frequent; 25min–1hr 10min).

Toulon to: Marseille (frequent; 1hr–1hr 5min).

Buses

Aix to: Apt (2 daily; 2hr 20min); Arles (6 daily; 1hr 15min); Avignon (6 daily; 1hr–1hr 15min); Bandol (2 daily in summer; 1hr 5min); Brignoles (2 daily; 50min); Carpentras (3 daily; 1hr 50min); Cavaillon (3 daily; 1hr 10min); Marseille (frequent; 25min); Nice (5 daily; 2hr 15min–3hr 55min); St-Cyr (2 daily in summer; 55min); Salon (6 daily; 30min); Toulon (4 daily; 1hr 15min); Sanary (2 daily in summer; 1hr 15min); St-Maximin (2 daily; 25–30min); Six Fours (2 daily in summer; 1hr 25min). Other buses start from Marseille.

Marseille to: Aix (frequent; 25min); Arles (5 daily; 2hr 5min–2hr 30min); Aubagne (frequent; 30–40min); Bandol (6 daily; 1hr 30min); Barcelonnette (2 daily; 3hr 55min); Brignoles (1 daily; 1hr 20min); Carpentras (4 daily; 2hr 15min); Cassis (2 daily; 25min); Digne (2 daily; 2hr–2hr 40min); Forcalquier (3 daily; 1 hr 40min–1hr 55min); Gémenos (4 daily; 45min); Grenoble (1 daily; 3hr 55min); La Ciotat (6 daily; 45min); Les Lecques (6 daily; 1hr 10min); Manosque (5–6 daily; 1hr 30min); Martigues (10–11 daily; 1hr 15min–1hr 30min); Ollioules (4 daily; 1hr 55min); St-Chamas (3 daily; 1hr 20min); St-Maximin (1 daily; 1hr); Salon (6 daily; 1hr 20min–1hr 50min); Sisteron (5–6 daily; 2hr 25min); Toulon (frequent 45min).

Martigues to: Istres (5 daily; 25min); Marseille (10–11 daily; 1hr 15min–1hr 30min); Salon (4 daily; 1hr 10min).

Salon to: Aix (6 daily; 40min); Arles (7 daily; 1hr 5min–1hr 20min); Eyguières (7 daily; 15min); La Barben (3 daily; 15min); Les Baux (2 daily; 30min); Marseille (5 daily; 45min–1hr 15min); Martigues (4 daily; 1hr 10min); Miramas (4 daily; 20min).

Toulon to: Aix (4 daily; 1hr 15min); Bandol (every 30min; 50min–1hr); Brignoles (6 daily; 1hr 25min); Draguignan (5 daily; 2hr 10min); Hyères (every 30min; 35–50min); Le Brusc (6–7 daily; 25min); Le Pradet (every 30min; 20min); Marseille (frequent 45min); Méounes (2 daily; 50min); Nice (2 daily; 2hr 30min); St-Maximin (1 daily; 1hr 40min); St-Raphaël (4 daily; 2hr); St-Tropez (8 daily; 2hr 15min); Sanary (every 30min; 35–45min); Signes (2 daily; 1hr 15min); Six-Fours (every 30min; 25min). Other buses start from Marseille.

Ferries

Marseille to: Corsica (4–10 weekly; 8–12 hr).

Toulon to: Corsica (2–5 weekly; 7–11hr).

Flights

Marseille to: Paris (21 daily; 1hr 5min).

CHAPTER FOUR

THE COTE D'AZUR: HYERES TO THE ESTEREL

The **Côte d'Azur** is the most desirable and at the same time most detestable stretch of Mediterranean coast. The glimmering rocks along its shore and the translucent sea, the February mimosa blossom, the springtime scents of pine and eucalyptus or the golden autumn chestnut crop and reddening vines are woven by the Mediterranean light into a compulsive sensual magic. It can still cast the spell that attracted the Impressionist and Post-Impressionist painters at the turn of the century (whose paintings can be seen at St-Tropez), their Bohemian successors and the 1950s film world. But in summer it also has the worst traffic jams and public transport, the most crowded quaysides, campsites and hitching queues, the most short-tempered locals – and outrageous prices.

Unlike the Riviera further east, or the Toulon–Marseille stretch, the Côte d'Azur proper is off the main routes and has no major cities. Between the largest town, Hyères, and the conurbation of St-Raphaël-Fréjus, are a string of fishing villages turned yacht and pleasure ports. Pre-eminent among them is **St-Tropez**, or "St-Trop" as its aficionados like to call it, a brand-name for sea, sun, celebrity and sex.

There's such a tangle of resorts it's sometimes hard to distinguish one from another; but in the smaller **Cavalière**, **Pramousquier**, **Le Rayol** with its fabulous **garden**, and **Le Trayas** you can get glimpses of how this coast all once looked. There are even some stretches which have held out against the construction mania altogether: west of **Cap Bregançon**, the southern end of **St-Tropez**'s **peninsula**, little snatches of the **Corniches des Maures** and along the **Corniche d'Esterel** west of Le Trayas below the dramatic red volcanic crags of the **Massif d'Esterel**. But for real coastal wilderness you need to head out to sea to the gorgeous **Iles d'Hyères** where the region's rarest fauna and flora is seriously conserved and protected.

Of the proper towns, as opposed to sprawled resorts, **Hyères**, which attracted foreign visitors in the eighteenth century while Cannes was still a fishing village and Nice a border town of Savoy, thrives on its horticulture as much as on its

HOTEL ROOM PRICES

For a fuller explanation of these price codes, see the box on p.32 of *Basics*.

① Under 160F	② 160–220F	③ 220–300F	④ 300–400F
⑤ 400–500F	⑥ 500–600F	⑦ 600–700F	⑧ over 700F

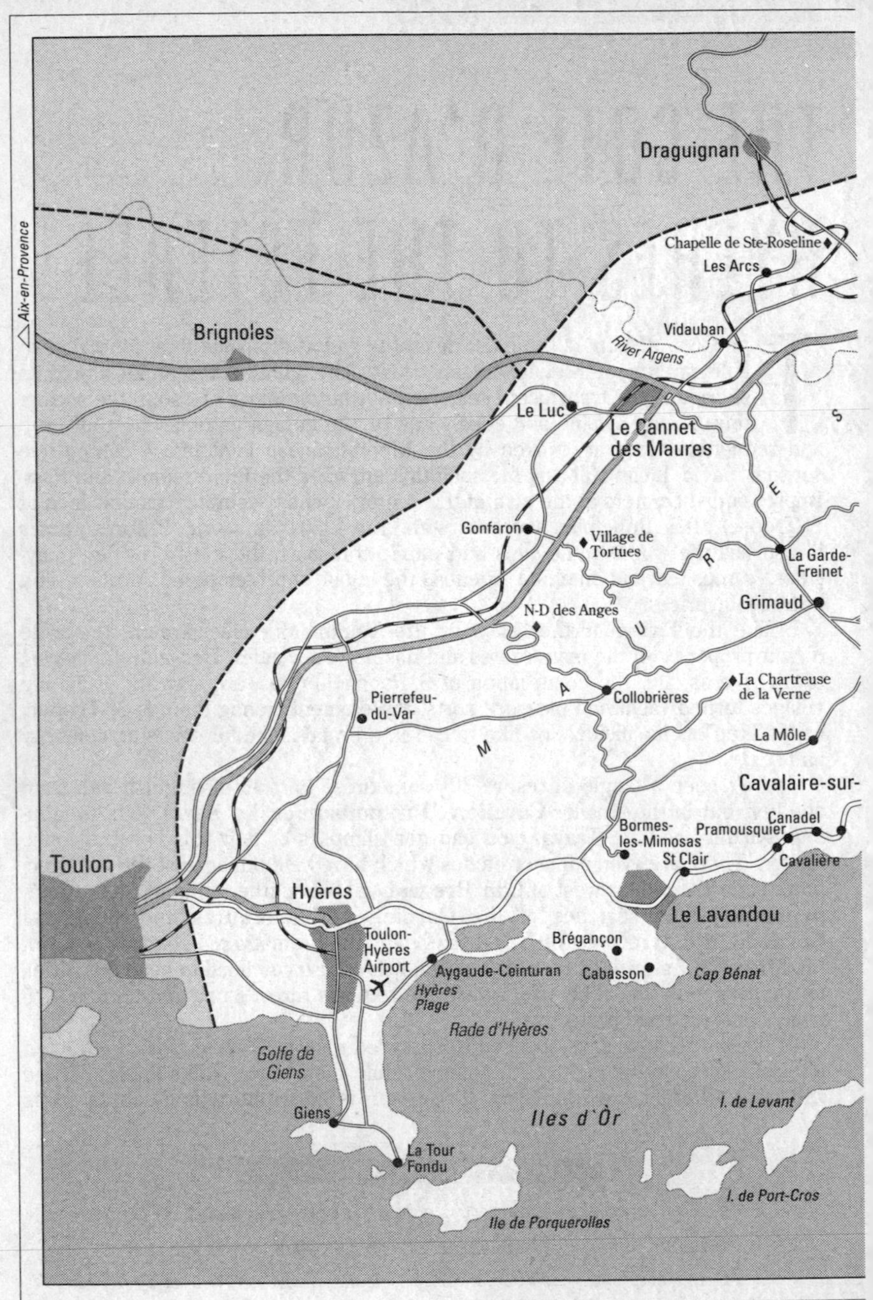
Draguignan
Chapelle de Ste-Roseline
Les Arcs
Aix-en-Provence
Brignoles
Vidauban
River Argens
Le Luc
Le Cannet
des Maures
S
E
Gonfaron
Village de
Tortues
La Garde-
Freinet
R
Grimaud
N-D des Anges
U
La Chartreuse
de la Verne
A
Pierrefeu-
du-Var
Collobrières
M
La Môle
Cavalaire-sur-
Canadel
Bormes-
les-Mimosas
Pramousquier
Toulon
St Clair
Cavalière
Hyères
Le Lavandou
Toulon-
Hyères
Airport
Brégançon
Aygaude-Ceinturan
Cabasson
Cap Bénat
Hyères
Plage
Rade d'Hyères
Golfe de
Giens
I. de Levant
Giens
Iles d'Òr
La Tour
Fondu
I. de Port-Cros
Ile de Porquerolles

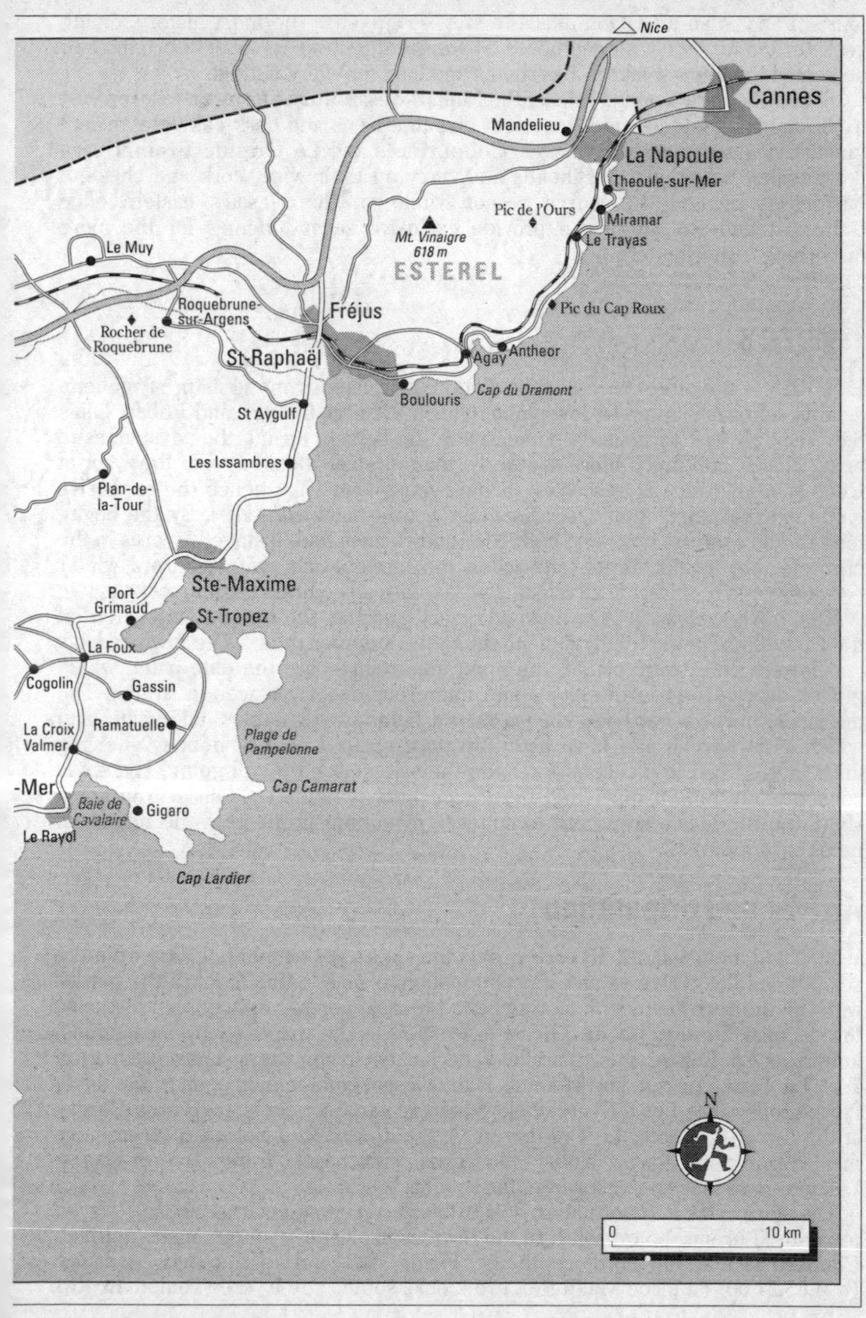
Nice
Cannes
Mandelieu
La Napoule
Theoule-sur-Mer
Pic de l'Ours
Miramar
Le Trayas
Mt. Vinaigre
618 m
ESTEREL
Le Muy
Roquebrune-
sur-Argens
Rocher de
Roquebrune
Fréjus
St-Raphaël
Pic du Cap Roux
Agay
Antheor
Boulouris
Cap du Dramont
St Aygulf
Les Issambres
Plan-de-
la-Tour
Ste-Maxime
Port
Grimaud
St-Tropez
La Foux
Cogolin
Gassin
Ramatuelle
La Croix
Valmer
Plage de
Pampelonne
-Mer
Cap Camarat
Baie de
Cavalaire
Gigaro
Le Rayol
Cap Lardier
N
0
10 km

tourism and is an affordable place to stay. **Fréjus** has the most history, dating back to Roman times; its neighbour **St-Raphaël** ignores its ancient origins but, dedicated to holiday-makers, has rooms and food for every budget.

Inland, the dark wooded hills of the **Massif des Maures** form a backdrop east to St-Raphaël. Hidden amid the sweet chestnut trees and cork oaks are ancient monasteries and medieval villages. **Collobrières** and **La Grande Freinet** have not forsaken traditional livelihoods and carry on their wine, cork and chestnut businesses beyond the tourist season while on the Massif's eastern edge **Grimaud** and **Rocquebrune** provide exclusive second homes for the more discerning Côte clientele.

Hyères

HYERES is the oldest resort of the Côte d'Azur, listing among its pre-twentieth-century admirers Empress Josephine, Queen Victoria, Tolstoy and Robert Louis Stevenson. It was particularly popular with the British, having the advantages of being closer, and much more southerly, than its rival Nice. In order to winter at Hyères in style it was necessary to have one's own villa, hence the expansive gardened residences that spread seawards from the *Vieille Ville*. By the beginning of this century, however, both Nice and Cannes had upstaged Hyères in the clientele they could attract, and when the foreign rich switched from winter convalescents to quayside strutters, Hyères, with no central seafront, lost out.

It is, nevertheless, a very popular resort, and has the unique distinction on the Côte of not being totally dependent on the summer influx. The town exports cut flowers and exotic plants, the most important being the date palm, which graces every street in the city – and numerous desert palaces in Arabia. The orchards, nursery gardens, vineyards and fields of vegetables, taking up land which elsewhere would have been developed into a rash of holiday shelving units, are crucial to its economy. Even the salt works are still going. Hyères is consequently rather appealing: the *Vieille Ville* is neither a tourist trap nor a slum and the locals aren't out to squeeze maximum profit from the minimum number of months.

Arrival and orientation

Walled and medieval **old Hyères** lies on the slopes of Casteou hill, 5km from the sea. Av des Iles d'Hyères and its continuation av Gal-de-Gaulle mark the border with the **modern town** with av Gambetta the main north–south axis. At the coast the peculiar **Presqu'île de Giens** is leashed to the mainland by an isthmus, known as **La Capte**, and a parallel sand bar enclosing the salt marshes and a lake. **La Tour Fondue** port at Giens is the closest embarcation point to the Ile de Porquerolles (see Iles d'Hyères below); Hyère's **main port** is at **Hyères-Plages** at the top of La Capte. **Le Ceinturon**, **Ayguade** and **Les Salins d'Hyères** are the village-cum-resorts along the coast northeast from Hyères-Plages; **L'Almanarre** is to the west where the sandbar starts.

The **gare SNCF** (information ☎94.91.50.50; reservations ☎94.38.82.97) is on place de l'Europe, 1.5km south of the town centre, with frequent buses to **place Clemenceau** at the entrance to the *Vieille Ville* and to the **gare routière** (☎94.65.21.00) on place Mal-Joffre, two blocks south. The Hyères-Toulon **airport**

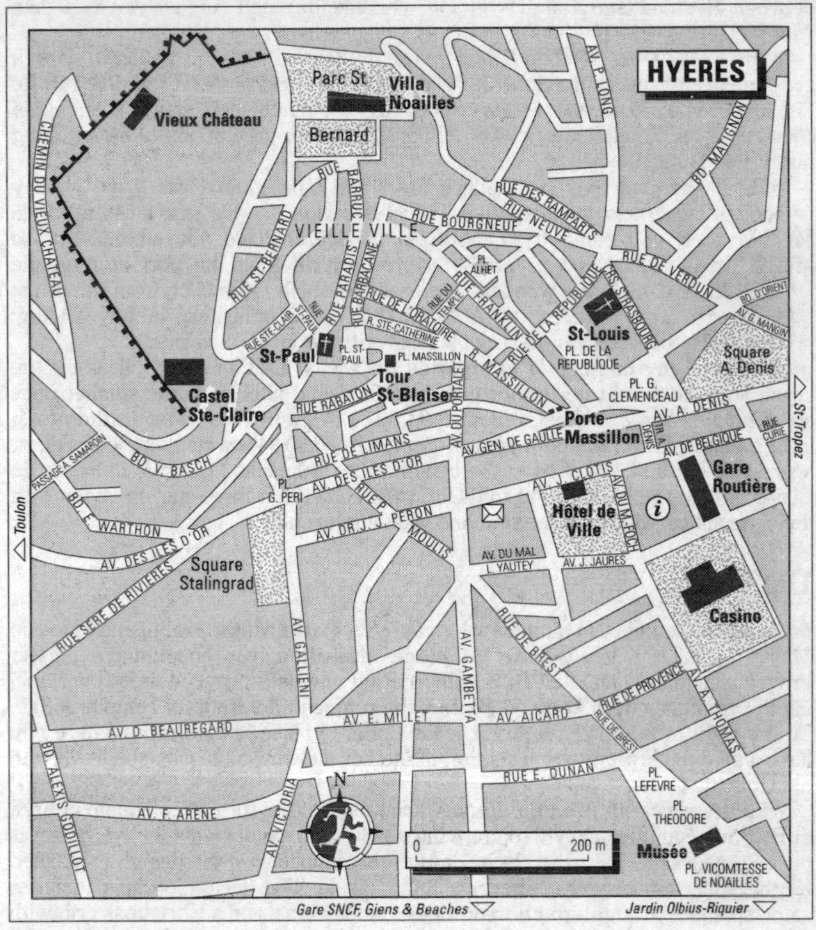

(☎94.22.81.60) is between Hyères and Hyères-Plage, 3km from the centre with a regular shuttle to the centre.

The **tourist office** is next door to place Mal-Joffre in the beautiful Rotunde Jean-Salusse on av de Belgique (daily 10am–noon & 2–5.30pm; ☎94.65.33.40) and will provide information on everything from archery and karate clubs to fishing and surfing competitions. **Bikes** and mopeds, which you may need, can be rented from *Holiday Bikes* on rte du Palyvrestre, between the airport and the *gare SNCF* (☎94.38.46.08), or the *Mistral Centre* on rte de Giens (☎94.58.26.87).

Accommodation

Hotels in Hyères are not expensive. There are only three in the *Vieille Ville* but plenty in the modern town and even more on La Capte and along the seafront between Hyères-Plage and L'Ayguade. Outside July and August you can take your pick.

In the *Vieille Ville, Hôtel du Soleil,* on rue du Rempart (☎94.65.16.26; ④), is well positioned high up at the foot of parc St-Bernard; *Hôtel du Portalet,* 4 rue de Limans (☎94.65.39.40; ③), is less appealing but much more central; and *Lion d'Hyères,* 2 rue République (☎94.65.25.55; ②), has no pretentions to be anything but basic.

Right in the centre of the modern town, the *Hôtel de la Poste,* 7 av Lyautey (☎94.65.02.00; ②), is an inexpensive reliable option. By the sea, at 36 av de la Méditerranée, you could try *Le Calypso* at Hyères-Plage (closed mid-Nov to March; ☎94.58.02.09; ④) or *La Reine Jane* overlooking the port at Ayguade (☎94.66.32.64; ④). On the wooded slopes of Costabelle, 1km back from the sea at L'Almanarre, *La Québécoise,* av Admiral (half-board obligatory in July & Aug; ☎94.57.69.24; ④), is quiet and very pleasant with a pool and sea views.

There are any number of **campsites** on Giens, La Capte and all along the coast, some of them catering for over one thousand pitches. Some smaller ones are: *Camping-Bernard* (Easter–Sept; ☎94.66.30.54), a two-star close to the beach in Le Ceinturon; *Le Capricorne* (April–Sept; ☎94.66.40.94) on rte des Vieux Salins, also a two-star and 1.5km from the beach at Les Salins; and *Clair de Lune,* av du Claire de Lune (mid-March to mid-Oct; ☎94.58.20.19), a three-star on Giens with diving facilities, windsurfs for rent and washing machines.

The Town

From place Clemenceau a medieval gatehouse, **Porte Massillon**, opens onto rue Massillon and the *Vieille Ville*. At **place Massillon**, you encounter a perfect Provençal square, animated by a daily market and with terraced cafés overlooking the twelfth-century **Tour St-Blaise**, the remnant of a Knights Templar lodge. To the right of the tower, a street leads uphill to place St-Paul, from where you have a panoramic view over a section of medieval town wall to Costabelle hill and the Golfe de Giens.

Wide steps fan out from the Renaissance door of the former collegiate church of **St-Paul** (summer daily 3–6pm; winter 2.30–5pm), whose distinctive belfry is pure Romanesque, as is the choir, though the simplicity of the design is masked by the collection of votive offerings hung inside. The decoration also includes some splendid wrought-iron horror-movie candelabras, and a Christmas crib with over-life-size *santons*. Today, the church is only used for special services – the main place of worship is the mid-thirteenth-century former monastery church of **St-Louis** on place de la République.

To the right of St-Paul, a Renaissance house bridges rue St-Paul, its turret supported by a pillar rising beside the steps. Through this arch you can reach rue St-Claire which leads past the neo-Gothic Porte des Princes to the entrance of **parc Ste-Claire** (8am–dusk; free), the exotic gardens around **Castel Ste-Clair**. The Castel was originally owned by the French archeologist Olivier Voutier, who discovered the Venus de Milo, was then home to the American writer and interior designer Edith Wharton and now houses the offices of the Parc National de Port Cros.

Cobbled paths lead up the hill via Rue St-Bernard towards the **parc St-Bernard** (8am–dusk; free), full of almost every Mediterranean flower known. Alternatively, from St-Paul you can head up to the parc via rue Paradis, where you'll find an exquisite Romanesque house at no. 6, now just an ordinary residence. Thankfully, the streets of old Hyères have managed to refrain from breeding arts and crafts and trinket shops, keeping their traditional feel. In the upper part of the *Vieille Ville* all the houses have a slight backward tilt as if to let even more light play on their old undistrubed facades.

At the top of the park, above montée des Noailles (which can be reached by car from cours Strasbourg and av Long), is the **Villa Noailles**, a Cubist mansion designed by Mallet-Stevens in the 1920s and enclosed within part of the old citadel walls. All the luminaries of Dada and Surrealism stayed here and left their mark, including Man Ray who used it as the setting for one of his most inarticulate films, *Le Mystère du Château de Dé*. It is gradually being restored and only open between the end of June and beginning of September when it's the setting for a major art exhibition (10am–noon & 3–7pm).

To the west of the park and further up the hill you come to the remains of Hyères' **Vieux Château** whose keep and the ivy-clad towers outreach the oak and lotus trees and give stunning views out to the Iles d'Hyères and east to the Massif des Maures.

The modern town

The switch from medieval to eighteenth- and nineteenth-century Hyères is particularly abrupt, with wide boulevards and open spaces, opulent villas, waving palm fronds and whitewashed walls instead of weathered stone. Erstwhile fantasy aristocratic residences now have administrative functions, a good example being the former palace-hotel behind the tourist office. One block south, however, the opulent **casino** has been restored to its glass-domed glory and to its original vice.

If you're keen on the ancient history of this coast, the **Musée d'Art et d'Archéologie** (Mon & Wed–Fri 10am–noon & 3–6pm; free) on place Lefèvre will be of interest. It displays the finds of the archeological digs at L'Almanarre, the point where the route de Sel from the Presqu'île de Giens joins the coast. Its name derives from the Arabic for "lighthouse", which is what the Saracens built higher up the slope after destroying a Benedictine monastery, leaving only the chapel of St-Pierre-de-la-Manarre. Merovingian graves have been unearthed, beneath them traces of a Roman city known from Classical texts by the wonderful name of Pomponiana, and beneath that the remnants of the Greek port of Olbia.

The museum also contains local paintings and natural history. But rather than looking at the collection of stuffed birds and fish, you would do better to wander around the **Jardins Olbius-Riquier** (daily 8am–5.30/7pm; free) at the bottom of av Gambetta. Incorporating a lake and a little zoo, these huge gardens have a spectacular array of cacti and palms as well as plants from southern latitudes.

Down to the coast

Hyères' coastal suburbs offer plenty of beaches to choose from. The eastern side of La Capte, the very built-up isthmus of the **Presqu'île de Giens** (L'Almanarre or Hyères-Plage bus), is one long sand beach, with very warm and shallow water and packed out in summer. Heading northeastwards, traffic fumes and the proximity of the airport take away the seaside charms between Hyères Plage and Le Ceinturon despite the pines and ubiquitous palms.

It's far more pleasant further up by the little fishing port of **Les Salins d'Hyères**. East of Les Salins, where the coastal road finally turns inland, you can follow a path between abandoned saltflats and the sea to a naturist beach. Alternatively, there's the less sheltered **L'Almanarre** beach to the west of the Presqu'île de Giens, where you can swim from a narrow crescent of sand: French sailing championships are sometimes held here and it's a popular venue for funboarding.

Just to the north of L'Almanarre is the Costabelle hill, topped by the 1950s **Notre-Dame-de-Consolation**. The church, a concrete, stone and stained-glass classic of its sorry architectural era, houses an ancient statue of Our Lady, the object of pilgrimage for almost a millennium. South of L'Almanarre the route du Sel leads down the sand bar on the western side of the Presqu'île, giving you glimpses of the saltworks and the lake with its flamingoes between the sand bar and the built-up La Capte.

Besides the peculiarity of Presqu'île's attachment to the mainland (last broken by storms in 1811) Giens is a fairly nondescript, up-market and over-populated resort, though it does have some fine cliffs facing the sea and in rough weather you can begin to understand why so many wrecks have been discovered here. **La Tour Fondue**, a Richelieu construction on the eastern side, overlooks the small port that serves the Iles d'Hyères.

Regular **buses** from Hyères' *gare routière* run to L'Almanarre, Hyères-Plage, Giens and Le Centurion.

Eating and drinking

For **eating** and **drinking** in Hyères, there are the terraced café-brasseries in place Massillon and, all around this corner of the *Vieille Ville*, a good choice of crêperies, pizzerias and little bistros that serve plats du jour for around 80F.

At *Le Haut du Pavé*, 2 rue du Temple (☎94.35.20.98), you can dine on every sort of mussels mixture for under 50F and on Saturday evenings listen to jazz in the basement. The best **restaurant** in the *Vieille Ville* has to be *Chez Ma-Mie*, 3 rue de l'Oratoire (closed Wed; evenings only; ☎94.35.39.20; menus 150–250F), with a cosy atmosphere and a wonderful chocolate fondue with fresh-fruit dips. *La Bergerie*, 16 rue de Limans (closed Sat & Sun midday, out of season also Sun evening), is a friendly and down-to-earth pizzeria, with excellent salads and pizzas that are cooked under your nose in a coal-fired oven.

On the edge of the new town, at *Les Jardins de Bacchus*, 32 av Gambetta (closed Mon, summer Sat midday, winter Sun evening; ☎94.65.77.63), you can try novel concoctions like pigeon with foie gras and caramelized pears on salmon with prawns and bacon; menus start at 140F, and à la carte at around 350F.

Overlooking the Port d'Hyères in Hyères-Plages is *La Parillada* (April–Oct; ☎94.57.44.82), with Spanish specialities based on fresh fish; menus from 150F. For the best **cakes and ice creams** try *Pâtisserie Blonna* at 1 place Clemenceau (Tues–Sun 6.30am–1pm & 3.30–7.30pm).

As well as the small daily **market** on place Massillion, there are food markets on place République on Tuesday and Thursday morning and on av Gambetta on Saturday morning; organic produce on place Vicomtesse de Noailles on Tuesday, Thursday and Saturday morning; arts, crafts and food on place Clemenceau on Saturday morning; and a fleamarket in La Capte on Sunday mornings.

The Iles d'Hyères

A haven from tempests in ancient times, then the peaceful habitat of monks and farmers, the **Iles d'Hyères** (also known as the Iles d'Or) from the Middle Ages onwards became a base for piracy and coastal attacks by an endless succession of assorted aggressors, against whom the tiny populations of the islands were ineffectual. Henri II hit upon an inspired solution to this problem in 1550: presumably intending to fight fire with fire he designated the islands as penal colonies. Convicted criminals arrived in droves but Henri's plans were thwarted when they turned to piracy themselves and even attempted to capture a ship of the royal fleet from Toulon. The islands are covered in forts – half-destroyed, rebuilt or abandoned – from the sixteenth century, when François I started a trend of under-funded fort building, to the twentieth century, when the German gun positions on Port-Cros and Levant were knocked out of action by the Americans.

Porquerolles and Levant are still not free of garrisons, thanks to the knack of the French armed forces for getting prime beauty sites for bases. In this case, the army only acquired its *terrain militaire* in 1971, when the French government bought most of the archipelago to save the islands from overdevelopment and to protect their unique fauna and flora. A contradictory move certainly, but it has prevented the otherwise inevitable Côte build-up, and in the non-military areas, the government, through the *Parc National de Port-Cros* and the *Conservatoire Botanique de Porquerolles*, has taken some sound **environmental initiatives**. On **Porquerolles**, the largest island, water is recycled using the natural means of sun-bred micro-organisms; some electricity is generated from gas produced from cane; the fertilizers used are compost not chemical; and cars are strictly limited.

GETTING TO THE ILES D'HYERES

There are Iles d'Hyères ferries, some operating only in summer, from six ports along the Côte d'Azur. If you just want to visit one of the islands, Le Lavandou is the port closest to **Port-Cros** (35min) and **Levant** (35min); La Tour Fondue to **Porquerolles** (20min).

Departures are from:

Cavalaire
(☎94.64.08.04).
Summer-only services to all three islands.

Le Lavandou
15 quai Gabriel-Péri (☎94.71.01.02).
Year-round daily services to Ile de Levant and Port Cros, three-weekly service to Porquerolles (daily from mid-July to Aug).

Port d'Hyères
(☎94.57.44.07).
Services to Port-Cros and Levant all year round and to all of the three islands (July–Aug).

Toulon
quai Stalingrad (☎94.62.41.14).
Services to all three islands (June–Sept).

La Tour Fondue
Presqu'île de Giens (☎94.58.21.81; bus #66 from the Port d'Hyères).
Summer services to all three islands; all year round to Porquerolles.

Port-Cros and its small neighbour **Bagaud** are just about uninhabited, so there the main problem is controlling the flower-picking, litter-dropping habits of visitors. On **Levant** the military rule all but a tiny morsel of the island.

Whatever measures are taken to protect them, the Iles d'Hyères still constitute a very fragile environment, situated as they are in one of the world's most polluted seas by one of the most overpopulated coastlines. But their hot, wild, scented greenery, fine sand beaches, sea and sun constitute the essence of what makes this part of the planet so desirable. If you want to **stay on them**, however, your only reasonable options are on Levant, and then you need to book months in advance. Accommodation on Porquerolles is limited to extremely pricey hotels and rented apartments; on Port-Cros it is almost non-existent.

Porquerolles

PORQUEROLLES is the most easily accessible of the Iles d'Hyères and has a permanent village around the port, with a few hotels and restaurants, plenty of cafés, a market and interminable games of *boules*. In summer its population explodes to over ten thousand, but there is some activity year-round. This is the only cultivated island and it has its own wine, *appellation Côtes des Iles*.

The origins of the ancient **Fort Sainte-Agathe** which overlooks the village are unknown, but it already existed in 1200, and was refortified in the sixteenth century by François I, who built a tower with five-metre thick walls to resist cannon-fire. The fort has a small **museum** (June–Sept daily 11am–6pm; 20F) dedicated to shipwrecks.

The **village** itself dates from a nineteenth-century military settlement. It still focuses around the central place d'Armes, named after its original function as a parade ground. Its first non-military notoriety came in the 1960s, when Jean-Luc Godard used the village, and the calanque de la Treille at the far end of the plage de Notre-Dame, for the bewildering finale of the film *Pierrot le Fou*. Recently the island has taken to hosting an artist in residence with works on show during the summer months at one of the hotels in the village.

Porquerolles is big enough to find yourself alone amid its stunning landscapes, and to get lost. The **lighthouse** due south of the village and the **calanques** to its east make good destinations for an hour's walk, though don't even think of swimming on this side of the island. The southern shoreline is all cliffs with scary paths meandering close to the edge through heather and exuberant Provençal growth. Gentle sandy **beaches** are to be found on either side of the village, with the nearest beach to the village just 1km away (continue away from the port past the *Arche de Noë* and take the first, well-signed right), known as the **plage d'Argent**, a 500-metre strip of white sand around a curving bay, backed by pine forests and a single restaurant. The longest beach is the **plage de Notre-Dame**, 3km northeast of the village, just before the *terrain militaire* that takes up the northern tip.

Practicalities

If you don't want to get around on foot, you can rent a **bike** from eight outlets in the village, including *La Becane* (☎94.58.30.20) to the left of the church or *L'Indien* (☎94.58.30.39) on place d'Armes, but a cheaper option is to pay for your bike with your ferry ticket in La Tour Fondue and pick it up when you disembark at Porquerolles. There's a small **information centre** (daily June–Sept 9am–12.30pm & 2.30–6pm) by the harbour where you can get basic maps of the island.

Hotels in Porquerolles cost 500F upwards and need to be booked months in advance. The most expensive and de luxe is *Le Mas du Langoustier* (May to mid-Oct; ☎94.58.30.09; ⑧) at the western end of the island. *Sainte-Anne* (mid-Feb to mid-Nov; ☎94.58.30.04; ⑥), *Auberge des Glycines* (☎94.58.30.36; ⑦) and *Relais de la Poste* (May–Oct; ☎94.58.30.26; ⑥) are all on place d'Armes in the village, and, with the exception of the *Relais de la Poste*, require you to take full-board. The island has no **campsite** and *camping sauvage* is strictly forbidden.

Most of the **cafés** and **restaurants** in the village are pure tourist fodder. The wealthy can snack on lobster at *Le Mas du Langoustier* (see above; menus from 300F) and the merely well-off on grilled fish at the *Auberge des Glycines* (see above; menus from 145F). *La Plage d'Argent* (May to mid-Sept; ☎94.58.32.48), overlooking the d'Argent beach, has a good midday menu for around 100F, but the best strategy is to picnic, so arrive in the morning to buy **provisions**.

Port-Cros

The dense vegetation and mini mountains of **PORT-CROS** make exploring this island considerably harder going than Porquerolles, even though it is less than half the size. Aside from ruined forts and the handful of buildings around the port, the only intervention on the island's wildlife are the classification labels on some of the plants and the extensive network of paths. You are not supposed to stray from these signposted routes and it would be very difficult to do so given the thickness of the undergrowth. **Staying** on Port Cros, sadly, is not much of an option. The sole island hotel is prohibitively expensive, as are the few restaurants around the port, though you can get a sandwich or a slice of pizza. Camping is forbidden.

The entire island is a protected zone – no smoking outside the port area, no picking of flowers – and, as the only member of the archipelago with natural springs, has the richest **fauna and flora**. Kestrels, eagles and sparrow-hawks nest here; there are shrubs that flower and bear fruit at the same time, and more common species like broom, lavender, rosemary and heather flourish in abundance. If you come armed with a botanical dictionary, the leaflet provided by the **Bureau d'Information du Parc** at the port will reveal all the species to be seen, watched and smelled.

It takes a couple of hours to walk from the port to the nearest beach, **plage de la Palu**; a similar time to cross the island via the **Vallon de la Solitude** or **Vallon de la Fausse-Monnaie**. You can also follow a ten-kilometre **circuit of the island**. At the Fort de Lestissac, on the way to the plage de la Palu, there is an exhibition on the island **marine life** which is also protected (July–Sept 10am–6pm; free). If you have a snorkel and flippers with you the shallow waters between Palu beach and the tiny offshore island are full of diverting fishes to flap at. More serious scuba divers explore the underwater world around the **Ilot de la Gabinière** off the southern shore.

Alternatively, an expensive "submarine" trip in a glass-bottomed boat called the *Seascope* is on offer around the islands. Be warned though, that, while enjoyable, it is not as exciting as its publicity makes out.

Ile de Levant

The **ILE DE LEVANT** – ninety percent military reserve – is almost always humid and sunny. Cultivated plantlife goes wild with the result that giant geraniums and nasturtiums climb three-metre hedges, overhung by gigantic eucalyptus trees and yucca plants.

The tiny bit of the island spared by the military is a **nudist colony**, set up in the village of **Heliopolis** in the early 1930s. About sixty people live here all the year round, joined by thousands who come just for the summer and tens of thousands of day-trippers. The residents' preferred street dress is *"les plus petits costumes en Europe"*, on sale as you get off the boat.

Visitors who come just for a couple of hours tend to be treated as voyeurs. If you stay, even for one night, you'll generally receive a much friendlier reception, but in summer without advance booking you'd be very lucky to find a room or camping pitch. There are three **campsites**: *Le Colombero* (Easter–Oct; ☎94.05.90.29), *La Joie de Vivre* (June–Sept; ☎94.05.90.49) and *La Pinède* (April–Oct; ☎94.05.90.47). The **hotels** range from the reasonable to the expensive, and again half-board is usually compulsory in summer with rooms needing to be reserved well in advance. *Le Gaëtan* (April–Oct; ☎94.05.91.78; ④) and *La Source,* chemin de l'Aygade (Easter to mid-Oct; ☎94.05.91.36; ④), both close to the port, or *La Brise Marine* (June–Sept; ☎94.05.91.15; ⑤), in the centre of the village, are the three best-value hotels, all small and very charming. For more luxury, there's the clifftop *Le Ponant* (June–Aug; ☎94.05.90.41; ⑥–⑦) and the very smart *Héliotel* (Easter–June; ☎94.05.90.63; ⑧).

Levant has a better choice of **restaurants** than the other islands; you can eat decently at *La Source* and *La Brise Marine* hotels (see above) with menus starting under 100F, or snack at the *Brasserie Ile de Beauté.*

The Corniche des Maures

The Côte really gets going with the resorts of the **Corniche des Maures**, the twenty-kilometre stretch of coast from Le Lavandou to the Baie de Cavalaire, as multi-million-dollar residences lurk increasingly in the hills, even more pricey yachts in the bays, and seafront prices start edging up. You can sip the divinest cocktail under the warmest moon, become obsessed with estate agents' windows, or have your luggage stolen while you're waiting at the lights. It is where the rich and famous go to seed: namely Douglas Fairbanks Jr (a house in Bormes), the late grand duke of Luxembourg and a host of titled names that *Tatler* readers are assumed to know. And though aristos and celebrities may not be renowned for their good taste, when it comes to locations for living, they can usually be relied upon.

The Corniche des Maures has beaches that shine silver from the mica crystals in the sand; tall dark pines, oaks and eucalyptus shading them and hiding garish villa balconies; glittering rocks of purple, green and reddish hue; and chestnut-forested hills keeping winds away. There are even stretches where it's possible to imagine what all this coast was like in bygone years, notably around **Cap de Brégançon**, at the **Domaine de Rayol gardens**, and between **Le Rayol** and the huge resort of **Cavalaire**.

Transport around the Corniche is the biggest problem. There are no trains and buses in high season are extremely slow, for the same reason that driving can be pretty hellish. Cycling is strenuous and hair-raising, and doesn't get you very far unless you're *Tour de France* material.

Bormes-les-Mimosas

BORMES-LES-MIMOSAS, like all good Provençal villages, 6km west of Hyères, is indisputably medieval, with a ruined but restored castle at the summit of its hill, protected by spiralling lines of pantiled houses backing onto short-cut flights of steps. Attractions include a **Musée d'Art et d'Histoire** at 65 rue Carnot (June–Sept Thurs, Sat & Sun 9am–noon & 3–5pm; Oct–May Thurs & Sun 10am–noon & 3–5pm; free), with its turn-of-the-century regional painting; a mindlessly ugly pleasure port down by **La Favière**, flanked by spot-the-spare-foot-of-sand beaches; and oddly named addresses in the *Vieux Village* such as "alleyway of lovers", "street of brigands", "gossipers' way", and "arse-breaker street".

The mimosas here, and all along the Côte d'Azur, are no more indigenous than the people passing in their Porsches. The tree that flowers in February in a myriad of tiny yellow pom-poms was introduced from Mexico in the 1860s, and the extension to the place-name dates from 1968. It has to be said, however, in Bormes' favour, that its bougainvillea and other luscious summer climbing flowers are spectacular and ubiquitous.

When you've had enough of exploring the immaculately paved alleyways or following the signed *circuits touristiques* up and down the steep slopes of the old village, you can head for the coast but be prepared for *Defense d'entrée* (No Entry) and *Propriété privée* (Private Property) signs at every turn. Private housing estates have entirely blocked road access to the extremity of **Cap Bénat** but you can reach it on foot along a coastal path from La Favière's beach. From Cap Bénat westwards to the hideous seaside extension of **La Londe**, vineyards and private woods will block your passage, as well as the security arrangements around the château at **Cap de Brégançon** which is the holiday home of the president of the Republic. Note also that you will be forced to pay on each of the three public tracks down to the shore off the road between La Londe and **Cabasson** (summer around 35F for a car, 7F for a bike and 4F for your feet; winter free). However, once you've reached the water you can wander along the georgeous beaches as far as you like, with no apartment buildings amongst the pinetrees, not even villas, just the odd mansion in the distance surrounded by its vineyards.

Practicalities

For more information, the **tourist office** in Bormes (daily 10am–noon & 2–6pm; ☎94.71.15.17) is on place Gambetta, near the top of the village and where **buses** arrive. Three reasonable **hotels** in old Bormes are *La Terrasse*, 19 place Gambetta (☎94.71.15.22; ②), with ordinary, clean rooms; *Le Provençal* on rue de la Plaine-des-Anes (☎94.71.15.25; ③), with a pool and seaside restaurant, if rather shabby rooms; and the *Bellevue* on place Gambetta (☎94.71.15.15; ③), a bit plain and old-fashioned. In Cabasson there's a very attractive and peaceful hotel *Les Palmiers*, 240 chemin du Petit Fort (half-board compulsory in summer; ☎94.64.81.94; ⑦), with its own path to the beach. By far the nicest **campsite** for miles around, and less than 500m to the sea, is the three-star *Au Bout du Monde* (April–Oct; book in July & Aug; ☎94.64.80.08), where you can buy wine from the *domaine* next door and a *boulangerie* van visits every day. Other campsites are all just below the main road or in La Favière, closer to Le Lavandou than to Bormes, and include the four-star *Clos Mas Jo*, 895 chemin de Bénat (open all year; ☎94.71.53.39), the two-star *La Célinette*, 30 impasse du Moux (April to mid-Oct; ☎94.71.07.98), and the two-star *Les Cyprès* on av de la Mer (Easter–Oct; ☎94.64.86.50). Book in advance in high season.

This being the Côte proper, **restaurants** become rather interesting, though often more costly than a hotel room. Bormes' star eating place is *Le Jardin de Perle-Fleurs*, 100 chemin de l'Orangerie (July–Sept Tues–Sun; ☎94.64.99.23) where traditional Provençal dishes like *soupe au pistou*, tomato raviolis, *bourride*, *panisses* and *daube* can't be bettered; menus unfortunately start from 240F; à la carte 330F upwards. *L'Escoundudo*, 2 ruelle du Moulin (closed Sat & Sun out of season; ☎94.71.15.53), is a lot more affordable with a delicious tomato and hot goat's cheese tart on the generous 135F menu; there's another menu for under 100F. *Pâtes ... et Pâtes* on place du Bazar (Mon & Wed–Sun) serves the best pasta for 100–150F. More ordinary dinners can be had at the hotels listed above and at *La Pastourelle*, 41 rue Carnot (☎94.71.57.78).

To reach Le Lavandou and La Favière on foot, follow bd de la République downhill, and at the first hairpin after it has become bd du Soleil, take a left to the sentier St-François. For Cabasson (7km from Bormes) take bd Jean-Jaurès from place du Bazar and at the main road turn left and right.

Le Lavandou

One of many Mediterranean fishing villages turned pleasure port, **LE LAVANDOU** has nothing wildly special to recommend it, apart from the seduction of its name (which comes from *lavoir* or wash-house rather than lavender), some tempting shops and a general Azur atmosphere. From the central promenade of quai Gabriel Péri the sea is hardly visible for pleasure boats moored at the three harbours and it's only the more upmarket restaurant demand that keeps the dozen or so fishing vessels still in business. The **beach** that port construction has spared is east-facing and backed by high-rise buildings to the west of town.

The whole conglomeration of the town, which merges with Bormes to the west and **Saint Clair** to the east (whose beach is more pleasant than Le Lavandou's), concentrates its charm in the tiny area between av du Gal-de-Gaulle and quai Gabriel-Péri where café tables sporting multicoloured goblets of cocktails and ice creams overlook the *boules* pitch and the traffic of the seafront road. Three narrow stairways lead back to rue Patron Ravello, place Argaud and rue Abbé-Helin where you can wander menu-browsing or window shopping. Place Argaud has a typical mixture: *Marie Boutique* selling desirable baskets and chinaware, an "*artisan-créateur*" jeweller with very original designs, and an inexpensive shop of flashy shoes called *La Puce Tropezienne*, as well as cafés and restaurants. If you're feeling more energetic or adventurous you can rent a surf-board or a boat, go water-skiing, take a trip to the Iles d'Hyères or try out deep-sea diving. But if you're after the fabled silver beaches you need to head out of town and east to the string of villages between Le Lavandou and Cavalaire-sur-Mer.

Practicalities

Buses arrive between quai Gabriel Péri and quai Baptistin Pins opposite the **tourist office** (Mon–Sat 8.30am–7.30pm, Sun 10am–noon & 4–7pm; ☎94.71.00.61). The unexotic **quai des Iles d'Or** juts out from here, a wide patch of tarmac dividing two of the ports. Boats to the Iles d'Hyères (daily), to St-

Tropez (every Tues) and to Brégançon (every Sun) leave from here; the *Ecole de Plongée* offers initiation deep-sea dives (turn up at noon; around 150F); and *Cap Sud* rents out motor boats. For escaping into the hills or vainly hunting out secluded beaches you can rent **bikes** from *Neway Waikiki*, 15 av des Ilaires (☎94.71.16.50).

In summer, if you haven't booked in advance, your chances of finding a **hotel room** are pretty slim. Prices are similar to Bormes with rather less charm at the bottom end of the range. Some less pricey addresses to try, all in the centre, include: *Neptune*, 26 av Général-de-Gaulle (☎94.71.01.01; ③); *Hôtel l'Oustaou*, 20 av Général-de-Gaulle (☎94.71.12.18; ④); and *L'Auberge Provençale*, 11 rue Patron Ravello (☎94.71.00.44; ④). For twice as much you could have a charming room overlooking the sea at St-Clair in the *Belle-Vue*, chemin du Four des Maures (April–Oct; ☎94.71.01.06; ⑦), or at *La Calanque*, 62 av du Gal-de-Gaulle (Feb–Sept & Dec; ☎94.71.05.96; ⑧) in a less attractive building but with views over the port and fishing and diving trips laid on. For **campsites**, there are those at Bormes (see above) or the *Camping St-Clair*, av André-Gide in St-Clair (March–Oct; ☎94.71.03.38), a three-star amidst bamboos for campervans and caravans only.

Sea-view gourmandise comes at a price at *L'Algue Bleue* (menus from 190F, à la carte from 300F), the **restaurant** of *La Calanque* (see above); the sea bass is particularly fine. The *Auberge Provençale*'s restaurant (see above; closed Tues & Thurs midday, plus Tues evening out of season) is a great place to be, though the food is still a touch expensive with *aïoli* at 99F and menus from 130F. At *Le Pêcheur*, quai des Pêcheurs (☎94.71.58.01), you can dine on fish caught by the restaurant's owner (around 120F). As for **café lounging** you can take your pick. On quai Gabriel-Péri *Le Rhumerie* has live music weekend nights and the most comfy terrace chairs; the *Brasserie du Centre* is the most restrained in style, and the cocktails pricier; *Chez Mimi* has good beers and perhaps the edge on the ice-cream front; *La Panthèse Bleue* is a smart piano-bar.

If you're determined to accelerate the rate your money parts company with you, Le Lavandou's **nightlife** will assist. *Le Paradis*, at résidence Marbello, bd du Front-de-Mer (April to mid-Oct 10.30pm–5am), is a **disco** which has been going strong for more than fifty years; *La Jamaïque*, quai Baptistin Pins (10.30pm–dawn), is a more laid-back nightclub with an older clientele and Afro-Caribbean sounds.

Along the Corniche: Lavandou to Cavalaire-sur-Mer

The road east out of Le Lavandou and St-Clair (av André-Gide or the D559) is lined with pink oleander bushes interspersed with purple bouganvillea, a classic feature of the Côte d'Azur corniche as it curves its way through the steep wooded hills that reach right down to the sea. The pines and eucalyptus hiding the estates of holiday villas, the geographical impossibility of a constant shore-line road, and the scented flowers go some way to compensate for the loss of countryside. There's also the old railway track of the *Ex-Voie Férée* line, the lengths of which you can walk along, running from **Pramousquier** to **Cavalaire-sur-Mer,** which brought the rich and curious to these parts at the turn of the century. For all the modern build-up of this stretch, it is, along with the St-Tropez peninsula it leads to, the most beautiful part of the Côte d'Azur.

The **beaches** here really are silvery and from Pramousquier, 7km from Le Lavandou, you can even look up from the turquoise water to woods undisturbed by roads and buildings. Between **AIGUEBELLE** and **CAVALIERE** before you reach Pramousquier, a path through the pines above **Pointe du Layet** gives you access to the tiny *calanques* around the headland that extends out from Plage du Rossignol and Plage du Layet. Cavalière has a long wide beach and hill horizons that easily outreach the highest houses. Though **LE CANADEL** and **LE RAYOL**, two joined villages 4km east of Pramousquier, have gradually colonized their upper slopes, they feel like villages and the climb up the D27 to the **Col du Canadel** has unbeatable views.

The best place of all, however, where you can totally forget what has happened to this coast in the last forty years, is the huge **Domaine du Rayol gardens** in **Le Rayol** (July & Aug Tues–Sun 9.30am–12.30pm & 4.30–8pm; April–June & Sept–Oct 9.30am–12.30pm & 2.30–6.30pm; 30F). The grounds extending down to the Figuier bay and headland originally belonged to a banker who went bust at the gaming tables of Monte Carlo in the 1930s. He built the Art Nouveau mansion through which you enter the gardens, the Art Deco villa, farmhouse and classical pergola to which a later owner added the dramatic long flight of steps lined with cypresses. Areas of the garden are dedicated to plants from different parts of the world that share the Mediterranean climate: Chile, South Africa, China, California, Central America, Australia and New Zealand. Apart from the extraordinary diversity in the forms and colours of the vegetation, some of which is left alone to spread and colonize at will, there's sheer brilliance in the landscaping that entices you to explore, to retrace your steps and get to know every path and every vista. You never see beyond the limits of the garden, even when you're looking at the sea, and as for gazing down below the shore through different depths of water at glittering rocks and swaying sea urchins, no superlatives are adequate. In July and August you can take a snorkelling tour of the "Jardin Marine" (reservation needed, preferably a week in advance but you could be lucky on the same day; ☎94.05.32.50; 60F). There are also highly informative and engaging guided tours (in French only) of the garden, given by its professional gardeners.

Heading east from Le Rayol and Le Canadel the corniche climbs away from the coast through 3km of open countryside, sadly scarred nearly every year by fires, where the only visible building is **La Maison Blanche**, a lone mansion donated by its heirless owner to the *commune* of Cavalaire, who have made all the land around it a protected site. As abruptly as this wilderness commences, it ends with the choking, hideous sprawl of **CAVALAIRE-SUR-MER**. Here the tiny beaches below steep inclines give way to a long stretch of sand and level land behind that has been exploited for the maximum rentable space. In its favour, Cavalaire is very much a family resort and not too stuck on glamour.

Practicalities

The helpful **tourist office** (July & Aug daily; Sept–June Mon–Sat 9am–noon & 3–7pm; ☎94.05.65.69) for Le Rayol and Le Canadel, on place Le Rayol opposite *Le Maurin des Maures* restaurant, has details of possible walks including the Ex-Voie Férée. Cavalaire-sur-Mer's **tourist office** (daily 9am–6pm; ☎94.64.08.28), on the corner of rue du Port and av Charles-de-Gaulle, close by the supremely ugly and unmissable *Maison de la Mer*, hands out lists of hotels and campsites. **Bikes** can be rented nearby at *Holiday Bikes*.

Finding **rooms** in this area outside July and August should not present a problem; if you get stuck there are a number of hotels in Cavalaire-sur-Mer. In

Cavalière the **hotel** with the best view is *Les Cigales*, rue des Ecoles (☎94.05.80.32; ⑤). Above the main road in Pramousquier and within easy walking distance of the beach, the *Hôtel Beau Site* (☎94.05.80.08; ④) has rooms with sea- view balconies, while *Le Mas* (☎94.05.80.43; ⑤), one street behind, has a pool and even better views. Between Pramousquier and Le Canadel *Le Karlina*, on chemin du Plageron (☎94.05.61.65; ⑦), has its own private beach front and boat. In Le Rayol you can stay in an apartment for four people from 320F to 480F a day at *Les Iles de la Mer*, close to the beach on av des Américains (☎94.05.63.76), or there are simple low-priced rooms at *Les Silaques* on the main road (☎94.05.60.13; ③).

The place to **eat** and **drink** is *Le Maurin des Maures* on the main road at Le Rayol (open till late in July & Aug; ☎94.05.60.11; Mon–Sat midday menu under 100F, otherwise 150F) serving fresh grilled fish, *bouillabaisse* and fried seafoods and genuinely popular with the locals. For **nightlife**, head down to Le Canadol's beach where *La Tropicana* **disco** keeps the night young (July & Aug only; from 10.30pm).

La Croix-Valmer

From Cavalaire's seafront, another exceptional sight of coastline, the **Domaine de Cap Lardier**, dressed only in its natural covering of rock and woodlands, greets you from the other side of the Baie de Cavalaire. This is a wonderful coastal conservation area around the southern tip of the St-Tropez peninsula; access to it is the main reason why **LA CROIX-VALMER** is a preferable base to Cavalaire, though the resort's centre is some 2.5km from the sea. That too adds charm, however, since some of the land in between is taken up by vineyards which produce a very decent *Côte de Provence*. Local legend maintains that Emperor Constantine stopped here with his troops on his way to Rome and had his famous vision of the sun's rays forming a cross over the sea which converted him, and therefore ultimately all of Europe, to the new religion; hence the "cross" in the name of the village which only came into existence in 1934.

La Croix-Valmer's **tourist office** is in Jardin de la Gare (daily 10am–noon & 2–6pm; ☎94.79.66.44), just up from the central junction place des Palmiers. A budget-priced **hotel** for this part of the world is *La Cigale* (half-board obligatory in season; ☎94.79.60.41; ②), right on the main road by place des Palmiers and consequently not very quiet; better value is *La Bienvenue* on rue L-Martin (☎94.79.60.23; ④), right in the centre of the village. At the other end of the scale is *Le Château de Valmer* on rte de Gigaro (☎94.79.60.10; ⑦), a seriously luxurious old Provençal manor house within walking distance of the sea. For a **campsite** with excellent facilities try the four-star *Selection* site on bd de la Mer (Easter–Sept; essential to book mid-summer; ☎94.79.61.97), 2.5km southwest of the town centre on the main road towards Cavalaire, and just 400m from the sea.

For the extravagant hungry there are some extremely tempting **restaurants** along the **beach**, the best of which is *Souleias* (☎94.79.61.91; 200F upwards). If you're on a budget, good, inexpensive pizzas are guaranteed at *Le Coin de l'Italien*, almost the last commercial outlet before the conservation area. The local **wine** is for sale at the *Cave Vinicole* on bd de Tabarin by place des Palmiers.

To reach **Plage du Gigaro** and the start of the paths to Cap Lardier, you need to take bd Georges Selliez from place des Palmiers (the D93), turn right into bd de Sylvabelle then left along bd de la Mer.

St-Tropez and its peninsula

The origins of **ST-TROPEZ** are not remarkable: a little fishing village that grew up around a port founded by the Greeks of Marseille, was destroyed by the Saracens in 739 and finally fortified in the late Middle Ages. Its sole distinction from the myriad other fishing villages along this coast was its inaccessibility. Stuck out on the southern shores of the Golfe de St-Tropez, away from the main coastal routes on a wide peninsula that never warranted real roads, St-Tropez could only easily be reached by boat. This held true as late as the 1880s, when the novelist **Maupassant** sailed his yacht into the port during his final high-living binge before the onset of syphilitic insanity. The Tropeziens were a little shocked but it was the beginning of their induction to bizarre strangers seeing paradise in their commonplace home.

Soon after Maupassant's fleeting visit, the painter and leader of the Neo-Impressionists, **Paul Signac**, sailed down the coast in his boat named after Manet's notorious painting *L'Olympia*. Bad weather forced him to moor in St-Tropez and, being an impulsive anarchist and rich, he instantly decided to have a house there. Eventually *La Hune* (on what is now rue Paul-Signac) was built for him, designed by his fellow painter Henri van de Velde. Signac opened his doors to impoverished friends who could benefit from the light, the beauty and the distance from the respectable convalescent world of Cannes and Nice. **Matisse** was one of the first to take up his offer (the locals were shocked again by Madame Matisse modelling in a kimono). **Bonnard**, **Marquet**, **Dufy**, **Derain**, **Vlaminck**, **Seurat**, **Van Dongen** and others followed, and by the eve of World War I, St-Tropez was fairly well established as a hang-out for Bohemians.

The 1930s saw a new influx of artists, this time writers as much as painters. **Jean Cocteau**, who went everywhere, came here. **Colette** bought a villa outside the village where she lived for fourteen years, describing the main concerns of her life there as "whether to go walking or swimming, whether to have rosé or white, whether to have a long day or a long night". **Anaïs Nin's** journal records "girls riding bare-breasted on the back of open cars … an intensity of pleasure …" and undressing between bamboo bushes that rustled with concealed lovers.

After World War II, St-Tropez was ready for another burst of singular animation. In 1956 Roger Vadim arrived, with crew, to film **Brigitte Bardot** in *Et Dieu Créa La Femme*. The international cult of Tropezian sun, sex and celebrities took off; even the Sixties hippies who flocked to the revamped Mediterranean mecca of liberation managed to look glamorous, and the resort has been big-money mainstream ever since.

The star-studded list of St-Tropez **property owners** includes Brigitte Bardot, Elton John, George Michael, Jean-Paul Belmondo as well as high-profile business types such as Mohammad Al Fayad, owner of *Harrods*. Bardot is almost an icon of the place, though in the summer of 1989 she announced to the world that a "black tide of human filth" was physically and morally polluting her beloved village. Europe's media descended on the *mairie* where the beleaguered mayor said yes, the summer influx has quadrupled in the last few years, and yes, they have to collect the rubbish twice a day and still can't keep the streets clean. "It is true that St-Tropez is a dying village," concluded the mayor, "but who brought all this vice and indecency here in the first place?"

In 1991 another disaster struck with the discovery that the famous hundred-year-old **plane trees** on place des Lices were rotting. Several had to be chopped down; the remainder have undergone intensive surgery and their hollow trunks

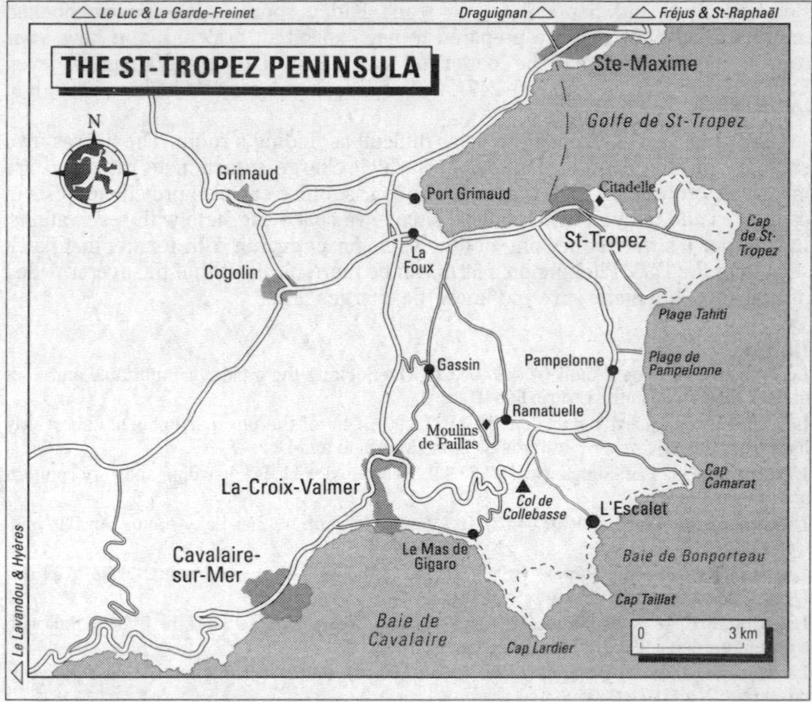

are now propped up with metal crutches. They are perhaps a fitting metaphor for St-Tropez itself. Bardot and her animal foundation are still there; rubbish bins have multiplied; the clientele with titanium-plated credit cards has not been abandoned, but the ordinary punter, who used to only stroll and gawp, is now catered for in run-of-the-mill rip-off fashion. The myth, of course, is hollow; yet it seems that nothing will stop people coming here and the old fabric of the village is still gorgeous if you bother to look up from the people-watching.

Arrival, information and accommodation

The road into St-Tropez from La Foux divides as it enters the village into av Général-Leclerc and av du 11 novembre 1918, with the **gare routière** between them and a tourist office annexe on av Général-Leclerc. The harbour here is the **Nouveau Port** for yacht overspill. On foot follow av du 8 mai past the **post office** and you'll hit the **Vieux Port**, with the *Vieille Ville* rising above the eastern quay. The main **tourist office** is on the *Vieux Port* at the start of quai Jean-Jaurès (summer daily 9am–8pm; winter Mon–Sat 9am–12.30pm & 2–6.30pm; ☎94.97.45.21). You can rent **bikes** and mopeds from *La Tropezienne* just before the Esso garage on av du 11 novembre 1918 or at 5 rue J-Quaranta.

The tourist office can help with **hotel** reservations, although with more and more people wanting to pay homage to St-Trop, accommodation is a problem.

Between April and September you won't find a room unless you've booked months in advance and are prepared to pay exorbitant prices. If you have your own transport, you may be better off staying in La Croix-Valmer or even Cavalaire-sur-Mer (see pp.246–247). Out of season you may be luckier, though in winter few hotels stay open.

Camping near St-Tropez can be as difficult as finding a room. The nearest two sites are on the plage du Pampelonne which charge extortionate rates and are massively crowded in high summer. The tourist office can also provide full lists of campsites and tell you which official sites have space and help with reservations. In summer it's worth checking out the signs for **camping à la ferme**, that you'll see along the D93. Pitching on a farm can be more pleasant that the overcrowded official sites, but make sure you know the charges first.

Hotels

Le Baron, 23 rue de l'Aïoli (☎94.97.06.57). Overlooking the citadel, comfortable and a bit quieter than those in the centre. Feb–Dec. ⑧

Les Chimères, quartier du Pilon (☎94.97.02.90). One of the cheaper options a short way back from the *gare routière* towards La Foux. March to mid-Dec. ④

L'Hermitage, av Paul-Signac (☎94.97.52.33). Above pl des Lices, charming and very comfortable. Open all year. ⑧

Laetitia, 52 rue Allard (☎94.97.04.02). In a central location but has poky rooms. April to mid-Oct. ⑥

Les Lauriers, rue du Temple (☎94.97.04.88). Small and very good value, close to pl des Lices. Open all year. ⑦

Lou Cagnard, 18 av Paul-Roussel (☎94.97.04.24). Dreary looking from the outside, but with a decent garden and night-time quiet. Open all year. ⑤

La Méditerranée, 21 bd Louis-Blanc (☎94.97.00.44). Rather scruffy and not on a glamourous street. March–Oct. ⑤

La Ponche, 3 rue des Ramparts (☎94.97.02.53) An old block of fishers' houses luxuriously kitted out and with a host of famous arty names in its guest book. ⑧

Le Roustidou, pl Gramont (☎94.97.01.37). Charmless rooms but is very central and open all year. ⑤

Le Sube, quai Suffren (☎94.97.30.04). Unique views over the port for over 1500F a night; decor to make you think you're in a yacht and mirrors everywhere. Open all year. ⑧

Campsites

La Croix du Sud, rte de St-Tropez (☎94.79.80.84). A four-star 3km towards the Plage de Pampelone from Ramatuelle (see p.254). May–Sept.

Camping Parc Montana, off the road to Bourrian near Gassin (☎94.56.12.49). A three-star site which also has caravans for rental. April–Sept.

Les Tournels on rte de Camarat (☎94.79.80.54). Vast site but well situated. Open all year.

The Town

Beware of coming to St-Tropez in high summer, unless by yacht and with limitless credit. The 5.5km of road from Le Foux (the mainland as it were) has summer traffic jams as bad as Nice or Marseille, and the pedestrian jams to the port are not much better. The hotels and restaurants are full and too expensive, and the beaches, while not quite as bad as Bardot's description of being covered in human turds, condoms and every other sort of rubbish, are certainly not the cleanest on the coast. So save your visit, if you can, for a spring or autumn day and you may understand why this place has had such history and such hype.

St-Trop has no need to advertise its medieval streets with *circuits touristiques* – you circulate spontaneously and the soft-coloured ancient weathered buildings appear such a natural backdrop to the commerce that you hardly notice them.

The **Vieux Port** is where you get the classic St-Tropez experience: the quay-side café clientele *face à face* with the yacht-deck Martini sippers, and the latest fashion looks parading in between, defining the French word *frimer* (derived from sham) which means exactly this – to stroll ostentatiously in places like St-Tropez. You may well be surprised at just how entertaining this spectacle can be, especially when added to the jugglers, fire-eaters and mimics that trade their art in the streets. Less appealing are the choc-box landscape artists, corny caricaturists and dreadful portrait painters that set up their easels along quai G-Péri.

The **yachts**, which in this restricted harbour space appear to share the scale of cross-Channel ferries, tend to be registered in Britain, the US, the Caribbean or France. Union Jacks normally predominate, with passengers sporting quasi-military casual dress. The Americans are always in Yves St-Laurent and Christian Dior, the Germans in pseudo-naval uniforms, making it hard to distinguish them from the crews who dress either as Dorchester *maître d'hôtel*s or as cinematic high-tech burglar teams. The French dress to show that they're at home – the odd yacht habitué has been known to cross the quayside in dressing gown and slippers to buy himself some *Gauloises*. The actual owners of these ugly floating fortunes are just as likely to be Manhattan or City of London banks as individual aristocrats or stars.

The other pole of St-Trop's life is **place des Lices**, southeast of the *Vieux Port*, with its sad but surviving plane trees and the benches and *boules* games underneath. The café-brasseries have become a bit too Champs-Elysées in style, and a new commercial block has been added near the northern corner, but you can still sit down for free and ponder the unchanged dusty surface that is so essential for the momentum of Provence's favourite pastime.

Between the port and place des Lices – rue Sibille, rue Clemenceau – and in the smaller lanes in the heart of the old village you can window-shop or buy haute couture, antiques, *objets d'art* and classy trinkets to your heart's content.

East from the port, from the top end of quai Jean-Jaurès, you pass the **Château Suffren** originally built in 980 by Count Guillaume 1er of Provence (now home to an antique shop and occasional art exhibitions) into place de l'Hôtel-de-Ville where the *mairie* with its attractive earthy pink facade and dark green shutters reminds you that this is a real town. A street to the left takes you down to the rocky **Baie de la Glaye**; straight ahead rue de la Ponche passes through an ancient gateway to place du Revelin above the **fishing port** with its tiny beach. Turning inland and upwards, struggling past continuous shop fronts, stalls and café tables, you can finally reach the open space around the sixteenth-century **citadel**. Its maritime museum is not much fun but the walk round the ramparts on an overgrown path has the best views of the gulf and the back of the town, views that have not changed since their translations in oil onto canvas before World War II.

These paintings can be seen at the **Musée de l'Annonciade** (Mon & Wed–Sun 10am–noon & 2–6pm or 3–7pm; closed Nov; 20F), reason in itself for a visit to St-Tropez. It was originally Signac's idea to have a permanent exhibition space for the Neo-Impressionists and Fauvists who painted here, though it was not until 1955 that collections owned by various individuals were put together in the deconsecrated sixteenth-century chapel on place Georges-Grammont just west of the port. The museum features representative works by Signac, Matisse and most of the other artists who worked here: grey, grim, northern scenes of Paris, Boulogne and Westminster, and then local, brilliantly sun-lit scenes by the same brush. Two winter scenes of St-Tropez by Dufy contrast with Camille Camoin's springtime *Place des Lices* and Bonnard's boilingly hot summer view. The museum is a real delight for its contents, unrivalled outside Paris for the 1890 to 1940 period, for the way it displays them, and for the fact that it's the least crowded place in town.

Eating and drinking

There are **restaurants** for every budget in St-Tropez, as well as plenty of snack bars and takeaway outfits, particularly on rue Georges-Clemenceau and place des Lices. Almost all are open every day of the week from June to September; many close altogether for the winter months. Place des Herbes has a Tuesday and Saturday morning fruit, veg and fish **market**.

Cafés and snacks

Café des Arts, pl des Lices. The number-one café-brasserie on the square. Old-timers still gather in the bar at the back. Menus from 200F.

Glaces Alfred, rue Sibille. Ice creams made on the premises.

Le Gorille, quai Suffren. Straightforward quayside fare of plats du jour and *frites*. Open 24hr in July & Aug. Under 100F.

La Patate, rue Clemenceau. Snack bar with omelettes, pasta, *pain beignats* and so forth.

Café Sénéquier, on the port. The top quayside café, horribly expensive, but selling sensational nougat (also sold in the shop at the back).

Snack Thierry et Roland, cnr bd Vasserot and rue F-Sibilli. Generous takeaway sandwiches for around 25F. In the same block of outlets you'll find pizzas, roast chicken and a charcuterie.

La Tarte Tropezienne, 1 rue G-Clemenceau. *Pâtissier* claiming to have invented this sponge and cream custard cake.

Restaurants

Chez Angèle, 1 rue des Charrons, an alleyway off rue Aillard (☎94.97.47.74). Tiny, homely and serving acceptable if very ordinary dishes. Plats du jour 80F, menu from 90F. Closed Wed & midday Sun.

Auberge des Maures, rue du Dr Boutin, off rue Aillard (☎94.97.01.50). Roast lamb, stuffed peppers and gooey chocolate cake at reasonable prices; menu from 130F.

Bistrot des Lices, 3 pl des Lices (☎94.97.29.00). Turn-of-the-century decor for traditional preening and spectacular food, from spider-crab soup to scallop *aïoli*, roasted turbot in ratatouille to stuffed shoulder of hare in a thyme sauce, and unbelievable chocolate puds; midday menu 175F, otherwise from 260F. The *Boeuf sur la Place* next door, run by the same establishment serves less exotic dishes for half the price.

La Citadelle, cnr rue Citadelle and rue Aire du Chemin. *Moules marinières*, fish soup, *pissaladières*, and other standard regional fare. Not brilliant, but reasonably priced with plats du jour for 58F.

L'Echalote, 35 rue du Allard (☎94.54.83.26). Rich meaty dishes and a great scallop salad to enjoy in the tranquillity of the garden; 150F menu.

Joseph, 5 rue Cepoun San Martin and 6 rue Sibille (☎94.97.03.90). Good *bouillabaisse*, *bourride* and desserts. Menus from 160F, à la carte 300F upwards.

Lou Revelen, 4 rue des Remparts (☎94.97.06.34). Grilled fish, *petits farcis*, fresh pasta and seafood dishes with a menu under 100F before 8.30pm.

Le Petit Charron, 6 rue des Charrons (☎94.97.73.78). Tiny terrace and dining room serving beautifully cooked Provençal specialities. Midday menu under 100F, otherwise from 130F.

La Table du Marché, 38 rue Clemenceau (☎94.97.85.20). Hard to get a table here but worth the wait for true bistro style gourmandize; 115F menu.

Nightlife

In season St-Tropez stays up late, as you'd expect. The **boules games** on place des Lices continue till well after dusk, the portside spectacle doesn't falter till the early hours and even the shops stay open well after dinner time. If you're insane enough to want to pay to see, and be seen with, the nightlife creatures of St-Trop, **clubs** include the currently young and fashionable *Le Papagayo* in the Résidence du Nouveau Port with world music and theme nights; *L'Esquinade*, which has been going strong for decades, and *La Spirale* on rue du Four; *Les Caves du Roy* in the flashy *Hôtel Byblos* on rue Paul-Signac, the most expensive and exclusive; and the **gay** disco *Le Pigeonnier*, 13 rue de la Ponche. All are open every night in summer, and usually Saturday only in winter.

The beaches

The beach within easy walking distance of St-Tropez is **Les Graniers**, below the citadel just beyond the Port des Pêcheurs along rue Cavaillon. From here a path follows the coast around the **Baie des Canoubiers** which has a small beach, to Cap St-Pierre, Cap St-Tropez, the very crowded **Salins** beach and right round to **Tahiti-Plage** (about 11km). This eastern area of the peninsula is where the rich and famous have their vast villas with helipads and artificial lakes in acres of heavily guarded grounds.

Tahiti-Plage is the start of the almost straight five-kilometre north–south **Pampelonne** beach, famous bronzing belt of St-Tropez and world initiator of the topless bathing cult. The water is shallow for 50m or so and exposed to the wind, and it's sometimes scourged by dried sea vegetation, not to mention slicks of industrial pollutants. But spotless glitter comes from the unending line of beach bars and restaurants, all with patios and sofas, and all serving cocktails and gluttonous ice creams (as well as full-blown meals), in addition to hiring out the luxurious beach mattresses and matching parasols. Though you'll find people in the nude on all stretches of the beach, only some of the bars welcome people carrying wallets and nothing else. *Club 55*, named for the year when Vadim's film crew scrounged food from what was then a family beach hut, is supposed to be a favourite with the celebrities (à la carte from 250F).

The beach ends with the headland of **Cap Camaret**, beyond which the private residential settlement of **Villa Bergès** grudgingly allows public access to the **Plage de l'Escalet**. Another coastal path leads to the next bay, the **Baie de Briande**, where you'll find the least populated beach of the whole peninsula. Beyond here the villas end and you can continue to **Cap Lardier** with a choice of paths upwards and downwards and along the gorgeous shore all the way round to La Croix-Valmer.

To **get to the beaches** from St-Tropez, there's a frequent minibus service from place des Lices to Salins, Tahiti and Pampelonne, and a bus from the *gare routière* to Tahiti, Pampelonne and L'Escalet. They make great bike rides too. If you're driving you'll be forced to pay high parking charges at all the beaches, or to leave your car some distance from the sea and easy prey to thieves.

The interior: Gassin and Ramatuelle

Though the coast of the St-Tropez peninsula sprouts second residences like a cabbage patch gone to seed, the **interior** is almost uninhabited, thanks to government intervention, complex ownerships and the value of some local wines. The best view of this richly green and flowering countryside is from the hilltop village of **Gassin**, its lower neighbour **Ramatuelle**, or the tiny road between them, where three ruined windmills could once catch every wind.

Gassin

GASSIN is the shape and size of a small ship perched on a summit; once a Moorish stronghold, it is now, of course, highly chic. It's a perfect place for a blow-out dinner, sitting outside by the village wall with a spectacular panorama east over the peninsula. Of the handful of **restaurants**, *Bello Visto*, 9 place des Barrys (☎94.56.17.30), has very acceptable Provençal specialities on a 120F menu and nine **rooms** at excellent prices for this brilliant setting (④). Cheapish crêpes and pizzas can be had at *Au Vieux Gassin* nearby, and plats du jour for 65F at *La Dame de Coeur* on the west side of the village.

Ramatuelle

RAMATUELLE is bigger than its neighbour, though just as old, and is surrounded by some of the best *Côte de Provence* vineyards (the top selection of wines can be tasted at *Les Maîtres Vignerons de la Presqu'île de St-Tropez* by the La Foux junction on the N98). The twisting and arcaded streets are inevitably full of arts and crafts of dubious talent, but it is very pleasant none the less. The most beautiful French actor ever to have appeared on screen, Gérard Philippe (1922–59), is buried in Ramatuelle's **cemetery** on the outskirts of the village. His ivy-covered tomb, shaded by a rose bush, is set against the wall on the right as you look down. The central Romanesque **Eglise Notre-Dame** that formed part of the old defences has heavy gilded furnishings from the Chartreuse de la Verne (see p.256) and an impressive early seventeenth-century door carved out of serpentine.

If you want to **stay**, *Chez Tony* (☎94.79.20.46; ③), on rue Clemenceau, is inexpensive and one of very few **hotels** within the village; the classier ones are all nearer to the beaches and very pricey. For something to **eat**, stop off for a dish of fresh pasta or the day's speciality at *Au Fil à la Pâte* at 27 rue Victor-Léon (closed Wed; ☎94.79.27.81; under 100F).

The Massif des Maures

The secret of the Côte d'Azur is that despite the gross conglomeration of the coast, Provence is still just behind, old, sparsely populated, village-oriented and dependent on the land for its produce as much as for its value as real estate.

Between Marseille and Menton, the most bewitching hinterland is the **Massif des Maures** that stretches from Hyères to Fréjus.

The highest point of these hills stops short of 800m but the quick succession of ridges, the sudden drops and views and then closure again, and the curling looping roads are pervasively mountainous. Where the lie of the land gives a wide bowl of sun-lit slopes, vines are grown. Elsewhere the hills are thickly forested, with Aleppo and umbrella pines, holly, cork oaks and sweet chestnut trees. On a windy autumn day chestnuts the size of grenades explode upon your head, while water from a thousand springs cascades down each face of rock. In the heat of summer there is always the darkest shade alternating with one-way light – the rocks that compose this massif absorb rather than reflect – and it's hardly surprising that its name derives from the Provençal and Latin words for dark, *mauram* and *mauro*.

Much of the Massif is inaccessible even to **walkers**. However, the **GR9** follows the most northern and highest ridge from Pignans on the N97 past **Notre-Dame-des-Anges**, La Sauvette, **La Garde-Freinet** and down to the head of the Golfe de St-Tropez. There are other **paths and tracks**, such as the one following the Vallon de Tamary from north of La Londe-Des-Maures to join one of the roads snaking down from the Col de Babaou to Collobrières. But few go very far and many are closed to the public in summer for fear of forest fires.

If you're **cycling**, the D14 that runs through the middle, parallel to the coast, from Pierrefeu-du-Var north of Hyères to **Cogolin** near St-Tropez, is manageable and stunning.

Collobrières

At the heart of the Massif is the ancient village of **COLLOBRIERES**. It is reputed to have been the first place in France to learn from the Spanish that a certain tree plugged into bottles allows a wine industry to grow. From the Middle Ages until very recent times **cork** production has been the major business of the village. Now it is *marrons glacés* and every other confection derived from sweet chestnuts.

On the terrace of the main *bar-tabac* that overlooks the stormy water of the Collobrier river, you can imagine that the forests that surround you go on for hundreds of miles, shutting out all the world of cost-accounting time and space. The church, the *mairie* and the houses don't seem to have been modernized this century. Yet on the other side of the river, at the eastern end of the village, a streamlined, no-nonsense, gleaming bright-blue construction, the **Confiserie Azurienne**, exudes efficiency and modern business skills. Workers clock in and out, production schedules are met, profits are made, all from the conker's sister fruit. The factory itself can't be visited but there's a shop (9/10am–1pm & 2–6/7pm) that sells chestnut ice cream, chestnut jam, chestnut nougat, chestnut purée, *chestnut glacées* and chestnut bonbons.

Practicalities

Collobrières' **tourist office** on bd Charles-Caminat (Mon–Thurs & Sat 10am–noon & 2–6pm; ☎94.48.08.00) is welcoming and can supply details of **walks** in the area. If you're too overdosed on sticky chestnut to move, or you've fallen in love with the place, there are two **hotels**, *Notre-Dame*, 15 av de la Libération (☎94.48.07.13; ④), and *Auberge des Maures*, 19 bd Lazare Carnot (☎94.48.07.10; ④), both small so need to be booked in advance. There's also a municipal **camp-**

site, the *St-Roch*, which is officially open from May to October but will let you camp outside this period (bookings through the *mairie* on ☎94.48.07.01). You might just get away with camping in the woods in late autumn or early spring, but when it's hot and dry don't even consider it (one stray spark and you could be responsible for a thousand acres of burnt forest).

For food, other than chestnuts, the **restaurant** *La Petite Fontaine*, 1 place de la République (closed Mon & Sun afternoon; last orders 9pm; ☎94.48.00.12), is congenial and affordable with one menu around 110F, but books up fast. South of the village signed off the D41 to Bormes at the Col de Babaou, the *Chèvrerir du Peïgros* (open midday all year, evening mid-May to mid-Sept; ☎94.48.03.83) is an isolated farmhouse serving its own produce on a 120F menu. If you want to buy some local **wines**, head for *Les Vignerons de Collobrières* close to the Hôtel Notre-Dame; local **market** day is Tuesday.

Around Collobrières: La Chartreuse de la Verne, Notre-Dame-des-Anges and le Village des Tortues

Writing at the end of the nineteenth century, Maupassant declared that there was nowhere else in the world where his heart had felt such a pressing weight of melancholy as at the ruins of **La Chartreuse de la Verne**. Since then a great deal of restoration work has been carried out on this Carthusian monastery, abandoned during the Revolution and hidden away in total isolation, 12km from Collobrières on a winding, untarmaced road off the D14 towards Grimaud (July–Oct daily 11am–6pm; Dec–June Mon & Wed–Sun 10am–5pm; 20F). It remains a desolate spot; the buildings of this once vast twelfth-century complex, in the dark reddish-brown schist of the Maures, combined for decorative effect with local greenish serpentine, appear gaunt and inhospitable, but the atmosphere is indisputable.

Another religious settlement concealed in these hills is **Notre-Dame-des-Anges**, between Collobrières and Gonfaron, almost at the highest point of the Maures. As a place of worship it goes back to pagan times, but in its nineteenth-century remodelled form it lacks the atmosphere of La Verne. Pilgrimages still head here – it's equipped with a **hostel** to receive the faithful – but the main point of a visit for anyone else is to take in the views encompassing the Alps and the sea.

A rare creature which populated a third of France a million years ago and now only just survives in the Massif des Maures is cared for and protected in **Le Village des Tortues**, a few kilometres east of Gonfaron on the D75 to Les Mayons (March–Nov daily 9am–7pm; 30F). This is not a tourist attraction but a serious conservation project to repopulate the native Hermann tortoise, under ever-increasing threat from urbanization, forest fires, theft of eggs and sale as pets. Other tortoises, like the yellow-shelled giant from Madagascar, have been rescued and brought here. The visit is both relaxed and educational (once you're past the clinic where wounds such as dog bites are treated in full view). A leaflet (available in English) guides you round the large enclosures where you'll see babies, "juveniles" and those soon to be released back into the wild. From March to May you can watch them mate, which they do for hours, making little squeaking noises, and in September see the eggs hatching.

La Garde-Freinet

For almost a hundred years, from 888 to 975, the Massif des Maures was occupied by invaders from the eastern and southern Mediterranean. The dreaded

Saracens, the name by which the people of Provence refer indiscriminately to Moors, Turks, Arabs or North Africans, and who are held responsible for everything that has failed to survive since the Dark Ages, had their headquarters in **LA GARDE-FREINET**, originally known as Le Fraxinet. The foundations of their **fortress**, from where attacks on the interior were made, are still visible above the village beside the ruins of a fifteenth-century castle. Follow the signs to the GR9 at the northern end of the village; a path leads from a car park down to a cross and then up to the fort, about 1km in all, and steep.

La Garde-Freinet also has the honour of a radical past in the insurrectionary days of Louis Napoléon's coup d'état. Not only did the cork workers form a highly successful co-operative in 1851, but in their struggle with the landowners, women played as strong a role as men. So much so that the prosecuting magistrate of Aix wrote to the minister of justice warning him that La Garde-Freinet, with its new form of socialism in which women took part, would encourage other villagers to abandon public morals and descend into debauchery.

Today the occupiers of the village include Oxbridge professors and other Anglos with time on their hands, but it still feels that it belongs to the locals (thanks to the regeneration of forestry business around cork and chestnut) and the number of young local children around is refreshing. It also has top-notch medieval charm; easy walks to stunning panoramas; markets twice a week (Wed & Sun) and tempting food shops and good local wines for sale at the *Cave des Vignerons* on rue Saint-Jacques; as well as reasonable accommodation possibilities.

For pigeon fanciers there's a special treat at **Le Mouron Rouge** pigeon breeders based 1km north of the village on the D558 (May–Sept Mon & Wed–Sun 10am–12.30pm & 3–6pm; Oct–April 2–5pm; 15F). As well as all the variety of pigeons to be seen, a **museum** deals with the intricacies of racing, different breeds and the history of these extraordinary birds as messengers, from 3000 BC in Egypt to 1815 in London when Rothschilds made a killing on European stock markets when news of the British victory at Waterloo was delivered by pigeon three days ahead of conventional communications.

Practicalities

The **tourist office** operates in summer from the Chapelle St-Eloi on the southern side of the village (Mon–Sat 9.30am–12.30pm & 3–7pm; ☎94.43.67.40) and in winter from the *mairie* (office hours; ☎94.43.60.01). It can provide details for all of the Maures region.

For **rooms**, *La Sarrasine*, on the D588 after it turns west at the top of the village (☎94.43.67.16 ③), *La Claire Fontaine* on place Vieille (☎94.43.60.36; ③) and *Le Fraxinois* on rue François-Pelletier (reception at the *Tabac-Presse*; Tues–Sun; ☎94.43.62.84; ③) are incredibly good value for this part of the world. The two three-star **campsites** are close at hand: the municipal *Saint-Eloi* (June–Sept; ☎94.43.62.40) opposite the municipal pool, and *La Ferme de Bérard* (Easter–Oct; ☎94.43.32.23) on the D558 towards Grimaud with its own pool and restaurant. **Walkers** can stay at a **gîte d'étape** on the GR51 towards the coast, the *Hameau de La Cour Basse* (☎94.43.64.63; ①).

Of an evening *Le Lézard* **restaurant** and **piano bar** on the exquisite place du Marché is the place to be (concerts Sat; ☎94.43.62.73; menus from around 100F). Second choice for a meal should be *La Grille* on place de la Vieille (closed Mon out of season & Wed; ☎94.43.69.13) with two menus under 100F. More elaborate food is served up in the rampant garden at *La Faucado* on the main road to the south (closed Tues out of season; booking essential; ☎94.43.60.41; midday menu Mon–Sat 120F, à la carte from 300F). Pigeon lovers beware as the bird sometimes features on the menu.

La Môle

Another village with its own life, and in this case, singularly free of tourist concerns, is **LA MOLE** on the fast N98 between Bormes and **Cogolin**, southeast of La Chartreuse de La Verne and north of Le Rayol and Le Canadel. It is in a fabulous bowl of meadows and vineyards with old farmhouses, rather than new villas, dotted along the lanes that lead into the hills. The three reasons to stop here are: the *Auberge de la Môle* **café** serving good strong coffee and decked out with old wooden fittings, ancient framed posters and a wonderfully old-fashioned petrol pump; the *Relais d'Alsace* **restaurant** (summer evenings only; closed Mon out of season & Sun; ☎94.49.57.02) with hearty specialities from northeast France on menus from 80F and dependable *steack-frites* for under 50F; and, best of all, the *Boulangerie Simon* that stays open day and night, baking the most amazing olive and raisin breads, cakes and flans, and selling goat's cheeses and jam (May–Oct). As you leave Le Môle for Cogolin, the perfect four-turreted residence appears on the left (with an aerodrome for the private plane on the right), and, more realistically, a small one-star **campsite**, *Les Caramagnols* (☎94.54.40.06) with caravans to rent.

Cogolin

What makes **COGOLIN** special is that the inevitable tourism base of its economy is combined with the traditional crafts of making reeds for wind instruments, pipes for smoking, cane and wrought-iron furniture, silk yarn and knotted wool carpets. These industries don't just thrive as a bygones crowd-puller. They are serious businesses for the one-off, made-to-order, high-quality and high-cost Côte d'Azur market. One immediate consequence is that Cogolin is alive all year round, so you might well want to stay here out of season, plus it's within 10km of St-Tropez.

Visits to the **craft factories** are easily arranged and free. The **tourist office** (see below) will provide you with a complete list of addresses and times, and help with making appointments. Or you can just wander down av Georges-Clemenceau and pop into the retail outlets. For **carpets**, the renowned *Manufacture de Tapis* just off av Clemenceau on bd Louis-Blanc (Mon–Fri 9am–noon & 2–6pm; by appointment on ☎94.54.66.17) re-creates designs by famous artists such as Léger and Mondrian. Every carpet is hand-made and can take up to a year to finish; the order book includes presidential residences, embassies and local palaces. The production of **pipes** from briar wood is on show at *Courrieu*, 58 av Clemenceau (Mon–Sat 8am–noon & 2–6pm). World-famous musicians visit *Rigotti* on rue Barbusse to replace the reeds of their oboes, bassoons and clarinets; unfortunately, they only open their doors to professionals. The **Maison du Liège**, 102 av Clemenceau (summer Mon–Sat 9am–8pm, Sun 10am–noon & 4–8pm; winter Mon–Sat 9am–noon & 2–7pm), demonstrates the extraordinary variety of uses for cork, one of the most important natural products of the Massif des Maures.

From place Bellevue, at the top of the town away from the bustling centre, you can see across the St-Tropez peninsula, to Gassin, Ramatuelle and St-Tropez itself. Having taken in that view, and seen enough of Cogolin's manufacturing businesses, the one thing left to do is try the **wines** which particularly pleased Julius Caesar. The *Cave des Vignerons* is on rue Marceau on the way out of town before you join the N98 heading westwards.

Practicalities

From the **gare routière** on av Clemenceau head upwards to the central place de la République where you'll find the **tourist office** (July & Aug Mon–Sat 9am–12.15pm & 2.30–7pm, Sun 9.30am–noon; Sept–June Mon–Fri 9am–noon & 2.30–6.30pm, Sat 9am–noon; ☎94.54.63.17).

Hotels are reasonable with *Le Golfe*, 13 av Clemenceau (☎94.54.40.34; ④), and *Le Coq* on rue Général-du-Gaulle (☎94.54.63.14; ⑤). *Le Clemenceau*, 1 rue Carnot (☎94.54.15.17; ③), has some low-priced rooms but is on a very noisy junction. For **eats** you can choose your own menu for under 100F at *La Grange*, 7 rue du 11 novembre (closed Mon & Sat midday; ☎94.54.60.97), or plump for a plat du jour (50F) at *Les Quat' Saisons* opposite. *La Taverne du Siffleur*, 9 rue Nationale (☎94.54.67.02), overlooks a fountain on a very quiet street and does an *aïoli* for 90F. If you want a **drink**, the *Bistrot de Cogolin* next to *Le Golfe* hotel has a fine beer selection and you can check what is being shown at the pretty **cinema** across the street, dedicated to the French film actor Georges Raimu.

Grimaud

GRIMAUD is a film set of a *village perché*, where the cone of houses enclosing the eleventh-century church and culminating in the ruins of a medieval castle appears as a single, perfectly unified entity, decorated by its trees and flowers. The most vaunted street in this ensemble is the arcaded **rue des Templiers** which leads up to the pure Romanesque **Eglise St-Michel** and a house of the Knights Templars. The views from the château ruins are superb.

It's an exclusive little village whose "corner shop" sells antiques and contemporary art. If you're on a budget and need food or a place to stay it makes sense to continue the tortuous climb to La Garde-Freinet. But if you do stop **to eat**, you can get crêpes and omelettes at *Le Boubou* on the fountained place du Cros (closed Wed); plats du jour (75F) at *L'Ecurie de la Marquise* at 3 rue du Gacharel (closed Sun evening & Wed); or more serious fare on the vine-covered terrace of the *Café de France* on place Neuve (Mon & Wed–Sun; ☎94.43.20.05; 125F menu). On the lower side of place Neuve the *Pâtisserie du Château* sells wonderful cakes and fresh nutty breads. Thursday is **market** day.

Port Grimaud

In the height of summer, the **junction at La Foux** generates the overheated fury and frustration that turn drivers into psychopaths. A gleeful bird's eye view of the tailbacks in all directions (still spectacular even after nightfall) can be had from the big wheel of the permanent **fun fair** between the roundabout and the sea (Mon–Sat 8.30pm–1/2am, Sun 4pm–1/2am; 20F). Avoiding it altogether is difficult if you're visiting **PORT GRIMAUD**, the ultimate Côte d'Azur property development that half stands and half floats at the head of the Golfe de St-Tropez just north of La Foux, and whose fortunate residents move around by boat not car.

It was created in the 1960s as a private lagoon pleasure city with waterways for roads and yachts parked at the bottom of every garden. All the houses are in exquisitely tasteful old Provençal style and their owners, Joan Collins for example, are more than a little well heeled. In a way it's surprising that the whole enclave isn't wired off and patrolled by Alsatian dogs. One can only assume that envious gawping tourists somehow add to the already over-inflated values.

The main visitors' entrance is 800m up the well-signed road off the N98. You don't have to pay to get in but you can't explore all the islands without hiring a boat (about 90F for half an hour) or taking a crowded boat tour (around 20F). Even access to the church is controlled by an automatic paying barrier (5F). However, if you want to **eat** and **drink**, there are rows upon rows of brasseries, restaurants and cafés, clearly designed for the visiting public rather than the residents, and not particularly good value though affordable enough.

Ste-Maxime

STE-MAXIME, which faces St-Tropez across its gulf, is the perfect Côte stereotype: palmed corniche and enormous pleasure boat harbour, beaches crowded with confident bronzed windsurfers and waterskiers, a local history museum in a defensive tower that no one goes to, and an outnumbering of estate agents to any other businesses by about ten to one. It sprawls a little too far – like many of its neighbours – but the magnetic appeal of the water's edge is hard to deny.

To enjoy the resort, however, requires money. If your budget denies you the pleasures of promenade cocktail sipping and seafood-platter picking (not to mention waterskiing, wet-biking and windsurfing), you might as well choose somewhere rather prettier to swim, lie on the beach and walk along the shore.

For the spenders, **Cherry Beach** or its five neighbours on the east-facing Plage de la Nartelle, 2km from the centre round the Pointe des Sardinaux towards Les Issambres, is the strip of sand to head for. As well as paying for shaded cushioned comfort, you can enter the water on a variety of different vehicles, eat grilled fish, have drinks brought to your mattress, and listen to a piano player as dusk falls. A further 4km on, **Plage des Eléphants** has much the same facilities but is slightly cheaper.

In addition to the beaches, Ste-Maxime's *Vieille Ville* has several good **markets**: a covered flower and food market on rue Fernand-Bessy (Mon–Sat 6am–1pm & 4.30–8pm); a Thursday morning market on and around place du Marché; bric-à-brac every Friday morning on place Jean-Mermoz; and arts and crafts in the pedestrian streets every afternoon and evening in summer from 4 to 11pm.

Ten kilometres north of town on the road to Le Muy, the **Musée du Phonographe et de la Musique Mécanique** at parc St-Donat (Easter to Sept Wed–Sun 10am–noon & 2.30–6pm; 25F) is the result of one woman's forty-year obsession with collecting audio equipment. She has one of Thomas Edison's "talking machines" of 1878, the first recording machines of the 1890s and an amplified lyre (1903). One of the first saucer-shaped amplifiers, made of paper, is on display, along with a 1913 audiovisual language teaching aid and the wonderfully neat portable record-players of the 1920s. In addition there's an extraordinarily wide selection of automata, musical boxes and pianolas. Almost half the exhibits still work. The main aim of the collection is to get kids to understand that their CD Walkmans didn't drop out of the sky after eighty years of silence. If you get a tour from Madame herself (she speaks a little English) you'll find it hard to resist her enthusiasm for the history of this branch of twentieth-century technology.

Practicalities

The **tourist office** on the promenade Simon-Lorrièrre (July–Sept daily 9am–7pm; Oct–June Mon–Sat 9am–noon & 1.30–6.30pm; ☎94.96.19.24) can give you all the relevant information on trips and pleasures. If you're heading for St-Tropez from Ste-Maxime, an alternative to the **bus**, and at not much greater cost, is to go by **boat**; the service from Ste-Maxime's **gare maritime** runs from July to September with frequent daily crossings of twenty minutes. **Bikes** can be rented at *Veloc Alain*, 1 rue Paul-Bert, or *Rent Bike*, 13 rue Magali.

The tourist office can advise on hotel vacancies which are very rare in summer. Among the cheaper **hotels** is the small *Castellamar*, 21 av G-Pompidou (☎94.96.19.97; ③), on the west side of the river but still close to the centre and the sea. For more pleasant and more expensive surroundings, the *Hôtel de la Poste*, 7 bd Frédéric-Mistral (☎94.96.18.33; ⑥), is an ugly modern construction but with very nice rooms and is right in the centre; *Les Palmiers*, on rue Gabriel-Péri in a quieter location by the church and Tour Carrée (☎94.96.00.41; ⑤); or the *Marie-Louise*, 2km west in the Hameau de Guerre-Vieille (☎94.96.06.05; ④), tucked away in greenery but in sight of the sea. For **camping**, *Les Cigalons*, in quartier de la Nartelle, is the three-star seaside option (June to mid-Sept; ☎94.96.05.51); or there's *La Baumette*, rte du Plan de la Tour (June to mid-Sept; ☎94.96.14.35) up in the hills off the D74.

For non-beach **eating**, the *Hostellerie de la Belle Aurore*, 4 bd Jean-Moulin (closed Wed midday & Oct to mid-March; ☎94.96.02.45; weekday midday menu 180F, otherwise from 240F), offers gourmet food on a sea-view terrace; or, for half the price, there's *Le Calypso*, 12 av Général-de-Gaulle (Mon & Wed–Sun ☎94.96.42.55; menus under 100F), serving traditional fish dishes. *Le Sarrazin*, 7 place Colbert (closed Tues & Wed out of season; ☎94.96.10.84; menus from 125F), is not bad either. The pedestrian streets are jam-packed with restaurants; one way of choosing from those on rue Hoche is to check them from the kitchen side along rue Fernand-Bessy.

Coastwards to St-Aygulf

Distinguishing **Val d'Esquières**, a suburb of Ste-Maxime, **Les Issambres**, the seaside extension of **Roquebrune**, and **St-Aygulf**, belonging to the *commune* of **Fréjus**, is hardly worth the effort. They all merge into one continuous lesser clone of Ste-Maxime. For all that, this stretch still has its attractions, revealing traditional white-washed, pantiled Provence architecture amid the filing-cabinet condominiums, and a shoreline of rocky coves and *calanques* alternating with golden crescents of sand. In Les Issambres there's even a narrow band of pines that almost lets you pretend that the corniche apartments and villas don't exist. If the seaside development gets too much, you can always head up and away into the empty eastern extremity of the Massif des Maures.

Practicalities

For **hotels** *La Quietude*, set back from the corniche (☎94.96.94.34; ④), and *La Bonne Auberge*, overlooking the sea (☎94.96.90.73; ③), are worth trying in Les

Issambres, along with *Le Catalogne*, av de la Corniche d'Azur (☎94.81.01.44; ⑦) with a pleasant shaded garden, and *Motel Defillet* (☎94.81.21.15; ③) at the start of the long straight beach to St-Raphaël in St-Aygulf, plus *La Caravelle* (☎94.81.24.03; ⑦) near Plage de la Gaillarde between the two. **Campsites** are plentiful and well signed off the corniche. **Bikes** can be rented from *Les Hippocampes* in St-Aygulf on the main road (519 av Corniche d'Azur; ☎94.81.35.94).

The *Villa St-Elme* is the fancy **restaurant** in Les Issambres, with elaborate and delicate fish dishes to be consumed while admiring the Golfe de St-Tropez from an exotic 1930s building directly above the sea (☎94.49.52.52; menus from 190F). At the other end of the scale, *Le Pointu*, on place de la Galiote in St-Aygulf, produces a brilliant *moules marinières* for under 50F. The St-Aygulf resort has a good daily **market** too, and great *poulets rotis* from a permanent stall overlooking the main square on bd Honoré-de-Balzac.

Inland: the Argens Valley

The **River Argens** meets the Mediterranean in unspectacular style between St-Aygulf and St-Raphaël. It is an important source of irrigation for orchards and vines, but as a waterway it has little appeal, being sluggish, full of breeding mosquitoes and on the whole inaccessible. The geographical feature that dominates the lower Argens Valley, and acts as an almost mystical pole of attraction, is the **Rocher de Roquebrune** between the village of **Roquebrune-sur-Argens** and the town of **Le Muy**.

Roquebrune-sur-Argens

ROQUEBRUNE-SUR-ARGENS lies on the edge of the Massif des Maures, 12km from the sea, facing the flat valley of the Argens opening to the northeast. Some of its sixteenth-century defensive towers and ramparts remain, and almost every house within them is four hundred years old or more, joined together by vaulted passageways, arcades and tiny cobbled streets. The largest mulberry tree in Provence shades the central square, while at the bridge over the Argens, just north of the village, M Vacherot grafts the rarest **orchids** in his nursery (visits by appointment only ☎94.45.48.59). *Vignerons* can make a good living here; you can taste beautiful red and rosé **wines** (phone first) at the *Domaine de Marchandise* (☎94.45.42.91), and at the *Domaine des Planes* (☎94.82.90.03). Or fill up with quality plonk at the *Coopérative Vinicole*. Delicious nougat can be bought from *Le Rocher Rose*, 37 av G-Péri, and there's a **market** Tuesday and Friday morning.

Between Roquebrune and Le Muy, a *Formule I* **hotel** is, for once, very conveniently situated (☎94.81.61.61; ①); otherwise two **chambres d'hôtes** to try are *L'Acacia* (M Mayer ☎94.45.71.92; ⑤) and *Vasken* (M & Mme Kuerdjian ☎94.45.76.16; ⑤). Between the village and St-Aygulf the road is lined with mega **campsites**; more sympathetic pitches are to be had on local farms; the **tourist office** on rue Jean-Aicard (July & Aug daily 9am–noon & 2–6pm; rest of the year closed Sun; ☎94.45.72.70) can provide addresses, as well as information on **walks** and **sports**. Of the rather disappointing **restaurants**, *Le Basilic*, 37 Grande Rue (closed Tues out of season; ☎94.45.49.00), has a lovely setting.

Rocher de Roquebrune

The rust-red mass of the **Roquebrune rock** erupts unexpectedly out of nothing, as if to some purpose. Even the *autoroute du soleil* thundering past its foot fails to bring it into line with the rest of the coastal scenery glimpsed from the fast lane. To reach it, coming from Roquebrune, take the left fork just after the village, signed to La Roquette; at the next fork you can go left or right depending which side of the mountain you want to skirt. The right-hand route runs alongside the highway giving you access, should you wish it, to **Notre-Dame-de-la-Roquette**, an erstwhile place of pilgrimage. The southern side is quieter but steeper.

From either side of the mountain several **paths** lead into the ancient woods encircling the rock and up through the fissured and pot-holed face. You may meet a latterday "hermit" (summer only) who is suspected by local people of luring young girls and boys to his cave; an accusation perhaps mixed up with the older generation's memories of coming up to a tunnelled passage here known as the *Saint-Trou* to lose their virginity as young lads and lassies. The summit has recently been crowned by some basic metal work resembling semaphore signals, the "art" of trendy sculptor Bernard Venet, who lives in **Le Muy** when he's not hobnobbing in Paris or New York. In case it isn't immediately obvious, these minimalist T, arrow and cross shapes are hommages to three great crucifixion paintings by Giotto, Grunewald and El Greco.

Le Muy

LE MUY is not a wildly exciting place but it's interesting politically, having had one of the sole surviving Communist mayors of the Côte d'Azur in the 1980s, switching to a coalition of right wing and *Front National* in 1989, and shifting now, in the mid-1990s, to a Socialist administration.

The town's political history and ideological leanings are often mirrored in the names of its streets, its buildings and architecture. One street is named after Maurice Lachâtre, a revolutionary writer, publisher and printer who escaped from the 1871 Paris commune and was sheltered in Le Muy. The *Provençal* **bar** that surrounds and hides the apse of the town's church was built during the 1930s period of militantly atheist socialism.

The **tour Charles-Quint** takes its name from the attempted assassination of the Emperor Charles V in 1536 by the people of Le Muy. Unfortunately they were not to know that the king was aware of his unpopularity and had rented a Spanish poet, Garcilaso de la Vega, to masquerade as him. Consequently the Muyoise killed the Spaniard, retreated to the tower, were told by the invader that they would be spared if they surrendered, came out with their hands up and were promptly massacred; the tower was renamed after their arch enemy. Today, the tower is used as a **cultural centre** with temporary art exhibitions.

Chapelle de Ste-Roseline

A short way up the road to **Draguignan** (see p.280) from Le Muy, the D91 leads left to the **Chapelle de Ste-Roseline** (June–Sept Tues–Sun 3–7pm; Oct–May 2–6/7pm; free). The old abbey buildings of which the chapel is part are a private residence, belonging to a wine grower, and today you can visit the cellars and taste the *cru classé* named after the chapel (Mon–Fri 8am–noon & 1–7pm, Sat & Sun 10am–noon & 2–6pm).

The chapel itself is really rather horrid. Saint Roseline was born in 1263 and spent her adolescence disobeying her father by giving food to the poor. On one occasion he caught her and demanded to see the contents of her basket; the food miraculously turned into rose petals. She became the prioress of the abbey and when she died her body refused to decay. It was paraded around the faithful of Provence until it got lost. A blind man found it and, supposedly, there it lies in a glass case in the chapel, shrivelled and dark brown but not quite a skeleton. What's worse are her eyes – one lifeless, the other staring at you – displayed in a separate, gaudy frame on a wall. Louis XIV is said to be responsible for the dead eye. On a pilgrimage here he reckoned the staring eyes smacked of sorcery so had his surgeon pierce one. Life immediately left it. Horror objects apart, the chapel has a fabulous mosaic by **Chagall** showing angels laying a table for the saint; some beautifully carved seventeenth-century choir stalls; and an impressive Renaissance rood-loft in which peculiar things happen to the legs of the decorative figures.

If you fancy a blow-out meal the **restaurant** *L'Orée du Bois* nearby, on the junction of the D91 and the N555, has a very good reputation (menus from 110F, à la carte 230F upwards).

Les Arcs-sur-Argens

LES ARCS is yet another picturesque medieval village, a Saracen look-out tower dominating its skyline, the sole standing remnant of its thirteenth-century castle. It is also one of the centres for the Var wine industry. On the main road from Le Muy, past the turning to the village and the bridge across the Argens you'll see the **Maison des Vins**. Here you can taste and buy wine and cheeses, in a rather snooty environment, and pick up details of local *vignerons* to visit and *routes du vin* to follow (daily 10am–7/8pm). The *Maison* also has a very beautiful restaurant, *Le Bacchus Gourmand*, which has become ridiculously upmarket and as a result rarely needs booking (closed Mon out of season & Sun evening; menus from 150F).

There are plenty of other **restaurants**, however, to choose from in the village, most notably in the **hotel** *Le Logis du Guetteur* (☎94.73.30.82; menus from 135F; ⑤) which commands the only access to the panoramic views by the Saracen tower on place du Château. Less expensive rooms are available at *L'Avenir*, av de la Gare (☎94.73.30.58; ③), by the **gare SNCF**, situated halfway between the village and the N7, and inexpensive food at the young and friendly *La Bonne Franquette* at 11 rue de la République (closed Sat, & Sun midday; ☎94.73.33.03). The best day to come to Les Arcs is Thursday for the busy **market** on the central square. The **tourist office** on place Gal-de-Gaulle (Mon–Sat 9am–noon & 2–6pm; ☎94.73.37.30) has information for the surrounding area.

Vidauban

If you're following the road west from Les Arcs the next village you come to, **VIDAUBAN**, is equally attractive, particularly at night when its old-fashioned lamps are lit. The village has a charming **restaurant** where the *petits farcis* are especially good: *Le Concorde*, 9 place Clemenceau (☎94.73.01.19; menus from 130F); and some wine *domaines* worth visiting including the *Vieux Château d'Astros* (☎94.73.02.56 for an appointment) where the *vigneron* has spent years of wine-growing in the United States, and the *Château St Julien d'Aille* (☎94.73.02.89 for an appointment) whose 1994 rosé is exceptional.

Fréjus and St-Raphaël

The major conurbation of **St-Raphaël** on the coast and **Fréjus**, centred 3km inland, has a history dating back to the Romans. Fréjus was established as a naval base under Julius Caesar and Augustus, St-Raphaël as a resort for its veterans. The ancient port at Fréjus, or *Forum Julii*, had 2km of quays and was connected by a walled canal to the sea, considerably closer then. After the battle of Actium in 31 AD, the ships of Anthony and Cleopatra's defeated fleet were brought here.

The area between Fréjus and the sea is now the suburb of **Fréjus-Plage** with a hideous 1980s development of a marina, **Port-Fréjus**. Both Fréjus and Fréjus-Plage merge with St-Raphaël, which in turn merges with **Boulouris** to the east.

Despite the obsession with facilities for the seaborne rich – there were already two pleasure ports at St-Raphaël before Port-Fréjus was built – this is no bad place for a stop-over. There's a wide price range of hotels and restaurants, some interesting sight-seeing in Fréjus, and good transport links with inland Provence and the coast eastwards along the Corniche d'Esterel.

Fréjus

The population of **FREJUS**, remarkably, was greater in the first century BC than it is today if you just count the residents of the town centre, which lies well within the Roman perimeter. But very little remains of the original **Roman walls** that once circled the city, and the **harbour** that made Fréjus an important Mediterranean port silted up early on and was finally filled in after the Revolution. It is the **medieval centre** that evokes a feel for this ancient town much more than the classical remants and has very lively shopping and café streets.

Arrival and information

About four trains a day also stop at **Fréjus gare SNCF** (☎94.51.30.53), just three to four minutes away from St-Raphaël. Buses between the two towns are much more frequent and take ten minutes on the St-Raphaël–Draguignan route. The Fréjus **gare routière** is at place Paul-Vernet (☎93.99.50.50) on the east side of the town centre, opposite the small Fréjus **tourist office**, 325 rue Jean-Jaurès (Mon–Sat 9am–noon & 2.30–6.30pm; ☎94.17.19.19). **Bikes** can be rented in Fréjus from *Holiday Bikes*, 943 av de Provence (☎94.52.30.65).

Accommodation

Hotels are not as plentiful in Fréjus as in St-Raphaël, but it's generally a quieter place to stay. There are several **youth hostels** in the vicinity, in particular the *HI Auberge de Jeunesse de Fréjus*, chemin du Counillier (closed 10am–6pm, 11pm curfew; ☎94.52.18.75; ①), 2km from Fréjus centre; a bus leaves for the hostel

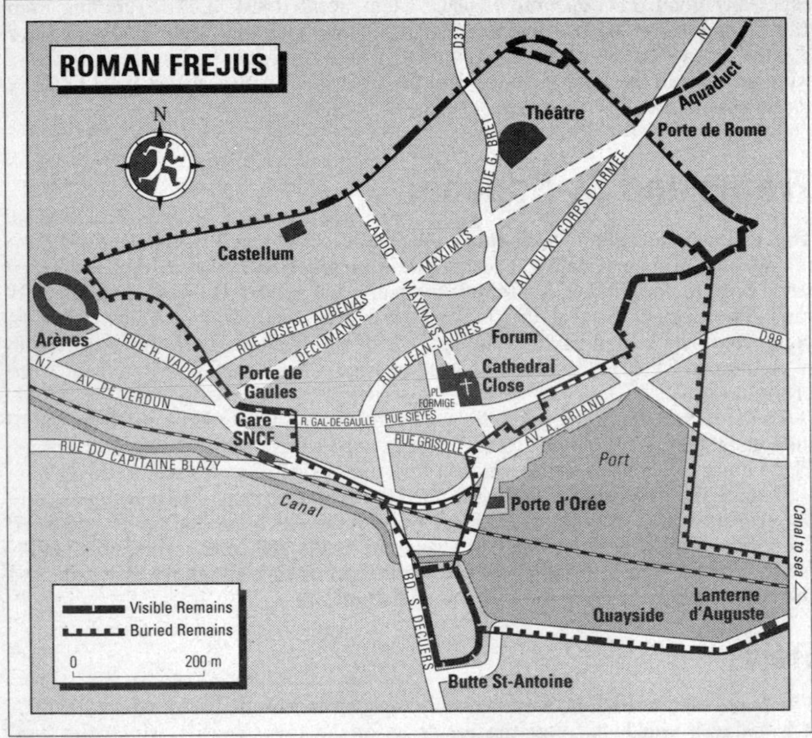

from St-Raphaël *gare routière*, *quai* 6 at 6pm in summer, *quai* 7 at 7pm in winter, Sunday *quai* 7 at 5.30pm, or you can take a regular bus #4, #8 or #9 from St-Raphaël or Fréjus, direction *L'Hôpital* to *Les Chênes* stop and walk up av du Gal-d'Armée Jean-Calies; the chemin du Counillier is the first left.

There are several **campsites** close to the sea between Fréjus and St-Aygulf but they are all on a giant scale and neither cheap nor friendly. The campsites in the woods north of Fréjus are preferable but charges are still high in mid-summer.

HOTELS

Aréna, 139 av Général-de-Gaulle (☎94.17.09.40). Pretty rooms, if a bit small, in a converted bank in Fréjus centre. Very friendly reception. ⑦

La Bellevue, pl Paul-Vernet (☎94.51.39.04). Not the quietest location but convenient and not expensive. ③

Résidences du Columbier, 1239 rte de Bagnols (☎94.51.45.92). A series of modern bungalows in a pine wood north of the town; all rooms have their own garden and terrace. ⑥

La Riviera, 90 rue Grisolle (☎94.51.31.46). Very small hotel in the centre of Fréjus. Not very modern, but clean and perfectly acceptable. ③

Sable et Soleil, 158 rue Paul-Alène, Fréjus-Plage (☎94.51.08.70). A pleasant, small, modern hotel 300m from the sea. ④

CAMPSITES

Le Dattier, rte de Bagnols (☎94.40.88.93). A three-star site 3.5km north of Fréjus. Easter–Sept.

Site de Gorge Vent, quartier de Bellevue, Fréjus (☎94.52.29.88). A two-star site off the N7 towards Cannes, 3km from the town centre.

Auberge de Jeunesse de Fréjus, a large campsite alongside the hostel (see p.265).

The Roman town

Doing a tour of the **Roman remains** gives you a good idea of the extent of *Forum Julii*, but they are scattered throughout and beyond the town centre and take a full day to get around. Turning right out of the *gare SNCF* and then right down bd Severin-Decuers brings you to the **Butte St-Antoine**, against whose east wall the waters of the port would have lapped, and which once was capped by a fort. It was one of the port's defences, and one of the ruined towers may have been a lighthouse. A path around the southern wall follows the quayside (odd stretches are visible) to the medieval **Lanterne d'Auguste**, built on the Roman foundations of a structure marking the entrance of the canal into the ancient harbour.

In the other direction from the station, past the Roman **Porte des Gaules** and along rue Henri-Vadon, you come to the **amphitheatre** (Mon & Wed–Sun 9/9.30am–noon & 2–4.30/6.30pm; 12F), smaller than those at Arles and Nîmes, but still able to seat around ten thousand. Today it's used for bullfights and rock concerts. Its upper tiers have been reconstructed in the same greenish local stone used by the Romans, but the vaulted galleries on the ground floor are largely original. The Roman **theatre** is north of the town, along av du Théâtre-Romain, its original seats long gone, though again it is still used for shows in summer. Northeast of it, at the end of av du XVème-Corps-d'Armée, a few arches are visible of the forty-kilometre **aqueduct**, once as high as the ramparts. Closer to the centre, where bd Aristide-Briand meets bd Salvarelli, are the arcades of the **Porte d'Orée**, positioned on the former harbour's edge alongside what was probably a bath complex.

The medieval town

The **Cité Episcopale**, or cathedral close, takes up two sides of **place Formigé**, the marketplace and heart of both contemporary and medieval Fréjus. It comprises the cathedral flanked by the fourteenth-century bishop's palace, now the hôtel de ville, the baptistery, chapterhouse, cloisters and archeological museum. Visits to the cloisters and baptistry are guided (April–Sept Mon & Wed–Sun 9am–7pm; Oct–March 9am–noon & 2–5pm; 21F including entrance to museum); access to the cathedral is free (9am–noon & 4–6pm); you can wander through the modern courtyard of the hôtel de ville but you get a better view of the orangy Esterel stone walls of the episcopal palace from rue de Beausset.

The oldest part is the **baptistry** built in the fourth or fifth century and so contemporary with the decline and fall of the city's Roman founders. Its two doorways are of different heights, signifying the enlarged spiritual stature of the baptized. Parts of the early Gothic **cathedral** may belong to a tenth-century church but its best features, apart from the coloured diamond-shaped tiles on the spire, are Renaissance: the choir stalls, a wooden crucifix on the left of the entrance, and the intricately carved doors with scenes of a Saracen massacre. Far the most beautiful and engaging component of the whole ensemble, however, is the **cloisters**. In a small garden of scented bushes, around a well, slender marble columns, carved in the twelfth century, support a fourteenth-century ceiling of wooden panels painted with apocalyptic creatures. Out of the original 1200 pictures, 400 remain, each about the size of this page. The subjects include multiheaded monsters, mermaids, satyrs and scenes of bacchanalian debauchery. The **Musée Archéologique** on the upper storey of the cloisters has as its star pieces a complete Roman mosaic of a leopard and a statue of double-headed Hermes.

Rue Jean-Jaurès, at the top of rue de Fleury, curves down to the shaded **place de la Liberté** which **rue Sieyes** links with place Formigé. Clothes, souvenirs and food shops are interspersed with cafés, and commercial arty life draws people down **rue St-François-de-Paule** off the bottom end of rue Jean-Jaurès: *Riquet Beaux-Arts* at no. 69 sells artists' materials; a photo gallery has free exhibitions at no. 108; plus there are antique shops and attractive bistros. Beyond place Agricola on the main road out of town, wonderful old distillery buildings house *La Fréjusienne* **wine co-op**.

Around Fréjus

Unlikely remnants of the more recent past come in the shape of a **Vietnamese pagoda** and an abandoned Soudanese-style **mosque**, both built by French colonial troops. The **Pagode Hong Hien** (daily 9am–noon & 2–5/8pm; free), still maintained as a Buddhist temple, is on the crossroads of the N7 to Cannes and rue Henri Giraud (bus #3), about 2km out of Fréjus. The **Mosquée Missiri de Djeanne** is on rue des Combattants d'Afrique du Nord, to the left off the D4 to Bagnols 2km from the RN7 junction. A strange, guava-coloured, fort-like building of typical West African style, it is decorated inside with fading murals of desert journeys gracefully sketched in white on the dark pink walls.

Fréjus has a **modern art gallery** (summer Tues–Sun 2–6/7pm; winter closed Sat & Sun) bizarrely located in the Zone Industrielle du Capitou just by turnoff 38 from the highway; from place Paul-Vernet, take bus #2 to Z.I. Capitou. It has no permanent collection but some quite interesting temporary exhibitions. Another venue for temporary exhibitions, this time of photography, is the ugly Neo-Classical **Villa Aurélienne** (Tues–Sun 2–6/7pm) in the Parc Aurélienne, north of av de l'Europe on the bus #4 line (details of what's on at both from the tourist office).

If you like **zoos** there's one just across the highway from Capitou (May–Sept daily 9.30am–6pm; Oct–April daily 10am–5pm; 57F, children 33F; bus #2). A kinder habitat, for the human young at least, is the **water amusement park**, *Aquatica* (July & Aug daily 10am–7pm; June & Sept 10am–6pm; 98F, children 55F; bus #19 or #29), off the RN98 to St-Aygulf. Water scooters, toboggans and pedal boats, chutes into an enchanted river, lakes, a huge swimming pool with artificial waves, a beach for the less energetic and an open-air cinema make up some of its main attractions. In the same entertainment zone there's a **funfair**, a **go-cart track** *Azur Karting* (mid-June to mid-Sept daily 11am–midnight; rest of year Mon & Wed–Sun 11am–9pm; 70F, children 40F), and a one-kilometre motorbike and quad circuit (daily 11am–9pm/midnight; 80F).

Eating and drinking

Fréjus is not a bad place for menu-browsing and café-lounging, with the cheaper **eateries** found on place Agricola, place de la Liberté and the main shopping streets. At Fréjus-Plage there's a string of eating houses to choose from, with more upmarket *plateau des fruits de mer* outlets at Port-Fréjus.

Aréna, 139 av Général-de-Gaulle, Fréjus (☎94.17.09.40). A hotel restaurant (see p.266) which is excellent for fish; menus start at 120F.

Café des Arts, on rue St-François-de-Paule. Reasonable café if you need a rest.

La Cave Blanche, on pl Calvini above the cathedral close (☎94.51.25.40). Offers a seafood cocktail on a menu for around 100F. Closed Mon & Sun evening.

Café de la Cité, 152 rue Jean-Jaurès. A nicely ordinary bar.

Les Potiers, 135 rue des Potiers (☎94.51.33.74). One of the best restaurants and located in a tiny backstreet, it serves dishes of fresh seasonal ingredients à la carte only for around 220F. Closed Mon midday.

Chez Vincent, on rue Desaugiers below pl Formigé (☎94.53.89.89). Has a good goats cheese salad and tiramisu pudding, with menus from 120F. Closed Mon midday.

St-Raphaël

A large resort and now one of the richest towns on the Côte, **ST-RAPHAEL** became fashionable at the turn of the century. It lost many of its *belle époque* mansions and hotels in the bombardments of World War II; some, like the *Continental* have recently been rebuilt, others have been restored more gradually. Meanwhile the tiny **old quarter** (*vieux quartier*) beyond place Carnot on the other side of the rail line has been starved of municipal funds.

Arrival and information

St-Raphaël's gare SNCF (☎94.91.50.50), in the centre of the town, is the main station on the Marseille–Ventigmilia line; the **gare routière** is on av Victor Hugo (☎94.95.16.71), just across the rail line opposite the *gare SNCF*. For information on St-Raphaël and all the surrounding region, go to the **tourist office** on rue W-Rousseau (daily 10am–noon & 2–5.30pm; ☎94.19.52.52): turn left out of the *gare SNCF* and you'll see it in front of you. **Bikes** can be rented from *Patrick Moto*, 260 av Général-Leclerc (☎94.53.65.99).

Accommodation

There are plenty of **hotels** in St-Raphaël from seafront palaces to backstreet cheapies. They can get very busy in summer, however, so it's worth booking in advance; if you get stuck the tourist office can help.

If you prefer to go **camping** try the area east of St-Raphaël along the Esterel coast (see p.272), which although preferable is still a little pricey in mid-summer. *Le Val Fleury*, on the N98 at Boulouris (☎94.95.21.52), is a large four-star site with all facilities and close to the beach.

The *Centre International Le Manoir*, chemin de l'Escale, Boulouris (closed 4–5pm; ☎94.95.20.58), is a luxurious and expensive **youth hostel**, 5km east of St-Raphaël close to the beach by the Boulouris *gare SNCF* (trains or buses every half-hour from St-Raphaël).

Beau Séjour, promenade Réné-Coty (☎94.95.03.75). One of the cheaper seafront hotels with pleasant terrace. ④–⑥

La Bellevue, 22 bd Félix-Martin (☎94.95.00.35). Good value for its central location. ④

La Bonne Auberge, 54 rue de la Garonne (☎94.95.69.72). A cheapie close to the old port. ③

Continental, promenade Réné-Coty (☎94.83.87.87). A classic seafront pile reconstructed to its 1900s ocean-liner glory. ⑦

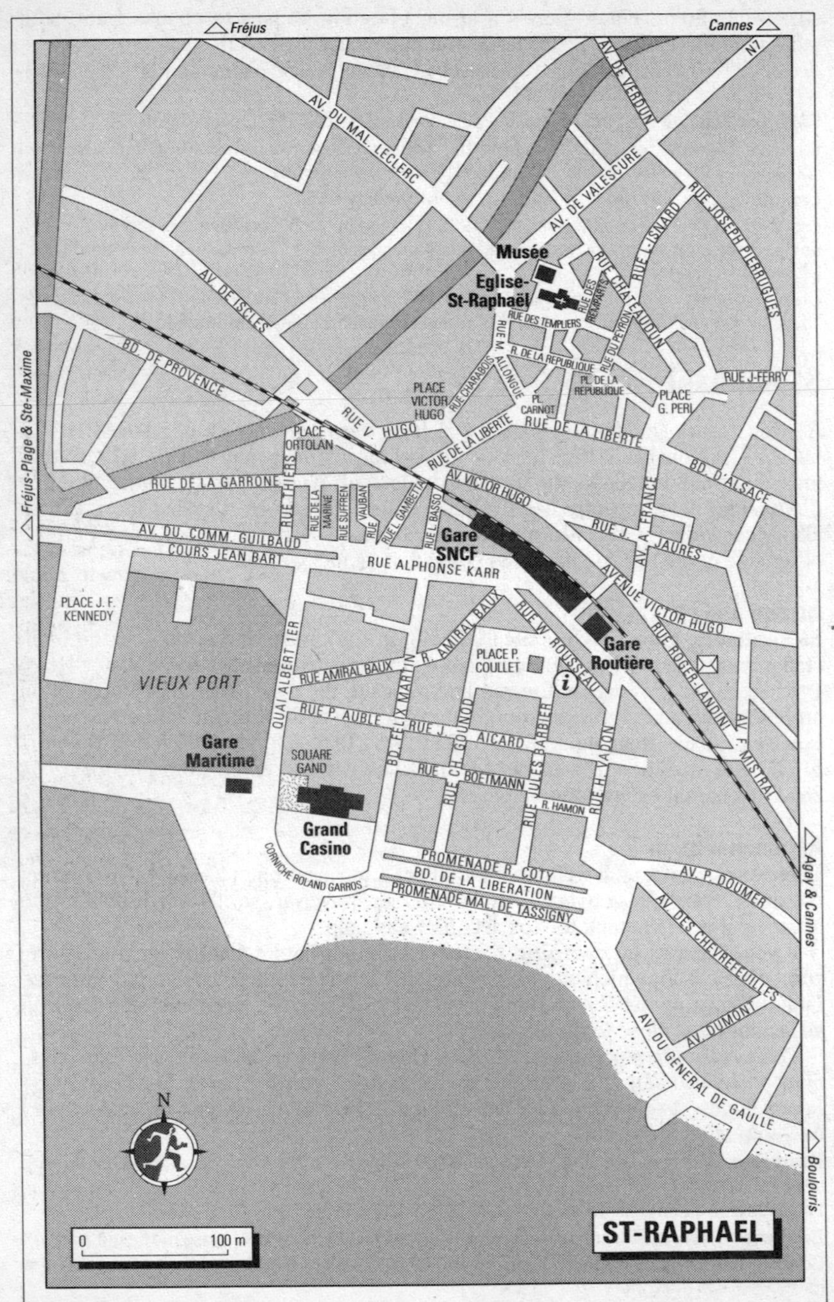

Fréjus
Cannes
N7
AV. DE VERDUN
AV. DU MAL. LECLERC
AV. DE VALESCURE
RUE JOSEPH PIERRUGUES
RUE L. ISNARD
Musée
Eglise-St-Raphaël
RUE CHATEAUDUN
RUE DES REMPARTS
RUE DES TEMPLIERS
RUE DU PEYRON
AV. DE ISCLES
BD. DE PROVENCE
RUE M. ALLONGUE
R. DE LA REPUBLIQUE
PL. DE LA REPUBLIQUE
PLACE VICTOR HUGO
RUE CHARABOIS
PL. CARNOT
PLACE G. PERI
RUE J-FERRY
RUE V. HUGO
RUE DE LA LIBERTE
PLACE ORTOLAN
BD. D'ALSACE
RUE DE LA GARRONE
AV. VICTOR HUGO
RUE THIERS
RUE DE LA MARINE
RUE SUFFREN
VAUBAN
RUE
RUE L. GAMBETTA
RUE L. BASSO
Gare SNCF
AV. A. FRANCE
RUE J. JAURES
AV. DU COMM. GUILBAUD
COURS JEAN BART
RUE ALPHONSE KARR
AVENUE VICTOR HUGO
Fréjus-Plage & Ste-Maxime
PLACE J. F. KENNEDY
R. AMIRAL BAUX
RUE W. ROUSSEAU
Gare Routière
PLACE P. COULLET
RUE ROGER-LANDINI
VIEUX PORT
QUAI ALBERT 1ER
RUE AMIRAL BAUX
BD. FELIX MARTIN
RUE P. AUBLE
RUE J. AICARD
RUE CH. GOUNOD
RUE JULES BARBIER
RUE H. VADON
AV. F. MISTRAL
Gare Maritime
SQUARE GAND
RUE BOETMANN
R. HAMON
Grand Casino
CORNICHE ROLAND GARROS
PROMENADE R. COTY
BD. DE LA LIBERATION
PROMENADE MAL. DE TASSIGNY
AV. P. DOUMER
Agay & Cannes
AV. DES CHEVREFEUILLES
AV. DUMONT
AV. DU GENERAL DE GAULLE
Boulouris
N
0
100 m
ST-RAPHAEL

Excelsior, promenade Réné-Coty (☎94.95.02.42). All mod cons overlooking the Plage du Veillat seafront of the town centre. ⑦

La Méditerranée, cnr of rue W-Rousseau and rue Vadon (☎94.19 07.67). Close to the station and nothing special. Closed noon–3pm. ②

Hôtel du Soleil, 47 bd du Domaine de Soleil, off bd Christian-Lafon (☎94.83.10.00). A small pretty villa with its own garden east of the centre. ④

Le Touring, 1 quai Albert 1er (☎94.95.01.72). Not very quiet but good value for the location. ③

The Town

On rue des Templiers a crumbling fortified Romanesque church has fragments of the Roman aqueduct that brought water from Fréjus in its courtyard along with a local history and underwater archeology **museum** that no one really visits (Mon & Wed–Sun 10am–noon & 2/3–5/6pm, closed Sun out of season; free). The streets in this *vieux quartier* are full of shops to let or for sale, unable to compete with the shopping malls in the seafront apartment buildings and hotels.

Back on **the seafront**, a stroll along the broad promenade Réné-Coty to the junction with rue Henri Vadon reveals St-Raphaël's preference for the loud and large in the grand hotels and the 1930s *Résidence Le Méditerranée* with mosaiced vases beneath the eaves at 1 av Paul-Doumer. Art Deco stucco flowers adorn *La Rocquerousse* apartment buildings next to the *Hôtel Beauséjour* and vestiges of the town's prewar clientele appear amidst the characterless modern constructions along av des Chevrefeuilles – a blue-domed but surprisingly plain Russian church, and on av Paul-Doumer a rather pretty English church and a turn-of-the-century villa.

The **beaches** stretch between the *Vieux Port* in the centre and the newer Port Santa Lucia, with opportunities for every kind of water sport. **Boats** leave from the *gare maritime* (☎94.95.17.46) on the south side of the *Vieux Port* to St-Tropez, Port Grimaud, the Iles d'Hyères and the islands off Cannes as well as the much closer *calanques* of the Esterel coast. When you're tired of sea and sand there's **bowling** at the *Bowling Raphaëlois* on promenade Réné-Coty (3pm–3am) and **billiards** close by at *Le Candy*. And if you want to lose whatever money you have left on slot machines or blackjack, the **Grand Casino** on Square de Grand overlooking the *Vieux Port* (whose director is also the mayor) will be only too happy to oblige (daily 11am–4am).

Eating and drinking

You'll find reasonably priced **brasseries** and any number of pizzerias, *crêperies* and **restaurants** of varying quality around Port Santa Lucia and along the promenades. **Cafés** such as *Le Victor-Hugo* on rue Victor-Hugo, which overlooks the market, are also a good cheaper option. For **snacks**, cakes, ice creams, **beers** and cocktails try *L'Emeraude*, 3 bd du Gal-de-Gaulle. **Food markets** are held every day on place Victor-Hugo and place de la République, with fish sold on place Ortolan.

Le Pastorel, 54 rue de la Liberté (☎94.95.02.36). This has been serving traditional dishes since 1922. Menus start around 160F; there are decently priced Provençal wines, *aïoli* on Fri and wonderful hors d'oeuvres. Closed Mon & Sun evening.

La Petite France, 57 rue Vauban (☎94.40.51.34). Friendly and inexpensive restaurant on a narrow street between rue Alphonse Karr and rue de la Garonne. *Moules-frites* for 45F; menu from 69F.

Le Poussin Bleu, cnr of Promenade and rue Charles-Gounod. Cheapish seafront brasserie.

Le Sirocco, 35 quai Albert Ier (☎94 95 39.99). Quite a smart restaurant specializing in fish, with a good menu for around 120F plus a view of the sea. The wine is expensive.

Le Tisonnier, 70 rue de la Garonne (☎94.95.28.51). Offers a Provençal menu for 89F with raviolis and salmon cooked with fennel.

La Voile d'Or, 1 bd du Gal-de-Gaulle (☎94.95.17.04). The *bourride Raphaëloise à la rouille* (fillet of sea bream in a seafood and saffron sauce) is the best of the fishy dishes on offer. Menus from 140F. Closed Tues, & Wed midday in July & Aug; Sept–June closed Tues evening & Wed.

Nightlife and entertainment

La Reserve on the Promenade is the stereotypical Côte d'Azur **disco**, with conventional red velvet and glitter decor and popular hits from the last twenty years. Be warned, however, as *tenue correcte* (you need to look expensive) is essential and the first drink 80F, thereafter from 50F. *Le Kilt*, 130 rue Jules-Barbier (11.30pm–dawn) is a little more exciting but not much.

For plain **drinking**, try the selection of beers at *Blue Bar* on the Promenade above Plage du Veillat (open till 4am in summer), or for sipping expensive cocktails to piano accompaniment there's the *Madison Club* at the casino (7pm–4am) or *Coco-Club* at Port Santa Lucia (till dawn). Motor-racing fanatics should try out the downmarket *Le Silverstone* on rue W-Rousseau (till 4.15am), next to the *Méditerranée* hotel.

At the end of June/beginning of July St-Raphaël hosts an international competition of New Orleans **jazz** orchestras, and in October, a festival of **Russian films** (the tourist office can supply details).

Listings

Boat rental *Club Nautique* at western end of Port Santa Lucia (☎94.95.11.66).

Car rental *ADA St-Raphaël Automobiles* (☎94.83.11.41); *Avis* (94.95.60.42) and *Europcar* (☎94.95.56.87), all on pl P-Coulet, St-Raphaël; *Holiday Bikes*, 943 av de Provence, Fréjus (☎94.52.30.65).

Currency exchange *Centre Commerciale de la Gare* in the St-Raphaël train station (June–Sept Mon–Fri 4–10pm, Sat & Sun 9am–10pm) or *Change Service*, 26 av du Commandant Guilbaud on the *Vieux Port*, St-Raphaël (July & Aug daily 9am–9pm). Most banks have cashpoint machines.

Emergency ☎15; *Hôpital Intercommunal Bonnet*, av André Léotard, Fréjus (☎94.40.21.21); *SOS Médecins* (☎94.95.15.25).

Laundry 5 rue Jules-Ferry; 34 av Général-Leclerc.

Pharmacy Call Police Municipale in St-Raphaël on ☎94.95.24.24 for late-night pharmacy.

Police Commissariat, av Amiral-Baux, St-Raphaël (☎94.95.00.17).

Post office *PTT*, Poste Principale, av Victor Hugo, St-Raphaël.

Taxi ☎94.95.04.25.

The Esterel

About a quarter of the 40km or so of the **Corniche de l'Esterel**, between **Anthéor** and **Le Trayas**, is still untouched by property development, the sole stretch of wild coast between St-Raphaël and the Italian border, its backdrop an arc of brilliant red volcanic rock tumbling down to the sea from the harsh crags of the **Massif de l'Esterel**. From the two major routes between Fréjus and **LA NAPOULE**, the coastal N98 and rail line, and the inland N7, minor roads lead into this steeply contoured and once deeply wooded wild terrain. The shoreline, meanwhile, is a mass of little **beaches**, some sand, some shingle, cut by rocky promontories.

The inland route

The high, hairpin **inland route** is a heart-rending drive. For every 2km of undisturbed ancient olive trees and gravity-defying rock formations, you have to suffer 1km of new motels and "residential parks" with real-estate hoardings. The Esterel is – or was – one of the most beautiful areas on the planet, as well as one of its oldest land masses. Unhappily, however, property sharks can get away not only with circumventing planning laws, but worse still, encouraging **fires**. No developer has ever been prosecuted for arson (given the regularity of forest fires here it would be nearly impossible to prove) but local people notice with bitterness the speed at which designs are ready for recently scorched land.

The interior of the Esterel had for centuries been uninhabited, save for reclusive saints, escaped convicts from Toulon and Resistance fighters. It has no water and the topsoil is too shallow for cultivation. Prior to the twentieth-century creation of the corniche, the coastal communities were linked only by sea routes. The N7, however, is ancient, part of the Roman *Via Aurelia*.

Many of the minor roads are barred to vehicles during the summer months, the worst season for the Esterel, and some are closed throughout the year. But that makes **walking** all the more enjoyable. The tourist office in St-Raphaël (see p.269) can provide details of paths and of the peaks that are the most obvious destinations. The highest point is **Mont Vinaigre**, which you can almost reach by road, turning left 8km out of Fréjus on the N7; a short signposted footpath leads up to the summit. At 618m it's not really a mountain – 600 million years of erosion have taken their toll – but the view is spectacular. Other peaks that don't require long treks (assuming you've got transport) are the **Pic de l'Ours**, inland from Le Trayas, and the **Pic du Cap Roux** above the promontory of the same name between Le Trayas and Anthéor.

The Corniche

With half a dozen train stations and hourly buses between St-Raphaël and La Napoule, this is a very accessible coastal stretch for non-drivers. Along the stretch between Anthéor and Le Trayas each easily reached beach has its summer snack-van, but by clambering over rocks you can usually find a near deserted cove.

Le Dramont, Agay and Anthéor

The merest snatch of clear hillside and brasserie-less beach distinguishes Boulouris from **LE DRAMONT**, 9km east from St-Raphaël's centre, where the landing of the 36th American division in August 1944 is commemorated. A cliff-top path around the **Cap du Dramont** headland gives fine views, though looking inland the most severe and recent encroachment on the Esterel is revealed. This is the designer "village" of **Cap Esterel**, created out of nothing but pure profit motive and squatting smugly on the ridge between Le Dramont and Agay.

Fenced off and with its security gates guarded night and day, it is a vast enclave of time-share apartments and hotels, huge swimming pools, a golf course, terraced gardens, "streets" of arty-crafty shops, and even a mock church divided into "studios" and "*appartements de luxe*". All very tastefully done of course, pastel shades and pantiled roofs, but totally unreal. No one lives there permanently; there's no history past or present, no depth and no diversity. If you want to take a look, there's free two-hour parking (no vehicles circulate in Cap Esterel) or buses from St-Raphaël.

In contrast, Le Dramont's close neighbour **AGAY** is one of the least pretentious resorts of the Côte d'Azur and beautifully situated around a deep horse-shoe bay edged by sand beaches, red porphyry cliffs and pines. Both Agay and its eastern neighbour **ANTHEOR** suffer from the creeping contagion of estates with friendly rural names like *Mas* and *Hameaux* edging ever higher up their hills but once you do get above the concrete line, at the **Sommet du Rastel** for example (signed up Agay's av du Bourg or bd du Rastel), you can begin to appreciate this wonderful terrain.

There are at least nine **campsites** in this area. Along the Valescure road near the Agay river you'll find the four-star *Les Rives d'Agay* (mid-Feb to Oct; ☎94.82.02.74) or, by the beach, *Agay-Soleil*, 1114 bd de la Plage (mid-March to mid-Nov; ☎94.82.00.79), and *Azur Rivage*, around the headland in Anthéor-Plage (mid-March to mid-Oct; ☎94.44.83.12). **Hotels** are also thick on the ground: Agay's *France Soleil* on bd de la Mer (Easter–Oct; ☎94.82.01.93; ⑥) and *Sol e Mar* (☎94.95.25.60; April to mid-Oct; ⑦) in Le Dramont both have sea views; a less expensive option is *Les Flots d'Or* in Anthéor (mid-Feb to mid-Oct; ☎94.44.80.21; ④). **Bikes** can be rented at the *Vallée du Paradis* campsite on av du Gratadis in Agay.

Le Trayas

LE TRAYAS is on the highest point of the Corniche and its shoreline is the most ragged, with wonderful inlets to explore. You can also trek to the Pic d'Ours from here (the path is signed from the *gare SNCF*, about 3hr).

The **hotel** *Relais des Calanques*, corniche d'Or (Jan–Oct; ☎94.44.14.06; ⑥) nestles above a cove, the water almost lapping at its terrace where good seafish is served. Less expensive rooms can be had at *Les Terrasses* on bd Théodore-Guichard (☎94.44.14.13; ③). Le Trayas also has an **HI youth hostel**, the *Villa Solange*, 9 av de la Véronèse (Feb–Dec; ☎93.75.40.23; ①), a two-kilometre uphill slog from the *Auberge Blanche* stop on the Cannes–St-Raphaël bus route or from Le Trayas *gare SNCF*. Once you've arrived you won't regret it – as long as you've booked in advance.

Miramar

At **MIRAMAR**, the proximity of Cannes begins to show: you can see the city's outskirts, and the local architecture is infected with its style. From the Pointe de l'Esquillon you get an unhindered view of the private residential estate at Porte-La-Galère on the neighbouring headland, a foul, reeling, drunken design by Jacques Couelle.

Staying at Miramar, one **hotel** worth trying out if you're not on a tight budget is the *Hôtel de la Corniche d'Or*, 10 bd de l'Esquillon (March–Oct; half-board compulsory in season; ☎93.75.40.12; ⑦), with a very good, and equally pricey, restaurant.

La Napoule

The fantasy castle, built onto the three towers and gateway of a medieval fort, that announces **LA NAPOULE** and heralds the Riviera, appears on the point of sinking under its own weight. The castle ranks high amongst the classic pre-World War I follies built by foreigners on the Côte, the creators, in this instance, being the American sculptor Henry Clews and his wife. The lovely gardens and the interior can be visited (guided tours only Mon & Wed–Sun 3pm & 4pm, plus 5pm in July & Aug; 25F) with its collection of Clews' odd and gloomy works, represented on the outside by the creatures on the gateway.

On the eastern side of the village, the River Siagne flows into the sea. If you follow it a short way upstream, you'll see an elegant arched rail bridge, which could hardly offer a more telling contrast to the Clews château, in terms of lightness, grace, and economy of design. Its creator was Gustave Eiffel of Tower fame.

The one **hotel** in La Napoule worth approaching is *La Calanque* on bd Henri-Clews (mid-March to Oct; half-board compulsory in summer; ☎93.49.95.11; ④), which has rooms with views of the château and the sea and a **restaurant** serving some fine fish dishes *à la Provençal* (menus from around 100F). If you get stuck, the characterless inland resort of **MANDELIEU-LA NAPOULE** has plenty of hotels, not to mention golf courses. The **tourist offices** on av de Cannes by the *autoroute* exit (☎93.49.14.39), and av Henri-Clews opposite La Napoule's port (☎93.49.95.31) will help.

Should 500–1000F seem like a reasonable price for a meal, *L'Oasis* **restaurant**, rue Jean-Honoré-Carle (book weeks in advance; ☎93.49.95.52), which ranks amongst the gourmets' Bible *Gault Millau*'s top one hundred French restaurants, is here. It offers a spectacular three-course lunch plus coffee, petits fours and wine for a mere 250F, but, choosing this, you don't get to taste the Asiatic specialities.

travel details

Trains

Les Arcs to: Draguignan (frequent; 5min); Fréjus (4 daily; 16min); Gonfaron (1–3 daily; 10min); St-Raphaël (frequent; 20min); Toulon (frequent; 40min–1hr 5min); Vidauban (1–3 daily; 5 min).

Hyères to: Toulon (4–6 daily; 20min).

St-Raphaël to: Agay (9 daily; 10 min); Anthéor (9 daily; 14min); Boulouris (9 daily; 4min); Cannes (frequent; 25–35min); Le Dramont (9 daily; 7min); Le Trayas (9 daily; 19min); Mandelieu-La Napoule (9 daily; 26min); Marseille (frequent; 1hr 45min); Nice (frequent; 1hr–1hr 20min); Théole-sur-Mer (9 daily; 23min); Toulon (frequent; 55min).

Buses

Hyères to: Bormes (frequent; 25min); La Croix-Valmer (8 daily; 1hr 15min); Le Lavandou (frequent; 35min); Le Rayol (8 daily; 55min); St-Tropez (8 daily; 1hr 35min–1hr 45min); Toulon (every 30min; 35–50min).

Le Lavandou to: Bormes (frequent; 10min); Cavalaire-sur-Mer (8–9 daily; 30min); Cavalière (8–9 daily; 10min); Cogolin (2 daily; 40min); Grimaud (2 daily; 45 min); Hyères (frequent; 35min); La Croix-Valmer (8–9 daily; 40min); La Garde Freinet (2 daily; 1hr); La Môle (2 daily; 30min); Le Rayol (8–9 daily; 20min); St-Tropez (8 daily; 55min–1hr 5min); Toulon (frequent; 1hr 10min).

Ste-Maxime to: Plan-de-la-Tour (2–4 daily; 15min).

St-Raphaël to: Cannes (8–9 daily; 1hr 10min); Cogolin (8 daily; 1hr–1hr 10min); Draguignan (10–12 daily; 1hr 15min–1hr 25min); Grimaud (8 daily; 50min–1hr); La Foux (8 daily; 1hr 5min–1hr 15min); Le Muy (12–14 daily; 50min); Les Issambres (8 daily; 20–30min); Rocquebrune (9–11 daily; 40min); Ste-Maxime (8 daily; 30–40min); Ste-Roseline (8–9 daily; 1hr); St-Tropez (8 daily; 1hr 15min–1hr 25min) .

St-Tropez to: Bormes (8 daily; 1hr 5min–1hr 15min); Cavalaire-sur-Mer (8–9 daily; 30min); Cavalière (8–9 daily; 50min); Cogolin (8 daily; 15min); Gassin (1 daily; 35min); Grimaud (8 daily; 20–35min); Hyères (8 daily; 1hr 30min–1hr 40min); La Croix-Valmer (8 daily; 20min); La Garde Freinet (1 daily; 45min); Le Lavandou (8 daily; 55min–1hr 5min); Le Rayol (8 daily; 40–55min); Les Issambres (8 daily; 55min); Ramatuelle (4 daily; 25min); Ste-Maxime (8 daily; 45min); St-Raphaël (8 daily; 1hr 15min–1hr 25min); Toulon (8 daily; 2hr 15min).

Flights

Hyères to: Lille (April–Sept 1 weekly; 1hr 25min); Paris (daily; 1hr 15 min).

CHAPTER FIVE

THE HEARTLAND OF PROVENCE

This chapter takes in the Upper Var (the northern half of the Var *département*) and the western section of the Alpes de Haute Provence. It is the heartland of Provence not because it is geographically central, but because it is here that you can escape the mindless devotion to the tourist industry and begin to discover the individuality and unsullied beauty of Provence. It is one of the least populated of France's non-mountainous areas.

Small towns and villages such as **Aups**, **Riez**, **Cotignac**, **Forcalquier** and **Simaine-la-Rotonde** still carry on their traditional occupations of cultivating lavender, making honey, tending sheep, digging for truffles and pressing olive oil. In isolated places like **Banon** and the hamlets around Sisteron, it's hard to believe this is the same country, never mind province, as the Côte d'Azur.

True, foreigners have bought second homes in the idyllic **Haut Var villages** but the tidal wave of new house building does not yet extend north of the *Autoroute Provençale*. The Marseille–Gap highway along the **Durance river** has not encouraged major industrialization of the valley; in many ways it has further isolated many of the towns and villages along its route; and prices here remain much, much lower than on the coast or in western Provence.

Landscapes are exceptional from the gentle countryside of the Haut Var or Pays de Forcalquier to the rolling plains and wide horizons of the **Plateau de Valensole** and the high harshness of the **Montagne de Lure**; the wild emptiness of the **Plateau de Canjuers**, the untrammelled forests east of Draguignan and, most spectacularly of all, Europe's largest ravine, the **Grand Canyon** (or Gorges) **du Verdon**, matched only in grandeur by the snow-capped mountains on the northern horizons.

Food here is fundamentally Provençal: lamb from the high summer pastures, goat's cheese, honey, almonds, olives and wild herbs. The soil is poor and water scarce, but the *Côtes de Provence* wine *appellation* extends to the Upper Var.

The towns, dull **Draguignan**, busy but parochial **Manosque** and the declining mountain gateway to Provence of **Sisteron**, are not the prime appeal. First and foremost this is an area for **walking** and **climbing**, or **canoeing** and **windsurfing**

HOTEL ROOM PRICES

For a fuller explanation of these price codes, see the box on p.32 of *Basics*.

① Under 160F	② 160–220F	③ 220–300F	④ 300–400F
⑤ 400–500F	⑥ 500–600F	⑦ 600–700F	⑧ over 700F

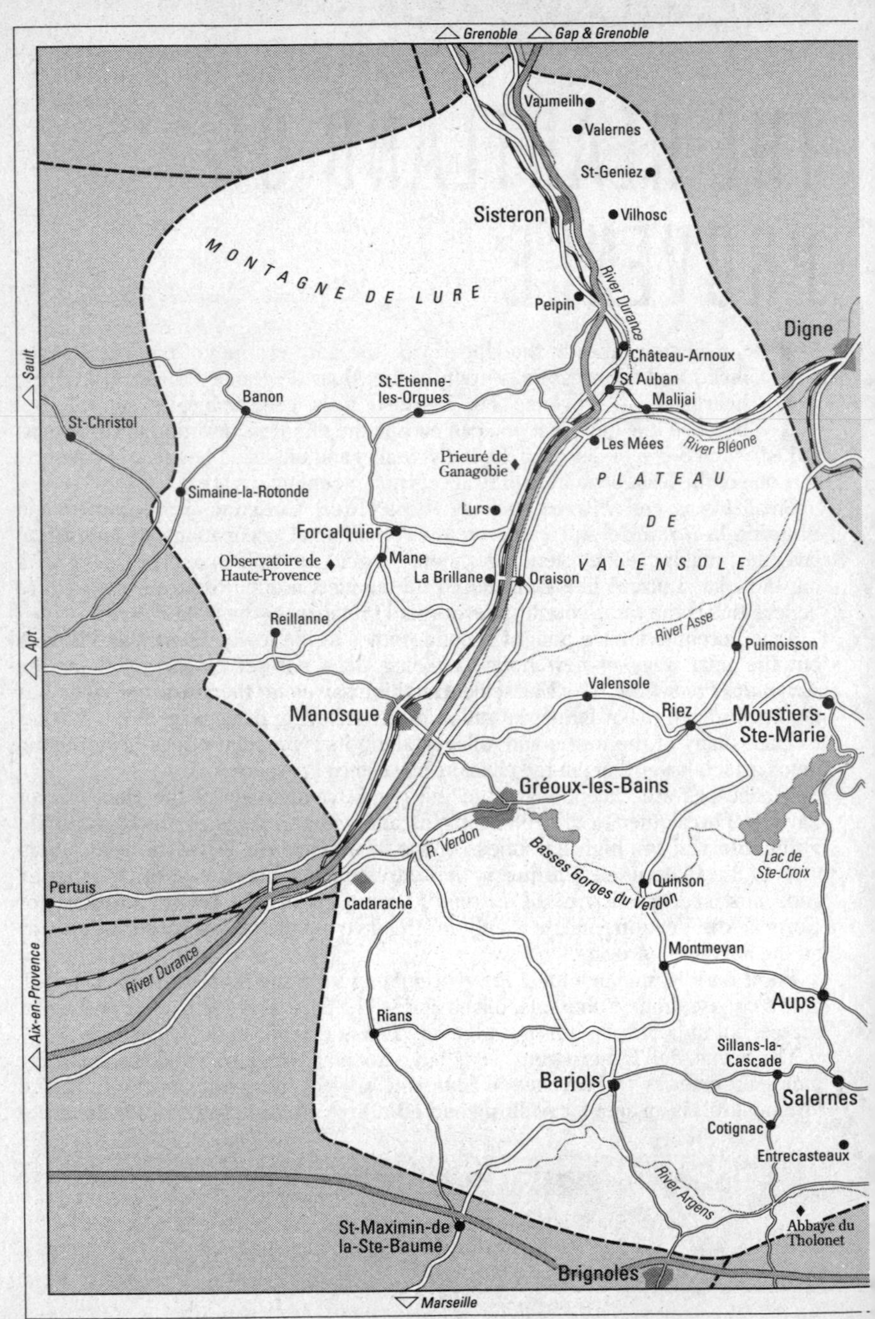
Grenoble
Gap & Grenoble
Vaumeilh
Valernes
St-Geniez
Sisteron
Vilhosc
MONTAGNE DE LURE
River Durance
Peipin
Digne
Château-Arnoux
St Auban
Malijai
Sault
Banon
St-Etienne-les-Orgues
St-Christol
Les Mées
River Bléone
Prieuré de Ganagobie
PLATEAU DE VALENSOLE
Simaine-la-Rotonde
Lurs
Forcalquier
Mane
Observatoire de Haute-Provence
La Brillane
Oraison
River Asse
Reillanne
Apt
Puimoisson
Valensole
Manosque
Riez
Moustiers-Ste-Marie
Gréoux-les-Bains
R. Verdon
Basses Gorges du Verdon
Lac de Ste-Croix
Pertuis
Quinson
Cadarache
Montmeyan
Aix-en-Provence
River Durance
Aups
Rians
Sillans-la-Cascade
Barjols
Salernes
Cotignac
Entrecasteaux
River Argens
Abbaye du Tholonet
St-Maximin-de la-Ste-Baume
Brignoles
Marseille

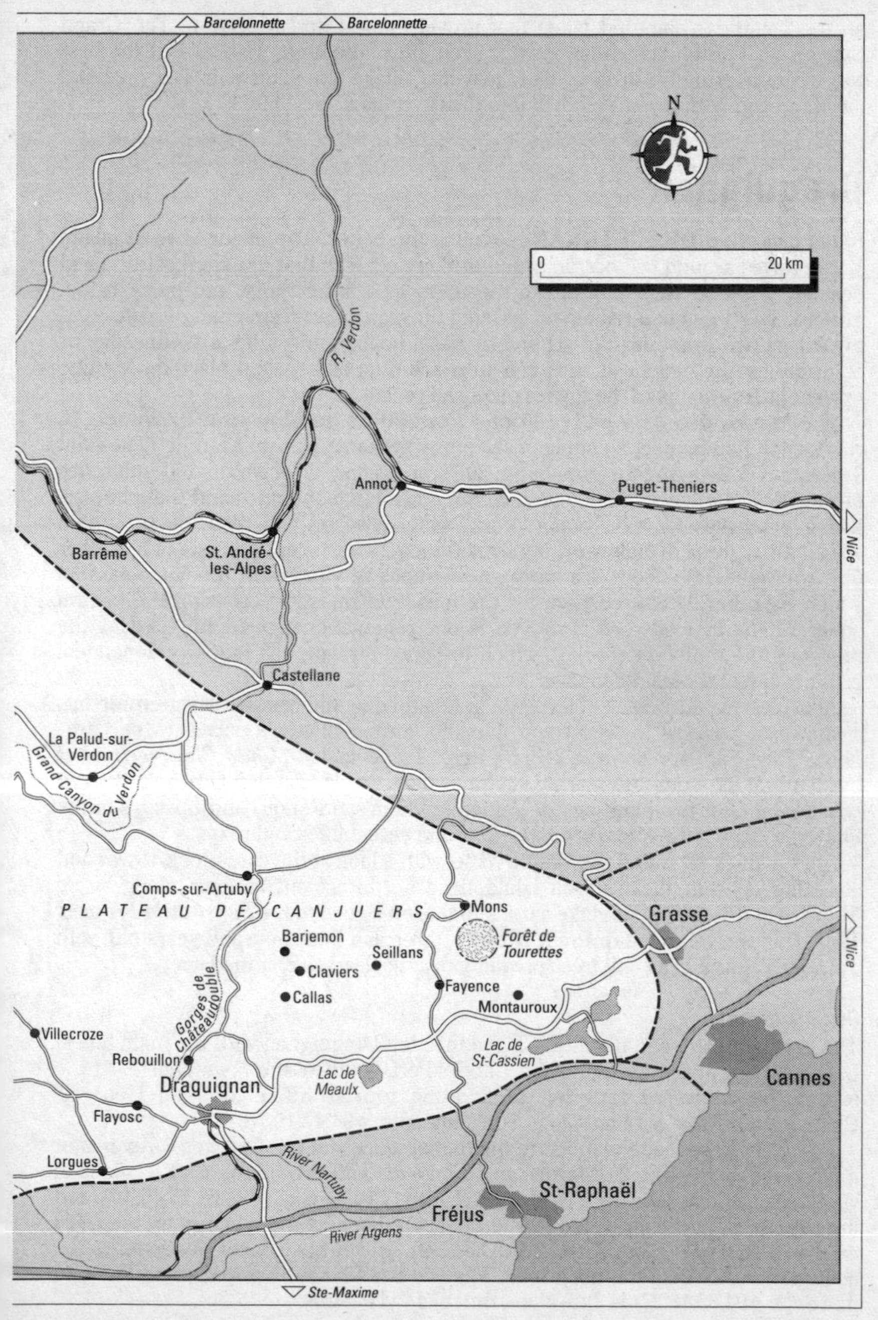
Barcelonnette
Barcelonnette
N
0
20 km
R. Verdon
Annot
Puget-Theniers
Nice
Barrême
St. André-les-Alpes
Castellane
La Palud-sur-Verdon
Grand Canyon du Verdon
Comps-sur-Artuby
PLATEAU DE CANJUERS
Mons
Grasse
Nice
Forêt de Tourettes
Barjemon
Seillans
Claviers
Callas
Fayence
Montauroux
Gorges de Châteaudouble
Villecroze
Lac de St-Cassien
Rebouillon
Lac de Meaulx
Cannes
Draguignan
Flayosc
River Nartuby
Lorgues
St-Raphaël
Fréjus
River Argens
Ste-Maxime

on the countless dammed lakes that provide power and irrigation. The Grand Canyon du Verdon is a must, even if seen only from a car or bus. But the best way of discovering the area is just to stay in a village that takes your fancy, eating, dawdling and letting yourself drift into the rhythms of local life.

Draguignan

If you can avoid **DRAGUIGNAN**, so much the better. The major town of inland Var revolves around the barracks and artillery schools that use the beautiful and desolate **Plateau de Canjuers** to the north as a firing range and mock battleground. The only good reason for passing through, apart from changing buses, is to visit its two **museums** of art and of social history, and if it's a Wednesday or Saturday for the benefit of an excellent **market** on and around place du Marché in what little remains of the town's medieval centre.

The **Musée des Arts et Traditions Populaires de Moyenne Provence**, 15 rue Joseph-Roumanille, a couple of streets away from place du Marché (Tues–Sat 9am–noon & 2–6pm, Sun 9am–noon; 20F), beautifully displays the old industries of the Var *département*. Nineteenth-century farming techniques and the manufacturing processes for silk, honey, cork, wine, olive oil and tiles are presented within the context of daily working lives (though some scenes are spoilt by rather dire wax models). There are early photographs of villages in the Var, many of which have hardly altered save for the means of transport crossing the central squares. The loss of trees, however, is one regional change highlighted by the museum: the mulberry tree, on which the once thriving silk industry depended, is today one of the rarest species.

Also close to the centre at 9 rue de la République, the **Musée Municipale** has a showcase window to tempt you into this former bishop's palace (Mon 9am–noon, Tues–Sat 9am–noon & 2–6pm; free). Treats include *Child Blowing Bubbles* by Rembrandt; a delicate marble sculpture by Camille Claudel; Greuze's *Portrait of a Young Girl*; two paintings of Venice by Ziem's; a Renoir; and upstairs in the library, a copy of the *Romance of the Rose* and early bibles and maps.

After a quick flit round the **Vieille Ville**, with a look at the cute **clock tower** and adjoining open-air theatre, you could head northwest out of town along av de Montferrat (the D995) and take a track to the left signed to the *Pierre de la Fée* after 1km. This is a very neat **dolmen** between three and four thousand years old, with the added charm of an oak tree spreading over it; clearly a charmed spot .

Practicalities

The **gare routière** and **gare SNCF** (connecting Draguignan with the main line at Les Arcs) are at the bottom of bd Gabriel-Péri, south of the town centre. At the top of the boulevard turn left to find the **tourist office** at 9 bd Georges-Clemenceau (Mon–Sat 9am–7pm, Sun 9am–1pm; ☎94.47.10.76).

Rue de la République just before the tourist office and rue Georges-Clisson after it both lead up to place du Marché and the *Vieille Ville*, where there's a a couple of very reasonable **hotels**, the *Touring Hôtel*, place Claude-Gay (☎94.68.15.46; ③), and the *Dracenois*, 14 rue du Cros (☎94.68.14.57; ②). For a bit more luxury try the *Hôtel du Parc*, 21 bd de Liberté (☎94.68.53.84; ④), which has rooms overlooking the courtyard rather than the main road. The two-star *La Foux* **campsite** (mid-June to mid-Sept; ☎94.68.18.27) is 2km along the road to Les Arcs.

There's a generous choice of cheap **eats** in the *Vieille Ville*, though nothing very special, and if you've come from the coast you'll be relieved to be back with cafés charging well under 10F for a sit-down terrace coffee. The *Bar de Négociants* amidst the flower stalls on place du Marché or the youth-oriented, traditional sawdust, mirrors and bar-football café, *Les Mille Colonnes* on place des Herbes are recommended. If sugary things are your passion, seek out the *Cabre d'Or confiserie* at 191 rue du Combat.

Northwards: Rebouillon and Châteaudouble

Continuing on from the *Pierre de la Fée*, you reach, after 5km or so, **REBOUILLON**, an exquisitely peaceful village built around an oval field on the banks of the Nartuby river. Almost immediately the scenery changes dramatically with the start of the **Gorges du Châteaudouble** whose serpentine cliffs are full of caves where skeletons of prehistoric animals that roamed these parts when the Mediterranean was dry have been found. Though a mere scratch compared to the great Verdon gorge, it has some impressive moments, not least when you see the village of **CHATEAUDOUBLE** hanging high above the cliffs. Nostradamus predicted that the river would grind away at the base until the village fell; he could yet be proved right. The gateway to the village is an arch cut out of a massive rock. Almost deserted except during the summer holidays, Châteaudouble consists of little more than a ruined tower and ramparts, which you can reach from a path beside the *Bar du Château*, two churches, a handful of houses, a potter's workshop, a bee-keeper and his hives, and *La Tour* restaurant (☎94.70.93.08; menu under 100F) with a terrace overlooking the gorge.

East to the Lac de St-Cassien

If you're meandering eastwards towards **GRASSE** from Draguignan a number of **medieval villages** north of the main Draguignan–Grasse road (the D562) might detain you. Sheltering below the inhospitable wilderness of the plateau of Canjuers, the settlements of **Callas**, **Claviers**, **Bargemon**, **Seillans**, **Mons**, **Fayence**, **Tourettes** and **Montauroux** were all virtually inaccessible less than a hundred years ago. Not so now, though they are still a far cry from the mega-villages nearer the coast. To the south of the D562 is a wonderful virtually uninhabited expanse of forest where between January and June you may see untended cattle with bells round their necks and sheep chewing away at the undergrowth. After a long period of campaigning farmers have managed to persuade the authorities to allow the animals to roam some of the old pasturing grounds of the transhumance routes, which has the great ecological benefit of maintaining the diversity of the forest fauna.

Callas, Claviers, Bargemon and Seillans

CALLAS, 12km northeast of Draguignan, has a lovely square by the church at the top of the village, and further down, on the shaded place Georges-Clemenceau, a very reasonable **hotel-restaurant**, *the Hôtel de France* (Mon & Wed–Sun; ☎94.76.61.02; ②). In the same *commune*, but 7km south, below the Draguignan–Grasse road on the D25 overlooking the Pennafort waterfalls, is the much grander *Hostellerie des Gorges de Pennfort* with its own pool, lake and olive grove (☎94.76.66.51; ⑦).

Steep narrow roads through luscious valleys connect **CLAVIERS** with Callas (3km) and Bargemon (6km), where very little happens other than gentle games of *boules* and slow sipping of local Côtes de Provence wine. Eastwards from Callas the road gently curves past woods and vineyards without a building in sight. If you turn right at the junction with the Draguignan–Grasse road you can stop after 1km and take a track to your left through more undisturbed cricket-chirping scrub and woods down to the Lac de Meaulx.

Within its four twelfth-century gates, **BARGEMON** is kept in summer shade by towering plane trees on every fountained square, and, in spring, the streets are adrift with orange petals and mimosa blossom. The fifteenth-century **Eglise St-Etienne** which forms part of the defences is now a **museum-gallery** with exhibitions of local painters (afternoons only). The two angel heads on the high altar are attributed to the great Marseillais sculptor Pierre Puget. There's a good place to **stay**, **eat** and **drink**, the *Auberge des Arcades*, 12 av Pasteur (☎94.76.68.33; menus from 100F; ③), which has a cosy sitting room, a piano-bar and a *salon de thé*.

Approaching **SEILLANS** from Bargemon (a distance of 13km), the long-distance view suddenly opens out eastwards to the mountains. The close-up view reveals Côte-style property inflation in an ugly rash of white villas. The *Vieux Village*, where the painter Max Ernst spent his last years, hides behind medieval walls and the inevitable *Porte Sarrasine*. Its most spectacular piece of artistry, however, is 1km away as you leave the village eastwards for Fayence. A Renaissance retable, sculpted by an inspired Italian monk, is housed in the Romanesque **Chapelle de Notre-Dame-de-l'Ormeau** (open Sun afternoon or Thurs morning; if not, ask at the Seillans **tourist office** on place du Valat; ☎94.76.96.04). The smart place to **stay** or **eat** in Seillans is the *Hôtel de France Clariond* (closed Wed out of season; ☎94.76.96.10; menus from 170F; ⑤) with its own pool and panoramic views. A few cheaper rooms are available at the equally pleasant *Les Deux Rocs* on the fountained place Font-d'Amont by the old wash house (☎94.76.87.32; ④), with good food as well (closed Tues & Thurs evening; menus from 140F).

Fayence

FAYENCE, one of the main centres for gliding in France, makes a sensible, if not the most inspiring base for this part of the world. It's livelier than its smaller neighbours, has a good selection of places to eat, as well as bus connections with Draguignan, 33km to its southwest, Grasse, 25km east, and Cannes. The **tourist office**, on place Léon-Roux (Mon–Sat 9.30am–noon & 2.30–6pm; ☎94.76.20.08), will provide information on the whole area, and if that isn't enough, the **English-language bookshop** at 1 rue St-Pierre near the car park (9am–12.30pm & 2.30–7pm; closed Mon morning & Sun), stocks a reasonable selection of local guides and maps.

Right in the centre of the village, five stunningly good-value well-equipped studio **rooms** for two to four people are available at *La Sousto*, rue du Paty (☎94.76.02.16; ④). The other pleasant place to stay is at the *Auberge de la Fontaine* (☎94.76.07.59; ③), over 3km away on the road to Fréjus, beyond the junction with the main Draguignan–Grasse road. Here, Provençal **cooking** with a menu under 100F adds to the attraction of its isolation. Just below the village, on the D19, you'll find the *Hôtel des Oliviers* (☎94.76.13.12; ⑤) which is perfectably acceptable but a touch characterless. For really special surroundings you need to book in at *Le Moulin de la Camandoule* (half-board compulsory mid-March to Oct; ☎94.76.00.84; ⑥), a converted mill on the little road out to Notre-Dame-des-Cyprès, and run by an English couple; the meals (menus from 180F) are prepared by a seriously skilled and inventive French chef.

Options for **camping** include the three-star *Lou Cantaire* (mid-March to mid-Oct; ☎94.76.23.77), 7km out on the road to Draguignan, or the two-star *Le Grillon* (April–Sept; ☎94.76.02.96), 4km towards Grasse, past the turning to Tourrettes.

For **food** other than in hotels, the *France* on the main street above the old gateway (closed Tues eve & Wed in winter; ☎94.76.00.14) has dependable chefs and menus for every budget. The tables below it belong to the café *Le Lord Byron* just opposite who do good ice creams. A few doors down is the best place for fish meals, *Au Bleu Marine* (Tues–Sun evenings only; ☎94.76.15.77) with *plateaux de fruits de mer* from 110F. Down the dark and narrow steps of rue Fort-de-Vin you'll find *Le Poëlon* (closed Mon & Sun evening; ☎94.76.21.64; menus from 80F), serving vast and rich plates of food. Equally copious and good is *Patin Couffin*, place de l'Olivier (Tues–Sun; ☎94.76.29.96; 125F menu). The most gourmet restaurant is *Las Castellaras* (closed Wed; ☎94.76.13.80; menus from 165F), signed off the Seillans road, where you can eat lobster, wild mushrooms, pigeon and courgette flowers by a rose garden. For a **drink** and a game of bar billiards try *Bar des Campagnes*, across the way from *Chez P'tit Louis*, a small and friendly *salon de thé* on place de l'Eglise.

Mons and Tourettes

If you want an energetic walk take the GR49 (off the D563 just north of Fayence) through the Fôret de Tourettes, across the valley of La Siagnole river and up to the truly perched village of **MONS** where you can reward yourself with a drink at one of the cafés on place St-Sébastien from where the views sometimes extend as far as Corsica and Italy.

The distinctly un-medieval **château** in **TOURETTES**, Fayence's close neighbour 1km to the east, needs some explanation. A copy of an early nineteenth-century cadet school set up in St Petersburg for Tsar Nicholas I by a French colonel who built this replica for his retirement, it's still a private residence and not open to the public.

Callian, Montauroux and the Lac de St-Cassien

CALLIAN and its larger neighbour **MONTAUROUX** have merged together, leaving only a tiny expanse of woods before the suburbs of Grasse begin. Callian is more obviously picturesque but Montauroux's large open place du Clos makes a pleasant change from narrow twisting medievalism, as does the grassy summit of the village with its fig tree, church and little chapel of St-Barthélémy whose ceiling and walls are covered in painted panels.

Montauroux's **tourist office** on place du Clos (Mon–Sat 9am–12.30pm & 3–7pm; ☎94.47.75.90) can advise on the many inexpensive hotels and campsites in the vicinity, and will point you in the right direction for the pleasant **youth hostel**, *Les Roses*, rue Ste-Brigitte (bus stop *L'Auberge*; ☎94.76.59.08; meals for 50F; ①) on the road leading east from place du Clos, which has very flexible hours, self-catering facilities and a small campsite. The tourist office also sells guide sheets for local walks. The obvious destination is the **Lac de St-Cassien** reservoir 4km to the south where you can swim (best access from the D37 after you've crossed the lake), go sailing or rowing, and eat pizzas, grills and ice creams at the various lakeside establishments. No motor boats are allowed and the water is very clean.

Haut Var villages

An overdose of picturesque medieval villages can become a problem for any determined traveller through the **Haut Var**, stretching from the Argens Valley to the Verdon Gorge. A point may be reached when one more serene square, one more massive gateway of ancient stone, or one more climb to a romantic vista of mountains, vines and *villages perchés* might induce cravings for high-rises or the grossness of the Côte, though it is highly unlikely. For this particular bit of the Haut Var, west of Draguignan, is the heart of Provence, with soft enveloping countryside of woods, vines, lakes and waterfalls, with streaks of cliffed hill ridges before the high plateaux and mountains further north.

To the outsider, the villages merge together; to see them properly you'd have to live here for winter after winter, limiting your world to just a few square miles. Familiarity would establish the individuality of each place and the stories of the older residents would connect the present with the past. For these villages, despite the half-year-empty second homes, hold on to their identity, however guarded it is from the casual eyes of visitors.

Flayosc, Lorgues and the Abbaye du Thoronet

From Draguignan you can head east through **FLAYOSC** or southeast through **LORGUES**, both excellent **eating** stops. *L'Oustaou* (closed Mon & Sun evening; ☎94.70.42.69; menus from 115F) on place Brémond, the main square of Flayosc, has a rare genuine Provençal atmosphere to go with the local specialities. *Chez Bruno* on rte de Vidauban in Lorgues (closed Mon & Sun evening out of season; ☎94.73.92.19; menu at 270F, à la carte around 400F) is in a different bracket but if you're prepared to pay the serious sums involved you can try wonderfully wild local ingredients in a chestnut and *chanterelle* soup and in the truffle and game dishes, followed by *crème brûlée* with figs in wine. M. Bruno is one of France's celebrity chefs and may well be away cooking dinners for presidents or royalty.

Further west, across the Argens, deep in the forest of La Daboussière, is the last of Provence's three great Cistercian monasteries, the **Abbaye du Thoronet** (April–Sept Mon–Sat 9am–7pm, Sun 9am–noon & 2–7pm; Oct–March 9am–noon & 2–5pm; 18F). Like Silvacane and Sénanque, it was founded in the first half of the twelfth century, and is the oldest of the group and the one that was completed in the shortest time, giving it a tight unity that emphasises its graceful austerity. Finally abandoned in 1791, it was kept intact during the Revolutionary era as a remarkable monument of history and art. Restoration started in the 1850s, and a more recent campaign has brought it to clear-cut perfection. As with the other two, it's the spaces – here delineated by walls of pale rose-coloured stone – that are the essence of the experience. The *abbaye* is off the D79 between the hamlet of Le Thoronet and **Cabasse** and not easy to reach without your own transport:

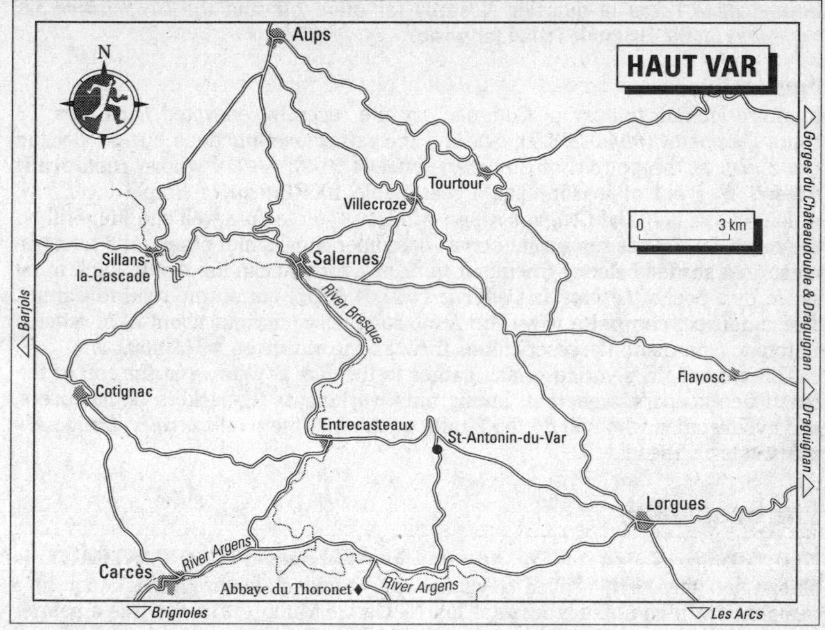

there are two buses weekly during school holidays and one daily in term time from Les Arcs or Lorgues.

Cotignac

Of all the Haut Var villages **COTIGNAC** would perhaps be the best to choose for a life of sensual exile. From its utterly photogenic place de la Mairie, rue de l'Horloge leads under the clock tower and on up to the church. From here a path takes you to the foot of the eighty-metre cliff that forms the village's back wall. At the summit stand two ruined towers of a long-abandoned castle, and in between the rock is riddled with caves and subterranean passages of white rock and stalactite formations. Rock falls have blocked the nerve-racking upward route of rusty iron rails and precarious ledges. Instead you can wander along the semi-abandoned gardens at the foot of the cliff or through the village's passageways and stairs bursting with begonias, jasmine and geranium before gravitating to the long shaded **cours Gambetta** where life in Cotignac revolves.

Centre-stage in the history of Cotignac are the now defunct tanning works, once a major industry of the Haut Var, and the miraculous Virgin in the **Chapelle de Notre-Dame-des-Grâces**, on the summit across the valley to the south. Long called upon as a saviour from the Plague, this Virgin finally hit the big time in 1638 when Louis XIII and Anne of Austria – married for 22 childless years – made their supplications to her. Nine months after the royal visit, the future Sun King let out his first demanding squall.

If you want to sample some of Cotignac's produce direct, don't miss *Les Ruchers du Bessillon* at 2 rue des Naïfs which sells an exceptional variety of

honey; *Réné Vacca* in quartier Nestuby for **olive oil**; and the *Coopérative des Vignerons* on the Brignoles road for **wine**.

Practicalities

If you're looking to **stay** in Cotignac, try the recently renovated *Du Cours*, 18 cours Gambetta (☎94.04.78.50; ③), and the rather over-unctious but good-value *Lou Calen* at the bottom of the *cours* (☎94.04.60.40; ④–⑤), whose **restaurant** (closed Wed out of season) has a reasonable 100F menu of simple local fare, which, with a bottle of *Cotignac rouge*, will leave you feeling well and full. Still on the *cours*, *La Falaise* restaurant serves cassoulet, steaks and other solid nourishment on a shaded balcony (menus from 110F). Or you can indulge in duck in fig sauce by a pool at *Le Mas de Cotignac* (☎94.04.66.57) out on the road to Carcès. The municipal **campsite** is on the Aups road on your right about 3km outside Cotignac (summer only; reservations through the *mairie* on ☎94.04.60.01).

The community's various clans gather in the *Bar de l'Union* at the top of the *cours*: bee keepers, *vignerons*, immigrants working as fig-packers or labourers, and even women who still do the family washing in the public *lavoirs*. Cotignac's **market** is on Tuesday.

Entrecasteaux

Nine kilometres east of Cotignac towards Lorgues, **ENTRECASTEAUX** is almost too tiny to be called a village. Its dominant feature owes a lot to a Scotsman with an unlikely history. Ian McGarvie-Munn (1919–81) was a painter who trained as a naval architect after World War II, but was shortly to be found running the National Workshops for Applied Arts in Colombia. Soon after his wife's father had become president of Guatemala, McGarvie-Munn took over as head of the Guatemalan navy, following that with a stint as the country's ambassador to London. In 1974, by now retired from diplomatic-military service, he found himself looking longingly at the ruined shell of Entrecasteaux's seventeenth-century **château**. He bought it, then spent the rest of his life and every last penny on the massive restoration job.

The family continued the work and it is now more or less complete. What makes it very different from other visitable French châteaux is that there has been no attempt to reinstate the original decor and furnishings. The spaces of the castle are light and open, minimally furnished with the sort of stuff you'd expect a fairly impecunious but cosmopolitan family to have, and decorated throughout with McGarvie-Munn's terrible paintings.

You can visit the château (July–Sept Mon & Wed–Sun 10am–noon & 2–6pm; Oct–June closes 5pm; Jan–March Mon & Wed–Sun 2–5pm; 30F), and the publicly owned **Le Nôtre** gardens of twenty-metre magnolias, box hedges and eucalyptus, separating the château from the village. A *chambre d'hôtes* is on offer in the château too, at luxury prices (☎94.04.43.95; ⑧).

If you don't fancy château-gazing, follow the pleasant walk along the river past the old *lavoirs* that are still used (there are steps down close to the château entrance).

Practicalities

If you're seeking a suitable base as an alternative to Cotignac, see if you can get one of the eight **rooms** in the very welcoming hotel-restaurant *Lou Cigaloun* (☎94.04.42.67; ③–④) in St-Antonin-Du-Var, Entrecasteaux's even smaller neighbour to the west. The **restaurant** (closed Mon out of season & Tues; weekday menu around 100F) offers simple but fine cooking and all the menus are good value.

Decent meals for around 120F can be had at *La Forchette*, up beyond the Entrecasteaux's château entrance (closed Mon & Sun evening; ☎94.04.42.78), or cheap pizzas below the château at *Lou Picateou*.

Salernes

Compared with Cotignac, **SALERNES**, 7.5km north of Entrecasteaux, is quite a metropolis, with its tile-making industry and enough near-level irrigated land for productive agriculture. Sunday and Wednesday are the best days to visit the **market** beneath the ubiquitous plane trees on the *cours*. There are also the pottery and tile workshops, selling a mix of designs you'd find in any home improvement shop as well as items with more local flair.

In the nineteenth century the workshops churned out those hexagonal terracotta floor tiles that have been reproduced in various synthetic materials ever since. You'll find shops in the centre of the town and larger *ateliers-magasins* on the outskirts: *Maurice Emphoux* and *Pierre Boutal* on the road to Draguignan; *Jacques Polidori* and *Alain Vagh* on the road to Entrecasteaux; and *Ateliers de la Baume*, 4km east on the D560. Remember if you want to carry home some originals, these are artisans' artefacts and priced accordingly.

The *Grand Hôtel Allègre* on the rte de Sillans (☎94.70.60.30; ③) is a classic old-fashioned hotel with a pretty garden or you can stay in a fourteenth-century farm house, *La Bastide Rose* (☎94.70.63.30; evening meal 100F; ④) across the Bresque river towards La Colle Riforan. There's a four-star **campsite**, *Les Arnauds* (May–Sept; ☎94.67.51.95), just outside the town on the Sillans road. **Cheap eats** in Salernes include *La Fontaine*, place du 8 mai 1945 (closed Wed, & Sun evening; ☎94.70.64.51), take-away pizzas at *La Cuillère* on rue Pierre Blanc (Tues–Sun), a range of cafés on the *cours* and a good selection of beers in the **bar** opposite the *mairie*.

Sillans

SILLANS, 6km west of Salernes, is not in itself overtly picturesque, but its **waterfall** down a delightful path signed from the main road (about 20min) is stunning. The water never dries up, falling into a turquoise pool that makes for a brilliant swim.

In 1992 the *commune* bought the **château** from the count of Castellane and are gradually renovating it, using its rooms for art exhibitions, craft sales and for the *mairie*. There's a good feel to the place, probably because it's not a chicly restored village. If you want to **stay**, there's *Les Pins* hotel-restaurant (☎94.04.63.26; ③), *chambres d'hôtes* at *La Dame d'Argent* beyond the waterfall (☎94.04.63.23; ③) or the **campsite** and **gîte**, *Le Relais de la Bresque* (☎94.04.64.89; ①), 1km out along the road to Aups, which has a restaurant, swimming pool, bar, horse-riding, *pétanque* and ping-pong, and is open all year round.

Villecroze

Five kilometres northeast of Salernes, **VILLECROZE**, like Cotignac, sits beneath a water-burrowed cliff. The gardens around the base are delightfully un-Gallic (though walking on the lawns is not allowed) and the same lack of formality extends throughout the town. It's an attractive place, with lovely vaulted arcades down rue des Arcades and rue de France, and a Romanesque church with a wall of bells.

In the 1970s, an early radical ecologist by the name of Jean Pain ran his heating, lighting and 2CV on compost made from the undergrowth of the surrounding woods, material otherwise destroyed to avoid the risk of fire. Pain's compost gave back nutrients to the forest soil and agricultural land of this harsh terrain, and his methods of generating power from compost have been taken up in Canada, California and Senegal. He died in 1979, having lived off his patents and never paid any bills for unrenewable energy.

If Villecroze tempts you to **stay**, try to get one of the eight rooms at the *Auberge des Lavandes* on place du Général-de-Gaulle (☎94.70.76.00; ②), one of the cheapest deals in the region, or at the secluded and very comfortable *Au Bien Etre* in quartier Les Cadenières (☎94.70.67.57; ⑤), 3.5km south along the D557, which also has a decent **restaurant** with a generous menu for around 115F. The other restaurant of some repute is *Le Colombier* on rte de Draguignan (closed Mon out of season; ☎94.70.63.23; midday menu around 115F). For three-star **camping** there's *Les Cadenières* (open all year; ☎94.70.60.31) and *Le Ruou* (April–Sept; ☎94.70.67.70), both on the D560 towards Flayosc.

Tourtour

TOURTOUR sits 300m higher than Villecroze, atop a ridge from which the view extends to the massifs of Maures, Ste-Baume and Ste-Victoire. The village has a seemingly organic unity, soft-coloured stone growing into stairways and curving streets, branching to form arches, fountains, and towers. The ruin of an old mill looks as if it has always been like this; the elephant-leg towers of the sixteenth-century bastion stand around the *mairie* and the post office as if of their own volition, while the twelfth-century **Tour du Grimaldi** might have erupted spontaneously from the ground. The two elms on the main square, planted when Anne of Austria and Louis XIII visited Cotignac, are almost as enormous as the bastion towers, but are beginning to show signs of decrepitude.

Having said this, Tourtour is all a bit unreal, full of *résidences secondaires*, pandering artisanerie and *salons de thé* selling expensive fruit-juice cocktails. It also has this region's most upmarket **hotel-restaurant**, the *Bastide de Tourtour* (☎94.70.57.30; ⑦), specializing in classic cuisine combined with current dietary concerns, and has jacuzzis, tennis courts and a gym to go with the rooms.

Aups

As a base for visiting the villages of Haut Var or the Grand Canyon du Verdon, the village of **AUPS**, 10km north of Salernes, is ideal, as long as you have your own transport. Though only 500m or so above sea level, it was considered by the ancients to be the beginning of the Alps; the Romans called it Alpibus which became Alps then Aups. The chief town of one of the Ligurian tribes and the location for a Roman army hospital, it then thrived in the Middle Ages, and by the eighteenth century its prosperity was inducing delusions of grandeur in the local abbot. Having mathematically proved Aups to be at the centre of Europe, he drew a map of the continent on the tiles of his house to illustrate the fact. He also erected a column in his garden inscribed with the scientific knowledge of his day and was responsible for one of the seven sundials that decorate the village.

Arrival, information and accommodation

Coming from Sillans, Salernes or Villecroze, you enter **Aups** along av Georges-Clemenceau which ends with place Frédéric-Mistral and place Martin-Bidouré. The very helpful **tourist office** is to your left on av Georges-Clemenceau (Mon–Sat 10am–noon & 3–6pm; ☎94.70.00.80) with the **post office** next door. The *Vieille Ville* is in front of you with the church to the right.

All the **hotels** in Aups are good value: *Le Provençal* on place Martin-Bidouré (☎94.70.00.24; ①) is the cheapest; the *Grand Hôtel* on place Duchâtel (May–Sept; ☎94.70.10.82; ②–③) is the most expensive. More luxury is to be had at *L'Escale du Verdon*, 1km out on the rte de Sillans-la-Cascade (May–Sept; ☎94.84.00.04; ④). There are two three-star **campsites** close to town: *Camping Les Prés*, to the right off allée Charles-Boyer towards Tourtour (all year; ☎94.70.00.93), where you can also rent **bikes**; and *Saint Lazare* 2km along the Moissac road (April–Oct; ☎94.70.12.86), which has a pool.

The Town

On place Martin-Bidouré a monument commemorates a period of republican resistance all too rarely honoured in France. Its inscription reads: "To the memory of citizens who died in 1851 defending the republic and its laws", the year being that of Louis Napoléon's coup d'état. Peasant and artisan defiance was strongest in Provence, and the defeat of the insurgents, who flew the red flag because the tricolour had been appropriated by the usurper, was followed by a massacre of men and women alike. At Aups, the badly wounded Martin Bidouré escaped, but was found soon afterwards being succoured by a peasant, and instantly shot dead.

This event might explain the strident "*République Française, Liberté, Egalité, Fraternité*" sign on the **Eglise St-Pancrace**, proclaiming the supremity of state before religion (a common feature of French churches but usually more discreet). The church was designed by an English architect five hundred years ago and has had its doors restored in the last ten years by two resident British carpenters. The Renaissance portal is in good shape, there are some altarpieces inside and the attractive nineteenth-century stained-glass windows have all been cleaned up and repaired.

Another plus for Aups is its **museum of modern art**, the *Musée Simon Segal*, in the former convent chapel on av Albert-1er (mid-June to mid-Sept 10.30am–noon & 3–6pm; 10F). The best works are by the Russian-born painter Simon Segal, but there are interesting local scenes in the other paintings, such as the Roman bridge at Aiguines, now drowned beneath the artificial lake of Ste-Croix.

Unfortunately *La Fabrique*, the mad *abbé*'s house, is a private residence and can't be visited. But the old streets, the sixteenth-century clock tower with its campinale, and the Wednesday and Saturday morning **market** which fills place Martin-Bidoué, all make this a very appealing place to be. Aups has become more geared to tourism in recent years but its living still comes from agriculture and there's prime local produce to be had in the shops. Along with honey, the Aups speciality is truffles, and if you're here on a Thursday between November and mid-March you'll witness the **truffle market**. The local lamb has a gourmet reputation:

marinaded and roasted with thyme is the traditional preparation. Other delicacies include small birds cooked with juniper berries; the gun shops in the main street explain the ready supply. For **food shopping**, Bernard Georges sells honey and truffles (in season) from his farm, *Mas du Vieux Moulin*, on rue de la Piscine east of place Martin-Bidouré; André Goin has a honey and nougat shop at 3 rue Maréchal-Foch; and, on the same street, *L'Herbier* sells soaps, liqueurs and dried flowers. The best place for bread and cakes (olive oil *fougasses* in particular) is the *Boulangerie-Pâtisserie Canut* on place du Marché. On av Albert 1er the *Domaine Valryoisine* has a shop where you can buy wine *en vrac*.

If you want to go **riding**, *Le Mas des Jonquières* (☎94.70.06.86) on the road to Moissac organizes treks to the Gorges du Verdon and can put people up for the night. The tourist office has details of local **walks** (special treats in autumn for fungophiles).

Eating, drinking and entertainment

For **meals**, your first choice should be the hotel-restaurant *St-Marc* (closed second & third week of June, Tues evening & Wed; ☎94.70.06.08; ③), a nineteenth-century mill on rue Aloisi. Serving local dishes, truffles and boar in season, it offers a very cheap midday menu and evening menus for around 100F. There's also the good-value *Framboise* on place Maréchal-Foch (closed evenings out of season) and for snacks *La Pizza boulangerie-pâtisserie* on place Général-Giraud (May–Sept). The **bar** opposite the church is the place to sip *pastis*, or, if you just want to relax, you can sit on the benches by the church and watch the lively local life at the bar. The tourist office has details of theatre, film and other **entertainment** to be had at the *Centre Culturel*.

Barjols

For all its springs, streams and fountains, **BARJOLS**, 16km west of Cotignac, is a depressing place. Many of the people at the Saturday **market** on place Emile-Zola seem as glum as characters from a Zola novel. In January a strange **festival** takes place in which a saint and a cow's intestines are celebrated: the cow gets killed and roasted to the accompaniment of flutes and tambourines and the refrain "Saint Marcel, Saint Marcel, the little tripe, the little tripe".

Cattle skins used to be the main business of Barjols, and the town has still not recovered from the closure of its tanneries. The rickety buildings of this ancient industry have been taken over by artists and craft workers; you can visit their studios (follow signs to *Art-Artisanal*) down the *ancienne route de Brignoles*, east of the *Vieille Ville*. Looking back upwards from here at the industrial ruins is a good spooky night-time experience. If it is dark, the only place you're likely to find life is by the huge mossy fountain opposite the hôtel de ville. *Le Logis de la Fontaine* here serves drinks, cheap meals and has a few very basic **rooms** (②).

The Grand Canyon du Verdon

From Aups the road north skirts the military terrain of the Camp de Canjuers and crosses the Verdon river as it leaves the gorge to fill the vast artificial basin of the **Lac de Ste-Croix**. This is the quickest approach from the south to the **Grand Canyon du Verdon**, but not the most dramatic.

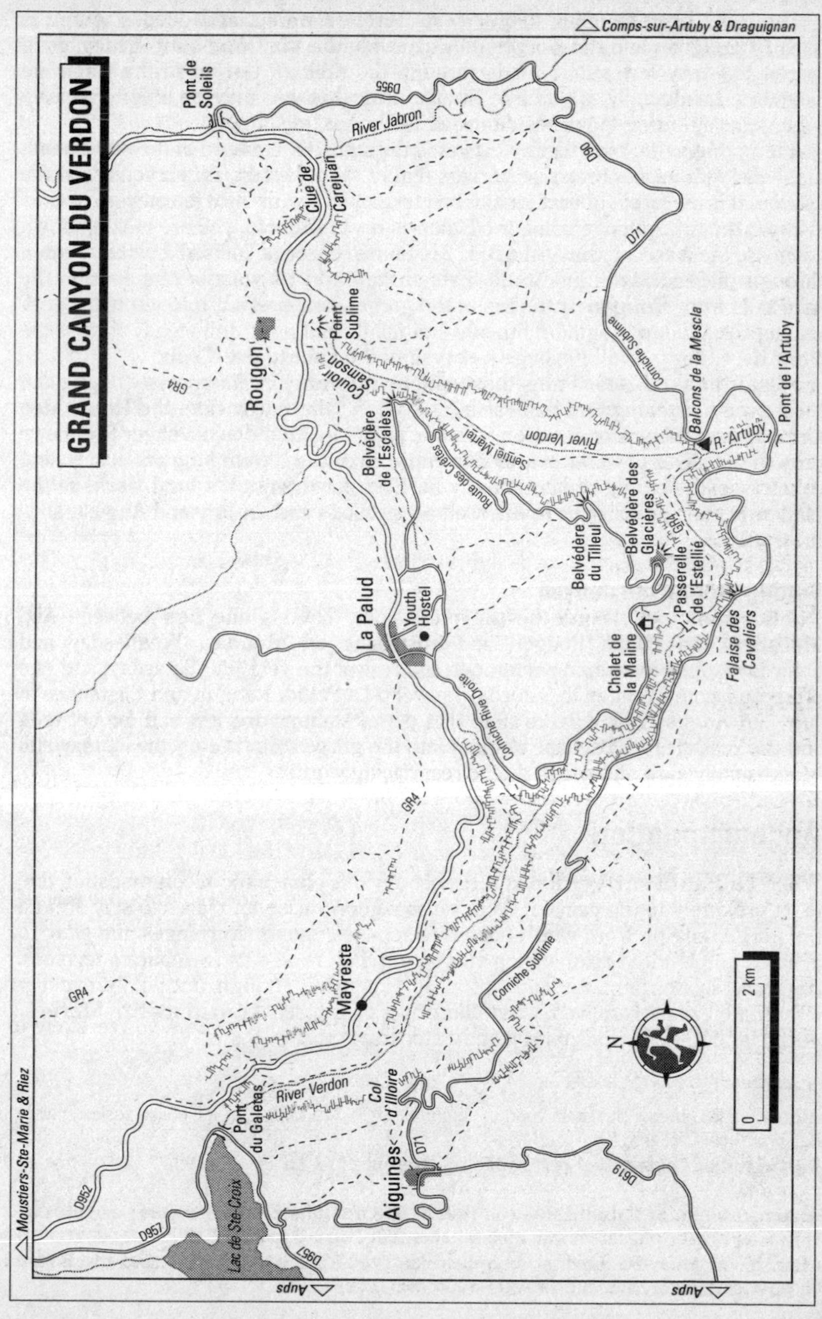
GRAND CANYON DU VERDON
Comps-sur-Artuby & Draguignan
Pont de Soleils
D955
River Jabron
Clue de Carejuan
D90
D71
Point Sublime
Rougon
GR4
Couloir Samson
Belvédère de l'Escalès
Corniche Sublime
Balcons de la Mescla
Pont de l'Artuby
R. Artuby
River Verdon
Sentier Martel
Route des Crêtes
Belvédère du Tilleul
Belvédère des Glacières
GR4
Passerelle de l'Estellié
La Palud
Youth Hostel
Chalet de la Maline
Falaise des Cavaliers
Corniche Rive Droite
GR4
Mayreste
Corniche Sublime
GR4
N
0
2 km
Moustiers-Ste-Marie & Riez
River Verdon
Col d'Illoire
Pont du Galetas
D952
D957
Aiguines
D71
D19
Lac de Ste-Croix
Aups
Aups

The most heart-stopping approach to Europe's widest and deepest gorge is from Draguignan and the Gorges de Châteaudouble via Comps-sur-Artuby along one of the very few public roads through the military terrain of the Camp de Canjuers. Incidentally, if you like bizarre postcards you may be able to pick up such gems as "firing tanks beside the almond trees" at Comps.

After Comps, the road turns westwards through 16km of end-of-the-earth heath and hills, with each successive horizon higher than the last. When you reach the canyon, it is as if a silent earthquake had taken place while you journeyed.

From the first vantage point, the **Balcons de la Mescla**, you are looking down 250m to the base of the V-shaped, 21-kilometre gorge incised by the Verdon through piled strata of limestone. Ever-changing in its volume and energy, the river falls from **Rougon** at the top of the gorge, disappearing into tunnels, decelerating for shallow languid moments and finally exiting in full steady flow at the **Pont de Galetas** to fill the huge resorvoir of the **Lac de Ste-Croix**.

West from the Balcons runs the **corniche sublime**, built expressly to give the most breath-catching and hair-raising views. On the north side, the **Route des Crêtes** serves the same function, at some points looking down a sheer 800-metre drop to the sliver of water below. The entire circuit is 130km long and it's cycling country solely for the preternaturally fit. Even for drivers it's hard work, as the hidden bends and hairpins in the road are perilous and, in July and August, so is the traffic.

Getting around the canyon

Public transport around the canyon is poor. There's one **bus** between Aix, Moustiers, La Palud, Rougon and Castellane on Monday, Wednesday and Saturday from July to mid-September, the rest of the year just Saturday; and one other bus from Monday to Saturday between La Palud, Rougon and Castellane in July and August. For **drivers** note that petrol stations are few and far between and the road from Castellane coming into the gorge from the northeast may still be extremely slow and rough due to resurfacing works.

Accommodation

While **La Palud-sur-Verdon** is the most obvious choice for accommodation due to its proximity to the canyon, there's also a good variety of places to stay around the gorge ranging from youth hostels, campsites, mountain refuges and *gîtes*, to isolated hotels with breath-taking views from their rooms and restaurant terraces. **Aiguines** is not far away and not at all expensive, though not wildly exciting either; a bit more removed, **Castellane** is a possibility; **Moustiers-Ste-Marie** is not as far but is a serious tourist and traffic trap.

Hotels

Altitude 823, below the main road in Aiguines (☎94.70.21.09). Rather characterless place; half-board compulsory. ④

Auberge des Crêtes, 1km east towards Castellane from La Palud (☎92.77.38.47). Just 12 rooms. ④

Auberge du Point Sublime, Rougon (☎92.83.60.35). At the head of the gorge and lives up to its name; rustic restaurant with menus under 100F. Open April–Nov. ③

Chez M. & Mme Richard, pl de la Fontaine (☎94.70.21.26). *Chambre d'hôtes* with very cheap beds; 2 nights minimum stay. Has a lock-up for bikes. ①

Les Gorges du Verdon, La Palud (☎92.77.38.26). All mod cons and beautifully isolated, further down from the youth hostel; half-board compulsory. March–Sept. ⑦

Grand Hôtel du Verdon, Falaise des Cavaliers, halfway between Aiguines and Comps (☎94.76.91.31). Comfortable rooms with balconies and a dining terrace overlooking the 300-metre drop down the gorge. May to mid-Oct. Restaurant closed Fri except mid-July to mid-Sept; menus from 125F. ⑤

Le Panoramic, rte de Moustiers, La Palud (☎92.77.35.07). Not as panoramic as others, but agreeable enough. ⑤

Le Provence, rte de la Maline, La Palud (☎92.77.36.50). A stunning position below the village. ④

Du Vieux Château, on the main road in Aiguines (☎94.70.22.95). Hotel-restaurant with breakfast included. ②

Hostels, gîtes, refuges and campsites

HI youth hostel *Le Trait d'Union* (☎92.77.38.72). Half a kilometre below La Palud with **camping** in its grounds. Walks and horse rides organized. March–Nov. ①

L'Etable gîte, rte des Crêtes, La Valdenay (☎92.77.30.63). Dormitory beds and rooms, billiards, climbing wall and restaurant. ①

Le Wapiti gîte, La Palud (☎92.77.30.02). 12 rooms. April to mid-Nov. ①

Chalet de la Maline, rte des Crêtes, La Maline (☎92.77.38.05). Mountain refuge run by the Club Alpin Français; half-board available and snacks. ①

Camping de Carajuan, Rougon (☎92.83.70.94). Gorgeous two-star by the Verdon above the gorge. April–Sept.

Camping Municipal, two-star 800m to the west of La Palud (☎92.77.38.13).

Les Galetas, on the D957, Aiguines (☎94.70.20.48). A two-star campsite almost within diving distance of the lake, a long way down from the village. April–Nov.

Exploring the gorge

By far the best way to explore the canyon, if your legs are strong enough, is in its depths. To follow the river **by foot** from Rougon to Mayreste on the **Sentier Martel** takes two days, and its accessibility depends on the French electricity board, which controls the volume of the Verdon. Anyway, it must be done in a guided group (see box overleaf), as crossing the torrent by rope is no simple matter on your own. It's possible to walk just the section between Rougon and Les Malines, a trek of about eight hours. Unaccompanied shorter excursions into the canyon include the fairly easy descent from the **Falaise des Cavaliers** (west of the Balcons), crossing via the **Passerelle de l'Estellié** and ascending to the *Chalet de la Maline*, about two hours one-way. Another walk of similar length can be done from the **Point Sublime**, passing though the **Couloir Samson**, a 670-metre tunnel with occasional "windows" and a stairway down to the chaotic sculpture of the river banks.

LA PALUD-SUR-VERDON is the closest village to the gorge and the best base in terms of information and organizations for exploring the area (see box overleaf). La Palud **tourist office** (mid-June to mid-Sept Tues–Fri 10am–noon & 4.40–6.30pm, Sat 10am–noon; ☎92.77.32.02), on the main road, will help. You should also get details of the route and advice on **weather conditions** (recorded information ☎92.64.90.60 or 36.68.02.04) before you set out. You'll need drinking water, a torch/flashlight (for the tunnels), and a jumper for the cold shadows of the narrow corridors of rock. Always stick to the path and don't cross the river except at the *passerelles* as the *EDF* (electricity board) may be opening dams upstream.

INFORMATION AND GUIDES: A CHECKLIST

There are plenty of organizations and individual guides with whom you can arrange expeditions on foot, horseback, raft, canoe or in the air, as well as rock climbing. The *Bureau des Guides*, the *Cabanou Verdon* and *Le Perroquet Vert* will also give advice if you don't want to be part of a group. Prices vary with the season and the number of people taking part, but they are reasonable.

Bureau des Guides, La Palud (Mon–Sat 10am–12.30pm & 2–5.30pm; ☎92.77.30.50). Information and guides on walks and rock-climbing.

Cabanon Verdon, La Palud (☎92.77.38.58). Information on all Verdon activities; maps and books; contact point for J.F. Bettus, professional and educational all-year-round walking guide.

Bruno Potié, La Palud (☎92.77.32.07). Professional walking guide and rock-climber.

Le Perroquet Vert, La Palud (☎92.77.33.39). Climbing shop.

Ranch Les Pioneers, La Palud (☎92.77.38.30). Horse rides with your own guide.

Verdon Animation Nature, La Palud (☎92.77.31.95). Canoeing and rafting with the help of a trained guide.

Verdon Insolite, La Palud (☎92.77.33.57). Rafting, canoeing, kayak and mountain biking made easier with a professional guide.

Verdon Passion, Moustiers (☎92.74.69.77). Hang-gliding and bi-planes.

Verdon Sensation, La Palud (☎92.77.30.50). Rock-climbing and canoeing.

Canoeing or **rafting** the entire length of the gorge should not be attempted unless you are very experienced and strong, as you will have to carry your craft for long stretches. However, you can pay (quite a lot) to join a group to tackle certain stretches of the river. Because of the *EDF*'s operations these trips aren't always possible, so be prepared for disappointment. A cheaper, though less exciting option, is to paddle about on the last stretch of the gorge: you can rent canoes and pedalos at the Pont du Galetas. **Rock-climbing** is also possible as is **horse riding** on the less precipitous slopes around the gorge. Finally, for the ultimate buzz, there's **hang-gliding**.

Villages around the gorge

AIGUINES, at the western end of the Corniche Sublime, is perched high above the Lac de Ste-Croix, with an enticing château (closed to public) of pepperpot towers that dazzle with their coloured tiles and a history of wood-turning. The *boules* for *pétanque* made from ancient box wood roots used to be Aiguines' speciality; in the 1940s the industry sustained a population of six hundred people. Women would bang the little nails into the *boules* to give them their metal finish, inventing intricate and personalized designs. There's a tiny **Musée des Tourneurs sur Bois** (Mon & Wed–Sun 10am–noon & 2–6pm; 10F) devoted to the intricate art of wood-turning, and some very expensive and beautiful woodwork to be viewed at the **Infiniment Rond** gallery on rue Haute (daily March–Sept). Walking around Aiguines you'll notice a great sense of openness and of being up in the air; even its old streets follow the ridge rather than clustering in the usual spiral.

Every conceivable water sport is practised on the Lac de Ste-Croix, and you should find gear available for rental at Les Salles-sur-Verdon or Ste-Croix-du-Verdon and at other outlets around this enormous reservoir. Swimming is good with easy access from the D957 between Aups and Moustiers, though sometimes when the water levels are low it's a bit muddy round the edges.

Given the choice, **MOUSTIERS-STE-MARIE** is one place to avoid, particularly in the height of summer when it can take several hours to get by car or bus to the Pont du Galetas, a distance of 7km. It's glutted with *ateliers* making and selling glazed pottery – Moustiers' traditional speciality – and with hotels, restaurants and souvenir stalls where service is given as a reluctant favour. The pottery, like the village before its commercial metamorphosis, is pastel and pretty; it's on sale in *Liberty's* and *Bloomindales* but if you want to lug plates or jugs home with you, here's your chance. The **tourist office** at the *mairie* will dole out leaflets by the bagful should you wish to do the rounds. But the sole curiosity is the star suspended on a chain between two enormous cliffs above the village; it derives from a vow made by a local baron while a prisoner during the Crusades. The current 200m of chain and 17kg of star date from 1957, a bit of a sham, like most of Moustiers.

Eating and drinking

Apart from taking **half-board** while staying at one of the isolated hotels, you'll find the majority of *crêperies*, pizzarias and brasseries in La Palud. Here, the centre of life is *Lou Cafetier* bar-restaurant, where conversation is inevitably thick with stories of near-falls, near-drownings and near-death from exposure. For picnic provisions there's a **market** on Wednesday morning.

Riez and around

The perfect antidote to Moustiers is **RIEZ**, one of the least spoilt small towns of inland Provence, located a little over 20km from the Grand Canyon to the west of the Lac de Ste-Croix. There are a couple of pottery workshops in the town, but the main business comes from the lavender fields that cover this part of Provence. Just over the river on the road south, less than 1km down, is a **lavender distillery**, a building strangely reminiscent of 1950s Soviet architecture, which produces essence for the perfume industry.

At the other end of Riez, 1km along the road to Digne, is the **Maison de l'Abeille** (House of the Bee; daily 10am–12.30pm & 2.30–7pm; free), a research and visitors' centre where you can buy various honeys and hydromel (the honey alcohol of antiquity). If you show enthusiasm you will be regaled with fascinating accounts of bee physiology, bee anthropology, bee sociology, bee sexuality (the mating of French and English bees has yet to succeed), and get introduced to the bees themselves. The people here are very keen for you to share their obsession.

In size Riez is more a village than a town but it soon becomes clear that it was once more influential than it is now. Some of the houses on Grande Rue and rue du Marché, the two streets above the main allées Louis-Gardiol, have rich Renaissance facades, and the hôtel de ville on place Quinconces is a former episcopal palace. The cathedral, which was abandoned four hundred years ago, has been excavated just across the river from allées Louis-Gardiol. Beside it is a

baptistry, restored in the nineteenth century, but originally constructed, like the cathedral, around 600 AD (key from the tourist office). If you recross the river and follow it downstream you'll find the even older and much more startling relics of four **Roman columns** standing in a field.

A rather more strenuous walk, first heading for the clock tower above Grande Rue and then taking the path past the cemetery and on upwards (leaving the cemetery to your left), brings you to a cedar-shaded platform at the summit of the hill where the pre-Roman and post-Roman *Riezians* lived. The only building now occupying the site is the eighteenth-century **Chapelle St-Maxime**, with a patterned interior that is gaudy or gorgeous, depending on your taste.

On the main road between the fountained *place*, where the medieval Porte d'Aiguière marks the former entry to the town, and the hôtel de ville, there's a small **museum**, *Nature en Provence* (Mon & Wed–Sun 10am–noon & 2–5pm; 12F), which from time to time has very good exhibitions on local ecology or crafts. The permanent exhibition is of the over-crowded glass-case variety, with stuffed birds and insects, pressed flowers and so forth, and one extraordinary exhibit of a 35-million-year-old fossil of a wading bird.

Practicalities

Riez is in danger of losing its out-of-the-way charm. Pedestrian precincts have recently been introduced and restoration work has started on the medieval quarter. The **tourist office**, a fairly recent innovation, is at 4 cours allées Louis-Gardiol (June–Sept Tues–Sat 2–6pm; ☎92.77.76.36); when closed try the hôtel de ville (office hours; ☎92.74.51.81 or 92.77.80.21) which can also provide information.

Carina, the ugly executive-style **hotel** across the river in the quartier St-Jean (☎92.77.85.43; ④), has lovely views from its rooms. The musty old *Hôtel des Alpes* (☎92.77.80.03; ③), overlooking the allées Louis-Gardiol, is still going strong at 2 av de Verdon. You'll also find the **restaurant** *Les Abeilles* on allées Louis-Gardiol (Tues–Sun; ☎92.77.89.29), which is a real treat with specialities like *aïoli* and imaginative menus including wine that start well below 100F. A municipal two-star **campsite** is across the river, on rue Edouard-Dauphin (June–Sept; ☎92.77.75.45).

The Plateau de Valensole

Riez is situated on the southern edge of the **Plateau de Valensole**, which continues as far as the Bléone and Durance rivers and is cut in two by the wide stony course of the River Asse. Roads and villages north of the river are sparse. It's a beautiful landscape, a wide uninterrupted plain whose horizons are the sharp high edges of mountains.

The most distinctive sight of the plateau is row upon row of lavender bushes like sleeping hedgehogs, green in early summer, turning purple in July. Every farm advertises *lavandin* (a hybrid of lavender used for perfume essence) and *miel de lavande* (lavender honey). There are fields of golden grain, of almond trees blossoming white in early spring, and the gnarled and silvery trunks of olive trees. Even for Provence, the warm quality of the light is exceptional: the ancient town of **Valensole**, midway between Riez and Manosque, the village of **Puimoisson** on the road to Dignes, and the tiny hamlets along the **Asse** exude warmth from it even on wintry days.

This is well off the beaten track; hotels, though not thick on the ground, are unlikly to be booked up, and you can ask farmers if you can camp on their land.

The Lower Verdon

Southwest of Riez, along the Colostre and the last stretch of the Verdon, the land is richer and more populated. People commute to the Cadarache nuclear research centre at the confluence of the Durance and the Verdon, or to the new high-tech industries that are very gradually following the wake of the Marseille–Grenoble *autoroute*. Visitors tend to be the affluent ill, coming to take the cure at the long-established spa of **Gréoux-Les-Bains**.

On the much more attractive route south from Riez towards Barjols, **QUINSON** sits at the head of the **Basses Gorges du Verdon**. If you have not yet explored the Verdon's Grand Canyon, these 500-metre depths should strike you as quite dramatic, although, unfortunately, they are not as accessible. The river, restrained upstream by barrages and artificial lakes, rushes down here to one last reservoir and dam before rolling resignedly past Gréoux and down to the Durance. From Quinson the path from the road as it crosses the Verdon shortly comes to an end with steps down to a bathing place. The GR99 makes a short detour to the south side of the gorge a couple of kilometres downstream, and there are paths from the road between Quinson and Esparron that lead to the edge and go no further.

The nicely old-fashioned *Relais Notre-Dame* **hotel** (mid-March to mid-Dec; ☎92.74.40.01; ③) on the main road just south of Quinson, close to the river before it enters the gorge, also rents out **bikes**.

Seven kilometres south of Quinson, **MONTMEYAN** is a beautifully unspoilt Provençal village with fabulous views of the Valensole Plateau and the Alps. You could stop for something to eat at the one restaurant but there's nowhere to stay. As you leave the village heading south you can feel envious of its towered château nestling in the fields to the right of the main road.

Manosque

MANOSQUE, 33km west of Riez, is a very ancient town, strategically positioned just above the right bank of the Durance. Its small, compact old quarter is surrounded by ever-spreading industrial units linked by roads designed for container lorries. It is a major population centre in the *département* of Alpes-de-Haute-Provence and busy profiting from the new corridor of affluence that follows the Durance. Many of its residents work at the Cadarache atomic centre, or in Aix, or even in Marseille now that the highway gives speedy access.

For the French Manosque is most famous as the home town of the author **Jean Giono** who was born here in 1895. As well as mementoes to the writer, the town also contains an extraordinary work of art on the theme of the Apocalypse by the Armenian-born painter, **Jean Carzou**. These may or may not appeal, but there's a certain up-beat provincial atmosphere to the town and it's an economical place to stay with good transport links.

Arrival, information and accommodation

The **gare SNCF** (☎92.51.50.50) is 1.5km south of the centre with regular **buses** up av Jean-Giono, the main route into town which ends at Porte Saunerie. From the **gare routière** (☎92.87.55.99), on bd Charles-de-Gaulle, turn left then right onto av Jean-Giono. The **tourist office** (Mon–Sat 9am–noon & 2–6pm;

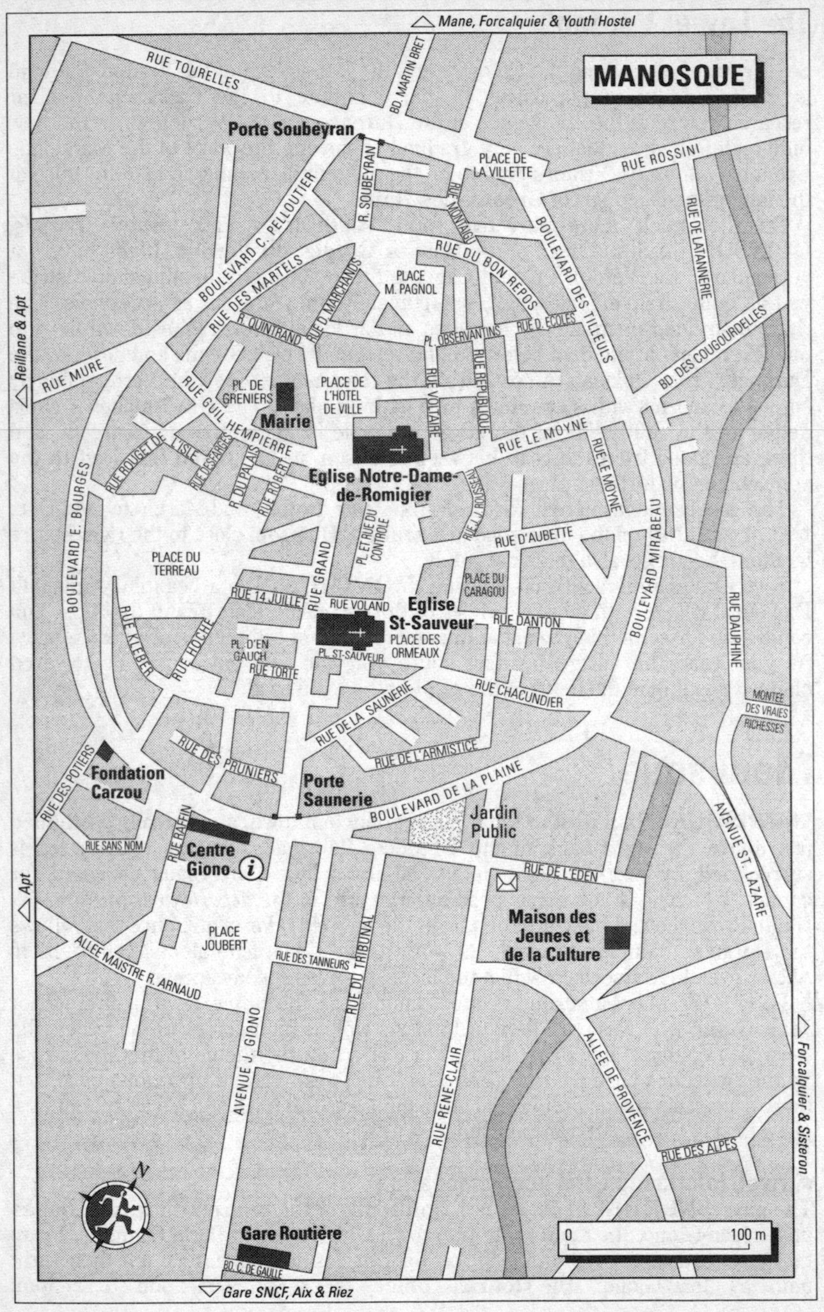

MANOSQUE
Mane, Forcalquier & Youth Hostel
Reillane & Apt
Apt
Forcalquier & Sisteron
Gare SNCF, Aix & Riez
RUE TOURELLES
BD. MARTIN BRET
Porte Soubeyran
PLACE DE LA VILLETTE
RUE ROSSINI
R. SOUBEYRAN
RUE MONTAGU
BOULEVARD C. PELLOUTIER
BOULEVARD DES TILLEULS
RUE DE LATANNERIE
RUE DU BON REPOS
PLACE M. PAGNOL
RUE DES MARTELS
R. QUINTRAND
RUE D. MARCHANDS
PL. OBSERVANTINS
RUE D. ECOLES
BD. DES COUGOURDELLES
RUE MURE
PL. DE GRENIERS
Mairie
PLACE DE L'HOTEL DE VILLE
RUE VOLTAIRE
RUE REPUBLIQUE
RUE GUIL HEMPIERRE
RUE LE MOYNE
RUE ROUGET DE L'ISLE
RUE DESARGES
R. DU PALAIS
RUE ROBERT
Eglise Notre-Dame-de-Romigier
RUE J.J. ROUSSEAU
BOULEVARD E. BOURGES
PL. ET RUE DU CONTROLE
RUE D'AUBETTE
BOULEVARD MIRABEAU
PLACE DU TERREAU
RUE GRAND
PLACE DU CARAGOU
RUE 14 JUILLET
RUE VOLAND
Eglise St-Sauveur
RUE DANTON
RUE DAUPHINE
RUE KLEBER
RUE HOCHE
PL. D'EN GAUCH
RUE TORTE
PL. ST-SAUVEUR
PLACE DES ORMEAUX
RUE CHACUNDIER
MONTEE DES VRAIES RICHESSES
RUE DE LA SAUNERIE
RUE DE L'ARMISTICE
RUE DES PRUNIERS
RUE DES POTIERS
Fondation Carzou
Porte Saunerie
BOULEVARD DE LA PLAINE
Jardin Public
AVENUE ST. LAZARE
RUE RAFFIN
RUE SANS NOM
Centre Giono
RUE DE L'EDEN
Maison des Jeunes et de la Culture
PLACE JOUBERT
ALLEE MAISTRE R. ARNAUD
RUE DES TANNEURS
RUE DU TRIBUNAL
AVENUE J. GIONO
RUE RENE-CLAIR
ALLEE DE PROVENCE
RUE DES ALPES
N
Gare Routière
BD. C. DE GAULLE
0
100 m

☎92.72.16.00) is to the left on place du Dr Joubert just before you reach Porte Saunerie.

Staying in Manosque presents few problems. For low-priced rooms in the centre, you could try *Chez Artel*, 8 place de l'Hôtel-de-Ville (☎92.72.13.94; ②), or *Peyrache*, 37 rue Jean-Jacques-Rousseau (☎92.72.07.43; ③). Outside the *Vieille Ville*'s ring of boulevards, are the *Grand Hôtel de Versailles*, 17 av Jean-Giono (☎92.72.12.10; ④), and, a little way out on the rte de Sisteron, the charming *Rose de Provence* (☎92.87.56.28; ⑤). The most pleasant, and costly, hotel is the *Hostellerie de la Fuste* (☎92.72.05.95; ⑥) across the Durance and 1km along the D4 towards **Oraison**. There's an **HI youth hostel** (☎92.87.57.44) 750m north of the *Vieille Ville* along bd Martin-Bret and av de l'Argile, in the Parc de la Rochette; take bus #35 to *La Rochette*. It's near a covered swimming pool and the three-star municipal **campsite** on av de la Repasse (April–Oct; ☎92.72.28.08).

The Vieille Ville

Vieux Manosque is scarcely half a kilometre across. You can enter it through two of its remaining fourteenth-century gates, **Porte Saunerie** from the south and **Porte Soubeyran**, which sports a tiny bell suspended within the iron outline of an onion dome, from the north. Another bell tower of more intricate design graces the **Eglise de Saint-Sauveur**. Neither this nor the **Eglise de Notre-Dame-de-Romigier** is a particularly stunning church, though the latter's Black Virgin (black due to the effect of gold leaf on wood) has a lengthy *curriculum vitae* of miracles. The charm of Manosque lies not in architectural set-pieces, but rather in its small decorative details, like the pattern in brick and flints in front of the seventeenth-century **Hôtel de Ville**, the Renaissance door frame of Notre-Dame, and the superb statue, "*Le Froid*", by Bloche on Promenade Aubert-Millot.

There's nothing pretentious about the shops lining **rue Grande**, **rue des Marchands** and **rue Soubeyran** which link the two gates. The streets are busy with fruit and vegetable **markets** on Monday, Wednesday and Friday, and the big weekly market every Saturday, which is even bigger in the first week of the month. Stall-holders and bargain-seekers come in from all the surrounding villages and you'll find moving through the central streets a very slow but entertaining business. If you can find a seat in the **bar-tabac** *Le Cigaloun* beside the church on place Hôtel-de-Ville, grab it fast and watch the animation from there.

Around the Vieille Ville

The attractive eighteenth-century house that is now the **Centre Jean Giono** (Tues–Sat 9am–noon & 2–6pm; 15F), on bd Elémir-Bourges by Porte Saunerie, was the first house to be built outside the old town walls. As well as manuscripts, photos, letters and a library of translations of Giono's work, the centre has an extensive video collection of films based on his novels, films he contributed to as well as interviews and documentaries. Giono himself did not live here; his home was at **Le Paraïs** (30-min guided tours Fri 2.30–5.30pm; 10F), off Montée de la Vrais Richesses 1.5km north of the *Vieille Ville*, which gives a more immediate sense of the man than the *Centre*.

Giono who was imprisoned at the start of World War II for his pacifism, and again after liberation because the Vichy government had promoted his belief in the superiority of nature and peasant life over culture and urban civilization as appropriate Nazi propaganda. Giono was far from being a fascist; his pacifism came from his experience of the trenches in World War I. He was a passionate ecologist and believed that to live close to nature was to be in touch with the cosmic essence of things and with essential human goodness. The countryside around Manosque, its hills and streams, its wildlife, sun, storms and winds do more than just feature in his novels, but actually play as strong a part as the characters that they shape. World War II embittered him, and his later novels are less idealistic. Giono never left Manosque and died here in 1970.

Jean Carzou, Giono's contemporary, confronts the issues of war, technology, dehumanization and the environmental destruction of the planet head on in an extraordinary monumental work, **L'Apocalypse**, composed of painted panels and stained-glass windows in the former church of the **Couvent de la Présentation**, on bd Elémir-Bourges just up from the Centre Giono (Mon & Wed–Sun 10am–12.30pm & 3–7pm; 25F). Nuclear and chemical weaponry, Pol Pot's massacres, Stalin's gulags, Hitler's concentration camps, the genocide of the Armenians by the Turks, the extermination of the American Indians, the Terror of the French Revolution, cities in ruins, scorched earth, civilizations destroyed . . . it's all portrayed in nightmarish style, presided over by the worst symbolism of woman as Madonna or whore.

Eating, drinking and entertainment

Restaurants in the *Vieille Ville* are generally great value. Simple but satisfying meals for 100F or less can be had at *La Barbotine* on place de l'Hôtel-de-Ville (Mon–Sat; ☎92.72.57.15) or *Chez André* (closed Mon, Sun evening out of season & end of June; ☎92.72.03.09) on place du Terreau, where there are many more restaurants to choose from. If you want a change from Provençal cuisine, the Chinese *Le Royal Orient*, 12 bd Elémir-Bourges (Tues–Sun; ☎92.72.42.57), Vietnamese *Le Viet-Nam*, 98 av de Lattre-de-Tasigny (☎92.72.16.49), and Thai *Thanh Binh*, 7 bd Casimir Pelloutier (☎92.87.36.83), are all excellent though not cheap. *La Source* on rte de Dauphin (closed Mon & Sat midday; ☎92.72.12.79) serves an ace chocolate pud.

Entertainment after dinner is not diverse. Aside from sipping cognacs till the cafés close, your only option is the movies at the *Utopia* **cinema**, 2 av St-Lazare.

Forcalquier and its pays

In contrast with Manosque, **FORCALQUIER**, 17km to the north, is a very low-key town. It's not on any rail line and it seems surprising that the main road that ascends to place du Bourguet should take the trouble at all. The *place* can be deserted, the bars empty, and the masonry of the ancient houses is fraying at the edges. So it comes as no surprise to learn that it is the past glories of the town, and the surrounding soft, hilly countryside, that are the real attraction.

That said, things are a good deal livelier on a Monday when it's **market day**, which on the first week in every month becomes a *foire* and really rouses this sleepy place. In July and August there's a flea market every Sunday, and over the first two weeks of August a general glut of arts and crafts fairs and exhibitions in the *Festival de Haute-Provence*.

Arrival, information and accommodation

Buses will drop you off at place Bourguet, where you'll find the **tourist office** on the north side at no. 8 (June–Sept Mon–Fri 9am–noon & 2–6pm; Oct–May afternoons only; ☎92.75.10.02). You can **rent bikes** from the *Association du Pays de Forcalquier* in the *Moulin du Sarret* (☎92.75.01.77) and from the campsite (see below).

The best place **to stay** is the *Auberge Charembeau* (mid-Feb to mid-Nov; ☎92.75.05.69; ⑤) out of town at the end of a long drive signed off the road to Niozelles. *Le Colombier* (☎92.75.03.71; ⑤) is another attractive countryside retreat, 3km south of Forcalquier off the D16. In town, the *Hostellerie des Deux Lions,* next door to the tourist office at 11 place du Bourguet (closed Mon out of season & Sun evening; ☎92.75.25.30; ⑤) is a seventeenth-century coach house, with comfortable rooms and an excellent restaurant serving gorgeous game and fowl dishes flavoured with all the herbs of Provence. *Le Grand Hôtel,* 10 bd Latourette (☎92.75.00.35; ③), is the low-budget option and perfectly acceptable. The municipal **campsite** (April–Oct; ☎92.75.27.94) is on the road to Sigonce past the cemetery and rents out caravans.

The Town

Despite its slumbering air, Forqualquier's **public buildings** suggest that this was once a place of some significance. In the **twelfth century** the counts of Forcalquier rivalled those of Provence, with dominions spreading south and east to the Durance and north to the Drôme. Gap, Embrun, Sisteron, Manosque and Apt were all ruled from the **citadel** of Forcalquier, which even minted its own currency. When this separate power base came to an end, Forcalquier was still renowned as the *"Cité des Quatre Reines"*, since the four daughters of Raimond Béranger V, who united Forcalquier and Provence, all married kings. One of them, Eleanor, became the wife of Henry III of England, a fact commemorated by a modern plaque on the Gothic fountain of place Bourguet.

Not much remains of the ancient citadel at the summit of the rounded, wooded hill that dominates the southern half of the town. Beside the ruins of a tower, sole vestige of the counts of Forcalquier's castle, and the half-buried walls of the original cathedral, stands a nineteenth-century chapel, **Notre-Dame-de-Provence**. In two octagonal tiers decorated in Byzantine style, it's the sort of edifice that Classicist painters liked to position on an Arcadian hill. From the surrounding bowl of land, tilting down to the Durance, Notre-Dame plays precisely such an ordered aesthetic role.

On the opposite side of the town, along the road to Sigonce, is the town's **cemetery**, in a much better state of repair than the houses of the living. Many of the oddly conical vaults were used for habitation until this century, like the Neolithic *bories* they resemble. The elegant staircase leading down to the geometric paths, the clipped yews and high box hedges, and the detailed inscriptions on many of the tombs make this an especially appealing place.

In the town centre the former **Cathédrale Notre-Dame** with its asymmetric and defensive exterior, a finely wrought Gothic porch and Romanesque nave is slowly being restored. South of the cathedral you enter the **Vieille Ville** where the houses date from the thirteenth to the eighteenth century. From place Vieille or rue Mercière you can bear right for place St-Michel and the ancient street fronts of Grande Rue, rue Béranger, place du Palais and rue du Collège. Place St-Michel has another fountain, which has details of activities currently banned under biblical sanction in 25 states of the USA.

At the top and to the left of rue Passère, running south off place Vieille, and with more crumbling historic facades, you reach the start of montée St-Mary, which leads up to the citadel. The one remaining gateway of the *Vieille Ville*, the Porte des Cordeliers, is further down, east of place Vieille. The old synagogue on rue des Cordeliers marks the former Jewish quarter of Forcalquier. The superior power of the Catholic Church is represented by the **Couvent des Cordeliers** at the end of bd des Martyrs. Built between the twelfth and fourteenth centuries, it bears the scars of wars and revolutions but preserves a beautifully vaulted scriptorium and a library with its original wooden ceiling. It's used for concerts and exhibitions (programme from the tourist office) and is open for guided visits (July to mid-Sept Mon & Wed–Sun 11am, 2.30, 4.30 & 5.30pm; May, June, & mid-Sept to Oct Sun & holiday afternoons only; closed Nov–April; 15F).

Eating and drinking

After the *Deux Lions*, next choice for **dinners** is either *La Crêperie*, 4 rue des Cordeliers, which does great salads, grills, ice creams, and crêpes, or *Le Commerce* (closed Mon evening & Tues out of season) on place du Bourguet, with a wide price range of menus. This is a good place to have local lamb, which you should try before leaving Forcalquier. The soil in this high region is extremely poor, and not much other than grass will grow. The sheep, who winter in the Crau, are brought back here for summer, with many flocks still herded by shepherds on the ancient drove roads.

Another product of the town, based on fruits and nuts from further south, is **exotic alcohol**. The *Distillerie de Haute-Provence*, that has its shop on av St-Promasse just down from the touritst office, sells cherries, pears and mixes of different fruits and nuts pickled in liqueur. Of its fruit wines, the *de brut de pêche*, a sparkling peach aperitif, needs to be tasted to be believed. For ordinary café drinking, the *Snack Bar Moderne* on place St-Michel is a friendly locals' watering hole and there are plenty of cafés on place Bourguet.

Mane and around

The village of **MANE**, 4km south of Forcalquier at the junction of the roads from Apt and Manosque, still has its feudal citadel (a private residence closed to the public) and Renaissance churches, chapels and mansions remarkably intact. The most impressive building is a former Benedictine priory, **Notre-Dame-de-Salagon**, half a kilometre out of Mane off the Apt road. It comprises fifteenth-century monks' quarters, seventeenth-century stables and farm buildings, and an enormous fortified twelfth-century Romanesque church with traces of fourteenth-century frescoes and sculpted scenes of rural life. Archeological digs in the choir have revealed the remnants of an earlier, sixth-century church. Three **gardens**, one of aromatic plants, another of medicinal plants, and one cultivated as the medieval monks would have used it, have been re-created to illustrate the relationship with nature of earlier time. A number of exhibitions and activities are organized each year by the *Conservatoire du Patrimoine Ethnologique* of the Alpes de Haute Provence *département* which runs the site (July & Aug daily 10am–noon & 2–7pm; April–June 2–6pm; Oct–Nov Sat & Sun 2–6pm; 25F).

If you need somewhere to **stay** in Mane try *La Reine Rose*, on Grand Chemin (☎92.75.35.30; ②) with cold tiles in the rooms but offering a friendly welcome and a bargain fixed menu.

In the same direction from Mane, past a medieval bridge over the River Laye, you come to a palatial residence that has been called the Trianon of Provence.

The pure eighteenth-century ease and luxury of the **Château de Sauvan** (guided tours June–Sept Mon–Fri & Sun 3.30pm; Oct–May Sun & hols only; 30F) come as a surprise in this harsh territory, leagues from any courtly city. Though there are hundreds of mansions like it around Paris and along the Loire, the residences of the rich and powerful in Haute-Provence tend towards the moat and dungeon, not to French windows giving onto lawns and lake. The furnishings are predictably grand and ugly, though the hall and stairway would take some beating for light and spaciousness. What's best is the setting: the swans and geese on the square lake, the peacocks strutting by the drive, the views around and the delicate solidity of the aristocratic house.

The Observatoire de Haute-Provence

The tourist literature promoting the **pure air** of Haute-Provence is not just hype. Proof of the fact is the National Centre for Scientific Research **observatory** on the wooded slopes west of Mane, sited here because it has the fewest clouds, the least fog and the lowest industrial pollution in all France. Visible from miles around, it presents a peculiar picture of domes of gleaming white mega-mushrooms pushing up between the oaks. It's open for visits (April–Sept Wed every half-hour 2–4pm, and on first Sun of month 9–11am; Oct–March Wed only 3pm; 15F), so you get to see some telescopes and blank monitors, and the mechanism that opens up the domes and aims the lens. It's more fun than it sounds, but it's a shame the opening hours aren't at night. As recompense you can buy wonderful postcards of stars, comets and nebulae.

Simaine-la-Rotonde, Banon and the Montagne de Lure

The gentle countryside of the Pays de Forcalquier gives way to the north to the great barrage of the **Montagne de Lure** and to the west, past **Simaine-la-Rotonde** and **Banon**, to the desolate Plateau d'Albion (see *The Eastern Vauclause*). The more northern villages, including Banon, are where you're likely to hear Provençal being spoken and see aspects of rural life that have hardly changed over centuries. It was in a tiny place on the Lure foothills due north of Banon called Le Contadour where Jean Giono (see under "Manosque") set up his summer commune in the 1930s to expostulate the themes of peace, ecology and the return to nature.

Simaine-La-Rotonde

The spiralling cone of **SIMAINE-LA-ROTONDE** marks the horizon with an emphasis greater than its size would warrant. However many *"villages de caractère"* (Simaine's official classification) you may have seen, this is one to reseduce you. Neither over-spruce nor on the verge of ruin, it gives the feeling of a place that people love and are prepared to work for.

The *faubourg*, where you'll find the post office, the banks, *boulangerie* and bars, lies in the plain by the D51, cleany separated from the old village's winding streets of honey-coloured stone in which each house is part of the medieval defensive system. The zigzags end at the **Rotonde** (mid-June to mid-Sept Mon–

Sat 10am–12.45pm & 3–7pm, Sun 3–7pm; April to mid-June & end Sept Mon & Wed–Sun 3–5.30pm; 12F), a huge domed building that was once the chapel of the castle but looks more like a keep. Nineteenth-century restoration work added smooth limestone to its rough-hewn fortress stones, but the peculiar feature is the asymmetry between its interior and exterior, being hexagonal on the outside and irregularly dodecagonal on the inside. The set of the stones on the domes is wonderfully wonky and no one knows what once hung from or covered the hole at the top. In July and August the Rotonde is used for diverse cultural functions and can be visited between 3 and 6pm.

Beyond the Rotonde there's a path to the chapel of **Notre-Dame-de-Pieté**, which stands amongst old windmills. Descending back through the village are all sorts of architectural details to catch the eye: heavy carved doors with stone lintels in exact proportion, wrought-iron street lamps, the scrolling on the dark wooden shutters of the *Café-Restaurant de la Rotonde*. Simaine's most stunning building is the **halles couvertes** opposite the café. With its columns framing open sky, it almost overhangs the hillside on the steepest section of the village. No longer used as a market-place, it's where people stop in their daily rounds to pass the time of day or stare into the middle distance, where cats stretch out in the sun, and where, each July 14, the **village dance** is held.

Practicalities

Tourism is not Simaine's main preoccupation, so it's not surprising that it doesn't have an official **tourist office**; if you need information go to the *mairie* in the upper village. There's only one **hotel**, the *Auberge du Faubourg* (March–Oct; ☎92.75.92.43; ②), which has just eight rooms and insists on half-board. The only other accommodation options are a **gîte**, *Le Chaloux* (c/o M Rider; mid-March to Dec; ☎92.75.99.13; ①), with horses to ride and a two-star **campsite**, *Camping de Valsaintes*, on the main road (June–Sept; ☎92.75.91.46).

The only **eaterie** besides the *Café-Restaurant de la Rotonde* (Sun–Fri), is *Chez Mimile/Le Restaurant St-Hubert* in the quartier des Gîtes in the *faubourg* (closed Wed & Sun evening).

Banon

Like Simaine, the houses of the *Haute Ville* of **BANON** form a guarding wall. Within the fortified gate, the protective huddling of the buildings is even closer, forcing one street to tunnel underneath, and creating the sense that the entire village is set to face an invasion.

You do not have to come here to sample the produce for which it is famed: the *plateau des fromages* of any half-decent Provence restaurant will include a round goat's cheese marinaded in brandy and wrapped in sweet chestnut leaves. But there's nothing like tasting different ages of *Banon* cheese, sliced off for you by the *fromager* at a market stall on place de la République. As well as ensuring that you taste the very young and the well-matured varieties, they may give you an accompaniment in the form of a sprig of savory, an aromatic local plant of the mint family. The *boulangerie* on the square sells the local variety of *fougasse* bread, stuffed with *Banon*.

Practicalities

The **market** in Banon is on Tuesday mornings, but if you come on another day you can still taste the untravelled **cheese** as part of a pleasant and reasonably priced meal at the **hotel-bar-restaurant** *Les Voyageurs* (☎92.76.21.02; ③). The only other concession to visitors is *La Braserade* pizzeria and *crêperie*, open only at the weekend out of season, and a **campsite**, *L'Epi Bleu* (May–Sept; ☎92.73.30.30) with a pool and **bikes** for rental.

The Montagne de Lure

Roads north of Banon peter out at the lower slopes of the **Montagne de Lure**. To reach the summit of the Lure, by road or the GR6, you have to head east to St-Etienne-Les-Orgues, 12km north of Forcalquier. The footpath avoids the snaking road for most of the way, but you're walking through relentless pine plantation and it's a long way without a change of scenery (about 15km). Just below the summit you'll see **ski-lifts** and the *Hôtel-Restaurant Montagne de Lure* (mid-July to mid-Sept & mid-Dec to March; ☎92.75.04.88; ②).

When the trees stop you find yourself on sharp and rubbly stones without a single softening blade of grass. The summit itself is a mass of telecommunications aerials and dishes; a grimmer high-perched desert would be hard to find. That said, the point of the climb is that the Lure has no close neighbours, giving you 360 degrees of mountainscape, as if you were airborne. The view of the distant snowy peaks to the north is the best; those with excessive stamina can keep walking towards them along the GR6 to Sisteron.

Up the Durance river

The Marseille–Grenoble *autoroute* now speeds along the Durance river, bypassing the industrial town of **St-Auban** and its older neighbour **Château-Arnoux**, famous for a superb restaurant. The views from the fashionable little village of **Lurs** and the ancient **Prieuré de Ganagobie** have not been affected, nor their isolation. **La Brillane** is the nearest **gare SNCF** to Lurs; Ganagobie is between La Brillane and Peyruis with no public transport links.

Lurs

Situated on a narrow ridge above the west bank of the Durance, **LURS** is another of the "*villages de caractère*" but much more keen on its picturesque status than Simaine-la-Rotonde. Immaculately restored houses stand amid immaculately maintained ruins; commerce extends no further than *Le Séminaire* **hotel-restaurant** (☎92.79.94.19; ④) in the old summer residence of the bishops of Sisteron, and *La Bello Visto* restaurant (closed Wed; ☎92.79.95.09), a printer's and a café, all around the compulsory visitors' car park on place de la Fontaine. Once you surface at the top of the village, however, you have to admit it's worth the fuss. Across the wide, multi-branching river you have the abrupt step up to the Plateau de Valensole, with the snowy peaks beyond. To the south the land drops before rising again in another high ridge along the river. To the west and north the views are as extensive, from the rolling hills around Forcalquier to the Montagne de Lure.

The best way to appreciate this geography is to follow the paths to the small chapel of **Notre-Dame-de-Vie** along the narrowing escarpment. The right-hand path goes through the woods and is less clearly defined than the eastern path, the **Promenade des Evêques**, which is marked by fifteen small oratories.

In the late 1940s Lurs was deserted save for the passing bandit. With no electricity or running water except that which poured through gaping roofs, it was well on its way to joining the other ghost villages of Provence. Oddly enough, it was not architects or builders who rescued Lurs, but graphic artists and printers, including the author of the universal nomenclature for typefaces. Hence the *imprimerie* (printer) on place des Feignants, and the **Rencontres Internationales de Lure** that brings in practitioners of the graphic arts from calligraphers to computer-aided-design consultants for the last week in August.

The Prieuré de Ganagobie

About 7km north of Lurs are examples of complex design skills that long predate the invention of printing. The floor of the church of the twelfth-century **Prieuré de Ganagobie** is covered with mosaics composed of red, black and white tiles. They show fabulous beasts with tails looping through their bodies, and the four elements represented by an elephant for Earth, a fish for Water, a griffon for Air and a lion for Fire. Interlocking and repeating patterns show a strong Byzantine influence, and there's a dragon slain by a Saint George in Crusader armour. The porch of the church is also an unusual sight, its arches carved to a bubbly pattern that might be an imitation of medieval bunting.

Tours of the priory are given by one of the monks (30min; summer Tues–Sun 3–5pm; winter Tues–Sat 3–4pm & Sun 11am; 20F). As well as the church, you are shown the refectory, where patches of fresco reveal more mythical creatures, and the cloisters with their sturdy columns. If you have to wait, you can pass the time walking through the oaks and broom, pines and lavender eastwards along the allée des Moines to the edge of the Plateau de Ganagobie on which the priory stands, 350m above the Durance, or westwards following the allée de Forcalquier for views to the Montagne de Lure and beyond Forcalquier to the Lubéron.

St-Auban and Château-Arnoux

The impending confluence of the Durance and Bléone is announced by the **Pénitents des Mées**, a long line of pointed rocks on the east bank, which look like anything from sacks of nuts to a Ku Klux Klan gathering. The official image is of cowled monks, literally petrified for desiring the women slaves some local lord brought back from the Crusades.

The approach to Château-Arnoux is not very promising. Petrochemical factories cover the right bank of the Durance at **ST-AUBAN**, a suburb of grid-plan barrack houses set up in 1916. St-Auban does have one attraction, the national **gliding** centre, based at the *aérodrome de Château-Arnoux/St-Auban* (details on ☎92.64.17.24 or 92.64.19.53).

At **CHATEAU-ARNOUX** itself the hills once more close in on the Durance, blocking off St-Auban's plain from view. The river takes on a smoother and more majestic prospect, as a seven-kilometre-long artificial lake ending at the barrage just south of Château-Arnoux. An imposing Renaissance **castle** (July & Aug Tues–Fri 4pm only; free) dominates the centre of the town, now serving as the *mairie*. With two round towers at the back, two square ones at the front and a hexagonal tower in the middle, this is a mighty building. The tower staircase is carved from one block of stone, all 84 steps of it. The roofs are covered in tiles of different colours, with gargoyles glaring from below the eaves. If the castle has closed the doors to visitors, you can still take a wander in its **park**, which has the best and most diverse collection of trees in Haute-Provence: Chinese mulberries, bananas, Judas trees, different ivies and ebony, as well as native species.

A more energetic walk is to the **Chapelle St-Jean** above the town, with the usual stunning views of this part of the world; from place Jean-Jaurès take chemin de l'Oratoire, cross over to rte des Reservoirs de St-Jean, then follow the footpath signed to the left.

Exercise might be in order as Château-Arnoux is a centre of **gourmandise**, with *La Bonne Etape*, on chemin du Lac (closed Mon out of season & Sun evening; ☎92.64.00.09; menus 200–600F; à la carte 300F upwards), one of the best **restaurants** in Provence. It's expensive naturally (though nowhere near as bad as its handful of coastal rivals), needs booking in advance and has the sort of château decor that recommends (though never requires) smartish clothes. Pierre Gleize, the co-owner with his son Jany, belongs to the exclusive band of master chefs of France. A dream of a meal is assured, and one that celebrates the produce of the region without any trendy foreign influences. If you do treat yourself, take a look at the collection of *santons* in the restaurant, made by Liliane Guiomar, one of the greatest living practitioners of this Provençal art. It includes the easily recognizable figure of Monsieur Gleize senior dangling a hefty salmon.

Château-Arnoux practicalities

For information, the **tourist office** (Mon–Fri 9am–noon & 2–6pm; ☎92.64.02.64) is at 1 rue Victorin-Maurel, the main street of the *Vieille Ville*. **Bikes** can be rented at *Cycles BARO* on place du Commerce (to the left as you're leaving northwards, where av Général-de-Gaulle becomes av Calendal).

Hotels here range from the deluxe *La Bonne Etape* (⑧) to *La Taverne Jarlandine* (☎92.64.04.49; ②), an old-fashioned cheapie in the centre of the village. Rooms overlooking the Château-Arnoux lake at the *Hôtel du Lac*, 12 allées des Erables (☎92.64.04.32; ③), are very pleasant and not exorbitant.

The place for a low-cost meal is the excellent *Casa Mia* pizzeria on av Général-de-Gaulle. For **snacks** and ice creams there's the *Tchin-Tchin* bar on the central place Camille-Reymond, where the clientele is young and the music loud. Or there's the *Café Biz-Art* in the **Centre Culturel des Lauzières** on av Jean-Moulin, the main road coming in from the south, where you'll also find a cinema and exhibition space.

Sisteron

The last Provençal stretch of the **Route Napoléon**, the road following the path taken by the returning emperor and a small band of followers in March 1815 (see p.340), runs from Château-Arnoux to **SISTERON**. If you can choose which road you take, follow Napoléon's footsteps via the D4 on the left bank of the Durance. The first sight of Sisteron reveals its strategic significance as the major mountain gateway of Provence. The site has been fortified since time immemorial and even now, half-destroyed by the Anglo-American bombardment of 1944, its **citadel** stands as a fearsome sentinel over the city and the solitary bridge across the river.

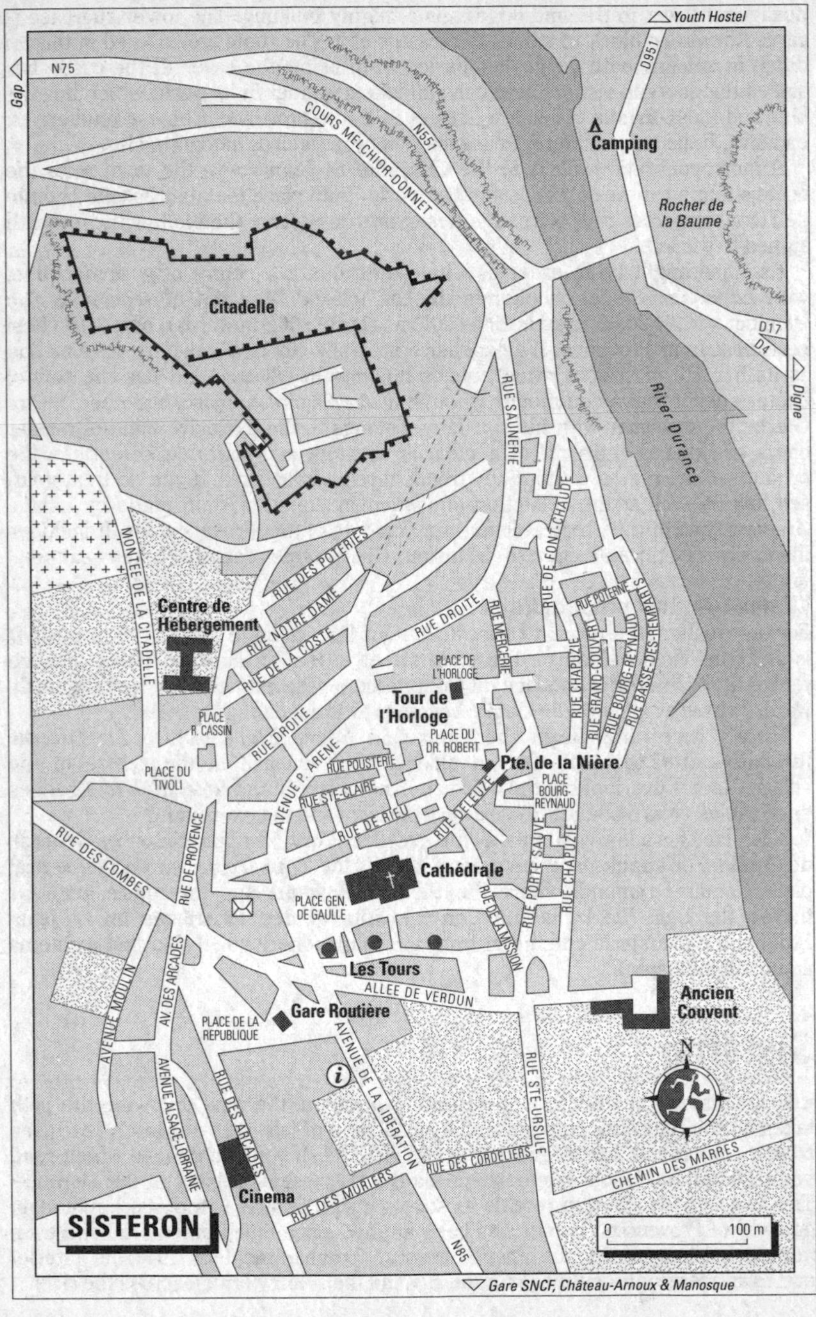
SISTERON
Youth Hostel
Gap
N75
D951
COURS MELCHIOR-DONNET
N551
Camping
Rocher de la Baume
Citadelle
D17
D4
Digne
River Durance
RUE SAUNERIE
RUE DE FONT-CHAUDE
MONTEE DE LA CITADELLE
RUE DES POTERIES
RUE NOTRE DAME
RUE DE LA COSTE
RUE DROITE
Centre de Hébergement
PLACE DE L'HORLOGE
Tour de l'Horloge
RUE MERCERIE
RUE POTERNE
RUE CHAPUZIE
RUE GRAND-COUVERT
RUE BOURG-REYNAUD
RUE BASSE-DES-REMPARTS
PLACE R. CASSIN
PLACE DU DR. ROBERT
Pte. de la Nière
PLACE DU TIVOLI
AVENUE P. ARENE
RUE POUSTERIE
RUE STE-CLAIRE
RUE DE RIEU
RUE DELEUZE
PLACE BOURG-REYNAUD
RUE PORTE SAUVE
RUE DES COMBES
RUE DE PROVENCE
Cathédrale
PLACE GEN. DE GAULLE
RUE DE LA MISSION
AV. DES ARCADES
AVENUE MOULIN
Les Tours
ALLEE DE VERDUN
Ancien Couvent
PLACE DE LA REPUBLIQUE
Gare Routière
AVENUE DE LA LIBERATION
RUE STE-URSULE
N
AVENUE ALSACE-LORRAINE
RUE DES ARCADES
RUE DES CORDELIERS
CHEMIN DES MARRES
RUE DES MURIERS
Cinema
N85
0
100 m
Gare SNCF, Château-Arnoux & Manosque

Sisteron gave Napoléon something of a headache. Its mayor and the majority of its population were royalist, and given the fortifications and geography of the town, it was evidently impossible for him to pass undetected. However, luck was still with the Corsican in those days as the military commander of the *département* was a sympathizer and removed all ammunition from Sisteron's arsenal. Contemporary accounts say Napoléon sat nonchalantly on the bridge, contemplating the citadel above and the tumultous waters below, while his men reassembled and the town's notables, ordered to keep their pistols under wraps, looked on impotently. Eventually Napoléon entered the city, took some refreshment at a tavern and received a tricolour from a courageous peasant woman before rejoining his band and taking leave of Provence.

Sisteron today feels a bit grey and abandoned. The promise of prosperity that builders of new highways always hold out has yet again proved false; fewer people stop here now; shops and restaurants have closed; the old quarter has become even more run down. A new museum dedicated to Baden-Powell and the scout movement is unlikely to attract the crowds. One advantage, however, of the downturn in the town's fortunes, is the hotel prices, some of the cheapest anywhere in Provence.

Arrival, information and accommodation

Arriving by train at Sisteron, turn right out of the **gare SNCF** (☎92.61.00.60) along av de la Libération until you reach place de la République. Here you'll find the **gare routière**, **post office** and **tourist office** (July & August Mon–Sat 9am–12.30pm & 1.30–7.30pm, Sun 10am–noon & 2–5pm; Sept–June Mon–Sat 9am–noon & 2–6pm; ☎92.61.12.03 or 92.61.36.50), which can provide details of good walks and advise on **bike rental**, if the garages on av de la Libération have none left. If you prefer a **horse** for transport, make enquiries at the *gîte La Fenière* (☎92.62.44.02) at **Peipin**, halfway between Sisteron and Château-Arnoux.

For **rooms** in Sisteron that are more economical than a youth hostel, try the run-down *Hostellerie Provençale* (☎92.61.02.42; ①) and nearby *Les Andrônes* (☎92.61.01.68; ①), both on av Jean-Moulin just up from place de la République. *La Citadelle* overlooking the river at the end of rue Saunerie (☎92.61.13.52; ③), the *Tivoli,* 21 place du Tivoli (☎92.61.15.16; ③), and the three-star genteel and old-fashioned *Grand Hôtel du Cours,* allée de Verdon (☎92.61.04.51; ④), are all exceptionally good value too. The four-star **campsite**, *Les Prés-Hauts* (March–Nov; ☎92.61.19.69), is over the river and 3km along the D951 to the left. Equipped with a pool, it also organizes horse rides, walks and a variety of sports including hang-gliding.

The Town

To visit the **citadel** (July & Aug daily 8am–7pm; mid-March to June & Sept to mid-Nov 9am–6pm; 18F) can easily take up half a day. There are no guides, just tape-recordings in French attempting to re-create historic moments, such as Napoléon's march and the imprisonment in 1639 of Jan Kazimierz, the future king of Poland. Most of the extant defences were constructed after the Wars of Religion, added to a century later by Vauban when Sisteron was a front-line fort against neighbouring Savoy. No traces remain of the first Ligurian fortification nor of its Roman successor, and the eleventh-century castle was destroyed in the mid-thirteenth century during a pogrom against the local Jewish population.

As you climb up to the fortress, there seems no end to the gateways, courtyards and other defences. The outcrop on which the fortress sits abruptly stops at the look-out post, **Guérite du Diable**, 500m above the narrow passage of the Durance, and affording the best views. On the other side of the ravine, the vertical folds of the **Rocher de la Baume** provide a favourite training ground for local mountaineers. In the distance, as the perspective draws them closer, the rock's dark and dangerous crevices resemble the ridged skin of an enormous reptilian creature.

In the fortress grounds, a **festival** known as *Nuits de la Citadelle* takes place throughout July and August, with open-air performances of music, drama and dance. There is also a **museum** on the history of the citadel with a room dedicated to Napoléon, and temporary art exhibitions in the vertiginous late medieval chapel, **Notre-Dame-du-Château**, restored to its Gothic glory and given very beautiful subdued stained-glass windows in the 1970s.

Back down at ground level the most striking feature of Sisteron are the three huge **towers** which belonged to the ramparts built around the expanding town in 1370. Though one still has its spiralling staircase, only ravens use them. Beside them is the much older former **Cathédrale Notre-Dame-des-Pommiers**, whose strictly rectangular interior contrasts with its riot of stepped roofs and an octagonal gallery adjoining a square belfry topped by a pyramidal spire. The altarpiece incorporates a Mignard painting; other seventeenth-century works adorn the chapels.

From the church you can follow a signposted route through the lower town. The tall houses enclose narrow passages with steps and ramps that interconnect through vaulted archways, known here as **andrônes**. In the upper town, on the other side of rue Saunerie and rue Droite, the houses, like the citadel above them, follow the curves of the rock. In some places the third or fourth storeys become ground floors on the succeeding street. Old Sisteron can take on a sinister aspect at night, as not all the *andrônes* and alleyways are well lit, unlike the troubled days in 1568 (during the Wars of Religion), when sixty lanterns were put in place to deter conspiracies and plots.

Place de l'Horloge, at the other end of rue Deleuze from the church, is the site for the Wednesday and Saturday **market**, where stalls of sweet and savoury *fougasse*, lavender honey, nougat and almond-paste *calissons* that rival those from Aix congregate. On the second Saturday of every month the market becomes a **fair**, and there are likely to be flocks of sheep and lambs, and cages of pigeons as well as stalls of clothes and bric-à-brac.

Eating and drinking

Sisteron has no outstanding **restaurants** though you can certainly have a filling meal without paying over the odds. Of the hotel restaurants *La Citadelle* has a menu below 100F and a terrace above the river where you can eat; the *Grand Hôtel du Cour* serves copious meals with the renowned *gigot d'agneau de Sisteron* included on a 110F menu. Otherwise you'll find *crêperies*, brasseries and pizzerias along rue Saunerie and on the squares around the clock tower. The best nougat and *calissons* come from *Canteperdrix* on place Paul-Arène which also runs *Le Grand Salon*, a *salon de thé* serving salads as well as cakes and ice creams. For anchovy *fougasse* head for *Boulangerie Bernaudon*, 37 rue Droite, and for *charcuterie* to *Traiteur des Gourmets*, 136 rue Droite. *Le Mondial* **bar** at the top of rue Droite stays open late, as does *Le Primerose* on place de l'Horloge.

Around Sisteron

If you're staying in Sisteron for several days there are some worthwhile expeditions into the wilds. To the east along the D17 you come to **VILHOSC** where the priory has an eleventh-century crypt hidden in its walls; a few kilometres further on, the graceful fourteenth-century **Pont de la Reine Jeanne** crosses the Vançon. Though the roads beyond lead to nowhere, and the villages that remain are almost all abandoned and in ruins, you may choose to continue onwards and upwards by foot on the GR6.

Ten kilometres to the north of Sisteron, through Valernes off the D951 in the village of **VAUMEILH**, is the *Aérodrome de Vaumeilh* (☎92.62.17.45), which can arrange for you to go **flying**, either in a glider or microlight, and **stay** or camp at *Le Janus* (☎92.62.15.23; ①).

travel details

Trains

Draguignan to: Les Arcs (frequent; 5min).

Manosque to: Aix (5–6 daily; 40min); Château-Arnoux–St-Auban (4–5 daily; 25min); La Brillane (4–5 daily; 12min); Marseille (5–6 daily; 1hr 15min); Sisteron (4–5 daily; 35min).

Buses

Aups to: Aiguines (1–2 daily; 1hr 10mins); Brignoles (1–2 daily; 45min); Cotignac (1–2 daily; 20min); Draguignan (1–2 daily; 1hr–1hr 20min); Salernes (1–2 daily; 10min); Sillans (1–2 daily; 10min); Tourtour (1–2 daily; 20min).

Banon to: Aix; (1 daily; 2hr 5min); Marseille (1 daily; 2hr 40min); Simaine (2 daily; 10min).

Draguignan to: Aix (2 daily; 2hr 25min); Aups (1–2 daily; 1hr–1hr 20min); Bargemon (1–2 daily; 20min); Barjols (1–2 daily; 1hr 40min); Brignoles (2 daily; 55min); Callas (1–2 daily; 20min); Entrecasteaux (1–2 daily; 40min); Fayence (2 daily: 45min); Grasse (3–4 daily; 1–2hr); Les Arcs (frequent; 15–20min); Lorgues (1–2 daily; 15min); Moustiers-Ste-Marie (1 daily; 2hr); Nice (1–2 weekly; 1hr 30min); St-Raphaël (10–12 daily; 1hr 15min–1hr 25min); Salernes (1–2 daily; 1 hr); Seillans (1–2 daily; 45min); Toulon (5 daily; 2hr 10min); Tourtour (1–2 daily; 1hr); Villecroze (1 daily; 55min).

Fayence to: Draguignan (2 daily; 45min); Grasse (2–3 daily; 1hr); Seillans (1–2 daily; 20min).

Forcalquier to: Apt (2 daily; 1hr); Avignon (2 daily; 2hr 10min); Château-Arnoux (2 daily; 45min); Digne (2 daily; 1hr 10min); La Brillane (2 daily; 10min); Lurs (2 daily; 15min); Mane (2 daily; 5min); Peyrius (2 daily; 25min); St Auban (2 daily; 40min); St Michel l'Observatoire (2 daily; 10min).

Manosque to: Aix (5 daily; 40min–1hr); Château-Arnoux (5 daily; 45min); Digne (5 daily; 45min–1hr); Lurs (3 daily; 25min); Marseille (5 daily; 1hr 5min–1hr 25min); Riez (1 daily; 1hr 15min); St Auban (5 daily; 40min); Sisteron (5 daily; 1hr 5min).

Riez to: Barjols (1–2 daily; 45min); Digne (1 daily; 1hr 30min); Manosque (1 daily; 1hr 15min); Moustiers-Ste-Marie (1 daily; 25min).

Sisteron to: Aix (3 daily; 1hr 10min–2hr 5min); Château-Arnoux (9 daily; 15min); Château-Arnoux–St-Auban *gare SNCF* (3 daily; 10min); Digne (1 daily; 45min); Lurs (3 daily; 40min); Manosque (4 daily; 40min); Marseille (3 daily; 1hr 25min–1hr 45min); Nice (1 daily; 3hr 45min); Peipin (3 daily; 15min).

CHAPTER SIX

THE RIVIERA: CANNES TO MENTON

The seventy-odd kilometres of coast between Cannes and the Italian border known as the **Riviera** was once an inhospitable shore with few natural harbours, its tiny local communities preferring to cluster around feudal castles high above the sea. It is now an almost uninterrupted promenade, lined by palms and mega-buck hotels, with speeding sports cars on the corniche roads and yachts like minor ocean liners moored at each resort. The sea is speckled with boats, boards, bikes and skis; the beaches, many of them shingle or made from imported sand, form a gaudy pattern of parasols and beds. The occasional breaks in the garish, grotesque and intermittently gorgeous facades overlooking the Mediterranean are filled by formal parks or gardens, and, where vertical contours limit construction, roads and rail lines have been cut on the water's edge. Just when it seemed that construction could go no further, plans were announced for a new *autoroute* to run from Le Muy through Grasse and Vence to Monaco, a new expressway from Cannes to Grasse, two more lanes on the existing *autoroute*, a forty-kilometre *métro* from Nice to Sophia-Antopolis, and a *TGV* line.

The largest city, **Nice**, became fashionable as a winter resort in the eighteenth century. The fishing village of **Cannes** was discovered in the 1830s by a retired British chancellor who couldn't get to Nice because of a cholera epidemic. Up until World War I, aristocrats and royals from all ends of Europe built their Riviera mansions, and artists, including **Renoir**, sought warm retreats here while the local population continued to farm and fish. The inter-war years saw the advent of more artists – **Picasso**, **Matisse**, **Dufy**, **Bonnard**, **Miró** – and the beginnings of a switch from winter to summer as the favoured season.

By the 1950s **mass summer tourism** started to take off and the real transformation began. It became far more profitable to service the new influx of visitors than to make a living from the land or sea. Property speculation and despoiling the environment went hand in hand – only in the 1970s were any serious controls implemented, by which time no wild Riviera coast was left. Today, for all their glamorous air of luxury living, the towns are hotbeds of quick money, crime and tourist rip-offs.

HOTEL ROOM PRICES

For a fuller explanation of these price codes, see the box on p.32 of *Basics*.

① Under 160F	② 160–220F	③ 220–300F	④ 300–400F
⑤ 400–500F	⑥ 500–600F	⑦ 600–700F	⑧ over 700F

Attractions, however, still remain, most notably in the legacies of the **artists** who stayed here: Picasso in **Antibes** and **Vallauris**; Léger in **Biot**; Matisse in **Nice** and **Vence**; Renoir in **Cagnes-sur-Mer**; Cocteau in **Villefranche** and **Menton**; Chagall in **Nice**; and all of them in **St-Paul-de-Vence** and **Haut-de-Cagnes**. The relatively unspoilt villages in the Nice hinterland, too, guard superb artworks from the medieval School of Nice in their churches and chapels. There are the thrills of the **corniches** running across the mountains between Nice and Menton; the good times to be had in Vieux Nice; and the vicarious pleasures of the two major excrescences of the Riviera, **Cannes** and the independent principality of **Monaco**. Finally, for those with the requisite gourmet greed, this region has some of the world's best **restaurants**, catering for some of the world's most loaded clientele.

Speedy and inexpensive **train connections** make it easy to visit all the coastal towns and villages without committing yourself to staying overnight.

Cannes

Movies and their stars are what normally bring the name of **CANNES** to people's lips: this year's winner of the Palme d'Or award or the youngest, richest director and most photographed young star; the latest producers' takeover; the death or rebirth of each country's film industry; the favoured clothes designer; the eminently forgettable quotes from all the unforgettable old-timers . . . Cannes might be more than its film festival, but it's still a grotesquely over-hyped urban blight on this once exquisite coast, a contrast sublimely reinforced by the **Iles de Lérins**, a short boat ride offshore.

The film industry, and all manner of business junketing, represent Cannes' main source of income in an ever-multiplying calendar of festivals, conferences, tournaments and trade shows. The spin-offs from servicing the day and night needs of the jetloads of agents, reps, dealers, buyers, pen-pushers, cheque-pushers and celebrities are even more profitable than providing the strictly business facilities. The main venue for all the big events is the **Palais des Festivals**, an orange concrete mega-bunker on the prime seaside spot between the *Vieux Port* and La Croisette, the seafront promenade and the main focus of Cannes life.

Arrival, city transport and information

The central **gare SNCF** (information ☎93.99.50.50; reservations ☎93.90.33.50) is on rue Jean-Jaurès; the **gare routière** (☎93.39.11.39) is on place B-Cornut Gentille overlooking the *Vieux Port* between the *mairie* and Le Suquet, the hill overlooking modern Cannes from the west. The central axis of the town is **rue d'Antibes**, halfway between rue Jean-Jaurès and La Croisette, becoming rue Félix-Faure behind the *Vieux Port*. With just five blocks between rue Jean-Jaurès and the seafront, central Cannes is not particularly big, though it manages to look daunting. **Urban buses** run from outside the *mairie*, and you can buy individual **tickets** for 6.80F, a carnet of ten for 48F and a weekly pass, the *Carte Palm'Hebdo*, for 50F. A useful service is the **minibus shuttle** along the seafront from place Frédéric-Mistral, west of Le Suquet, to *Palm Beach Casino* on Pointe Croisette, at the other end of the bay. If you prefer to cycle, **bikes** can be rented from *Cannes Locations*, 5 rue Allieis (☎93.39.46.15) or *FRL*, 14 rue Clemenceau (☎93.39.33.60).

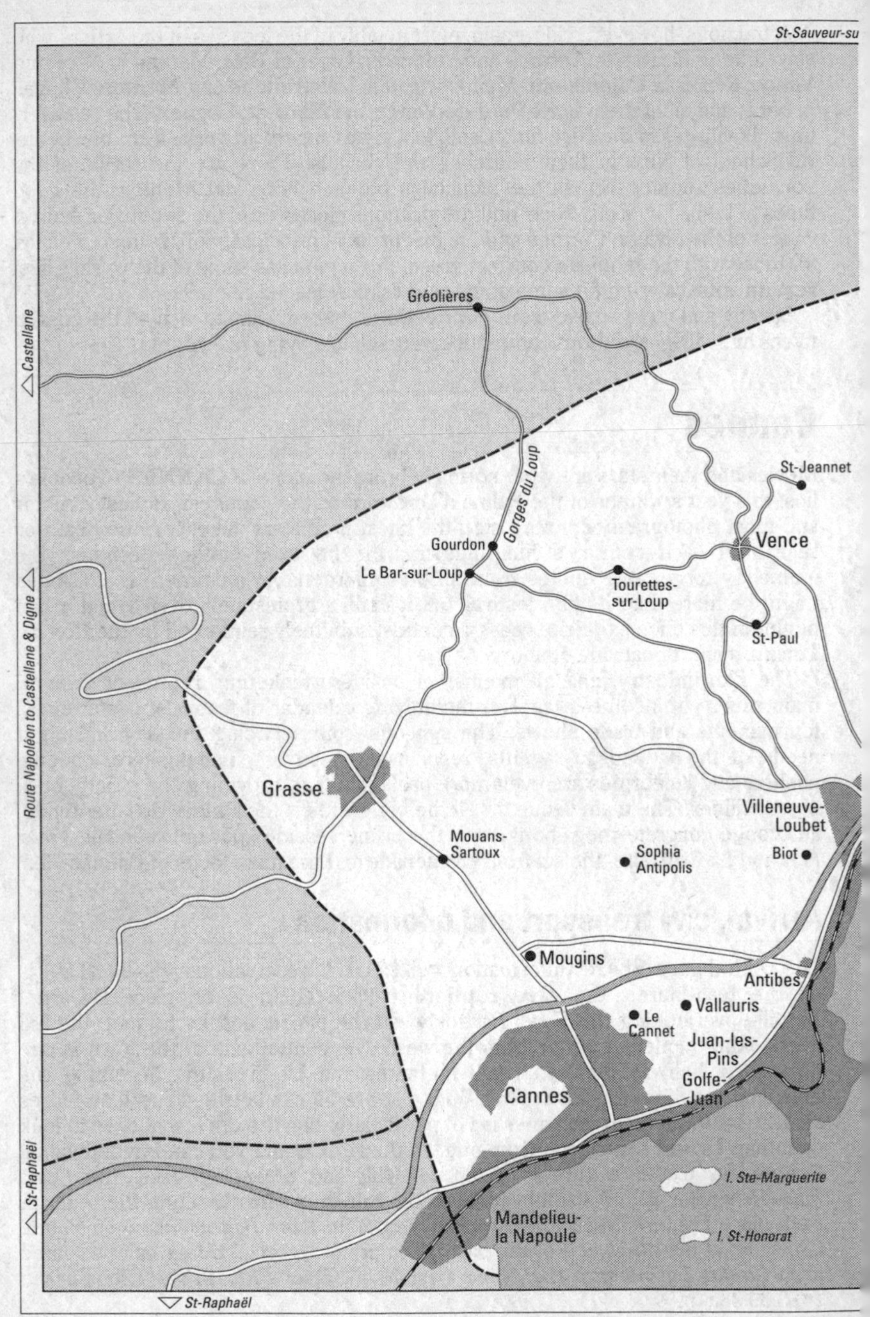
St-Sauveur-su
Castellane
Route Napoléon to Castellane & Digne
St-Raphaël
Gréolières
Gorges du Loup
Gourdon
Le Bar-sur-Loup
Tourettes-sur-Loup
St-Jeannet
Vence
St-Paul
Grasse
Villeneuve-Loubet
Mouans-Sartoux
Sophia Antipolis
Biot
Mougins
Antibes
Le Cannet
Vallauris
Juan-les-Pins
Golfe-Juan
Cannes
I. Ste-Marguerite
Mandelieu-la Napoule
I. St-Honorat
St-Raphaël

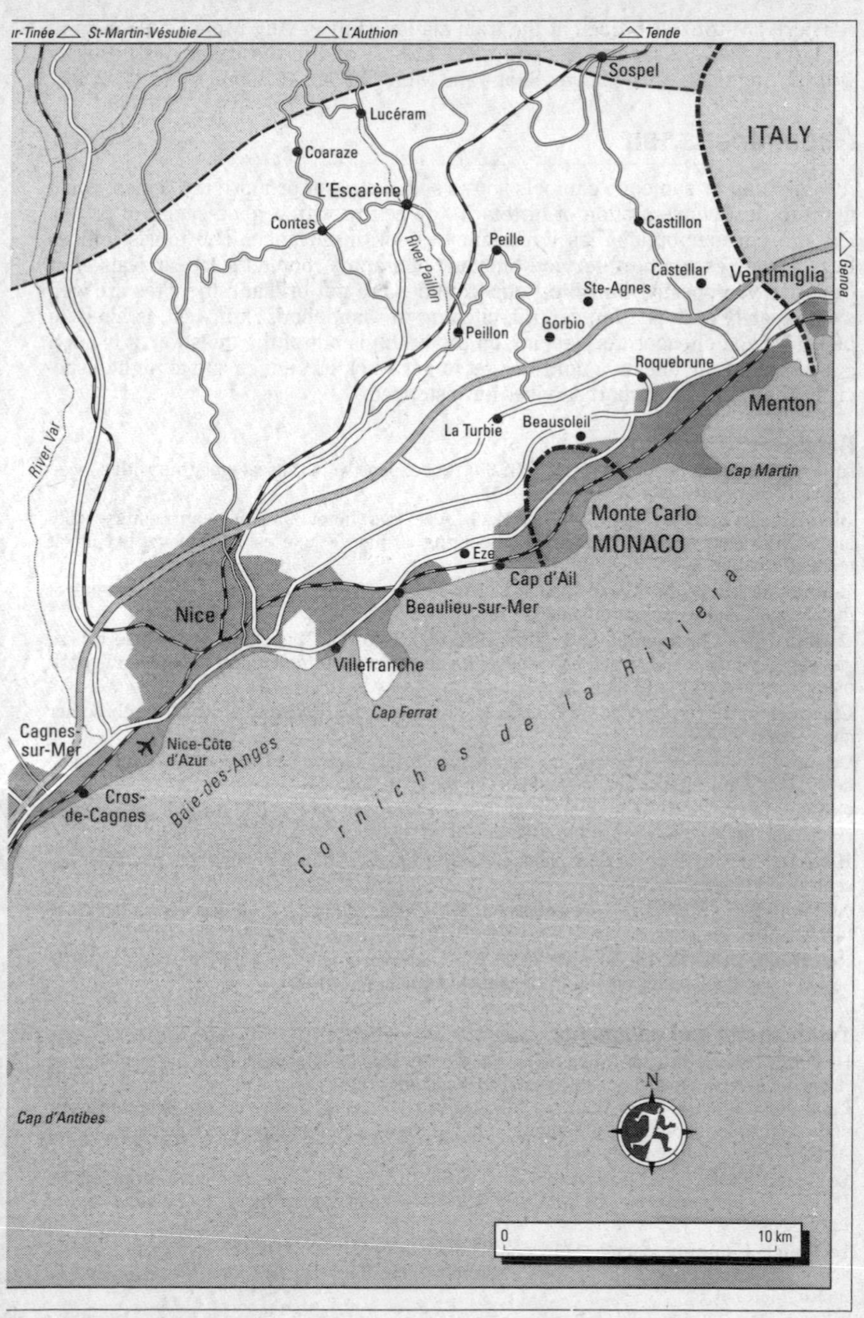
St-Martin-Vésubie
L'Authion
Tende
Sospel
ITALY
Lucéram
Coaraze
L'Escarène
Contes
Castillon
Peille
River Paillon
Castellar
Ventimiglia
Genoa
Ste-Agnes
Gorbio
Peillon
Roquebrune
Menton
La Turbie
Beausoleil
River Var
Cap Martin
Monte Carlo
MONACO
Eze
Cap d'Ail
Beaulieu-sur-Mer
Nice
Villefranche
Cap Ferrat
Corniches de la Riviera
Cagnes-sur-Mer
Nice-Côte d'Azur
Baie-des-Anges
Cros-de-Cagnes
Cap d'Antibes
N
0
10 km

There are **tourist offices** at the train station (July & Aug Mon–Fri 9am–7pm; Sept–June 9am–12.30pm & 2–6pm; ☎93.99.19.77) and in the Palais des Festivals (July & Aug daily 9am–7.30pm; Sept–June Mon–Sat 9am–6.30pm; ☎93.39.24.53).

Accommodation

If something or someone compels you to spend a night or more in Cannes, you'll find the best concentration of **hotels** in the centre with a good range of prices. For the cheaper options it's important to book in advance. The tourist offices have a free **reservation service** but can't guarantee rooms for late arrivals or at the price you specify. **Camping** opportunities are not brilliant: the sites are well over capacity and far from central; pitching in Mandelieu, 7km west, is likely to be easier and cheaper. As sleeping on the beach is out of the question, it is not a good idea for anyone on a tight budget to get stuck in Cannes late at night, especially after public transport services have stopped.

Hotels

Alnea, 20 rue Jean-de-Riouffe (☎93.39.39.90). Not expensive in this category but with service and style that puts it in a class above. ④–⑤

Bleu Rivage, 61 La Croisette (☎93.94.24.25). A seafront hotel in a nineteenth-century building with its own stretch of beach, neighbouring all the de luxe establishments but much more affordable. ⑤–⑦

Bourgogne, 13 rue du 24-Août (☎93.38.36.73). Neither friendly nor very appealing but one of the cheapest and very central. Jan–Nov. ③

Carlton Inter-Continental, 58 La Croisette (☎93.06.40.06). This is the palace-hotel where you stay if you're a Hollywood big-timer or if you've just won the lottery. Rooms at the back in low season start from 1220F. ⑧

Chanteclair, 12 rue Forville (☎93.39.68.88). By the *Vieille Ville* and a cut above the other cheapies. ③

Cristal, 13 rond-point Duboys-d'Angers (☎93.39.45.45). Just off La Croisette but with palatial decor. Panoramic restaurant, bar and pool on the sixth floor. ⑥–⑧

Cybelle, 14 rue du 24-Août (☎93.38.31.33). Only 10 rooms and well known for its excellent restaurant. ③

Hôtel le Florian, 8 rue du Commandant-André (☎93.39.24.82). Without much character but central and reasonable. ③

National, 8 rue Maréchal-Joffre (☎93.39.91.92). Clean, adequate, a bit depressing but close to the station. ③

Ruc Hôtel, 15 bd de Strasbourg (☎93.38.30.61). Away from the central hubbub to the north-east of town. Pool, tennis court and elegant old furnishings. ④–⑧

Youth hostel and campsites

HI youth hostel, 35 av de Vallauris (☎93.99.26.79). Five minutes walk from the train station; rooms for 4–6 people and not cheap at 75–80F a night.

Camping Bellevue, 67 av Maurice-Chevalier (☎93.47.28.97). Three-star site 3km northwest of the centre in the suburb of Ranguin; bus #10 from La Bocca, direction Cimitière Annexe Abadie, stop *Le Plateau*. Feb–Oct.

Le Grand Saule, 24 bd Jean Moulin (☎93.90.55.10). Three-star site 2km out of town, off the D9 towards Pérgomas; bus #9 from *gare SNCF*, direction Lamartine, stop *Le Grande Saule*. April–Sept.

Le Ranch Camping, chemin St-Joseph l'Aubarède (☎93.46.00.11). Three-star site 2km out and very close to the highway; bus #1 from *mairie*, direction Les Pins Parasols, stop *Le Ranch*. March–Oct.

The Town

Though the centre of Cannes is neatly defined by the loop of the rail line tunnelled beneath the expressway and the sea, the town's urban sprawl stretches west to **Mandelieu-La-Napoule**, north past **Mougins** and **Mouans-Sartoux** more or less to **Grasse**, and east to **Vallauris** and **Juan-les-Pins**. It incorporates the erstwhile village of **Le Cannet** on the heights just below the highway, a good place to escape to if you find yourself staying longer than a day. If you're just popping into Cannes for a quick look – the most sensible option – the seafront **La Croisette** is the bit to experience. An afternoon's visit could take in **Le Suquet**, the old town to the west of the *Vieux Port*. The **Iles de Lérins** should definitely be seen though as you don't have to embark from Cannes to get to them, there's no reason to come here for that purpose.

The seafront

You'll find nonpaying **beaches** to the west of Le Suquet, along the Plages du Midi and just east of the Palais des Festivals. But the sight to see is **La Croisette**, the long boulevard sweeping along the seafront. In season, the fine sand **beach** below it, cleaned and raked overnight, looks like an industrial production line for parasols with neat rows extending the length of the shore, changing colour with each change of concession. It is possible to find your way down to the beach without paying, but not easy (you can of course walk along it below the rows of sunbeds). The bits of beach plus jetties owned by the deluxe palace-hotels on La Croisette, the *Majestic*, the *Martinez*, the *Carlton Intercontinental* and the *Noga Hilton*, are where you're most likely to spot a face familiar in celluloid or a topless hopeful, especially during the film festival, though you'll be lucky to see further than the sweating backs of the paparazzi buzzing around them.

The buildings behind, which used to form the most famous skyline of bulbous belle époque hotels, now include modern monstrosities, most notably the *Noga Hilton* and the *Hôtel de la Reine* next to the rather beautiful but overshadowed **La Malmaison** at no. 47, which has an excellent palm tree mural on its side wall. This is the home of the city's cultural affairs department, where temporary exhibitions of modern and contemporary art are often staged.

Having watched the Rolls Royces and Ferraris unloading pig-skin luggage in the hotel foyers – or taken a rest on the little blue chairs provided for free on the wide pavement above the beach – you can wander along to the **Vieux Port**. Here you'll find millionaires eating meals served by white-frocked crew on enormous yacht decks, feigning oblivion of landborn spectators a crumb's flick away. As an alternative to watching langoustines disappear down overfed mouths, you can buy your own food in the Forville **covered market** two blocks behind the *mairie*, or wander through the day's flower shipments on the allées de la Liberté just back from the port.

Le Suquet

The old town is known as **Le Suquet** after the hill on which it stands. Back in the eleventh century it became the property of the Iles de Lérins monks and a **castle** with a high watchtower, built by the *abbé* in 1088, is still there as evidence, alongside the white stone twelfth-century Romanesque **Chapelle de Ste-Anne**. After several centuries in which a small town took root around the religious settlement, a dispute arose between the monks and the townsfolk who wanted their own

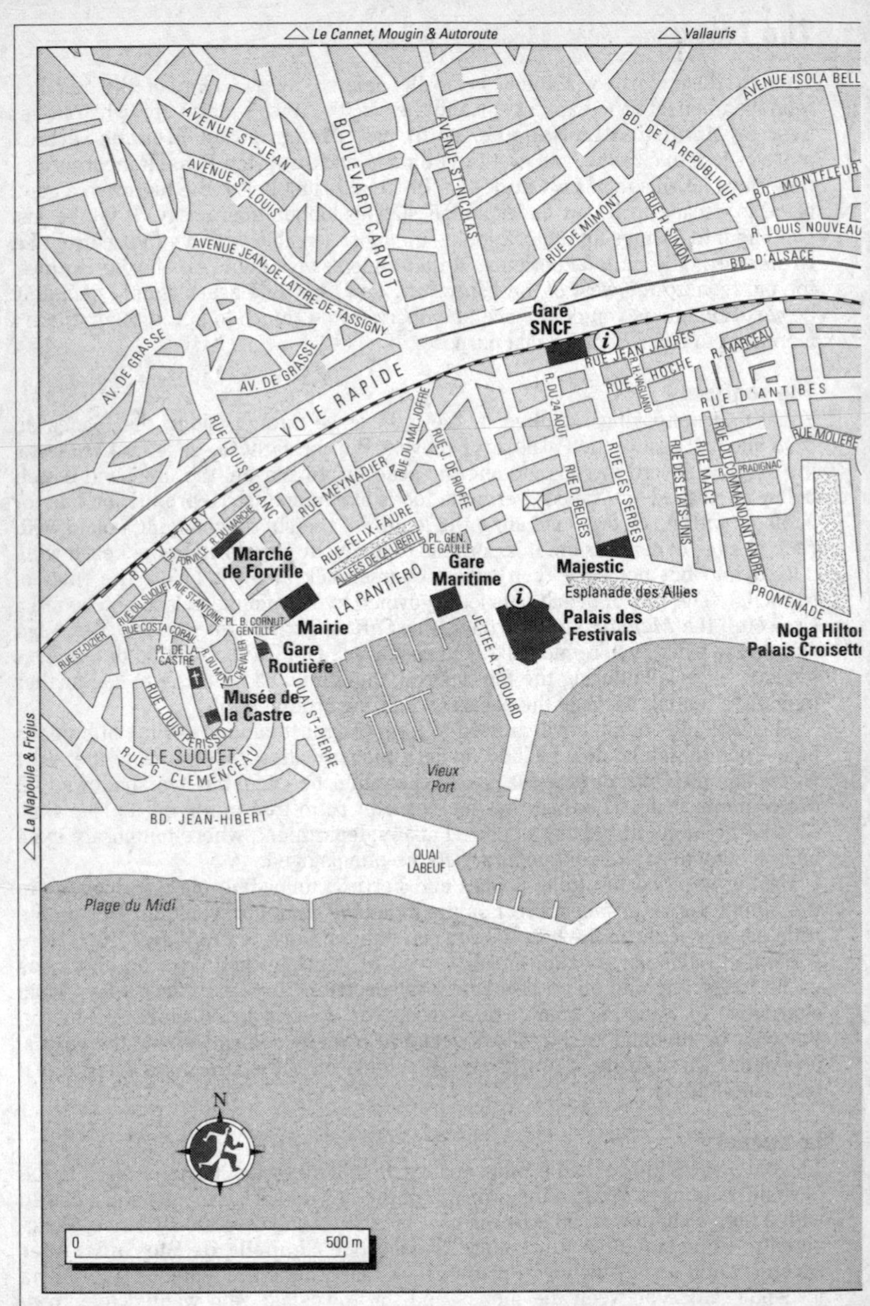

Le Cannet, Mougin & Autoroute
Vallauris
La Napoule & Fréjus
AVENUE ISOLA BELL
BD. DE LA REPUBLIQUE
BD. MONTFLEURY
R. LOUIS NOUVEAU
BD. D'ALSACE
AVENUE ST-JEAN
AVENUE ST-LOUIS
BOULEVARD CARNOT
AVENUE ST-NICOLAS
RUE DE MIMONT
RUE H. SIMON
AVENUE JEAN-DE-LATTRE-DE-TASSIGNY
AV. DE GRASSE
AV. DE GRASSE
VOIE RAPIDE
Gare SNCF
RUE JEAN JAURES
R. MARCEAU
RUE HOCHE
R. H. VAGLIANO
RUE D'ANTIBES
R. DU 24 AOUT
RUE MOLIERE
RUE LOUIS BLANC
RUE DU MAL JOFFRE
RUE J. DE RIOUFFE
RUE MEYNADIER
RUE FELIX-FAURE
ALLEES DE LA LIBERTE
PL. GEN. DE GAULLE
RUE D. BELGES
RUE DES SERBES
RUE DES ETATS-UNIS
RUE MACE
RUE DU COMMANDANT ANDRE
PRADIGNAC
BD. V. TUBY
R. DU MARCHE
R. FORVILLE
Marché de Forville
LA PANTIERO
Gare Maritime
Majestic
Esplanade des Allies
Palais des Festivals
PROMENADE
Noga Hilton
Palais Croisette
RUE DU SUQUET
RUE ST-ANTOINE
RUE COSTA CORAIL
PL. B. CORNUT GENTILLE
Mairie
RUE ST-DIZIER
PL. DE LA CASTRE
R. DU MONT CHEVALIER
Gare Routière
JETTEE A. EDOUARD
Musée de la Castre
QUAI ST-PIERRE
RUE LOUIS PERISSOL
LE SUQUET
RUE G. CLEMENCEAU
Vieux Port
BD. JEAN-HIBERT
QUAI LABEUF
Plage du Midi
N
0
500 m

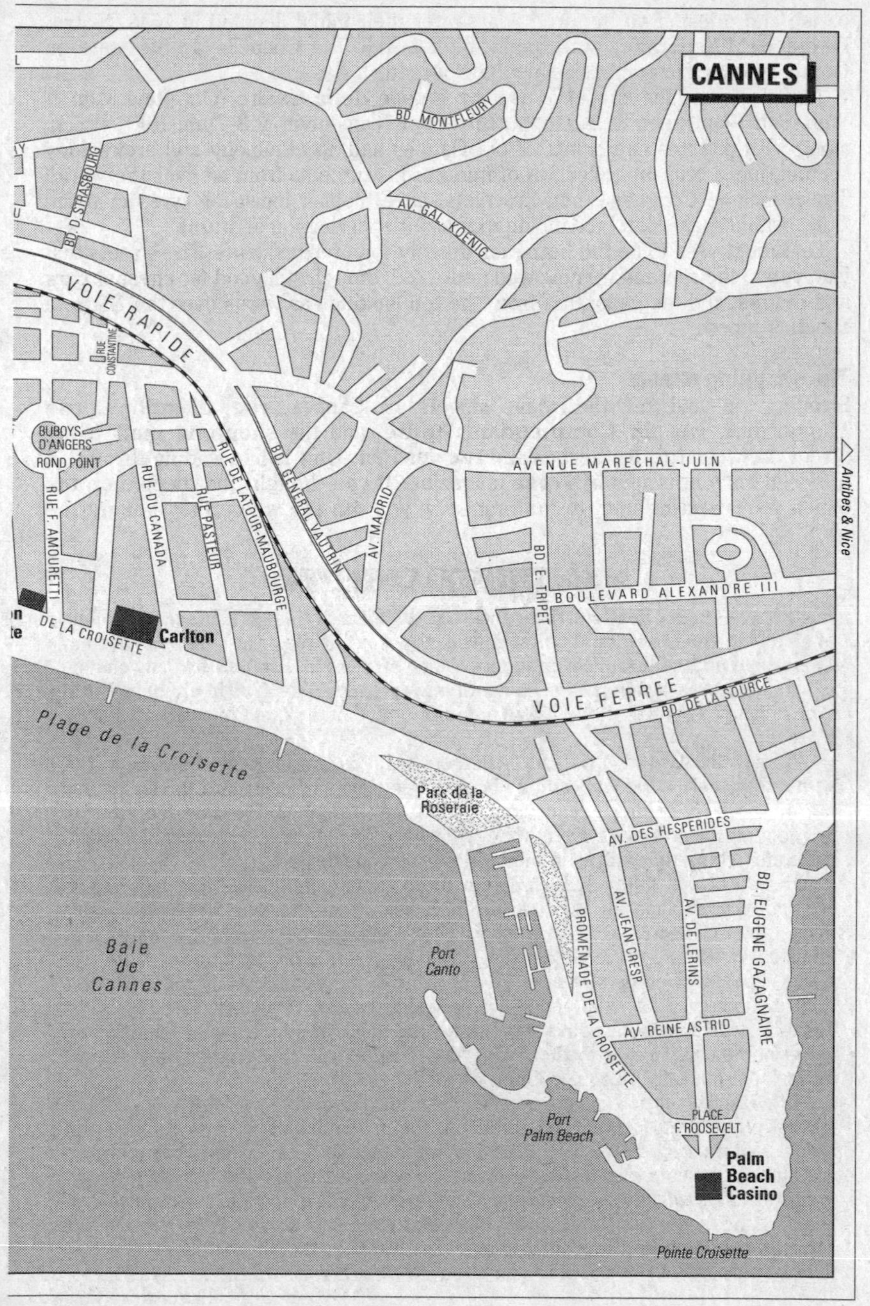

CANNES
BD. MONTFLEURY
BD. D. STRASBOURG
AV. GAL. KOENIG
VOIE RAPIDE
RUE CONSTANTINE
BUBOYS D'ANGERS
ROND POINT
RUE F. AMOURETTI
RUE DU CANADA
RUE PASTEUR
RUE DE LATOUR-MAUBOURGE
BD. GENERAL VAUTRIN
AV. MADRID
AVENUE MARECHAL-JUIN
BD. E. TRIPET
BOULEVARD ALEXANDRE III
Antibes & Nice
DE LA CROISETTE
Carlton
VOIE FERREE
BD. DE LA SOURCE
Plage de la Croisette
Parc de la Roseraie
AV. DES HESPERIDES
BD. EUGENE GAZAGNAIRE
AV. JEAN CRESP
AV. DE LERINS
PROMENADE DE LA CROISETTE
Baie de Cannes
Port Canto
AV. REINE ASTRID
Port Palm Beach
PLACE F. ROOSEVELT
Palm Beach Casino
Pointe Croisette

parish and priest. Two hundred years after their initial demand in 1648, **Notre-Dame de l'Espérance** was finally built beside the Chapelle de Ste-Anne, in Gothic style as if to emphasize just how overdue it was.

The castle and the chapel house the **Musée de la Castre** (Oct–June Mon & Wed–Sun 10am–noon & 2–5/6pm; July–Sept 10am–noon & 3–7pm; 10F), which, along with pictures and prints of old Cannes and an ethnology and archeology section, has a brilliant collection of musical instruments from all over the world. These include Congolese bell bracelets, an Ethiopian ten-string lyre, an Asian "lute" with a snake-skin box and an extraordinary selection of drums.

Le Suquet used to be the home for the city's poorer residents. The streets that lead you to the summit are now well gentrified, though still good for cheaper **eats** and **drinks**, and the panorama from the top looking eastwards over the 12km of beach is superb.

The shopping streets

Strolling on and off the main streets of Cannes, **rue d'Antibes**, **rue Meynardier**, **rue du Commandant André**, and the **shopping mall** "Gray Street" between rue des Serbes and rue des Etats-Unis is like wading through a hundred current issues of *Vogue* magazine. If you thought that people on the beach were wearing next to nothing, now you can see where they bought the

THE FILM FESTIVAL

Each May sees the **Festival International du Film** at Cannes. This most famous of all movie media events was first conceived when the major festival was based at Venice and under Mussolini's influence. Since only pro-fascist films had any chance of winning prizes, an alternative competition was planned for 1939 in Cannes. World War II dictated otherwise and it was not until 1947 that the first Cannes festival took place.

Winning the **Grand Prix** can't compete with Oscars for box-office effect, but within the movie world you can't do better. Some years it seems as if the big names are all too busy talking finance in LA to come to Cannes; the next they are all begging for the accolades. Even if the Hollywood moguls keep their new blockbusters under wraps, they still send minions to wheel and deal.

There are over thirty thousand film professionals, journalists and hangers-on who get accreditation for the festival. In classic French fashion, **credentials** are divided into categories which confer varying access to the screenings and events. Spouses/lovers/escorts/couple-posing friends of someone with credentials can wangle passes given persistence. Ten percent of the **tickets** to the official selections are reserved for local people – they elect the *Prix Populaire*. The *Palais des Festivals* sells tickets for some screenings one week in advance, and hands out a select number of **passes** to those considered to be true cineastes (a student card for an internationally recognized film school is helpful).

Cultivating contacts through food, booze and sex reaches a high pitch as the festival progresses; forged credentials no doubt pass hands for major sums; and casual visitors are left well excluded. However, not all the new films being shown are official entries to the festival, nor are all screened within the heavily guarded *Palais des Festivals*. Every cinema and conference hall in town is a **venue** and at some of these you can buy tickets, but don't expect to do so on the day. As for **programme details**, they blow about La Croisette, are strewn about the café floors, or can be obtained in mint condition from the *Palais*.

sunglasses and swimsuits, the suntan lotion, the jewels, and the collar and the leash for little Fou-Fou.

Note that though walking around town in swimsuits or bikini bottoms used to be the norm in Cannes, there's now a fine of around 80F for "indecent" dress on the streets and anywhere other than the beaches themselves. Cannes being Cannes, the police are entitled to make personal judgements on the offensiveness or otherwise of a person's attire.

Eating, drinking and nightlife

Being glitter city, Cannes **restaurants** tend to stay open late, so getting a meal at 4am is no great problem. There are hundreds of eateries, covering the whole range from 75F fixed menus to 500F blow-outs, and, though quality is patchy, the vigour of the *Forville* **market** means that every chef in town has access to the finest and freshest ingredients. The best areas for less expensive dining are **rue Meynardier, Le Suquet** and **quai St-Pierre** on the *Vieux Port*, with nothing but **brasseries** and **cafés**. Reserving a table is advisable at almost all of the restaurants listed below.

Restaurants

Au Bec Fin, *Hôtel Cybele*, 12 rue du 24-Août (☎93.38.35.86). Traditional cooking with an excellent choice of plats du jour and generous portions. Menus around 100F. Closed Sat evening & Sun.

Le Bouchon d'Objectif, 10 rue de Constantine (☎93.99.21.76). An excellent local bistro serving *aïoli*, monkfish terrine, duck à l'orange and other staple dishes with admirable simplicity. Menus from 85F and very generous helpings on the 125F menu. Closed Sun & mid-Nov to mid-Dec.

La Brouette de Chez Grand-Mère, 9 rue d'Oran (☎93.39.12.10). A single menu (around 200F) that includes an aperitif and as much wine as you want, with filling dishes such as a 5-meat stew, quails in grapes, or Bresse chicken steamed in tarragon for the main course. Closed midday & Sun.

La Croisette, 15 rue du Commandant-André (☎93.39.86.06). Grilled fish is the speciality here, cooked to perfection. If the supplements on some of the fish dishes irritate you, take a look at the *Forville* market to see just how few fish are caught; around 150F. Closed Tues.

La Grande Brasserie, 81 rue d'Antibes (☎93.39.06.26). A good standby for meals and snacks, including gorgeous puddings in classic Art Nouveau brasserie surroundings. Menus from around 110F. Closed Sun.

Le Lion d'Or, 46 bd de la République (☎93.38.56.57). On the north side of the rail tracks with no pretensions to gourmandise but edible and filling home-made food all the same. Menus from 75F. Closed Sat.

Lou Souléou, 16 bd Jean-Hibert (☎93.39.85.55). A fish specialist serving a good range of seafood on very reasonably priced menus in view of the sea west of Le Suquet. Menus from 115F. Closed Mon, Tues & Wed evening out of season.

La Mère-Besson, 13 rue des Frères-Pradignac (☎93.39.59.24). Each day has a different speciality: *estouffade, aïoli* and *lottes niçoises* (tiny fried monkfish) among them. Menu at 130F. Closed Sat midday & Sun.

La Palme d'Or, *Hôtel Martinez*, 73 La Croisette (☎92.98.74.14). Cannes' temple of taste, where you'd celebrate a film festival prize with some of the most exquisite and original food this coast has to offer. A la carte over 500F and a weekday midday menu around 300F; wine included.

La Pizza, 3 quai St-Pierre (☎93.39.22.56). The major pizzeria of the *Vieux Port*. Menus from 120F, but slices of pizza also available – the seafood one is excellent. Open till 4am in season.

Nightlife

As elsewhere along this coast, bouncers pride themselves on their prejudice and lack of humour. The clientele that step off their yachts or out of a festival prize-giving disappear behind closed doors: the more private and unmarked a club is, the more it's raking in. The late-night restaurants can be the most congenial after-dark venues, but there are **bars** and **clubs** where you can get through the evening and still have change from 300F. If you are determined to lose money, choose from **casinos** at the *Palais des Festivals*, the *Carlton Intercontinental* and the *Noga Hilton*.

Blue Bar, 42 La Croisette. Recently reopened; expensive and fashionable place to be seen in.

La Brasserie des Artistes, 48 bd de la République. Disco for young vanities.

Le Blitz, 22 rue Macé. Disco and live pub music with very reasonable rates (open from 9pm). Closed Mon & Tues out of season.

Le Whisky à Go-go, 115 av des Lérins. The disco where everyone beneath the jet set goes to sweat and pound to mind-numbing music. Open from 11pm.

Roxburg Salon, 36 bd de Lorraine. Expensive late-night bar for the *haute* designed crowd.

Le Zanzi-Bar, 85 rue Félix-Faure. An old favourite with Cannois gays; drinks are cheaper before 10pm but the ambience gets better later. Open 5pm–6am.

Listings

Airlines *Air France*, 2 pl du Général-de-Gaulle (☎93.39.39.14).

Banks Most banks on rue d'Antibes have cash dispensers.

Boat terminal *Gare maritime*: Jetée Albert-Edouard (☎93.39.11.82).

Bookshop *Librairie Anglaise*, 11 rue Bivouac-Napoléon (☎93.99.40.08), sells new and secondhand English-language books.

Bus terminals *Gare routière*: for Grasse, Mougins and Vallauris you need the station by the *gare SNCF*; for Juan-les-Pins, Antibes, Nice, La Napoule and St-Raphaël, buses leave from the hôtel de ville.

Car rental *Avis*, 68 La Croisette (☎93.94.15.86); *Budget*, 160 rue d'Antibes (☎93.99.44.04); *Europcar*, 3 rue du Commandant-Vidal (☎93.39.75.20).

Currency exchange *Office Provençal*, 17 av Maréchal-Foch (Mon–Fri 8am–7pm; 9am–noon & 2–7pm out of season).

Emergencies ☎18 or ☎15; *SOS médecins* (☎93.38.39.38); *Hopital des Broussailles*, 13 av des Brousailles (☎93.69.70.00).

Parking Cheap overnight parking between 8pm and 8am beneath Palais des Festivals and *gare SNCF*.

Pharmacy Call ☎93.68.33.33 for the address of 24-hr pharmacy.

Police Commissariat Central de Police, 15 av de Grasse (☎93.39.10.78).

Post office *PTT*, 22 rue Bivouac-Napoléon, Cannes 06400.

Taxis At the *gare SNCF* (☎93.38.30.79), on La Croisette (☎93.38.09.76 or 93.99.52.10 or 93.94.13.39), at Pointe Croisette (☎93.43.41.44), and at the hôtel de ville (☎93.39.60.80).

Iles de Lérins

The **Iles de Lérins** would be lovely anywhere, but a fifteen-minute ferry ride from Cannes, they're not far short of paradise facing purgatory. Known as Lerina or Lero in ancient times, the two islands have powerful historical associations, although very little evidence of the contemporary world.

Getting to the islands

Boats leave from the *gare maritime* in the *Vieux Port* (summer 9 crossings daily 7.30am–4.15pm; winter 5 daily), with the last boats back leaving St-Honorat at 4.45pm and Ste-Marguerite at 5 or 6pm (summer and winter times). You can also reach the islands from **Golfe-Juan** between Cannes and Juan-les-Pins (quai St-Pierre ☎93.63.45.94). **Tickets** are a bit more expensive but car parking by the *gare maritime* is free at Golfe-Juan.

Taking a **picnic** is a good idea as the handful of restaurants and snack outlets on the islands have a lucrative monopoly.

St-Honorat

ST-HONORAT, the smaller southern island, has been owned by monks almost continuously since its namesake and patron founded a monastery here in 410 AD. Honoratus, a Roman noble turned good, is said to have chosen the isle of Lerina because of its reputation for being haunted, full of snakes and scorpions, and lacking any fresh water. Quickly divining a spring and gradually exterminating all the vipers, the saint and his two companions found themselves with precisely the peace and isolation they sought. In time, visitors started to increase in frequency and numbers; the monastic order was established to structure a growing community. By the end of Honoratus's life the Lérins monks had monasteries all over France, held bishoprics in cities such as Arles and Lyon, and were renowned throughout the Catholic world for their contributions to theology. Saint Patrick was one of the products of the Lérins bishops' seminary, training here for seven years before setting out for Ireland.

The present **abbey** buildings are mostly nineteenth century, though some vestiges of the medieval and earlier constructions remain in the church and within the cloisters. Behind them, on the sea's edge, stands an eleventh-century **fortress**, a monastic bolthole that was connected to the original abbey by a tunnel, and used to guard against the threat of invaders, especially the Saracens. Of all the protective forts built along this coast, this is the only one that looks as if it might still serve its original function, but at the same time it shows its age without cosmetic reconstruction or picture postcard ruin. If there is anywhere in Provence that can give a ghostly sense of the Dark and Middle Ages, it is here.

The other buildings on St-Honorat are the churches and chapels that served as retreats. **St-Pierre**, beside the modern monastery, **La Trinité**, on the eastern end of the island, and **St-Sauveur**, west of the harbour, are more or less unchanged. By **St-Cabrais**, on the eastern shore, is a furnace with a chute for making cannonballs, evidence that the monks were not without worldly defensive skills.

Today, the main attractions of this island are peace and silence within the sound of pine leaves stirring and the sea mapping out its minuscule tide. There are no cars or shops or bars or hotels: just cultivated vines, lavender, herbs and olive trees mingled with wild poppies and daisies; and pine and eucalyptus trees shading the paths beside the white rock shore and mixing with the scent of rosemary, thyme and wild honeysuckle.

Ste-Marguerite

STE-MARGUERITE can be a bit of a let-down after St-Honorat. The water is sludgy round the port, the lagoon at the western end is stagnant and the Aleppo pines and evergreen oak woods are so thick that many of the paths are in semi-darkness. It is still beautiful, though, and large enough for vistors to find seclusion. The **Chemin de la Chasse** from the harbour crosses to the southern shore where an arc of rocky inlets provides good bathing points. The **Chemin de la Ceinture** follows the island's edge for about 3km till it reaches the battery on the eastern headland. Returning via the northern shore is not so agreeable, dogged as it is by insistent views of Cannes.

The dominating structure and crowd-puller of the island is the **Fort Ste-Marguerite**, a Richelieu commission which failed to prevent the Spanish occupying both Lérin islands between 1635 and 1637. Later, Vauban rounded it off, presumably for Louis XIV's glory, since the strategic value of enlarging a fort facing the mainland, rather than the sea, is pretty minimal. The main interest in the Fort Ste-Marguerite for the French today is the identification of one cell as having held the **Man in the Iron Mask**, a mythical character given credence by Alexandre Dumas, author of *The Three Musketeers* and *The Count of Monte Cristo*, and by Hollywood. Other cells undoubtedly held the prisoners attributed to them, mostly Huguenots held for refusing to submit to Louis XIV's vicious suppression of Protestantism. Also housed in the fort is the **Musée de la Mer** (both museum and fort: Mon & Wed–Sun 9.30/10.30am–noon & 2pm till the last boat; 10F), containing mostly Roman local finds, and including remnants of a tenth-century Arab ship.

There's free access to the grassy ramparts of this vast construction, where you're likely to find French tourists, having done their sightseeing duty, relaxing with guitars and playing games of *boules* and even cricket.

Le Cannet

The upper part of **Le Cannet** along rue St-Sauveur has the charm of a medieval village, far removed from the city of Cannes just 3km away and spread below you from the *terrasse* of **place Bellevue**. Circled by seven hills, the land originally belonged to the Iles de Lérins monks who summoned 140 families from Genoa to come to cultivate the orange trees. These original "Le Cannois" are commemorated by the mural of portraits and orange trees on place Bellevue. If you approach the *place* from the south (bus stop *place Leclerc*) you'll pass the tiny fifteenth-century **Chapelle de St-Sauveur** (Mon–Fri 9am–noon & 2–5pm, Sat & Sun 10am–12.30pm & 3–6pm; free; key from *mairie* annexe at no. 74), decorated by the contemporary artist Tobiasse and, further up a street, a mural by Peynet of a bride, bridegroom and cherubs floating away to wedded bliss.

Below place Bellevue, on bd Sadi-Carnot is the stridently Côte d'Azurian *belle époque* **Hôtel de Ville**, with more fancy turn-of-the-century villas down rue Cavasse opposite, which leads to an open-air theatre and a children's library, decorated with yet more murals. To the east is another ancient little chapel, the **Espace Bonnard**, named after the painter who spent his last years here, which hosts temporary art exhibitions (winter 2–6pm; summer 3–7pm). Le Cannet's streets are wonderfully sleepy and relaxed, particularly between rue de Cannes, with its proud medieval tower, and the old **quartier Ste-Cathérine** over to the west around the sixteenth-century **Eglise Ste-Catherine** and **Chapelle St-Bernardin**. You can even hear birds singing in the gardens, and though it may not feel exclusive, this is an understandably desirable part of the Cannes conglomeration to live.

Practicalities

Le Cannet is easily reached from the centre of Cannes on **bus** #4 from the *gare SNCF* or bus #5 from the *mairie*, both of which will drop you off at the muralled *Hôtel-de-Ville* stop or at *place Leclerc*. There's a **tourist office** annexe on bd Carnot just above the start of rue St-Sauveur (open Mon–Fri 10am–noon), much more accessible than the main office south of the centre on place de Benidorm.

For **dining**, Le Cannet has an excellent Caribbean restaurant, *Le Pezou*, 346 rue St-Sauveur (closed Wed, & Sun evening out of season; ☎93.69.32.50), with menus from 80F, and a *pâtisserie-salon-de-thé, La Minaudière*, 25 bd Carnot, which does a wicked *tarte au citron*. *La Wapiti* **bar** on rue St-Sauveur above place Bellevue is a nicely ordinary café with a lovely painting of the street inside.

Vallauris, Mougins and Mouans-Sartoux

Within easy reach of Cannes, **Vallauris** 4km to the northeast (with a direct bus from Cannes' *gare SNCF*), is famous for **pottery** and has some striking works by **Picasso**. **Mougins** and **Mouans-Sartoux**, both to the north, are also of note: the former has exclusive and expensive village life plus a **car museum**, while the latter hosts important **contemporary art** exhibitions in its château.

Vallauris

It was in 1946, when **Picasso** was installed in the castle at Antibes, that he met some of the few remaining potters of **VALLAURIS**. The town's association with this craft goes back to Roman times, but it was in the early sixteenth century, after the Plague had decimated the population, that **pottery** became its major industry. The bishop of Grasse rebuilt the village from its infested ruins and settled Genoese potters to exploit the clay soil and the fuel from the surrounding forests. By the end of World War II, however, aluminium was the cheap and easy material for pots and plates, and redundancy was setting in.

Picasso was invited to Vallauris by the owner of a ceramics studio, Georges Ramié. The mega-man of twentieth-century art, who turned his hand to every visual medium, got hooked on clay and spent the next two years working at Ramié's **Madoura workshop**. The result, apart from adding pages to the catalogue of the Picasso *oeuvre*, was a rekindling of the age-old industry of this little town in the hills above Golfe-Juan. Today the main street, av Georges-Clemenceau, sells nothing but pottery, much of it the garishly glazed bowls and figurines that could feature in souvenir shops anywhere. The *Madoura* pottery is on av des Anciens Combattants d'AFN, to the right as you come down av Clemenceau, and still has sole rights on reproducing Picasso's designs, for sale, at a price, in the shop (Mon–Fri only).

A bronze **Man with a Sheep**, Picasso's gift to the town, stands in the main square and market-place, place de la Libération, beside the church and castle. The municipality had some misgivings about the sculpture but decided that the possible affront to their conservative tastes was outweighed by the benefits to tourism of Picasso's international reputation. In the end they need not have worried; the statue looks quite simply like a shepherd boy and sheep.

The local authorities then offered him the task of decorating the early medieval deconsecrated **chapel in the castle courtyard** (July & Aug Mon & Wed–Sun 10am–12.30pm & 2–6.30pm; Sept–June 10am–noon & 2–6pm; 13F), which he finally did in 1952. The space is tiny and, with the painted panels covering the vault, has the architectural simplicity of an air-raid shelter. Picasso's subject is *La Guerre et la Paix* (War and Peace). At first glance it's easy to be unimpressed (as many critics still are) – it looks mucky and slapdash with paint runs on the unyielding plywood surfaces. Stay a while, however, and the passion of this violently drawn pacifism slowly emerges. On the War panel a music score is trampled by hooves and about to be engulfed in flames; a fighter's lance tenuously holds the scales of justice and a shield that bears the outline of a dove; from a deathly chariot escape contagious, disintegrating microbes or bits of skeletons. Peace is represented by Pegasus the winged horse of poetry; people dancing and suckling babies; trees bearing fruit; owls; books – and the freedom of the spirit to mix up images and concepts with innocent mischief.

The **ticket** for the chapel also gives admission to the **Musée Municipal** (same hours) in the castle, which for some years has exhibited many of the ceramics Picasso made at the *Madoura* and a collection of paintings by Alberto Magnelli.

Picasso and pottery apart, not much happens in Vallauris.

Practicalities

Buses for Cannes and Golfe-Juan *gare SNCF* arrive and depart by the castle on place de la Libération. If you need any information, the **tourist office** is at the bottom of av Clemenceau on place du 8 mai 1945 (Mon–Sat 9am–noon & 2–5/6pm; ☎93.63.82.58). You can **eat** for very little at *La Grupi*, 47 av Clemenceau, and very well at *La Gousse d'Ail*, 11 av de Grasse (closed Tues, & Wed evening out of season; ☎93.64.10.71; menus from 105F).

Mougins

Those who live in **MOUGINS** are not going to let any quick-buck entrepreneur come and sully their exquisitely tasteful setting. House painters, tile-makers, French polishers, orchid specialists, other skilled artisans, and even the new expressway passing in close proximity, yes, but not *fast foude* merchants or souvenir vendors. They occasionally have to suffer the embarrassment of press interest in some of the residents of the luxurious villas that surround the village – the exiled dictator of Haiti, Baby Doc, for example, who finally fled his creditors after running up astronomical phone, jewellery and nightclub bills. But on the whole, people with homes here can be relied upon to be connoisseurs of discretion and good taste.

There's an excellent **photography museum** (July & Aug daily 2–11pm; Sept–June Wed–Sun 1–7pm; 20F), just beyond the Porte Sarrasin, with changing exhibitions every two months. It has its own small collection, among which are pictures of Jacques Lartigue (who lived in the neighbouring village of Opio) and rather too many portraits of Picasso. The old wash house, **La Lavoir** (March–Oct), at the top end of the village on av Charles Mallet, forms another exhibition space for the visual arts, its wide basin of water playing reflecting games with the images and the light, and the **Musée Municipal** (July & Aug daily 10am–noon & 2–6pm; Sept–June Mon–Fri 10am–noon & 2–6pm) on place de la Mairie holds very classy exhibitions of art and design.

Practicalities

The frequent Cannes–Grasse buses stop at Maugins (20min). If price is no object then you should **stay** at *Les Muscadins*, 18 bd Courteline, the last word in relaxed luxury (⑧). A less extravagant choice of hotel would be *Les Liserons de Mougins*, 608 av St-Martin (☎93.75.50.31; ④).

Mougins has some very fine **restaurants**, none of them cheap. The best is *Les Muscadins* (closed Tues out of season; ☎93.90.00.43; midday weekday menu under 120F, otherwise from 170F) which needs booking well in advance. Less grand is the congenial *Bistrot de Mougins* on place du Village (closed Wed; ☎93.75.78.34; menus from 125F) serving Provençal specialities, and *Le Zinc*, the bistro annexe to *Le Relais à Mougins*, place de la Mairie (☎93.90.03.47), where you can get plats du jour for under 70F. *Le Feu Follet*, on place de la Mairie (Tues–Sun; ☎93.90.15.78; menus from 150F), and *L'Estaminet des Ramparts*, 24 rue Honoré-Henri (closed Mon evening & Tues; ☎93.90.05.36; menus from 125F), are both dependable with pleasant atmospheres.

The Musée de l'Automobiliste

Between Mougins and Cannes, just by the D3's slip-road onto the highway, is a museum that will delight even those who don't share the passion of its subject, the **Musée de l'Automobiliste** (daily 10am–6/7pm; 40F). No expense has been spared on this indulgent dedication to the motorcar and its two-wheeled relations. Sculptures made of shiny tangled exhaust pipes line the pathway to the hangar-like exhibition space. Inside, entire scenes bigger than an average stage set portray a kitchen in the 1950s – a motorbike in its mass design context – and a creepily realistic Mercedes and Bugatti garage of 1939. There are glamour cars – a 1933 Hispano-Suiza; toy cars; German army vehicles; record-breaking racing cars; a simulation of the traffic control room for the Nice–Menton *autoroute*; bizarre prototypes; and films of classic races.

If you can't wait to put your foot down on a throttle after this, the **Buggy Cross à Mougins** (July & Aug daily till dusk; Sept–June Sat & Sun till dusk), opposite the museum, has a racing track and small but whippy go-carts. If you disapprove entirely of internal combustion engines, they have horses too.

Mouans-Sartoux

The build-up along the Cannes–Grasse road is such that it's easy to miss **MOUANS-SARTOUX** altogether. The old village lies to the west of the main road and is designed on a grid pattern (accessible on the Grasse bus from Cannes; 30min), with the residential streets running north to south and the commercial streets east to a high wall at the west end, all to protect the good citizens from the Mistral wind.

The **Centre Culturel** has one of the biggest collections of literature in the Provençal language, but the main focus for a visit is the **château**, rebuilt to its medieval design in the nineteenth century. The château is one of twenty provincial venues in France chosen by the Socialist former minister for culture, Jack Lang, to be a centre for modern and contemporary art. Since the municipality already had a collection of Concrete art, it was decided to concentrate on this rationalist form of art defined by Théo Van Doesburg as "concrete rather than abstract because nothing is more real than a line, a colour or a surface". **L'Espace de l'Art Concret** (June–Sept Mon & Wed–Sun 11am–7pm; Oct–May Thurs–Sun 11am–6pm), the name of the château's beautiful space of white galleries, stages three exhibitions a year. The staff are very keen to welcome visitors and to help them appreciate the art on show: you can get a personal guided tour just by asking.

Grasse

From a distance it did not make a particularly grand impression. There was no mighty cathedral towering above the houses, just a little stump of a church steeple, no commanding fortress, no magnificent edifice of note. The walls appeared anything but defiant . . . It was as if the place had been overrun and then retaken so often that it was weary of offering serious resistance to any future intruders – not out of weakness, but out of indolence, or maybe even out of a sense of its own strength. It looked as if it had no need to flaunt itself. It reigned above the fragrant basin at its feet, and that seemed to suffice.

So eighteenth-century **GRASSE** appears to Grenouille, the murderous scent-gifted monster of Patrick Süskind's novel, *Perfume*. Grasse then was the capital of the perfume industry, as it still is today. These days it most surely flaunts itself, promoting its perfumed image and medieval heart, its site with an uninterrupted view of the sea, and its environment of acres of scented flowers.

Making **perfumes** is usually presented as a mysterious process, an alchemy, turning the soul of the flower into a liquid of luxury and desire. The reality, including traditional methods of *macération* – mixing the blossoms with heated animal fat – and *enfleuration* – placing the flowers on cold oil, then washing the result with alcohol and finally distilling it into the ultimately refined essence – are far more vividly described in *Perfume* than in the perfume factories in Grasse. Since the 1920s synthetic ingredients have been added to the perfumeries' repertoire but locally grown jasmine and roses are still used, with the industry preferring to keep quiet about modern innovations and techniques.

Arrival, information and accommodation

Grasse's **gare routière** is to the north of the *Vieille Ville* at the *Parking Notre-Dames-des-Fleurs*. Head downhill on av Thiers becoming bd du Jeu de Ballon and you'll find the old casino on cours Honoré-Cresp, now converted into a Palais des Congrès which houses the **tourist office** (July & Aug daily 9am–7pm; Sept–June Mon–Sat 9am–noon & 2–6pm; ☎93.36.66.66).

Two possible **hotels** at the cheaper end of the market are: *Napoléon,* 6 av Thiers (☎93.36.05.87; ③), close to the *gare routière* and *Pension Michèle,* 6 rue du Palais-de-Justice (half-board obligatory; ☎93.36.06.37; ②), right in the centre of the old town. More expensively, the *Panorama* on place du Cours (☎93.36.80.80; ⑥) offers rooms with a view and all mod cons. Even more comfortable, if less well located, is the *Hôtel du Patti*, place du Patti (☎93.36.01.00; ⑤), which has two rooms designed for **wheelchair users**.

The Vieille Ville

Vieux Grasse, despite its touristy shops and full range of restaurants, is surprisingly humble, a working-class enclave where lines of washing festoon the high,

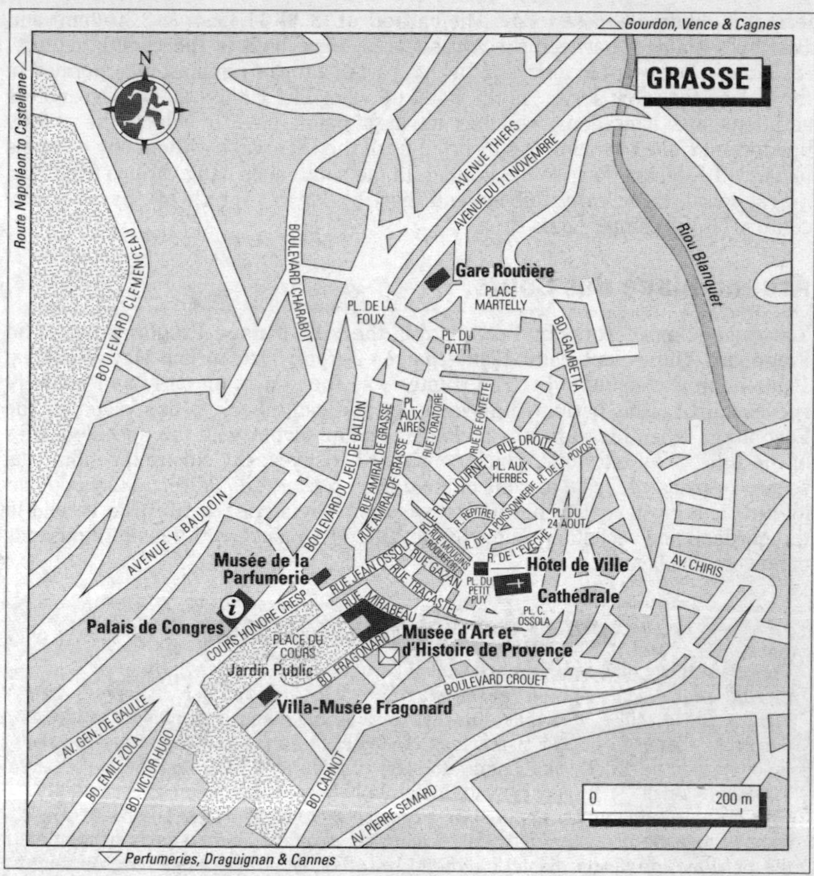

narrow streets. The mansions of sixteenth-century tanning merchants, seventeenth-century perfumed glove manufacturers and eighteenth-century *parfumiers* have been turned into museums and municipal offices or divided into apartments. The inhabitants say it's like a village where everyone knows each other, and out of season that is certainly the atmosphere that prevails. The rich all live in **Mougins**, **Cabris** and the surrounding countryside that gets progressively less rural every year. Even when Grasse was part of the aristocratic tourist boom of the late nineteenth century, the desirable addresses, Queen Victoria's among them, were all east of the *Vieille Ville*.

Place des Aires, at the top of the *Vieille Ville*, is the main meeting point for all and sundry and the venue for the **daily flower and vegetable market**. It is ringed by arcades of different heights with an elegant wrought-iron balcony on the Hôtel Isnard at no. 33, and at one time was the exclusive preserve of the tanning industry.

Spiritual power was concentrated at the opposite end of Vieux Grasse, around place du Petit-Puy and place du 24 Août, one of the most dark and deserted quarters of night-time Grasse today. The **cathedral** (8.30–11.45am & 2.30–6pm) and **Bishop's Palace**, between the two squares, were built in the twelfth century, replacing a 200-year-old fortress of which part of a tower remains, incorporated in the palace that now serves as the hôtel de ville. The cathedral, despite endless additions and alterations, still has its high gaunt nave in which the starkly unadorned ribbed vaulting is supported from the side walls without any columns to carry the design down to the ground. In the south aisle hang various paintings, a Fragonard, three early Rubens and, best by far, a triptych by the sixteenth-century Niçois painter Louis Bréa.

Around place des Cours

You can see more works by Fragonard in the **Villa-Musée Fragonard** at 23 bd Fragonard (June–Sept daily 10am–1pm & 2–7pm; Oct & Jan–May Wed–Sun 10am–noon & 2–5pm; 10F). The painter was the son of an early and not very successful Grassois perfumed glove-maker and came back to this villa after the Revolution, when his work was no longer finding favour with the new ideologies of the time. Why his work, which consists of wishy-washy coloured sentimental scenes to please delicate patrons of the *ancien régime,* should retain any popularity now is a mystery. During the last week of May a **rose exhibition** is held in the gardens and reception rooms of the Villa Fragonard, with tens of thousands of flowers displayed.

THE PERFUME FACTORIES

There are thirty major **parfumeries** in and around Grasse, most of them producing the different essences-plus-formulas which are then sold to Dior, Lancôme, Estée Lauder and the like, who make up their own brand-name perfumes. One litre of pure rose essence can cost as much as 125,000F. Perfume contains twenty percent essence (eau de toilette and eau de Cologne considerably less) and the bottles are extremely small. The major cost to this multi-billion pound business is marketing, with over £10 million a year spent on advertising alone. The grand Parisian couturiers, whose clothes, on strictly cost-accounting grounds, serve simply to promote the perfume, go to inordinate lengths to sell their latest fragrance. As you might imagine, however, the rates paid to those who pick the raw materials, mostly in the Third World, are notoriously low.

A good place to get an overview, and a fairly close-up look at the production, is the **Parfumerie Fragonard** (summer daily 9am–6.30pm; winter Mon–Sat 9am–12.30pm & 2–6pm; free), actually two venues, one in the centre of town at 20 bd Fragonard and the other 3km towards Cannes at Les Quatre Chemins. The first shows traditional methods of extracting essence and has a collection of bejewelled *flagons* through the ages. The one outside town is more informative and does admit to modernization of the processes. A map of the world shows the origins of all the various and strange ingredients: resins, roots, moss, beans and bark join civet (extract of cat genitals) and ambergris (intestine goo from whales), bits of beaver and musk from Tibetan goats in the array of scents the "nose" – as the creator of the perfume's formula is known – has to play with.

Other parfumeries to tour include *Galimard*, 73 rte de Cannes (summer daily 9am–6.30pm; winter daily 9am–12.30pm & 2–6pm; free), and *Molinard* at 60 bd Victor-Hugo (summer daily 9am–6.30pm; winter Mon–Sat 9am–12.30pm & 2–6pm; free). All have shops and give frequent tours in French and English.

Another museum to quickly flit through is the **Musée d'Art et d'Histoire de Provence**, 2 rue Mirabeau (June–Sept daily 10am–1pm & 2–7pm; Oct & Jan–May Wed–Sun 10am–noon & 2–5pm; 10F), set in a luxurious town house commissioned by Mirabeau's sister for her social entertainment duties. As well as all the gorgeous fittings and the original eighteenth-century kitchen, the historical collection adds a nice eclectic touch. It includes wonderful eighteenth- to nineteenth-century faïence from Apt and Le Castellet, Mirabeau's death mask, a tin bidet, six prehistoric bronze leg bracelets; costumes, *santons* and oil presses.

Also in this part of town is the **Musée International de la Parfumerie**, 8 place du Cours (Oct & Jan–May Wed–Sun 10am–noon & 2–5pm; June–Sept daily 10am–7pm; 15F), whose main display is lots of perfume bottles from the Romans to the present via Marie-Antoinette. There's also a greenhouse full of roses, jasmine and vanilla and you can take a test on recognizing perfumes.

If you're around on a Friday, more relaxed flower-smelling can be done at the **Jardin de la Villa de Noailles**, 59 av Guy de Maupassant (Fri 10.30am–2.30pm; 50F) to the west of the town centre: take rue Jeanne-Jugan off av Gal-de-Gaulle, then left down Chemin Noailles, and left again. Camelias, magnolias and peonies are the star attractions here.

Eating and drinking

Bars and **restaurants** in the *Vieille Ville* are good value. *Le Vieux Bistrot*, 5 rue des Moulinets (closed Sun; midday only), serves great, simple food. The *Crêperie Bretonne* (till 11pm; closed Sun), *La Galerie Gourmand* and *Casablanca*, all on rue Fabrières, are good stand-bys and you'll find many more menus to choose from on rue de la Fontette. *Pierre Baltus*, 15 rue de la Fontette (closed Mon, second half Feb & first week March; ☎93.36.32.90; menus from around 100F), is well reputed for its fine cooking based on dependably fresh ingredients. At the *Maison Venturini*, 1 rue Marcel Journet (closed Sun & Mon), you can buy fabulous savoury *fougasses* or sweet *fougassettes*, flavoured with the Grasse speciality of orange blossom. Takeaway pizzas and *socca* won't break the bank at *La Socca*, 1 rue Paul-Goby.

The **bars** on place aux Aires give the most opportunity for encounters with the locals; the spit and sawdust *Bar-Tabac L'Ariel* is a good place to start.

Around Grasse

The countryside around Grasse is pleasant for a day or two, especially if you're driving. To the north is the **Plateau de Calern**, almost deserted save for the British archeologists who arrive every September to map the changing patterns of land use and ownership by the commune of **Cipières**. Running northwest is the **Route Napoléon** and to the northeast, the gorges of the **Loup river** pass the cliff-hanging stronghold of **Gourdon** and the mortality reminders of **Le-Bar-sur-Loup**. To the west, towards the Upper Var, there are good dinners to be had at **Cabris** and musical caves to witness at **St-Cézaire**.

The Route Napoléon: St-Vallier-de-Thiey

Heading north from Grasse you can once again inhale air free from perfume if not from exhaust fumes. The road is the **route Napoléon**, the path taken by the emperor in March 1815 after his escape from Elba, in pursuit of the most audacious recapture of power in French history. In typically French fashion the road was built in the 1930s specifically to commemorate their greatest leader's journey.

Inevitably the route does not follow the imperial boot tracks precisely, going miles off course in some places, but it serves a useful communications purpose. After several kilometres of zigzagging bends you get fantastic views of Grasse, its basin and the coast. At the first village, **ST-VALLIER-DE-THIEY**, 12km from Grasse, you'll find three **campsites**, plus Napoleonic souvenirs, and prehistoric ones in the form of dolmens and tumuli. The **tourist office** on place du Tour (Mon–Fri 9am–noon & 2.30–5.30pm, Sat 10am–noon; ☎93.42.78.00), has walking maps for these sites and the true path taken by Napoléon. The place to **eat** and **stay** is *Le Préjoly* at place Rougière (half-board obligatory in summer; ☎93.42.60.86; menus from around 100F; ③–④).

Beyond St-Vallier, the Route Napoléon heads, almost uninterrupted by settlement, towards **Castellane** (see p.408). Wayside stalls sell honey and perfume; each little hamlet has a petrol station and hotel-restaurant, and every so often you see a commemorative plaque carved with Napoléon's winged eagle.

Cabris

CABRIS, just 6km from Grasse, has all the trappings of a picture postcard village: a ruined château providing panoramas from the Lac de St-Cassien to the Iles de Lérins, sometimes even Corsica, and arty residents for those who no longer find it fashionable to live in Grasse. If you're stopping here the warm and welcoming *Le Petit Prince* **restaurant** at 15 rue Frédéric-Mistral (closed Mon evening & Thurs; ☎93.60.51.40), overlooking the park lined with chestnut trees, is a treat, with a weekday menu of around 100F. The puddings are gorgeous, as is the smoked salmon *mille feuilles* and the wild mushroom dishes. If you want to **stay**, the *chambre d'hôtes* at *L'Ecurie du Château* (☎93.60.56.19; ④) in the courtyard of the old château on place Mirabeau offers large tasteful rooms, decorated with watercolours and has wonderful views.

The Grottes de St-Cézaire and Gouffre des Audides

Just outside St-Cézaire-sur-Siagne (signed off the Cabris road) are the **Grottes de St-Cézaire** (tours: July & Aug daily 10.30am–6.30pm; June & Sept daily 10.30am–noon & 2.30–6pm; mid-Feb to May & Oct daily 2.30–5/5.30pm; Nov to mid-Feb Sun only 2.30–5pm; 25F). The visit to the caves does not involve a very deep descent, and visually it is not a great treat because of the uniform rust-red colour of all the natural sculptures. What is special is the aural experience of the stalagmites and stalactites, with the most iron in them. The guide plays them like a xylophone, with an eerie resonance in this most irregular of acoustic chambers.

At the **Gouffre des Audides** on the road from Cabris to St-Vallier (tours 10am, 11am, 3pm, 4pm & 5pm; July & Aug daily; Sept & June Mon & Wed–Sun; Oct–May Wed–Sun afternoons only; 40F) you descend 60m into caves that were neolithic dwellings. Scenes of prehistoric life have been re-created including stone tools found in the caves.

Along the Gorges de Loup

From Grasse the main approach to the Gorges de Loup is via **LE-BAR-SUR-LOUP**. The little **Eglise de St-Jacques** here contains an altarpiece attributed to Louis Bréa and a fifteenth-century *Danse Macabre* painted on a wooden panel at the west end of the nave. The latter is a tiny but detailed illustration of courtly dancers being picked off by Death's arrows, their souls gathered up by devils, failing Saint Michael's test of blessedness and being thrown into the teethed and tongued mouth of hell. Alongside is a poem, in Provençal, warning of mortality and of the heavy risk involved in committing sins as grievous as dancing.

To cheer yourself up after this, you can follow the **gorges road**, through dark, narrow twists of rock beneath cliffs that look as if they might tumble at any minute, through the sounds of furiously churning water, to corners that appear to have no way out. Alternatively, you could miss out Le-Bar-sur-Loup and take the D3 from **Châteauneuf-Grasse** up along the northern balcony of the *gorges* to **Gourdon**.

Gourdon

Like every *village perché* in striking distance of the coast, **GOURDON** has turned itself into an unofficial theme park. It stinks of perfume even more than Grasse, and is fatally infected with the related commerce. Only the iron-willed can leave without having bought soap, scented oil, crystal glass or an olive-wood figurine.

The village's **château** (June–Sept daily 11am–1pm & 2–7pm; Oct–May Mon & Wed–Sun 2–6pm; 25F) is the one escape, an immaculately restored private residence, containing a historical museum and a collection of naïve paintings. The first houses the better art: a self-portrait by Rembrandt (not always on show) and religious paintings of the early sixteenth century, as well as Saracen helmets made in Damascus, a writing desk used by Marie-Antoinette and letters signed by Henri IV. After this miscellany, the naïve art seems very one-track-minded. In fact the owner of the château has an immense art collection, but for insurance purposes these are the cheapest ones to exhibit permanently. You're allowed out to the terraced garden from where you can enjoy the heights and depths and distance of the view, but not the swimming pool and tennis courts added to the formal pattern.

Antibes, Cap d'Antibes and Juan-les-Pins

Antibes, or rather its promontory the **Cap d'Antibes**, is one of the select places on the Côte d'Azur where the *really* rich and the very, *very* successful still live, or at least have residences. However, even in this world the recession has taken its toll. A château on the Cap whose past residents include the duke of Windsor, Onassis and Niarchos had to drop its price from $50 million to a mere $27 million. Graham Greene, on the other hand, lived the last years of his life in a small apartment in Antibes. Shortly before his death he revealed the simple reason for his choice: to be near the woman he loved. But for the rest it's not so obvious why this area should be so desirable. It is as built up as the rest of the Riviera, with no open countryside separating Golfe Juan, **Juan-les-Pins** and Antibes, nor is Antibes spared the high-rise apartments from the decades scorned by the old Côte aristocrats for allowing ordinary tourists a taste of this coast. The southern end of the Cap, however, still has its woods of pine, in which the most exclusive mansions hide, and with yacht or helicopter access, one could no doubt pretend that little had changed in the last forty years.

For visitors, the Cap offers walks and intermittent access to the wonderful rocky shore as well as one garden that isn't private, the **Jardin Thuret**. Antibes is animated by street upon street of bars and restaurants, has one of the finest **markets** on the coast, and a superb **Picasso collection** in its ancient seafront castle. Juan-les-Pins is pretty low on glamour these days, though there's any number of nightclubs, discos and hotels. But its **jazz festival** is still a treat and the beach more attractive than Antibes'.

Antibes

The centre of **ANTIBES** remains predictably pretty, though very little of its medieval centre is left thanks to border squabbles from the fifteenth century to the Revolution when Antibes belonged to France and Nice to Savoy. Yachts and fishing boats moor in a harbour designed by sixteenth- and seventeenth-century military architects to be under the dependable protection of the vast **Fort Carré**, enlarged by Vauban to an impregnable eight-pointed star of bastions. This is the dominant landmark of Antibes if you approach from Nice and Cagnes. Seventeenth-century ramparts still separate the port from the *Vieille Ville* whose key focus is the solidly rectangular medieval masses of the **Château Grimaldi** and the belfry of the former **cathedral** rising above the sea wall.

Arrival, information and accommodation

The *Vieille Ville* fits in the triangle formed by the coast, the ramparts along bd de l'Aiguillon, and av Robert-Soleau and bd Albert 1er, with the **gare SNCF** (☎93.99.50.50) at the apex, a block back from the head of the port at the junction of av Robert-Soleau and rte du Bord-de-la-Mer. Place du Général-de-Gaulle separates av Robert-Soleau and bd Albert-1er with the **tourist office** at no. 11 (July & Aug Mon–Sat 9am–8pm, Sun 10am–1pm; Easter–June & Sept Mon–Fri 9am–12.30pm & 2–7pm, Sat 9am–noon & 2–6pm, Sun 10am–noon; Oct–Easter Mon–Fri 9am–12.30pm & 2–6.30pm, Sat 9am–noon & 2–6pm; ☎92.90.53.00). The **gare routière** is off the adjoining place Guynemer (☎93.34.37.60) with frequent buses to and from the *gare SNCF*, except on Sundays. Bus #2A goes to Cap d'Antibes; bus #1A and #3A to Juan-les-Pins. **Bikes** can be rented from *Midi Location Service*, Galarie du Port, rue Lacan (☎93.34.48.00) and *Holiday Bikes*, 93 bd Wilson (☎93.61.51.51).

From the *gare routière*, rue de la République leads down through place des Martyrs into the heart of Vieux Antibes around **place Nationale**. Rue Sade links this *place* with **cours Masséna**, the limit of the original Greek settlement and the daily **market-place**. The castle and cathedral lie between cours Masséna and the sea.

Though cheap **hotels** are thin on the ground, there are plenty of rooms to be had in and around Antibes and a **youth hostel** on the Cap. Booking in advance for the summer is recommended. All of Antibes' **campsites** are 3 to 5km north of the city in the quartier de La Brague (bus #10a or one train stop to *Gare de Biot*).

HOTELS

Brasserie Nouvelle, 1 av Niguet (☎93.34.10.07). Close to the *gare routière* and very economical, with just 5 rooms. ②

La Gardiole, 74 chemin de la Garoupe (☎93.61.35.03). Lovely location on a lane in Cap d'Antibes, friendly, quiet and with a terrace overlooking the garden on which to dine. April–Sept. ⑦

Hôtel du Levant, 50 chemin de la Plage (☎92.93.72.99). On Cap d'Antibes with woods behind and the sea in front. Mid-April to Oct. ⑧

Mas Djoliba, 29 av Provence (☎93.34.02.48). Between the *Vieille Ville* and the main beach, with a large garden; very pleasant. ⑥

Le Nouvel Hôtel, 1 av du 24-août (☎93.34.44.07). Not a bad location close to the *gare routière* and the rooms at the top have good views. ③

Le Ponteil, 11 impasse Jean-Mensier (☎93.34.67.92). Quiet location at the end of a cul-de-sac close to the sea. ④

Auberge Provençale, 61 pl Nationale (☎93.34.13.24). Right in the centre of Vieux Antibes and only 7 rooms so book in advance. ⑥

HOSTELS AND CAMPING

Relais International de la Jeunesse, bd de la Garoupe, Cap d'Antibes (☎93.61.34.40). Youth hostel which needs booking well in advance. Open June–Sept; closed 10am–5.30pm; midnight curfew; bus #2a from *gare routière* to *La Bouée* and head north along bd de la Garoupe to junction with av de l'Antiquité.

Logis de La Brague, rte de Nice (☎93.33.54.72). Three-star campsite, the closest to Biot's station. May–Sept.

Idéal-Camping, rte de Nice (☎93.74.27.07). Two-star site south of Biot's station; and close to the sea. March–Oct.

The Town

The most atmospheric and uncrowded approach to the castle and cathedral is from the south through the distinctive **quartier du Safranier**. The place du Safranier and the little residential streets off rue de la Tourraque and rue de l'Esperon, including rue de Lavoir with its old public **wash house**, have a very appealing villagey atmosphere, and commerce is minimal. By turning right on rue de l'Orme (rather than continuing straight into cours Masséna) and left on rue du Bateau, you'll find yourself on place Marie Jol, in front of the **Château Grimaldi**, rebuilt in the sixteenth century but still with its twelfth-century Romanesque tower.

In 1946 Picasso had returned from Paris and was living with Françoise Gilot in an apartment in Juan-les-Pins which had very little space for him to work. He met the director of the museum who suggested he use the castle as a studio. Several extremely prolific months followed before he moved to Vallauris, leaving all his Antibes output to what is now the **Musée Picasso** (June–Sept daily 10am–6pm; Oct–May Tues–Sun 10am–noon & 2–6pm; 20F). Although Picasso donated other works later on, the bulk of the collection belongs to this one period. At this time, the artist was involved in one of his better love relationships; his friend Matisse was just up the road in Vence; the war was over; and the 1950s had not yet arrived to change the Côte d'Azur for ever. There's an uncomplicated exuberance in the numerous still-lifes of sea urchins, the goats and fauns in Cubist nondisguise, and the wonderful *Ulysses et ses Sirènes*, a great round head against a mast around which the ship, sea and sirens swirl. The materials reveal postwar shortages – odd bits of wood and board instead of canvas, and boat paint rather than oils. Picasso is also the subject here of other painters and photographers, including André Villers, Brassai, Man Ray and Bill Brandt. The photo of him holding a sunshade for Françoise Gilot catches the happiness of this period in the artist's life.

By contrast, on the second floor, in Picasso's old studio, the anguished works of Nicholas de Staël, who eventually killed himself, are displayed. He stayed in Antibes for a few months from 1954 to 1955, painting the sea, gulls and boats with great washes of grey. A disturbing red dominates *Le Grand Concert* and purple the *Still Life with Candlestick*. Works by other great twentieth-century artists are included in the museum's **modern art** collection, with thirteen special commissions for the tenth anniversary of Picasso's death. The terrace overlooking the sea is adorned by Germaine Richier sculptures along with works by Miró, César and others, and a violin hommage to Picasso by Arman. The combination of the terrace, the beautifully cool, light space of the galleries with their hexagonal terracotta floor tiles and windows over the sea, make this an exceptional setting for the superb work within it.

Alongside the castle is the **cathedral**, built on the site of an ancient temple. The choir and apse survive from the Romanesque building that served the city in the Middle Ages while the nave and stunning ochre facade are Baroque. Inside, in the south transept, is a sumptious altar-piece by Louis Bréa surrounded by immaculate panels of tiny detailed scenes.

One block inland, the **covered market** on cours Masséna overflows with Provençal goodies including a particularly good line in differently prepared olives, and a profusion of cut **flowers**, the traditional and still flourishing Antibes business (June–Aug daily 6am–1pm; Sept–May Tues–Sun 6am–1pm). On Friday and Sunday (plus Tues & Thurs Easter–Sept) a **craft market** takes over in the afternoon. When the stalls are all packed up, café tables take their place.

There's a museum of local history and traditions in a medieval tower at the southern end of cours Masséna, the **Musée de la Tour** (Wed, Thurs & Sat 3/4–5/7pm; 10F). Though it's not wildly interesting it does have the first ever water skis, invented in Juan-les-Pins in the 1930s.

Further south, beyond the quartier du Safranier, where the coast ramparts end, the Bastion St-André houses the **Musée d'Histoire et d'Archéologie** (Mon–Fri 9am–noon & 2–6pm; closed Nov; 10F), which gathers together the Greek, Roman, medieval and later finds of the region. Modern art is Antibes' strength: alongside the archeological museum, at 24 Promenade Amiral de Grasse, there's a **gallery of contemporary art** with temporary exhibitions. Of the town's **commercial galleries**, *Albert 1er*, 7 bd Albert 1er; *Pams*, 25 cours Masséna; *Fersen*, 27 rue de Fersen; and *Galerie Domus*, at 3 rue Thuret, offer a varied and sometimes outstanding selection of current work.

One Antibes artist who can't compete with Picasso, but who is honoured with his own museum, is **Peynet**, a cartoonist whose most famous creation was the 1940s series of "the lovers", a truly old-fashioned conception of romance which, if you're not careful, may even induce nostalgia. The **Musée Peynet** is on place Nationale (mid-June to mid-Sept Tues–Sun 10am–6pm; mid-Sept to mid-June Tues–Sun 10am–noon & 2–6pm; 20F).

Finally, there's the very pleasant **Heidi's English Bookshop** at 24 rue Aubernon (daily 10am–7pm), just north of cours Masséna, which is the cheapest English-language bookshop on the coast and a meeting place for ex-pats.

Eating and drinking

Place Nationale and cours Masséna are lined with **cafés**; rue James Close has nothing but **restaurants** and rue Thuret and its side streets also offer numerous menus to browse through. If you've missed the market, you'll find excellent **food shops** on rue du Sade, including the *Charcuterie Lorraine* at no. 15.

Auberge Provençale, 61 pl Nationale (☎93.34.13.24). Fish grills and seafood served in the covered garden of this welcoming hotel; one menu under 100F. Closed Mon, Tues midday, mid-April to mid-May & mid-Nov to mid-Dec.

Restaurant de Bacon, bd de Bacon, Cap d'Antibes (☎93.61.50.02). The best restaurant in the region, overlooking Vieux Antibes and serving fabulous fish soups and stews, including a superb *bouillabaisse*. Menus at 250F and 400F. Closed Mon & Nov–Jan.

L'Eléphant Bleu, 28 bd de l'Aiguillon (☎93.34.28.80). Thai and Vietnamese specialities with good vegetarian dishes. Midday weekday menu under 80F, otherwise from 120F. Closed Mon & Tues midday.

La Famiglia, 34 av Thiers (☎93.34.60.82). A cheap family-run outfit serving good pizzas and pasta. Closed Wed.

Il Giardino, 21 rue Thuret. Ace pizzas though you may have a long wait to be served.

La Marmite, 20 rue James-Close, (☎93.34.56.79). One of the best on this street; around 120F. Closed Mon out of season.

Le Marquis, 4 rue Sade (☎93.34.23.00). Traditional Provençal food in a charming setting; midday weekday menu under 100F, otherwise from 130F. Closed Mon & Tues midday.

Chez Olive, 2 bd Maréchal Leclerc (☎93.34.42.32). Provençal specialities, around 150F. Closed Sun evening & Mon out of season.

Café Pimms, cnr of rue de la République and pl Guynemer. Brasserie with carousel decor and friendly atmosphere. Closed Sun.

Café de la Porte du Port, bd de l'Aiguillon by the archway through the ramparts. One of many lively cafés in the rampart arcades; serves good Guinness.

Le Romantic, 5 rue Rostan (☎93.34.59.39). Charming, small restaurant with an excellent 120F menu on which the grilled sardines are delicious. Closed Wed midday & Tues.

Taverne da Cito, in the covered market. Café with a wide selection of beers; *moules marinières, frites* and beer for 65F. Open 3pm–midnight.

Les Vieux Murs, near the castle at av Amiral de Grasse (☎93.34.06.73). Very classy food such as oysters cooked in champagne and a perfect setting on the ramparts. Menu 200F, à la carte from 300F.

Nightlife

Many **cafés** and **bars** stay open late, but if you want to dance at several venues of a night, you'd be better off in Juan-les-Pins (see below).

For post-prandial energetics, the most frequented **nightclub** is *La Siesta*, between Antibes and La Brague on the route du Bord-de-la-Mer. There are seven dance floors with a choice of night-time sky for ceilings and drinks at over 150F a go. At *Sommersby*, a Tex-Mex brasserie at 1 av Maizière next to the Bastion St-André, you can drink beer, watch cable TV, play billiards, and listen to fairly mainstream live rock on Friday and Saturday nights (open till 2am).

Cap d'Antibes

Plage de la Salis, the longest Antibes beach, runs along the eastern neck of **Cap d'Antibes** and is free to anyone who wants to sunbathe on the sand. It's an amazing rarity on the Riviera, with no artificial landscaping and without the rows of big hotels owning mattress exploitation rights. The success of Juan-les-Pins spared this side of the Cap from wild development in the days before all coastal promontories became protected by more stringent planning laws.

A second beach, **Plage de la Garoupe**, equally public and untrammelled, is along bd de la Garoupe before the promontory of Cap Gros. From here a **footpath** follows the shore for quite some way but *propriété privée* prevents it joining up with chemin des Douaniers. To reach the most southern point, the Pointe de l'Ilette, you have to take chemin de la Mosquée from av J-F-Kennedy, passing the superstars' favourite hang-out, the *Hôtel du Cap*. At the end of av J-F-Kennedy is one of the very few public buildings on the Cap, the **Musée Naval et Napoléonien** (Mon–Fri 9.30am–noon & 2.15–6pm, Sat 9.30am–noon; closed Oct; 20F), documenting the great return from Elba (see under "Juan-les-Pins") along with the usual Bonaparte paraphernalia of hats, cockades, and signed commands; and presents models of seventeenth- and eighteenth-century ships. It also allows you frustrating views over the woods of the southern Cap, all parcelled up into large private domains.

Another public building is the **Eglise de la Garoupe**, at the top of chemin du Calvaire above the southern end of plage de la Salis (9.30/10am–noon & 2.30–5/6pm), which is full of ex-votos for deliverances from accidents that range from battles with the Saracens to collisions with speeding Citroëns. It also contains a Russian Byzantine medieval icon and a painting on silk, both spoils from the Crimean War. Next to the church is a viewing platform and an immensely powerful lighthouse whose beam is visible 70km out to sea.

In the middle of the Cap, on bd du Cap between chemins du Tamisier and G-Raymond, is the **Jardin Thuret** (Mon–Fri 8/8.30am–5/6pm; free), established in the mid-nineteenth century by a famous botonist and now belonging to *INRA*, a national research institute which, amongst other things, tests out and acclimatizes subtropical trees and shrubs in order to diversify the Mediterranean plants of France. You can wander around freely; don't expect anything other than Latin names on the labels; but whether you're a botanist, forester or complete amateur, you are sure to be surprised by some of the trees and shrubs growing here.

Walking, or **cycling** between the Jardin Thuret and the Musée Naval along the western side of the cap along bd du Maréchal-Juin, is very pleasant, with rocks and jetties, little sand beaches, high walls around gardens on the inland side of the road, and the tiny **Port de l'Olivette** near the Musée Naval with nothing but small, unflashy boats.

Juan-les-Pins

JUAN-LES-PINS, just 1.5km west of Antibes, is another of those overloaded Côte d'Azur names. It's the legendary summer night-time playground for the most expensively outfitted and consistently photographed celebrities who retreat at dawn, like supernatural creatures, to their well-screened cages on Cap d'Antibes.

Arrival, information and accommodation

Walking from the **gare SNCF** on av de l'Esterel down av Dr Fabre and rue des Postes you reach the carrefour de Nouvelle Orléans, beyond which is La Pinède; by bus from Antibes the most central stops are *Pin Doré* and *Palais des Congrès*. The **tourist office** is at 51 bd Guillaumont on the seafront at the western end of the town (July & Aug Mon–Sat 9am–8pm, Sun 10am–1pm; Easter–June & Sept Mon–Fri 9am–12.30pm & 2–7pm, Sat 9am–noon & 2–6pm, Sun 10am–noon; Oct–Easter Mon–Fri 9am–12.30pm & 2–6.30pm, Sat 9am–noon & 2–6pm; ☎92.90.53.05).

If you haven't booked a **hotel** the two streets to try are av Gallet between av de l'Esterel and the seafront, and av Alexandre III which crosses it. *Hôtel de Noaille*, 17 av Georges-Gallice (☎93.61.11.70; ④), has some cheap rooms and is right by La Pinède; the *Parisiana*, 16 av de l'Esterel (☎93.61.27.03; ③), is close to the station. For more than just the basics, try *Pré-Catalan*, corner of av des Palmiers and av des Lauriers (☎93.61.05.11; ⑤), or the very upmarket and beautiful *Hôtel du Parc*, corner of av Maupassant and av Gallet (☎93.61.61.00; ⑧).

The Town

Beyond the image, Juan-les-Pins has very little in the way of history. Unlike St-Tropez it was not a fishing village, just a pine grove by the sea, which tried to become fashionable in the late nineteenth century with the help of one of Queen Victoria's sons. It had a casino built in 1908, but only took off in the late 1920s as the original summer resort of the Côte d'Azur. Revealing swimsuits, as opposed to swimming "dresses", were reputedly first worn here in the 1930s; its trail-blazing style and attraction for global aristocrats and royals, fashionable writers and dancers, and the star creations of the film world continued unabated through the 1950s and 1960s. Now, like so much of the Côte, it's so overcrowded and over-built that it's impossible to see what all the fuss is about – or to imagine it as a pine forest. But its **jazz festival** is the best in the region.

The main venue for the jazz festival, and what's left of the pine forest is the **Jardin de La Pinède** (known simply as La Pinède) and **Square Gould** above the beach by the casino and divided by bd Edouard-Baudon. The pines are very old and very beautiful but a wood it most certainly is not. This urban park and the 2km of sheltered sand beach are all that Juan-les-Pins has to offer for free, apart from the dizzying array of architectural styles along its streets.

Eating and drinking

La Terrasse overlooking La Pinède on av Gallice (☎93.61.20.37) is one of the **star restaurants** on this coast, and needs booking several weeks in advance. It will set you back at least 400F though there is a midday 250F menu, but the original 1930s decor, the exquisite fish and seafood dishes, mouth-melting desserts and the high culinary art of the whole meal, may make it worth starving several days for. That apart, Juan-les-Pins is not blessed with dependable restaurants, so take pot luck from the countless menus on offer on the boulevards around La Pinède. You can get brasserie food, crêpes, pizzas and similar snacks from street stalls till the early hours, and many shops and bars also keep going in summer till 3 or 4am.

Nightlife

The fads and reputations of the different **discos** in Juan-les-Pins change by the month (and all the starry *boîtes* are members only). In general, however, opening hours are 11pm to dawn and you can count on paying at least 100F for your first drink. Some to try are: *Joy's Club*, 142 bd Président Wilson; *Les Pêcheurs* at Port Gallice and *Voom-Voom*, 1 bd de la Pinède.

Le Pam–Pam, 137 bd Wilson, is the most popular music venue with live Brazilian **bands** (cocktails from 60F), but go early to get a seat. *Le Festival* opposite at 146 bd Wilson also offers Latin American sounds but lacks the cachet of *Le Pam-Pam*. In the basement of the *Beachôtel* on av Alexandre III there's a piano-bar, *Le Madison*, with jazz bands several nights a week; or you can listen to small jazz combos or solists in the much less flashy *Le Jazzman*, on 5 bd de la Pinède.

The Côte d'Azur Festival International de Jazz

The best jazz event on the Côte d'Azur, the **Festival International de Jazz**, takes place during the **last two weeks of July** in the open air of La Pinède and Square Gould. The 35th jazz festival in 1995, celebrating a hundred years of jazz, featured B.B. King, Chuck Berry, Keith Jarrett, Didier Lockwood, the Newport

THE ROUTE NAPOLEON

The pines and silver sand between Juan-les-Pins and Cannes, now **Golfe-Juan,** witnessed Napoléon's famous return from exile in 1815. The emperor knew the bay well, having been in command of the Mediterranean defences as a general in 1794 with Antibes' Fort Carré as his base. This time, however, his emissaries to Cannes and Antibes were taken prisoner upon landing, though the local men in charge decided not to capture him. The lack of enthusiasm for his return was enough to persuade the ever-brilliant tactician to head north, bypassing Grasse, and take the most isolated snowbound mule paths up to Sisteron and onwards – the path commemorated by the modern **Route Napoléon**. By March 6 he was in Dauphiné. On March 19 he was back in the Tuileries Palace in the capital. One hundred days later he lost the battle of Waterloo and was finally and absolutely incarcerated on St Helena.

An anecdote relates that on the day of landing at Golfe-Juan, Napoléon's men accidentally held up the prince of Monaco's coach travelling east along the coast. The Revolution incorporated Monaco into France but the restored Louis XVIII had just granted back the principality. When the prince told the former emperor that he was off to reclaim his throne, Napoléon replied that they were in the same business and waved him on his way.

For **continuations of the Route Napoléon**, see "Grasse", "Sisteron" and "Castellane".

Jazz Festival All Stars, George Benson, Wynton Marsalis and Sonny Rollins. The music is always chosen with serious concern for every kind of jazz, both contemporary and traditional, rather than commercial popularity. Programme details and **tickets** (120–200F) are available from the Maison de Tourisme at 11 place de Gaulle, Antibes (☎92.90.53.00) or 51 bd Guillaumont, Juan-les-Pins (☎92.90.53.05); tickets can also be bought from *FNAC* and *Virgin* shops.

Biot and Sophia-Antipolis

Twenty years ago, the area inland from Antibes above the *autoroute* was still the more-or-less untouched Forêt de la Brague, stretching from Mougins in the west to Biot in the east. Now transnational companies have offices and laboratories linked by wide roads cut through the forest. Biot has become one of the most visited places on the Côte, for its *village perché* charm, its glassworks and its monumental museum to Fernand Léger.

Biot

The village of **BIOT**, above the coast 8km north of Antibes, is extremely beautiful and oozes with art in every form, architectural, sculpted, ceramic, jewelled, painted and culinary. It's inevitably packed out in high season but it's not a place to miss if you can help it.

Arrival, information and accommodation

The **gare SNCF** for Biot is by the sea at La Brague. It's a four-kilometre steep climb to the village, so it's far better to catch one of the Antibes buses (10 daily to Biot). From the bus stop in the village head up Chemin Neuf and you'll find rue St-Sébastien, the main street, running off to your right. The **tourist office** (Mon–

Fri 2.30–6pm, Sat & Sun 10am–noon & 2.30–6pm; ☎93.65.05.85) is on place de la Chapelle at the far end of rue St-Sébastien, and can provide copious lists of art galleries, should you need them.

There's not a lot of **accommodation** in Biot. If you book well in advance you could stay at the very reasonable *Hôtel des Arcades*, 16 place des Arcades (☎93.65.01.04; ⑤), full of old-fashioned charm and with huge rooms in the medieval centre of the village. There are plenty of **campsites** in the vicinity; three to try are the two-star *Le Mistral*, 1780 rte de la Mer (April–Sept; ☎93.65.61.48); the two-star *Typhas*, 144 chemin de la Romaine (☎93.65.10.07); and the four-star *L'Eden*, chemin du Val-de-Pome (May to mid-Sept; ☎93.65.63.70).

The village

Fernand Léger lived in Biot for a few years at the end of his life. A stunning collection of his intensely life-affirming works can be seen at the purpose-built **Musée Fernand Léger**, just southeast of the village (summer Mon & Wed–Sun 10am–noon & 2.30–6.30pm; winter 10am–noon & 2–5pm; 27F). It was the experience of fighting alongside "the entire French populace . . . miners, labourers, artisans who worked in wood or metal", and the sight of "the breechplate of a 75-mm cannon lying in the open sun, the magic of the light on the polished metal" in World War I that turned Léger away from the abstraction of Parisian painters. Not that he favoured realism, but he wanted his paintings to, as he put it, share the toughness and directness of the working class and have a popular appeal. He was vocal on the politics of culture, arguing for museums to be open after working hours; for public spaces to be adorned with art in the way of "incidental background", on which he collaborated often with Le Corbusier; and for making all the arts more accessible to working people.

Few painters have had such consistency and power in their use of space and colour and the ability to change the relations between objects or figures without ever descending to surrealism. Without any realism in the form and facial expressions, the people in such paintings as *Four Bicycle Riders* or the various *Construction Workers* are forcefully present as they engage in their work or leisure, and are visually on an equal footing with the objects. Of the *Construction Workers*, Léger describes seeing a factory being built and men like fleas balancing on the steel beams: "this is what I wanted to depict: the contrast between man and his creations, between the worker and this whole architecture of metal". *Mona Lisa with Keys* speaks of his deep concern about the relationship between works of art and ordinary people.

Léger's art has the capacity for instant pleasure – the pattern of the shapes, the colour, particularly in his ceramic works – though he can also draw it back to harsh horror as with the charcoal black to brown on off-white paper in *Stalingrad*. It's instructive to compare Léger's life and work with that of Picasso, his fellow pioneer of Cubism and long-time comrade in the Communist Party. While Legér's commitment to collective working-class life never wavered, Picasso only waved at it when he needed it. Picasso wanted to embrace the whole world and be embraced in return. He chose a complex, dominating and sometimes perverted persona through which to do it, while Léger stuck within the reality of himself and the world, an outlook captured by Alexander Calder's wire sculpture portrait of Léger in the museum.

It was the **potteries** that first brought Léger to Biot, where one of his old pupils had set up shop to produce ceramics of his master's designs. After Léger's death five years later in 1956, the Biot glassworks were established. Today, you can watch the glass-blowers at work, visit an *Eco-musée du Verre*, and see some extraordinary and extravagant glass creations in the *Galerie Internationale du Verre* in the **Verrerie de Biot** on chemin des Combes, the third turning off the D4 after the Léger museum (June–Sept Mon–Sat 8am–7pm, Sun 10am–1pm & 3–7pm; rest of the year Mon–Sat 8am–6pm, Sun 10.30am–1pm & 2.30–6.30pm; free). There are several other glass makers in the same area, all keen for you to visit and buy their products.

If **children** are getting bored with street wandering and window gazing there are a number of attractions – all expensive – back on the main sea road. They include the performing dolphins of *Marineland*, the water toboggans, chutes and slides of the neighbouring *Aquasplash* and a fun fair, *Antibesland*.

Eating and drinking

Among the **restaurants**, *Le Galerie des Arcades* belonging to the hotel (see p.341) is a very appealing combination of café, art gallery and resto with traditional Provençal cooking (closed Sun evening & Mon; 160F menu). *L'Auberge du Jarrier*, 30 passage de la Bourgade (closed Tues evening & Wed; ☎93.65.11.68; menus from 200F), serves up Biot's best dinners; *Le Bistro du Jarrier*, next door at no. 28 (closed Sun evening & Mon; ☎93.65.53.48; around 100F), is a lot more affordable and excellent value.

Sophia-Antipolis

If Cap d'Antibes symbolizes the old wealth of land and business, then **SOPHIA-ANTIPOLIS** represents the diverse multi-billion dollar power of current multinationals. When labour and production can be shifted round the world, why not have your communications centre, your researchers and most skilled technicians, or just your most sophisticated inorganic intelligence, in the planet's most desirable corner, the hills above Antibes?

IBM, *Wellcome*, *Toyota*, *Dow Chemicals* and *Air France* are just a few of the hundreds of companies who have set up operations just west of Biot in this **industrial park** with a difference. A large expanse of forest has been cut by wide, smooth roads named after ancient greats in science, music and literature. Behind them lurk heavily fenced buildings that make the promenade hotels look like cottages. In the ground, miles of fibre-optic cable whizz real-time moving images and unreal electronic money back and forth. They say that productivity goes up. What's certain is that business income now outstrips tourism in the Côte d'Azur.

The *parc* is expanding towards **Valbonne** and a *métro* line from Nice airport is being built. In the meantime, the only way to see it is with your own wheels (signed off the D4 from Biot or from the Antibes highway exit). Some of the architecture is spectacular though you can only admire the exterior shapes and facades of the extravagant buildings.

Villeneuve-Loubet and Cagnes

Villeneuve-Loubet and **Cagnes** flash past on the speedy train and road connections between the conurbations of Cannes, Antibes and Nice. Glimpses in transit suggest these places are the direst consequence of late twentieth-century coastal planning consents, but the seaside extensions have little to do with Cagnes and Villeneuve-Loubet proper. Both are worth a look: Villeneuve for its castle from the Middle Ages and place in culinary history; Cagnes for its artistic connections with Renoir in particular and wonderfully preserved medieval quarter.

Villeneuve-Loubet

Villeneuve-Loubet-Plage is dominated by a gigantic **marina**, constructed in the 1970s to a design of André Minangoy with petrified sails topped by vicious points, inescapably visible from Cap d'Antibes to Cap Ferrat. When the French government started to mind about the despoliation of the Côte d'Azur, apartments in this marina were changing hands for far too much for it to be knocked down. So there it stays, snubbing its nose at all the older artistry of this coast.

On the other side of the main road and highway, following the last stretch of the Loup river, you reach the tiny, quiet village of **VILLENEUVE-LOUBET** itself, grouped around its undamaged twelfth-century castle. The borders of the river are park and pastures and a stopover point for migrating birds.

The castle here, which was once François I's residence, is not open to the public, but you can visit the house where a king of culinary arts was born in 1846, now the **Musée de l'Art Culinaire** (Tues–Sun 2–6/7pm; closed Nov; 10F). The son of a blacksmith, **Auguste Escoffier** began his career in restaurants aged thirteen, skivvying for his uncle in Nice. By the end of the century he had reached the top in a business the French value as much as design or art. In London he was the *Savoy*'s first head chef, then the *Carlton*'s, and had fed almost every European head of state. *Pêche melba* was his most famous and lasting creation, but his significance for the history of indulgent and expensive eating was in breaking with the tradition of health-hazard richness and quantity. He also showed concern for those who would never be his clients, publishing a pamphlet in 1910 proposing a system of social security to eliminate starvation and poverty.

It must be said that the **Musée de l'Art Culinaire** (summer daily 2–6pm; winter Tues–Sat 2–6pm) does not have much appeal unless the subject fascinates you – for a start there's nothing to eat. But there are videos of great chefs demonstrating recipes; extraordinary models made of sugar and flour and a portrait in chocolate; photographs of chefs and famous clients; menus, letters and bills; and the original kitchen of the house.

Cagnes

The various parts of **CAGNES** are somewhat confusing: the nondescript coastal district is known as **Cros-de-Cagnes**; **Cagnes-sur-Mer** is inland, above the *autoroute*, and constitutes the town centre; while **Haut-de-Cagnes**, the original medieval village, overlooks the town from the northwest heights. Cros-de-Cagnes has plenty of beach, and for horse fanatics there's racing from December to March and trotting in July and August at the *Hippodrome* on the seafront to the west of the resort. Cagnes-sur-Mer, pleasant enough as a bustling town, is only really notable for Renoir's house. Haut-de-Cagnes, however, has a stunning **castle** containing the fabulous **Donation Suzy Solidor** (see p.345) and a changing array of contemporary art.

Arrival, information and orientation

The **gare SNCF Cagnes-sur-Mer** (☎93.22.46.47; one stop from the *gare SNCF* Cros-de-Cagnes) is southwest of the centre alongside the *autoroute*. You need to turn right on the northern side of the *autoroute* along av de la Gare to reach the town centre. If you want to rent an ordinary **bike**, take the second right, rue Pasqualini, where you'll find *Cycles et Cyclomoteurs Marcel* at no. 5 (☎93.20.64.07) or the fifth right into rue du Logis where *Location 2 Roux* at no. 3 rents scooters and mountain bikes. The sixth turning on your right, rue des Palmiers, leads to the **tourist office** at 6 bd Maréchal-Juin (mid-June to mid-Sept Mon–Sat 8.45am–12.30pm & 3–7pm; rest of year Mon–Sat 8.30am–12.15pm & 2.30–6.30pm; ☎93.20.61.64).

Bd Maréchal-Juin, which becomes av de l'Hôtel-des-Postes and then av Mistral, is the **main street**, running parallel to av de la Gare, which becomes av Renoir. The central **place de Gaulle** lies between the two, and at the top, where av Renoir veers eastwards, **place Bourdet** is where you'll be dropped if you're arriving from Cannes or Nice by bus. From here bus #7 runs to the *gare SNCF*; bus #2 to Cros de Cagnes and the seafront, and bus #9 to Haut-de-Cagnes, a steep ascent along rue Général-Bérenger, which forks left at the end of av de la Gare and turns into montée de la Bourgade.

Accommodation

Cros-de-Cagnes has the greatest choice of **hotels**; two of the most economical are *La Caravelle*, 42 bd de la Plage (☎93.20.10.09; ①) on the seafront, and *Le Saratoga*, 111 av de Nice (☎93.31.05.70; ①–②) on the busy N7. Up in the hills close to Renoir's house, *Les Collettes*, 38 chemin des Collettes (☎93.20.80.66; ④–⑤), has a pool, garden, and very pleasant rooms with views of the sea; some have a kitchenette for self-catering. In Haut-de-Cagnes, if you have the budget, try the ultra-luxurious *Le Cagnard*, rue Pontis-Long (☎93.20.73.21; ⑥–⑦), the ancient guard room for the castle to which twentieth-century comforts have been added without touching the authentic medieval architecture and decor. Alternatively there are seven rooms at the less exciting but well-situated *Le Grimaldi*, place du Château (☎93.20.60.24; ③).

Campsites are not marvellous, though there are plenty of them. The four-star *Panoramer*, chemin des Gros-Buaux (April–Sept; ☎93.31.16.15), about 1km northeast of Cagnes-sur-Mer, is well equipped but overpriced. Less expensive are the two-star *La Rivière* (all year; ☎93.20.62.27) on the chemin des Salles, 4km north of the town, and the two-star *Le Todos* (April–Oct; ☎93.31.20.05), similarly distant at 159 Vallon des Vaux.

Renoir's house

Les Collettes, the house that **Renoir** had built in 1908 and where he spent the last twelve years of his life, is now a memorial museum, the **Musée Renoir**, chemin des Collettes (Mon & Wed–Sun 10am–noon & 2/2.30–5/6pm; garden 10am–5/7pm; 20F), which you are free to wander around. You can also explore the olive and rare orange groves that surround it; Renoir was captivated by the olive trees and by the difficulties of rendering "a tree full of colours". Remarking on how a gust of wind would change the tree's tonality, he said "The colour isn't on the leaves, but in the spaces between them". One of the two studios in the house, north-facing to catch the late afternoon light, is arranged as if Renoir had just popped out. Despite the rheumatoid arthritis that had forced him to seek out a warmer climate than Paris, he painted every day at *Les Collettes*, strapping the brush to his hand when moving his fingers became too painful. There are portraits of him here by his closest friends: a painting by Albert André, *A Renoir Peignant*, showing the ageing artist hunching over his canvas; a bust by Aristide Maillol; and a crayon sketch by Richard Guido. Bonnard and Dufy were also visitors to *Les Collettes* and there are works of theirs here, including Dufy's *Hommage à Renoir*, transposing a detail of *Moulin de la Galette*. Renoir himself is represented by several sculptures including two bronzes – *La Maternité* and a medallion of his son Coco – some beautiful, tiny watercolours in the studio, and ten paintings from his Cagnes period (the greatest, the final version of *Les Grandes Baigneuses*, hangs in the Louvre).

To **get to Les Collettes**, take bus #5 from place Bourdet or, on foot, follow av Renoir eastwards and turn left up passage Renoir; coming by bus from Antibes or Nice get off at *Béat-Les Collettes*.

Haut-de-Cagnes

HAUT-DE-CAGNES, a favourite haunt of successes in the contemporary art world, as well as those of decades past, lives up to everything dreamed of in a Riviera hilltop village: no architectural excrescences to spoil the perfection of tiers of tiny streets hanging on the rock, where the light shifts from brilliant sunshine to darkest shadow at every turn. Even the flowers spilling over earthenware pots or climbing the soft stone walls never seem to die or show the slightest defect.

The ancient village backs up to a crenellated feudal **château**, which houses museums of local history, fishing and the cultivation of olives, along with the **Musée d'Art Moderne Méditerranéen** and the **Donation Suzy Solidor** (July–Sept daily 10am–noon & 2.30–7pm; mid-Nov to June Mon & Wed–Sun 10am–noon & 2–5/6pm; closed mid-Oct to mid-Nov; 20F in summer, otherwise 5F). The castle's Renaissance interior is itself a masterpiece, with tiers of arcaded galleries, vast frescoed ceilings, stuccoed reliefs of historical scenes and gorgeously ornamented chambers and chapels. The *Donation Suzy Solidor* consists of wonderfully diverse portraits of the cabaret star, whose career in Paris and on the Côte spanned the 1920s to the 1970s; almost all the great painters of the period are represented. Suzy Solidor was quite a character: extremely talented, totally independent and immensely sexy. She declared herself a lesbian years before the word, let alone the preference, was remotely acceptable, and, incidentally, inspired the music hall and pub song "If you knew Suzy, like I know Suzy". The qualities that most endeared her to each artist, or the fantasies she provoked, are clearly revealed in every one of the canvases, giving a fascinating insight into the art of portraiture as well as a multi-faceted image of the woman. The stylistic signatures are apparent too: Dufy, Cocteau, Laurençin, Foujita, Friesz, Van Dongen and Kisling, among others.

The *Musée d'Art Moderne Méditerranéen* is dedicated to all the painters who have worked on the coast in the last hundred years, Chagall, Matisse and many of the painters of Solidor's portraits. Their works, however, are not always on show, because of temporary exhibitions featuring an individual artist in December, craft work at Easter, and from the end of June to mid-September the *Festival International de la Peinture*. The latter is the big event of the year, with entries from forty-odd countries, representing highly disparate strands in painting. The selection is made by an august body, similar to Britain's Royal Academy.

Eating and drinking

Cagnes' best eating places are in **Haut-de-Cagnes** or **Cros-de-Cagnes**, and for **café lounging**, place du Château or place Grimaldi, to either side of the castle, are the obvious spots.

In Haut-de-Cagnes, montée de la Bourgade is the main **restaurant** street: *Restaurant des Peintres* at no. 71 (closed Wed; ☎93.20.61.01; from 200F) is not the cheapest but has an excellent reputation; *Le Clap*, just off the street at 4 rue Hippolyte-Guis (closed Wed; ☎92.02.06.28; one menu under 100F) serves very reasonably priced southwest France specialities. If you want to spend lots of money, *Le Cagnard* (see p.344) has a predictably smart restaurant (closed Thurs midday; menus from 300F) or there's *Josy-Jo*, place Planastel (closed Sat midday & Sun, & mid-July to mid-Aug; ☎93.20.68.76; from 330F), with Provençal delicacies served in the space that served as Soutine's workshop in the inter-war years.

In Cros-de-Cagnes, a couple of places serve good seafood: *La Bourride* (closed Wed; ☎93.31.07.75; menus from 150F) and *La Villa du Cros* (closed Sun evening out of season; ☎93.07.57.83; menus from 120F), next to each other on the port.

Nightlife

Haut-de-Cagnes is the centre of the town's **nightlife**. On place du Château is the famous and expensive *Jimmy's* restaurant and members-only piano-bar with a marbled interior where, if you can manage to get in, you can relax luxuriously amongst the *habitués* (the *terrasse* café-bar is open to everyone in the afternoon). *Le Vertigo*, on the opposite corner of the *place*, is a very reasonably priced **disco** but without much charm; *Le Quatre*, also on the *place*, is a bit more expensive and livelier (open from midnight). Haut-de-Cagnes also has a crowded calendar of cultural events, including free **jazz concerts** on place du Château in mid-July and a bizarre **square boules** competition on montée de la Bourgade at the beginning of August.

St-Paul-de-Vence

Further into the hills, halfway between Cagnes or Villeneuve-Loubet and **Vence**, the fortified village of **ST-PAUL-DE-VENCE** is home to the remarkable **Fondation Maeght** (daily July–Sept 10am–7pm; Oct–June 10am–12.30pm & 2.30–6pm; 45F), the artistic centre that most fully represents the link between the Côte d'Azur and modern European art. The foundation was created in the 1950s by Aimé and Marguerite Maeght, art collectors and dealers who knew all the great artists who worked in Provence. They commissioned the Spanish architect José Luis Sert, along with a number of the painters, sculptors, potters and designers on their books for the decoration. Both structure and ornamentation were conceived as a single project with the aim of creating a museum in which the concepts of entrance, exit and *sense de la visite* would not apply. It worked.

Once through the gates, any idea of dutifully checking off a catalogue of priceless museum pieces crumbles. Giacometti's *Cat* is sometimes stalking along the edge of the grass; Miró's *Egg* smiles above a pond and his totemed *Fork* is outlined against the sky. It's hard not be bewitched by the Calder mobile swinging over watery tiles, by Léger's flowers, birds and a bench on a sun-lit rough stone wall, by Zadkine's and Arp's metallic forms hovering between the pine trunks, or by the clanking tubular fountain by Pol Bury. And all this is just a portion of the garden.

The building itself is a superb piece of architecture: multilevelled and flooded with daylight, with galleries opening on to terraces and courtyards, blurring the boundaries between inside and outside. The collection it houses – sculpture, ceramics, paintings and graphic art by Braque, Miro, Chagall, Léger, Kandinsky, Dubuffet, Bonnard, Dérain and Matisse, along with more recent artists and the young up-and-comings – is undeniably impressive. Not all the works are exhibited at any one time, however, and during the summer, when the main annual exhibition is mounted, the only ones on show are those that make up the decoration of the building.

There are several major **exhibitions** every year, from retrospectives to shows on contemporary themes, along with workshops by musicians or writers with strong links to the visual arts, concerts, theatre and dance, and films screened daily throughout the summer until mid-October. The **library** of ten thousand books, including the catalogues of the world's top collections, is open year round. And as if that was not enough, the *fondation* contains etching, ceramics and experimental film studios.

The Nice–Vence **bus** that stops at *place de Gaulle* in Cagnes-sur-Mer has two stops in St-Paul; the *fondation* is signed from the second. By **car or bike**, follow the signs just before you reach the village, off the D7 from **La-Colle-sur-Loup** or the D2 from Villeneuve. Admission includes the permanent and temporary exhibitions, bookshop, library and cinema, and it's worth every last *centime*.

The village

Despite its *village perché* claims, there's little point hanging about in St-Paul itself, unless you've got a great deal of spare cash. If you're prepared to spend more than 1000F for a room or 400F for a mediocre meal, you can sit at the **Colombe d'Or** restaurant-hotel on place du Général-de-Gaulle, beneath Dufys, Dérains, Bonnards, Braques, Modiglianis, Matisses and Picassos, most of them acquired by the establishment from the painters themselves, settling their bills in the lean years post-World War I. This is, in fact, one of the biggest private collections of modern art in the country; if you haven't got the cash, you'll have to make do with a view through the grille of Léger's mural, unless you're confident enough to walk in and order a glass of pastis (that will probably cost more than a bottle) at the bar.

A wander around the sixteenth-century citadel will confirm that *La Colombe d'Or* is not alone in demanding *tenue très correcte* (however snooty it seems, bear in mind that by French law you can't be refused entrance on grounds of dress) – it's a place characterized by shops with pretensions to being artists' studios staffed by assistants dressed as fashion models selling paper serviettes with mock artistic squiggles for 200F a pack. To be fair, you will also find *crêperies* and normal restaurants where you can eat for less than 120F, and there are one or two people who will see you rather than look you up and down in mindless disdain. The great square **church**, with the only plain exterior in St-Paul, is nice, but beyond the *Fondation Maeght* there's little to detain you from heading straight on for Vence.

Vence

Set 10km back from the sea, and with abundant water and the sheltering Pre-Alpes behind, **VENCE** has always been a significant city. Its Ligurian inhabitants, the Nerusii, put up stiff opposition to Augustus Caesar, but to no avail. Roman funeral inscriptions and votive offerings from the period remain embedded in the fabric of the old cathedral. In the Dark Ages of Visigoth and Ostrogoth invasions, the bishop of Vence, **Saint Véran** from the St-Honorat seminary, was as effective in organizing the defence of the city as in rebuilding its moral fabric. When he died in 481 he was canonized by popular request – in those days the democratic principle of *vox populi vox Dei* (the voice of the people is the voice of God) operated. But the people of Vence had no spiritual or temporal power to call on to save them from the Saracens who razed Saint-Véran's cathedral to the ground and the town with it.

In the twelfth century the second patron saint of Vence, St-Lambert, took up residence at the same time as the baron **Romée de Villeneuve**, chief minister of Raymond Béranger IV, count of Provence. It was Villeneuve who arranged the powerful marriages of Béranger's four daughters, as part of his strategic scheming (see pp.300–301 "Forcalquier and its pays"). From then on, until the Revolution, Vence was plagued by rivalry between its barons and its bishops. During the Wars of Religion a bomb was put under the bishop's throne in the cathedral; in the early eighteenth century, in the farcical *Affaire des Poissons*, the two sides spilt blood in the cathedral over who had first choice of the fish brought up from the coast.

In the 1920s Vence became yet another haven for **painters and writers**, for André Gide, Paul Valéry, Soutine, Dufy and D.H. Lawrence (who died here, in 1930, of tuberculosis contracted in cold England). Near the end of World War II **Matisse** moved to Vence to escape the Allied bombing of the coast and his legacy is the town's most famous and exciting building, the **Chapelle du Rosaire**, built under his exclusive design and direction. **Vieux Vence** too has its charms, with its ancient houses, gateways, fountains and chapels as well as the **St-Véran Cathedral**.

Arrival and information

From Cagnes there are two **roads into Vence**. One enters the town as av Maréchal-Leclerc, leading straight up to the eastern end of the old walled city. The other, along with the roads from Grasse, St-Paul and the north, arrives at place du Maréchal-Juin and the two main avenues of the modern town, av de la Résistance and av des Poilus/Henri-Isnard. Coming by bus you'll be dropped at the **gare routière** on place du Grand-Jardin, next door to place du Frêne and the western gateway of Vieux Vence. On place du Grand-Jardin you'll find the **tourist office** (Mon–Sat 9am–noon & 2–6.30pm; ☎93.58.06.38) and *Vence Motocycles* for **bike rental**.

Accommodation

Being very much on the tourist circuit as well as a proper town, Vence has a good choice of **places to stay**, though as ever it would be as well to book ahead in the summer.

Hotels

Hôtel des Alpes, 2 av Général-Leclerc (☎93.58.13.30). On the eastern edge of Vieux Vence, rather down-at-heel, but the most economical option. ①

La Closerie des Genêts, 4 impasse Maurel, off av M-Maurel to the south of Vieux Vence (☎93.58.33.25). Pleasant rooms and very welcoming. Closed Sun evening. ③

Diana, av des Poilus (☎93.58.28.56). A modern building in a quiet location. ⑤

La Victoire, pl du Grand-Jardin (☎93.58.61.30). A bit noisy but very central. ④

La Roseraie, 14 av H-Giraud (☎93.58.02.20). Classic rich Provençal homestead with ancient cedars and magnolias overhanging the terrace on the road to the Col de Vence northwest of town. Charming reception and lovely pool in the garden. ⑤

Auberge des Seigneurs, pl du Frêne (☎93.58.04.24). Just within Vieux Vence with rooms named after the painters who lodged there. ④

Campsites

La Bergerie, rte de la Sine (☎93.58.09.36). Three-star site 3km west off the road to Tourettes-sur-Loup. Mid-March to Oct.

Les Cents Chênes, rte de Gattières, St-Jeannet (☎93.24.95.73). Three-star site 6.5km northeast of Vence.

The Town

Vieux Vence certainly has its fair share of the chic boutiques and arty restaurants that tell you this is an *haut-lieu* of the current Côte aristocracy. But it also has an everyday feel about it with ordinary people going about their business, seeking out the best market deals, stopping for a chat and a *petit verre* at run-of-the-mill cafés. The **castle** and the **cathedral** are the two dominant buildings; in the modern town, **Matisse's chapel** (with its very limited opening hours) and the **Centre d'Art Vaas** both provide a welcome diversion.

Vieux Vence

The 450-year-old ash tree that gives its name to **place du Frêne** stands in front of Vence's castle, the **Château de Villeneuve** (July–Sept daily 10am–7pm; Oct–June Tues–Sun 10am–noon & 2–6pm; 15F), built just outside the city walls in a calm period of fifteenth-century expansion. It was rebuilt in the seventeenth century and renovated in 1992 to become a beautiful temporary exhibition space for the works of artists like Matisse, Dufy, Dubuffet and Chagall associated with the town, along with other modern and contemporary art.

The **Porte du Peyra** and its sheltering tower that adjoins the castle have remained more or less untouched from the twelfth century and provide the best entry into Vieux Vence. **Place du Peyra**, within the medieval *enceinte*, has the town's oldest fountain (though not in its present urn form). The narrow **rue du Marché** off to the right is a wonderfully busy street of tiny and delectable food shops, all with stalls on the cobbles. Behind rue du Marché you'll find **place Clemenceau**, which centres on the **cathedral** and hosts the main Tuesday and Friday **market**, spilling into place Surian.

The **Cathédrale** is a tenth- and eleventh-century replacement for the church St Véran presided over in the fifth century, which in turn was built on the ruins of a Roman temple to Mars and Cybele. Like so many of the oldest Provençal churches, it is basically square in shape, with an austere exterior appearance of monastic exclusion. Over the centuries bits have been demolished and other bits added, leaving none of the clear lines of Romanesque architecture. But with each project, including the initial construction, fragments of the Merovingian and Carolingian predecessor and Roman Vence were incorporated. In the chapel beneath the belfry two reliefs from the old church show birds, grapes and an eagle. More stone birds, flowers, swirls of leaves and interlocking lines are embedded in the walls and pillars throughout the church. Roman inscriptions from an aqueduct adorn the porch and more have found their way into the walls of the southwestern tower. The purported **tomb of St Véran**, in the southern chapel nearest the altar, is a pre-Christian sarcophagus. He and his fellow patron saint of Vence, St Lambert, survive in reliquary form in the neighbouring chapel. Of later adornments there are Gothic carved choir stalls and, in the baptistry, a **Chagall mosaic**. Church-as-museum devotees can have a field day examining all the treasures, but those who go for a sense of awesome space will probably be disappointed.

On the east side of the cathedral is **place Godeau**, almost totally medieval save for the column in the fountain that was given to the city, along with its twin on place du Grand-Jardin, by the Republic of Marseille some time in the third century. Rue St-Lambert and rue de l'Hôtel-de-Ville lead from place Godeau down to the original eastern gate, the **Porte du Signadour**, with another fifteenth-century fountain just outside on place Antony-Mars celebrating the town's expansion. In the thirteenth century the only other gate was the Portail Levis on the opposite corner of the city to Porte du Signadour.

The fountain on **place Vieille**, between the Portail Levis and the cathedral, was redesigned in 1572, this time to celebrate the town getting the better of both its feudal and spiritual lords. The predecessor of the bishop who escaped death by explosion in the cathedral had been condemned as a heretic for his dabblings with the new religion. The people of Vence kicked him out not because of his Protestantism but because he'd sold his seigneurial rights to Baron Villeneuve, who now had exclusive jurisdiction over them. Using the courts both of Rome and of Provence, the town acquired the illegally transferred rights itself. What is more, when the baron laid siege to Vence with Protestant troops in 1592, the town held out. But the townspeople didn't like it when Rome sent a new envoy the same year. They only accepted him after he had won the approval of the new "Paris is worth a Mass" king in 1594. Which goes to show how adept the *Vençois* were at playing off powers without worrying about religious affiliations.

Matisse's Chapelle du Rosaire

Henri Matisse was never a Christian believer, though some have tried to explain the **Chapelle du Rosaire**, 466 av Henri-Matisse, on the road to St-Jeannet from the Carrefour Jean-Moulin at the top of av des Poilus (Tues & Thurs only 10–11.30am & 2.30–5.30pm; Sunday Mass at 9am; closed Nov to mid-Dec; 5F), as a late-life conversion. "My only religion is the love of the work to be created, the love of creation, and great sincerity," he said in 1952, when the five-year project was completed.

A serious illness in 1941 had left Matisse an invalid. In August 1943, during his convalescence in Vence, where he was nursed by the Dominican sisters who were to involve him in the design of the chapel, he wrote to Louis Aragon: "I am an elephant, feeling, in my present frame of mind, that I am master of my fate, and capable of thinking that nothing matters for me except the conclusion of all these years of work, for which I feel myself so well equipped."

The artist moved back to his huge rooms in Nice in 1949 in order to work on the designs using the same scale as the chapel. There is a photograph of him in bed drawing studies for the figure of St Dominic on the wall with a paintbrush tied to a long bamboo stick. It's not clear how much this bamboo technique was a practical solution to his frailty, and how much a solution to an artistic problem. You rather suspect that Matisse was capable of drawing in whatever style he chose, whether wielding a six-metre pole or not. According to some critics, Matisse wanted to pare down his art to the basic essentials of human communication, and to do this he needed to remove his own stylistic signature from the lines.

The drawings on the **chapel walls** – black outline figures on white tiles – succeed in this to the extent that many people are bitterly disappointed, not finding the "Matisse" they expect. The east wall, which is not the altar end, is the most shocking. It shows the *Stations of the Cross*, each one numbered and scrawled as if it were an angry doodle on a pad. Matisse described the **ceramic murals** as "the visual equivalent of an open book where the white pages carry the signs explaining the musical part composed by the stained-glass windows". The **full-length windows** in the west and south walls are the aspect of the chapel most likely to live up to expectations. They are the only source of colour in the chapel, changing with the day's light through opaque yellow, transparent green and watery blue, and playing across the black and white murals, floor and ceiling.

Every part of the chapel is Matisse's design (with some architectural input from Auguste Pérret): the high cross with oriental leanings on the roof; the vestments, chasubles, crucifix and candelabra; the layout of the chapel; the decoration on the floors, steps and roof. It is a total work and one with which Matisse was content. It was his "ultimate goal, the culmination of an intense, sincere and difficult endeavour".

The Centre d'Art VAAS

The **Centre d'Art VAAS**, 14 traverse des Moulins, just north of Vieux Vence (Tues–Sat 11am–1pm & 2.30–7pm; free), takes its name from the first letters of the Latin words for truth, love, art and spirituality. You walk through a garden of sculptures into what was, from 1955 to 1970, Jean Dubuffet's studio. It feels like a house – the resident cat, Crocus, comes to say hello, as does a member of staff. As well as a gallery of figurative art belonging to its founder, Marion Duteurtre, this is a space for artists to meet and work, for amateurs to learn techniques from practising artists, for performances of theatre, poetry and music, and, most importantly, a place where people usually denied access to the arts are welcomed. For details of the centre's programme and of the painting and drawing classes, phone ☎93.58.29.42.

Eating and drinking

You'll find plenty of **cafés** in the squares of Vieux Vence. *La Clemenceau* on place Clemenceau is the big *café-brasserie-glacier* but you might find *Harry's Bar* on place de Peyra more congenial. *La Régence* on place du Grand-Jardin serves excellent coffee to sip beneath its stylish parasols. Rue du Marché is the place for **picnic** food; *Au Poivre d'Ane* at no. 12 specializes in **cheeses** and serves cheese dishes at the back. For **wine** *en vrac*, including Var table wine, *Côtes de Provence* and *Côtes du Rhône*, there's *Les Bons Vins de France* at 38 av Colonel-Meyère.

Restaurants

Château Saint-Martin, rte de Coursegoules (☎93.58.02.02). The most extravagant and beautiful place to eat, a rock-perching Templars' castle with a stunning panorama. Classic French food served with due pomp and ceremony. Weekday midday menu 300F, otherwise from 430F. Closed Wed out of season & Nov–March.

La Closerie des Genêts (see "Hotels"; p.349). Cosy and very welcoming with excellent food. Menus from 130F; closed Sun evening.

La Farigoule, 15 av Henri-Isnard (☎93.58.01.27). Not always brilliant food but a great atmosphere. Menus from 115F. Closed Fri.

Le Matisse, 7 av de la Résistance (☎93.24.66.15). Open midday only for salads, sandwiches and the like. Very good value.

Le Pêcheur du Soleil, 1 pl Godeau (☎93.58.32.56). An astounding choice of pizzas. Around 80F. Closed Fri lunchtime.

La Vieille Douve, 10 av Henri-Isnard (☎93.58.10.02). Lovely *terrasse* with a view of the zigzagging blue roof of the Chapelle du Rosaire. Menu 100F. Closed Thurs.

Around Vence

LA GAUDE, 3km due east of Vence but only accessible by road via **St-Jeannet** to the north, has the simple attraction of being a *village perché* which hasn't been turned into a showpiece. You can **stay** at the *Trois Mousquetaires* just outside the village on rte de St-Laurent (☎93.24.40.60; ②–③) and **eat** cheap and delicious pasta at *La Romane.* The local **wine** is very good if you get the chance to try it; unfortunately there are only four or five vineyards, who tend to produce it for friends and family only.

In total contrast, **TOURETTES-SUR-LOUP**, 6km west of Vence, is an artisans' paradise and a strong contender for picturesque prizes. The three towers from which its name derives and its rosy stone houses clinging to their high escarpment, almost all date from the fifteenth century. Its Grande-Rue consists of nothing but *ateliers* for sculpture, jewellery, weaving, pottery, papier-mâché puppets, cushions, decorated doors and dressers, murals and a hundred other desirable and incredibly expensive designer household items.

If you want more information on what's going on in Tourettes, the **tourist office**, 2 rte de Vence (Mon–Sat 10.15am–12.30pm & 2.30–5.30pm; ☎93.24.18.93), should help. A reasonable **hotel** close to the village centre is *La Grive Dorée*, 11 rte de Grasse (☎93.59.30.05; ②–③). **Campsites** around the village include the three-star *La Camassade*, rte de Pie Lombard (☎93.59.31.54), and the three-star *Les Rives du Loup*, rte de la Colle (April to mid-Oct; ☎93.24.15.65).

A diverting place to **eat** in Tourettes, without breaking the bank, is *Le Médiéval* at 6 Grande Rue (closed Thurs; ☎93.59.31.63; menu around 100F), or try *Le Petit Manoir* at 21 Grande Rue (closed Sun evening & Wed; ☎93.24.19.19; weekday menu around 100F, otherwise from 150F).

Nice

The capital of the Riviera and fifth-largest town in France, **NICE** scarcely deserves its glittering reputation. Living off inflated property values and fat business accounts, its ruling class has hardly evolved from the eighteenth-century Russian and English aristocrats who first built their mansions here; today it's the *rentiers* and retired people of various nationalities whose dividends and pensions give the city its startlingly high ratio of per capita income to economic activity.

Their votes ensured the monopoly of municipal power held for decades by a right-wing dynasty, whose corruption was finally exposed in 1990 when Mayor Jacques Médecin fled to Uruguay. He was finally extradited and jailed. Despite some 400 million francs of tax-payers' money having disappeared, public opinion remained in his favour. From his Grenoble prison cell, Médecin, who had twinned Nice with Cape Town during the height of South Africa's apartheid regime, backed the former Front National member and close friend of Jean-Marie Le Pen, Jacques Peyrat in the 1995 local elections. Peyrat won with ease.

Politics apart, Nice has other reasons why it should qualify as one of the most loathsome cities on the Riviera: it's a pickpocket's paradise; the traffic is a nightmare; the Mardi Gras carnival is a commercial fraud; miniature poodles would appear to be mandatory; the public phones are always vandalized; and the beach isn't even sand. Yet, all that said, Nice manages to be delightful. The sun and the sea and the laid-back, affable Niçois cover a multitude of sins. A thousand sprinklers keep the grass lush in the numerous green spaces of the city as temperatures soar into the thirties. Fountains ease the harshness of new prestige developments and every park is full of flowers. Along the famous seafront the frayed but sturdy palms survive against all odds the fumes of speeding cars. On summer nights the old town buzzes with contented crowds. It's very hard not to love Nice.

Recent architectural aberrations apart, the city has retained its historical styles almost intact: the medieval rabbit warren of **Vieux Nice**, the Italianate facades of **modern Nice** and the rich exuberance of **turn-of-the-century residences** from when the city was Europe's most fashionable winter retreat. It has also retained mementoes from its ancient past, when the Romans ruled the region from here, and earlier still, when the Greeks founded the city. The city's **museums** are a treat for art lovers with the **Musée Matisse**, the **Musée d'Art Moderne**, the **Musée des Beaux Arts**, **Musée Dufy**, Chagall's **Message Biblique** and the numerous private and municipal art galleries with their changing exhibitions. A great many of the artists represented by these collections have a direct connection to the city.

Arrival and information

Arriving by **air**, you can get a bus (every 20min; 21F) from outside the end door of Terminal I to the junction of av Gustav V and the promenade des Anglais, or on to the **gare routière** (☎93.85.61.81) if you're continuing your journey straight out of town. The *gare routière* is very central, close to the *Vieille Ville* beneath the promenade du Paillon on bd Jean-Jaurès; the **gare SNCF** (☎93.87.50.50) is a little further out, a couple of blocks west of the top end of av Jean-Médecin.

You'll find the main **tourist office** beside the *gare SNCF* on av Thiers (daily 8am–7/8pm; ☎93.87.07.07). It's one of the most useful and generous of Côte tourist offices and has annexes at 2 rue Massenet (☎93.87.60.60) and at Nice-Ferber (☎93.83.32.64) on the promenade des Anglais near the airport (both July to mid-Sept Mon–Sat 8am–8pm, Sun 8am–noon; rest of year Mon–Sat 8am–7pm) and another at Terminal 1 of the airport (daily 8am–10pm; ☎93.21.44.11). Any of these offices can supply you with a free listings magazine, *Le Farfe Lu*, which comes out every Wednesday and covers the whole Riviera.

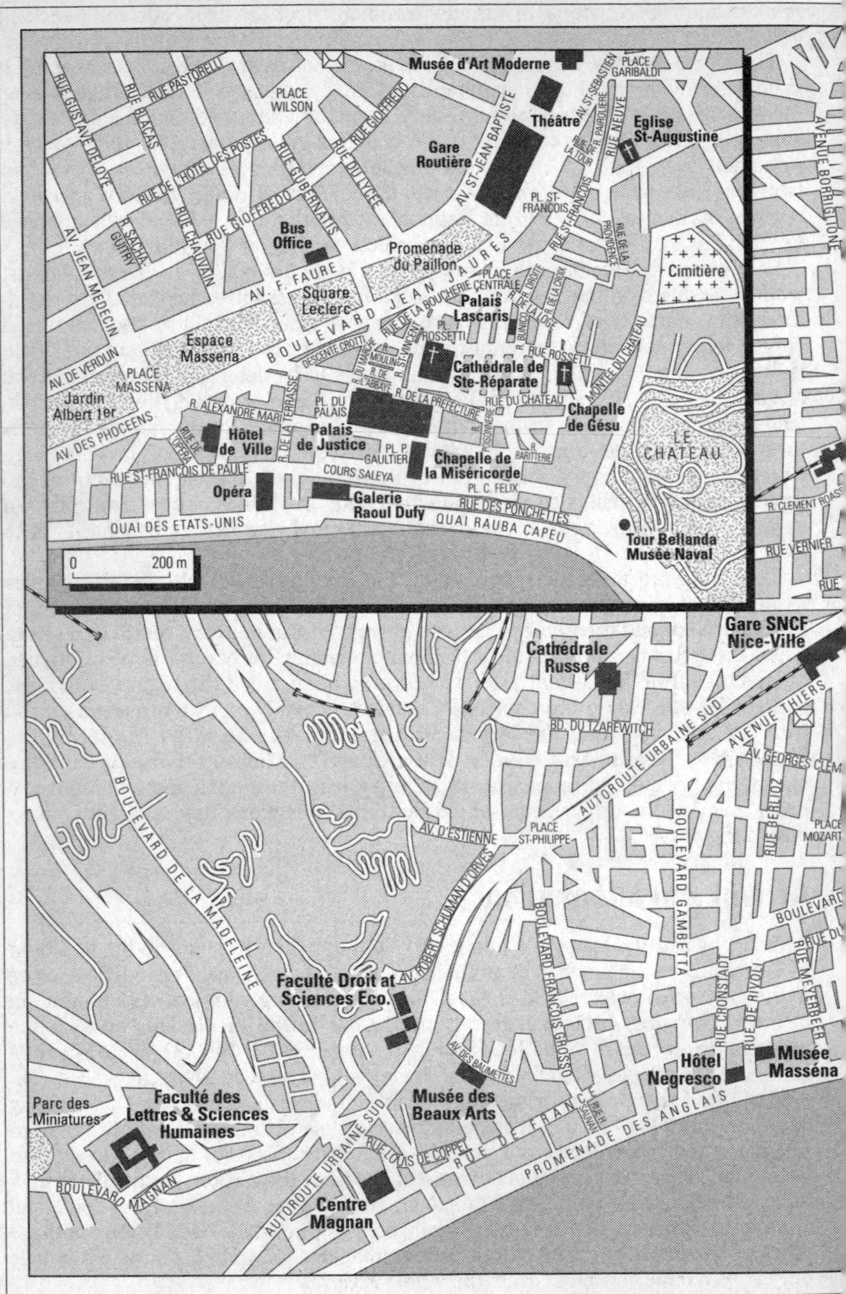

Musée d'Art Moderne
Théâtre
Eglise St-Augustine
Gare Routière
Bus Office
Promenade du Paillon
Square Leclerc
Palais Lascaris
Espace Massena
Cathédrale de Ste-Réparate
Chapelle de Gésu
Jardin Albert 1er
Hôtel de Ville
Palais de Justice
Chapelle de la Miséricorde
Opéra
Galerie Raoul Dufy
Tour Bellanda Musée Naval
LE CHATEAU
Cimitière
0 200 m
PLACE GARIBALDI
PLACE WILSON
PLACE MASSENA
PLACE CENTRALE
PL. ST-FRANCOIS
PL. DU PALAIS
PL. P. GAULTIER
PL. C. FELIX
PL. ROSSETTI
RUE PASTORELLI
RUE GUSTAVE DELOYE
RUE BLACAS
RUE DE L'HOTEL DES POSTES
RUE GIOFFREDO
RUE GUBERNATIS
RUE DU LYCEE
AV. ST-JEAN BAPTISTE
AV. ST-SEBASTIEN
RUE NEUVE
RUE ST-FRANCOIS
AV. JEAN MEDECIN
R. SACHA GUITRY
RUE CHAUVAIN
AV. F. FAURE
BOULEVARD JEAN JAURES
RUE DE LA BOUCHERIE
R. DROITE
R. DE LA LOGE
RUE ROSSETTI
MONTEE DU CHATEAU
DESCENTE CROTTI
R. ST-VINCENT
R. DE LA PREFECTURE
RUE DU CHATEAU
R. ALEXANDRE MARI
R. DE LA TERRASSE
AV. DE VERDUN
AV. DES PHOCEENS
RUE ST-FRANCOIS DE PAULE
COURS SALEYA
RUE DES PONCHETTES
QUAI DES ETATS-UNIS
QUAI RAUBA CAPEU
R. CLEMENT ROASSAL
RUE VERNIER
AVENUE BORRIGLIONE
Gare SNCF Nice-Ville
Cathédrale Russe
BD. DU TZAREWITCH
AUTOROUTE URBAINE SUD
AVENUE THIERS
AV. GEORGES CLEMENCEAU
RUE BERLIOZ
PLACE MOZART
BOULEVARD DE LA MADELEINE
AV. D'ESTIENNE D'ORVES
PLACE ST-PHILIPPE
AV. ROBERT SCHUMAN
BOULEVARD GAMBETTA
BOULEVARD FRANCOIS GROSSO
Faculté Droit at Sciences Eco.
RUE CRONSTADT
RUE DE RIVOLI
RUE MEYERBEER
Hôtel Negresco
Musée Masséna
AV. DES BAUMETTES
Musée des Beaux Arts
RUE DE FRANCE
PROMENADE DES ANGLAIS
Parc des Miniatures
Faculté des Lettres & Sciences Humaines
BOULEVARD MAGNAN
RUE LOUIS DE COPPET
Centre Magnan

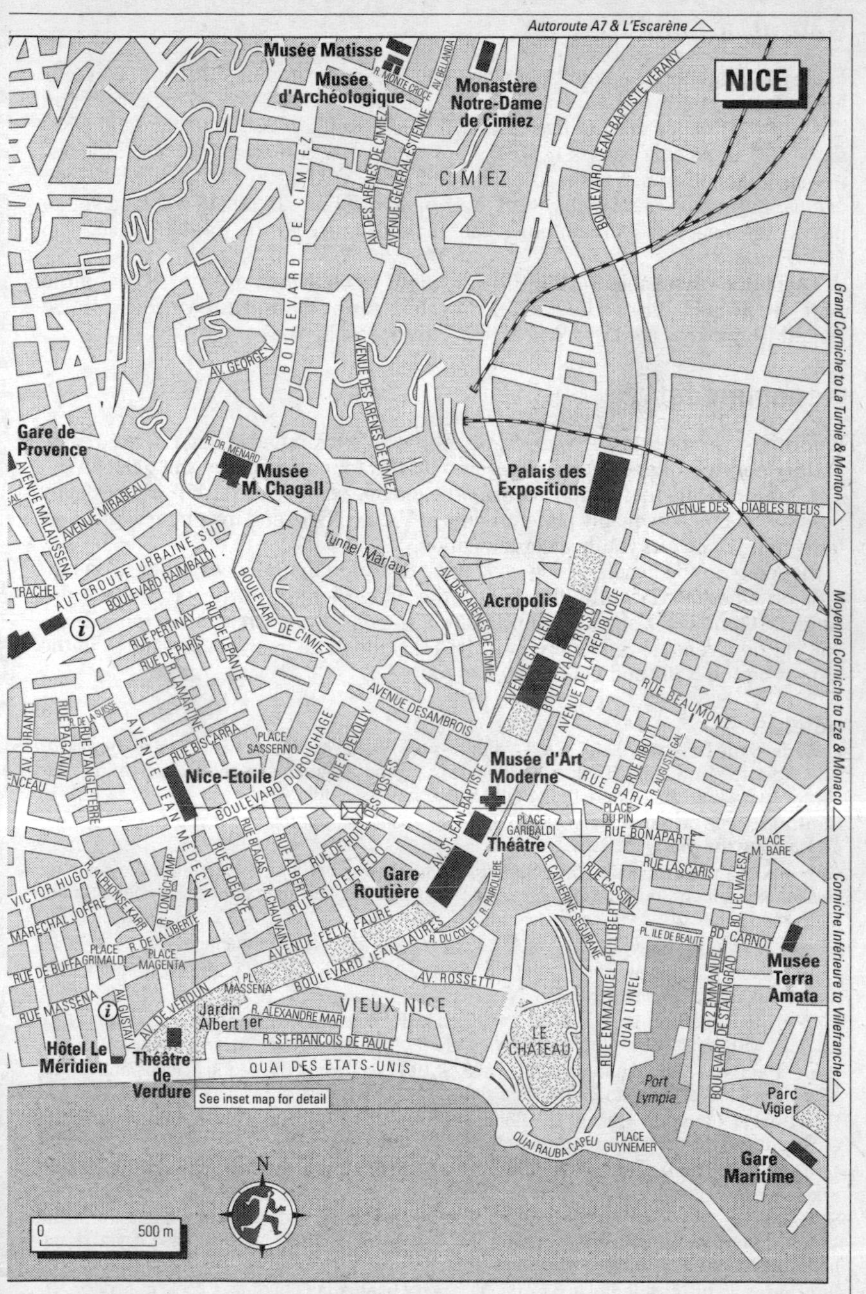

Autoroute A7 & L'Escarène
NICE
Musée Matisse
Musée d'Archéologique
Monastère Notre-Dame de Cimiez
CIMIEZ
BOULEVARD DE CIMIEZ
AV. DES ARENES DE CIMIEZ
AVENUE GENERAL ESTIENNE
BOULEVARD JEAN-BAPTISTE VERANY
AV. GEORGE V
AVENUE DES ARENES DE CIMIEZ
Gare de Provence
Musée M. Chagall
R. DR. MENARD
Palais des Expositions
AVENUE DES DIABLES BLEUS
Grand Corniche to La Turbie & Menton
AVENUE MALAUSSENA
AVENUE MIRABEAU
AUTOROUTE URBAINE SUD
BOULEVARD RAIMBALDI
Tunnel Marlaux
TRACHEL
RUE PERTINAY
RUE DE PARIS
RUE DE LEPANTE
BOULEVARD DE CIMIEZ
Acropolis
AVENUE GALLIENI
BOULEVARD RISSO
AVENUE DE LA REPUBLIQUE
RUE BEAUMONT
Moyenne Corniche to Eze & Monaco
AVENUE DESAMBROIS
R. LAMARTINE
RUE PAGANINI
RUE D'ANGLETERRE
AV. DURANTE
AVENUE JEAN MEDECIN
RUE BISCARRA
PLACE SASSERNO
BOULEVARD DUBOUCHAGE
RUE P. DEVOLUY
RUE DE L'HOTEL DES POSTES
Nice-Etoile
Musée d'Art Moderne
AV. ST-JEAN-BAPTISTE
RUE BARLA
PLACE DU PIN
PLACE GARIBALDI
RUE BONAPARTE
Théâtre
RUE LASCARIS
PLACE M. BARE
Gare Routière
RUE CASSINI
R. CATHERINE SEGURANE
VICTOR HUGO
R. ALPHONSE KARR
R. LONGCHAMP
RUE G. DELOYE
RUE ALBERT
RUE GIOFFREDO
R. CHAUVAIN
MARECHAL JOFFRE
R. DE LA LIBERTE
PLACE GRIMALDI
PLACE MAGENTA
RUE DE BUFFA
AVENUE FELIX FAURE
BOULEVARD JEAN JAURES
R. DU COLLET
R. PAIROLIERE
AV. ROSSETTI
PL. MASSENA
RUE MASSENA
AV. DE VERDUN
AV. GUSTAV V
Jardin Albert 1er
R. ALEXANDRE MARI
VIEUX NICE
R. ST-FRANCOIS DE PAULE
LE CHATEAU
Hôtel Le Méridien
Théâtre de Verdure
QUAI DES ETATS-UNIS
See inset map for detail
RUE EMMANUEL PHILIBERT
QUAI LUNEL
PL. ILE DE BEAUTE
BD. CARNOT
BOULEVARD DE STALINGRAD
BD. LEC WALESA
Musée Terra Amata
Port Lympia
Corniche Inférieure to Villefranche
Parc Vigier
QUAI RAUBA CAPEU
PLACE GUYNEMER
Gare Maritime
N
0
500 m

Getting around

For getting around the city, **buses** are frequent and run until 12.15am, with four lines running until 1.10am. Fares are flat rate and you can buy a single ticket on the bus (8F) or a carnet of five tickets (31F). There are also one-day (21F), five-day (87F) or weekly passes (117F), all of which can be bought at *tabacs*, kiosks, newsagents and from *Sunbus*, the transport office at 10 av Félix-Faure, where you can pick up a free route map. From the *gare SNCF* bus #12 or #15 will take you to place Masséna; bus #15 continues the short distance to the *Sunbus* office, stop *Félix-Faure*.

Taxis are reasonable during the day; night rates, which operate from 7pm to 7am, are around 10F per kilometre. **Bicycles, mopeds and motorbikes** can be rented from *Nicea Location Rent* at 9 av Thiers, just by the *gare SNCF*.

Accommodation

Before you start doing the rounds, it's well worth taking advantage of the **reservation service** offered, for a small fee, by the tourist office by the *gare SNCF*. The area around the station teems with cheap, seedy hotels, but it's perfectly possible to find reasonably priced rooms in **Vieux Nice**, and in summer, there's a fairly good choice of youth accommodation.

Sleeping on the beach, which used to be common though always illegal, is now difficult since it's brightly illuminated the whole length of the promenade des Anglais. Options for official **camping** are also poor: the nearest is *Camping Terry*, 768 rte de Grenoble St-Isodore (☎93.08.11.58; open all year), 6.5km north of the airport on the N202 and not on any bus route.

Hotels

Canada, 8 rue Halevy (☎93.87.17.12). Nothing very special but central and close to the sea. ③

Le Capitole, 4 rue de la Tour (☎93.80.08.15). A good if potentially noisy location in Vieux Nice with a warm atmosphere though not overgenerous rooms. ⑤

Central, 10 rue de Suisse (☎93.88.85.08). Very small, and not too bad if you can get a room overlooking the courtyard. ③

Cronstadt, 3 rue Cronstadt (☎93.82.00.30). Hidden away one block away from the seafront; charming *patronne*; free parking on street; old-fashioned clean and comfortable rooms; amazingly good value. ③

Meurice, 14 av de Suède (☎93.87.74.93). Very central with pleasant manager. ④

Les Orangers, 10 bis av Durante (☎93.87.51.41). A cheapie that all American students head for and unfailingly recommend. ③

La Pérouse, 11 quai Rauba-Capeu (☎93.62.34.63). A wonderful location at the foot of Le Château with views across the bay. Very comfortable and spacious. ⑦

Petit Palais, 10 av Emile-Bieckert (☎93.62.19.11). Turn-of-the-century mansion on the heights of Cimiez. Quiet and very comfortable. ⑦

Hôtel de la Place du Pin, 10 rue Bonaparte (☎93.56.42.19). Not a bad location between pl Garibaldi and the port. Rooms are reasonable, if a little dingy. ③

Le Relais de Rimiez, 128 av de Rimiez (☎93.81.18.65). Up in the hills north of Cimiez with pleasant rooms giving great views from the balconies, and an easy bus ride into the centre. ④

St-François, 3 rue St-François (☎93.85.88.69). On a busy pedestrian thoroughfare in the *Vieille Ville*, above a restaurant hosting live jazz on Fri nights. An ideal base if you're not bothered by noise or by basic amenities. ②

Vendôme, 26 rue Pastorelli (☎93.62.00.77). A very handsome building. Excellent service. ⑦

Windsor, 11 rue Dalpozzo (☎93.88.59.35.). Where the stars of Truffaut's *Day for Night* were filmed having their off-set hysterics. Chinoiserie in the foyer and a swimming pool in the verdant courtyard at the back. ⑧

Hostels

Clairvallon Relais International de la Jeunesse, 26 av Scuderi (☎93.81.27.63). Slightly cheaper than the youth hostel but 10km north of the centre and with a 10.30pm curfew. Location apart, it's pleasantly informal and has a pool; take bus #15 or #25, stop *Scudéri*. Reception till 6pm. ①

HI youth hostel, rte Forestière du Mont-Alban (☎93.89.23.64). Nice's hostel is 4km out of town and, for 2 people, not a lot cheaper than sharing a hotel room. The last bus from the centre leaves at 7.30pm and there's a curfew at 11.30pm. No card required. Take bus #14 from pl Masséna, direction *pl du Mont-Boron*, stop *L'Auberge*. Reception 7–10am & 5–11pm. ①

MJC Magnan, 31 rue Louis-de-Coppet (☎93.86.28.75). This hostel is not too far from the centre and close to the beach. Take buses #3, #9, #10, #12, #22 or #24, stop *Magnan*. Mid-June to mid-Sept. ①

Résidence Les Collinettes, 3 av R-Schuman (☎93.97.06.64). Much more central than the *Clairvallon* but around 100F a night, in individual rooms. Bus #17 from *gare SNCF* or #14 from the centre, direction *Square Daudet* stop *Châteauneuf* and walk down av Schuman to Law Faculty complex. July & Aug only; 4–10pm. ①

The City

It doesn't take long to get a feel for the layout of **Nice**. Shadowed by mountains that curve down to the Mediterranean east of its port, it still breaks up more or less into old and new. Vieux Nice, the old town, groups beneath the hill of **Le Château**, its limits signalled by boulevard Jean-Jaurès, built along the course of the **River Paillon**. Along the seafront, the celebrated **promenade des Anglais** runs a cool 5km until forced to curve inland by the sea-projecting runways of the airport. The central square, **place Masséna**, is at the bottom of the modern city's main street, **avenue Jean-Médecin**, while off to the north is the exclusive hill-side suburb of **Cimiez**.

MUSEUM CHARGES

Up until the end of 1995 all Nice's museums, with the exception of the Musée Matisse, Musée d'Art Moderne et Contemporaine and the Musée Marc Chagall, had free **admission**. The decision, made in January 1996, to charge for entry reflects the city's financial troubles since Médecin's embezzling reign. The new rates were not available at the time of writing, but the tourist office's "Guide to the Museums of Nice" will give details.

Le Château

For initial orientation, with brilliant sea and city views, fresh air, a cooling water-fall and the scent of Mediterranean vegetation, the best place to make for is the **Château park** (daily 7am–7pm). There's no château; the city's fortress was destroyed by the French in the early eighteenth century when Nice belonged to Savoy. But this is where Nice began as the ancient Greek city of Nikea: hence the mosaics and stone vases in mock Grecian style. Excavations have revealed Greek and Roman levels beneath the foundations of the city's first, eleventh-century cathedral on the eastern side of the summit. Rather than ruin spotting, however, the real pleasure here lies in looking down on the scrambled rooftops and gleaming mosaic tiles of Vieux Nice, on the yachts and fishing boats in the port on the eastern side, along the sweep of the promenade des Anglais, and of course at the sea itself in the smooth arc of the Bay of Angels between Antibes and the rock on which you stand. At the top of the hill a viewing platform usefully points you towards St Petersburg among other places. In the cemetery to the north of the park are buried the two great Niçois revolutionaries, Giuseppe Garibaldi and Léon Gambetta.

To reach the park, you can either take the lift by the **Tour Bellanda**, at the eastern end of quai des Etats-Unis – which also houses a small naval museum (Wed–Sun 10am–noon & 2–5/7pm) – or climb the steps from rue de la Providence or rue du Château in Vieux Nice.

Vieux Nice

Only a handful of years ago, any ex-pat or police officer would tell you that **Vieux Nice** was a dangerous place, brimming with drug-pushers, "dark-skinned" muggers and car thieves. That was always a gross exaggeration, but it still reveals how much the *quartier* has changed of late. In the early 1980s, an upmarketing process started with the renovation of low-rent apartments. Rents then went up and the first batch of old residents were moved out to high-rise hutches on the city's perimeter. Then the town hall moved in on the private sector, giving itself first option on any property for sale, on the grounds that it could then ensure renovation. What in practice it ensured was more money for the municipal (or rather Médecin's) coffers, higher prices and a selection process of would-be buyers. The Arab, Chinese and other ethnic communities are now almost entirely absent from Vieux Nice. However, though the expensive boutiques, art galleries, and mass of restaurants, bars and clubs make the area as crowded at night as it is by day, gentrification hasn't fully taken over. A fair number of the old residents remain, and co-existing with the glitzier places, little hardware stores still sell brooms and bottled gas, clothes lines are strewn high across the streets and tiny cafés are packed with blue-overalled men.

The streets of Vieux Nice are too narrow for buses, and though the natives insist on driving round and round looking for parking space, it's an area made for walking. The central square, where you tend to surface from random wanderings, is **place Rosetti** where the soft-coloured Baroque **Cathédrale de St-Réparate** (daily 8am–7pm), currently being restored, just manages to be visible in the concatenation of eight narrow streets. There are cafés to relax in, with the choice of sun or shade, and a magical ice-cream parlour, *Fenocchio*, with an extraordinary choice of flavours. Head to the neighbouring **place du Palais de Justice** on a Saturday, and you'll be able to browse through a jumble of old paintings, books and post cards.

The real magnet of Vieux Nice is the **cours Saleya** and adjacent places Pierre-Gautier and Charles-Félix. These wide-open, sun-lit spaces, lined with grandiloquent municipal buildings and Italianate chapels, are also the site of the city's main **market** (Tues–Sun 6am–1pm), where there are gorgeous displays of fruit, vegetables, cheeses and sausages, along with cut flowers and potted roses, mimosa and other scented plants till 5.30pm. On Monday the stalls sell bric-à-brac and secondhand clothes. On summer nights café and restaurant tables fill the *cours*, with literally thousands of people enjoying the warmth and extraordinary animation.

A collection of exotic shells is displayed in the **Galerie de Malacologie** at 2 cours Salaya (Tues–Sat 10.30am–1pm & 2–6pm). Equally alluring is the display of different flavoured olive oils, soaps, dried fruit and flowers at the shop *Aux Allées de la Côte d'Azur*, 1 rue St-François-de-Paule, run in old-fashioned style by two courteous old gentlemen. Further up the street, which runs west from the *cours*, is the suitably grand *belle époque* **Opéra**. On the north side of Vieux Nice, the narrow **rue du Marché** and its continuations – rue de la Boucherie, rue du Collet, rue St-François-de-Paule and rue Pairolière – have the atmosphere of a covered market, lined with food stores and invitingly laid out clothes, with permanent special offers and sales. The **fish market** is in place St-François (Tues–Sun 6am–1pm), its odours persisting till late at night when all the old streets are hosed down with enough water to go paddling.

If you want to feast your eyes on Baroque splendour, pop into the **chapels** and **churches** of Vieux Nice: La Chapelle de la Miséricorde on cours Saleya (open for Sunday Mass 10.30am or by contacting the Palais Lascaris); L'Eglise du Gesu (9am–6pm) on rue Droite; or L'Eglise St-Augustine on place St-Augustine which also contains a fine Pietà by Louis Bréa (open for Mass Sat 4pm & Sun 9am). For contemporary graphic and photographic art some of the best **art galleries** in Vieux Nice include *Autothèque*, 4 rue St-Réparate (Tues–Sat 10.30am–9pm; closed Aug), a municipal gallery that loans out works to schools and institutions; *Galerie Municipale Renoir* on the corner of rue de la Loge and rue Droite; and, diagonally opposite at 14 rue Droite, the *Galerie du Château* (Tues–Sat 10.30am–6pm; closed Aug to mid-Sept).

Also on rue Droite is the **Palais Lascaris** (Tues–Sun 9.30am–noon & 2.30–6pm; closed Nov), a seventeenth-century palace built by a family whose arms, engraved on the ceiling of the entrance hall, bear the motto "Not even lightning strikes us". It's all very noble, with frescoes, tapestries and chandeliers, along with a collection of porcelain vases from an eighteenth-century pharmacy.

In contrast, the light and joyous art of Raoul Dufy can be seen at the **Musée Dufy/Gallerie des Ponchettes** between cours Saleya and the sea at 77 quai des Etats-Unis (Tues–Sat 10am–noon & 2–6pm, Sun 2–6pm). Temporary exhibitions, changing every three months, display the town's considerable collection of Dufy's works, including many painted in Nice. Nearby, at 59 quai des Etats-Unis, is the less appealing collection of the **Musée Alexis et Gustav Adolf Mossa** (Tues–Sat 10am–noon & 2–6pm, Sun 2–6pm), both figures of the Nice establishment. Alexis initiated the Carnival and painted it in vapid watercolours; his son Gustav, who died in 1971, produced lurid symbolist paintings that reek of misogyny.

Place Masséna and the course of the Paillon

The stately, red-ochre **place Masséna** is the hub of the new town, built in 1835 across the path of the River Paillon, with good views north past fountains and palm trees to the mountains. A balustraded terrace and steps on the south of the square lead to Vieux Nice; the new town lies to the north. It's a pretty and spacious expanse, without being very significant – the only thing of interest here are the sundry ice-cream vendors who shelter their goods under the arcades during summer. To the west, the **Jardins Albert-1er** lead down to the promenade des Anglais, where the *Théâtre de Verdure* hosts concerts and theatre.

The covered course of the Paillon to the north of place Masséna has provided the sites for the city's more recent municipal prestige projects. At their worst, up beyond traverse Barla, they take the form of giant packing crates for high-tech goods, in the multi-media, mega-buck conference centre grotesquely called the **Acropolis**. Though theoretically a public building, with exhibition space, a cinema and bowling alley (11am–2am), international business often limits casual entry. There are, however, various modern sculptures outside the building on which to vent your critical frustration.

Downstream from the Acropolis is the vast 1980s monument to the ambitions of the city's former leader, composed of four towers clad with streaky marble and linked by glass-panelled steel girders. The **Musée d'Art Moderne et d'Art Contemporain** or MAMAC (Mon, Wed, Thurs, Sat & Sun 11am–6pm, Fri until 10pm; 25F) has a rotating exhibition of its collection of the avant-garde French and American movements of the 1960s to the present. **Pop Art** highlights include Lichtenstein cartoons and Warhol's Campbell's soup tin, while the **French New Realists** take the detritus or mundane objects of everyday life and smash them, tear them up, burn them, squash them (César's favourite action), trap them in glass or reflect them in mirrors (Spoerri), or, in the case of Christo, wrap them. Arman's *The Birds II* is a flock of flying wrenches; telephone boxes, wastepaper-basket contents, furniture and the remains of a meal all feature; Jean Tinguely has cogwheels creakingly moving a blade and a weight. The founder of the movement, Yves Klein, is particularly well represented, with two massive sculptures on the roof terrace, *Mur de Feu* and *Jardin d'Eden* as well as numerous huge canvases of monochrome blue or torched paper. The **Supports-Surfaces** group (Alocco, Bioulès, Viallat) take paintings themselves as objects, concentrating on the frame, the texture of the canvas, the back of the canvas, and there are also sections on the **Fluxus International** artists like Ben, who were into "Happenings", street life and graffiti. The collection also includes American Abstractionists and Minimalists, and the 1980s return to Figurative Art. It's a very masculine collection, and leaves you feeling sometimes that the works are little more than sterile by-products of the various intellectual theories upheld by the different schools, but it's good fun nonetheless, with huge, light galleries that are hardly ever crowded.

The next block down from the museum, above the *gare routière*, the "hanging gardens" of the **promenade du Paillon** fulfil the exclusive needs of the city's heroin users and gay cruisers, but things improve from here to place Masséna, and beyond in the Jardin Albert 1er, with benches, flower beds and fountains on a mammoth scale enjoyed by the city's massive sedentary population.

The modern city centre

Running north from place Masséna, **avenue Jean-Médecin** is the city's main **shopping** street, named after a former mayor, father of corrupt mayor Jacques Médecin. The late nineteenth-century architecture and trees don't distinguish it from any other big French city high street; the cafés are not particularly inviting; the cinemas show predictable blockbusters; street stalls sell overpriced bags and costume jewellery; and the traffic fumes have no escape. The *Nice-Etoile* shopping complex between rue Biscarra and bd Dubouchage has all the mainstream clothes and household accessory chains, plus *FNAC* for books and records, and you'll find other big department stores along the street.

Couturier shops are concentrated west of place Masséna on rue du Paradis and av de Suède. Both streets lead to the pedestrianized **rue Masséna** and the end of **rue de France** where tourists are supposed to congregate – and they do.

It's all hotels, bars, restaurants, ice-cream and fast-food outlets, with no regard for quality or style. Skirting this, the chief interest in the modern town is in the older architecture: eighteenth- and nineteenth-century Italian Baroque and Neo-classical, florid *belle époque*, and unclassifiable exotic aristo-fantasy. The trophy for the most gilded, exotic and elaborate edifice goes to the **Russian Orthodox Cathedral**, off bd Tsarewitch at the end of av Nicolas II (summer 9am–noon & 2.30–6pm; winter 9.30am–noon & 2.30–5pm; closed Sun morning; 12F; buses #14 or #17, stop *Tsarewitch*).

The promenade des Anglais

The point where the Paillon flows into the sea marks the beginning of the world-famous palm-fringed **promenade des Anglais**, which began as a coastal path created by nineteenth-century English residents for their afternoon's sea-breeze stroll. Today it's the city's unofficial high-speed racetrack, bordered by some of the most fanciful architecture on the Côte d'Azur.

Past the first promenade building, the glittery *Casino Ruhl*, is the 1930s Art Deco facade of the **Palais de la Méditerranée**, all that remains of the original municipal casino, closed for the usual reasons of intrigue and corruption, and finally demolished. A commercial centre is being constructed behind the old facade. Nearby, at 2 rue Congrès, the art gallery *Ferraro* has a permanent collection of New Realists Ben, César, Arman and Yves Klein.

The most celebrated of all the promenade buildings is the opulent **Negresco Hotel** at no. 37, filling up the block between rues de Rivoli and Cronstadt, built in 1906, and one of the great surviving European palace-hotels, where self-made millionaires rubbed shoulders with royalty. There's nothing to stop you wandering in past the flunkies in ludicrous operatic dress to take a look at the *Salon Louis XIV* and the *Salon Royale*. The first, on the left of the foyer, has a seventeenth-century painted oak ceiling and mammoth fireplace plus royal portraits that have all come from various French châteaux. The *Salon Royale* in the centre of the hotel is a vast collonaded oval room with a dome built by Gustav Eiffel's workshops. The stucco and cornices are decorated with 24-carat gold leaf, the carpet is the largest ever made by the Savonnerie factory and the bill for it accounted for a tenth of the total cost of the hotel. The chandelier is one of a pair commissioned from Baccarrat by Tsar Nicholas II – the other hangs in the Kremlin. You can also take a peep at *La Rotonde*, the smaller of the hotel's two restaurants, all done up as a childhood fantasy with carousel horses, cupids and puppets beneath a chandelier of grapes and a ceiling of circus scenes. Also within the hotel, with an entrance on rue de Rivoli, the *Gye Jacquot* art gallery specializes in Impressionists and Post-Impressionists. You don't have to be a potential buyer to have a look.

Just before the Negresco, with its entrance at 65 rue de France, the **Musée Masséna** (April–Sept Tues–Sun 10am–noon & 2–6pm; Oct–March closes 5pm) is one of those dire historical museums committed to making its subjects as inaccessible and uninteresting as possible. There's a section on Garibaldi, who fought against oppression in Italy, France, Brazil and Uruguay, which leaves you with no impression of his unbelievable life. Details of the plebiscite in 1860 on Nice becoming part of France, opposed by Garibaldi and Gambetta, leave you wondering why the vote was so close in the city and so massiveiy in favour in the countryside. There's predictable Napoleana – busts, drawings and paintings – and, in addition, medieval artworks and bits and pieces from just about every other era.

Set back from the promenade at no. 59 is an example of the modern equivalent of the turn-of-the-century palace-hotel, where Western arms dealers might rub shoulders with Third World defence ministers. It's the **Elysée Palace Hotel**, distinguished, if the word is applicable, by black glass, multinational flags and a monumental sculpture of a bare-breasted Venus clamped in concrete.

A kilometre or so down the promenade and a couple of blocks inland at 33 av des Baumettes in a house built by a Ukrainian princess in 1878 is the **Musée des Beaux-Arts** (Tues–Sun May–Sept 10am–noon & 3–6pm; Oct–April 10am–noon & 2–5pm; bus #38, stop *Chéret*). It has too many whimsical canvases by Jules Chéret, who died in Nice in 1932, a great many *belle époque* paintings to go with the building, a room dedicated to Van Loos, plus modern works that come as unexpected delights: a Rodin bust of Victor Hugo and some very amusing Van Dongens, such as the *Archangel's Tango*. Monet, Sisley – one of the famous poplar alleys – and Degas also grace the walls.

If you're a fan of naïve art, the **Musée International d'Art Naif Anatole Jakovsky** is behind the promenade and the expressway a further kilometre west in the Château Ste-Hélène, av Val-Mairie (Mon & Wed–Sun 10am–noon & 2–5/6pm; buses #9, #10 or #12, stop *Fabron* then bus #34 to Art Naïf). The six hundred examples of the genre here from the eighteenth century to the present day include works by Vivin, Rimbert, Bauchant and the Yugoslavian masters of the art, Yvan, Generalić and Lačković. Not far from here is the Parc des Miniatures (see overleaf).

The beaches and the port

Though mostly public with showers provided, the **beach** below the promenade des Anglais is all pebbles, not particularly clean and riddled with broken glass. There are, of course, the mattress, food and drinks concessionaries, but nothing like to the extent of Cannes.

There's a small, more secluded beach, **Plage de Païola**, on the west side of Le Château below the sea wall of the port with big blocks of concrete to sunbathe on and a little café for drinks and ice creams. But the best, and cleanest, place to swim, if you don't mind rocks, is the string of coves beyond the port that starts with the **Plage de la Reserve** opposite Parc Vigier (bus #32 or #3). From the water you can look up at the nineteenth-century fantasy palaces built onto the steep slopes of the Cap du Nice. Further up, past **Coco Beach** (bus #3 only, stop *Villa La Côte*), rather smelly steps lead down to a coastal path that continues around the headland. Towards dusk this becomes a gay pick-up place.

The **port**, flanked by gorgeous red to ochre eighteenth-century buildings and headed by the Neoclassical Notre-Dame du Port, is full of bulbous yachts but has little quayside life despite the restaurants along quai Lunel. On the hill to the east, prehistoric life in the region has been reconstructed on the site of an excavated fossil beach in the **Musée de Terra Amata**, 25 bd Carnot (Tues–Sun 9am–noon & 2–6pm; bus #32 from the port).

Cimiez

Nice's northern suburb of **Cimiez** has always been a posh place. Its principal streets, av des Arènes-de-Cimiez and bd de Cimiez, rise between plush, high-walled villas to what was the social centre of the town's elite some 1700 years ago, when the city was capital of the Roman province of *Alpes-Maritimae*. Part of a small amphitheatre still stands, and excavations of the Roman baths have revealed enough detail to distinguish the sumptuous and elaborate facilities for the top tax official and his cronies, the plainer public baths and a separate complex for women. The **archeological site** is overlooked by the impressive, modern **Musée d'Archéologie**, on rue Monte-Croce, which displays all the finds and illustrates the city's history up to the Middle Ages (Tues–Sat 10am–noon & 2–5/6pm, Sun 2–6pm; closed Nov; buses #15, #17, #20 or #22, stop *Arènes*).

The seventeenth-century villa between the excavations and the amphitheatre is the **Musée Matisse**, 164 av des Arènes (Mon & Wed–Sun April–Sept 11am–7pm; Oct–March 10am–5pm; 25F). Matisse spent his winters in Nice from 1916 onwards, staying in hotels on the promenade (from where *La Tempête à Nice* was painted) and then from 1921 to 1938 renting an apartment overlooking place Charles-Félix. It was here that he painted his most sensual, colour-flooded canvases featuring models got up as oriental odalisques posed against exotic draperies. In 1942, when he was installed with his tropical birds and plants in the *Régina* palace-hotel in Cimiez, he said that if he had gone on painting up north "there would have been cloudiness, greys, colours shading off into the distance". As well as the Mediterranean light, Matisse loved the cosmopolitan aspect of Nice, the rococo salons of the hotels, the times he spent rowing at the *Club Nautique*, the Carnival, and the presence of fellow artists Renoir, Bonnard and Picasso in neighbouring towns. He returned to the *Régina* from his stay in Vence in 1949, having developed his solution to the problem of "drawing in colour" by cutting out shapes and putting them together as collages or stencils. Almost all his last works in Nice were these cut-out compositions, with an artistry of line showing how he could wield a pair of scissors with just as much strength and delicacy as a paintbrush. He died in Cimiez in November 1954, aged 85.

The museum's collection includes work from every period, a great number of drawings and an almost complete set of his bronze sculptures. There are sketches for one of the *Dance* murals; models for the Vence chapel plus the priests robes he designed; book illustrations including those for a 1935 edition of Joyce's *Ulysses*; and excellent examples of his cut-out technique, of which the most delightful are *Les Abeilles* and *La Danseuse Créole*. Among the paintings are the 1905 portrait of Madame Matisse; *La Tempête à Nice* (1919–20) which seems to get wetter and darker the further you step back from it; *Odalisque Casquette Rouge* from the place Charles-Félix years; the 1947 *Nature Morte aux Grenades*; and one of his two earliest attempts at oil painting, *Nature Morte aux Livres* painted in 1890.

The Roman remains and the Musée Matisse back onto an old **olive grove**, one of the best open spaces in Nice and venue for the July **jazz festival** (see p.367). At its eastern end on place du Monastère is the **Monastère Notre-Dame de Cimiez** (church daily 8.30am–12.30pm & 2.30–7pm), with a pink flamboyant Gothic facade of nineteenth-century origin topping a much older and plainer porch. Inside there's more gaudiness, reflecting the rich benefactors the Franciscan order had access to, but also three masterpieces of medieval art: a *Pietà* and *Crucifixion* by Louis Bréa and a *Deposition* by Antoine Bréa. The sixteenth-century **monastic buildings** (guided tours Mon–Fri 10.30am, 3.30pm & 4.30pm) include two cloisters, the sacristy and the oratory which has extraordinary murals above the heavy wood panelling, full of alchemical symbols. You can see a copy of a 1687 engraving of Nice viewed from the monastery garden (to which there's public access), showing the walled city with its fortress and fields leading up from the River Paillon to Cimiez. To the north of the monastery is the **cemetery** where Matisse and Raoul Dufy are buried.

At the foot of Cimiez hill, just off bd Cimiez on av du Docteur-Menard, **Chagall's Biblical Message** is housed in a perfect custom-built museum (Mon & Wed–Sun Oct–June 10am–12.30pm & 2–5.30pm; July–Sept 10am–7pm; 35F; bus #15 stop *Musée Chagall*) opened by the artist in 1972. The rooms are light, white and cool, with windows allowing you to see the greenery of the garden beyond the indescribable pinky red shades of the *Song of Songs* canvases. The seventeen paintings are all based on the Old Testament and complemented with etchings and engravings. To the building itself, Chagall contributed a mosaic and stained-glass window.

The Villa Arson

In the district of **St-Barthélemy**, also in the north of the city but well over to the west from Cimiez, is the unlikely mix of a seventeenth-century mansion surrounded by a 1960s college constructed of concrete rendered with pebbles. The **Villa Arson**, 20 av Stephen-Liégeard (July–Sept daily 11am–7pm; Oct–June Wed–Sun 2–6pm; bus #36 stop *Arts Décoratifs*), is a national school for the plastic arts and an international centre for the teaching of contemporary art. Along with several exhibitions a year and displays of work by pupils, the school has fantastic views over the city to the sea, a pleasant garden to lounge about in, a cafeteria, bookshop and a very friendly, unelitist atmosphere.

Two blocks to the east of the Villa Arson, at 59 av St-Barthélemy, the **Prieuré du Vieux Logis** (Wed, Thurs, Sat & first Sun of month 3–5pm; bus #5, stop *Gorbella*) contains a collection of fourteenth- to sixteenth-century furniture, household objects and works of art in a sixteenth-century farm turned into a priory by a Dominican father in the 1930s.

Theme and leisure parks

Right out by the airport is a vast tourist attraction, the **Phoenix Parc Floral de Nice**, 405 promenade des Anglais (April–Sept 9am–7pm; Oct–March 9am–5pm; closed Jan & Mon except bank hols & school hols; 40F; exit St-Augustin from the highway or bus #9, #10, #23, #24 or #26 from Nice). It's a cross between botanical gardens, bird and insect zoo, and a tacky theme park: a curious jumble of automated dinosaurs and mock Maya temples, alpine streams, ginkgo trees, butterflies and cockatoos. The greenhouse full of fluttering butterflies is the star attraction, but the assumption that the world's fauna and flora are yours to admire may make you feel a bit uneasy.

Halfway between the city and the airport on bd Impératrice-Eugénie, and more manageable in size, is the **Parc des Miniatures** (mid-Dec to mid-Nov daily 9.30am–5.30/7pm; 47F or 60F combined entrance with *Musée des Trains Miniatures*; bus #22), with scaled models of Côte d'Azur buildings, past and present. The new **Musée des Trains Miniatures** within the park consists of model train sets with all the scenery and rolling stock from steam to *TGV* (same hours; 30F or 60F combined ticket).

Eating and drinking

Nice is a great place for **food** indulgence, whether you're picnicking on market fare, snacking on **Niçois specialities** of *pain beignet* (a bun stuffed with tuna, salad and olive oil), *salade niçoise*, *pissaladière* (onion tart with anchovies) and *socca* (a chick-pea flour pancake), or dining in the palace hotels. The **Italian** influence is strong in all restaurants, with pasta on every menu; **seafood** and **fish** are equally staple, with good *bourride* (fish soup), *estocaficada* (stockfish and tomato stew), and all manner of sea fish grilled with fennel or *herbes de Provence*. The local *Bellet* wines from the hills behind the city provide the perfect light accompaniment. For **snacks**, many of the cafés sell sandwiches with typically Provençal fillings such as fresh basil, olive oil, goat's cheese and mesclum, the unique green-salad mix of the region. If you want to buy the best **bread** or *croissants* in town, seek out *Espuno André*, at 22 rue Vernier in the old town (closed Sun afternoon & Mon). For **wines** at very decent prices there's the *Caves Caprioglio*, 16 rue de la Préfecture.

Most areas of Nice reveal excellent **restaurants**. Vieux Nice has a dozen on every street catering for a wide variety of budgets; the port quaysides have excellent, very pricey, fish restaurants, and the streets behind are very good for low budget meals. From June till September it's wise to **reserve** tables, or turn up before 8pm, especially in Vieux Nice.

Restaurants

L'Ane Rouge, 7 quai des Deux-Emmanuel (☎93.89.49.63). Lobster is the speciality of this portside gourmet's palace, grilled, baked or stuffed into little cabbages. Sea bass on a bed of fresh asparagus, turbot with salmon eggs, and the creamiest *bourride* are some of the other delights. Classic, classy and very expensive. Menus from 400F. Closed weekends and from mid-July to the end of Aug.

L'Antre d'Or, 19 av Audiffret. Good and affordable Chinese and Vietnamese food. Closed Wed, & Thurs midday.

L'Arbalète, 8 rue Jules-Gilly (☎93.80.58.28). Family run cosy and low priced pizzeria. 80F.

L'Avion Bleu, 10 rue Alphonse Karr (☎93.87.77.47). Theme nights for would-be jet-setters against a background decor inspired by the early days of aviation. Good grilled meat and fish. Weekday lunch menu 70F, otherwise from 100F. Open till midnight; last orders 11pm.

Le Bateleur, 12–14 cours Saleya (☎93.85.77.15). Generous and delicious pizzas for under 50F, plus live bands of dubious talent. Open till 2.30am.

Chantecler and La Rotonde, *Hôtel Negresco*, 37 promenade des Anglais (☎93.88.39.51). *Chantecler* is the best restaurant in Nice and well over 500F à la carte, but chef Dominique Le Stanc provides a lunchtime menu, wine and coffee included, for 250F, which will give you a good idea of how sublime Niçoise food at its best can be. At *La Rotonde* you can taste less fancy but still mouth-watering dishes on a 150F lunchtime menu or plats du jour for 75F. A la carte around 250F. Closed mid-Nov to mid-Dec.

Chez Flo, 4 rue Sacha-Guitry (☎93.80.70.10). Huge brasserie behind *Galeries Lafayette*, serving *choucroute*, *confit de canard*, seafood and great *crème brûlée*. Around 200F; after 10pm 95F menu including wine. Last orders 12.30am.

Chez René Socca, 2 rue Miralhéti, off rue Pairolière. The cheapest meal in town: you can buy helpings of *socca*, *pissaladière*, stuffed peppers, pasta or calamares at the counter and eat with your fingers on stools ranged haphazardly across the street; the bar opposite serves the drinks. Closed Mon.

Chez Thèrese, 28 rue Droite and also a market stall on the north side of cours Saleya, between rues St-Gaeten and Ste Marie. Superb *socca* to take away; 7.30am–1pm.

Le Comptoir, 20 rue St-François-de-Paule (☎93.92.08.80). Very chic 1930s-style brasserie by the Opéra. Superb sea bass in salt crust. 120F menu; à la carte 250F upwards. Evenings only until 1am, closed Sun.

Don Camillo, 5 rue des Ponchettes (☎93.85.67.95). A strong Italian influence, and ingredients straight from the cours Saleya market. Menus from 200F. Closed Sun.

Dounia-Zed, 7 rue Assalit (93.80.40.91). Excellent cous-cous and a warm welcome. Very good quality for the price. Around 110F.

L'Estrilla, 13 rue de l'Abbaye (☎93.62.62.00). Reservations essential in summer for this popular restaurant that serves superb *petites fritures* and paella in huge earthenware pots. Around 150F; menu around 100F before 8pm. Closed Mon midday and Sun.

La Grange, 7 rue Bonaparte (☎93.89.81.83). Good-value and well-prepared food in a congenial atmosphere. Around 100F.

Grigi Panini, 5 rue St-Réparate. Hot Italian sandwiches known as *paninis* from the counter, plus plats du jour. Very inexpensive.

La Mérenda, 4 rue de la Terrasse (no phone). The menu scribbled up on a blackboard will probably include courgette fritters, fresh pasta with pestou, *trulle* (a Niçois black pudding) and gorgeous chocolate mousse. A la carte only, from 180F. Closed Mon, Sat & Sun, Feb & Aug.

Nissa La Bella, 6 rue Ste Réparate (☎93.62.10.20). *Socca*, pizzas and other Niçois specialities. From 75F.

La Noisetine, cours Saleya, near rue Gassin. One of the cheapest places to eat on the cours Saleya, with generous and tasty crêpes, huge salads, nice desserts and fresh fruit juices. Open till midnight.

Prum-Bayon, 8 rue Dr-Pierre-Richelmi (☎93.26.69.80). Brilliant Cambodian, Chinese and Thai food; especially recommended are the *fruits de mer au fromage de soya* and *salade de papaye aux crevettes*. Around 120F.

Socca d'Or, 45 rue Bonaparte (☎93.56.52.93). A few blocks back from the port; cheap and very *sympa*. Summer Wed–Sun 10am–2.30pm & 5.30–9.30pm; winter 4.30–8.30pm.

Le Table de Chine, 57 quai des Etats-Unis (☎93.80.94.70). Chinese cuisine amid stunning decor including aquariums in the floor, plus view of the sea. From 150F.

Virginie, 2 pl A-Blanqui (☎93.55.10.07). Excellent *plateau des fruits de mer*. From 100F.

Cafés and bars

Bar des Oiseaux, 9 rue St-Vincent. Named for the birds that fly down from their nests in the loft and the pet parrot and screeching myna bird that perch by the door. Serves delicious and copious baguette sandwiches. Erratic opening hours, sometimes closed all afternoon; live jazz some evenings.

Caves Ricord, 2 rue Neuve. Old-fashioned wine bar with faded peeling posters and drinkers to match. A wide selection of wine by the glass, plus pizzas and other snacks. Open till 7pm.

La Douche à l'Etage, 34 cours Saleya. A cybercafé with four terminals linked up to the internet. Upstairs there really is a shower, plus comfortable settees, billards and music. Open till 12.30am.

Grand Café de Lyon, corner of avs Jean-Médecin & Maréchal Foch. One of the more attractive big *terrasse* cafés on the main street.

Pauline Tapas, 14 rue Emma-Tiranty. Bar/resto with music, cocktails and a pleasant easy-going atmosphere. Open till 2am.

Les Ponchettes and La Civette du Cours, cours Saleya. At Le Château end of the market-place, neighbouring cafés with cane seats fanning out a good 50m from the doors. Open late in summer.

Nightlife

Pubs have long been a very popular element of the Nice night scene, particularly with the young. For the older, more staid and affluent generation the luxury **hotel bars** with their jazzy singers and piano accompaniment have held sway for decades, and so they should as an essential ingredient of Riviera night life. There are plenty of **discos** too, and, particularly in Vieux Nice, a wide choice of venues for drinking and dancing, though the music tends not to be very novel. As for the **clubs**, bouncers judging your wallet or exclusive membership lists are the rule.

B52, 8 Descente Crotti. Small dance floor, young clientele and good value. Daily 10.30pm–4am, free entry until 1am.

Le Baby Doll, 227 bd de la Madeleine. Lesbian disco, not exclusively female. Daily from 10pm.

Le Baccara, *Hôtel Méridien*, 1 promenade des Anglais. Be-bop, blues, rock'n'roll or old French *chansons* sung to piano accompaniment. Very stylish. Music 11pm–1pm.

Banana Republic and Banana Club, 26 quai Lunel. Bar and mainstream disco; no entry charge and low-priced drinks. Open 9pm–5am; closed Tues.

Le Blue Boy, 9 rue Jean-Baptiste Spinétta. Lesbians and heteros are welcome at this, Nice's best gay venue off bd François-Grosso. There are two bars, two dance floors, DJs who know what's what, and a floorshow every Wed night. Daily 11pm–dawn; entrance charge on Wed and weekends.

Chez Wayne, 15 rue de la Préfecture. Popular bar on the edge of Vieux Nice run by an ex-pat who shares the French penchant for good old rock'n'roll. Live bands, of greatly varying quality, Fri and Sat nights. Daily 10am–midnight.

L'Iguane, 5 quai des Deux-Emmanuel. Very stylish night bar with dance floor for the poseurs. Open till 6am.

Pub Oxford, 4 rue Mascoïnat. English-style pub (in theory); excellent range of beers; live music every evening from 9.30pm; open 7pm–2.30am.

Le Salon, 2 rue Bréa. A fashionable late-night bar.

Scarlet O'Hara, 22 rue Droite. Tiny Irish folk bar on the corner of rue Rosetti serving the creamiest Guinness this side of the Irish Sea. Warmth, laughter, resonant heart-plucking folk music, spontaneous singing. Open 7pm–12.30am; closed Mon & first half of July.

Subway, 19 rue Droite. Reggae, soul and rock; reasonably priced; Tues–Sat from 11.30pm.

Le Zoom, 6 cours Saleya. Tapas bar with live soul and acid jazz Thurs–Sat; reasonable prices. Open from 6pm.

Entertainment and festivals

Of Nice's many **festivals** – which begin with the Mardi Gras **Carnival** in February – probably the most worthwhile are the **Festival de Jazz** in the amphitheatre and gardens of Cimiez, in the second week in July, and the **Festival International du Folklore** with traditional dance and music performed in the Théâtre de Verdure, in mid-July.

Nice's mainstream **opera**, *Opéra de Nice*, 4 and 6 rue St-Françoise-de-Paule (☎93.85.67.31), and **theatre**, *Théâtre de Nice*, promenade des Arts (☎93.80.52.60), have no special reputation; of the small independent theatres, *Théâtre de la Cité*, 3 rue Paganini (☎93.16.82.69), stages the most exciting shows. The best **cinema** is *Le Nouveau Mercury*, 16 place Garibaldi (☎36.68.81.06); the *UGC Rialto*, 4 rue de Rivoli (☎93.88.08.41), and *UGC Variétés*, 7 bd Victor-Hugo (☎93.87.74.97), show recent releases in the original language; the *Cinémathèque de Nice*, Acropolis, 3 Esplanade Kennedy (☎92.04.06.66), may have old classics showing.

Other than looking through the **listing mag** *Le Farfe Lu*, the best place to find out about concerts, plays, films and so on is *FNAC* in the Nice-Etoile shopping complex on av Jean-Médecin, where you can also buy **tickets**. Full details of municipal events, in particular festivals, are available from the *Comité des Fêtes*, 5 promenade des Anglais (☎93.87.16.28). For the jazz festival the main office is the *Abela Hôtel*, 223 promenade des Anglais (☎93.21.10.00).

The biggest sporting event is the **Triathlon de Nice** in early June when competitors from all round the world swim 4km in the Baie des Anges, cycle 120km in the hills behind the city and run 30km ending up along the promenade des Anglais.

Listings

Airlines *Air France* ☎93.18.89.89; *Air Inter* ☎93.14.84.84; *British Airways* ☎93.21.47.01.

Airport information ☎93.21.30.12.

Boat trips *Trans Côte d'Azur*, quai Lunel (☎92.00.42.30), run summer trips to Iles de Lérins, Cannes, Monaco, St-Tropez, Villefranche and Cap Ferrat.

Bookshop *The Cat's Whiskers*, 26 rue Lamartine, is an English-language bookshop.

Car breakdown *Dépannage Côte d'Azur Transport* 24-hr service ☎93.29.87.87.

Car parks Acropolis; rue Rossini; promenade du Paillon; *gare SNCF*; pl Masséna; pl de la Préfecture; cours Saleya.

Car rental Major firms represented at the airport. Otherwise try: *ADA*, 24 av Clemenceau (☎93.82.27.00); *Avis*, 2 av Phocéens (☎93.80.63.52); *Budget*, quai Lunel (☎93.56.45.50); *Europcar*, 89 rue de France (☎93.88.64.04); *Hertz*, 12 av de Suède (☎93.87.11.87).

Consulate USA, 31 rue Maréchal Joffre (☎93.88.89.55).

Currency exchange *American Express*, 11 promenade des Anglais (May–Oct Mon–Fri 9am–6pm, Sat 9am–noon; Nov–April Mon–Fri 9am–noon & 2–6pm); *Change Halévy*, 1 rue Halévy (daily 8am–7pm); *Change d'Or Charrière*, 10 rue de France (summer daily 8am–midnight; winter 8am–8pm).

Emergencies ☎15 or 93.92.55.55; *S.O.S. Médecins* (☎93.85.01.01) or *Nice Médecins* (☎93.52.42.42); *Hôpital St-Roch*, 5 rue Pierre-Dévoluy (☎92.03.33.75).

Ferries to Corsica *SNCM gare Maritime*, quai du Commerce (☎93.13.66.66).

Laundry *Taxi-Lav*, 24 av St-Augustine (7am–8pm); *France Lav*, 2 rue Provana de Leyni; *Lavomatique*, 11 rue du Pont-Vieux.

Lost property 10 cours Saleya (☎93.80.65.50). *SOS Voyageurs* for help with lost or stolen luggage at *gare SNCF* (Mon–Fri 9am–noon & 3–6pm; ☎93.16.02.61).

Pharmacy 7 rue Masséna 7.30pm–8am (☎93.87.78.94).

Police Commissariat Central de Police, 1 av Maréchal Foch (☎92.17.22.22).

Post office *PTT*, pl Wilson, 06000 Nice.

Taxis ☎93.80.70.70.

Trains Information ☎93.87.50.50; reservations ☎93.88.89.93. For the line to Digne: *Chemins de Fer de Provence*, 4 bis rue Alfred Binet (☎93.82.10.17).

Niçois villages

The **foothills of the Alps** come down to the northern outskirts of Nice, and right down to the sea on the eastern side of the city: a majestic barrier, snowcapped for much of the year, beyond which crest after crest edges higher while the valleys get steeper and livelihoods more precarious. From the sea, the wide course of the Var to the west appears to be the only passage northwards. But the hidden river of Nice, the **Paillon**, cuts its way southwestwards through the mountains, its course an ancient route connecting small communities still living in the defensive architecture of the Middle Ages. The **Nice–Turin railway line** follows the Paillon for part of its way – one of the many spectacular train journeys of this region. If you have your own transport this is hard hairpin-bend country where the views are a serious distraction. **Buses** from Nice to its villages are on the whole very good.

With their proximity to the metropolis, the perched villages of **Peillon**, **Peille**, **Lucéram**, **Coaraze**, **Contes** and **L'Escarène** are no longer entirely peasant communities, though the social make-up remains a mix. You may well hear

Provençal spoken here and the **traditional festivals** are still communal affairs, even when the participants include the well-off Niçois escaping from the coastal heat. The links between the city and its hinterland are strong: the villagers still live off the land and sell their olives and olive oil, goat's cheese or vegetables and herbs in the city's markets; many city dwellers' parents or grandparents still have homes within the mountains and for every Niçois this wild and underpopulated countryside is the natural remedy for city stress.

Peillon

For the first 10km or so along the River Paillon, after you leave the last of Nice, the valley is marred by quarries, supplying the city's constant demand for building materials. However, once you reach Peillon's *gare SNCF*, the road begins to climb, looping for 3km through olive groves, pine forest and brilliant pink and yellow broom before you reach the gates of **PEILLON**'s medieval enclave.

Peillon is beautifully maintained, right up to the lovely place de l'Eglise at the top. There is very little commerce save for the gallery of Gabriel Mariani's bronze and wood sculptures in *Le Vieux Logis* and *Les Lutins*, the *salon de thé* and post-card shop at the village entrance. Just outside the village stands the *Chapelle des Pénitents Blancs*, decorated with violent fifteenth-century frescoes similar to those by Jean Canavesio at La Brigue (to visit ask at the *mairie*; ☎93.79.91.04). From the chapel a path heads off across the hillside northwards to Peille. It's a two-hour walk or so along what was once a Roman road, and a lot more direct than going via the valley.

Practicalities

Peillon has an extremely glamourous **hotel-restaurant**, *Auberge de la Madonne* (booking essential; ☎93.79.91.17; ⑧), with balconies overlooking the valley and a very good restaurant offering a *Menu Peillonnais* of local quails, hare and fresh goat's cheese salad flavoured with herbs from the garden (closed Wed; 200F, also 130F menu). If you're on a tight budget, there's a two-star **campsite**, *La Laune*, at the *Moulins de Peillon*, chemin des Prés (May–Oct; ☎93.79.91.61).

Peille

PEILLE has a very different atmosphere to Peillon. Historically it has always been a bit bolshy. Excommunicated several times for refusing to pay its bishop's tithes, the republicanism of this small town was later manifested by the domed thirteenth-century Chapelle de St-Sébastien being turned into the **Hôtel de Ville**, and the Chapelle des Pénitents Noirs into a communal **oil press**. Peille claims to be the birthplace of the Roman emperor Pertinax who was assassinated within thirteen weeks of his election on account of his egalitarian and democratic tendencies.

In the Romanesque **church** at the eastern end of the village you can see a painting of the village in medieval times, the count of Provence's castle – in ruins now – standing guard above the ravine. This and the other fourteenth- and sixteenth-century adornments will be shown to you by someone from the hospice next door to the church – you cannot visit unaccompanied. The main square, **place A. Laugier**, is graced with a Gothic fountain and two half-arches supporting a Romanesque pillar; on rue St-Sébastien the former salt tax office, the **Hôtel de la Gabelle**, still stands; on place de Colle the medieval **court house** bears a plaque recalling Peille's transfer of its rights over Monaco to Genoa. Peille's only minus is its views, destroyed by the quarrying around La Grave, its suburb down in the valley by the rail line. You can, however, take labyrinthine winding routes to **Ste-Agnes** and **L'Escarene** from the village, on which precipitous panoramas are assured.

Practicalities

Peille is 6.5km of hairpins above its *gare SNCF*, with fairly regular buses making the connection. If you want to **stay** you'll need to have booked in advance at Peille's one **hotel-restaurant**, *Le Belvédère* (☎93.79.90.45; ③) at the western entrance to the village. *Chez Nana* on place Carnot (☎93.79.90.41; around 100F) does a great Sunday lunch with real Provençal cooking and a generous choice of hors d'oeuvres; *La Fenière*, rue de la Tour (closed Thurs; ☎93.91.90.01), offers a set meal for 80F, and you can snack at *Le Serre* or *L'Absynthe* bars at the end of rue Centrale.

L'Escarène and Lucéram

At **L'ESCARENE** the rail line leaves the Paillon and heads northeast to **Sospel**. In the days before rail travel, this was an important staging post on the road from Nice to Turin, when drivers would rig up new horses to take on the thousand-metre Braus pass, which the rail line tunnels under. The village's single-arched bridge (rebuilt after its destruction in World War II) was the crucial river crossing, yet the people who first lived beside it obviously mistrusted all travellers; their houses had no windows overlooking the river, nor any doors, and access was by retractable ladders.

If you want to stop off head for the beautiful **place de l'Eglise** surrounded by pale yellow, green and ochre houses; opposite the great Baroque church is the *Café de l'Union* bar.

Upstream to Lucéram

Following the Paillon upstream for 6km, you pass the fifteenth-century **Chapelle de St-Grat** with frescoes by Jean Beleison, a colleague of Louis Bréa. Just 1km distant, **Lucéram** clings to the side of the valley, the walls of its interlocking houses showing the erosion of their age. Above the houses, the belfry of **Ste-Marguerite** rises in defiance, its cupola glittering with polychrome Niçois tiles. Within are some of the best late medieval artworks in the Comté de Nice, though several have been removed and taken to the Musée Masséna in the city.

All these works belong to the School of Nice and both the *Retable de Ste-Marguerite*, framed by a tasteless Baroque baldaquin, and the painting of Saints Peter and Paul, with its cliff-hanging castle in the distance, are attributed to Louis Bréa. There are more local landscapes in the *Retable de St-Antoine*, painted on flamboyant Gothic panelling, with generous additions of gold, and said to be by Jean Canavesio. Popular art is present in a thirteenth-century plaster *Pietà*, probably by a local craftsman, to the left of the choir, and the black and red processional lanterns kept in the choir.

To have the works illuminated you need to apply to the *presbytère* to the right of the church. The priest can also give you the keys to the **Chapelle St-Grat** and the **Chapelle de Notre-Dame-de-Bon-Coeur**, 2km northwest of the village off the road to the St-Roch pass. The walls and ceilings in this chapel are also painted by Jean Beleison.

Lucéram

The **village** of **LUCERAM** itself has the friendliness of a still-peasant community, full of well-fed cats and mangy dogs. The communal oil press remains in service and at the start of the olive season in October the villagers dip their traditional *brissaudo* – toasted garlic bread – in the virgin oil. At Christmas the shepherds bring their flocks into the church and after mass make their offerings of dried figs and bread.

Like L'Escarène, Lucéram has no hotels but you can get an excellent huge plat du jour for under 50F at *Le Pin* (open daily), perched above the main road opposite the steps leading up past the pink *mairie* into the medieval village.

Coaraze

COARAZE overlooks the valley of the Paillon de Contes, a tributary running west of the main Paillon. From Lucéram and the pass of St-Roch the road hangs over near-vertical descents, turning corners onto great open views of these beautiful but inhospitable mountains.

The population is less than five hundred, though this is one of the more chic Niçois villages, with many an artist and designer in residence. The facades of the post office and *mairie*, and place Félix-Giordan near the top of the village are decorated with **sundials** signed by various artists including Cocteau and Ponce de Léon. The latter decorated the **Chapelle Notre-Dame du Gressier** just north of the village in 1962, known now as the *Chapelle Bleu* from the single colour he used in the frescoes. Place Félix-Giordan also has a **lizard mosaic** and a Provençal poem engraved in stone. The church, destroyed and rebuilt three times, is famous for the number of angels in its interior decoration, 118 in all.

Unlike the other Niçois villages, Coaraze goes so far as to have a volunteer-run **tourist office**, or rather a *Syndicat d'Initiative* on place A-Mari below the village (no fixed hours; ☎93.79.37.47), which has the key to the church and chapel.

Coaraze has one excellent **hotel-restaurant**, the *Auberge du Soleil* (closed mid-Nov to mid-March; ☎93.79.08.11; ④), with wonderful views from the rooms and the dining terrace. Access to it is on foot only but you won't have to drag your cases up yourself.

Contes

The story always told about **CONTES**, 9km downstream from Coaraze, is of its **caterpillar plague** in 1508, which was so bad the bishop of Nice had to be called in to exorcise the leaf-eating army. With the full weight of ecclesiastical law the caterpillars were sentenced to exile on the slopes of Mont Macaron on the other side of the valley. A procession to the mountain was organized with all the villagers plus saintly relics, holy oil and so forth, and lo and behold, every last caterpillar joined the ranks and never bothered Contes again.

Whatever persuaded the caterpillars to move, snails in Contes would seem to suffer a more direct approach if the illumination of the *Fête-Dieu* at the end of

May is anything to go by. For this night-time procession, the streets of Contes are lit by lamps made from snail shells found on all the window ledges.

The **church** of medieval Contes has another prime example of the rich colour and pure lines of the fifteenth-century Nice School in the *Retable de Ste-Madeleine* attributed to François Bréa. The central panel has disappeared – perhaps eaten by the caterpillars. Outside the church is a two-tiered Renaissance fountain.

Contes has spread down the valley from its old village, and is quite a major town in these parts with a population of over four thousand. The **tourist office** is on place A-Olivier in the modern town (Mon–Sat 2–6pm); buses #300 and #302 leave from the *place* for Haute Contes. There are **places to stay** in the modern town: *Le Chaudron*, bd Raiberti (closed Sun evening; ☎93.79.11.00; ③), and *Le Relais de la Vallée* next door (☎93.79.01.03; ②), both on the main Nice road and not much to write home about.

Châteauneuf-de-Contes

Across the river from Contes a road winds up the mountainside to **CHATEAUNEUF-DE-CONTES**, a hilltop gathering of houses around an eleventh-century Romanesque church. About 2km further on a path to the left leads to a more recent but **ruined village**, also called Châteauneuf-de-Contes, which was last inhabited before World War I. That this Châteauneuf was abandoned gradually is evident from the varying degrees of building decay and vegetation growth. Ivy-clad towers and crumbling walls rise up among once-cultivated fig trees and rose bushes, and insects buzz in the silence and butterflies flit about the wild flowers that have replaced the gardens. The crescent of walled terraces where the people grew their vegetables is still clearly defined. The passing of time rather than some cataclysm saw its decline – there are no ghosts, nor even a whiff of eerieness; just immense unthreatening horizons on either side.

Apart from the odd railings around the most insecure bits of masonry, there are no gates or fences and you can wander around at any time of the day or night. On the Monday of Pentecost the inhabitants of the older surviving village make a pilgrimage to the ruins which finishes with a communal meal.

The corniches

Three **corniche roads** run east from Nice to the independent principality of Monaco and to Menton, the last town of the French Riviera. Napoléon built the **Grande Corniche** on the route of the Romans' *Via Julia Augusta*. The **Moyenne Corniche** dates from the first quarter of the twentieth century, when aristocratic tourism on the Riviera was already causing congestion on the coastal road, the **Corniche Inférieure**. The upper two are the classic location for executive car commercials, and for films where people driving them are killed. Real deaths occur too: most notoriously Grace Kelly, princess of Monaco, who died when she took a bend on the Moyenne Corniche too fast.

Buses take all three routes; the **train** follows the lower corniche; and all three are superb means of seeing the most mountainous stretch of the Côte d'Azur. For the long-distance panoramas you follow the Grande Corniche, for precipitous views the Moyenne Corniche, and for close-up encounters with the architectural riot of the continuous coastal resort, you take the Corniche Inférieure. There's

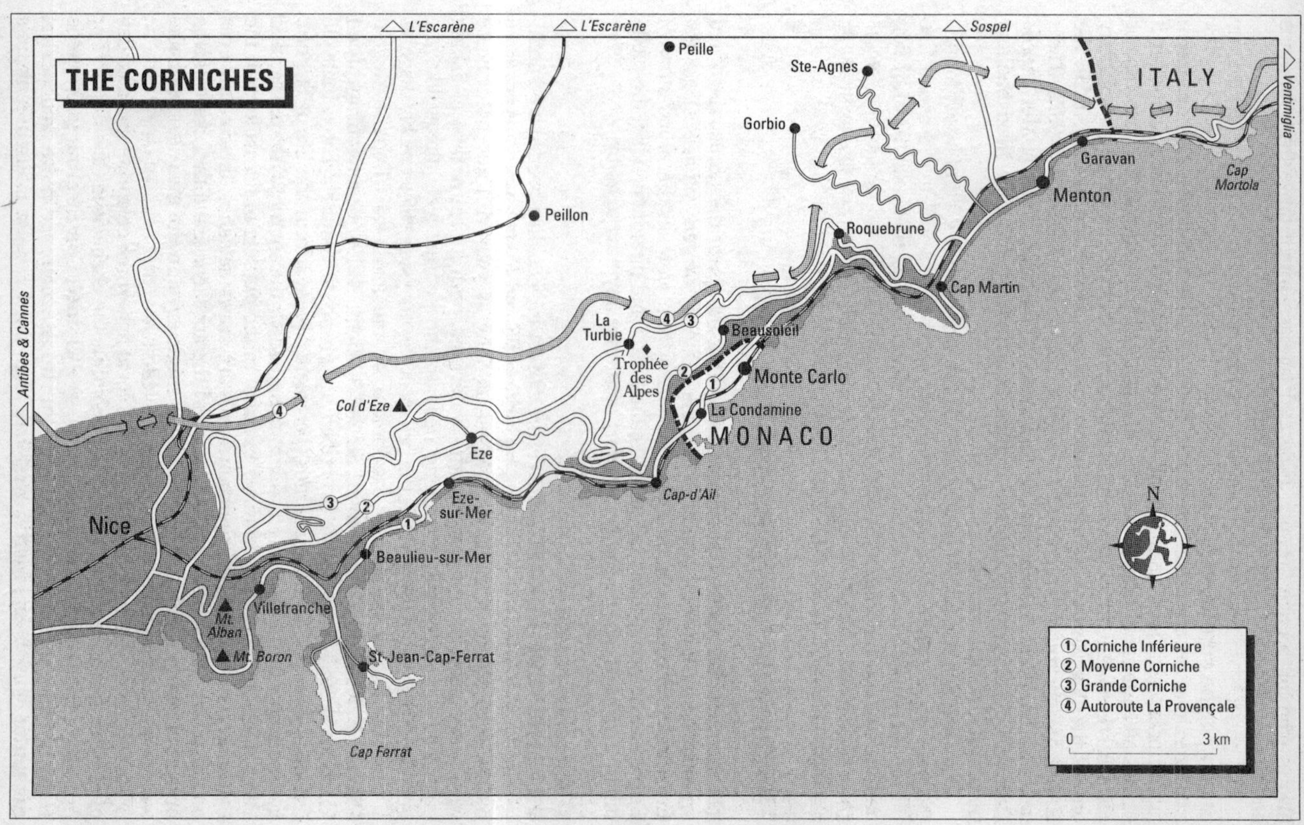
THE CORNICHES
L'Escarène
L'Escarène
Sospel
Peille
Ste-Agnes
Gorbio
ITALY
Ventimiglia
Garavan
Menton
Cap Mortola
Peillon
Roquebrune
Cap Martin
Antibes & Cannes
La Turbie
Trophée des Alpes
Beausoleil
Monte Carlo
La Condamine
MONACO
Col d'Eze
Eze
Cap-d'Ail
Eze-sur-Mer
Nice
Beaulieu-sur-Mer
Villefranche
Mt. Alban
Mt. Boron
St-Jean-Cap-Ferrat
Cap Ferrat
N
① Corniche Inférieure
② Moyenne Corniche
③ Grande Corniche
④ Autoroute La Provençale
0
3 km

also a hydrofoil service between Nice and Monaco which takes thirty minutes and costs around 100F return (☎92.16.15.15).

Staying in the corniches

Staying along the corniches, anywhere between Nice and Menton, is expensive and impractical if you haven't booked well in advance. On a limited budget it makes more sense to base yourself in Menton or Nice and treat the corniches as pleasure-rides. Still, if you do want to stay somewhere in the area, you could try one of the two **youth accommodation** centres by the sea in **Cap d'Ail**: the *Centre Méditerranéen*, chemin des Oliviers (half-board obligatory; ☎93.78.21.59; ①), and the *Relais International de la Jeunesse "Thalassa"*, bd de la Mer (April–Oct; ☎93.78.18.58; ①). Rates are higher than hostels and they need booking months ahead for summer.

Camping is again not an easy option. There's no secluded bit of beach to hide out on, and the campsites charge exorbitant rates in season. There's one at **Eze** off the Grande Corniche, the two-star *Les Romarins* (April–Sept; ☎93.01.81.64), and at Roquebrune there's the two-star *Fleur de Mai*, 67 val de Gorbio, on the D23 (April–Sept; ☎93.57.22.36) and the three-star *Toraca*, 14 av du Général-Leclerc (Feb–Nov; ☎93.35.62.55) just north of the *mairie*.

The Corniche Inférieure and Cap Ferrat

The characteristic **Côte d'Azur mansions** that represent the unrestrained and stylistically incompatible fantasies of the original owners parade along the **Corniche Inférieure**. Or they lurk screened from view on the promontory of **Cap Ferrat**, their gardens full of man-eating cacti and piranha ponds if the plethora of *"Défense d'entrer – Danger de Mort"* signs are anything to go by.

Villefranche-sur-Mer

VILLEFRANCHE-SUR-MER, the resort closest to Nice, has been spared architectural eyesores only to be marred by lurking US and French warships attracted by the deep waters of the bay. However, as long as your visit doesn't coincide with shore leave, the old town on the waterfront, with its active fleet of fishing boats and its **rue Obscure** running beneath the houses, feels almost like the genuine article, an illusion which the prices at the quayside cafés quickly dispel.

The tiny fishing harbour is overlooked by the medieval **Chapelle de St-Pierre** (Tues–Sun 9.30am–noon & 2–4.30/6pm; 12F), decorated by **Jean Cocteau** in 1957 in shades he described as "ghosts of colours". The colours fill drawings in strong and simple lines, portraying scenes from the life of St Peter and homages to the women of Villefranche and to the gypsies. Above the altar Peter walks on water supported by an angel to the outrage of the fishes and the amusement of Christ. The fishermen's eyes are drawn as fishes; the ceramic eyes on either side of the door are the flames of the apocalypse and the altar candelabras of night-time fishing forks rise above single eyes. In the guide to the chapel written by Cocteau, the artist invites travellers to enter without any aesthetic preconceptions. On June 29 each year the local fishermen celebrate the feast day of St Peter and St Paul with a mass, the only time the chapel is used.

To the west of the fishing port, the massive **Citadelle de St-Elma** shelters the Hôtel de Ville, an open-air cinema and theatre, a conference centre and two **art museums** (July & Aug Mon & Wed–Sat 10am–noon & 3–7pm, Sun 3–7pm; June

& Sept 9am–noon & 3–6pm; Oct–May 10am–noon & 2–5pm; closed Nov; free). One is dedicated to the Villefranche sculptor **Volti**, whose bronze woman lies in the fountain outside the citadel gates; the other, dedicated to the couple **Henri Goetz** and **Christine Boumeester**, contains two works by Picasso and one by Miró.

PRACTICALITIES

Villefranche's **tourist office** is in the Jardins François-Binon (July & Aug daily 8.45am–7pm; Sept–June Mon–Sat 9am–noon & 2–6.30pm; ☎93.01.73.68), just below the corniche as it changes from bd Princesse-Grace-de-Monaco to av Albert-1er.

For **hotels** in the area, a good-value low-budget possibility is *Pension Patricia*, on chemin des Pépinières, Pont St-Jean (☎93.01.06.70; ③). *Hôtel Welcome*, 1 quai Amiral-Courbet (☎93.76.76.93; ⑦), the former convent where Cocteau used to stay in the prime position overlooking the port, is highly recommended. *La Résidence Carlton*, 9 bis av Albert-1er (☎93.01.06.02; ⑦), has pretty rooms with balconies, 200m from the sea.

Of the fresh-fish **restaurants** on quai Amiral-Courbet *Le Saint-Pierre* (☎93.76.93.93; menus from 150F) is the most desirable; *Le Nautic* (closed Sun evening & Mon; ☎93.01.94.45) and *Lou Roucas* (closed Tues; ☎93.01.90.12) are good, and rather more affordable.

Cap Ferrat

Closing off Villefranche's bay to the east is **Cap Ferrat**, the Côte d'Azur's most desirable address. Its one town, **ST-JEAN-CAP-FERRAT**, departs little from the Riviera tradition of old houses overlooking modern yachts in a fishing port turned millionaires' resort.

East of St-Jean's new port you can follow av Jean-Mermoz then a **coastal path** out along the little peninsula, past the Plage Paloma to **Pointe Hospice**, where a nineteenth-century chapel cowers behind a twelve-metre-high turn of the century metal Virgin and Child. From av Claude-Vignon back in St-Jean another coastal path runs right round to chemin du Roy on the opposite side of the peninsula. At the southernmost point of the Cap you can climb a **lighthouse** (9.30am–noon & 3–4/7pm) for an overview of what you cannot reach – most of Cap Ferrat. Two exceptions to the formidable restrictions of passage are the **zoo** at the northern end of bd Général-de-Gaulle (9.30am–7pm; July & Aug till 11pm; 40F), in the park of King Leopold of Belgium's old residence, and the Villa Ephrussi on the road from the mainland.

The **Villa Ephrussi** (mid-Feb to Oct daily 10am–6/7pm; Nov to mid-Feb Mon–Fri 2–6pm, Sat & Sun 10am–6pm; last entry 30min before closing; 40F) was built in 1912 for Baroness Ephrussi née Rothschild, a woman of unlimited wealth and highly eclectic tastes. The result is a wonderful profusion of decorative art, paintings, sculpture and artefacts ranging from the fourteenth to the nineteenth centuries and from European to Far Eastern origin. Among the highlights are a fifteenth-century d'Enghien tapestry of fabled hunting scenes; paintings by Carpaccio and other works of the Venetian Renaissance; Dresden porcelain; Ming vases; Mandarin robes; and canvases by Monet, Sisley and Renoir. Visits to the villa are unguided, giving you time to make your own selection of favourites. In order to make the **gardens** the baroness had a hill removed to level out the space in front and then had tons of earth brought back in order that her formal French design could grow above the rock. She named the house after an ocean liner, the *Ile de France*, and had her 35 gardeners wear sailors costumes. They tended Spanish, English, Japanese and Florentine gardens all on a grand scale with attendant statuary and pools. One part of the park, the eastern slope, remained wild Provençal growth, because funds did eventually run out. In 1915 the baroness divorced and moved to Monaco, after just three years in her extraordinary creation.

PRACTICALITIES

The St-Jean **tourist office** is at 59 av Dénis-Séméria (July & Aug daily 9am–6pm; Sept–June Mon–Fri 9am–noon & 1–5pm; ☎93.76.08.90). A not too frequent **bus** service does the circuit of the promontory.

The cheapest **hotel** option is *La Fregate*, av Denis-Séméria (☎93.76.04.51; ③). For rooms with good views of the sea try *La Bastide*, 3 av Albert-1er (☎93.76.06.78; ④), or *La Costière*, av Albert-1er (☎93.76.03.89; ④), with its own garden. *Brise Marine*, 58 av J-Mermoz (March–Sept; ☎93.76.04.36; ⑦) has spacious rooms 100m from the sea, while the pleasant *Clair Logis*, 12 av Centrale (☎93.76.04.57; ⑥), boasts a lovely large garden and balconies to each room.

The best **dinners** to be had are both on the pleasure port: *Le Sloop* (closed Wed out of season; ☎93.01.48.63; 155F menu) serves prime fish in delicate and original flavours; and the hotel *La Voile d'Or* (closed Nov to mid-March; ☎93.01.13.13; menus from 250F) which provides very sophisticated and imaginative Mediterranean cuisine; the welcome and comfort at both are exceptional too. For plats du jour, salads and pasta for less than 80F head for *Le Pirate*, also on the port (closed Thurs; ☎93.76.12.97).

Beaulieu

On the east side of the Cap Ferrat peninsula, overlooking the pretty Baie des Fourmis and accessible by foot from St-Jean along the promenade Maurice-Rouvier, is **BEAULIEU**, sheltered by a ring of hills that ensure its temperatures are amongst the highest on the Côte. The most interesting thing in town is undoubtedly the **Villa Kerylos** (mid-March to June & Oct daily 10.30am–12.30pm & 2–6pm; July–Sept daily 10am–7pm; Dec–March Tues–Fri 2–5.30pm, Sat & Sun 10.30am–12.30pm & 2–5.30pm; 35F), a near perfect reproduction of an ancient Greek villa, just east of the casino on av Gustave-Eiffel. The only concessions made by Théodore Reinach, the archeologist who had it built, were glass in the windows, a concealed piano, and a minimum of early twentieth-century conveniences. He lived here for twenty years, eating, dressing and behaving as an Athenian citizen, taking baths with his male friends and assigning separate suites to women. However perverse the concept, it's a visual knockout, with faithfully reproduced frescoes, ivory and bronze copies of mosaics and vases, authentic antiquities and lavish use of marble and alabaster.

Beaulieu's modern-day residents are as long in the tooth as their bank balances are high in the black. The 1930s **casino** provides concerts and shows from a bygone age and tables for the last thrill left. For those tempted to **stay** overnight, two economical options are the simple but decent *Hôtel France*, 1 montée des Orangers (☎93.01.00.92; ④), and *Select*, 1 place Gén-de-Gaulle (☎93.01.05.42; ③), which is basic but clean, comfortable and excellent value for this part of the world.

For **food**, *La Réserve* at 5 bd du Général-Leclerc (closed Nov–March; ☎93.01.00.01; midday menu 310F) features the grand old dishes of French cuisine. *Le Maxilien*, 43 bd Marinoni (closed Oct to mid-April; ☎93.01.47.70;

menus from 155F), still expensive but no way near as outrageous as *La Réserve*, serves classic dishes with panache.

Eze-sur-Mer and Cap d'Ail

The next stop on the train is **EZE-SUR-MER**, the seaside extension of **Eze** village on the Moyenne Corniche, with a narrow shingle beach and less pretensions than its western neighbours. For reasonable **accommodation**, *Mimosa Cottage*, av de la Liberté (closed mid-Nov to mid-Dec ☎93.01.54. 82; ③), is on the corniche but not quite as charming as the name suggests.

CAP D'AIL feels equally informal though it suffers from the noise and congestion of the lower and middle corniches running closely parallel. Having said that, its tiny eastern promontory has for years maintained one of the few open public spaces left on the Riviera, around M. Jeannot's little cabin **bar-restaurant** on Cap Fleuri, which serves its faithful customers who come down here to fish, play *boules* or just look out to sea. A short coastal path leads from here to **Monaco**.

Hôtel la Cigogne on rte de la Plage-Mala (closed Nov–March; ☎93.78.29.60; ④) is nothing very special but comfortable.

The Moyenne Corniche

The first views from the **Moyenne Corniche** are back over Nice as you grind up Mont Alban, which, with its seaward extension, Mont Boron, separates Nice from Villefranche. Two forts command these heights: **Fort Boron** which is still in naval service, and **Fort Alban**, as endearing a piece of military architecture as is possible to imagine, which though now overgrown still remains in one piece, with its four tiny turrets glimmering in glazed Niçois tiles. The fort was continually taken by the enemies of Villefranche, who could then make St-Elme surrender in seconds. You can wander freely around the fort and see why Villefranche's citadel, so unassailable from the sea, was so vulnerable from above. To reach it you turn sharp right off the corniche along rte Forestière before you reach the Villefranche pass. The #14 bus from Nice stops at *Chemin du Fort* from which the fort is signed.

Once through the pass, the cliff-hanging car-chase stretch of the Moyenne Corniche begins, with great views, sudden tunnels and little habitation.

Eze

EZE is unmistakable long before you arrive, its streets wound around a cone of rock below the corniche, whose summit is 470m above the sea. From a distance the village has the monumental medieval unity of Mont St-Michel, but seen up close, its secular nature exerts itself. There is no other *village perché* in all of Provence so infested with antique dealers, pseudo artisans and other caterers to the touristic rich. It takes a mental feat to recall that the labyrinth of tiny vaulted passages and stairways was designed not for charm but from fear of attack.

The ultimate defence, the castle, no longer exists, and a cacti **Jardin Exotique** (summer daily 9am–8pm; winter daily 9am–noon & 2–7pm; 12F) replacing it offers the only respite from the commerce below. The one other place to visit where nothing is on sale is the **Chapelle des Pénitents Blancs** on place du Planet, where the crucifix, of thirteenth-century Catalan origin, has Christ smiling down from the cross.

From place du Centenaire, just outside the old village, you can reach the shore through open countryside, via the **sentier Frédéric-Nietzsche**. The philosopher Nietzsche is said to have conceived part of *Thus Spoke Zarathustra* on this path –

which is not quite as hard going as the book. You arrive at the Corniche Inférieure at the eastern limit of **Eze-sur-Mer** (coming upwards it's signposted to *La Village*).

PRACTICALITIES
Eze's **tourist office**, on place du Gal-de-Gaulle by the first car park you come to (July & Aug daily 9am–6pm; Sept–June Mon–Sat 9am–noon & 2–6pm; ☎93.41.26.00), can supply a map of the many **footpaths** through the hills linking the three corniches.

For **rooms** with a sea view, the *Auberge des Deux Corniches* on the D46, 1km from the village (closed Nov; ☎93.41.19.54; ④), is worth checking out. *Hôtel le Beleze*, place de la Colette on the Moyenne Corniche (☎93.41.19.09; ③), is a bit noisy but reasonable for the price.

Eze's top **restaurant** is the *Château Eza* (closed Nov–March; ☎93.41.12.24; menus from 150F), where a fortune can be spent on ravioli stuffed with white truffle or *langoustine*, and the like. More affordably, there's *La Taverne*, rue du Barri (closed Mon; ☎93.41.00.17; midday menu around 100F) also known as *Le Grill du Château*, serving grills and pizzas, and, very good value, *Au Nid d'Aigle* (closed Wed; ☎93.41.19.08; menus from 125F), at the very top of the village.

The Grande Corniche

At every other turn on the **Grande Corniche** you're invited to park your car and enjoy a *belvédère*, and at certain points, such as **Col d'Eze**, you can turn off upwards for even higher views. For drivers the main danger, apart from being tempted by the views, is the switches between dazzling light and darkness as you go in and out of the tunnels.

Col d'Eze

The upper part of Eze is backed by the **Parc Forestier de la Grande Corniche**, a wonderful oak forest covering the high slopes and plateaux of this coastal range. Paths are well signed; there are picnic and games areas, orientation tables ... in fact it's rather over managed, but at least it isn't built on. If you take a left (coming from Nice) to cross the *col* and keep following rte de la Réserve, you come, after 1.5km or so, to an observatory, **Astrorama** (April–June & Sept Tues & Fri 6.30–11pm; July & Aug daily 6.30–11pm; Oct–May Tues & Fri 20F) where you can look at the evening and night sky through telescopes.

If you're on a low budget, the *Hôtel L'Hermitage*, on the corniche (closed mid-Dec to mid-Jan; ☎93.41.00.68; ③), has magnificent views, passable meals and a **restaurant** (closed from mid-Nov to mid-Feb).

La Turbie

After eighteen stunning kilometres from Nice, you reach **LA TURBIE** and the **Trophée des Alpes**, a sixth-century monument to the power of Rome and the total subjugation of the local peoples. Originally a statue of Augustus Caesar stood on the 45-metre plinth which was inscribed with the names of 44 vanquished tribes and an equally long list of the emperor's virtues. In the tenth century the descendants of the suppressed were worshipping the monument, to the horror of St Honorat who did his best to have the graven image destroyed. However, it took several centuries of barbarian invasions, quarrying, and incorporation into military structures before the trophy was finally reduced to rubble in the early eighteenth century. Its painstaking reconstruction was undertaken in the 1930s, and it now stands, statueless, at 35m.

Viewed from a distance along the Grande Corniche, however, the *Trophée* can still hold its own as an imperial monument. If you want to take a closer look and see a model of the original, you'll have to buy a ticket for the fenced-off plinth and its little museum (April–Sept daily 9am–7pm; Oct–March daily 9am–noon & 2–5pm; 20F).

In the town, just west of the *Trophée*, the eighteenth-century **Eglise de St-Michel-Archange** is a Baroque cream tea of marble, onyx, agate and oil paint, with pink the overriding colour, and, among the paintings, a superb *St Mark writing the Gospel* attributed to Veronese. The rest of the town is less colourful, with rough-hewn stone houses, most of them medieval, lining rue Comte-de-Cessole, the main street which was part of the *Via Julia* leading to the *Trophée*.

If you're thinking of **staying** here, try *Hôtel Napoléon*, 7 av de la Victoire (closed Tues out of season; ☎93.41.00.54; ⑤), set in an attractive building, with views onto the *Trophée* and very good **food**.

Roquebrune Cap Martin

As the corniche descends towards Cap Martin, it passes the eleventh-century castle of **ROQUEBRUNE** and its fifteenth-century village nestling round the base of the rock. The **castle** (summer daily 10am–noon & 2–7pm; winter closed Fri 10am–noon & 2–5pm; 12F) might well have become yet another Côte-side architectural aberration, thanks to its English owner in the 1920s. He was prevented from continuing his "restorations" after a press campaign brought public attention to the mock-medieval tower by the gateway, now known as the *tour anglais*. The local authority has since made great efforts to kit the castle out in an authentic medieval fashion.

The village itself is a bit too good to be true, especially if you wander its streets in winter, when the caterers of deluxe trinketry are on holiday. It's a real maze of passages and stairways that eventually lead either to one of the six castle gates or to dead ends. If you find yourself on rue de la Fontaine you can leave the village by the Porte de Menton and find, on the hillside about 200m beyond the gate, an olive tree that was perhaps one hundred years old when the count of Ventimiglia first built a fortress on Roquebrune's spur in 870 AD.

Southeast of the old village, just below the joined middle and lower corniches and the station, is the peninsula of **Cap Martin**, with a **coastal path**, giving you access to a wonderful shoreline of white rocks and wind-bent pines. The path is named after **Le Corbusier**, who spent several summers in Roquebrune and died, tragically, by drowning off Cap Martin in 1965. His grave – a work of art designed by himself – is in the cemetery (square J near the flagpole), high above the old village on promenade 1er DFL, and his beach house (visits through tourist office only) is on the shore just east of Plage du Buse, the beach just below the station.

Roquebrune Cap Martin's main **beach** is the Plage de Carnolès, a great long stretch of east-facing sand running northeast from Cap Martin. Close by the tourist office, at the junction of the Via Aurelian and Via Julia, is a remnant from the Roman station. Known as the **Tombeau de Lumone**, it comprises three arches of a first-century BC mausoleum, with traces of frescoes still visible under the vaulting.

PRACTICALITIES

To get to Roquebrune's *Vieux Village* from the **gare SNCF**, some way away, turn east and then right up av de la Côte d'Azur, then first left up escalier Corinthille, across the Grande Corniche and up escalier Chanoine JB Grana. Between the station and the beach, on the main road av Paul Doumer you'll find the **tourist office** in the *mairie* at no. 20 (July & Aug daily 9am–6pm; Sept–June Mon–Fri 9am–noon & 2–5.30pm; ☎93.35.62.87).

Hotels to try in Roquebrune are *Westminster*, 14 av Louis-Laurens (☎93.35.00.68; ③–④), close to the sea, west of the station, and *Reine d'Azur*, 29 promenade du Cap (☎93.35.76.84; ④), overlooking the Plage de Carnolès.

Good **restaurants** in Roquebrune involve hefty bills that aren't really justified. If you don't mind what you spend, see if *La Dame Jeanne*, 1 chemin Ste-Lucie (closed Sun evening out of season; ☎93.35.10.20), or *Piccolo Mondo*, 15 rue Grimaldi (☎93.35.19.93), both in the *Vieux Village* and around 220F upwards, takes your fancy. If not, the **bar** *La Grotte* on place des Deux-Frères (closed Tues) serves generous plats du jour for around 60F.

Monaco

Though you may miss the signs telling you you've entered **MONACO** it will be instantly clear from the dramatic switch to over-pristine streets and hideous buildings scrubbed of every spot of grime.

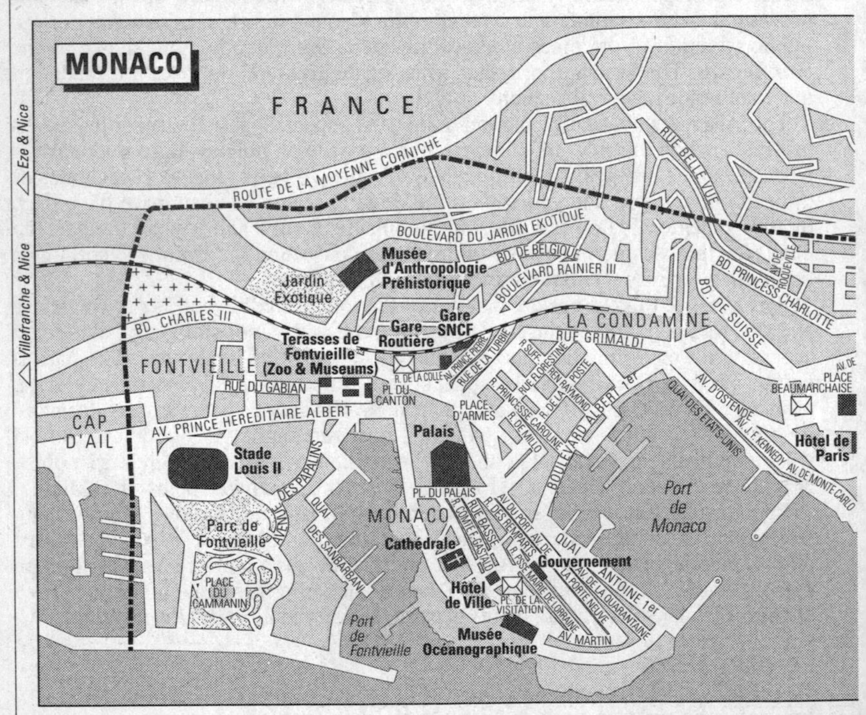

Monstrosities are common on the Côte d'Azur, but nowhere, not even Cannes, can outdo Monaco. This tiny independent principality, no bigger than London's Hyde Park, has been in the Grimaldi family's hands since the fourteenth century, save for the two decades following the French Revolution, and, legally, Monaco would again become part of France were the royal line to die out. For the last hundred years the principality has lived off gambling and catering for the desires of the idle international rich. While still carrying out these functions it has also become one of the most rampant property speculation sites in the world, a sort of Manhattan-on-sea without the saving aesthetic grace of the skyscrapers rising from a single level.

Finding out about the workings of the regime is not easy, but it is certainly true that **Prince Rainier** is the one constitutionally autocratic ruler left in Europe. There is a parliament, but it is of limited function and elected only by Monégasque nationals, about sixteen percent of the population. A copy of every French law is automatically sent to it, reworded and put to the prince. If he likes the law it is passed, if not, it isn't. The only other power is the *Société des Bains de Mer* (*SBM*), which owns the casino, the opera house, four of the grandest hotels, a handful of the most expensive cafés, restaurants, nightclubs and sports clubs, and large chunks of land including the Monte Carlo beach. The principality is the major shareholder and the director is usually a former minister, in other words

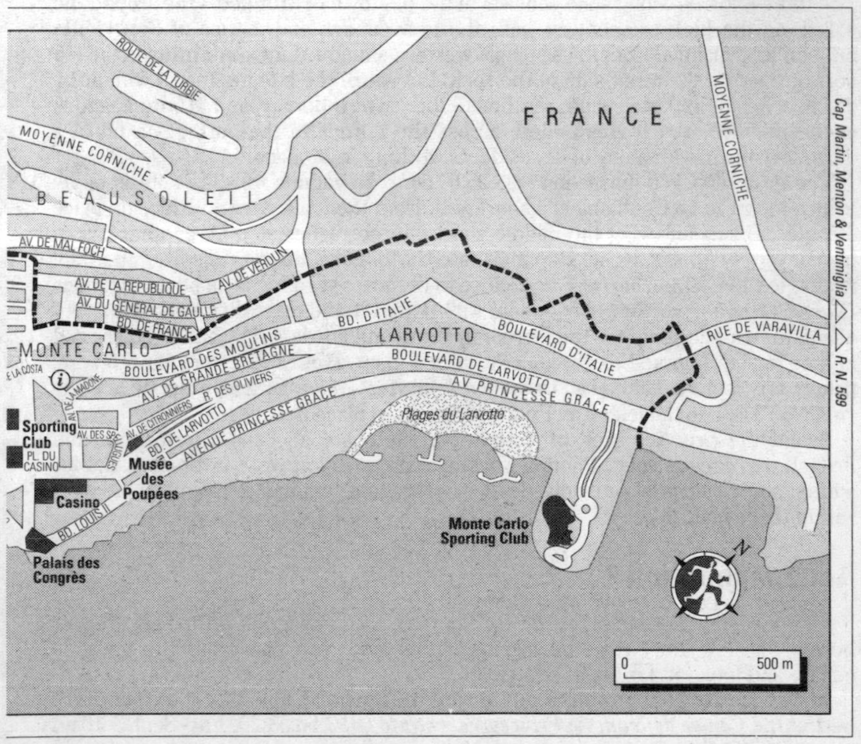

someone very close to Rainier. What the precise distinction is between the *SBM* and the state is a matter of legal and financial intricacies beyond innocent human understanding.

There is no opposition to the ruling family. What the citizens and residents like so much is that, despite living in the most densely populated country in the world, they pay no income tax and their riches are protected by rigorous security forces. There are more police per square metre than in any other country in the world, and probably more closed-circuit television cameras too. Unlike France, where hotel registration forms are a widely ignored formality, here they are strictly enforced, collected nightly and filed. Such efficient surveillance can have its embarrassments for the state, as in the case of an Italian wanted for his involvement in the Ambriosi affair who was extradited even though his actual crime was the Monégasque way of life – tax evasion. Should you feel tempted to take up residence, $1 million is about the minimum you need for a very small apartment.

One time to avoid Monaco – unless you're a motor-racing enthusiast – is the second week in May, when racing cars burn around the port and casino for the **Formula 1 Monaco Grand Prix**. Every space in sight of the circuit is inaccessible without a ticket, making casual sightseeing out of the question.

Arrival, orientation and information

The three-kilometre-long state consists of the old town of **Monaco-Ville** around the palace on the high promontory, with the new suburb and marina of **Fontvieille** built on land claimed from the sea in its western shadow. **La Condamine** is the old port quarter on the other side of the rock; **Larvotto**, the bathing resort with artificial beaches of imported sand, reaches to the eastern border, and **Monte Carlo** is in the middle. French **Beausoleil**, across the border to the north, is a bit of a dormitory town, with many of its residents working in Monaco.

The **gare SNCF** (information ☎93.25.54.54; reservations ☎93.30.74.00) is on av Prince-Pierre in La Condamine, a short walk from the main **gare routière** on place d'Armes. Buses following the middle and lower corniches stop here; other routes have a variety of stations; all stop in Monte Carlo. Local bus #4 runs from the train station to the *Casino-Tourisme* stop, close to the **tourist office** at 2a bd des Moulins (Mon–Sat 9am–7pm, Sun 10am–noon; ☎92.16.61.16) and place du Casino. One very useful free public service is the incredibly clean and efficient **lifts** linking lower and higher streets (marked on the tourist office's map). **Buses** run from 7am to 9pm; tickets are flat rate. **Bikes** can be rented from *Auto-Motos* garage, 6 rue de la Colle (☎92.05.73.88), to the left off av Prince-Pierre from place d'Armes.

As for the **practicalities of statehood**, there are no border formalities and French currency is valid. Phones work exactly as if you were in France, and for letters and postcards you only need Monégasque stamps if the destination is within the principality.

Accommodation

If you must stay more than one day in Monaco, La Condamine is the best area for **hotels**, though don't expect bargains. Otherwise, you can cross the invisible border and look for a room in Beausoleil.

Arriving early enough in the day means you may be able to get a **dormitory bed** at the *Centre de Jeunesse Princess Stéphanie* (☎93.50.83.20; July–Sept 7–10am

& 2pm–1am; ①), near the station at 24 av Prince-Pierre on the junction with bd Rainier III. You must be between 16 and 26 years old or a student under 31, and be prepared to hang about all morning before you know whether one of the forty beds is yours.

Monaco has no **campsite** and **caravans** are illegal in the state (as are bathing costumes, bare feet and chests once you step off the beach). Camping vehicles must be parked at the *Parking des Ecoles* in Fontvieille which is only open during the day (8am–8pm).

Hotels

Balmoral, 12 av Costa (☎93.50.62.37). An elegant old building in Monte Carlo, if you want somewhere classy to stay. ⑦

Boeri, 29 av Général-Leclerc, Beausoleil (☎93.78.38.10). A cheapish option with reasonably sized rooms, some with sea views. ④

Cosmopolite, 4 rue de la Turbie (☎93.30.16.95). Characterless but very clean and respectable; near the station. ④

Hôtel de France, 6 rue de la Turbie (☎93.30.24.64). Cheerful rooms and good value for the principality. ④

Helvetia, 1 rue Grimaldi (☎93.30.21.71). A reasonable option. Clean and comfortable, but fairly basic. ④

Monte Carlo

The **Casino** of **Monte Carlo** must be seen if nothing else. Entrance is restricted to those over 21 and you may have to show your passport; dress code is rigid, with shorts and T-shirts frowned upon, and skirts, jackets, ties and so forth more or less obligatory for the more interesting sections. Any coats or large bags involve hefty cloakroom fees.

In the first gambling hall, the *Salons Européens* (open from noon; 50F), slot machines surround the American roulette, craps and blackjack tables, the managers are Vegas-trained, the lights low and the air oppressively smoky. Above this slice of Nevada, however, the decor is turn-of-the-century Rococo extravagance, while in the adjoining *Pink Salon Bar*, female nudes smoking cigarettes adorn the ceiling.

The heart of the place are the *Salons Privés* (open from 4.15pm), through the *Salles Touzet*. You must look like a gambler, not a tourist (no cameras), to get in, and dispense with 100F at the door. More richly decorated than the *Salons Européens* and much bigger, the atmosphere in the early afternoon or out of season is that of a cathedral. No clinking coins, just quiet-voiced croupiers and sliding chips. Elderly gamblers pace silently, fingering 500F notes (the maximum unnegotiated stake here is 500,000F), closed-circuit TV cameras above the chandeliers watch the gamblers watching the tables, and no one drinks. On midsummer evenings the place is packed out and the vice loses its sacred and exclusive touch.

Charles Garnier, the nineteenth-century architect of the Paris Opera, designed both the casino and the neighbouring **Opera House** which is not open to the public save for ticket holders during the January to March season. Its interior is only what you would expect: a Baroque excess of gold and marble with statues of pretty Grecian boys, frescoed classical scenes and figures waving palm leaves.

From the terraces behind the casino you look down onto the **Centre de Congrès Auditorium** which juts out over the sea and has a blazingly coloured hexagonal roof designed by Vasarely.

Around place du Casino are more **casinos** and the city's **hôtels-palais** and **grands cafés**, all owned by the *SBM* monopoly. The *American Bar* of the *Hôtel de Paris* is, according to its publicity, the place where "the world's most elite society" meets. As long as you dress up and are prepared to be outraged (in English) if asked why you haven't ordered a 200F drink, you can entertain yourself, free of charge, watching tedious humans with fascinating bank accounts against the background of *belle époque* decadence.

People here really do live up to their stereotypes. The stones around their necks or on their cuffs are the real things – those shaded men in blue with revolvers at their hips can be relied upon. You may not catch sight of Caroline and Stéphanie, but you can be sure of a brilliant fashion parade of clothes and jewels, cars and luggage. You can even see how much they cost, if you're interested, in the shops and showrooms along bd des Moulins.

The **Musée National**, 17 av Princesse Grace (Easter–Oct daily 10am–6.30pm; Nov–Easter daily 10am–12.15pm & 2.30–6.30pm; 26F), dedicated to the history of dolls and automata from the eighteenth century to Barbie dolls in not quite the latest haute couture, might appeal to some. Some of the dolls' house scenes and the creepy automata are fun.

Monaco-Ville

After the casino, the amusements of the glacé-icing **Monaco-Ville** where every other shop sells Prince Rainier mugs and assorted junk, are less rewarding. You can trail gasping round the state apartments of the **Palace** (daily June–Sept 9.30am–6pm; Oct 10am–5pm; closed Nov–May; 30F); look at waxwork princes in **L'Historial des Princes de Monaco**, 27 rue Basse (daily Feb–Oct 9.30am–7pm; Nov–Jan 10.30am–5pm; 24F); watch a dreadful slideshow on different aspects of this revolting place in the **Monte Carlo Story** (hourly; daily July & Aug daily 11am–6pm; March–June, Sept–Oct 11am–5pm; Nov–Feb 2–5pm; 38F) or traipse around the tombs of the former princes and Princess Grace in the Neo-Romanesque-Byzantine **cathedral**. A reredos by Louis Bréa in the right-hand transept is the one genuine treasure inside this cake-like building.

For those who don't need to be turned into raving republicans, one very good, though pricey visit is to the aquarium in the basement of the **Musée Océanographique**, av St-Martin (June–Aug 9am–8pm; April, May 7 & Sept 9am–7pm; March & Oct 10pm–7pm; Nov–Feb 10am–6pm; 60F), where the fishy beings outdo the weirdest Kandinsky, Hieronymous Bosch or Zandra Rhodes creations. Films by the famous underwater explorer Jacques Cousteau are screened in the museum's conference hall.

Bus #1 or #2 will take you to Monaco-Ville; by car head for the *Parking du Chemin des Pêcheurs* from where there's a lift up to av St-Martin by the Musée Océanographique. Only Monégasque- and Alpes Maritimes-registered cars are allowed in Monaco-Ville.

Fontvieille, the Jardin Exotique and La Condamine

Below the rock of Monaco-Ville by the Port de Fontvieille a whole new complex, the **Terrasses de Fontvieille** (bus #5), has been built to house more museums. These include the **prince's collection of private cars**, everything from Cadillacs and Rollers to Trabants, Morris Minors and US jeeps (10am–6pm;

closed Fri & Nov; 30F); a **Musée Naval** (daily 10am–6pm; 25F) containing His Serene Highness's toy ships; a **zoo** (June–Sept 9am–noon & 2–7pm; Oct–May 10am–noon & 2–5/6; 20F); and a museum of stamps and coins, the **Musée des Timbres et des Monnais** (due to open). Below all these, a very discreet MacDonalds forgoes its normal red and yellow colours in favour of racing green awnings and parasols. Also in Port de Fontvieille, there's a **bric-à-brac market** every Saturday (9.30am–5.30pm).

Surrounded by car parks (spotlessly clean and with a range of cars almost as impressive as the prince's collection) the **Parc de Fontvieille** and Princess Grace's **rose garden** on the west side of the port are rather more rewarding than the museums. The prime garden in Monaco, however, is the **Jardin Exotique** full of bizarre cacti emerging from the hillside high above Fontvieille on bd du Jardin Exotique (mid-May to mid-Sept 9am–7pm; otherwise 9am–6pm; 35F; bus #2). Admission also includes entry to the **Musée d'Anthropologie Préhistorique**, tracing the history of the human race from Neanderthal man to Grimaldi prince, and the **Grotte de l'Observatoire**, prehistoric caves with illuminated stalagmites and stalactites.

The yachts in the **Port de Monaco** in **La Condamine** are, as you might expect, gigantic. If the idea of getting on one and sailing out of the harbour gives you a buzz, there are mini **cruises** on the *Monte-Carlo* catamaran, quai des Etats-Unis, which has a glass hull for underwater viewing (☎92.16.15.15; around 70F) and day cruises on the *Winnaretta Singer* yacht, at the eastern end of quai Albert 1er (☎93.25.36.33; around 480F). A much more exciting vessel to try out, however, is the **Seabus**, a genuine submarine that takes you down 35m past old wrecks and all the fauna and flora of the edge of the Mediterranean bed. The trip lasts 45 minutes and is not cheap (around 300F); departures from quai des Etats-Unis at the outer end of the port (hourly 10am–6pm, 9pm & 10pm; reservations on ☎92.16.18.20).

Eating and drinking

La Condamine and Monaco-Ville are replete with **restaurants**, **brasseries** and **cafés** but good food and reasonable prices don't exactly match. The best-value cuisine is Italian, and it's really not worth going upmarket in Monaco unless you're prepared to hit 900F-a-head bills, in which case you dine in the *belle époque* glory of the *Louis XV* in the *Hôtel de Paris*. As for **food shopping**, you can buy caviar, champagne and smoked salmon without any problem on and around av St-Charles, but finding *boulangeries* can be difficult. There are **markets** at place d'Armes and bd de France but they're minimal affairs. Better to go to rue du Marché in Beausoleil.

Restaurants

Bacchus, 13 rue de La Turbie (☎93.30.19.35). Generous pizzas, close to the station; menu around 80F. Closed Sat, Sun & mid-June to mid-July.

Castelroc, pl du Palais (☎93.30.36.68). Crowded but convenient place if you've been doing the palace tours to recover with Monégasque specialities; menus from 120F; midday only. Closed Sat.

La Cigale, 18 rue de Millo (☎93.30.16.14). Between the station and the Port de Monaco; decent menu under 80F. Closed Sat, Sun & mid-July to Aug.

Le Pinocchio, 30 rue Comte F-Gastaldi (☎93.30.96.20). Dependable Italian in Monaco-Ville; menus from 110F. Open till midnight in summer.

Polpetta, 2 rue Paradis (☎93.50.67.84). Attractive terrace and vaulted dining hall in Monte Carlo; Italian food; menu at 150F. Closed Tues & Sat midday.

Pulcinella, 17 rue du Portier (☎93.30.73.61). Traditional Italian cooking in Monte Carlo; menu at 135F. Closed Wed out of season.

Nightlife, entertainment and festivals

There are better places to throw money away on **nightlife** than Monaco, and the top discothèques like *Jimmy'z* in the Monte-Carlo Sporting Club are not going to let you in unless you're dripping with real jewels. American- or British-style bars and pubs abound but since human atmosphere is lacking in the entire principality you're not likely to find it in any of its venues.

The **opera season** (Jan–March) is pretty exceptional, the *SBM* being able to book up star companies and performers before Milan, Paris or New York gets hold of them. The programme of **theatre**, **ballet** and **concerts** throughout the year is also impressive, with the **Printemps des Arts de Monte Carlo** in April and May seeing performances by famous classical and contemporary dance troupes from all over the world. The main booking office for ballet, opera and concerts is the casino foyer, place du Casino, Monte-Carlo (Tues–Sun 10am–12.30pm & 2–5pm; ☎92.16.22.99); for theatre, the *Théâtre Princesse Grace*, 12 av de l'Ostende, Monte-Carlo (Mon–Sat 10am–12.30pm & 3–6.30pm; ☎93.25.32.27).

Monaco's **festival calendar** is spectacular, especially the **International fireworks Festival** at the end of July and the beginning of August at the Port de Monaco, though these can be witnessed from Cap d'Ail or Cap Martin. The end of January sees vast trailers entering Monaco for the **International Circus Festival** at the Espace Fontvieille, a rare chance to witness the world's best in this underrated performance art (details on ☎92.05.23.45). **Holidays** in Monaco are as in France plus January 27 (*Fête de Ste-Dévote*) and November 19 (*Fête Nationale Monégasque*).

The **Monte-Carlo Automobile Rally** takes place at the end of January and the **Formula 1 Grand Prix** in mid-May. Every space in sight of the circuit which runs round the port and the casino is inaccessible without a ticket (☎93.15.26.00). Monaco also has a first-division **football team**, *AS Monaco*, whose home ground is the enormous Stade Louis II in Fontvieille, 2 av du Prince Héréditaire Albert (☎93.15.40.00).

Listings

Banks Most banks have a branch in Monaco, and congregate on bd des Moulins, av de Monte-Carlo and av de la Costa; opening hours are Mon–Fri 9am–noon & 2–4.30pm.

Bookshop *Scruples*, 9 rue Princesse-Caroline, sells English-language books.

Car park Ubiquitous. Free for first hour; 2hr 18F; 5hr 39F.

Consulates *Denmark*, 74 bd d'Italie (☎93.50.02.03); *Holland*, 24 av de Fontvieille (☎92.05.15.02); *Ireland*, 1 pl Ste-Dévote (☎93.15.70.00); *Norway*, Palais Héraclès, 17 bd Albert-1er (☎93.50.91.01); *Sweden*, 7 av de Grande-Bretagne (☎93.50.75.60); *United Kingdom*, 33 bd Princesse-Caroline (☎93.50.99.66). The nearest US consulate is in Nice.

Currency exchange *Crédit Foncier de Monaco*, 11 bd Albert-1er, has a 24-hr automatic currency exchange machine; change offices open daily can be found at the station and the parking des Pêcheurs.

Emergencies ☎18 or 93.30.19.45; *Centre Hospitalier Princesse Grace*, av Pasteur (☎93.25.98.69).

Pharmacy Call ☎141 or 93.25.33.25 from public phones.
Police 3 rue Louis Notari (☎93.15.30.15).
Post office *PTT* Palais de la Scala, Place Beaumarchais (Mon–Fri 8am–7pm & Sat 8am–noon).

Menton

Of all the Riviera resorts **MENTON**, the warmest and the most Italianate, is the one that most retains an atmosphere of aristocratic tourism. Today it is even more of a rich retirement haven than Nice, and it's precisely that genteel, slow promenading pace of the town that makes it easy to imagine the stultifying presence of arch duchesses, grand dukes, tsars and other autocrats, as well as sick artists such as Guy de Maupassant and Katherine Mansfield. Menton does not go in for the ostentatious wealth of Monaco nor the creativity cachet of Cannes or some of the hilltop towns. What it chiefly glories in is its climate and its all-year-round lemon crops. Ringed by protective mountains, hardly a whisper of wind disturbs the sun-trap of the city. Winter is when you notice the difference most, with Menton several vital degrees warmer than St-Tropez or St-Raphaël.

The town's history, like that of Monaco, almost took an independent path. In the revolutionary days of 1848, Menton and Roquebrune, both at the time under Monaco's jurisdiction, declared themselves an independent republic under the protection of Sardinia. When the prince of Monaco came to Menton in the hope that his regal figure would sway the people he had to be rescued by the police from a furious crowd and locked up overnight for his own protection. Eventually, following an 1860 vote by Roquebrune and Menton to remain in France, Grimaldi agreed the sale of the towns to the French state for four million francs.

Arrival and information

Roquebrune and Cap Martin merge into Menton along the three-kilometre shore of the **Baie du Soleil**. The modern town is arranged around three main streets parallel to the promenade du Soleil. The **gare SNCF** (information ☎93.87.50.50; reservations ☎93.88.89.93) is on the top one, bd Albert-1er, from which a short walk to the left as you come out brings you to the north–south avenues de Verdun and Boyer, between which are the **Jardins Biovès**, central location for citrus sculptures during the February **Fête du Citron**. The **tourist office** (mid-June to mid-Sept Mon–Sat 8.30am–7.30pm, Sun 8.30am–12.30pm; rest of year Mon–Sat 8.30am–12.30pm & 2–6pm, Sun 10am–12.30pm; ☎93.57.57.00) is at 8 av Boyer in the **Palais de l'Europe**, which has given up being a casino and, along with various cultural activities, hosts annual contemporary art exhibitions and an international art *biennale*.

The **gare routière** (☎93.35.93.60) and the **urban bus station** are between the continuation of the two avenues north of the rail line on the esplanade de Carei. All the local bus lines (flat rates) pass through the *gare routière*. The *Vieille Ville* lies further east, above the old port and the start of the Baie de Garavan. The district of Garavan, further east again, is the most exclusive residential area and overlooks the modern marina.

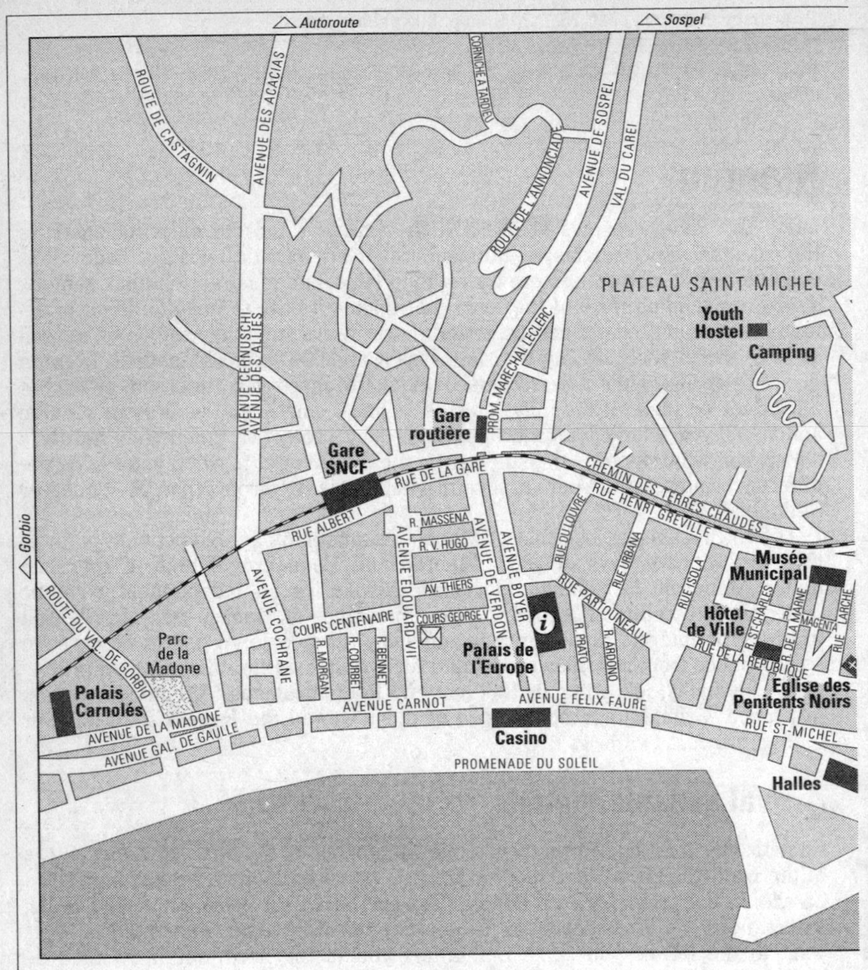

Accommodation

Accommodation, though good value, is difficult to find. Menton is no less popular than the other major resorts, so in summer you should definitely book ahead. The tourist office won't make reservations for you, though they will tell you where there are rooms for no charge.

Hotels

L'Aiglon, 7 av de la Madonne (☎93.57.55.55). Spacious rooms in a nineteenth-century residence surrounded by a large garden. ⑤

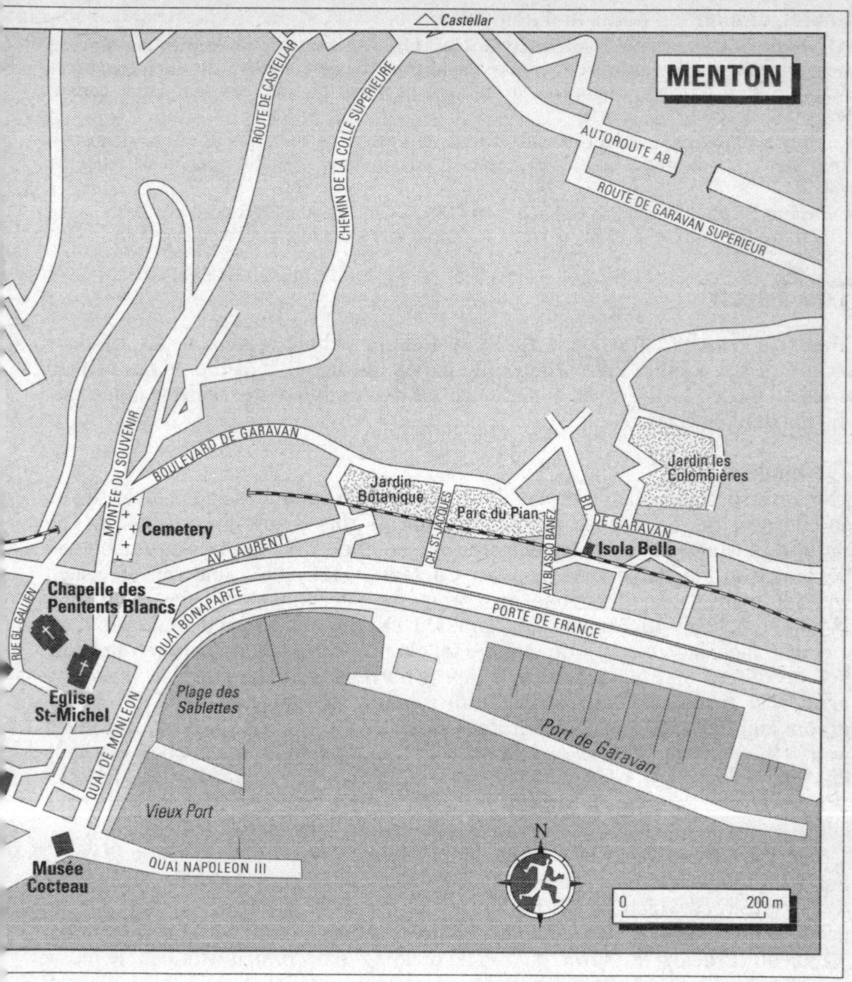

Auberge Provençale, 11 rue Trenca (☎93.35.77.29). Centrally located and reasonable enough. ③

Beauregard, 10 rue Albert-1er (☎93.35.74.08). Classically furnished rooms and no attempt to foist breakfast on you. Closed Oct–Dec. ③

Belgique, 1 av de la Gare (☎93.35.72.66). A bit mundane but clean and conveniently close to the station. Closed Dec. ④

Chambord, 6 av Boyer (☎93.35.94.19). Large rooms and well located. ⑤

Napoléon, 29 porte de France, Garavan (☎93.35.89.50). Wonderful views from the rooms. ⑥

Terminus, pl de la Gare (93.57.69.87). The cheapest rooms in Menton. ②

Viking, 2 av Gal-de-Gaulle (☎93.57.95.85). No beauty but with comfortable rooms and on the seafront. ⑥

Hostel, chambre d'hôtes and campsite

HI youth hostel, plateau St-Michel (☎93.35.93.14). The hostel is up a gruelling flight of steps from behind the *gare SNCF*, or take bus #6 from the *gare routière*, direction *Ciappes de Castellar*, stop *Camping St-Michel*. No advance booking, no card needed, 11pm curfew. Reception closed 10am–5pm. ①

Chambre d'hôtes, M. Paul Gazzano, 151 rte de Castellar (☎93.57.39.73). Two kilometres from Menton, a delightful house with a terrace looking down over the wooded slopes to the sea. ③

Camping St-Michel, plateau St-Michel (☎93.35.81.23). Reasonably priced campsite in the hills above the town, with plenty of shade and good views out to sea. Closed Dec–Feb.

The Town

Menton's greatest attraction is not its seafront or pebble beach, but the fabulous facade of the **Vieille Ville** around the parvis St-Michel; and the works of Jean Cocteau owned by the town, in particular his decoration of the registry office, and the **gardens** in Garavan.

The modern town

Menton's speciality should be weddings rather than widowers and widows. If you should ever need a French marriage certificate this is the place to get it. The **Salle des Mariages** (registry office) in the hôtel de ville on place Ardoiono was decorated in inimitable style by **Jean Cocteau** (1889–1963) and can be visited without matrimonial intentions by asking the receptionist by the main door (Mon–Fri 8.30am–12.30pm & 1.30–5pm; 5F). On the wall above the officials' desk a couple face each other, with strange topological connections between the sun, her headdress and his fisherman's cap. A *Saracen wedding party* on the right-hand wall reveals a disapproving bride's mum, the spurned girlfriend of the groom and her armed vengeful brother amongst the cheerful guests. On the left wall is the story of *Orpheus and Eurydice* at the doomed moment when Orpheus has just looked back. Meanwhile on the ceiling are *Poetry rides Pegasus*, tattered *Science juggles with the Planets* and *Love*, open-eyed, waiting with bow and arrow at the ready. Just to add to the confusion the carpet is mock panther-skin.

There are other works by Cocteau in the **Musée Jean Cocteau** (Mon & Wed–Sun mid-June to mid-Sept 10am–noon & 3–7pm; mid-Sept to mid-June 10am–noon & 2–6pm; free) which he set up himself in the most diverting building on the front, an unmenacing seventeenth-century bastion with tiled turrets on quai Napoléon III below the *Vieille Ville*. The building is decorated with pebble mosaics conceived by Cocteau and contains more Mentonaise lovers in the *Inamorati* series, a collection of delightful *Animaux Fantastiques* and the tapestry of *Judith and Holopherne* simultaneously telling the sequence of seduction, assassination and escape. The walls are also hung with photographs, poems, a portrait by his friend Picasso and ceramics.

Close to the museum are the pretty **market halls** and **place du Marché** off quai de Monléon where food and flowers are sold every morning. Behind place du Marché is the attractive **place des Herbes** with a bric-à-brac market every Friday morning, and the pedestrianized rue **St-Michel**, lined with cafés and restaurants and citrus trees, linking the old and modern towns.

At the far western end of the modern town, on av de la Madone, an impressive collection of paintings from the Middle Ages to the twentieth century can be seen in the sumptuous **Palais Carnolès** (Mon & Wed–Sun mid-June to mid-Sept

10am–noon & 3–7pm; mid-Sept to mid-June 10am–noon & 2–6pm; free; bus #3 or #7 to *Madone Parc*), the old summer residence of the princes of Monaco. Of the early works, the *Madonna and Child with St Francis* by Louis Bréa is exceptional; there are excellent Dutch and Venetian portraits; and an anonymous sixteenth-century Ecole Français canvas of a woman holding a scale. The small modern and contemporary collection includes a wonderful Suzanne Valadon and works by Graham Sutherland, who spent some of his last years in Menton. The downstairs of the building is given over to temporary exhibitions and there's a **jardin des sculptures** in the adjoining lime, lemon and orange grove.

If you've dragged little ones around the palace, treat them to **Koaland**, a funfair with go-karts, mini-golf and other attractions, just east of the sculpture garden at 5 av de la Madone (July & Aug daily 10am–noon & 3pm–midnight; Sept–June Mon & Wed–Sun 10am–noon & 2–7pm).

The other museum in Menton is the **Musée de Préhistoire Régionale** at the top of rue Lorédan-Larchey close to the hôtel de ville (Mon & Wed–Sun mid-June to mid-Sept Mon & Wed–Sun 10am–noon & 3–7pm; mid-Sept to mid-June 10am–noon & 2–6pm; free), which is one of the best on the subject. There are good videos to watch, lifesize re-created scenes of early human life, and the famous 27,000-year-old skull of "Menton Man" found in a cave near the town, encrusted with shells and teeth from his head gear.

The Vieille Ville

As the *quai* bends round the western end of the Baie de Garavan from the Cocteau museum, a long flight of black and white pebbled steps leads to the **parvis St-Michel** and the perfect pink and yellow proportions of the **Eglise St-Michel**. The interior of the church (Mon–Fri & Sat 10am–noon & 3–5pm) is a stupendous Italian Baroque riot of decoration, with an impressive vast organ casing, a sixteenth-century altarpiece in the choir by Antonio Manchello and a host of paintings, sculptures, gilded columns, stucco and frescoes.

From the church, take a few more steps up to another square and the apricot and white marbled **Chapelle des Pénitents Blancs** (Mon–Sat 3–5pm), home to a collection of processional lanterns and with a fine *trompe-l'oeil* over the altar. All this, as well as the pastel campaniles and disappearing stairways between long-lived houses, are a sure sign that you've arrived at the most Italianate and beautiful of the Riviera's *Vieille Villes*.

The **Ecomusée La Forge** at 2 rue du Grenadier, the steep stepped street running south from the Chapelle des Pénitents Blancs, is an old smithy filled with a ramshackle and cluttered display of tools, traditional kitchenware, costumes and hideous objects sculpted from gourds, and not really worth the entrance fee. Instead head north, or uphill, from the *parvis*, which is far more rewarding. The *Vielle Ville* has no commerce, just bright window boxes and cacti poking over walls in the stepped and cobbled lanes. At the top you'll reach the **Cimetière du Vieux Château** which is low on gloom and high on views, with cream-coloured mid-nineteenth-century sculpted stone and diverse foreign names ranging from Russian princes to William Webb-Ellis, credited, in language redolent of public schools, with the invention of rugby.

Garavan

If it's cool enough to be walking outside, the public **parks** up in the hills and the **gardens** of **Garavan's** once elegant villas make a change from shingle beaches.

From the *Vieux Cimetière* you can walk or take bus #8 along bd de Garavan past houses hidden in their large, exuberant gardens.

The first public garden you come to is the **Jardin Botanique** (June–Sept Mon & Wed–Sun 10am–noon & 3–6pm; Feb–May 10am–noon & 2–5pm; 20F) which surrounds the Villa Val Rameh. Though there's a good variety of plants it's not brilliantly maintained and you can get the same views from the **Parc du Pian**, an olive grove with free access below the boulevard just past the Jardin Exotique. Further on, down av Blasco-Ibanez and north up rue Webb-Ellis and chemin Wallaya, is the **Isola Bella** where Katherine Mansfield stayed. Above here, up rte des Colombières from bd de Garavan, are the **Jardins Les Colombières** (Jan–Sept daily 10am–noon & 2–6pm; bus #8, direction *bd de Garavan*, stop *Colombières*; 20F) which used to be the best of all the Garavan gardens. They have been allowed to fall into ruin but plans are always afoot to resuscitate them, so you might be lucky. Designed by the artist Ferdinand Bac, they lead you through every Mediterranean style of garden. There are staircases screened by cypresses; balustrades to lean against for the soaring views through pines and olive trees out to sea; fountains, statues and a frescoed swimming pool.

Eating, drinking and entertainment

Surprisingly Menton is not blessed with streets of inviting Provençal **restaurants** so most people usually cross into Italy for a blow-out meal. If you're not that bothered what you eat as long as it's cheap, the pedestrianized rue St-Michel is promising ground. There are plenty of snack bars among the burger houses, as well as outlets for omelettes or steak and chips and occasionally interesting plats du jour. For a proper restaurant meal in very elegant surroundings, there's *La Veranda* in *Hôtel Les Ambassadeurs*, 2 rue du Louvre (☎93.28.75.75), with an evening bistro menu for 160F. *Piccolo Mondo* at 10 rue Trenca (closed Wed; ☎93.57.53.11) offers a light Italian lunchtime menu for under 100F. *L'Orchidée*, 2 rue Masséna (closed Mon evening, Tues, & July; ☎93.35.90.17), tucked away in the back streets by the station, is basic but good value with two menus under 100F.

As well as the covered market there's the **marché du Carei** on promenade du Mal-Leclerc. Good bread and *fougasse* can be got from the *Midi Boulangerie* on rue St-Michel.

The town's **lemons** are celebrated in the citrus fruit extravaganza every February. Have no illusions, however, about cheap local produce: a *citron pressé* served in a Menton bar still costs twice as much as an imported Belgian beer.

In August the pebbled mosaic of the Grimaldi arms on the *parvis* is covered by chairs, music stands, pianos and harps for the **Festival de Musique de Chambre**. The nightly concerts are superb and can be listened to from the quaysides without buying a ticket. If you want a proper seat make a reservation at the tourist office.

Villages around Menton

In the hills above Menton and Roquebrune are the tiny villages of **Gorbio** and **Ste-Agnes**, and on the road to Sospel, **Castellar** and **Castillon**. All give god's-eye views over steep, forested slopes to the sea.

Gorbio and Ste-Agnes

Ten kilometres west of Menton, **GORBIO** is an exquisite hilltop village with very few arts and crafts boutiques or other tourist fodder. The locals are traditionally known as *les nébuleux* because of the mists that often engulf the village. Three buses daily (#901) climb up from Menton's *gare routière*, a thirty-minute journey; it's best to time it so that you can have a **meal** at the *Auberge du Village* at 8 rue Gambetta (Tues–Sun; ☎93.35.87.83; from 130F). After feasting on vegetable fritters, seafood salad, raviolis and courgette flowers you can sit on the benches of place de la République at the entrance to the mottled grey medieval quarter, watching kids play and soaking up the sun and the view.

In contrast, **STE-AGNES**, 2km northeast of Gorbio, is milling with crystal engravers, painters, herbalists, jewellers and leather workers. It perches at the foot of a cliff, again with enchanting views, but its atmosphere isn't a patch on Gorbio's. Though the two villages are close, the roads between them meet below the *autoroute*. Walkers can take a more direct route: a path from Gorbio joins the road south from Ste-Agnes after about 1500m. Three buses run daily from Menton to Ste-Agnes (bus #902; 30min).

Castillon and Castellar

A railway used to run along the **Carei valley** from Menton up to Sospel. Though the tracks and tunnels are still there, there's been no incentive for over forty years to revive it, which is a great pity as this valley offers one of the best roller-coasting descents to the sea. The villages are few and far between and much of the valley is thickly forested. The Sospel bus from Menton passes through Castillon; for Castellar there's a local bus (#903; 5 daily; 25min).

CASTILLON, a few kilometres south of Sospel, has twice been destroyed and rebuilt, by an earthquake in 1887 and by bombing in 1944. The current village, a short way down from Vieux Castillon, dates from the 1950s with **Les Arcades des Serres**, a terrace of artists' and crafts workers' studios added in the 1980s. Its status as an artists' village – the turning from the main road is marked by a dazzling ceramic – is not based on the normal Riviera riches market; the studios and galleries are provided at low rents in a genuine attempt to help local practitioners; and the works you see are very original and of a high standard. There's also a primary school so it's not just single creative spirits that make up the community. If you want to stop for a **meal**, the restaurant/ *salon de thé St-Julien* (☎93.04.18.04) has low-priced *formules* and a menu from 120F. *La Bergerie* **hotel-restaurant** (Jan–Sept; ☎93.04.00.39; ④), on the southern edge of the village, is in hideous rustic style but has great views and pleasant rooms.

To the east of the Carei valley, and closer to Menton, **CASTELLAR** marks the point where the pines start to take over from the lemon groves and the sea is all-visible. Castellar is another old *village perché*, very beautiful and not overrun by tourist commerce. It's also good for **walks**, with several paths radiating out into the hills around it as well as the **GR52** from Gorbio and Ste-Agnes, which turns north along the Italian border to Sospel. Details of paths, rooms and food can be had from the *Hôtel des Alpes*, place Georges-Clemenceau (☎93.35.82.83; ③) and you can sip a coffee or beer on the edge of the rock spur at *La Renaissance bar-tabac*.

travel details

Trains

Cannes, Antibes, Nice, Monaco and Menton are the main stops on the **Ventimiglia line** along the Riviera coast. There are 3–4 fast trains daily stopping at all these stations with 20 more stopping at all stations. There is also an express service between Cannes and Nice (frequent; 25 min).

Cannes to: Antibes (9–13min); Biot (17min); Cagnes-sur-Mer (24min); Cros-de-Cagnes (27min); Golfe Juan-Vallauris (6min); Juan-les-Pins (10min); Marseille (frequent; 1hr 5min); Nice (29–38min); St-Raphaël (frequent; 25–35min); Villeneuve-Loubet-Plage (20min).

Nice to: Annot (4 daily; 1hr 45min); Beaulieu (13min); Breil-sur-Roya (4 daily; 1hr 5min–1hr 10min); Cap d'Ail (24min); Cap Martin-Roquebrune (37min); Digne (4 daily; 3hr 10min); L'Escarène (4 daily; 35–45min); Eze-sur-Mer (18min); Entrevaux (4 daily; 1hr 30min); Marseille (frequent; 2hr 45min–3hr 15min); Menton (24–35min); Monaco (21–25min); Peille (4 daily; 25–30min); Peillon (2 daily; 25min); Puget-Théniers (4 daily; 1hr 20min); St-Raphaël (frequent; 1hr–1hr 20min); Sospel (4 daily; 45–50min); Tende (2 daily; 2hr 5min); Touët-sur-Var (4 daily; 1hr 10min); Villars-sur-Var (4 daily; 1hr); Villefranche (9min).

Note that due to floods and rock-falls the timetable of the Chemin de Fer de Provence from Nice to Dignes is subject to change.

Buses

Buses along the coast are slower, more expensive and less frequent than trains.

Cannes to: Aéroport Nice-Côte-d'Azur (hourly; 45min); Golfe-Juan (5 daily; 10min); Grasse (frequent; 50min); Mouans-Sartoux (frequent; 30min); Mougins (frequent; 20min); St-Raphaël (8–9 daily; 1hr 10min); Vallauris (frequent; 15min).

Grasse to: Le-Bar-sur-Loup (2 daily; 20min); Cabris (5 daily; 15min); Cannes (frequent; 50min); Mougins (4 daily; 20min); Nice (1 daily; 2hr 40min); St-Cézaire (5 daily; 35 min); Tourettes-sur-Loup (2 daily; 45min); Vence (4 daily; 1hr).

Menton to: Nice (14 daily; 50min); Sospel (3 daily; 50min).

Nice to: Aix (5 daily; 2hr 15min–3hr 55min); Beaulieu (14 daily; 15 min); Cagnes-sur-Mer (frequent; 20min); Cap d'Ail (14 daily; 25min); Châteauneuf-de-Contes (2 daily; 1hr 10min); La Colle-sur-Loup (frequent; 35min); Coaraze (2 daily; 1hr 25min); Contes (hourly; 40min); Cros-de-Cagnes (frequent; 15min); Digne (5 daily; 2hr 55min–3hr 15min); Draguignan (1–2 weekly; 1hr 30min); L'Escarène (6 daily; 1hr); Eze-sur-Mer (14 daily; 20min); Eze-Village (7 daily; 20min); Grasse (1 daily; 2hr 40min); Lucéram (4 daily; 1hr 35min); Menton (14 daily; 50min); Monaco (14 daily; 30min); Peille (3 daily; 1hr); Peillon (3 daily; 50min); Roquebrune (14 daily; 40min); Saint-Paul (frequent; 40min); Sisteron (1 daily; 3hr 45min); Toulon (2 daily; 2hr 30min); La Turbie (4 daily; 40min); Vence (frequent; 55min); Villefranche (14 daily; 10min).

Ferries

Nice to: Corsica (April–Sept daily; Oct–May 1 daily–3 weekly; 2hr 30min–11hr 30min).

Flights

Nice to: Amsterdam (2 daily; 2hr 5min); Birmingham (2 weekly; 2hr 5min); Dijon (1 weekly; 1hr 20min); Dublin (1 weekly; 2hr 30min); East Midlands (2 weekly; 2hr 5min); Lille (1daily; 1hr 30min); London (9–10 daily; 2hr 5min); Lyon (4–6 daily; 50min); Manchester (1 weekly; 2hr 10min); Marseille (1 daily; 45min); New York (4–6 daily; 9hr); Ottowa (2 weekly; 8hr 30min); Paris (frequent; 1hr 20min); Rome (2–4 daily; 2hr); Strasbourg (3–4 daily; 1hr 10min); Toulouse (2–4 daily; 1hr).

CHAPTER SEVEN

HAUTE PROVENCE

Haute Provence, the mountainous northeastern corner of Provence, is a different world in different seasons. In winter the sheep and shepherds retreat to warmer pastures, leaving the snowy heights to antlered mouflons and chamois, and the perfectly camouflaged ermine. The villages where the shepherds came to summer markets are battened down for the long cold haul, while modern conglomerations of Swiss-style chalet houses, sports shops and discotheques come to life around the ski lifts. From November to April many of the mountain road passes are closed, cutting off the dreamy northern town of **Barcelonnette** from its lower neighbours.

In spring the fruit trees in the narrow valleys blossom, and melting waters swell the **Verdon**, the **Vésubie**, the **Var**, the **Tinée** and the **Roya**, sometimes flooding villages and carrying whole streets away. In summer and early autumn you move from the valleys to the peaks through groves of chestnut and olive trees, then pine forests edged with wild raspberries and bilberries, up to moors and grassy slopes turned every colour from white to gold by alpine flowers. Above the line where vegetation ceases there are rocks with eagles' nests and snowcaps that never melt.

This is not an easy place to live. Abandoned farms and overgrown terraced slopes bear witness to the declining viability of mountain agriculture. But the ski resorts bring in money and summer brings the dedicated trekkers, naturalists and climbers. One area, covering 75km from east to west, protected as the **Parc National du Mercantour**, has no permanent inhabitants at all. It's crossed by numerous paths, with refuge huts providing basic food and bedding for trekkers.

Running along the edge of the southern limit of the Alps is the **Nice–Digne** rail line, known as the *Chemin de Fer de Provence*, the only remaining segment of the region's turn-of-the-century narrow-gauge network. One of the great train rides of the country, it takes in the isolated Var towns of **Puget-Théniers** and **Entrevaux**, and ends at **Digne**, a low-key but intriguing regional capital that serves as the centre of the lavender industry.

For centuries the border between Provence and Savoy ran through this part of France, a political divide embodied by the impressive fortifications of Entrevaux and **Colmars**, the principal town of the Haut Verdon. To this day most of the region is not considered to be part of Provence. The French refer to it by the geographical term, the **Alpes Maritimes**, which is also the name of the *départe-*

HOTEL ROOM PRICES

For a fuller explanation of these price codes, see the box on p.32 of *Basics*.

① Under 160F	② 160–220F	③ 220–300F	④ 300–400F
⑤ 400–500F	⑥ 500–600F	⑦ 600–700F	⑧ over 700F

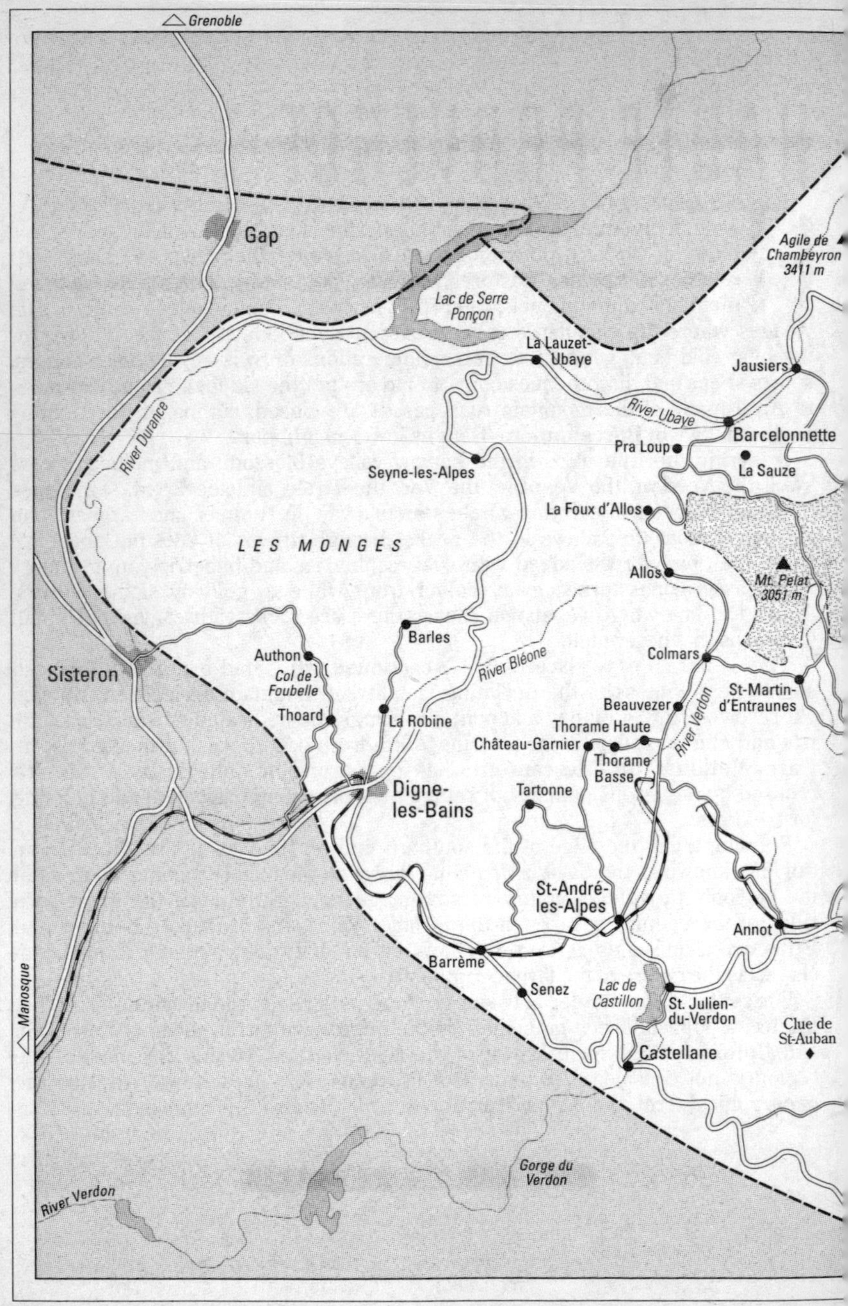
Grenoble
Gap
Lac de Serre Ponçon
La Lauzet-Ubaye
Agile de Chambeyron 3411 m
Jausiers
River Ubaye
Barcelonnette
Pra Loup
La Sauze
River Durance
Seyne-les-Alpes
La Foux d'Allos
LES MONGES
Allos
Mt. Pelat 3051 m
Barles
Authon
Col de Foubelle
Sisteron
River Bléone
Colmars
St-Martin-d'Entraunes
Beauvezer
Thoard
La Robine
Thorame Haute
Château-Garnier
Thorame Basse
River Verdon
Digne-les-Bains
Tartonne
St-André-les-Alpes
Annot
Barrème
Senez
Lac de Castillon
St. Julien-du-Verdon
Clue de St-Auban
Castellane
Manosque
Gorge du Verdon
River Verdon

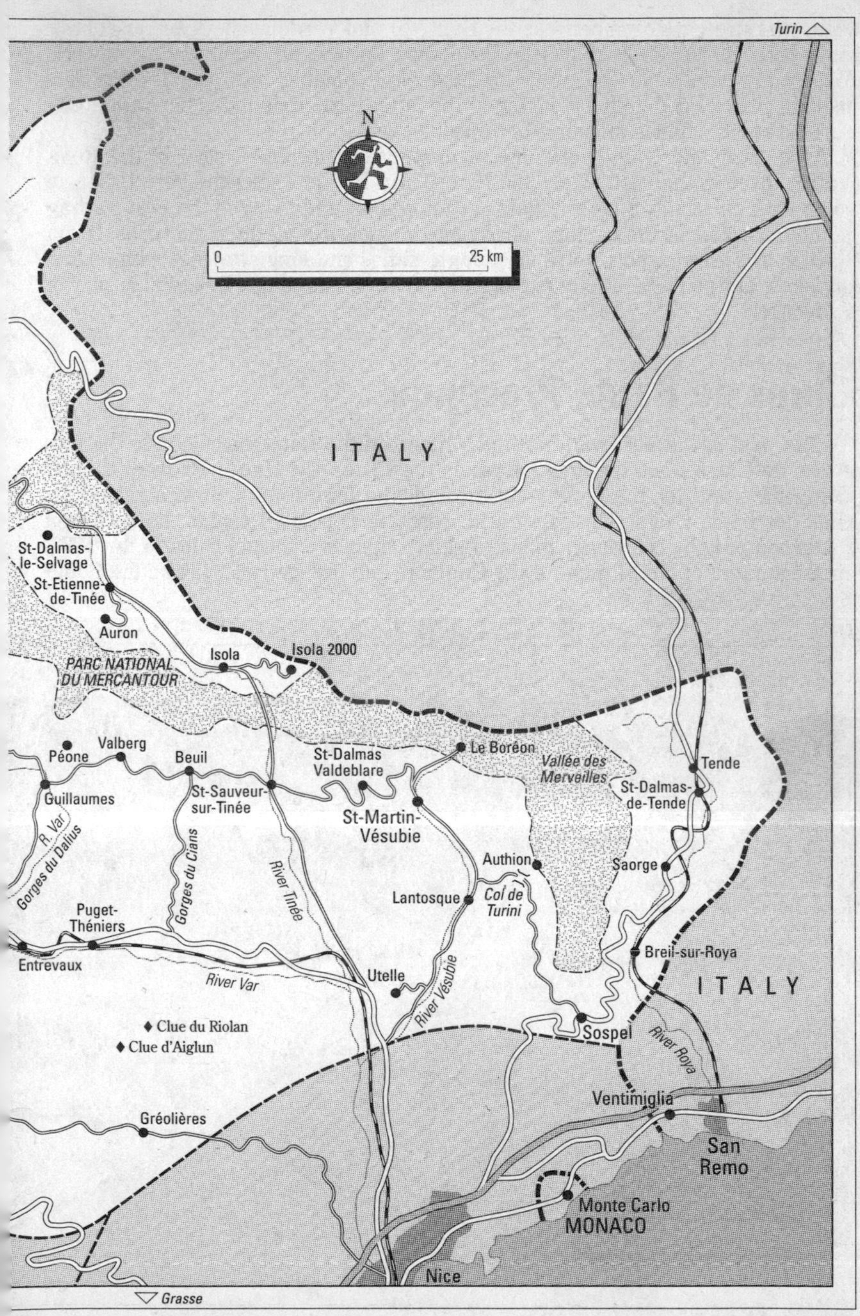
Turin
N
0
25 km
ITALY
St-Dalmas-le-Selvage
St-Etienne-de-Tinée
Auron
PARC NATIONAL DU MERCANTOUR
Isola
Isola 2000
Péone
Valberg
Beuil
Guillaumes
St-Sauveur-sur-Tinée
St-Dalmas Valdeblare
Le Boréon
St-Martin-Vésubie
Vallée des Merveilles
Tende
St-Dalmas-de-Tende
R. Var
Gorges du Dalius
Gorges du Cians
River Tinée
Authion
Saorge
Lantosque
Col de Turini
Puget-Théniers
Entrevaux
Breil-sur-Roya
River Var
Utelle
River Vésubie
ITALY
Clue du Riolan
Clue d'Aiglun
Sospel
River Roya
Ventimiglia
Gréolières
San Remo
Monte Carlo
MONACO
Nice
Grasse

ment that stretches from between the Haut Var and Verdon valleys and just above the source of the Tinée Valley to the Italian border, and includes the Riviera. Where Provence ends and the Alps begin is debatable, with the Tinée Valley usually cited as definitely belonging to the latter – the mountains here are pretty serious and the Italian influence becomes noticeable.

Away from the Nice–Digne line, **transport** is a problem save in the **Roya Valley**, over in the east, where the Nice–Turin rail line links the very Italianate towns of **Tende** and **Sospel**. Buses are infrequent and many of the best starting points for walks or the far-flung pilgrimage chapels are off the main roads. If you have your own transport, you'll face tough climbs and long stretches with no fuel supplies, but you'll be free to explore the most exhilaratingly beautiful corner of Provence.

Clues de Haute Provence

To the west of the Var river, north of Vence and the Route Napoléon in the Pre-Alpes de Grasse, lies the area known as the **Clues de Haute Provence**, *clues* being the word for the gorges cut through the limestone mountain ranges by their torrential rivers. This is an arid, sparsely populated region, its seclusion disturbed only by the winter influx of skiers from the coastal cities to the 1777-metre summit of the **Montagne du Cheiron**, and the car rallies along the Route

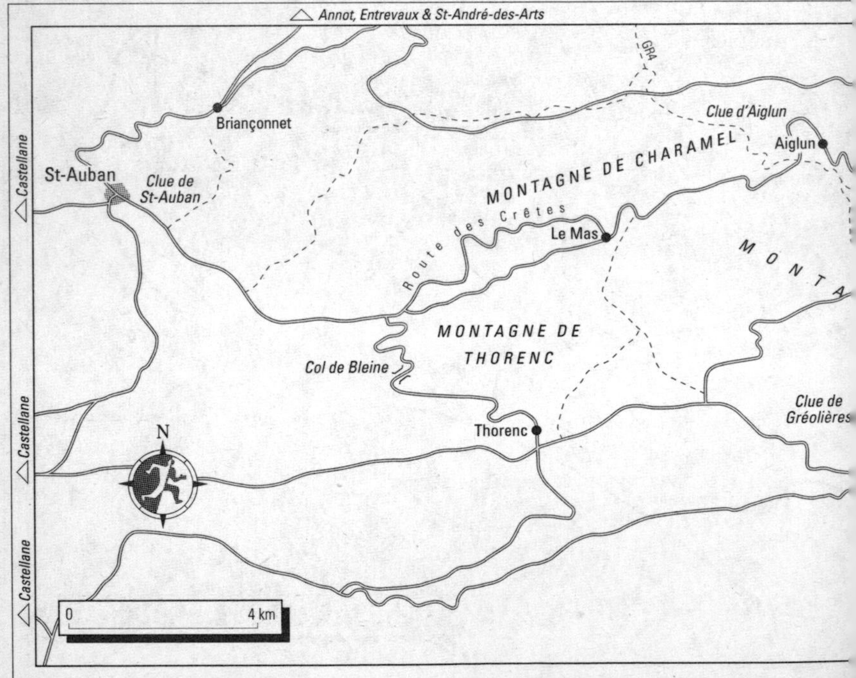

des Crêtes, which follows the contours of the Montagne de Charamel and the Montagne St-Martin between the Cols de Bleine and Roquestéron.

Each claustrophobic and seemingly collapsible *clue* opens onto a wide and empty landscape of white and grey rocks with a tattered carpet of thick oak and pine forest. The horizons are always closed off by mountains, some erupting in a space of their own, others looking like coastal cliffs trailing the **Cheiron**, the **Charamel** or the 1664-metre-high **Montagne de Thorenc**. It's the sort of scenery that fantasy adventure games take place in, with wizards throwing laser-bolts from the mountains.

To appreciate it though, you really need your own **transport**. Not all the passes are open during the winter – notices on the roads forewarn you of closures – and you should keep an eye on the fuel gauge, as garages are infrequent. Routes that go through the *clues* rather than over passes are manageable for cyclists: this is gorgeous, clean-air, long-freewheeling and panoramic terrain. There are plenty of footpaths, with the **GR4** as the main through-route for walkers from Gréolières to Aiglun across the Cheiron.

Accommodation isn't plentiful. What hotels there are tend to be very small, with a faithful clientele booking them up each year. Campsites are also thin on the ground, though there are a variety of *gîtes* scattered about. Even winter accommodation at **Gréolières** and **Gréolières-les-Neiges** is fairly minimal, as people tend to come up for a day's skiing or have their own weekend places. Most of the villages offer tourist information at the *mairie*. If you get stuck, the towns of Vence, Grasse, Puget-Théniers, Castellane or Nice are not far away.

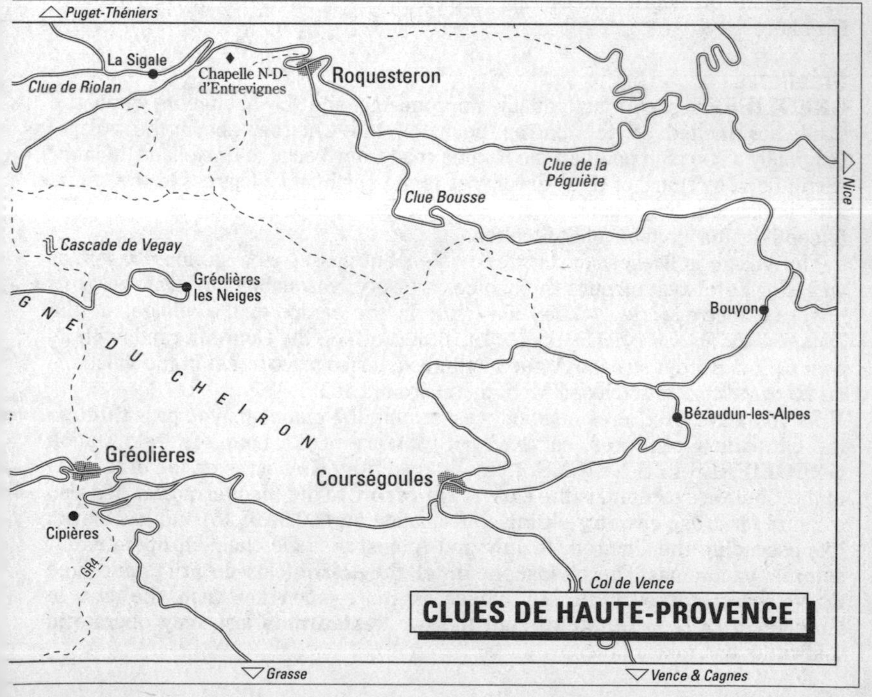

Courségoules and Gréolières

Coming **from Vence** you approach the *clues* via the **Col de Vence**, which brings you down to Courségoules; **from Grasse** and the Loup Valley the road north leads to Gréolières, 11km west of Courségoules.

Courségoules

The bare white rocks that surround **COURSEGOULES** are not the most hospitable of sites for a village, so it's no surprise that many of the smartly restored houses here are now used as second homes. The population has steadily declined, reaching its present level of a hundred or so people who don't need to eke a living from the soil-scoured terrain. In the village **church** the two obscure patron saints of the village have been honoured by Louis Bréa who painted them on each side of St John the Baptist (open, in theory, 10am–3pm; the light switches are to the left as you enter).

Accommodation possibilities here, all of which have superb views, are a *chambre d'hôtes* 400m from the village (c/o M et Mme Walverens, Le Brec; ☎93.59.10.53; ②), the hotel *L'Auberge de l'Escaou* on the lovely place des Tilleuls in the old village (closed All Saints to Easter; ☎93.59.11.28; ③) and the *Saint-Antoine* **campsite** (May to mid-Sept; ☎93.59.12.36). Courségoules has a *crêperie* and small bistro but for a proper **meal**, your best bet is to head northeast to the *Auberge Les Lavandes* in **Bezaudun-les-Alpes** (midday only; closed Thurs; ☎93.59.01.08; menus from 120F), which serves a very generous succession of courses featuring excellent local fare, or move west to Gréolières.

Gréolières

GREOLIERES seems an equally unpromising site for habitation when the snow has melted on the barren peaks of the Cheiron, above the village. Originally a stopping point on the Roman road from Vence to Castellane, it's now surrounded by ruins, of Haut-Gréolières to the north and a fortress to the south. The parish church, opposite the fortress, has a Romanesque facade and a fifteenth-century retable of St Stephen.

The village is liveliest during the winter, but passes as a summer resort as well. For **hotel-restaurants** the choices are very reasonable: *La Vieille Auberge* on place Pierre-Merle (☎93.59.95.07; ②) in the centre of the village, or the *Domaine du Foulon* (☎93.59.95.02; ③), 4km south on the Gourdon road, with its own park and trout stream. A good and inexpensive place to **eat** in the village is *La Barricade* pizzeria (closed Mon; menu around 100F).

As you leave Gréolières heading west around the mountain, you pass through the **Clue de Gréolières**, carved by a tributary of the Loup. The ski station **GREOLIERES-LES-NEIGES**, 18km by road from Gréolières on the other side of the Cheiron's summit, is the closest **ski resort** to the Mediterranean. It's also a centre for **cross-country skiing** (information on ☎93.59.95.16) and has eleven lifts ascending the Cheiron. In July and August a single chair lift operates for summer panoramas. There's just one **hotel**, the *Alpina* (closed April to mid-June & Nov–Dec; ☎93.59.70.19; ④), which is more upmarket than the two in Gréolières. *Le Gréo* **nightclub** and the two **restaurants** also only operate in midwinter and midsummer.

Thorenc, St-Auban and Briançonnet

The attractions of **THORENC**, lying at a dead end off the D2 road 13km west of Gréolières, are that it's not on the way to anywhere and has two very pleasant small **hotel-restaurants**: *Des Voyageurs*, 13 av du Belvédère (closed mid-Nov to Jan; ☎93.60.00.18; ③), and *Les Mesiriers*, 24 av du Belvédère (☎93.60.00.23; ③). It's a popular hang-gliding and cross-country-skiing area, and was created as a winter resort by English and Russians at the turn-of-the-century, an origin reflected in the style of the older buildings. There's been a lot of new development and it's a lively place during the winter and summer seasons.

To the north, the D5 crosses the **Montagne de Thorenc** by the **Col de Bleine** and then the D10 takes over for the ascent of **Charamel**, without a moment's pause in the looping climb. The D10 leads to **Aiglun** while the D5 takes the easier westward route to **ST-AUBAN** and its *clue*. St-Auban rests against the grassy slope of the mountainside, its wide southern views making up for the plainness of the village itself. The gash made by the Esteron river has left a jumble of rocks through which the water tumbles beneath overhanging cliffs riddled with caves and fissures. There's one ski lift and a *gîte equestre* where you can stable yourself and your horse, or rent a mount (all year; reservations through the *mairie*; ☎93.60.41.23 or 93.60.43.20). St-Auban's two **hotel-restaurants** are *Le Tracastel* (☎93.60.43.06; ③) in the village and the *Auberge de la Clue* (April–Nov; ☎93.60.43.12; ③) in the *clue*.

Above the Esteron further downstream, **BRIANCONNET** has one of the most stunning positions in the whole of inland Provence. This is best appreciated at the cemetery, from where the views stretch southwards past the edge of the Montagne de Charamel across miles of uninhabited space. The Romans had a settlement here and the present houses are built with stones from the ancient ruins with odd bits of Latin still decipherable in the walls. There's just one street with one *boulangerie* and one tiny **hotel-restaurant**, *Le Chanan* (☎93.60.46.75; ③), and a small museum of local history. The **church** contains a retable of *The Madonna of the Rosary* by Louis Bréa, showing Mary protecting the ecclesiastical and secular potentates in her cloak.

From here you can head north across the **Col de Buis** (usually closed Nov to mid-April) to Entrevaux or Annot (see pp.404 and 405), or east towards the Clue d'Aiglun and the Clue de Riolan.

The Route des Crêtes

Clinging to the steep southern slope of the Montagne de Charamel, the switchback **Route des Crêtes** (D10) almost defies you to take it at breakneck speed, burning tyres on every bend. For long stretches there are no distracting views, only thick forest matted with mistletoe. After Le Mas, which hangs on the edge of a precipitous spur below the road, trees can no longer get a roothold in the near-vertical golden and silver cliffs; the narrowing road crosses high-arched bridges over cascading streams which fall to smoothly moulded pools of aquamarine.

Just before **St-Aiglun** you cross the Esteron as it shoots out from the high-pressure passage (too narrow for a road) that splits the Charamel and the Montagne St-Martin. This is the most formidable of all the *clues* and is impossible to explore. You can, however, follow the GR4 southwards from the D10, 1.5km west of the *clue*, to the **Vegay waterfall**, halfway between Aiglun and Gréolières-les-Neiges, where water destined for the Esteron plummets down a vertical cliff-face.

In the village of **ST-AIGLUN** you can **stay**, if you're lucky, in one of the six rooms at the *Auberge de Calendal* (closed Feb; ☎93.05.82.32; half-board compulsory; ②), or there's dormitory-style accommodation in a *gîte communale* on the GR4 (c/o Mme Broussard; ☎93.05.82.32). East from St-Aiglun the campanile and silvery olive groves of the ancient fortified village of **LA SIGALE** flicker into view. Halfway between La Sigale and **Roquésteron**, the **Chapelle Notre-Dame-d'Entrevignes** has preserved fragments of fifteenth-century frescoes including the unusual scene of Mary, ready to give birth, with Joseph expressing deep suspicion. To visit apply to La Sigale's *mairie* (☎93.05.83.52) or to Mme Gioanni, 13 rue de la Fontaine. To the west La Sigale overlooks the Clue de Riolan, again inaccessible, though visible from the road from St-Aiglun.

ROQUESTERON, about 10km east of St-Aiglun, was divided for a hundred years by the France–Savoy border, which followed the course of the Esteron, and is now divided between two French *départements*. There's one **hotel** here, the *Passeron* at 25 bd Salvago (open all year; ☎93.05.91.01; ②). From Roquésteron you have the choice of following the D17 above the Esteron to the river's confluence with the Var, or taking the tangled D1, through passages of rock seamed in thin vertical bands to **BOUYON**, from where the D8 takes you back to Courségoules. Both routes take you from one eagle's-nest village to another. At Bouyon you'll find an excellent **hotel-restaurant**, the *Catounière* in place de la Mairie (closed Fri, first half June & first half Sept; ☎93.59.07.15; ②).

The Lower Var Valley

From Nice both the *Chemin de Fer de Provence* and the road stick closely to the left bank of the Var, which is wide, turbulent and not greatly scenic downstream of its confluence with the Esteron. Past the confluence with the Vésubie, a short way further north, you enter the **Défilé de Chaudan**, a long gorge between vertical cliffs through which the rail line and road have to tunnel. At the northern extremity of the gorge, the Tinée river comes rushing out of the **Gorges de la Mescla** to join the Var in a twisted semi-subterranean junction of rock and water. From here the course of the Var runs almost due west for 40km, passing tiny medieval villages and the towns of **Puget-Théniers** and **Entrevaux**. The main road and the rail line then continue west along the Vaïre river to **Annot**.

THE CHEMIN DE FER DE PROVENCE

Due to floods and landslides damaging the tracks, and tight budgets these days for repairs, some stretches of the *Chemin de Fer de Provence* line may be closed and the timetable reduced. For up-to-date **information** call the station in Digne (☎92.31.01.58) or in Nice (☎93.82.10.17).

Villars-sur-Var

VILLARS-SUR-VAR, 11km west of the Gorges de la Mescla, may have the northernmost vineyards of the *Côtes de Provence appellation*, but the quantity of wine produced is only just sufficient for local consumption, so you'll be lucky to get a glass of it in one of the two cafés.

The reason for stopping off here – apart from the charm of a *village perché* with stepped streets – is to see the **Eglise de St-Jean-Baptiste** and wander down the **allée des Grimaldi**. The carefully restored Baroque church is decorated with *trompe l'oeil* frescoes and an eighteenth-century ex-votive painting to "*Saint Patron de la Bonne Mort*", thanking him for killing off only 66 residents in the previous year's plague. The main altar has a striking retable, with another on the left wall from the Nice School. A door to the right of the church leads into the allée des Grimaldi, a flowering alleyway formed by a trellis supported on stone columns. At the end you come to a platform with views over the Var Valley.

Touët-sur-Var and the Gorges du Cians

Crammed against a cliff 10km west of Villars-sur-Var, **TOUET-SUR-VAR** also has a church that's rather special, though for a very different reason: it's built over a small torrent, visible through a grill in the floor of the nave. The village's highest houses look as if they are falling apart, but in fact the gaps between the beams are open galleries where the midday sun can reach the rows of drying figs.

Touët has a very good **restaurant**, the *Auberge des Chasseurs*, on the road from Nice (closed Tues & Feb, & out of season Fri evening & Sat; ☎93.05.71.11; menus from 110F) serving local fare which in autumn involves game and wild mushrooms. The specialities of the area are squash ravioli with nut sauce and *tartes des blettes* (Swiss chard tarts). For a **place to stay** try *Chez Paul*, also on the main road (closed Dec & Jan; ☎93.05.71.03; ③).

The Cians river joins the Var a short way west of Touët. The road along this tributary, the D28, leads to the ski resort of **Beuil**, passing first through the Gorges Inférieure du Cians, close to the confluence, and then the **Gorges du Cians** proper, a chaos of water tumbling over red schist rocks. This and the Gorges de Dalius to the west (see p.422) are a well-signed tourist circuit, so be prepared for traffic.

Puget-Théniers

Arriving by train at the small, dilapidated town of **PUGET-THENIERS**, the first monument you see is a statue of a powerful woman with her hands tied behind her back. It commemorates **August Blanqui**, who was born here in 1805. Blanqui was one of the leaders of the Paris Commune of 1871, and spent forty years of his life in prison for – as the inscription states – "his fidelity to the sacred cause of workers' emancipation". There are few French revolutionaries for whom the description "heroic defender of the proletariat" is truer, and none who came from a more isolated and unindustrialized region.

Sculpted by Maillol and titled *L'Action Enchaînée*, the monument immediately stirred up controversy in the town. It was first placed behind the church, but the priest was not going to have processions passing by a naked woman. So it was moved to the vicinity of the *Monuments des Morts* of World War I, but the veterans objected. Its next home was the abattoir. Only after World War II, from which French Communism emerged with a fairly unblemished record of resistance, was the monument finally placed on the *cours* below the old town.

The **Vieille Ville**, on the right bank of the Roudoule river, is full of mangy cats and thirteenth-century houses, some bearing the symbols of their original owners' trades on the door lintels. Across the Roudoule, the town is dominated by the great semicircular apse of the Romanesque **church**, outreaching even the ancient cedar alongside it, and suggesting a fort or prison more than a religious building. It's not a pretty structure by any standards, but it contains a brilliantly realistic Flemish *Entombment*, painted in the 1500s and an expressive calvary sculpted in wood.

Exploring the **Pays de la Roudoule** is the best reason for being in Puget-Théniers. In **PUGET-ROSTANG**, 5.5km northeast of Puget-Théniers, the **Ecomusée du Pays de la Roudoule** on place des Tilleuls (May–Sept Tues–Sun 10am–noon & 3–6pm) is not a museum as such but a centre for the discovery, preservation and animation of the natural and social heritage of the locality. The activities undertaken by the *écomusée* range from running an experimental agricultural station (planting aromatic plants at different altitudes and in different soils), to demonstrations by producers of local produce such as the *fromagerie communale* of the village of **St-Léger**. As well as a video workshop and a shop, the *écomusée* has information on local walks, and organizes guided tours concentrating on geology, botany, architecture, mycology (mushrooms) and so forth.

Practicalities

In summer there's a **tourist office** on the main road by the **gare Chemin de Fer de Provence** which has information on **walks**, **canoeing** and the **steam trains** that run between Puget-Théniers and Annot; otherwise the *mairie* (☎93.05.02.81) can supply details.

Puget-Théniers is not generously endowed with **hotels**, though with its surrounding area it offers a good range of accommodation. The *Laugier* at 1 place A-Conil (☎93.05.01.00; ④) is the best; cheaper possibilities are the *Coste* (☎93.05.00.20; ②), above a café, and *L'Univers* (☎93.05.02.81; ②). Up the Roudoule gorge along the D16, between La Croix-sur-Redoule and Léouvé, is the *Hostellerie des Tilleuls* (closed Nov–April; ☎93.05.02.07; ④), a beautifully situated hotel with a large swimming pool and views of the surrounding hills. Puget's two-star municipal **campsite** is by the river (Feb–Nov; ☎93.05.04.11) and there's a very well provisioned nudist three-star campsite 2km along the main road to Entrevaux, the *Club Origan Côte d'Azur* (☎93.05.06.00).

For a small *haut-pays* town, Puget-Théniers is not quite as dead as it might be. On summer evenings the **cafés** and **restaurants** on place A-Cornil in the *Vieille Ville* and down along the Roudoule towards the Var manage to get some custom, but don't expect a ball.

First choice for **meals** should be *Les Acacias*, (closed Mon; ☎93.05.05.25), 1km east of Puget-Théniers on the main road, with an excellent menu for around 120F plus a midday menu for around 80F (except Sun). *La Guinguette* at 18 rue du 4 Septembre in the centre (☎93.05.09.97; menus from 80F) specializes in trout and seafood with marinaded sea-trout sometimes on the menu. Excellent old-fashioned *boulangeries*, *charcuteries* and *fromageries* can be found in the old quarter of Puget-Théniers. If you happen to be here at Pentecost, La Croix-Sur-Redoule has a communal feast of bean soup cooked in a vast cauldron.

Entrevaux

Upstream from Puget-Théniers the valley widens, allowing space for pear, apple and cherry orchards. After 13km you reach **ENTREVAUX** whose striking feature is the fortification sealing the old town on the north bank of the river. Built on the site of a Roman city, this was a key border-town between France and Savoy.

The single-arched drawbridge across the Var – the only access – was fortified by Vauban, and both this and the gun turrets above the river are very attractive in the way anachronistic military features can sometimes be. It is Vauban's linking of the town with the ruined **Château** (permanent access through paying turnstyle; 10F; guided visits in July & Aug 9am–noon & 3–6pm; 25F) that gives the site its menacing character. Perched 135m above the river at the top of a steep spur, the château originally could be reached only by scrambling up the rock. By the seventeenth century this had become unacceptable, perhaps because soldiers leaving the garrison on their hands and knees did not do much for the army's image. Consequently, Vauban built the double-walled ramp, plus attendant bastions, that zigzags up the rock in ferocious determination. Trying out the cardiovascular system on the half-hour ascent is inevitably the primary requirement of all visitors to Entrevaux.

The former **cathedral** (July & Aug daily; Sept–June apply to the tourist office), the other focus of Entrevaux history, is well integrated into the military defences, with one wall forming part of the ramparts and the belfry a fortified tower. The interior, however, is all twirling Louis Quinze, with misericords, side altars and organ as overdecorated as they could possibly be. Just beyond the church, through the **Porte d'Italie**, you can escape from Baroque opulence and military might to wander along a path beside the river. The old town, much of which dates from Vauban's redevelopments, is little different from its medieval neighbours, with dark narrow passageways that seem to smell of age. Renovation of key buildings has now begun, and twentieth-century engineering is celebrated in a collection of working motorbikes from 1901 to 1967 at the **Musée des Motos** in rue Sénéquier (May–Sept daily 10am–12.30pm & 2–7pm; free).

Practicalities

The **gare Chemin de Fer de Provence** is just downstream from the bridge on the south bank, and the **tourist office** (summer only; ☎93.05.46.73) is in the left-hand tower of the drawbridge.

For places to stay, there's the rudimentary **hotel** *Hostellerie Vauban*, 4 place Moreau (☎93.05.42.40; ②) in the modern extension south of the river, and two **gîtes d'étapes**, the *Gîte des Moulins* (☎93.05.46.73; ②) and the *Gîte de la Caserne* (☎93.05.46.73; ①), both open all year.

For **food and drink** stops you could choose the *Bar au Pont-Levis* opposite Vauban's bridge where English-speaking tourists congregate or head up to place Charles-Panier where you'll find *L'Echauguette* (☎93.05.46.89; menus from 70F), a restaurant specializing in trout, pasta and the local dry beef sausage known as *secca de boeuf*, and *La Planète* snack-bar, serving omelettes, *pains beignets* and pizzas. The *Lovera charcuterie* (closed Mon) next door to *La Planète* sells *secca de boeuf* if you want to try it as picnic food, though it's best seasoned with lemon and olive oil. On place du Marché there's an *épicerie* selling gorgeous honey.

Annot

ANNOT promotes itself as a holiday centre, on the strength of its climate, pure health-giving waters, clean air and so forth. There are excellent **walks** up past strange sandstone formations to rocky outcrops with names like *Chambre du Roi* (the King's Chamber) and *Dent du Diable* (the Devil's Tooth). Annot is also useful as a transit town, where buses link the *Chemin de Fer de Provence* with Castellane and the Route Napoléon. It's grouped around a large open space lined by plane trees – the *cours* – with the medieval quarter to the north. The **Vieille Ville**, if not outstanding, does have some pretty arcades and a Renaissance clock tower on its church. The **gare Chemin de Fer de Provence** is to the southeast, at the end of av de la Gare, which leads to the *cours*. The **tourist office** on place du Revely (Mon–Sat 10am–noon & 3–6pm, Sun 10am–noon; ☎92.83.23.03) will load you down with details of walks, rides, sports facilities, the *Train des Pignes* steam train to Puget-Théniers, exhibitions and local festivities. It also rents **bikes**.

Accommodation is very easy to come by in Annot, all of it very reasonably priced. Of the **hotels**, budget options include the crumbling *La Cigale* (☎92.83.20.24; ①) on bd St-Pierre to the north; and the *Beauséjour*, by the entrance to the *Vieille Ville* on place du Revely (☎92.83.21.08; ②). The *Hôtel du Parc* on place du Germe (closed Oct–April; ☎92.83.20.03; ③) is an old house on the western side of the *cours* with a large garden and a good restaurant (menus from 80F). The hotel on av de la Gare, *L'Avenue* (April–Oct; ☎92.83.22.07; ③), has small cosy rooms and its **restaurant** is the best in town (menus from 75F). For **campers** there's a very pleasant two-star site, *La Ribière*, on the road to Fugeret (☎92.83.21.44; mid-Feb to mid-Nov) just north of the town.

St-André-les-Alpes, Castellane and the Route Napoléon

From Annot, the *Chemin de Fer de Provence* heads due north before tunnelling through to the Verdon Valley and **Thorame-Haute**'s station where you can take buses further north up the Verdon. The rail line turns south again with the next major stop at **St-André-les-Alpes**. St-André stands at the head of the **Lac de Castillon**, one of the Verdon's many artificial lakes, stretching a good 10km southwards to the Barrage de Castillon and the smaller Lac de Chaudanne from where the Verdon descends dramatically into **Castellane**, the most significant town on the **Route Napoléon** after Grasse.

The main road along the Var Valley, the N202 from Entrevaux, skirts Annot and heads west to the Lac de Castillon at **St-Julien-du-Verdon**, then takes over from the D955 as the lakeside corniche up to St-André. The road and rail line run parallel again west from St-André along a beautiful stretch of rock, river and forest to meet the Route Napoléon at Barrême.

With good train and road access, plenty of accommodation and well-organized facilities for outdoor activities, particularly water and airborne sports, this is an easy corner of Haute Provence to explore. Castellane and St-Julien can feel a bit too subservient to entrepreneurial tourism, but traditional Provence is never far away, as the sight of sheep taking over the roads on their way to or from their summer pastures may well remind you.

St-André-les-Alpes

ST-ANDRE-LES-ALPES is both very charming and rather boring, unless you're into gliding and hang-gliding. It has a sleepy, old-fashioned feel to it with none of the tight protective huddling of so many Provençal villages. Instead its streets and squares are open to the air, and to the magnificent views of the surrounding mountains and the lake. Accommodation and food are cheap; the only difficulty is choosing which of the beautiful routes out from St-André to explore.

Gliding and **hang-gliding** are done on the thermals around Mont Chalvet to the west of the village, with short flights for the less experienced in the morning. It's very well organized and regulated to ensure maximum safety by the **Ecole de Vol Libre "Aerogliss"** at the Base de Loisirs des Iscles to the south of the village (☎92.89.11.30), which charges around 400F for an initiation flight (price includes equipment rental). **Bikes** can be rented at *Pro-Verdon Activités Nature* on rue Basse (☎92.89.04.19); they also organize **walks**, and **rafting** and **canoeing** on the Lac de Castillon and the Gorges de Verdon.

Practicalities

The **gare Chemin de Fer de Provence** is right by the village centre, and the **tourist office** on place Marcel-Pastorelli, the square to the south of the station and north of the main car park (Mon, Tues, Thurs & Fri 9am–noon & 2–5pm, Wed 9am–noon; ☎92.89.02.39), is very helpful, with information on the surrounding area, including St-Julien, Thorame and Moriez.

Of the seven **hotels** in and around St-André the *Lac et Fôret* on the road to St-Julien (March–Sept; ☎92.89.07.38; ③) has the best views over the lake; the *France* has budget rooms right in the centre of the village on place de l'Eglise (☎92.89.02.09; ②), where you'll also find the *Auberge du Parc* (☎92.89.00.03; ②) offering very decent comfort for the price and a dependable **restaurant** (menus from 80F). The two-star municipal **campsite**, *Les Iscles*, by the confluence of the Verdon and the Issole on the road to St-Julien (April–Sept; ☎92.89.02.29) has good facilities. If you prefer a **gîte d'étape**, try the one in Moriez, the next stop on the *Chemin de Fer de Provence* or a five-minute drive west of St-André, which offers rooms for two to six people for 55F a night, excluding sheet rental and breakfast (☎92.89.13.20). There's a good choice of **beers** at *Le Commerce* bar on place de l'Eglise.

North to Château-Garnier and Thorame

Following the **Issole river** north from St-André along the D2 is extremely pleasant. The narrow road stays close to the banks most of the time, with well-signed **footpaths** leading off into the wooded hills. After 8km you can turn left towards **Tartonne** where there's a pleasant **gîte d'étape** with a good restaurant (menus at 55F and 75F), *Les Robines* (c/o Mme Pascale Reybaud; ☎92.34.26.07; ②), or keep going to **La Bâtie** where the valley opens out. Between La Bâtie and **CHATEAU-GARNIER**, on the left along the footpath to Tartonne, is the twelfth-century **Chapelle St-Thomas**, decorated with medieval frescoes (the key is available from the first farm on the right after the turning). The main reason to stop in Château-Garnier, however, is to visit the serious and dedicated **honey** business of M Rémy Chauvin at the further end of the village on the left (daily 9am–noon & 2–6pm, till 5pm at weekends). Though only groups are given tours of the hives, you may see the gleaming machinery in action, and you can certainly buy superb honey with such flavours as rosemary, acacia, "thousand flowers", sunflower, pine and lavander, plus nougat, sweets, candles and medicinal derivatives.

From Château-Garnier the road veers east through **THORAME BASSE**, where the church has an unlikely train station-style clock on the spire and the *Café du Vallée* serves inexpensive plats du jour, then through wide open meadows to **THORAME HAUTE** where there's a pizzeria (Fri–Sun), a *charcuterie* and a one-star municipal **campsite** down by the Verdon, *Fontchaude* (May–Oct; ☎92.83.90.86).

These quiet back roads are well off the beaten tourist tracks and *camping sauvage* is very possible.

South along the Lac de Castillon

Depending on the water levels the **Lac de Castillon** can be a bit grungy at the St-André end but you don't have to go far down the N202 to find places to **swim** and **rent boats**. The landscape gets more dramatic after the road crosses over the lake and the hills start to close in.

ST-JULIEN-DU-VERDON was a casualty of the creation of the lake. It's now a tiny place with a two-star **campsite**, *Camping du Lac* (mid-June to mid-Sept; ☎92.89.07.93), and a **hotel**, *Lou Pidanoux* (☎92.89.05.87; ②), but nothing to suggest that this was once *Sanctus Julienetus*, on the Roman road from Nice to Digne. Still, it's a pleasant quiet spot if you just want to laze about by calm, clear water with a gorgeous backdrop of mountains.

The main road heads east to Annot from St-Julien, a fabulous ride through the dramatic *clues* of Vergons and Rouaine, and passing the exquisite Romanesque chapel of **Notre-Dame de Valvert**.

Continuing south from St-Julien towards Castellane, there are more opportunities for bathing and boating. The gleam of gold up in the hills on the opposite bank that might catch your eye is the decoration of the Buddhist centre of Mandaron.

Castellane

Being the nearest town to the upper part of the Gorges du Verdon, some 17km away (see *The Heartland of Provence*), **CASTELLANE** has long since stopped behaving as anything else but a tourist camp. When not inveigling you to enter its medieval *enceinte* as the "gateway to the gorge" it poses the indigestible question: "Napoléon stopped here; why not you?" The place where Napoléon dined on March 3, 1815 is now the **Conservatoire des Arts et Traditions Populaires de Castellane et Moyen Verdon**, 34 rue Nationale, which has temporary exhibitions of variable interest. Your reason for stopping is likely to be for the range of restaurants, hotels and cafés which in summer gives the town an animation rare in these parts.

The only distinguishing and omnivisible feature of Castellane is the abrupt and massive rock topped by a **chapel** dedicated, predictably enough, to Our Lady of the Rock. Since there's little else to do you might as well climb up to it. The path begins behind the modern church set back at the head of place de l'Eglise from the central place Marcel-Sauvaire, and wends its way up past the *Vieille Ville* and the machicolated **Tour Pentagonal**, standing uselessly on the lower slopes. Twenty to thirty minutes should see you at the top, from where you cannot actually see the gorge, but you do get a pretty good view of the river disappearing into it and the mountains circling the town.

Practicalities

Castellane's **tourist office** at the top of rue Nationale (summer Mon–Sat 9am–noon & 2–6pm; ☎92.83.61.14) can provide a full list of hotels and campsites.

The best **hotel** deals in Castellane are the *Hostellerie du Roc*, place de l'Eglise (☎92.83.62.65; ③), *Le Verdon*, bd de la République (☎92.83.62.02; ③), and the *Auberge Bon Accueil*, place Marcel-Sauvaire (April–Sept; ☎92.83.62.01; ③). The *Nouvel Hôtel du Commerce* in place de l'Eglise (April–Oct; ☎92.83.61.00; ④) is the most upmarket, with rather awful plastic decor but wonderful **food** served in the garden, and a 115F menu of seriously sophisticated and elegant dishes. You can get cheap pasta dishes at *La Main à la Pâte* on rue de la Fontaine and there's a pleasant ice-cream bar at the end of the same street. Wednesday and Saturday are **market** days and there's a good wine shop between the tourist office and *Aqua-Verdon* (see below).

There are at least eleven **campsites** within 3km of the town. The closest is *Le Frédéric-Mistral* (open all year; ☎92.83.62.27), by the river on the rte des Gorges du Verdon. Further on down the same road you'll see the caravans and bungalows of the *Camping Notre-Dame* (April–Oct; ☎92.83.63.02), and 1.5km out of town the four-star *Camp du Verdon* (mid-April to mid-Sept; ☎92.83.61.29) which offers **horse rides**. In summer all the sites along this road are likely to be full. A good one further afield and away from the gorge is *La Colle* (May–Sept; ☎92.83.61.57) on the GR4 off the rte des Gorges.

For **canoeing** and **rafting** on Lac de Castillon and the Gorges de Verdon, *Agence Aqua-Verdon* at 9 rue Nationale (☎92.83.72.75) and *Verdon Rafts* just down from the tourist office (☎92.77.33.57) are the places to get information. *Aqua-Verdon* also rents out **bikes**. If you need any camping gear *L'Echoppe* at 36 rue Nationale is a useful address.

Moving on from Castellane, in July and August, there are two **buses** a day into the Gorges du Verdon (one hour to La Maline) and two to the Lac de Castillon.

Along the Route Napoléon

North of Castellane the barren scrubby rocks lining the Route Napoléon need the evening light to turn them a more becoming pinkish hue. The town's landmark remains visible all the way up the zigzags to the **Col de Leque**. Here, in the night-time cold of over 1000m above sea level, you can find a bed at the **hotel-restaurant** *Les Peyrascas* (☎92.83.61.28; ③), assured of a sublime view to greet you in the morning.

From the Col de Leque the Route Napoléon traverses the **Clue de Taulanne**, then opens out onto a marvellous northward view of a circle of crests. The tourist blitz is over. Though the emperor's hat or eagle still appears on signposts, and **Barrème** has its "Napoléon slept here", his image only appears on faded Courvoisier ads.

To either side of the road lie some of the most obscure and empty quarters of Provence. The populations of villages such as **Blieux** and **Majastres**, on the slopes of the Mourre ridge to the west, have dwindled close to the point of desertion. Life here is rural poverty at its starkest, for all the seeming promise of the springtime or early summer land to a non-agricultural eye.

Back on the only significant road, the village of **SENEZ** speaks of the same decline, with its vast Romanesque ex-cathedral that could easily accommodate ten times the present number of residents. The episcopal see established here in the fourth century, one of the earliest in France, was throughout the centuries one of the poorest bishoprics in the country. The church is only open on Sunday, unless you get the key from the *presbytère* in Barrême, 8km down the road. If you get stuck here, a very cheap and friendly hotel-bar-restaurant is *La Cathédrale* (summer only), just by the church.

Digne-les-Bains

The capital of the Alpes-de-Haute-Provence *département*, **DIGNE-LES-BAINS**, is by far the largest town in northeastern Provence, with about 17,000 inhabitants. However, despite its status and superb position between the Durance Valley and the start of the real mountains, it can be a dispiriting place. This is partly due to its curative **baths**, visited by those afflicted with rheumatism and respiratory disorders, and partly due to the overdose of administrative offices in what is a very small city. Despite brand new architecture around the central place Gal-de-Gaulle, and some tasteful modern infill to the crumbling *Vieille Ville*, Digne is a dull place to explore.

On the other hand, it has a bursting calendar of **festivals** and celebrations of **lavender cultivation** (see p.416 for a full run-down), two interesting **museums**, a **Tibetan foundation** that has been visited by the Dalai Lama, and a **geology reserve** of some significance which encompasses a huge area surrounding the town. Every odd year Digne runs a **Symposium International de la Sculpture** with the works exhibited throughout the town. Digne also has an excellent choice of places to stay and eat, and, if you have your own transport, there are great trips to be made into the mountains.

Arrival, information and accommodation

From the Durance Valley the Route Napoléon enters Digne along the west bank of the Bléone, arriving at the rond-point du 4 Septembre, with the **gares SNCF** (☎92.31.00.67) and **Chemin de Fer de Provence** (☎92.31.01.58) just to the west, along av Paul-Sémard. Avenue de Verdon continues to Grand Pont, the main bridge, over which you reach the rond-point du 11 Novembre 1918 where you'll find the **tourist office** (Mon–Sat 9am–noon & 2–5/6pm; ☎92.31.42.73), **gîtes de France** office and the **gare routière** (☎92.31.50.00). From the south the Route Napoléon comes in along the east bank of the river to the rond-point du 11 Novembre 1918. From the *rond-point*, the main street, **boulevard Gassendi**, leads up to **place Gal-de-Gaulle**; av Thiers, becoming av du 8 mai 1945, leads towards the **Etablissement Thermal** 3km east of the town; and the **old town** lies between the two. **Bikes** can be rented from *Gallardo*, 8 cours des Arès (☎92.31.05.29), or *Sport 2000*, 31 bd Gassendi (☎92.31.51.40).

The best-value **hotels** are the simple but nicely done-up *Le Petit Saint-Jean*, 14 cours des Arès (☎92.31.30.04; ③) with a restaurant serving local and Spanish specialities (menus from 70F), and the *Origan*, 6 rue Pied-de-la-Ville (☎92.31.62.13; ②), which also has good food (Tues–Sat; menus from 100F). The *Mistre*, 63 bd Gassendi (☎92.31.00.16; ⑤), is very comfortable and central, with excellent local specialities at its restaurant (closed Sat out of season; menus from 130F). At the top end of the market there's the very luxurious *Le Grand Paris*, 19 bd Thiers (☎92.31.11.15; ⑤–⑧), a seventeenth-century former convent with tastefully decorated large rooms and Digne's top gourmet restaurant (closed Sun evening & Mon out of season; 150F midday menu Mon–Sat, otherwise from around 200F).

The two-star municipal **campsite** *Notre-Dame du Bourg* is 2km out from the centre along the D900 to Seynes-les-Alpes (April–Oct; ☎92.31.04.87); take av Ste-Douceline left from the top of bd Gassendi and then turn right into av du Camping. Or there's the more pleasantly situated three-star *Camping des Eaux Chaudes*, rte des Thermes, 1.5km out towards the Etablissement Thermal (April–Oct; ☎92.32.31.04).

Vieux Digne

Late medieval Digne had **two centres**: the area to the north around Notre-Dame-du-Bourg, the original cathedral, where pre-Roman Digne developed; and the existing *Haute Ville* where the Cathédrale St-Jérôme was built as a small church at the end of the fifteenth century, to be successively enlarged as it took over the functions of Notre-Dame.

Standing in splendid isolation, **Notre-Dame** is typical of Provençal Romanesque, save for the vastness of its dimensions and the lightness of its yellowy stone. Built between 1200 and 1330, it contains fragments of early medallions and late medieval murals, the least faded illustrating the Last Judgement. Archeological digs have revealed a first-century construction and a fifth-century church from which a Merovingian altar and a mosaic floor remain. The edifice is currently being turned into a museum which should be open soon (for hours apply to the tourist office).

The Haute Ville

In the *Haute Ville* the present, fifteenth-century **Cathédrale St-Jérôme** (May–Nov Tues, Thurs, Sat & Sun 3–6pm) is in dire need of repair. Death by falling masonry is the closest thought of a spiritual nature that's likely to pass your mind in here. Having said that, the Gothic facade is impressive and the features inside, in particular the Gothic stained-glass windows, clearly indicate that this was once an awesome place of worship. Work will no doubt be carried out on the cathedral, along with the streets of Vieux Digne which are gradually being restored. **Rue Trou du Four** and the **montée St-Charles** that lead up to St-Jérôme are certainly atmospheric and **rue de l'Hubac** is now very pretty, even if its pastel tints would look dull to the medieval eye.

At the top of rue de l'Hubac the former residence of **Monseigneur de Miollis** still stands. He was the bishop of Digne, who from 1805 to 1838 laid out the plans for the cathedral's last enlargement, and was the inspiration for Victor Hugo's epitome of true virtue, Monseigneur Bienvenu in *Les Misérables*. Early in the novel the bishop walks into the mountains in search of a dying atheist revolutionary whom all the district has shunned. The man has no wish for priests or last rites and harshly accounts for his life in his own moral terms. He finishes by asking why he should need a bishop's blessing, at which point Monseigneur Bienvenu goes down on his knees and asks for his.

The Wednesday and Saturday **markets** bring animation to the otherwise rather clinically modernized **place Général-de-Gaulle**, with lots of lavender products, including honey, on sale. A statue of **Pierre Gassendi**, seventeenth-century *Dignois* mathematician and astronomer, stands within the balustrades

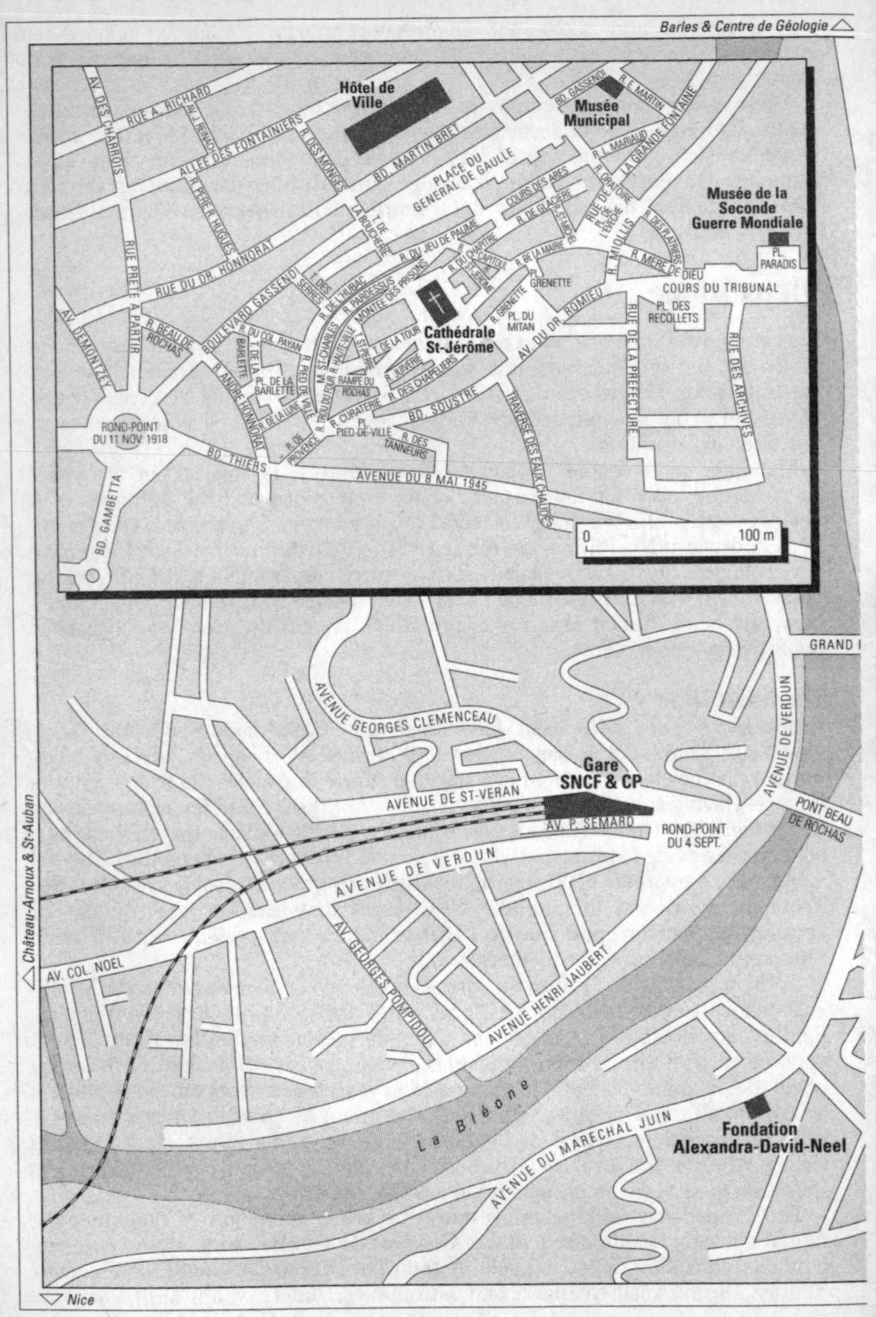
Barles & Centre de Géologie
Hôtel de Ville
Musée Municipal
Musée de la Seconde Guerre Mondiale
Cathédrale St-Jérôme
RUE A. RICHARD
AV. DES CHARROIS
ALLEE DES FONTAINIERS
BD. MARTIN BRET
PLACE DU GENERAL DE GAULLE
COURS DES ARES
R. DE GLACIERE
RUE DU DR. HONNORAT
RUE PRETE A PARTIR
BOULEVARD GASSENDI
R. BEAU DE ROCHAS
AV. DEMONTZEY
ROND-POINT DU 11 NOV. 1918
BD. GAMBETTA
BD. THIERS
AVENUE DU 8 MAI 1945
BD. SOUSTRE
AV. DU DR. ROMIEU
TRAVERSE DES EAUX CHAUDES
RUE DE LA PREFECTURE
RUE DES ARCHIVES
COURS DU TRIBUNAL
PL. DES RECOLLETS
PL. PARADIS
R. MERE DE DIEU
R. MIOLLIS
LA GRANDE FONTAINE
PL. GRENETTE
PL. DU MITAN
PL. PIED-DE-VILLE
R. DES TANNEURS
R. CURATERIE
R. ANDRE HONNORAT
PL. DE LA BARLETTE
0
100 m
AVENUE GEORGES CLEMENCEAU
Gare SNCF & CP
AVENUE DE ST-VERAN
AV. P. SEMARD
ROND-POINT DU 4 SEPT.
AVENUE DE VERDUN
PONT BEAU DE ROCHAS
GRAND
AV. COL. NOEL
AV. GEORGES POMPIDOU
AVENUE HENRI JAUBERT
La Bléone
AVENUE DU MARECHAL JUIN
Fondation Alexandra-David-Neel
Château-Arnoux & St-Auban
Nice

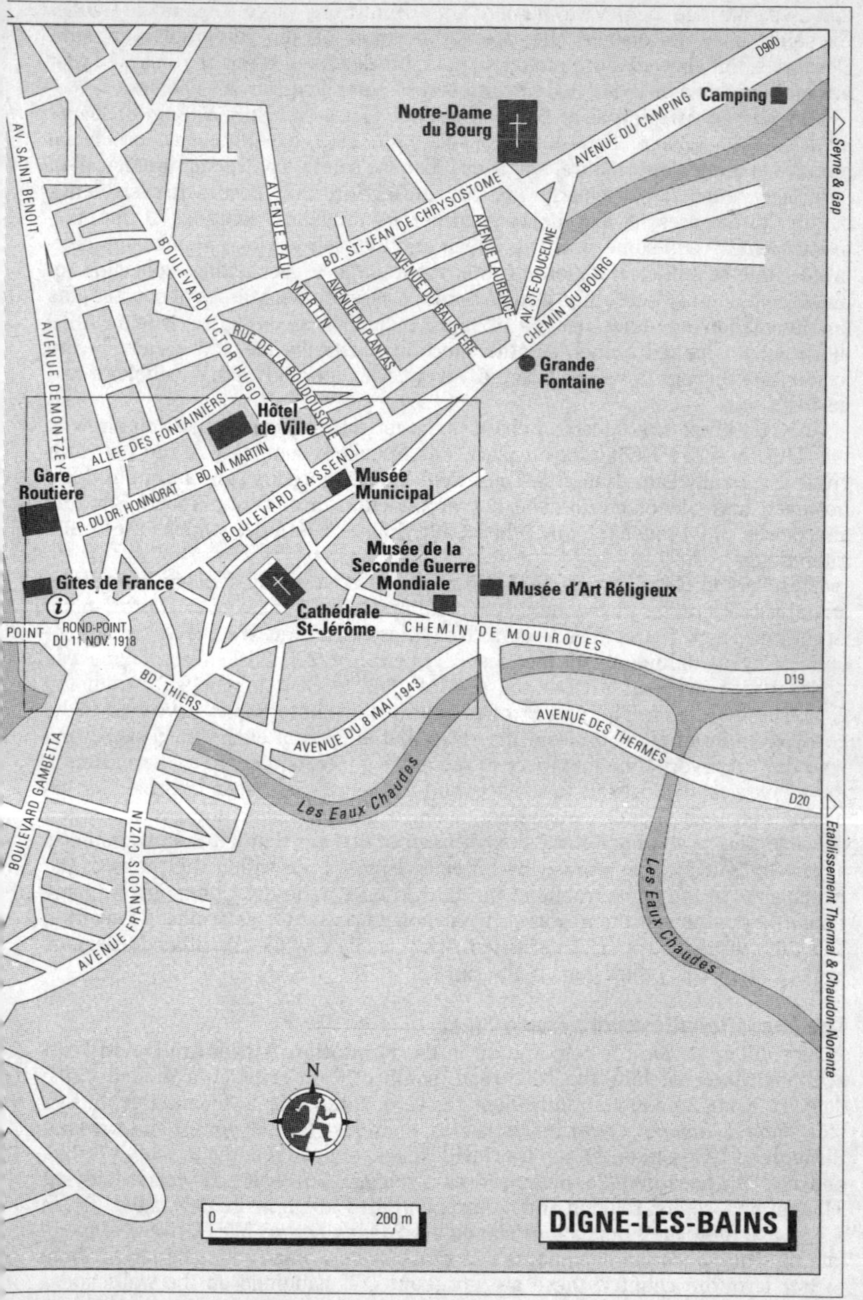

Notre-Dame du Bourg
Camping
D900
AVENUE DU CAMPING
Seyne & Gap
AV. SAINT BENOIT
AVENUE PAUL MARTIN
BD. ST-JEAN DE CHRYSOSTOME
AVENUE LAURENCE
AV. STE-DOUCELINE
CHEMIN DU BOURG
BOULEVARD VICTOR HUGO
AVENUE DU PLANTAS
AVENUE DU BALLSTÈRE
RUE DE LA BOUDOUSQUE
Grande Fontaine
AVENUE DEMONTZEY
ALLEE DES FONTAINIERS
Hôtel de Ville
BD. M. MARTIN
Gare Routière
R. DU DR. HONNORAT
BOULEVARD GASSENDI
Musée Municipal
Musée de la Seconde Guerre Mondiale
Gîtes de France
Musée d'Art Réligieux
Cathédrale St-Jérôme
POINT
ROND-POINT DU 11 NOV. 1918
CHEMIN DE MOUIROUES
D19
BD. THIERS
AVENUE DU 8 MAI 1943
AVENUE DES THERMES
BOULEVARD GAMBETTA
Les Eaux Chaudes
D20
Etablissement Thermal & Chaudon-Norante
AVENUE FRANCOIS CUZIN
Les Eaux Chaudes
N
0
200 m
DIGNE-LES-BAINS

that separate the boulevard named after him from place Général-de-Gaulle. Gassendi used to dispute the precise location of the immortal soul with Descartes, but showed more materialism on his deathbed when he remarked that he would not now be dying had he not been so compliant with his doctors.

The **Musée Municipal** at 64 bd Gassendi (Tues–Sun July & Aug 10.30am–noon & 1.30–6.30pm; Sept–June 1.30–5.30pm; 15F) has the usual provincial mixture of archeology, natural and social history, painting and sculpture. It's all of surprising quality, particularly the **art collection** that covers the sixteenth century to the present, and includes numerous Provençal paintings of the nineteenth century and some stunning Italian and Flemish works. The museum celebrates the scientific tradition of the town with a fascinating collection of nineteenth-century **scientific instruments**, Gassendi mementoes of course, plus documentation on other natives of note, including an engineer who in 1880 designed a Channel tunnel. Another section illustrates life and society in the lower Alps through a **reconstructed street** with its goldsmith's, cobbler's and barber's shop.

The collection of reliquaries, chalices, priest robes and crucifixes on show at the **Musée d'Art Réligieux** on place des Récollets southeast of the old town (June–Sept daily 9am–1pm & 3–7pm; free) is less inspiring. The museum does, however, have videos on Romanesque architecture throughout France, Baroque altarpieces in Provence, and the Cathédrale St-Jérôme, which are quite interesting.

Close by, on place Paradis, is the **Musée de la Seconde Guerre Mondiale**, an individual's rather than a municipal creation (July & Aug Wed & Thurs 2–6pm; April–June, Sept & Oct Wed 2–6pm; Nov–March the first Wed of the month 2–6pm; or by appointment with Jacques Teyssier on ☎92.31.28.95; free). Digne was under Italian occupation from the end of 1942 to September 1943, when the Germans took over. The names of people in the photographs have had to be covered up in an effort to avoid the rows that still erupt over who resisted and who did not. Every time members of the older generation come to the museum, the ideological battles start to surface, and the curator has been criticized for his position on Jean Giono's collaboration. For a foreign visitor, however, this is a fascinating exposé of one town's experience of the war that left the people here, as throughout France, scarred by bitter divisions, even within the ranks of the Resistance. In the photographs of the Liberation Parade the Communists (many Polish Jews amongst them) march with their Lorraine Cross armbands inverted and their weapons on the left, in Red Army fashion, while the other Resistance organizations carry their guns to the right.

The Fondation Alexandra-David-Neel

A very different world is conjured up in the **Fondation Alexandra-David-Neel** at 27 av Maréchal Juin, the Nice road, south of the centre (1-hr guided visits: daily 10.30am, 2pm & 4pm; July–Sept 10.30am, 2pm, 3.30pm & 5pm; free; bus #3 stop *Stade J. Rolland*). A writer, musician, anarchist (in her youth) and traveller throughout Indo-China, Alexandra David Neel spent two months in Tibet's forbidden city of Lhasa in 1924, disguised as a beggar. She spent 25 years studying Tibetan philosophy, religion and culture, and died in Digne in 1969, aged 101, in the house (now the Foundation) she called *Samten Dzong*, her "fortress of meditation". The *Fondation* documents this remarkable woman's life and pays tribute to her favourite country; there are gorgeous silk hangings on the walls and a shop where you can buy current Tibetan products, all blessed by the Nobel-Prize-winning Dalai Lama who has visited twice.

The Réserve Naturelle Géologique de Haute Provence

The **Réserve Naturelle Géologique de Haute Provence** is the biggest protected geological area in Europe. It covers an area of 150 square kilometres stretching from north of Digne to the Gorge du Verdon. Its sites include imprints and fossils of various Miocene creatures – crabs, oysters, ammonites, an ichthyosaurus – recording the time before the Alps had forced the sea southwards. Just outside Digne, 3.5km north of the rond-point du 11 Novembre 1918 on the road to Barles, you can see, on the left of the road, **a wall of ammonites**, the fossils of shells whose creatures lived off these rocks 185 million years ago. Further on, the road forks with the left turning signed to **La Robine**. From the car park near La Robine's school at the further end of the village, a path is signed with the logo of an ichthyosaurus. After a 45-minute to one-hour's walk you'll come to the extraordinarily well-preserved **fossilized skeleton of an ichthyosaurus**, a 4.5-metre-long reptile that was swimming around these parts while dinosaurs lumbered about on land. Closer to Digne than both these sites, at the end of the road off to the left after the bridge across the Bléone, is the **Centre de Géologie** (April–Oct daily 9am–noon & 2–5.30pm, closing Fri 4.30pm; rest of the year Mon–Fri only; 13F; bus #2 stop *Champourcin*; 15-min walk from car park to Centre) which has extremely good videos, workshops and exhibitions on the Réserve. If all this has really whetted your appetite for things geological, there are *jours de découverte* (discovery days) in July and August on Thursdays and Sundays, plus half days on Wednesday afternoons (days may change from year to year) where you go off with a guide to different sites in the Réserve (bookings at the tourist office; around 85F).

Along the Eaux Chaudes

The sulphurous water between 29°C and 49°C whose health-giving properties have been known since antiquity, spouts out of the Falaise St-Pancrace just east of the town above av des Thermes; the stream called Eaux Chaudes, which runs alongside the avenue, however, is as cold as any mountain stream. If you want to take a cure, the **Etablissement Thermal** (☎92.32.32.92) will be only to happy to oblige, and if you're not sure what it entails there's a guided tour every Wednesday at 2pm from April to October (bus #1, stop *Thermes*).

If you're more interested in stunning landscapes, the D20 along the Eaux Chaudes which meets the Route Napoléon at **Chaudon-Norante** is a great route to follow. Meadows contrast with the great wall of mountain to the north; acacia trees give way to larch forests as you climb to the Col du Corobin where the views open up to a vast expanse southwards. Near Digne you may notice women wearing floral scarves and long skirts of a distinctly un-Provençal style. They are likely to be Albanians, one of several foreign communities who have settled in this harsh and marginalized environment.

Eating, drinking and entertainment

The best **meals** to be had in Digne are at the hotels *Le Grand Paris*, the *Origan* and the *Mistre* (see p.410 "Arrival, information and accommodation"). Or you could try the hotel *La Bourgogne's* restaurant, 3 av de Verdon (closed Mon out of season; ☎92.31.00.19; menus from 90F), with specialities from Burgundy as well as Provence. Boulevard Gassendi has plenty of cafés and brasseries to chose from; *Le Tampinet* café on place du Tampinet opposite the tourist office is cheap and cheerful; and there's a lively brasserie at 43 bd Victor-Hugo, the *Happy Hours* (closed Sun; ☎92.31.00.37).

For evening **entertainment**, the *Centre Culturel Pierre Gassendi*, 45 av du 8 Mai 1945 (☎92.30.87.10), puts on shows, concerts and has a cinema. If you want to bop, head out towards **Aiglun**, 12km west from Digne along the N85 on rte de Marseille, where there are two **discos**, *Le Santos* (☎92.34.61.36) and *Les Douze Chênes* (☎92.34.65.10).

The first weekend in August sees the **Corso de la Lavande**, a jamboree with parades of floats celebrating the lavender crop and its two key products, honey and perfume. The **Foire-Exposition de la Lavande** at the end of August and the beginning of September is more commercially minded but excellent for buying pots of goodies to take back home. July sees a **jazz** festival; in September the **Journées Tibétaines** celebrate all things Tibetan; and there are special **film** seasons in March, July, October and November.

Listings

Car rental *Avis*, rte de Marseille (☎92.32.19.66); *Europcar*, rue Antoine Lavoisier, Zone Industrielle St-Christophe (☎92.32.04.89); *Toyota*, rte de Nice (☎92.31.14.26).

Currency exchange *BNP*, 5 bd Gassendi; *Crédit Lyonnais*, 69 bd Gassendi: both have automatic money distributers.

Emergencies ☎15; *Centre Hospitalier Charles Romieu*, rue Pasteur (☎92.30.15.15).

Laundry 99 bd Gassendi and 4 pl du Marché.

Pharmacy Call *Gendarmerie* on ☎92.30.11.00 for the *pharmacie de garde*.

Police Commissariat de Police, rue des Monges (☎92.30.86.60).

Post office *PTT*, 4 rue André-Honnorat, 04000 Digne (Mon–Fri 8am–7pm, Sat 8am–noon).

Taxis ☎92.31.26.02.

Massif les Monges and north to Seyne

North of Digne the mountains that reach their highest peak at Les Monges (2115m) form an impassable barrier, as far as roads go, between the valleys running down to Sisteron and the Durance and those of the Bléone's tributaries. There are footpaths, for serious walkers, (which begin at Digne on the west bank of the Bléone north of the Grand Pont) and just one road loop south of Les Monges linking Digne and Sisteron via **Thoard** and **Authon** across the **Col de Font-Belle**. Fantastic forested paths lead off past vertical rocks from the pass.

THOARD is a pretty village to base yourself with a **gîte d'étape** c/o Mme Bregou (☎92.34.63.74; ①) and two **chambres d'hôtes** outside the village: c/o M & Mme Charles Agniel, La Bannette (☎92.34.68.88; ③) and c/o M Claude Verchot, Hameau Les Bourres (☎92.34.63.92; ②).

The D900a, which follows first the course of the Bléone then the Bès torrent, passes many of the protected sites of the *Réserve Naturelle Géologique de Haute Provence*, where shrubs, flowers and butterflies are now the sole visible wildlife. After heavy rain the waters tear through the **Clues de Barles and Verdaches** like a boiling soup of mud in which it's hard to imagine fish finding sustenance.

Making any decent livelihood from the land here is difficult. A lot of "*marginaux*" (hippies or anyone into alternative lifestyles) manage to survive, making goat's cheese and doing seasonal work; the indigenous *paysans* are more likely to be opening *gîtes* and servicing the increasing numbers of city dwellers who come for trekking or skiing trips. But it's still very wild and deserted, with little accommodation other than *gîtes* and *chambres d'hôtes*; petrol stations are also few and far between.

Seyne-les-Alpes

To the west of the Clues de Barles, beyond the close horizon, the GR6 from Sisteron winds from valley to crest miles from any road or habitation on its route to **SEYNE-LES-ALPES**, some 40km north of Digne. Backed by forests of pine edging up towards the snowy summits, the sudden wide valley of the Blanche at Seyne is covered with cow pastures and fields where mules and horses are bred. The cows have bells round their necks, the houses have steep chalet roofs – if it were not for its general air of irregularity, it could almost be in Switzerland. A battered **Vauban fort** (July & Aug 9am–5pm; 10F) looks down on the equally dilapidated Romanesque **Eglise Notre-Dame de Nazareth**, graced with an old sundial, a Gothic porch and rose window.

Seyne's main influx of visitors is in winter, when its three skiing stations, **St-Jean**, **Chabanon** and **Le Grand Puy**, are in operation. The rest of the year the town is quieter, but still has plenty of accommodation on offer and scope for walking and riding into the mountains. It also has the only surviving **horse fair** in southeast France, held in October, and a **mule breeder**'s **competition** at the beginning of August.

Practicalities

The **tourist office** on Grande-Rue (Mon–Fri 9am–noon & 2–5pm; ☎92.35.11.00), which runs past the church, provides skiing and walking information and a list of places to **hire horses**. Also on Grande-Rue, you'll find *La Chaumière* **hotel-restaurant** (☎92.35.00.48; ②), somewhat over-rustic but comfortable enough. *Au Vieux Tilleil* (mid-April to Sept & Dec–Jan; ☎92.35.00.04; ③), 1km from the town centre at Les Auches, is in similar vein and has a pool/skating rink. Below the town, on each side of the river, are two two-star **campsites**, *Les Prairies* (☎92.35.10.21) and *Camping de la Blanche* (☎92.35.02.55) both open all year. The best place to **eat** is *Les Alisiers* (closed Tues & Wed except during school holidays; ☎92.35.30.88; menus from 70F) on the D207 at the top of the old village.

From Seyne **buses** run north to **Espinasse** on the Durance, from where there are connections to Gap and Barcelonnette, and, the other way, to Marseille via Digne and the lower Durance Valley.

Along the Ubaye to Barcelonnette

From the northern border of Provence at the Lac of Serre-Ponçon, the D900 follows the Ubaye river, where every near-level plot of ground is a tiny irregular field and the silhouettes of the mountains at the head of the valley imitate Dracula castles. There are **campsites** on the river bank in each village, and **canoe**, **raft** and **hydrospeed** bases at Le Lauzet-sur-Ubaye and Meolans-Revel. The

Aérodrome de Barcelonnette-St-Pons is announced by a grounded aeroplane transformed into a **restaurant** (☎92.81.02.77).

Snow falls on **BARCELONNETTE** around Christmas and stays till Easter, yet, despite the proximity of several ski resorts, summer is the main tourist season. The town is immaculate, with cobbled streets, sunny squares and snowcapped mountains visible at the end of every avenue. A more ideal spot for doing nothing would be hard to find. The central square, **place Manuel**, has café tables from which to gaze at the blue sky and a white clock tower commemorating the centenary of the 1848 revolution. Some of the larger houses on av de la Libération have a strongly un-European appearance; their Latin American style dates from the nineteenth century, when many of Barcelonnette's inhabitants emigrated to Mexico. Being expert sheep farmers and wool merchants several made their fortunes and returned home to build their dream houses. The Spanish association of the town's name, "Little Barcelona", is due to the town's foundation in the thirteenth century by Raimond Béranger IV, count of Provence, whose family came from the Catalan city.

One of the Mexican-style villas, *La Sapinière*, at 10 av de la Libération, houses the **Musée de la Vallée** (July & Aug daily 10am–noon & 3–7pm; school holidays and rest of the year daily 3–7pm; term time Wed, Thurs & Sat 3–6pm; 17F) which details the life and times of the people of the Ubaye Valley, the emigration to Mexico and the travels of a nineteenth-century explorer from the town. In summer, the ground floor becomes an information centre for the **Parc National du Mercantour** (July & Aug Mon–Sat 10am–noon & 3–7pm; June & first half Sept 3–7pm; ☎92.81.21.31), a national reserve stretching from the mountain passes south of Barcelonnette almost to **Sospel** (see map p.423). They can provide maps, advise on walks and mountain refuges, and tell you about the fauna and flora of the area.

SKIING

The tourist office in Barcelonnette has brochures for all the local ski resorts, which can also be contacted direct: Pra-Loup, the biggest, (☎92.84.10.04); Sainte-Anne/La Condamine (☎92.84.32.88); Jausiers (☎92.81.21.45); Le Sauze/Super-Sauze (☎92.81.05.61); and Larche (☎92.84.32.97). During the skiing season a **free bus** does the rounds of the resorts from Barcelonnette. Pra-Loup's pistes link up with La Foux d'Allos (see opposite under "The Haut-Verdon Valley").

Practicalities

Barcelonnette is very small. **Buses** from Marseille or Gap (information on ☎92.81.00.20) arrive on place Aimé-Gassier, from where the main street, rue Manuel, leads up to place Manuel, beyond which is place F-Mistral where you'll find the **tourist office** (Mon–Sat 9.30am–noon & 3–5/6pm; ☎92.81.04.71). **Bikes** can be rented from *Roro Sport*, place Aimé-Gassier (☎92.81.38.12), or at *RocknRaft*, 1 rue Manuel, whose main business is organizing **canoeing** and **rafting** trips.

The best **place to stay** in the centre of town if you're on a low budget is the *Grand Hôtel* (June to mid-Oct & Jan to mid-May; ☎92.81.03.14; ②), overlooking place Manuel at no. 6, an old-fashioned and comfortable place with creaky linoleum. Or there's the slightly pricier *Cheval Blanc*, just down the road at 12 rue

THE MOUNTAIN VALLEYS

From Barcelonnette there are four routes across the watershed of Mont Pelat, La Bonette, Chambeyron and their high gneiss and granite extensions. The Col d'Allos leads into the **Haut-Verdon** Valley; the Col de la Cayolle into the **Haut-Var** Valley; the road across the summit of La Bonette to the **Tinée** Valley; and the Col de Larche into Italy. All but the last are snowed up between November and April, and can sometimes be closed as late as June. Further east the **Vésubie** rises just below the Italian border; like the Tinée and the Verdon it runs into the Var.

Grenette (☎92.81.00.19; ③). The deluxe *Grande Eperviére* at 18 rue des Trois-Freres-Arnaud (☎92.81.00.70; ④), surrounded by its own park, is very good value, while *L'Azteca*, 3 rue François-Arnaud (☎92.81.46.36; ⑤), is extremely pleasant in a Mexican-style house with superb views of the mountains. There are two **campsites** on av Emile-Aubert, the D902 leading to the Col de la Cayolle: the closer, three-star *Camping Caravaneige du Plan* (mid-May to Sept; ☎92.81.08.11) is 500m out of town; the two-star *Le Tampico* (mid-Dec to Sept; ☎92.81.02.55) is 1km further out.

Beautifully prepared and delicious **food** is to be had at *La Mangeoire*, place des Quatre-Vents (closed Mon, Tues, second half May & Nov; ☎92.81.01.61; menus from around 100F), in the rustic setting of an old sheep barn. *Le Troubadour* on place Frédéric-Mistral (closed Tues evening & Wed; ☎92.81.24.24; menus from under 100F) serves more simple dishes, usually very good. Pizzas and lunchtime plats du jour are available for very little on the corner of place St-Pierre and rue Bellon (July & Aug only), and Tex-Mex snacks at *El Coco-Loco*, 2 rue Grenelle.

Wednesday and Saturday are the **market** days, where you'll see spread out on place Aimé-Gassier and place St-Pierre all manner of sweets, jams and alcohol made from locally picked bilberries, pâtés made from local birds – thrush, partridge, pheasant – and the favourite liqueurs of this part of the world, distilled from Alpine plants and nuts.

The Haut-Verdon Valley

The most westerly route from Barcelonnette crosses the **Col d'Allos** at 2250m to join the Verdon river just a few kilometres from its source. A mountain *refuge, Col d'Allos* (mid-June to mid-Sept; ☎92.83.00.89) on the pass marks the junction with the GR56, which leads west to the Ubaye Valley and Seyne-les-Alpes, and east to the Col de Larche and the Tinée Valley. In late June pale wild pansies and deep blue gentians flower between patches of ice. The panorama is magnificent though once you start backstitching your way down the side of the pass to the Verdon, the hideous vast hotels of **La Foux d'Allos** come into view.

La Foux d'Allos

If you're going to **ski**, **LA FOUX D'ALLOS** is probably the cheapest Provençal resort to do it. The lifts and *pistes* join up with **Pra-Loup** to the north and, for cross-country skiers, with **Allos Le Seignus** 7km to the south, giving the largest area in the southern Alps in which to lose yourself or break your neck. La Foux d'Allos is also quite high (1800–2600m), so melting snow shouldn't be a problem.

La Foux d'Allos and its neighbours are also keen to promote themselves as summer resorts, with all kinds of activities on offer, from **trapeze training** to **horse riding**, **archery**, courses in **wildlife photography**, and **water sports** at the *Parc de Loisirs* in Le Seignus. The **tourist offices** at La Foux (☎92.83.80.70) and Le Seignus (☎92.83.80.70), both open daily in high summer and winter, can provide all the details. For **rafting, canoing and kayaking** on the Verdon contact M Demoulin at the *Maison Forestière* in Allos (☎92.83.03.89). The Parc du Mercantour has an information point on rue de la Placette (July & Aug daily 9am–noon & 3–7pm; ☎92.83.04.18).

The best deal is to stay in the **youth hostel**, *HI La Foux d'Allos* (Dec–May & June–Sept; ☎92.83.81.08), which must be booked well in advance. Other options include the **hotels** *Le Sestrière* (mid-Dec to April & mid-June to mid-Sept; ☎92.83.81.70; ④) and *Le Toukal* (Dec–May & July–Sept; ☎92.83.82.76; ③) or the *Hameau de la Foux* **chalets** (☎92.83.82.26; weekly rents 2300–3200F for 2–6 people). For details of the ski-school, phone the *Ecole de Ski de La Foux d'Allos* (☎92.83.81.64) or the *Ecole de Ski du Seignus* (☎92.83.00.65).

Allos and its lake

The medieval village of **ALLOS**, 8.5km south of La Foux d'Allos, was all but destroyed by fire in the eighteenth century. One tower of the ramparts half-survived and was turned into the current clocktower. The old livelihoods of tending sheep and weaving woollen sheets only just made it past the turn of the century when tourism began with the discovery of the **Lac d'Allos**, 14km east and 800m above Allos. Once skiing became an established pastime the agricultural days of Allos were numbered. But for all its *résidences secondaires*, it's not a bad place to spend a day or two, and the lake is not too hard a destination, thanks to the French passion for building roads to beauty spots. If you want to walk the whole way, a path starts by the church.

The road stops short of the lake, leaving you with a half-hour or so's walk to reach what was once the head of a glacier. Round and blue, reflecting the high amphitheatre half-circling it, the lake nourishes trout and char in its pure cold waters. Looking in the direction of the one-time glacier flow, you can just see the peak of **Mont Pelat**, the highest mountain in the Parc du Mercantour. Though there are always people dutifully reading the pedagogic noticeboards, there's no limit to the space in which to escape the crowds.

Practicalities

For information on paths, weather conditions and so forth, the Parc de Mercantour has a *Maison du Parc* at Allos on rue de la Placette (☎92.83.04.18), or there's the **tourist office** (summer and winter Mon–Sat 8.30am–noon & 2–6.30pm, Sun am only; ☎92.83.02.81) at the northen end of the old village. Note that the only **bank** in this stretch of the valley is the *Crédit Agricole* on the main road (Tues–Sat).

Hotels include the run-down but very cheap *Pascal* (☎92.83.00.04; ②) and *Les Gentianes* (☎92.83.03.50; half-board obligatory; ②), both in the old village, and the more upmarket but characterless *Plein Soleil* (☎92.83.02.16; ④) in Super-Allos, the modern extension northeast of the village. There's a very comfortable **chambre d'hôtes**, *La Ferme* (walkers only; ☎92.83.04.76; ①) or a **gîte d'étape**, the *Chalet Auberge L'Autapie* (☎92.83.06.31; ①). Walkers can also stay at the *Refuge* *du Lac d'Allos* on the lake itself (☎92.83.00.24; ①) for which booking well in advance is advisable.

The best **meal** to be had in Allos is at *Les Gentianes* hotel (see above) with beautiful table settings, a delicious steak with wild mushrooms flambéed in cognac, and menus at 75F and 110F. Upmarket picnic food, in the form of local cheeses and sausages that look like stones, can be bought from *La Ferme Gourmande* opposite the tourist office. A more useful place to shop, for food and anything else you might need, is the *Shopi* supermarket on the main road (Mon–Sat 8.45am–12.15pm & 4–7pm).

Colmars-les-Alpes

The next town downstream from Allos is **COLMARS-LES-ALPES**, an extraordinarily well-preserved stronghold, whose name comes from a temple to Mars built by the Romans on the hill above the town. The sixteenth-century ramparts with their arrow slits and small square towers are almost too good to be true. They are not in fact complete and the two entrances, the Porte de France and Porte de Savoie, have been reduced to just gateways, but the impression is still that this is a perfect architectural-historical model. The ramparts were constructed on the orders of François 1er of France to reinforce the defences that had existed since 1381 when Colmars became a border town between Provence and Savoy. When Savoy declared war on France in 1690, Vauban was called in to make the town even more secure. He designed the **Fort de Savoie** and the **Fort de France** at either end of the town.

Having passed through the Porte de France, the Porte de Savoie or the opening halfway between them – all adorned with climbing roses – you find yourself in an exquisite old and quiet Provençal town with cobbled streets and fountained squares. There's not a lot to do here except soak up atmosphere. The Fort de Savoie is open for visits in summer (2–6.30pm daily; 20F) when exhibitions of art or local traditions are set up beneath the magnificent larch-timbered ceilings. Or you can take a twenty-minute walk east of the town to the Lance waterfall.

Colmars is on the junction of the Verdon Valley road with the D78 which climbs up between the Frema and Encombrette mountains and descends to the Var Valley at **St-Martin-d'Entraunes**. Six kilometres along the road, signed left, is the **Ratery ski-station** (☎92.83.40.92) which in summer rents out **bikes** and **ponies**. You can trek from here over the Encombrette to the Lac d'Allos or east across the Col des Champs to the Var at **Entraunes**.

Colmars has a very scenic **campsite** by the river, *Le Bois Joly* (May–Oct; ☎92.83.40.40); a **gîte d'étape**, the *Gassendi*, in a twelfth-century Templar hospice (☎92.83.42.25; ①); and two **hotels**, *Le Vauban* (☎92.83.40.49; ②) and *Le Chamois* (closed mid-Nov to mid-Dec; ☎92.83.43.29; ③). For **food** there's *Le Lézard* restaurant and *salon de thé* serving *raclette* on the corner of Grande Rue and place Neuve; a *boulangerie*, *charcuterie* and wine shop on Grande Rue; and the *Café de l'Union* on place J-Girieud by the *mairie*. The **tourist office** is by the *café* (close to the Porte de Savoie entrance; Tues, Wed, Thurs & Sat 8am–noon & 2–5pm, Mon & Sun 8am–noon; ☎92.83.41.92).

Beauvezer

If you're heading south towards Thorame, Annot or St-André (see pp.405–408), you can follow the D908 5km to **BEAUVEZER** in the Haut-Verdon Valley (experienced cross-country skiers can take a looping route through the Fôret de Monier and across the summit of the Laupon). The road sticks to the Verdon, a wide dramatic torrent in winter or spring, a wide messy track of scattered boulders and branches in summer. Beauvezer perches high above its right bank, a wonderful ancient village smelling of old timbers whose business used to be making linen. Beside the beautiful ochre church is one of the prettiest **hotel-restaurants** in Haute Provence, *Le Bellevue*, place de l'Eglise (☎92.83.51.60; ③). On the lower street of the village, rue Capitaine Bouscary, is the *Café de France* **jazz bar**, serving pizzas and fresh pasta.

The Haut-Var Valley

The route to the Haut-Var Valley from Barcelonnette first follows the **Bachelard** river through its gorge then east following its course between Mont Pelat to the south and the ridge of peaks to the north whose shapes have given them the names *Pain de Sucre* (Sugarloaf), *Chapeau de Gendarme* (Gendarme's Hat) and *Chevalier* (Horseman). At the **Bayasse refuge** (open all year; ☎92.81.07.31), the main road turns south towards the **Col de la Cayolle**, while a track (and the GR56) continues east towards La Bonette and the Tinée Valley. There's another **refuge** just before the pass, the *Refuge de la Cayolle* (July–Sept; ☎92.81.07.02), which, at over 2000m, is a multi-starred place to stay.

The baby Var makes its appearance below the Col de la Cayolle and pours southwards through **Entraunes** and **St-Martin-d'Entraunes** to **Guillaumes** and on down through the **Gorges de Daluis** to Entrevaux. Its banks are punctuated with **chapels** built before and after disasters of avalanches, floods, landslides and devastating storms. Many are superbly decorated, like the Renaissance **Chapelle de St-Sébastien**, just north of **ENTRAUNES** (key from Mme Sayan in Entraunes; ☎93.05.51.47), and the church at **ST-MARTIN-D'ENTRAUNES**, with its **Bréa retable** (key from the *mairie*; ☎93.05.51.04).

GUILLAUMES, the minor metropolis and favourite with cyclists in summer, is a traditional resting place for sheep on their way between the Haut-Var summer pastures and Nice. Though most flocks now travel by lorry, the old **sheep fairs** on September 16 and October 9 are still held in the village. Winter sees a migration in the opposite direction, as the Côte d'Azur's multicoloured padded bundles flock to the ski resorts of **Valberg** and **Beuil**, to the east of Guillaumes, on the fabulous road that climbs over to the Tinée Valley. Two neighbouring villages of Guillaumes, the dilapidated **SAUZE** up an exhausting series of hairpin bends to the west, and **PEONE** on the GR52A to the north-east which huddles under a line of rocks like spires, are both worth exploring.

About 5km south of Guillaumes, the Var enters the dramatic red-rocked **GORGES DE DALIUS**. Bungee-jumpers are fond of the seventy-metre fall from the Pont de la Mariée across the gorge; for those on wheeled propellants, note that traffic going upstream has the better views while the downstream carriageway is in tunnels much of the way.

Practicalities

The Nice–Entraunes **bus** visits each of the villages of the Haut-Var Valley daily; from Guillaumes to Sauze there's a bus on Thursday and Saturday only, and no bus to Péone. The biggest **tourist office** is in hideous Valberg (daily 9am–noon & 2–6pm; ☎93.02.52.77); Guillaume has a "chalet du tourisme" on the main road

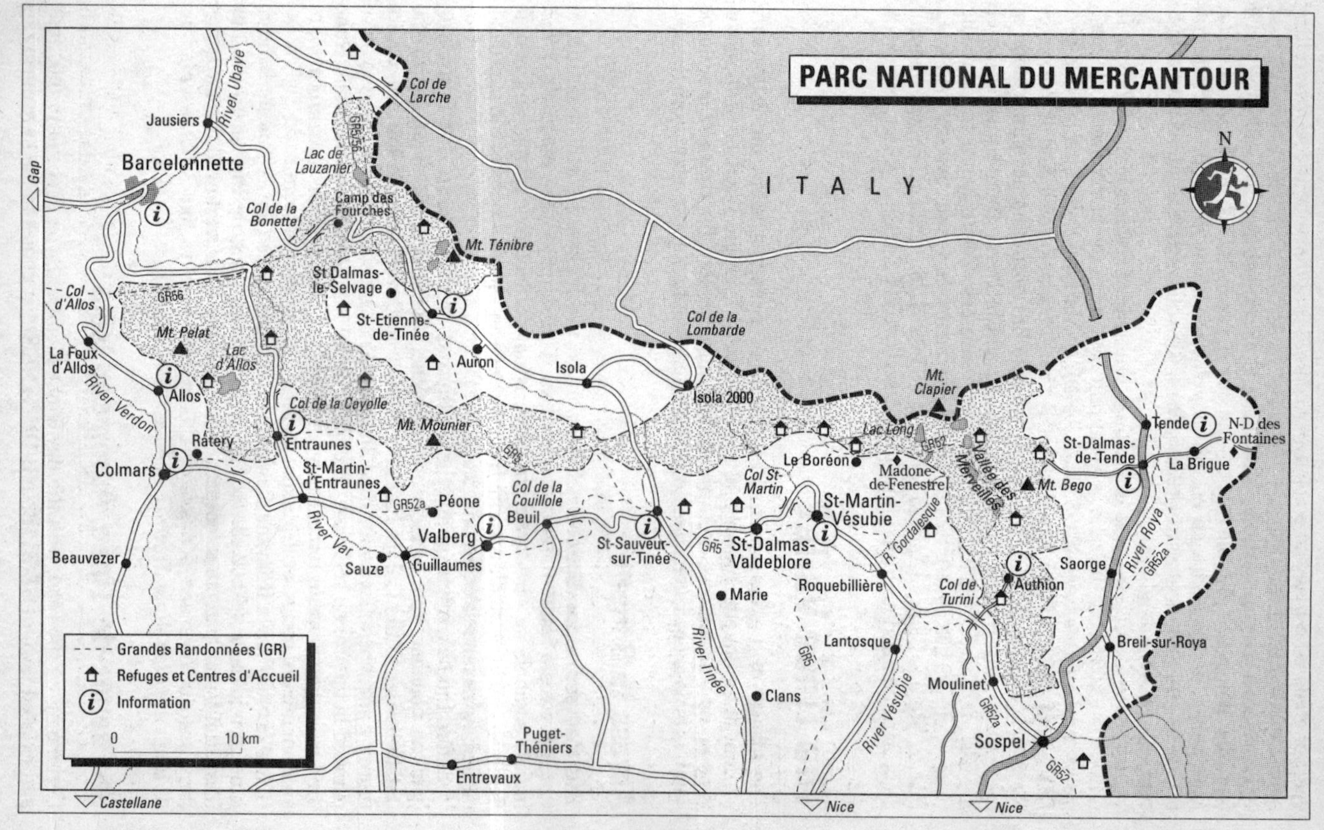
PARC NATIONAL DU MERCANTOUR
N
ITALY
Col de Larche
Jausiers
River Ubaye
GR5/56
Barcelonnette
Gap
Lac de Lauzanier
Camp des Fourches
Col de la Bonette
Mt. Ténibre
St Dalmas-le-Selvage
St-Etienne-de-Tinée
Auron
Col d'Allos
GR56
Mt. Pelat
Lac d'Allos
La Foux d'Allos
Allos
River Verdon
Col de la Cayolle
Ratery
Colmars
Entraunes
St-Martin-d'Entraunes
Mt. Mounier
GR5
Col de la Lombarde
Isola
Isola 2000
Mt. Clapier
Lac Long
GR52
Le Boréon
Madone-de-Fenestre
Vallée des Merveilles
Mt. Bego
Tende
N-D des Fontaines
St-Dalmas-de-Tende
La Brigue
River Roya
GR52a
Saorge
Authion
Col de Turini
Breil-sur-Roya
Moulinet
GR52a
Sospel
GR52
Nice
Nice
Col St-Martin
St-Martin-Vésubie
R. Gordalesque
St-Dalmas-Valdeblore
GR5
Roquebillière
Lantosque
River Vésubie
Marie
Clans
River Tinée
St-Sauveur-sur-Tinée
Col de la Couillole
Beuil
Péone
GR52a
Valberg
Guillaumes
Sauze
River Var
Beauvezer
Puget-Théniers
Entrevaux
Castellane
Grandes Randonnées (GR)
Refuges et Centres d'Accueil
Information
0
10 km

operating sporadic hours in season (☎93.05.57.76), otherwise the *mairie* (office hours; ☎93.05.50.13) can help.

There are **accommodation** possibilities at all the villages. In Guillaume you'll find the hotels *Les Chaudrons* on the main road (☎93.05.50.01; ③) and *La Renaissance*, an old-fashioned establishment 100m up to your right just past the bridge as you look upstream (☎93.05.50.12; ②) with a restaurant serving a five-course meal for around 70F.

Just below the Cayolle pass in the tiny commune of **Estenc** is the *Relais de la Cayolle* (☎93.05.51.33; ③), whose restaurant has one of the best views in the business, and *La Cantonnière* (☎93.05.51.36; ②). St-Martin d'Entraunes offers a *gîte*, *Le Prieuré* (☎93.05.51.25; open all year); in Entraunes you'll find the *Auberge Roche Grande* hotel (☎93.05.51.83; ③); Sauze has dormitory accommodation at the *Auberge Communale* (☎93.05.57.70; ①); and in Péone there's a small hotel, the *Col de Crous* (☎93.02.58.37; ③). For **campers**, Péone has a two-star site (May–Oct; ☎93.02.59.89); St Martin d'Entraunes has two two-star sites: *Le Prieuré*, rte des Blancs (April to mid-Oct; ☎93.05.51.25), and *La Bérarde*, quartier de la Bérarde Inférieure (mid-June to mid-Sept; ☎93.05.54.93).

The Tinée Valley

The longest of the Var's tributaries, the Tinée rises just below the 2800-metre summit of La Bonette, higher and more northerly than the Var itself. The mountains on its left bank rise up to the Italian border before the river's course turns south at Isola to cut a steep narrow valley before joining the Var 30km from the sea.

Across La Bonette

The road across **La Bonette**, claimed to be the highest stretch of tarmac in Europe, gives a feast of high-altitude views. The summit of the mountain, a ten-minute scrabble up scree from the road, is not particularly exciting, and is uglified by its military training camp. But the green and silent spaces of the approach, circled by barren peaks, are magical.

Before the hairpins begin for the southern descent, at **Camp des Fourches**, you can abandon your wheels and take the **GR5/56** north parallel with the Italian border to the Col de Larche and then northwest towards **Larche**, where there's a *gîte*, open all year (☎92.84.30.80). It's not exactly a stroll but once you've climbed to the Col de la Cavale (after 5km or so) it's more or less downhill all the way, with the Ubayette torrent as your guide, and the **Lac de Lauzanier** (5km on from the Col de la Cavale) a spot you may never want to leave.

A short way down from the Camp des Fourches is the *Gîte de Bousiéyas* (mid-June to mid-Sept; ☎93.02.42.20). About 5km on, a track on the left to the tiny hamlet of **Vens** leads to a footpath that follow the Vens torrent to the further of the Lacs de Vens and a *refuge* at 2380m (mid-June to mid-Sept; reservations through the *Club Alpin Français* in Nice ☎93.62.59.99).

St-Etienne-de-Tinée, Auron and Isola

Continuing on the road, with the tiny Tinée alongside, you descend to the small and isolated town of **ST-ETIENNE-DE-TINEE** that comes to life only during its

sheep fairs, held twice every summer and the **Fête de la Transhumance** at the end of June. The **tourist office**, 1 rue des Communes-de-France (July, Aug & Dec–April daily 9am–noon & 2–5.30pm; rest of year same times Wed & Sat only; ☎93.02.41.96), organizes tours of the town's **chapels**, which are decorated with frescoes illustrating naval battle scenes, Adam and Eve, and the usual saintly exploits, and the town's **museums** of milk-making, traditional crafts and of the old school (3pm same days as tourist office; 20F).

The two **hotel-restaurants** on offer are the *Pinatelle*, bd d'Auron (☎93.02.40.36; ③), and *Des Amis*, 1 rue Val Gélé (☎93.02.40.30; ②).

On the west side of the town off bd d'Auron, a **cable car** ascends to the summit of La Pinatelle from where there are good walks (or skiing but only for the experienced) including a path to the **ski resort** of **AURON**. Though ugly without snow, as ski resorts inevitably are, Auron prides itself on its summer activities which cover everything from hang-gliding and aerobics to tennis, pony rides and swimming. There are more cable cars, that operate in summer as well as winter, taking you further into the mountains for some serious high treks. By road, Auron is 7km south of St-Etienne, on a dead-end spur from the main road.

After the turning to Auron, there's nothing but the white quartz and white heather of the valley, with only the silvery sound of crickets competing with the river's roar. **ISOLA**, 14km south of St-Etienne, is slowly dying. Only the needle-sharp belfry maintains an upright permanence, while groups of old men and women sit around and chat, suspicious cats sniff for food and the external murals on the chapels slowly fade. Nothing could be a more dramatic contrast to **ISOLA 2000**, the zappy ski resort to which the road through the village leads.

St-Sauveur-sur-Tinée and downstream

Between Isola and **ST-SAUVEUR-SUR-TINEE** the drop in altitude is marked by sweet chestnut trees taking over from the pines. Another medieval needle belfry dominates St-Sauveur, which perches above the river in Mediterranean rather than Alpine fashion. The adornments of the Romanesque gargoyled church include a rather fine fifteenth-century retable behind the over-bloodied crucifix and a fifteenth-century statue of St Paul outside above the side door. The houses around the church have survived several centuries and those on the main street, av des Blavets, have more recent charm: the *Eaux et Fôrets* building at no. 5, for example, with its pretty tiles below the eaves.

There's not a lot to do here other than sitting in the sun above the river or heading off along the GR52A, but it's an attractive place to stop. The centre of life is the *Café du Centre bar-tabac* and resto; the *boulangerie* on the corner of place de la Mairie sells provisions like cereals and tinned food as well as scrumptious *tourtes de blettes* (closed Tues & 1–4pm).

The *Auberge de la Gare* at the southern end of the village (☎93.02.00.67; ①) has very cheap **rooms** and the *Relais d'Auron*, 18 av des Blavets (☎93.02.00.03; ③), offers *demi-pension* for around 170F. The two-star municipal **campsite** is in quartier Les Plans (mid-June to mid-Sept; ☎93.02.03.20).

The D30 towards Valberg and the Haut-Var Valley starts from St-Sauveur, a dramatically precipitous climb. A few kilometres south of St-Sauveur you can head east along the D2565 to **Valdeblore** and the **Vesubie Valley**.

Sticking with the Tinée, the perched villages of **MARIE**, **CLANS** and **LA TOUR** all have their charms as small mountain communities, with medieval decorations in their chapels and churches, and, at Marie, a pleasant place for a meal *Le Panoramique* (menus from 100F), with a few rooms as well, (closed Thurs out of season; ☎93.02.03.01; ②).

The Vesubie and Bevera valleys

The ancient town of **St-Martin-Vésubie** stands at the head of the **River Vésubie**, which is formed by two torrents, **Le Boréon** and **La Madone de la Fenestre**, descending from the north and east. The only through route to St-Martin comes from the Tinée Valley to the west, via **St-Dalmas-Valdeblore** with its ancient church. From St-Martin road and river head towards the Var, passing the flood-ridden *commune* of **Roquebillière**, the perched village of **Lantosque**, and the approach to the pilgrimage chapel of **Madonne d'Utelle**. An alternative southern route from the valley crosses east to the **Col de Turini** and down the **Bévéra** river towards Sospel.

St-Martin-Vésubie

ST-MARTIN-VESUBIE is only crowded in July and August, though a few winter visitors pass through on their way to the ski resorts. In late spring and early autumn, the best times for quiet nights and long daytime walks, St-Martin is a perfect base for exploring the surrounding mountains. Even in the height of summer it's not jam-packed, and in winter, if you're not up to the cross-country skiing routes that pass through the town, you can still go for wonderful walks in snow-shoes.

The main artery of the old quarter of St-Martin, the **rue du Docteur-Cagnoli**, is a single-file cobbled street of Gothic houses with overhanging roofs and balconies, through which flows a channelled stream designed in the fifteenth century for sewage and now charged with rainwater or melting snow. To the background sound of swift-moving water, the noises of domestic arguments, a television soap show, feet on stairs and closing doors are as audible as if this street were a stage.

Halfway down rue du Docteur-Cagnoli, on the left as you descend, is the **Chapelle des Pénitents-Blancs** decorated with eighteenth-century paintings. At the end of the street is St-Martin's **church**, with works attributed to Louis Bréa, a mirror on the high altar reflecting the stained glass window above the door, and a venerated polychrome wooden statue of the Madonna that is taken up to the Chapelle de Madone de Fenestre (see opposite) at the beginning of July and brought back towards the end of September. Southeast of the church you can look down at the Madone de Fenestre torrent from place de la Frairie. In the opposite direction a narrow lane leads to the junction of rue Kellerman and the main road, beyond which is the old wash house and *Le Vieux Moulin*, the town's one **museum** (summer Mon & Wed–Sun 2–6pm; 20F), which illustrates the traditional way of life of the *Vésubiens*.

Heading back towards the main **place Félix-Fauré** along rue Kellerman, you'll pass the *Villa des Iris* at no. 8 which is the **Maison du Parc** with occasional wildlife exhibitions as well as information about the Parc du Mercantour (summer daily 9am–12.30pm & 2–6.30pm; free).

If you want to drink health-giving mountain water, the **fountain** on allées de Verdun, the *cours* in front of place Félix-Fauré, has a placard detailing its mineral contents and citing the ministerial declaration of 1913 that the water has negative pathogenic germs.

Practicalities

You arrive in St-Martin on place Félix-Fauré to the west of the old town, along the allées de Verdun if you're coming from the Tinée Valley or av de la Gare from the south. The **gare routière** is on place de la Gare where av de la Gare loops south into av de Caqueray. The **tourist office** is on place Félix-Fauré (Mon–Sat 10am–noon & 3–6pm, Sun 10am–noon; ☎93.03.21.28) along with the *mairie*, post office and a bank.

The tourist office has lists of **gîtes** and mountain *refuges* for St-Martin and the surounding area posted up outside, plus lists of walking guides and weather information. On rue du Dr-Cagnoli, just below place du Marché, you'll find the *Bureau des Guides et Accompagnateurs de la Haute Vésubie* (☎93.03.44.30) which organizes **walks** including winter expeditions with snow-shoe rental and can give advice for your own expeditions, and the *Guides du Mercantour* (☎93.03.31.32) which can arrange **canoeing, climbing, horse rides, walks** and **skiing**. Maps, compasses and the like can be purchased from *Aux Milles Articles*, 52 rue du Dr-Cagnoli.

Accommodation possibilities in St-Martin are plentiful. The least expensive of the five **hotels** is *Les Etrangers* (☎93.03.21.81; ①) at 27 rue du Dr-Cagnoli. The nicest, *La Bonne Auberge* (closed mid-Nov to Jan; ☎93.03.20.49; ③) and *La Châtaigneraie* (closed Oct to mid-June; ☎93.03.21.22; ⑤), are both a short way up the allées de Verdun. The closest **campsite** is the two-star *Ferme St-Joseph* (open all year; ☎93.03.20.14) on the rte de Nice by the lower bridge over La Madone. Further down the same road, the two-star *Le Touron* camping (open all year; ☎93.03.21.32) is rather overpriced; its *gîte d'étape* is better value. In the opposite direction out of town, on the rte de la Colmiane, there's the one-star *La Mério* (April–Sept; ☎93.03.30.38) and, to the southwest, on the rte de Venanson, the two-star *Le Champouns* (open all year; ☎93.03.23.72), which has apartments to let, dormitory accommodation and a campsite.

For **meals**, *La Mavorine café-boulangerie* on place Félix-Fauré serves *bruschettas*, filling hot open sandwiches for around 30F, plus ice creams, crêpes and cakes. The nicest **restaurant** in St-Martin is *La Trappa* on place du Marché (closed Mon in term-time) offering a pasta-based four-course meal for around 100F. *La Bonne Auberge* (see hotels above) is also a good choice (menus from around 100F).

Finally, there's an après-ski **disco**, *Le Piolet* (☎93.03.22.21) off rue du Dr-Cagnoli on the east slope of the old town.

Around St-Martin

The **Chapelle de Madone de Fenestre** lies 12km northeast of St-Martin, above the treeline in a setting of barren rocks, just within the borders of the Parc du Mercantour. Half a dozen gloomy rough-hewn stone buildings, one of them a refuge/restaurant, surround the little nineteenth-century chapel in a thousand-year-old sanctuary. The name *fenestre* comes from the hole in the rock above the site through which you can see the sky. Floral murals and a bright blue ceiling add some welcome colour to this desolate little hamlet, but it's hardly worth coming all the way up here unless you join the procession or intend to trek

WILDLIFE OF THE MERCANTOUR

The least shy of the mammal inhabitants of these mountains is the **marmot**, a cream-coloured, badger-sized creature often to be seen sitting on its haunches in the sun. Chamois, mouflon and ibex are almost equally unwary of humans, even though it was not so long ago that they were hunted here. The male **ibex** is a wonderful big solid beast with curving, ribbed horns that grow to a metre long; the species very nearly became extinct, and it is one of the successes of the park that the population is now stable. Another species of goat, the **chamois**, is also on the increase. The male is recognizable by the shorter, grappling-hook horns and white beard. The **mouflon**, introduced to the Mercantour in the 1950s, is the ancestor of domestic sheep. Other animals that you might see include **stoats**, rare species of **hare**, and **foxes**, now the dominant predators since the wolves, bears and lynxes became extinct in the region.

The Mercantour is a perfect habitat for **eagles**, who have any number of crags on which to build their nests, and plenty to eat – including marmots. Pairs of **golden eagles** are now breeding, and a rare vulture, the **lammergeier**, has been successfully reintroduced to the region. Other birds of prey, **kestrels**, **falcons** and **buzzards**, wing their way down from the scree to the Alpine lawn and its torrents to swoop on lizards, mice and snakes. The **great spotted woodpecker** and the black and orange **hoopoe** are the most colourful inhabitants of the park. **Ptarmigan**, which turn snowy-white in winter, can sometimes be seen in June parading to their would-be mates on the higher slopes in the north. **Blackcocks**, known in French as *tétras-lyre* for their lyre-shaped white tails, burrow into the snow at night and fly out in a flurry of snowflakes when the sun rises.

The **flowers** of the Mercantour are an unmissable glory, with over two thousand species represented, about forty of which are unique to the region. The moment the snow melts, the lawn between the rocky crags and the treeline begins to dot with golds, pinks and blue. Rare species of **lily** and **orchid** grow here, as do the elusive **edelweiss** and the wild ancestors of various cultivated flowers – pansies, geraniums, tulips, gentian violets. Rarest of all is the **multi-flowering saxifrage** (*saxifraga florulenta*), a big spiky flower that looks as if it must be cultivated, though it would hardly be popular in suburban gardens since it flowers just once every ten years. Wild strawberries, raspberries and bilberries tempt you into the woods.

Camping, lighting fires, picking flowers, playing ghetto-blasters or doing anything that might disturb the delicate environment is strictly outlawed.

onwards. The GR52 passes by the sanctuary and leads eastwards to the Vallée des Merveilles (see p.434). This is not the shortest route but it's a very dramatic path that rarely descends below 2000m.

One main purpose for heading north from St-Martin to **LE BOREON**, also just inside the National Park, is to eat trout, either caught yourself or by those who supply the clutch of **restaurants** and **hotels** at this small and impeccably scenic mountain retreat. During the fishing season, from mid-March to early September, you can get a licence from the hotels here or from most of the bars in St-Martin. If fishing is not your passion, you can just sit down and order smoked trout, ***truite au bleu***, ***truite meunière*** or other local specialities such as crayfish, wild boar with *cèpes* mushrooms, and lamb. The two **hotel-restaurants** are *Le Boréon* (March–Oct; ☎93.03.20.35; menus from 90F; ③) and *Le Cavalet* (☎93.03.21.46; menus from 85F; half-board obligatory; ②), with a **gîte** (mid-June to mid-Sept; ☎93.03.27.27; ①) further up. Walks from half-hour strolls to half-day treks are signposted from the *gîte*, and the scenery does a very good job of enticing you to follow them.

In summer there are regular **buses** three times a week from St-Martin to Le Boréon, and one, on Wednesday, to Madone de Fenestre.

St-Dalmas-Valdeblore

West of St-Martin, along the D2565 to the Tinée Valley lies the Commune de Valdeblore which starts with La Colmiane ski resort, where you can take a chair-lift for stunning views from the **Pic de Colmiane** (July Sat, Sun & holidays; 10am–6pm; Aug daily same times; 21F). To the west are the medieval hamlets of La Bolline and La Roche, now suffering chalet rashes, and in the middle, the ancient village of **ST-DALMAS**, built on the remains of a Roman outpost. It lies on the strategic crossroads between the most accessible southern route across the lower Alps, linking Piedmont with Provence, and a north–south route through the mountain range linking Savoy with the sea.

The importance of the fertile Blore Valley (Val de Blore) is clear from the striking dimensions of the **Eglise Prieurale Bénédictine**, whose construction possibly started as early as the tenth century. The extraordinary wonky columns and vaults in the **crypt** are thought to date from then. A gruesome tomb under glass in the floor of the church reveals a 900-year-old skeleton; more appealing are the fragments of fourteenth-century frescoes in the north chapel. The current structure is Romanesque, plain and fierce with its typically Alpine pointed bell-tower and rounded apsidal chapels on which eleventh-century Lombardian decoration is still visible on the external masonry.

The church is open from 11am to 6pm; if your French is good it's worth getting a guided tour from Jean Alcoy (☎93.02.82.29) who may be found at the **museum** just up from the church (daily 11am–noon & 3.30–6pm; 20F) which along with traditional agricultural tools and household items has a working model train set.

Downstream to Madone d'Utelle

South from St-Martin on the other side of the valley, but approached by a circuitous route that heads north out of the town, is the little village of **VENANSON**, which declares itself, most appropriately, to be a "zone of silence". It has just the one pizzeria, *Chez Ma-Ma*, one hotel-restaurant, *Bella-Vista* (☎93.03.25.11; ①), a chapel too dark to see its Baleison frescoes, and an excellent vantage point over St-Martin.

Back on the left bank you come to the scattered village of **ROQUEBILLIERE**, which since the Dark Ages has been rebuilt six times after catastrophic landslides and floods. The last major disaster was in 1926, with a less lethal upheaval in the 1980s. Apart from the archeological interest of the leftovers of superseded settlements and the beauty of the frequently rebuilt church, the new village on the right bank has a wonderful *boulangerie*, *Chez Somiani* (closed Sun pm) on the main street, av C-Moulinie, where bread is baked in animal, plant and musical instrument shapes.

The road along the **Gordolesque Valley** above old Roquebillière heads north for 16km with paths leading off eastwards towards the Vallée des Merveilles. Where the road ends you can continue upstream past waterfalls and high crags to Lac de la Fous where you meet the GR52 running west to Madone de la Fenestre and east to the northern end of the Vallée des Merveilles (see p.434). This triangle between the **Mont Clapier** on the Italian border (3045m), **Mont Bego** (2873m) to the east and **Mont Neiglier** (2785m) to the west is a fabulous area for walking, but not to be taken lightly. All the mountain **refuges** here belong to the *Club Alpin Français* and may well be unsympathetic if they're booked up and you find yourself caught in a thunderstorm.

From the southern limit of Roquebillière, the D70 leaves the Vésubie Valley to head east through the chic resort of La-Bollène-Vésubie to the Col de Turini (see below). Staying with the Vésubie you reach **LANTOSQUE**, which, like Roquebillière, has had its share of earth tremors and was flooded badly in 1993. Yet it survives in picturesque if faded and partly crumbling form, a pyramid of winding stepped streets full of nervous cats, with a wonderful *café-brasserie*, the *Bar des Tilleuls*, on the lower *place* serving copious and delicious plats du jour for around 50F. There is a swish **hotel** on the other side of the river here, the *Hostellerie de L'Ancienne Gendarmerie* (☎93.03.00.65; ⑧) with an excellent restaurant (closed Mon midday; menus from 165F).

A short way before the river starts to pick up speed through the gorge leading to the confluence with the Var, you can detour westwards and upwards to yet another far-flung chapel, dedicated to **La Madone d'Utelle**. It stands on a plateau above the village of Utelle, high enough to be visible from the sea at Nice. According to legend, two Portuguese sailors lost in a storm in about the year 850 navigated safely into port by a light they saw gleaming from Utelle. They erected the first chapel, rebuilt as it stands today in 1806. Pilgrimages still take place on Easter Monday, the Monday of Pentecost, August 15 and September 8, and are concluded with a communal feast on the grassy summit. If you can't partake of one of these meals, you'll find reasonable fare in the village at *La Bellevue* **hotel-restaurant** (June to mid-Oct; ☎93.03.17.19; menus from 70F; ③).

The Col de Turini and Bévéra Valley

At the **Col de Turini**, 15km east of Roquebillière, you know you're in a popular spot from the litter, tacky restaurants and snack bars. Four roads and two tracks meet at the pass, all giving access to the **Forêt de Turini**, which covers the area between the Vésubie and Bévéra valleys. Larches grow in the highest reaches of the forest, giving way further down to firs, spruce, beech, maples and sweet chestnuts. The road north from the *col* to the small ski resort of **L'AUTHION** gives the strongest impression of limitless space, following the curved ridge between the two valleys and overlooking a hollow of pastures. So many directions tempt you to walk that it's impossible to choose, but the sun, the flowers and the wild strawberries and raspberries are so pleasant you might as well just pick any patch of grass and listen to the cow-bells.

If you want to **stay** in L'Authion, there's *Le Relais du Camp d'Argent* (closed first two weeks in Nov & first two weeks in June; ☎93.91.57.58; half-board compulsory; ③), where you can also have **a meal** for very little.

Between the Col de Turini and Sospel there's one possible place to stop off for a coffee or a bite to eat by the banks of the Bévéra. **MOULINET** has all the charm of an ordinary Provençal village, a dusty square with *boules* being played beneath the plane trees, a couple of chairs slung outside the café, scented flowers in the gardens, no chalet-style architecture and an overriding sense of indolence.

Sospel and the Roya Valley

The most easterly valley of Provence, the **Roya**, is also the most accessible, being served by train lines from Nice (via Sospel) and from Ventimiglia in Italy which converge just south of Breil-sur-Roya. When Nice became part of France in 1860, the upper Roya Valley was kept by the newly appointed King Victor Emmanuel II of Italy to indulge his passion for hunting despite a plebiscite in which only one person in Tende and La Brigue voted for the Italian option. It was not until 1947 that the valley was finally incorporated into France. As you would expect from the result of the vote, everyone speaks French, though they do so with a distinctly Italian intonation.

Sospel

The road and rail line into the Roya valley meet the road from St-Martin-Vésubie and Moulinet at **SOSPEL**, a dreamy Italianate town spanning the gentle River Bévéra. You may find it over-tranquil after the excitements of the high mountains or the flashy speed of the Côte d'Azur, but it can make a very pleasant break.

The main street, **avenue Jean-Médecin**, follows the river on its southern bank before crossing the most easterly of the three bridges to become bd de Verdun heading for the Roya Valley. The central bridge, the **Vieux Pont** with its tower between the two spans for collecting tolls, was built in the early eleventh century to link the town centre on the south bank with its suburb across the river.

The Vieux Pont is the linchpin of Sospel's townscape, a scene made yet more alluring by the balconied houses along the north bank which back on to the grimy rue de la République. The banks are lush with flowering shrubs and trees, and one house even has a *trompe-l'oeil* street facade. Viewed from the eastern end of av Jean-Médecin, with the hills to the west and the bridge tower reflected in the water, this scene would be hard to improve.

Yet there's another vista in the town that rivals the river scene. For maximum effect it's best approached down rue St-Pierre from the eastern place St-Pierre. The street is deeply shadowed and gloomy with equally uninviting alleyways running off it. Then suddenly it opens into **place St-Michel** and you have before you one of the most beautiful series of peaches-and-cream Baroque facades in all Provence. In front of you is the **Eglise St-Michel** with its separate austere Romanesque clock tower. To the left are the **Chapelle des Pénitents Gris** and the **Chapelle des Pénitents Rouges**, and to the right are the medieval arcades and *trompe-l'oeil* decoration of the **Palais Ricci**. St-Michel contains an **altarpiece** by François Bréa in which the background to the red and gold robes of the Madonna is a bewitching river landscape of mountains, monasteries and dark citadels. On the right-hand panel Saint Martha has the snarling *Tarasque* well under control on a lead, while the saint on the left has a face that might have been painted by Leonardo.

The road behind the church, rue de l'Abbaye, which you can reach via the steps between the two chapels, leads up to an ivy-covered **castle ruin**, from which you get a good view of the town. Further up, along chemin de St-Roch, an even better view can be had from the **Fort St-Roch**, part of the ignominious inter-war Maginot Line, which houses the **Musée de la Résistance**, illustrating the courageous local resistance movement during World War II (June–Sept Tues–Sun 2–6pm; April & May Sat & Sun 2–6pm; 10F). The French–Italian armistice followed ten days after the capitulation to the Germans in June 1940, but during the short period of heavy fighting on France's southeastern frontier, Sospel held out against the vastly superior Italian forces. Under Italian occupation the town hall continued to fly the French flag; when the Germans took over in 1943 life became much nastier. Only a few of the Jews who had taken refuge here managed to escape south to Monaco. After Menton was liberated in September 1944 the Allied force advanced north, carrying out airborne attacks on Sospel, but orders came to stay put within 5km of the town. The town was left to the mercy of the Germans, with American and Canadian artillery attacks adding to the casualties. At the end of October the Germans were forced to retreat, but not far enough, and the battle for Sospel continued until April 1945.

Practicalities

The **gare SNCF** is southeast of the town on av A-Borriglione, which becomes av des Martyrs-de-la-Résistance, before leading down to the park on place des Plantanes opposite place St-Pierre. Sospel's **tourist office** is housed in the Vieux Pont (Mon–Sat 10am–noon & 2.30–6pm; ☎93.04.18.44).

If you want to **stay**, the *Auberge du Pont-Vieux*, 3 av J-Médecin (☎93.04.00.73; ②), is Sospel's cheapest hotel. The *Auberge Provençale*, on rte du Col de Castillon 1.5km uphill from the town (☎93.04.00.31; ④), is much nicer, with a pleasant garden and terrace from which to admire Sospel. The *Hôtel des Etrangers* at 7 bd de Verdun (☎93.04.00.09; ③) has tacky decor but pleasant service, the use of a pool and **bikes** to rent. Behind the *Hôtel des Etrangers* there's a **gîte d'étape** for trekkers (☎93.04.00.09; ①). There are five **campsites** around the town, the closest of which is *Le Mas Fleuri* in quartier La Vasta (open all year; ☎93.04.03.48), with its own pool, 2km along the D2566 to Moulinet following the river upstream.

There are various **eating places** along av J-Médecin including *Chez Fredy* which serves *pains beignets*, pizzas and flans. At *L'Escargot d'Or*, 3 rue de Verdun (☎93.04.00.43; closed Fri), just across the eastern bridge, you can eat for between 100F and 150F on a terrace above the river; the restaurant of the *Hôtel des Etrangers* next door (see above) is good value (menus from 85F). A Thursday **market** is held on place des Platanes; on Sunday local produce is sold on place du Marché. You can find wines and Alpine liqueurs at the *Caves Sospellois* on av Jean-Médecin near *Chez Fredy*.

Upstream from Sospel: Breil, Saorge and Fontan

By the time it reaches **BREIL-SUR-ROYA** the river has picked up enough volume to justify a barrage and to provide swift white water for canoeing. A town of modest industries (leather, olives and dairy products), Breil spreads back from both banks in an easy undefensive manner, with the old town on the eastern edge. A Renaissance chapel with a golden angel blowing a trumpet from its rooftop cross faces the river, while in the centre of *vieux* Breil stands the **Eglise Santa-Maria-in-Albis**, a vast eighteenth-century edifice topped by a belfry with shiny multicoloured tiles and containing an impressive organ loft. On the road out towards Tende in a former *SNCF* depot, the **Ecomusée du Haut Pays** (July & Aug Mon &Wed–Sun 10am–noon & 3.30–6.30pm; May, June, Sept & Oct Sat &

Sun same hours; 15F) presents interesting exhibitions on the history and wildlife of the Roya Valley set up in old railway carriages, including a section on hydro-power, a steam train, tramway and trolleybus.

Several good **walks** are signed from the village; if you just want a short stroll, follow the river downstream past the barrage and the wash houses, then fork upwards through an olive grove to a tiny chapel and an old Italian gatehouse. The path eventually leads up to the summit of the Arpette, which stands between Breil and the Italian border.

If you want to battle with white water by **canoeing** up through the Gorges de Saorge, or paddle more gently through the village, the *Base USBTP* (☎93.04.46.66) north of the village on the right bank before you reach the *gare SNCF* is the place to go.

The **hotel** *Castel du Roy*, chemin de l'Aigara, off the rte de Tende (closed Nov–Feb; ☎93.04.43.66; ④), is the most luxurious of the two in town and has a very good **restaurant** (closed Tues out of season; menus from 100F). The other is the much more central *Hôtel du Roya* on place Biancheri (closed Fri out of season; ☎93.04.48.10; half-board obligatory in July & Aug; ③), overlooking the barrage, with a decent restaurant (menus from 80F). The municipal two-star **campsite** (open all year; ☎93.04.46.66) is by the river, just upstream from the village.

Saorge and Fontan

From the river, **SAORGE** reveals an unaesthetic clutter of houses in grey and mismatched shades of red. Only the shimmering gold Niçois tiles on its church and chapel towers entice you to climb the 1.5km from the train station it shares with Fontan (buses are very irregular) to the gateway into the village. But Saorge is much prettier at close quarters than from a distance: almost nothing is level, and vertical stairways turn into paths lined with bramble and old man's beard. There's just the one main horizontal street, and even that goes up and down flights of steps and through arches formed by the houses. At the end of the street a path leads across the cultivated terraces to **La Madone del Poggio**, an eleventh-century monastery guarded by an impossibly high bell-tower topped by an octagonal spire (guided tours by appointment; ☎93.04.50.22). Back in the village, there's a seventeenth-century **Franciscan convent** (Sat 2–4pm, Sun 10am–noon & 2–4.30pm) with rustic murals around its cloisters; and the **Eglise St-Sauveur** (daily 10am–5pm) has rich examples of ecclesiastical art over many centuries. Incidentally, if you hear French that sounds a bit strange but isn't Provençal, it will be the village's old dialect, which preserves words from the language spoken by the pre-Roman inhabitants.

Staying here, the only option is a **chambre d'hôtes** and **gîte** chez M & Mme Chimène, quartier Bergeron (☎93.04.55.49; ①). For **food**, *Lou Pountin*, rue Revelli (closed Wed), serves delicious pizzas, ravioli and other pasta dishes for under 100F; and there's one *bar-tabac*, *Chez Gillou*.

FONTAN, a couple of kilometres upstream and with another shining Niçois-tiled belfry, has a couple of **hotels** to fall back on. The *Terminus* (☎93.04.50.05; ③), overlooking the Roya at the north end of the village, has cheapish rooms and several reasonably priced menus to eat beneath a beautifully painted ceiling. Or try the *Auberge de la Roya* (☎93.04.50.19; ③), a little noisier but closer to the heart of the village. At both hotels and at the **restaurant** *Les Plantanes*, opposite the *Auberge de la Roya*, the main speciality is fresh trout from the river.

La Brigue and Notre-Dame-des-Fontaines

Six kilometres south of Tende is the small and very appealing village of **LA BRIGUE**, lying on an eastern tributary of the Roya surrounded by pastures and with the perennial snowcap of **Mont Bego** visible to the west. Its Romanesque church, the **Eglise St-Martin**, is full of medieval paintings, including several by Louis Bréa, most of them showing hideous scenes of torture and death. But the church, and the octagonal seventeenth-century **Chapelle St-Michel** alongside it, pale into insignificance compared with the sanctuary of **Notre-Dame-des-Fontaines**, 4km east of the village.

From the exterior this seems to be a plain, graceful place of retreat, but inside it's something more akin to an arcade of video nasties. Painted in the fifteenth century by Jean Baleison (the ones above the altar) and Jean Canavéso (all the rest), the sequence of restored **frescoes** contains 38 episodes. Each one, from Christ's flagellation, through the torment on the Cross to devils claiming their victims, and, ultimate gore, Judas's disembowelment, is full of violent movement and colour. Worship in medieval times was no quiet withdrawal into prayer: it was a battering of threats and exhortations in the one medium that every member of the congregation could understand.

The chapel is open all year but the opening hours vary so you should check with the *mairie* or any of the restaurants in La Brigue before you set out. There's no bus but it's a very pleasant walk up the D43 for 2km, then turning right over the **Pont du Coq**, built, like the chapel, in the fifteenth century.

If you want **to stay** at La Brigue, there's the *Auberge St-Martin* (closed Tues out of season & Dec–Feb; ☎93.04.62.17; ③) and the *Fleurs des Alpes* (closed Wed out of season & mid-Nov to Feb; ☎93.04.61.05; ②) both on place St-Martin by the church and with **restaurants** serving very satisfying meals for under 100F. The more upmarket *Le Mirval* (closed Nov–March; ☎93.04.63.71; ④), downstream from place St-Martin on rue Vincent-Ferrier, has rooms overlooking the Levenza stream. If you have no luck you can try the *Hôtel Terminus*, rue Martyres-de-la-Résistance (closed Nov–April; ☎93.04.60.10; ③) in **ST-DALMAS-DE-TENDE**, the preceding train stop, back on the Roya. During the summer you may need to book, as St-Dalmas is the nearest town to the Vallée des Merveilles.

The Vallée des Merveilles

The **Vallée des Merveilles** lies between two lakes over 2000m up on the western flank of Mount Bego. The first person to record his experience of this high valley of lakes and bare rock was a fifteenth-century traveller who had lost his way. He described it as "an infernal place with figures of the devil and thousands of demons scratched on the rocks". What his contemporary readers must have imagined to be delusions brought on by the terror of the place were no imaginings. The rocks of the valley are carved with thousands of images, of animals, tools, people working and mysterious symbols, dating from some time in the second millennium BC. More are to be found in the **Vallée de Fontanable** on the northern flank of Mont Bego, and west from the Vallée des Merveilles across the southern slopes of Mont des Merveilles. Very little is known about them and the instruments that fashioned them have never been found – this not being the easiest location to carry out an archeological dig.

Over the centuries other travellers, shepherds and eventually tourists have added their own engravings to the collection, the more recent offerings inevitably the most vandalistic, often done on top of the prehistoric works. As a result explorations of the Vallée de Fontanable are restricted to the one path unless accompanied by an official Mercantour guide with the same applying to the Mont des Merveilles area.

The easiest route to the Vallée des Merveilles is the ten-kilometre trek (6–8hr) that starts at *Les Mesces Refuge*, about 8km west of **St-Dalmas-de-Tende** on the D91. The first part of the climb is through woods full of wild raspberries, mushrooms and bilberries, not all of it steeply uphill. Eventually you rise above the treeline and the **Lac Long** comes into view. A few pines still manage to grow around the lake, and in spring the grass is full of flowers, but encircling you is a mountain wilderness. From the *Refuge des Merveilles* by the lake, where you can get sustenance and stay over, you continue up through a fearsome valley where the rocks turn from black to green according to the light. From here to just beyond the **Lac des Merveilles** you can start searching for the engravings. For the Vallée de Fontanable the path starts 4.5km further up the D91 from the *Mesces Refuge*, just before the Casterino information point.

Val des Merveilles, 10 rue du Château, Tende (☎93.04.77.73), organizes **guided walks** (July & Aug daily; June & Sept Sun; 35F), as does the *Bureau des Guides* in St-Martin-Vésubie (see above) and *Destination Merveilles* in St-Dalmas-de-Tende (☎93.89.88.98). These are all recommended: it's no fun being on your own when blue skies and sun suddenly turn into violent hailstorms and lightning, and it's perfectly possible to miss the engravings altogether.

Tende

TENDE, the highest town on the Roya, guards the access to the Col de Tende, which connects Provence and Piedmont but is now bypassed by a long road tunnel. Though not especially attractive, Tende is quite a busy place, with plenty of cheap accommodation, places to eat, bars to lounge around in and shops to browse through.

The town's old and gloomy rows of houses, built with green and purple schist, are blackened by fumes of heavy goods vehicles shunting beer and building materials between Italy and France. Above them rise the stridently cherry-coloured belfry of the **collegiate church**, the peachy-orange clock towers and belfries of various Renaissance **chapels**, and a twenty-metre needle of wall which is all that remains of a château destroyed by the French in the seventeenth century. An Italian-style terraced cemetery extends beyond the ruins. The **Musée des Merveilles**, on av du 16 Septembre 1947, is due to open during 1996, promising dioramas of prehistoric life with fancy lighting, sound and wind effects.

The **Vieille Ville** is fun to wander through, looking at the symbols of old trades on the door lintels, the overhanging roofs and the balconies on every floor. On place de l'Eglise, the **Collégiale Notre-Dame de l'Assumption** is more a repository of the town's wealth than a place of contemplation, with Baroque excess throughout, though the Apostles wearing their halos like lids on the Renaissance porch and the lions supporting the two Doric columns are rather nice. The more interesting church is **St-Michel** at the other end of town near the station on place du Grande Marché. This former convent was entirely remodelled in the 1960s, when the chevet was replaced by a wall of glass looking onto the trees and shrubs of the former convent gardens. It's decorated with dream-inspired paintings of a semi-symbolist, semi-surrealist nature by a contemporary local artist, some dreadful, others striking an eerily appropriate note. Local folklore has it that a dragon lives under the tombstones.

Between the neighbouring square of place de la République and the old town, **rue de France** is a good street for browsing, with craft shops, art galleries and potteries.

Practicalities

The **gare SNCF** is set back from the top of the main street, **avenue du 16 Septembre** (becoming av Aimable-Gastaud and av Georges-Bidault as it runs southwards), at the end of av Vassalo. Turning right out of the station you'll see the **tourist office** (May–Sept 9am–noon & 2–6pm, closed Thurs & Sun; Oct–April 9.30am–noon & 2.30–5pm; ☎93.04.73.71) at the back of the *mairie* on your left before you reach the avenue. This central axis leads down left towards place de la République; the *Vieille Ville* is further down on your right to either side of the Roya's tributary.

Hotels in Tende are not at all expensive: there's the *Miramonti* at 5–7 av Vassalo (☎93.04.61.82; ②), just by the station; the *Hôtel du Centre*, 12 place de la République (☎93.04.62.19; ②); and the bit more upmarket *Cheval Blanc*, 18 rue Maurice-Sassi (☎93.04.62.22; ③) just off the *place*. If you follow chemin Ste-Catherine, off rue St-Jean past the cathedral, you'll come to the edge of the town and the **gîte d'étape** *Les Carlines* (April–Sept; ☎93.04.62.74; ①), which has gorgeous views down the valley. The one-star municipal **campsite** is 500m down a path to the left of the *gare SNCF* (June–Oct; ☎93.04.76.08).

Restaurants are to be found on av du 16 Septembre and rue de France: nothing very special but plenty of Italian dishes. *La Marguería* pizzeria on av du 16 Septembre, with beams strung with dried herbs and garlic, and stuffed foxes on the walls, is the most popular.

travel details

Trains

Chemin de Fer de Provence **(Nice–Digne)**

Nice to: Annot (4–5 daily; 1hr 55min); Barrême (4–5 daily; 2hr 50min); Digne (4–5 daily; 3hr 20min); Entrevaux (4–5 daily; 1hr 30min); Puget-Théniers (4–5 daily; 1hr 25min); St-André-des-Alpes (4–5 daily; 2hr 35min); Thorame-Verdon (4–5 daily; 2hr 20min); Touët-sur-Var (4–5 daily; 1hr 10min); Villars-sur-Var (4–5 daily; 1hr 5min).

From Annot an *SNCF* bus meets some trains for the connection to Castellane (45min) and St-Julien (25min).

From Digne a regular *SNCF* bus links the *Chemin de Fer de Provence* with the *SNCF* Marseille–Sisteron line at St-Auban–Château-Arnoux (30min).

From Thorame-Verdon an *SNCF* bus meets each train for the connection to Beauvezer (20min); Colmars-les-Alpes (30min); Allos (45min); La Foux-d'Allos (1hr 10min).

Nice–Tende–Cuneo *SNCF* line

Nice to: Breil-sur-Roya (4–5 daily; 1hr–1hr 10min); La Brigue (4–5 daily; 1hr 35min–1hr 50min); Saorge-Fontan (4–5 daily; 1hr 15min–1hr 35min); St-Dalmas-de-Tende (4–5 daily; 1hr 30min–1hr 45min); Sospel (4–5 daily; 50min); Tende (4–5 daily; 2hr 5min–2hr 10min).

Buses

Barcelonette to: Gap (3 daily; 1hr 20min); Digne (1 daily; 1hr 45min); Marseille (2 daily; 3hr 55min).

Digne to: Avignon (2 daily; 3hr 30min); Barcelonnette (1 daily; 1hr 55min); Castellane (2 daily; 1hr 15min); Grenoble (2 daily; 4hr 30min); Manosque (5 daily; 45min–1hr); Marseille (2 daily; 2hr–2hr 40min); Nice (5 daily; 2hr 55min–3hr 15min); Puget-Théniers (1–2 daily; 1hr 55min); Pra-Loup (1 daily; 2hr 10min); St-André-les-Alpes (1–2 daily; 45min); Seyne-les-Alpes (1 daily; 55min); Sisteron (1 daily; 45min).

Gréolières to: Courségoules (1 daily; 10min); Grasse (2 daily Tues & Fri; 1hr).

Puget-Théniers to: Annot (4 daily; 20min); Barrême (1–2 daily; 1hr 25min); Digne (1-2 daily; 1hr 55min); Entraunes (1 daily; 1hr 10min); Entrevaux (4 daily; 10min); St-André-les-Alpes (1–2 daily; 1hr); St-Martin-d'Entraunes (1 daily; 55min); Thorame-Haute (4 daily; 50min).

St-André-les-Alpes to: Allos (3 daily; 1hr 5min); Barrême (2 daily; 15min); Beauvezer (3 daily; 45min); Colmars-les-Alpes (3 daily; 50min); Digne (1–2 daily; 45min); La Foux d'Allos (3 daily; 1hr 30min); Nice (1 daily; 2hr); Puget-Théniers (1–2 daily; 1hr); Thorame-Verdon (3 daily; 25min).

St-Etienne-de-Tinée to: Auron (2–3 daily; 15min); Isola (2–3 daily; 25min); La Tour (2–3 daily; 1hr 15min); Nice (2–3 daily; 2hr 10min); St-Sauveur-de-Tinée (2–3 daily; 40min).

St-Martin-Vésubie to: Lantosque (1–3 daily; 40min); Nice (1–3 daily; 1hr 40min); Roquebillière (1–3 daily; 20min); St-Dalmas (2–3 daily; 10–20min).

Sospel to: Menton (3 daily; 50min); Moulinet (2–3 daily; 30min).

PART THREE

THE CONTEXTS

THE HISTORICAL FRAMEWORK

FROM THE BIG BANG TO THE CELTO-LIGURIANS

Almost all the great discoveries of **Stone Age** life in France have been made in the southwest of the country. In Provence a few Paleolithic traces have been found at Nice and in Menton (the skull of "Grimaldi man", for example) but nothing to compare with the cave drawings of Lascaux. It's assumed, however, that the area, including large tracts now submerged under the sea, was equally populated.

The development of farming, characterizing the **Neolithic Era**, is thought to have been started in Provence around 6500 BC with the domestication of the indigenous wild sheep. Around 3000 BC the **Ligurians** came from the east, settling throughout southern France and cultivating the land for the first time. It is to these people that the carvings in the *Vallée des Merveilles*, the few megalithic standing stones, and the earliest *bories* – dry stone huts – belonged. It's also thought that certain Provençal word-endings in place-names and names of rivers and mountains like *-osc*, *-asc*, *-auni* and *-inc*, derive from the Ligurian dialects having passed through Greek and Latin.

At some later point the **Celts** from the north moved into western Provence, bringing with them bronze technology. The first known fortified hilltop retreats, the *oppidi* (of which traces remain in the Maures, the Lubéron, the upper Durance and the hills in the Rhône Valley), are attributed to this new ethnic mix, the **Celto-Ligurians**.

THE ANCIENT GREEKS DISCOVER PROVENCE

As the Celto-Ligurian civilization developed, so did its trading links with the other Mediterranean peoples. The name of the River Rhône may have been given by traders from the Greek island of Rhodes (in French the name can be made into an adjective, *Rhodien*). Etruscans, Phonecians, Corinthians and Ionians all had links with Provence. The eventual **Greek** colonies set up along the coast, starting with **Massalia** (Marseille) around 600 BC, were not the result of military conquest but of gradual economic integration. And while Massalia was a republic with great influence over its hinterland, it was not a base for wiping out the indigenous peoples. Prestige and wealth came from its port, and the city prided itself on its independence which was to last well into the Middle Ages.

The Greeks introduced olives, figs, cherries, walnuts, cultivated vines and money. During the two hundred years following the foundation of Massalia, **colonies** were set up in La Ciotat, Almanarre (near Hyères), Bréganson, Cavalaire, St-Tropez (known as *Athenopolis*), Antibes, Nice and Monaco. *Mastrabala* at St-Blaize and *Glanum* by St-Rémy-de-Provence developed within Massalia's sphere of influence. The **Rhône** was the corridor for commercial expeditions, including journeys as far north as Cornwall to acquire tin. Away from the coast and the Rhône Valley, however, the Celto-Ligurian lifestyle was barely affected by the advantages of Hellenic life, continuing its harsher and more basic battle for survival.

ROMAN CONQUEST

Unlike the Greeks, the **Romans** were true imperialists, imposing their organization, language and laws by military subjugation on every corner of their empire. During the third century BC Roman expansion was concentrated on Spain, the power base of the Carthaginians (from where Hannibal had set off with his elephants to cross the Rhône somewhere above Orange and the Alps, in what is now the

Hautes-Alpes *département,* in order to attack the Romans in upper Italy). During this time Massalia nurtured good diplomatic relations with Rome which stood the city in good stead when Spain was conquered and the Romans decided to secure the land routes to *Iberia*.

This they achieved in a remarkably short time. From 125 to 118 BC, ***Provincia*** (the origin of the name Provence) became part of the Roman Empire. It encompassed the whole of the south of France from the Alps to the Pyrenees, stretching as far north as Vienna and Geneva, and with Narbonne as its capital.

While Massalia and other areas remained neutral or collaborated with the invaders, many Ligurian tribes fought to the death, most notably the Salyens, whose ***Oppidum d'Entremont*** was demolished and a victorious new city, *Aquae Sextiae* (Aix), built at its foot in 122 BC. *Pax Romana* was still a long way off, however. **Germanic Celts** moving down from the Baltic came into conflict with the ruling power, managing to decimate several Roman legions at Orange in 105 BC. A major campaign was undertaken to prevent the Barbarians from closing in on Italy. The northern invaders were defeated, as were local uprisings. Massalia exploited every situation to gain more territories and privileges; the rest of Provence knuckled under, suffering the various battles and the requisitions and taxes to pay for them. Finally from 58 to 51 BC all of Gaul was conquered by **Julius Caesar**.

It was then that Massalia finally blew its hitherto successful diplomatic strategy by supporting Pompey against Caesar, who then laid siege, defeated the city and confiscated all its territories which had stretched from the Rhône to Monaco. Unlike earlier emperors, Julius Caesar started to implant his own people in Provence (St-Raphaël was founded for his veterans). His successor Octavian followed the same policy. While the coastal areas duly latinized themselves, the **Ligurians in the mountains**, from Sisteron to the Roya Valley, refused to give up their identity without a fight. Fight they did, keeping Roman troops busy for ten years until their inevitable defeat in 14 BC, which the **Trophie des Alpes** at La Turbie gloats over to this day.

This monument to Augustus Caesar was erected on the newly built **Via Aurelia**, which linked Rome with Arles, by way of Cimiez, Antibes, Fréjus and Aix, more or less along the route of the present-day N7. The **Via Agrippa** went north from Arles, through Avignon and Orange. Only the rebellious mountainous area was heavily garrisoned. Western Provence, with Arles as its main town (Narbonne was still the capital of *Provincia*), dutifully served the imperial interests, providing oil, grain and, most importantly, ships for the superpower that ruled western Europe and the borders of the Mediterranean for five centuries.

Christianity appeared in Provence during the third century and spread fairly rapidly in the fourth when it had become the official religion of the Roman Empire. The **Lérins Monastery** was founded around 410 AD and the **Abbey of St-Victor** in Marseille about six years later.

ROME FALLS: MORE INVASIONS

For a while in the early fifth century, when the Roman Empire was beginning to split apart, the invasions by the Germanic tribes bypassed Provence. But by the time the Western Roman Empire was finally done for in 476 AD Provence was under the domination of both the **Visigoths**, who had captured Arles and were terrorizing the lower Rhône valley, and the **Burgundians** (another Germanic tribe) who had moved in from the east. The new rulers confiscated land, took slaves and generally made life for the locals, save those of Roman extraction, even more miserable than usual.

Over the next two hundred years **Goths** and **Franks** fought over and partitioned Provence; famine, disease and bloodshed diminished the population; lands that had been drained returned to swamp; intellectual life declined. Under the **Merovingian dynasty** in the eighth century Provence was, in theory, part of the **Frankish empire.** But a new world power had emerged – **Islam** – which had spread from the Middle East into North Africa and most of Spain. In 732 a Muslim army had reached as far as Tours before being defeated by the Franks at Poitiers. At this point the local ruler of Provence rebelled against the central authority, and called on the **Saracens** (Muslims) to assist. Armies of Franks, Saracens, Lombards (allies of the Franks) and locals rampaged through Provence, putting the Franks back in control.

Though the ports had trouble carrying on their lucrative trade while the Mediterranean was controlled by Saracens, agriculture developed under the Frankish **Carolingian dynasty**, particularly during the relatively peaceful years of **Charlemagne's rule**. But when, during the ninth century, Charlemagne's sons and then grandsons started squabbling over the inheritance, Provence was once again easy prey to all and sundry.

Normans took over the lower Rhône, and the **Saracens** returned, pillaging Marseille and destroying its abbey in 838, doing over Arles in 842, and attacking Marseille again in 848. For a century they maintained a base at *Fraxinetum* (La Garde-Freinet), from where they controlled the whole Massif des Maures.

The domestic **conflicts of the Frankish empire** did not spare Provence either. Its borders switched and shifted as its status within or without the empire changed. It even became a separate kingdom at one point but there was no cohesive power to assert any identity or withstand the battery of invasions.

The **hilltop villages** along the coast are commonly explained as the frightened response to the Saracens, though few date back this far. Well inland, people were just as prone to retreat to whatever defensive positions were available. In the cities this would be the strongest building (the Roman theatre at Orange, for example). The Rhône Valley villagers took refuge in the Lubéron and the Massif de la Ste-Baume.

For all the terrors and bloodshed, the period was not without its evolution. The Saracens introduced basic medicine, the use of cork-bark, resin extraction from pines, flat roof tiles and the most traditional Provençal musical instrument, the tambourine.

THE COUNTS OF PROVENCE

The Saracens were expelled for good at the end of the tenth century by **Guillaume Le Libérateur**, count of Arles, who claimed Provence as his own feudal estate. After several centuries of anarchy a period of relative stability ensued. Forestry, fishing, irrigation, land reclamation, vine cultivation, bee-keeping, salt-panning, river transport and renewed learning (under the auspices of the Benedictine monasteries) began pulling Provence out of the Dark Ages.

Politically, Guillaume and his successors retained considerable independence from their overlords (first the kingdom of Burgundy then the Holy Roman Empire). In turn they tended to confine their influence to the area around Arles and Avignon, while local lords held sway throughout the rest of the countryside and the cities developed their own autonomy. The Rhône formed the border between France and the **Holy Roman Empire** but for much of the time this political division failed to cut the old economic, cultural and linguistic links between the two sides of the river.

In the **twelfth century**, Provence passed to the counts of Toulouse and was then divided with the counts of Barcelona, while various fiefdoms – amongst them Forcalquier, Les Baux and Beuil on the eastern side of the Var – refused integration. Power was a bewildering, shifting pattern but sporadic armed conflicts apart (confined mainly to the lower Rhône Valley), the titleholder to Provence hardly affected the ordinary people who were bound in serfdom to their immediate *seigneur*.

As a consequence of the **Crusades**, **maritime commerce** flourished once again, as did **trade along the Rhône**, giving prominence to Avignon, Orange, Arles and, most of all, Marseille. In Nice, then under the control of the Genoese Republic, a new commercial town started to develop below the castle rock. The cities took on the organizational form of the Italian *consulates*, increasingly separating themselves from feudal power.

Troubadour poetry made its appearance in the *langue d'oc* language that was spoken from the Alps to the Pyrenees (and from which **Provençal** developed as a dialect). Church construction looked back to the Romans for inspiration, producing the great **Romanesque** edifices of Montmajour, Sénanque, Silvacane, Thoronet and St-Trophime in Arles.

Raymond Béranger V, Catalan count of Provence in the early thirteenth century, took the unprecedented step of spending time in his domains. While fighting off the count of Toulouse and the Holy Roman Emperor, he made Aix his capital, founded Barcelonnette and travelled throughout the Alps and the coastal regions. Provence became, for the first time since the Romans, an organized mini-state with a more or less **unified feudal system** of law and administration.

THE ANGEVINS

After Béranger's death, Provence reoriented towards France, with the **house of Anjou** gaining control and holding it until the end of the fifteenth century. The borders changed: Nice, Barcelonnette and Puget-Théniers passed to Savoy in 1388 and remained separate from Provence until 1860. New extraneous powers claimed or bought territories within the country – the **popes** at **Avignon** (see p.71) and in the ***Comtat Venaissin***, the **Prince of Nassau** in Orange. Though armed conflicts, revolts and even civil war in 1388 chequered its medieval history, Provence was at least spared the devastations of the Hundred Years' War, which never touched this corner of the future France.

By the end of this period the established trading routes from the Orient to Genoa and Marseille, and from Marseille to Flanders and London, were forming the basis of **early capitalism**, and spreading new techniques and learning. Though Marseille was not a great financial centre like Antwerp or Florence, its expanding population became ever more cosmopolitan. Away from the coast and the Rhône, however, feudal villages continued to live in isolation, unable to survive if a harvest failed. For a shepherd or forester in the mountains, life in Marseille or in the extravagant papal city of Avignon would have appeared to belong to another planet, or more likely a corner of Hell.

Provençal Jews exercised equal rights with Christians, owning land and practising a wide variety of professions in addition to finance and commerce. Though concentrated in the western towns, they were not always ghettoized. But the moment any kind of disaster struck, like the **Black Death** in the mid-fourteenth century, latent hostility would violently manifest itself. The Plague, however, made no distinctions between Jew or Christian, rich or poor, in its victims: around half the population died from the recurring epidemics.

In **cultural and intellectual** life the dominant centres were the **papal court at Avignon**, and later **King Réné of Anjou's court at Aix**. However, despite the area's key position between Italy and northern Europe, and the cosmopolitan influence of the popes, Angevin rulers and foreign trade, art and architecture remained surprisingly unmarked by the major movements of the time. The popes tended to employ foreign artists and it was not until the mid-fifteenth century that native art developed around the **Avignon School** – represented by such works as Nicolas Froment's *Le Buisson Ardent* and *La Couronnement de la Vierge* by Enguerrand Quarton. At the same time the **School of Nice** developed, more directly under Italian influence, represented by the frescoes of Canavesio and Baleison and the paintings of Louis and François Bréa. Avignon was the chief city of endowment for great **Gothic architecture** – the Palais des Papes and many of the churches – but outside this city the only major examples of the new style were Tarascon's castle and the basilica of St-Maximin-de-la-Sainte-Baume.

The **legends of the saints** fleeing Palestine and seeking refuge in Provence began to take root around this time, too, with pilgrimages to the various shrines bringing glimpses of the outside world to small towns and villages. Equally significantly, the popes founded a **university** in Avignon in 1303 which became famous for jurisprudence; Aix university was established a century later and in the mid-fourteenth century the first paper mills were in use. By King Réné's time, French was the language of the court.

UNION WITH FRANCE

The short-lived Charles III of Provence, Réné's heir, bequeathed all his lands to **Louis XI of France**, a transfer of power that the *parlement* of Aix glossed over and approved in 1482. Within twelve months every top Provençal official had been sacked and replaced by a Frenchman; the castles at Toulon and Les Baux were razed to the ground; garrisons were placed in five major towns.

The *parlement* protested in vain, but after Louis XI's death a more careful approach was taken to this crucial border province. The **Act of Union**, ratified by *parlement* in 1486, declared Provence to be a separate entity within the kingdom of France, enshrining the rights to its own law courts, customs and privileges. In reality, the ever-centralizing power of the French state was to systematically erode these rights as it did with Brittany and the other once-autonomous provinces.

The **Jewish population** provided a convenient diversion for Provençal frustrations. Encouraged, if not instigated by the Crown, there were massacres, expulsions and assaults in Marseille, Arles and Manosque in the last two decades of the fifteenth century. The royal directive was convert or leave – some, such as the parents of Nostradamus, converted, many fled to the Comtat. During the sixteenth century more expulsion threats and special taxes were the rule. In 1570 the Jews lost their papal protection in the Comtat.

Meanwhile Charles VIII, Louis XII and François I involved Provence in their **Italian Wars**. **Marseille** became a **military port** in 1488, and in 1496 **Toulon** was fortified and its first **shipyards** opened. While the rest of the province suffered troop movements and requisitions, Marseille and Toulon benefited from extra funds and unchecked piracy against the enemies of France. Genoese, Venetian and Spanish vessels were regularly towed into Marseille's port.

The war took a more serious turn in the 1520s after the French conquest of Milan. **Charles V**, the new Holy Roman Emperor, retaliated by sending a large army across the Var and into Aix. The French concern was to protect Marseille at all costs – the rest of the province was left to fend for itself. After the imperial forces had failed to take Marseille and retreated, the city was rewarded with the pomp and carnival of a royal wedding between François' second son, the future Henri II, and Catherine de Medici. The **Château d'If** was built to protect the roadstead.

Another round in the war soon commenced. Charles V took back Milan, the French invaded Savoy and occupied Nice. In 1536 an even bigger **imperial army invaded**, and again the French abandoned inland Provence to protect Marseille and the Rhône Valley. The people of Le Muy stopped the emperor for one day with fifty local heroes hanged for their pains. Elsewhere people fled to the forests, their towns and villages pillaged by the invaders. Marseille and Arles held out; French troops finally moved south down the Durance; dysentery and lack of sure supply lines weakened the imperial army. Twenty thousand Savoyards were dead or imprisoned by the time the imperial troops were safely back across the Var.

One effect of the Italian Wars was that Provence now finally **identified itself with France**, making it easier for the Crown to diminish the power of the *Etats*, impose greater numbers of French administrators, and, in 1539, decree that all administrative laws were to be translated from Latin into French, not Provençal.

LIFE IN THE EARLY SIXTEENTH CENTURY

Sixteenth-century Provence was ruled by two royal appointees – a governor and *grand sénéchal* (the chief administrator) – but the **feudal hierarchy** failed to achieve the same command over the structure of society as it did elsewhere in France. Few nobles lived on their estates and those that did were often poorer than the **merchants and financiers** of the major cities. In remoter areas people cultivated their absent *seigneur's* land as if it were their own; in other areas towns bought land off the feudal owners. It is estimated that nearly half the population had their own **holdings**. Advances in **irrigation**, such as Craponne's canal through the Crau, were carried out independently from the aristocracy.

While not self-sufficient in grain, Provence had surpluses of wine, fish and vermilion from the Carmargue to export; growing **industries** in textiles, tanneries, soap and paper; and new **foods**, such as oranges, pepper, palm dates and sugar cane, introduced along the coast from across the Mediterranean. Olives provided the basic oil for food; orchards were being cultivated on a commercial scale; most families kept pigs and sheep; only vegetables were rare luxuries. People lived on their land, with the old fortified villages only populated in times of insecurity. Most small towns had weekly markets, and festivals celebrated the advance from survival being a non-stop struggle. Epidemics of the Plague continued, however, and sanitation left a lot to be desired – a contemporary noted that even in Aix it "rained shit as often as it did in Arles or Marseille".

Free **schools** were set up by some of the larger towns, and secondary colleges established in Aix, Marseille, Arles and Avignon. **Nostradamus** (1503–1566) achieved renown throughout France from the royal court down to his Salon and St-Rémy neighbours. His books had to be printed in Lyon though, as there was as yet no market for printers in Provence.

Châteaux such as La Tour d'Aigue, Gordes and Loumarin, with comfort playing an equal part to defence, were built at this time, as were the rich Marseille town houses of the *Maison Diamentée* and the *Hôtel Cabre*. The facade of St-Pierre in Avignon shows the **Renaissance** finally triumphing over Provence's artistic backwardness.

THE WARS OF RELIGION

Though the Italian Wars temporarily disrupted social and productive advances, they were nothing compared with the Wars of Religion that put all France in a state of **civil war** for most of the second half of the sixteenth century. The clash between the new reforming ideas of Luther and Calvin and the old Catholic order was particularly violent in Provence. **Avignon**, as papal domain, was inevitably a rigid centre of Catholicism. The neighbouring principality of **Orange** allowed Huguenots to practise freely and form their own organizations. **Haute Provence** and the **Lubéron** became centres for the new religion due to the influx of Dauphinois and Piedmontais settlers.

Incidents began to build up in the 1540s, culminating in the massacre of Lubéron Protestants and the destruction of Mérindol (see p.154). In Avignon heretics were displayed in iron cages while they died; in Haute Provence churches were smashed by the reformers while in Orange the Protestants pillaged the cathedral and took control of the city. The regent Catherine de Medici's **Edict of Tolerance** in 1562 only made matters worse. Marseille demanded and received an exemption; Aix promptly dispatched a Catholic contingent to massacre the Protestants of Tourves; Catherine's envoys prompted a massacre of Catholics at Barjols. The notorious Baron des Adrets, who had fought for the Catholics, now switched sides and carried out a series of terrifying attacks on Catholic towns and villages. The *parlement* resigned rather than ratify a new edict of tolerance in 1563, even though by this point Orange had been won back to the established Church, the garrison of Sisteron had been massacred for protecting the Protestants and the last armed group of reformers had fled north out of the province.

When Catherine de Medici and her son Charles XIV toured Provence in 1564, all seemed well. But within a few years fighting again broke out, with Sisteron once more under siege. In the mid-1570s trouble took a new turn with the rivalry between Henri III's governor and *sénéchal* adding to the hostile camps. This state of civil war was only terminated by another major outbreak of the **Plague** in 1580.

With the Protestant **Henri de Navarre** (the future Henri IV) becoming heir to the throne in 1584, the *Guerres de Religion* hotted up even more. The pope excommunicated Henri; and the leaders of the French Catholics (the de Guises) formed the **European Catholic League**, seized Paris and drove out the king, Henri III. Provence found itself with two governors – the king's and the League's appointees; two capitals – Aix and Pertuis; and a split *parlement*. After Henri III's assassination, Catholic Aix called in the duke of Savoy whose troops trounced Henri de Navarre's supporters at Riez. At this point the main issue for the Provençaux was loyalty to the French Crown against invaders, rather than religion. Even the Aix *parlement* stopped short of giving Savoy the title to Provence, and after Marseille again withstood a siege, the duke gave up and went back home to Nice in 1592. For another year battles continued between the Leaguers and the Royalists, with Marseille refusing to recognize either authority. Finally Henri IV said his mass; troops entered Marseille; and the war-damaged and impoverished Provence reverted back to **royal control**.

LOUIS XIII AND XIV

The **consolidation of the French state** initiated by Louis XIII's minister **Richelieu** saw the whittling away of Provençal institutions and ideas of independence, coupled with ever-increasing tax demands plus enforced "free gifts" to the king. The power and prestige of the *Etats* and *parlement* were reduced by force, clever negotiation or playing off the different cities' rival interests.

Political power switched from governors and *sénéchals*, who were part of the feudal structure, to ***intendants***, servants of the state with powers over every aspect of provincial life, including the military. The *Etats*, having refused to provide the royal purse with funds in 1629, were not convoked again. These changes, along with the failure of the aristocratic rebellions during Louis XIV's minority (the *Frondes*), and the increasing number of titles bought by the bourgeoisie, left the *noblesse d'épée* (the real aristos) disgruntled but impotent. The clergy (the First Estate) also lost a measure of their former power.

It was a time of **plague**, **famine**, further outbreaks of **religious strife** and **war**. To deal with opposition the Château d'If became a state prison. The **war with Spain**, for which Toulon's fortifications were upgraded and forts added to Giens and the Iles d'Hyères, increased taxation, decimated trade and cost lives. Marseille attempted to hold on to its ancient independence by setting up a rebel council in 1658. The royal response was swift. Troops were sent in, rebels were condemned to the rack or the galleys, a permanent garrison was established and the foundations laid for the Fort St-Nicolas to keep an eye on "*ce peuple violent et libertin*".

While the various upheavals and ever-multiplying tax burden caused untold misery, **progress in production** (including the faïence industry), **education** and **social provision** (mostly the work of the burgeoning *Pénitents* orders outside the Church establishment) carried on apace. The town houses of Aix, Marseille and Avignon, the *Hospice de la Charité* in Marseille, the Baroque additions to churches and chapels, all show the wealth accumulating, gained as ever by maritime commerce. But the greatest Provençal sculptor of the period, Pierre Puget, never received royal patronage and Provençal was still the language of all classes in society, though French for the first time was imposed on certain disciplines at Aix University.

As the reign of **Louis XIV**, the Sun King, became more grandiose and more aggressive, Provence, like all of France outside Versailles and Paris, was eclipsed. The **war with Holland** saw Orange and the valley of Barcelonnette annexed; Avignon and the papal Comtat swung steadily into the French orbit; attempts were made again to capture Nice. But for the Provençaux, the people of Orange, Avignon and the Comtat had always been their fellow countrymen and women, while Nice was a foreign city they had never wished to claim. Wars that involved the English navy blockading the ports were as unwelcome to the local bourgeois as they were to those who had to fight.

As the *ancien régime* slowly dug its own grave the rest of the country stagnated. The pattern for Provence of **wars**, **invasions and trade blockades** became entrenched. To add to the gloom, another outbreak of the Plague killed half the population of Marseille in 1720. The extravagance of **Louis XV's court**, where the Grassois painter **Fragonard** found his patrons, had few echoes in Provence. Aix had its grandiose town planning, Avignon its mansions, Grasse its perfume industry, but elsewhere there was complete stagnation.

THE REVOLUTION

Conditions were ripe for revolution in Provence. The region had suffered a disastrous silk harvest and a sharp fall in the price of wine in 1787, and the severe winter of 1788–89 killed off most of the olive trees. Unemployment and starvation were rife and the hurtling rise in the price of bread provoked serious rioting in the spring of 1789. There was no lack of followers for bourgeois *députés* exasperated by incompetent administration and the constant drain on national resources that the court represented.

So in July 1789, while the Bastille was stormed in Paris, **Provençal peasants** pillaged their local châteaux and urban workers rioted against the mayors, egged on by the middle classes. There was only one casualty, at Aups. The following year **Marseillaise revolutionaries** seized the forts of St-Jean and St-Nicolas, with again just one lashing of violence when the crowd lynched St-Jean's commander. **Toulon** was equally fervent in its support for the new order, and at **Aix** one counter-revolutionary lawyer and two aristocrats were strung up on lamp posts. In the **papal lands**, where the crucial issue was reunion with France, Rome's representative was sent packing from Avignon and a revolutionary municipality installed.

Counter-revolutionaries regrouped in Carpentras and there were several bloody incidents, including the ice-house massacre. However, 1792 saw Marseille's staunchly Jacobin National Guard, the ***Féderés***, demolish the counter-revolutionary forces in the Comtat and aristocratic Arles. Marseille's authorities declared that kingship was contrary to the principles of equality and national sovereignty. When the Legislative Assembly summoned all the *Féderés* to Paris to defend the capital and celebrate the third anniversary of the Bastille, five hundred Marseillaise marched north singing Rouget de Lisle's *Hymn to the Army of the Rhine*. It was written for the troops at the front in the war declared that April with Germany and Austria. But for the Parisian *sans-culottes* it was the ***Marseillaise*** and a major hit. Even more so after the attack on the Tuileries palace that was swiftly followed by the dethronement of the king. According to the Swedish ambassador of the time, "Marseille's *Féderés* were the moving force behind everything in August 1792".

Back in Provence (by now incorporating the papal states and divided into four *départements*) peasants were once again on the pillage, and still starving, while **royalists and republicans** fought it out in the towns. In 1793 the Var military commander was ordered to take Nice, a hotbed of émigré intrigue and part of the great European coalition out to exterminate the French Revolution. Twenty thousand people fled the city but no resistance was encountered. The Alpes-Maritimes *département* came into existence.

In the summer of 1793 political divisions between the various factions of the Convention and the growing fear of a dictatorship by the Parisian *sans-culottes* provoked the provincial **Federalist revolt**. The populace was fed up with conscription to the wars on every frontier, and a hankering after their old Provençal autonomy reasserted itself. Revolutionary cities found themselves fighting against government forces – a situation speedily exploited by the real **counter-revolutionaries**. In Toulon the entire fleet and the city's fortifications were handed over to the English. (In the battle to regain the city, the government's victory was secured by the young Napoléon.) Reprisals, in addition to the almost daily executions of the Terror, cost thousands of lives.

Much of Provence, however, had remained Jacobin, and so fell victim to the **White Terror** of 1795 that followed the execution of Robespierre. The prisons of Marseille, Aix, Arles and Tarascon overflowed with people picked up on the street with no charge. Cannons were fired into the cells at point blank range and sulphur or lighted rags thrown through the bars. By the time the Revolution had given up all hopes of being revolutionary in terms of its 1789 manifesto, anarchy reigned. Provence was crawling with returned émigrés who had no trouble finding violent followers motivated by frustration, exhaustion and famine.

NAPOLEON AND RESTORATION

Provence's experience of **Napoléon's reign** differed little from that of the rest of France, despite the emperor's close connection with the region (childhood at Nice; military career at Antibes and Toulon; then the escape from Elba). Order was restored and power became even more centralized, with *préfects* enlarging on the role of Louis XIV's *intendants*. The concordat with the pope re-establishing **Catholicism** as the state religion was widely welcomed, particularly since the new ecclesiastical authorities were not all the old First Estate, *ancien régime* representatives. However, secular power reverted to the old *seigneurs* in many places – the new mayor of Marseille, for example, was a marquise.

It was the **Napoleonic wars** that lost the emperor his Provençal support. Marseille's port was again blockaded; conscription and taxes for military campaigns were as detested as ever; the Alpes-Maritimes *département* became a theatre of war and in 1814 was handed over (with Savoy) to Sardinia. Monaco followed suit the following year, though with the Grimaldi dynasty reinstalled in their palace.

The **restoration of the Bourbons** after Waterloo unleashed another White Terror. Provence was again bitterly divided between royalists and republicans. Despite this split there was no major resistance to the **1830 revolution** which put **Louis-Philippe**, the "Citizen King" on the throne. The new regime represented liberalism – well tinged with anticlericalism and a dislike of democracy – and was welcomed by the Provençal bourgeoisie. Despite the ardent Catholicism of the *paysans*, and the large numbers of émigrés that had returned under the Bourbons' amnesties, the attempt by the duchess of Berry to bring back the "legitimate" royalty (which had some initial success in western France) failed totally here.

1848 AND 1851

The first half of the nineteenth century saw the first major **industrialization** of France, and, overseas, the **conquest of Algeria**.

In Provence, **Marseille** was linked by rail with Paris and expanded its port to take steam ships; iron bridges over the **Rhône** and new roads were built; many towns demolished their ramparts to extend their main streets into the suburbs. By the 1840s the **arsenal at Toulon** was employing over three thousand workers.

This emerging proletariat was highly receptive to the visit by the socialist and feminist Flora Tristan, who was doing the rounds of France in 1844. A year later all the different trades in the arsenal went on strike. Throughout industrialized Provence – the Rhône Valley and the coast – workers overturned their traditional *compagnons* (guilds) to form more radical **trade-union** organizations. Things hardly changed, however, in inland Provence, as protectionist policies hampered the exchange of foodstuffs, and the new industries' demand for fuel eroded *paysans'* forestry rights. In 1847 the country (and most of Europe) was in severe **economic crisis**.

News of the **1848 revolution** arrived from Paris before the representatives of the new republic. Town halls, common lands and forests were instantly and peacefully reclaimed by the populace. In the elections that followed, very moderate republicans were returned, though they included three manual workers in Marseille, Toulon and Avignon. Two months later, however, the economic situation was deteriorating again and newly won improvements in working hours and wages were being clawed back by the employers. A demonstration in Marseille turned nasty and the barricades went up (see p.177).

Elsewhere, the most **militant action** was in **Menton** and **Roquebrune**, both under the rule of Monaco, where the people refused to pay the prince's high taxes on oil and fruit. Sardinian military assistance failed to quell the revolt and the two towns declared themselves independent republics. With his main source of income gone, the Grimaldi prince turned the focus of his state shrewdly towards **tourism** – already well established in Nice and Hyères – and opened the casino at **Monte Carlo**.

The 1848 revolution turned sour with the election of **Louis-Napoléon** as president in 1850. A law was introduced which in effect annulled the 1830 universal male suffrage by imposing a residency requirement. Laws against "secret societies" and "conspiracies" followed. Ordinary *paysans* discussing prices over a bottle of wine could be arrested; militants from Digne and Avignon were deported to Polynesia for belonging to a democratic party. Newly formed **co-operatives** were seen by the authorities as hotbeds of sedition. All this inevitably accelerated politicization of the *paysans*.

When Louis-Napoléon made himself emperor in the **coup d'état of 1851**, Provence, as many other regions of France, turned again to **revolt**. Initially there were insufficient forces in the small towns and villages to prevent the rebels taking control (which they did without any violence). In order to take the *préfectures*, villagers and townspeople, both male and female, organized themselves into disciplined "*colonnes*" which marched beneath the red flag. Digne was the only *préfecture* they held, though, and then for only two days. Reprisals were bloody – another White Terror in effect, with thousands of the rebels caught as they tried to flee into Savoy. Of all the insurgents in France shot, imprisoned or deported after this rebellion, one in five were from Provence.

THE SECOND EMPIRE

The **Second Empire** saw greater changes in everyday life than in any previous period. **Marseille** became the premier port of France with trade enormously expanded by the **colonization** of North and West Africa, Vietnam, and parts of China. The **depopulation of inland Provence**, which had been gradually increasing over the last century and a half, suddenly became a deluge of migration to the coast and Rhône Valley. While the **railway** was extended along the coast – encouraging the nascent **Côte d'Azur tourism** – communications inland were ignored.

At the end of the **war for Italian unification** in 1860, **Napoléon III** regained the Alpes-Maritimes as payment for his support of Italy against Austria. A plebiscite in Nice gave majority support for **reunion with France**. To the north, Tende and La Brigue voted almost unanimously for France but the result was ignored: the new king of Italy wished to keep his favourite game-hunting grounds. Menton and Roquebrune also voted for France. While making noises about rigged elections, Charles of Monaco agreed to sell the two towns – despite their independence – to France. The sum was considerably more than the fledgling gambling and tourism industry was as yet bringing in and saved the principality from bankruptcy. **Monaco's independence**, free from any foreign protector, was finally established.

One casualty of this dispersal of traditional Provence, combined with the spread of national primary education, was the **Provençal language**. This prompted the formation of the ***Félibrige*** in 1854, by a group of poets including Frédéric Mistral – a nostalgic, backward-looking and intellectual movement in defence of literary Provençal. There were other, more popularist, Provençal writers at the time, but they too were conservative, railing against gas lighting and any other modern innovation. The attempt to associate the language with some past golden age of ultra-Catholic primitivism only encouraged the association of progress with French – particularly for the Left.

By the end of the 1860s the **socialism** of the **First International** was gaining ground in the industrial cities, and in Marseille most of all. Opponents of the empire had the majority in the town hall, and in the plebiscite of 1870, in which the country as a whole gave Napoléon III their support, the Bouches-du-Rhône *département* was second only to Paris in the number of *"nons"*. It was not surprising therefore that Marseille had its own *commune* (see p.180) when the Parisians took up arms against the right-wing republic established after the Prussians' defeat of France and the downfall of Napoléon III.

Honoré Daumier, the Marseillais caricaturist and fervent republican, was the great illustrator of both the 1851 and the 1871 events. In the middle of the century the **Marseille school of painting** developed under the influence of foreign travel and orientalism, attracting to the city such artists as Puvis de Chavannes and Félix Ziem. Provence's greatest native artist, **Cézanne**, though living in Paris from the 1860s to the 1880s spent a few months of every year in his home town of Aix, or in Marseille and L'Estaque. He was sometimes accompanied by his childhood friend **Zola**, and by **Renoir** whom he introduced to this coast.

THE THIRD REPUBLIC: 1890–1914

Under the **Third Republic**, the division between inland Provence and the coast and Rhône Valley accentuated. Port activity at Marseille quadrupled with the opening of new trade routes along the Suez Canal and further colonial acquisitions in the Far East. Manufacturing began to play an equal role with commerce. The orchards of the Rhône Valley were planted on a massive scale, and light **industries** producing clothes, foodstuffs and paper developed in Aix and other cities to export to the North African colonies. Chemical works in Avignon produced the synthetics that spelt the rapid **decline of the traditional industries** of the small towns and villages of the interior – tanning, dyeing, silk and glass. Wine production, meanwhile, was devastated by phylloxera.

The one area of brilliance connected with the climate but not with commerce was art – **painting** in particular. Following on from Cézanne and Renoir, a younger generation of artists were discovering the Côte d'Azur. The **Post-Impressionists** and **Fauvists** flocked to St-Tropez in the wake of the ever-hospitable Paul Signac. Matisse, Dufy, Seurat, Dérain, van Dongen, Bonnard, Braque, Friesz, Marquet, Manguin, Camion, Vlaminck and Vuillard were all intoxicated by the Mediterranean light, the climate and the ease of living. The escape from the rigours of Paris released a massive creative energy and resulted in works that, in addition to their radical innovations, have more *joie de vivre* than any other period in French art. Renoir retired to Cagnes for health reasons in 1907; for Matisse, Dufy and Bonnard the Côte d'Azur became their permanent home; and van Gogh, always a man apart, had a spell in Arles.

Ignoring these Bohemian characters, the **winter tourist season on the coast** was taking off. **Hyères** and **Cannes** had been "discovered" in the first half of the century (and **Nice** many years earlier). But increased ease of travel and the temporary restraint of simmering international tensions encouraged aristocratic mobility. The population of Nice trebled from 1861 to 1911; luxury trains ran from St Petersburg, Vienna and London; *belle époque* mansions and grand hotels rose along the **Riviera** seafronts; and gambling, particularly at **Monte Carlo**, won the patronage of the Prince of Wales, the Emperor Franz Joseph and scores of Russian grand-dukes.

The native working class meanwhile were forming the first French **Socialist Party**, which had its opening congress in Marseille in 1879.

Support came not just from the city but from towns and villages that had fought in 1851. In 1881 Marseille elected the first socialist *député*. By 1892 the municipal councils of Marseille, Toulon, La Ciotat and other industrial towns were in the hands of socialists. In Aix, however, the old legitimist royalists (those favouring the return of the Bourbons) still held sway, managing to block the erection of a monument to Zola in 1911.

WORLD WAR I AND THE INTER-WAR YEARS

The battlefields of **World War I** were in northern France and Belgium. In Provence, however, there was conscription. The socialists divided between pacifists and patriots, but when, in 1919, France took part in the attack on the Soviet Union, soldiers, sailors and workers joined forces in Toulon and Marseille to support the mutinies on French warships in the Black Sea. The struggle to have the mutineers freed continued well into 1920, the year in which the French **Communist Party** (*PCF*) was born; the party's adherents in Provence were again the heirs to the 1851 rebellion.

The casualties of the war led to severe depopulation in the already dwindling villages of inland Provence, some of which were actually deserted. **Land use** also changed dramatically, from mixed agriculture to a monocrop of vines in order to provide the army with its ration of one litre of wine per soldier per day. Quantity, thanks to the Provençal climate, rather than quality was the aim, leaving acres upon acres of totally unviable vineyards after demobilization. With the growth in tourism, it was easier to sell the land for construction rather than have it revert to former use.

The **tourist industry** recovered fairly quickly from the war. The *Front Populaire* of 1936 introduced paid holidays, encouraging native visitors to the still unspoilt coast. **International literati** – Somerset Maugham, Katherine Mansfield, Scott and Zelda Fitzgerald, Colette, Anaïs Nin, Gertrude Stein – and a **new wave of artists**, **Picasso** and **Cocteau** amongst them, replaced the defunct grand-dukes, even if anachronistic titles still filled the palatial Riviera residences.

Marseille during the inter-war years saw the evolution of characteristics that have yet to be obliterated. The activities of the fascist *Action Française* led to deaths during a left-wing counter-demonstration in 1925. Modern-style corruption snaked its way through the town hall and the rackets of **gangsters** on the Chicago model moved in on the vice industries. Elections were rigged and even revolvers used at the ballot boxes.

The increasing popularity of the Communist Party in the city was due to its anti-corruption platform. After the failure of the *Front Populaire* (which the great majority of Provençaux had voted for, electing several Communist *députés*), there were constant pitched battles between the Left and Right in Marseille. In 1939 a state administrator was imposed by Paris with powers to obstruct the elected council.

WORLD WAR II

France and Britain declared **war on Germany** together on September 3, 1939. The French Maginot line, however, swiftly collapsed, and by June 1940 the Germans controlled Paris and all of northern France. On June 22, Marshall Pétain signed the **armistice with Hitler**, which divided France between the Occupied Zone – the Atlantic coast and north of the Loire – and "unoccupied" **Vichy France** in the south. Menton and Sospel were occupied by the Italians, to whom the adjoining Roya Valley still belonged.

With the start of the British counter-offensive in 1942, Vichy France joined itself with the Allies and was immediately occupied by the Germans. The port of Toulon was overrun in November, with the French navy scuppering its fleet rather than letting it fall into German hands.

Resistance fighters and passive citizens suffered executions, deportations and the wholesale destruction of Le Panier quarter in Marseille (see p.176). The **Allied bombings** of 1944 caused high civilian casualties and considerable material damage, particularly to Avignon, Marseille and Toulon. The **liberation** of the two great port cities was aided by a general armed revolt by the people, but it was in the Italian sector – in Sospel and its neighbouring villages – that the fighting by the local populace was the most heroic.

MODERN PROVENCE

Before the Germans surrendered **Marseille** they made sure that the harbours were blown to bits. In the immediate **postwar years** the task of repairing the damage was compounded by a slump in international trade and passenger traffic. The nationalization of the Suez Canal was the next disaster to hit the city, spelling an end to its prime position on world trading routes. Company after company decamped to Paris leaving a growing problem of unemployment.

Marseille's solution was to orient its **port and industry** towards the Atlantic and the inland route of the Rhône. The oil industries that had developed in the 1920s around the Etang de Berre and Fos were extended. The mouth of the Rhône and the Golfe de Fos became a massive **tanker terminal**. Iron and steel works filled the spaces behind the new Port de Marseille that stretched for 50km beyond the *Vieux Port*. In the process, the city's population boomed. The urgent demand for housing was met by badly designed, low-cost, high-rise estates proliferating north and east from the congested city centre.

The **depopulation of inland Provence** was never halted, but considerably slowed by the massive irrigation schemes and development of hydroelectric power which greatly increased the agricultural and industrial potential of regions impoverished earlier in the century. The isolated ***mas*** or farmhouses, positioned wherever there happened to be a spring, were left to ruin or linked up to the mains. Orchards, lavender fields and olive groves became larger, the competition for early fruit and vegetables fiercer, and the market for luxury foods greater. The rich Rhône Valley continued to export fruit, wine and vegetables, while the river was exploited for irrigation and power, both nuclear and hydroelectric, and made navigable for sizeable ships.

After Algeria won back its independence in 1962, hundreds of thousands of French settlers, the ***pieds noirs***, returned to the mainland, bringing with them a virulent hatred of Arabic-speaking people. At the same time, the government encouraged immigration from its former colonies, North Africa in particular, with the promise of well-paid jobs, civil rights and social security, none of which were honoured. The resulting tensions, not just in Marseille but all along the coast, made perfect fodder for the

THE ASSASSINATION OF YANN PIAT

On February 25, 1994, Hyère's UDF *député*, Yann Piat, was returning to the city by car when a motorcyclist drew alongside and opened fire, leaving Piat dead and her chauffeur badly injured. It was clearly a hit job and the immediate suspects were the members of the Hyères mafia.

Piat, originally a *Front National député* (and Jean-Marie Le Pen's goddaughter), had switched to the *UDF* (*Union pour la Démocratie Française*) because of her unhappiness with the extreme right-wing policies of her former party. Piat's real crusade was against drugs and corruption, especially since Hyères had become known as the Chicago of the Côte or "Hyères-les-Bombes" after a series of bomb attacks in the new marina where different racketeering gangs were battling for control. In her attempts to clean up the marina, it's believed that Piat discovered links between local politicians and the underworld.

Piat was also opposed to the endless spread of new developments but as a *député* had little influence over this area. A year before her assassination she commissioned an opinion poll which showed a very good chance of her becoming mayor. More intriguingly, a letter written in 1992, kept in a locked drawer in the *Assemblée Nationale* in Paris, was found after her assassination stating that in the event of her sudden death, five people should be questioned: Bernard Tapie, at the time Socialist *député* in Marseille; Maurice Arreckx, mayor of Toulon, member of the French senate and head of the Var regional council; two business men; and Jean-Louis Fargette, godfather of the Toulon underworld who had fled to Italy and himself been assassinated a year before Piat died. Tapie, Arreckx and the businessmen were all ruled out as murder suspects though the investigation lead to the revelations about Arreckx's corruption which have since put him behind bars.

The identity of those behind Piat's killing remains a mystery. The one witness whose testimony might have nailed not only the assassins awaiting trial but those who paid them has died in suspicious circumstances. Piat's daughter is battling to get the murder investigation speeded up. Many believe that it is not just the involvement of local politicians that is blocking the investigation but also someone high up in Paris. The shock of the assassination has, however, given real impetus to local demands for a major clean-up of the Var *département*.

parties of the Right. From being a bastion of socialism at the end of World War II, Provence gradually turned towards intolerance and reaction.

MUNICIPAL FIEFDOMS, CORRUPTION AND VICE

The activities of the local mafia, known as the ***milieu***, with their invisible and inextricable ties to the town halls, have continued more or less unchecked since the 1920s. Not until the shocking assassination of the *député*, Yann Piat, in 1994 (see box) has the demand for a "clean hands" campaign really begun in earnest.

Drug trafficking became a major problem in Marseille in the early 1970s (providing solid material for the *French Connection* films) and is now prevalent all along the coast. Prostitution and protection rackets also flourish from Menton to Marseille, much of it controlled by the Cosonostra Italian mafia which has been spreading its tentacles westwards, taking advantage of the large numbers of Italians running businesses along the coast, the casinos and cash sales of high-priced properties for money-laundering, and the lack of specific anti-mafia laws in France.

As elsewhere in France, but particularly in Provence, **municipal fiefdoms** evolved – particularly with the huge budgets and planning powers that came with increasing decentralization – offering opportunities for patronage, nepotism and corruption, along with the financial muscle that ensured incumbents, until very recently, a more-or-less permanent position.

In **Marseille**, the town hall was controlled by **Gaston Defferre** for 33 years until his death in 1986. As well as being mayor, he was a socialist *député* and minister, and owned the city's two politically opposed regional newspapers. Though people had their suspicions about underworld links with the town hall, no one pointed the finger at Defferre.

In 1995, **Bernard Tapie**, the most popular politician in Marseille and millionaire owner of the town's football team, was unable to run for mayor because he'd just been sentenced to a year in prison for match-rigging his football team in the European Cup. A flamboyant businessman, député and European Member of Parliament for the Bouche-du-Rhône *département*, Tapie had already been disbarred from all public office until 1999 due to bankruptcy. He has also been investigated for tax evasion, shady financial dealings and insulting the police. None of which has diminished his popularity in the city.

Nice's police and judiciary were accused by Graham Greene in 1982 of protecting organized crime. Greene claimed he slept with a gun under his pillow after his *J'Accuse* was published (and banned in France) in which he detailed the corruption. **Jacques Médecin**, who succeeded his father as mayor of Nice in 1966, controlled just about every facet of public life until his downfall in 1990 for political fraud and tax evasion (see p.353) – only when Médecin fled to Uruguay were his mafioso connections finally discussed in public. But Médecin had so successfully identified his name with all the city's glamour that after his departure most Niçois gladly supported his sister Généviève Assemat-Médecin. Those who didn't, backed his daughter, Martine Cantinchi-Médecin, who claimed Le Pen was the rightful heir. Finally extradited in 1994 Médecin served a very short prison term and was able to use his popularity to back the successful candidate in the 1995 municipal elections – one Jacques Peyrat, a close friend of Le Pen and former member of the *Front National*.

Toulon was another classic fiefdom, run for four decades by **Maurice Arreckx** and his clique of friends with their underworld connections until he was put away when financial scandals finally came to light. Investigators are still looking for a Swiss bank account where some of the money paid to Arreckx's campaign fund in return for a major construction contract may have been secreted. His successor, and former director of finances, tried in vain to win back the voters but merely ran up more debts and lost to the *Front National* in 1995.

In neighbouring **La-Seyne-sur-Mer** a planning officer who attempted to stop a corrupt planning deal was murdered in 1986. More recently a British project for a World Sea Centre that would have provided much needed jobs after the closure of the shipyards was disbanded after the British refused to pay protection money to the tune of £1 million.

François Léotard the right-wing mayor of **Fréjus**, who held cabinet office (under Chirac in the late 1980s) and a seat in the *Assemblée*

Nationale, was investigated for financial irregularities but the case eventually ran out out of time and the charges were dropped. **Cannes**' mayor, **Michel Mouillot**, was disbarred from public office for five years and given a fifteen-month suspended sentence in 1989, then won his appeal and returned to the town hall only to be given an eighteen-month suspended sentence in 1996. **Pierre Rinaldi**, mayor of **Digne**, was investigated for fraud, **Jean-Pierre Lafond**, mayor of **La Ciotat**, for unwarranted interference, two successive mayors of **La Seyne** for corruption and abuse of patronage . . . and so the list goes on.

All these mayors were right-wingers; their exposure opened the way for the National Front gains in 1995, and for a return of the old industrial towns to their former favourites, the Communist Party.

THE RISE OF THE FRONT NATIONAL

The corruption, waste and general financial incompetence of right-wing municipal power has been one element in the rise of Jean-Marie Le Pen's neo-fascist **Front National** party. Another has been the significance of military bases to the region's economy. While the right-wing national government has made cuts in defence spending, Le Pen has trumpeted his ardent support for France retaining its maximum military capability. However, the most important factor has been the rampant racism of this area.

Cosmopolitan mixes of peoples have always been a feature of coastal Provence, and of Marseille in particular. But the experience of centuries has not bred tolerance. Algerians suffer the persecution meted out in the past to Jews, Armenians, Portuguese, Italians and other ethnic groups.

Jean-Marie Le Pen's *Front National* party developed its major power-base, after Paris, in Marseille, and in 1986 four *FN députés* were elected in the Bouches-du-Rhône *département*. They lost their seats when proportional representation was abandoned, but in 1989 the "respectable" parties of the Right joined forces with the *Front National* in Grasse, Le Muy and elsewhere to oust Socialist and Communist mayors.

That the *FN* failed to win outright control of any councils then was due not to any great counterbalance to racism but rather to the similarity in policies of Gaullists such as Jacques Médecin of Nice, and because of the unassailable fortresses of municipal power.

In 1995, however, the *Front National* won Toulon, the ninth-largest city in France, plus Orange and Marignane. The main electoral promise was "Priority for the French", by which, of course, they meant the ethnically pure French. Despite the fact that giving priority to white citizens over black citizens is illegal, there have already been instances in Toulon of people of Algerian origin being overtaken in the housing queue. The town hall has also used municipal grants to promote their political preferences. So, for example, a book fair lost its subsidy when the organizers refused to include ten far-right authors, including a historian who denies the holocaust took place. An AIDS charity has lost its grant along with many cultural organizations seen as threatening by Toulon's new masters. The former mayor's entertainment budget of 70 million francs is being used to quadruple the police force which may please some voters but not young French Algerians who are being stopped and searched far more frequently, accompanied by racist abuse. The Front's "clean" and "traditional" image has suffered a set-back since the elections: the deputy mayor has been murdered and investigations into his death revealed that he frequented Toulon's gay clubs.

Meanwhile Marseille has finally gone to the right; begging has been made illegal in Avignon and Carpentras; the Russian mafia has been buying up property around Nice; and the small left-wing pockets have been unable to get seats at the high table of regional government. During the winter strikes of 1995, however, there were a few small demonstrations in Nice, and in Marseille over a hundred thousand people took to the streets. Even Monaco's *Formula One Grand Prix* had to be abandoned.

MASS TOURISM AND THE ENVIRONMENT

A crucial factor in Provence's postwar history has been the development of **mass tourism**. Beginning with the St-Tropez boom in the 1960s, the number of visitors to the Côte d'Azur has steadily grown beyond manageable – in any sane sense – proportions. By the mid-1970s the coast had become a nearly uninterrupted wall of concrete, hosting eight million visitors a year. Agricultural land, save for a few profitable vineyards, was transformed into campsites, hotels and holiday housing. **Property speculation and construction** became the dominant economic activities while the flaunting of planning laws and the ever-increasing threat to the **environment** – the prime asset – were ignored.

When Brigitte Bardot started to complain that her beloved St-Tropez was becoming a mire of human detritus, the media saw it as a sexy summer story. But when ecologists began warning that the main **oxygenating seaweed** in the Mediterranean was disappearing because of yacht anchors damaging the sea bed, new jetties and marinas modifying the currents, and dust from building sites clouding the water, no one was particularly interested. The loss of *Posidonia oceanica* is now affecting fish, and a toxic algae has appeared, spreading out from Monaco. According to some experts, nearly half of all current developments need to be demolished and a total embargo put on new developments, if the sea is to recover.

Short-term financial gain is still, of course, the overriding principle, so new **marinas** are still being built and new private villages and estates edge into supposedly protected areas like the Esterel. An entirely new resort, Antibes-les-Pins, is to be built alongside Juan-les-Pins. As for the *pins* themselves, **fires** are responsible for destroying great swathes of forest every year.

URBAN EXPANSION ON THE COAST

If sun-worshipping set the region's tone for the first three postwar decades, the 1980s saw different forces at work. While the encouragement of summer tourism exacted its toll, a new type of visitor and resident was being encouraged: the expense-account delegate to business conferences and the well-paid employee of multi-national firms. Towns like Nice and Cannes lead the way in attracting the former, while the business park of Sophia-Antipolis north of Antibes showed how easy it was to persuade firms to relocate their *informatique* (information technology) operations to the beautiful Côte d'Azur hinterland. The result was a further erosion of Provençal identity and greater pressure on the environment. The Dutch, American, Parisian and Lyonnais employees of the **high-tech industries** needed more roads, more housing, more facilities. Sophia-Antipolis is to have not only its own new ring-road but a 25-kilometre *métro* line to Nice.

The business visitors, rather than countering the seasonal imbalance of tourism, made consumption and congestion an all-year-round factor. A black market even developed in game meat: venison and other game is shot with high-tech weaponry in areas such as the Clues de Haute Provence, and then sold to the promenade restaurants.

The rich Gulf Arabs decided Cannes and Monaco were the places to have palatial pied-à-terres. If hillsides needed shifting in order to get a better aspect for the gold and marble swimming pool then in came the heavy earth-moving equipment, invisible to planning objectors' eyes.

For the places that had always catered for flash extravagance, the last two decades have not seen a radical departure from what had gone before. The venues for commercial dealings have got uglier and more prominent, and the Kuwaiti sheiks, Bjorn Borgs and Jackie Collinses have increased their tendency to use finned or winged transport to reach their residences. In the big cities the distinctive Marseillaise and Niçois identities have recognizably remained, despite the dramatic changes in their economies. But elsewhere along the coast, and inland, continuities with the past have become ever harder to detect.

The money from **business services and industry** on the Riviera now outstrips the income from tourism. Economic growth is always visible while the recession hides in the back streets of Marseille and the villages of the interior that have never seduced the admen and the PR experts.

INLAND PROVENCE

Inland Provence has undergone a parallel transformation to the coast with second homes in the sun becoming a requisite for the high-salaried French (and other foreigners) from the 1960s onwards.

Though some villages were certainly saved from extinction by the new property buyers, all suffered from the out-of-season shutters syndrome. With the growth of **ski resorts**, however, the population of the Alpine valleys started to increase, reversing a centuries-old trend. The damage to trees, soil and habitats caused by the ski resorts has in part been offset by the creation of the Parc National du Mercantour, an enclave that has saved several Alpine animal and plant species.

In central Provence the Durance valley alongside the new Marseille–Grenoble *autoroute* has become the latest corridor for **sunrise industries**. Meanwhile the *paysans* keeping goats and bees, a few vines and a vegetable plot are all of pensionable age. The **cheeses** and **honey**, the **vegetables**, **olive oil** and **wine** (unless it's *A.O.C.*) must compete with Spanish, Italian and Greek produce, from land that doesn't have the ludicrously high values of Provence. In order to exploit the consumption patterns of the 1990s the scale has to be larger than the traditional peasant plots, and there must be speedy access to the biggest markets.

TRANSPORT MANIA

Fast access to the Côte d'Azur has become the obsession of planners in Paris. The world's fastest train, the **TGV**, is to have its special track extended down the Rhône Valley to Marseille and along the coast to Nice (at present it runs at low speeds on the existing lines). *SNCF* were determined that the journey time from Paris to Marseille had to be not a second over three hours, and planned the route accordingly. To their surprise protestors brought the entire region's rail services to a halt as they fought pitched battles with riot police. Amendments to the Rhône Valley route were made and the first section, to Valence, was completed on schedule. But environmental and residents' groups are now well organized all along the proposed coastal route and *SNCF*s financial problems have put all projects on hold.

As if the new train line and existing roads were not enough in a region that needs more visitors like a hole in the head, a brand new *autoroute* is planned. Unlike the Marseille–Grenoble *autoroute*, which has some logic to it (and on the whole follows existing main roads), the **A8 bis** is to shadow the A8 along the most congested stretch from Fréjus to Monaco. In addition there'll be an expressway linking Cannes and Grasse with both the A8 and the A8 bis. Almost every local councillor is opposed to the route Paris has chosen; every sane person is opposed to the whole endeavour.

CULTURE IN PROVENCE

In terms of cultural life, **Aix and Avignon**, historically the conservative cities of Provence, have maintained their strong artistic traditions, with **festivals** that draw in hordes of genuine admirers. And the region continues to attract people whose creative talents have made them lots of money. But Provence no longer inspires a flowering of the arts themselves, except in the unique environment of **Marseille**. Elsewhere, aside from the brilliant museum collections, the massive promotion of the arts and preservation of ancient monuments is clearly geared to commercial interests.

It is all part and parcel of the manic striving for **growth**. But the cost in terms of **quality of life** goes uncounted: this can be a stressful part of the world to live. Communities are over-stretched and split between outsiders and the old inhabitants; the Vaucluse has the highest crime and suicide rates of any rural region in France. The Provençal language has been lost and the environment, in what was once the most idyllic corner of Europe, is probably irreparably damaged. The **myth**-makers still ply their trade, partly because there's money in it, and partly because the myth has such enduring appeal. But Provence has to come to terms with its own direction – and lay the myth to rest – before any reversal of today's frightening trends can be envisaged.

BOOKS

HISTORY

Publishers are detailed below in the form of British publisher/American publisher, where both exist. Where books are published in one country only, France, UK or US follows the publisher's name.

Abbreviations: o/p (out of print); UP (University Press).

Edouard Baratier *Histoire de la Provence* (Privat, Toulouse, France). Huge, well-illustrated tome by a group of French academics, which covers the province in about as much detail as anyone could conceivably desire.

Robin Briggs *Early Modern France, 1550–1715* (Oxford UP, UK/US). Readable account of the period in which the French state started to assert control over the whole country. Strong perspectives on the provinces, including coverage of the Marseille rebellion of 1658.

Alfred Cobban *A History of Modern France* (3 vols: 1715–1799; 1799–1871; 1871–1962. Pelican, UK/US). Definitive account of three centuries of French political, social and economic life, from Louis XIV to mid-de Gaulle.

Margaret Crosland *Sade's Wife* (Peter Owen, UK). Expert on Provence's most notorious resident examines how Renée-Pélagie de Montreuil coped with being married to the Marquis de Sade.

Colin Jones *The French Revolution: A Companion* (Longman, UK). Original quotes and documents, good pictures and an unusually clear explanation of events. Good background on Marseille's *Fédéres* and Mirabeau.

John Noone *The Man Behind the Iron Mask* (Sutton/St Martin). Fascinating enquiry into the mythical or otherwise prisoner of Ste-Marguerite fort on the Iles de Lérins, immortalized by Alexander Dumas.

Jean Tulard *Napoléon – The Myth of the Saviour* (Methuen, UK). One of the classic French accounts of the rise and fall of the great man. Its interest is with the phenomenon rather than the personal life and characteristics of the man.

Theodore Zeldin, *France, 1845–1945* (5 vols, Oxford UP, UK/US). Five thematic and very accessible volumes on all matters French over the last century.

SOCIETY AND POLITICS

John Ardagh *France Today* (Penguin/Simon & Schuster). Comprehensive, journalistic overview of the country from World War II up until 1987, covering food, film, education and holidays, as well as politics and economics.

Roland Barthes *Mythologies* (Paladin/Hill & Wang). Brilliant analyses of how the ideas, prejudices and contradictions of French thought and behaviour manifest themselves, in food, wine, travel guides and other cultural offerings.

Mary Blume *Côte d'Azur – Inventing the French Riviera* (Thames and Hudson, UK). This attempt to analyse the myth only reconfirms it, mainly because the people Blume has interviewed have all at stake in maintaining the image of the Côte as cultured millionaires' dreamland. Great black and white photos.

Sean French *Bardot* (Pavilion, UK). Very intelligent biography, drawing on Simone de Beauvoir amongst others, of the former icon of St-Tropezian sun and sex, now associated with animal rights and the *Front National*.

Ann Tristan *Au Front* (Gallimard, France). Compelling report by a Parisian journalist who infiltrated Le Pen's *Front National* in Marseille in 1987. Excellent on detail of the working-class milieu of Front sympathizers, but ultimately unconvincing in its attempt to explain the phenomenon.

Lawrence Wylie *Village in the Vaucluse* (Harvard UP, US). Sociological study of Roussillon full of interesting insights into Provençal village life.

TRAVEL

John Flower and Charlie Waite *Provence* (George Philip/Sheridan, o/p). Waite's gorgeous photographs encompass landscapes, architectural details, markets, and images obscure and familiar. Flower's text draws on over thirty years of residence and visits.

Julian More *More about France: A Sentimental Journey* (Cape, UK). Entertaining tales of a lifetime's travel and sporadic residence, from the 1940s to the present, in the Côte d'Azur, Paris, Burgundy, Brittany, and the Midi.

James Pope-Hennessy *Aspects of Provence* (Penguin/Viking Penguin, o/p). Bitty account of travels made in the 1940s and early 1950s, prior to the arrival of mass tourism.

ART AND ARTISTS

Good introductions to the modern artists associated with Provence are published by Thames and Hudson (UK/US), Clematis and Phaidon (UK) and Abrams (US). Bracken Books (UK) publish a series *Artists by Themselves*, small, attractively produced books with extracts of letters and diaries to accompany the pictures, which includes Matisse, Picasso, Cézanne, van Gogh and Renoir. More substantial editions of artists' own writings include *Matisse on Art* (Phaidon/NAL-Dutton), *Chagall: My Life* (Peter Owen/Humanities, o/p), and *Cézanne by Himself: Drawings, Paintings, Writings* (Little/Brown).

Martin Bailey (ed) *Van Gogh: Letters from Provence* (Collins & Brown/Clarkson & Potter). Attractively produced in full colour. Very dippable and very good value.

Gilot *Matisse & Picasso: A Friendship in Art* (Bloomsbury, UK). A fascinating subject – two more different men in life and art would be hard to find.

D. and M. Johnson *The Age of Illusion* (Thames and Hudson/Rizzoli, o/p). Links French art and politics in the inter-war years, featuring Provençal works by Le Corbusier, Chagall and Picasso.

Jacques Henri Lartigue *Diary of a Century* (Penguin/Viking Penguin, o/p). Book of pictures by a great photographer from the day he was given a camera in 1901 through to the 1970s. Contains wonderful scenes of aristocratic leisure and Côte d'Azur beaches.

PROVENCE AND THE COTE D'AZUR IN LITERATURE

The Côte d'Azur has inspired many twentieth-century English, American and French writers, indulging in the highlife like Scott Fitzgerald, slumming it with the Bohemians like Anaïs Nin, or trying to regain their health like Katherine Mansfield. The two best-known Provençal writers of the twentieth century, Jean Giono and Maurice Pagnol, wrote about peasant life in inland Provence; many of their works have been turned into films. Nineteenth-century Provence features in Alexander Dumas' rip-roaring tale of revenge, *The Count of Monte Christo*, and in some of Aix-born Emile Zola's novels, while the horrors of eighteenth-century Provence are brought to life in Victor Hugo's *Les Misérables*.

Below is a selective recommendation of literary works in which the region plays a significant role, including poetry – spanning the ages from Petrarch troubadour songs through Mistral to the contemporary Bonnefoy and Mistral – and a play by Anouilh set in Marseille.

Jean Anouilh *Point of Departure*

Yves Bonnefoy *In the Shadow's Light*

Anthony Bonner (ed) *Songs of the Troubadours*

Colette *Collected Stories*

Alphonse Daudet *Letters from My Windmill*; *Tartarin de Tarascon* and *Tartarin of the Alps*

Alexandre Dumas (Père) *The Count of Monte Cristo*

Lawrence Durrell *The Avignon Quintet*

Scott Fitzgerald *Tender is the Night*

Jean Giono *To the Slaughterhouse*; *Two Riders of the Storm*; *Que ma Joie Demeure*; *Le Hussard sur le Toit*; and *La Femme du Boulanger*

Graham Greene *Loser Takes All*

Victor Hugo *Les Misérables*

Katherine Mansfield *Collected Short Stories*

Frédéric Mistral *Mirèio*

Anaïs Nin *Diaries*

Marcel Pagnol *Jean de Florette*; *Manon des Sources*, *The Time of Secrets*; *The Time of Love*; *Marius*; and *Fanny*

Francesco Petrarch *Songs and Sonnets*

Françoise Sagan *Bonjour Tristesse*

Patrick Süskind *Perfume*

Emile Zola *Fortune of the Rougons*, *Abbé Mouret's Transgression*; and *The Conquest of Plassans*

Nicholas Watkins *Matisse* (Phaidon, UK). A brilliant and accessible analysis of Matisse's use of colour with beautiful reproductions.

Barbara Ehrlich White *Renoir: His Life, Art and Letters* (Abrams, US). A thorough and interesting work.

Sarah Whitfield *Fauvism* (Thames and Hudson, o/p). Good introduction to a movement that encompassed Côte d'Azur and Riviera artists Matisse, Dufy and Van Dongen.

GARDENS AND FOOD

Robert Carrier *Feasts of Provence* (Weidenfeld & Nicholas, UK). Yummy cookery book.

Louisa Jones and Vincent Motte *Gardens in Provence* (Flammarion, France; Thames and Hudson, UK). The history and traditions of Provençal gardens as weil as gorgeous photographs of the edens behind the high walls and "No Entry" signs.

Timothy Shaw *The World of Escoffier* (Philip Wilson, UK). Biography of the famous chef who started his career on the Côte d'Azur.

GUIDES

Ely Boisson *Mystères et Histoires des Calanques* (Editions Terradou, France). Anecdotes, stories and legends abcut the *calanques,* with practical descriptions of walks plus maps.

James Bromwich *The Roman Remains of Southern France,* (Routledge UK/US). The only comprehensive guide to the subject; detailed, well illustrated and approachable. In addition to accounts of well-known sites, it will lead you off the map to all sorts of discoveries.

Duijker *Provence: A Wine Lover's Touring Guide* (Spectrum, UK). Useful Dutch guide.

W. Lippert *Fleurs des Montagnes, Alpages et Forêts* (Miniguide Nathan Tout Terrain, Paris). Palm-sized colour guide to flowers, available from French bookshops in the trekking areas.

Robyn Marsack (trans) *Walks in Provence* (Féderation Francaise de Randonnée Pedestre, France; Robertson McCarta, UK). Invaluable guide for trekking on the GRs in Provence.

LANGUAGE

French can be a deceptively familiar language because of the number of words and structures it shares with English. Despite this it's far from easy, though the bare essentials are not difficult to master and can make all the difference. Even just saying *"Bonjour, Madame/Monsieur"* and then gesticulating will usually get you a smile and helpful service. People working in tourist offices, campsites, hotels and so on, almost always speak English and tend to use it if you're struggling to speak French – be grateful, not insulted.

On the **Côte d'Azur** you can get by without knowing a word of French, with menus printed in at least four languages, and half the people you meet fellow foreigners. In **Nice**, **Sisteron** and the **Roya Valley** a knowledge of **Italian** would provide a common language with many of the natives. But if you can hold your own in French – however imperfectly – speak away and your audience will warm to you.

PROVENCAL AND ACCENTS

The one language you don't have to learn – unless you want to understand the meaning of street names – is **Provençal**. Itself a dialect of the *langue d'oc* (Occitan), it evolved into different dialects in Provence, so that the languages spoken in Nice, in the Alps, on the coast and in the Rhône Valley, though mutually comprehensible, were not precisely the same. In the mid-nineteenth century the *Félibrige* movement established a standard literary form in an attempt to revive the language. But by the time Frédéric Mistral won the Nobel Prize in 1904 for his poem *Mirèio*, Provençal had already been superseded by French in ordinary life.

Two hundred years ago everybody spoke Provençal whether they were counts, shipyard workers or peasants. Today you might, if you're lucky, hear it spoken by the older generation in some of the remoter villages. It just survives as a literary language: it can be studied at school and university and there are columns in Provençal in some newspapers. But unlike Breton or Occitan proper, it has never been the fuel of a separatist movement.

The French that people speak in Provence has, however, a very marked **accent**. It's much less nasal than northern French, words are not run together to quite the same extent, and there's a distinctive sound for the endings – *in*, -*en*, and for *vin*, and so on, that is more like *ung*.

LEARNING MATERIALS

Rough Guide French Phrasebook (Rough Guides). Mini dictionary-style phrasebook with both English–French and French–English sections, along with cultural tips for tricky situations and also a menu reader.

Mini French Dictionary (Harrap, UK/Prentice-Hall, US). French–English and English–French, plus a brief grammar and pronunciation guide.

Breakthrough French (Pan, UK; book and 2 cassettes). An excellent teach-yourself course.

French and English Slang Dictionary (Harrap, UK; National Textbook Co, US); ***Dictionary of Modern Colloquial French*** (Routledge, UK/US). Both volumes are a bit large to carry, but they are the key to all you ever wanted to understand.

A Vous La France; France Extra; France-Parler (BBC Publications, UK; EMC Publishing, US; each has a book and 2 cassettes). BBC radio courses, running from beginners' to fairly advanced language.

A BRIEF GUIDE TO SPEAKING FRENCH

PRONUNCIATION

One easy rule to remember is that **consonants** at the ends of words are usually silent. *Pas plus tard* (not later) is thus pronounced pa-plu-tarr. But when the following word begins with a vowel, you run the two together: *pas après* (not after) becomes pazapray.

Vowels are the hardest sounds to get right. Roughly:

a	as in h**a**t	*i*	as in mach**i**ne
e	as in g**e**t	*o*	as in h**o**t
é	between g**e**t and g**a**te	*o, au*	as in **o**ver
è	as in **air**	*ou*	as in f**oo**l
eu	like the **u** in h**u**rt	*u*	as in a pursed-lip version of **u**se

More awkward are the **combinations** in/im, en/em, an/am, on/om, un/um at the ends of words, or followed by consonants other than n or m. Again, roughly:

in/im	like the **an** in **an**xious	*on/om*	like the **don** in **Don**caster said by someone with a heavy cold
an/am, en/em	like the **don** in **Don**caster when said with a nasal accent	*un/um*	like the **u** in **u**nderstand

Consonants are much as in English, except that: ch is always sh, c is s, h is silent, th is the same as t, ll is like the y in yes, w is v, and r is growled (or rolled).

BASIC WORDS AND PHRASES

French nouns are divided into masculine and feminine. This causes difficulties with adjectives, whose endings have to change to suit the gender of the nouns they qualify. If you know some grammar, you will know what to do. If not, stick to the masculine form, which is the simplest – it's what we have done in this glossary.

today	*aujourd'hui*	that one	*celà*
yesterday	*hier*	open	*ouvert*
tomorrow	*demain*	closed	*fermé*
in the morning	*le matin*	big	*grand*
in the afternoon	*l'après-midi*	small	*petit*
in the evening	*le soir*	more	*plus*
now	*maintenant*	less	*moins*
later	*plus tard*	a little	*un peu*
at one o'clock	*à une heure*	a lot	*beaucoup*
at three o'clock	*à trois heures*	cheap	*bon marché*
at ten-thirty	*à dix heures et demie*	expensive	*cher*
at midday	*à midi*	good	*bon*
man	*un homme*	bad	*mauvais*
woman	*une femme*	hot	*chaud*
here	*ici*	cold	*froid*
there	*là*	with	*avec*
this one	*ceci*	without	*sans*

TALKING TO PEOPLE

When addressing people you should always use *Monsieur* for a man, *Madame* for a woman, *Mademoiselle* for a girl. Plain *bonjour* by itself is not enough. This isn't as formal as it seems, and it has its uses when you've forgotten someone's name or want to attract someone's attention.

Excuse me	*Pardon*	please	*s'il vous plaît*
Do you speak English?	*Vous parlez anglais?*	thank you	*merci*
		hello	*bonjour*
How do you say it in French?	*Comment ça se dit en Français?*	goodbye	*au revoir*
		good morning/afternoon	*bonjour*
What's your name?	*Comment vous appelez-vous?*	good evening	*bonsoir*
My name is . . .	*Je m'appelle . . .*	good night	*bonne nuit*
I'm English/Irish/Scottish/Welsh/American/Australian/Canadian/a New Zealander	*Je suis anglais[e]/irlandais[e]/écossais[e]/gallois[e]/américain[e]/australien[ne]/canadien[ne]/néo-zélandais[e]*	How are you?	*Comment allez-vous?/Ça va?*
		Fine, thanks	*Très bien, merci*
		I don't know	*Je ne sais pas*
		Let's go	*Allons-y*
		See you tomorrow	*à demain*
yes	*oui*	See you soon	*à bientôt*
no	*non*	Sorry	*Pardon, Madame/Monsieur je m'excuse*
I understand	*Je comprends*		
I don't understand	*Je ne comprends pas*	Leave me alone (aggressive)	*Fichez-moi la paix!*
Can you speak slower?	*s'il vous plaît, parlez moins vite*	Please help me	*Aidez-moi, s'il vous plaît*
OK/agreed	*d'accord*		

FINDING THE WAY

bus	*autobus, bus, car*	hitch-hiking	*autostop*
bus station	*gare routière*	on foot	*à pied*
bus stop	*arrêt*	Where are you going?	*Vous allez où?*
car	*voiture*		
train/taxi/ferry	*train/taxi/ferry*	I'm going to . . .	*Je vais à . . .*
boat	*bâteau*	I want to get off at . . .	*Je voudrais descendre à . . .*
plane	*avion*		
train station	*gare*	the road to . . .	*la route pour . . .*
platform	*quai*	near	*près/pas loin*
What time does it leave?	*Il part à quelle heure?*	far	*loin*
		left	*à gauche*
What time does it arrive?	*Il arrive à quelle heure?*	right	*à droite*
		straight on	*tout droit*
a ticket to . . .	*un billet pour . . .*	on the other side of	*l'autre côté de*
single ticket	*aller simple*	on the corner of	*à l'angle de*
return ticket	*aller retour*	next to	*à côté de*
validate your ticket	*compostez votre billet*	behind	*derrière*
		in front of	*devant*
valid for	*valable pour*	before	*avant*
ticket office	*vente de billets*	after	*après*
how many kilometres?	*combien de kilomètres?*	under	*sous*
		to cross	*traverser*
how many hours?	*combien d'heures?*	bridge	*pont*

QUESTIONS AND REQUESTS

The simplest way of asking a question is to start with *s'il vous plaît* (please), then name the thing you want in an interrogative tone of voice. For example:

Where is there a bakery?	*S'il vous plaît, la boulangerie?*
Which way is it to Avignon?	*S'il vous plaît, la route pour Avignon?*

Similarly with requests:

We'd like a room for two	*S'il vous plaît, une chambre pour deux*
Can I have a kilo of oranges?	*S'il vous plaît, un kilo d'oranges*

Question words

Where?	*où?*	When?	*quand?*
How?	*comment?*	Why?	*pourquoi?*
How many/ how much?	*combien?*	At what time?	*à quelle heure?*
		What is/which is?	*quel est?*

ACCOMMODATION

a room for one/two people	*une chambre pour une/deux personnes*	do laundry	*faire la lessive*
a double bed	*un lit double*	sheets	*draps*
a room with a shower	*une chambre avec douche*	blankets	*couvertures*
a room with a bath	*une chambre avec salle de bain*	quiet	*calme*
For one/two/three nights	*Pour une/deux/trois nuits*	noisy	*bruyant*
Can I see it ?	*Je peux la voir?*	hot water	*eau chaude*
a room on the courtyard	*une chambre sur la cour*	cold water	*eau froide*
a room over the street	*une chambre sur la rue*	Is breakfast included?	*Est-ce que le petit déjeuner est compris?*
first floor	*premier étage*	I would like breakfast	*Je voudrais prendre le petit déjeuner*
second floor	*deuxième étage*	I don't want breakfast	*Je ne veux pas le petit déjeuner*
with a view	*avec vue*	Can we camp here?	*On peut camper ici?*
key	*clef*	campsite	*un camping/terrain de camping*
to iron	*repasser*	tent	*une tente*
		tent space	*un emplacement*
		youth hostel	*auberge de jeunesse*

CARS

garage	*garage*	put air in the tyres	*gonfler les pneus*
service	*service*	battery	*batterie*
to park the car	*garer la voiture*	the battery is dead	*la batterie est morte*
car park	*un parking*	plugs	*bougies*
no parking	*défense de stationner/ stationnement interdit*	to break down	*tomber en panne*
		petrol can	*bidon*
petrol station	*poste d'essence*	insurance	*assurance*
petrol	*essence*	green card	*carte verte*
fill 'er up	*faire le plein*	traffic lights	*feux*
oil	*huile*	red light	*feu rouge*
air line	*ligne à air*	green light	*feu vert*

HEALTH MATTERS

doctor	*médecin*	stomach ache	*mal à l'estomac*
I don't feel well	*Je ne me sens pas bien*	period	*règles*
medicines	*médicaments*	pain	*douleur*
prescription	*ordonnance*	it hurts	*ça fait mal*
I feel sick	*Je suis malade*	chemist	*pharmacie*
headache	*J'ai mal à la tête*	hospital	*hôpital*

OTHER NEEDS

bakery	*boulangerie*	bank	*banque*
food shop	*alimentation*	money	*argent*
supermarket	*supermarché*	toilets	*toilettes*
to eat	*manger*	police	*police*
to drink	*boire*	telephone	*téléphone*
camping gas	*camping gaz*	cinema	*cinéma*
tobacconist	*tabac*	theatre	*théâtre*
stamps	*timbres*	to reserve/book	*réserver*

NUMBERS

1	*un*	11	*onze*	21	*vingt et un*	95	*quatre-vingt-quinze*
2	*deux*	12	*douze*	22	*vingt-deux*	100	*cent*
3	*trois*	13	*treize*	30	*trente*	101	*cent-et-un*
4	*quatre*	14	*quatorze*	40	*quarante*	200	*deux cents*
5	*cinq*	15	*quinze*	50	*cinquante*	300	*trois cents*
6	*six*	16	*seize*	60	*soixante*	500	*cinq cents*
7	*sept*	17	*dix-sept*	70	*soixante-dix*	1000	*mille*
8	*huit*	18	*dix-huit*	75	*soixante-quinze*	2000	*deux milles*
9	*neuf*	19	*dix-neuf*	80	*quatre-vingts*	5000	*cinq milles*
10	*dix*	20	*vingt*	90	*quatre-vingt-dix*	1,000,000	*un million*

DAYS AND DATES

January	*janvier*	November	*novembre*	August 1	*le premier août*
February	*février*	December	*décembre*	March 2	*le deux mars*
March	*mars*			July 14	*le quatorze juillet*
April	*avril*	Sunday	*dimanche*	November 23	*le vingt-trois novembre*
May	*mai*	Monday	*lundi*		
June	*juin*	Tuesday	*mardi*		
July	*juillet*	Wednesday	*mercredi*	1990	*dix-neuf-cent-quatre-vingt-dix*
August	*août*	Thursday	*jeudi*		
September	*septembre*	Friday	*vendredi*	1991	*dix-neuf-cent-quatre-vingt-onze*
October	*octobre*	Saturday	*samedi*		

FRENCH AND ARCHITECTURAL TERMS: A GLOSSARY

These are either terms you'll come across in the *Guide*, or come up against on signs, maps, etc while travelling around. For food items see *Basics*.

ABBAYE abbey

AMBULATORY covered passage around the outer edge of a choir of a church

APSE semicircular termination at the east end of a church

ARRONDISSEMENT district of a city

ASSEMBLEE NATIONALE the French parliament

AUBERGE DE JEUNESSE (AJ) youth hostel

BAROQUE High Renaissance period of art and architecture, distinguished by extreme ornateness

BASTIDE medieval military settlement, constructed on a grid plan

BEAUX ARTS fine arts museum (and school)

BORIE dry stone wall

CAR bus

CAROLINGIAN dynasty (and art, sculpture, etc) founded by Charlemagne, late eighth to early tenth century

CFDT Socialist trade union

CGT Communist trade union

CHASSE, CHASSE GARDEE hunting grounds

CHATEAU mansion, country house or castle

CHATEAU FORT castle

CHEMIN path

CHEVET east end of church, consisting of apse and ambulatory, with or without radiating chapels

CIJ (*Centre d'Informations Jeunesse*) youth information centre

CLASSICAL architectural style incorporating Greek and Roman elements – pillars, domes, colonnades, etc – at its height in France in the seventeenth century and revived in the nineteenth century as **NEOCLASSICAL**

CLERESTORY upper storey of a church, incorporating the windows

CODENE French CND

COL mountain pass

CONSIGNE luggage store

COTE coast

COURS combination of main square and main street

COUVENT convent, monastery

DEFENSE DE . . . It is forbidden to . . .

DEGUSTATION tasting (wine or food)

DEPARTEMENT county – more or less

DONJON castle keep

EGLISE church

EN PANNE out of order

ENTREE entrance

FAUBOURG suburb, often abbreviated to *fbg* in street names.

FERMETURE closing period

FLAMBOYANT florid form of Gothic (see below)

FN (*Front National*) fascist party led by Jean-Marie Le Pen

FO Catholic trade union

FOUILLES archeological excavations

FRESCO wall painting – durable through application to wet plaster

GALLO-ROMAN period of Roman occupation of Gaul (first to fourth century AD)

GARE station; **ROUTIERE** – bus station; **SNCF** – train station

GITE D'ETAPE basic hostel accommodation primarily for walkers

GOBELINS famous tapestry manufacturers, based in Paris; its most renowned period was in the reign of Louis XIV (seventeenth century)

GOTHIC architectural style prevalent from the twelfth century to the sixteenth century, characterized by pointed arches and ribbed vaulting

GRANDE RANDONEE (GR) long-distance footpath

HALLES covered market

HLM public housing development

HOTEL a hotel, but also an aristocratic town house or mansion

HOTEL DE VILLE town hall

JOURS FERIES public holidays

MAIRIE town hall

MARCHE market

MEROVINGIAN dynasty (and art, etc) ruling France and parts of Germany from the sixth to mid-eighth centuries

NARTHEX entrance hall of church

NAVE main body of a church

PCF Communist Party of France

PLACE square

PORTE gateway

PRESQU'ILE peninsula

PS Socialist party

PTT post office

PUY peak or summit

QUARTIER district of a town

RELAIS ROUTIERS truckstop café-restaurants

RENAISSANCE art-architectural style developed in fifteenth-century Italy and imported to France in the early sixteenth century by François I (see *Contexts*)

RETABLE altarpiece

REZ DE CHAUSSEE (RC) ground floor

RN (*Route Nationale*) main road

ROMANESQUE early medieval architecture distinguished by squat, rounded forms and naive sculpture

RPR Gaullist party led by Jacques Chirac

SANTON ornamental figure used especially in Christmas cribs

SI (*Syndicat d'Initiative*) tourist information office; also known as OT, OTSI and *maison du tourisme*

SNCF French railways

SORTIE exit

STUCCO plaster used to embellish ceilings, etc

TABAC bar or shop selling stamps, cigarettes, etc

TOUR tower

TRANSEPT cross arms of a church

TYMPANUM sculpted panel above a church door

UDF centre-right party headed by Giscard d'Estaing

VAUBAN seventeenth-century military architect – his fortresses still stand all over France

VIEILLE VILLE old quarter of town

VIEUX PORT old port

VILLAGE PERCHE hilltop village

VOUSSOIR sculpted rings in arch over church door

ZONE BLEUE restricted parking zone

ZONE PIETONNE pedestrian precinct

INDEX

around the world

Pacific Northwest	1-85828-092-3	9.99	14.95	19.99
Paris	1-85828-235-7	8.99	14.95	19.99
Poland	1-85828-168-7	10.99	17.95	23.99
Portugal	1-85828-180-6	9.99	16.95	22.99
Prague	1-85828-122-9	8.99	14.95	19.99
Provence	1-85828-127-X	9.99	16.95	22.99
Pyrenees	1-85828-308-6	10.99	17.95	23.99
Rhodes & the Dodecanese	1-85828-120-2	8.99	14.95	19.99
Romania	1-85828-305-1	10.99	17.95	23.99
San Francisco	1-85828-299-3	8.99	14.95	19.99
Scandinavia	1-85828-236-5	12.99	20.95	27.99
Scotland	1-85828-302-7	9.99	16.95	22.99
Sicily	1-85828-178-4	9.99	16.95	22.99
Singapore	1-85828-237-3	8.99	14.95	19.99
South Africa	1-85828-238-1	12.99	19.95	25.99
Soutwest USA	1-85828-239-X	10.99	16.95	22.99
Spain	1-85828-240-3	11.99	18.95	24.99
St Petersburg	1-85828-298-5	9.99	16.95	22.99
Sweden	1-85828-241-1	10.99	17.95	23.99
Thailand	1-85828-140-7	10.99	17.95	24.99
Tunisia	1-85828-139-3	10.99	17.95	24.99
Turkey	1-85828-242-X	12.99	19.95	25.99
Tuscany & Umbria	1-85828-243-8	10.99	17.95	23.99
USA	1-85828-307-8	14.99	19.95	25.99
Venice	1-85828-170-9	8.99	14.95	19.99
Vietnam	1-85828-191-1	9.99	15.95	21.99
Wales	1-85828-245-4	10.99	17.95	23.99
Washington DC	1-85828-246-2	8.99	14.95	19.99
West Africa	1-85828-101-6	15.99	24.95	34.99
More Women Travel	1-85828-098-2	10.99	16.95	22.99
Zimbabwe & Botswana	1-85828-186-5	11.99	18.95	24.99
	Phrasebooks			
Czech	1-85828-148-2	3.50	5.00	7.00
French	1-85828-144-X	3.50	5.00	7.00
German	1-85828-146-6	3.50	5.00	7.00
Greek	1-85828-145-8	3.50	5.00	7.00
Hungarian	1-85828-304-3	4.00	6.00	8.00
Italian	1-85828-143-1	3.50	5.00	7.00
Japanese	1-85828-303-5	4.00	6.00	8.00
Mexican	1-85828-176-8	3.50	5.00	7.00
Portuguese	1-85828-175-X	3.50	5.00	7.00
Polish	1-85828-174-1	3.50	5.00	7.00
Spanish	1-85828-147-4	3.50	5.00	7.00
Thai	1-85828-177-6	3.50	5.00	7.00
Turkish	1-85828-173-3	3.50	5.00	7.00
Vietnamese	1-85828-172-5	3.50	5.00	7.00
	Reference			
Classical Music	1-85828-113-X	12.99	19.95	25.99
European Football	1-85828-256-X	14.99	23.95	31.99
Internet	1-85828-288-8	5.00	8.00	10.00
Jazz	1-85828-137-7	16.99	24.95	34.99
Opera	1-85828-138-5	16.99	24.95	34.99
Reggae	1-85828-247-0	12.99	19.95	25.99
Rock	1-85828-201-2	17.99	26.95	35.00
World Music	1-85828-017-6	16.99	22.95	29.99

In the USA, or for international orders, charge your order by Master Card or Visa (US$15.00 minimum order): call 1-800-253-6476; or send orders, with complete name, address and zip code, and list price, plus $2.00 shipping and handling per order to: Consumer Sales, Penguin USA, PO Box 999 – Dept #17109, Bergenfield, NJ 07621. No COD. Prepay foreign orders by international money order, a cheque drawn on a US bank, or US currency. No postage stamps are accepted. All orders are subject to stock availability at the time they are processed. Refunds will be made for books not available at that time. Please allow a minimum of four weeks for delivery.

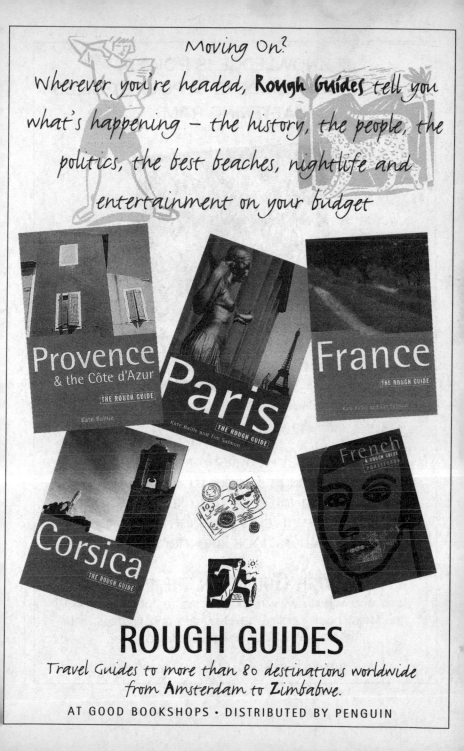